Financial Management: Concepts and Applications

Financial Management: Concepts and Applications

Edited by
Katlin McAndrew

Willford Press
www.willfordpress.com

Published by Willford Press,
118-35 Queens Blvd., Suite 400,
Forest Hills, NY 11375, USA

ISBN: 978-1-68285-582-9

Cataloging-in-Publication Data

Financial management : concepts and applications / edited by Katlin McAndrew.
p. cm.
Includes bibliographical references and index.
ISBN 978-1-68285-582-9
1. Finance--Management. 2. Corporations--Finance. 3. Business enterprises--Management.
I. McAndrew, Katlin.
HG173 .F56 2019
332--dc23

For information on all Willford Press publications
visit our website at www.willfordpress.com

Willford Press

Printed in China.

Contents

Preface....IX

Chapter 1 **Abnormal Returns to Shareholders of M&A Participating Firms: Evidence from the Kuwaiti Stock Market**....1
Mohammed Tarabay and Jamil Hammoud

Chapter 2 **Pension Fund Management: The case of Ethiopian Social Security Agency**....11
Kokobe Seyoum Alemu

Chapter 3 **Customer Metrics and how Store Performance is Related to them**....17
Bjorn P and Matteo A

Chapter 4 **Equity Prices and Real Output: Evidence from a Structural VAR for the MINT Economies**....33
Onikola HO

Chapter 5 **Granger Causality between Growth in the Education Sector and Social Economic Services in Nigeria**....43
Oluwapelumi A and Olaride OB

Chapter 6 **An Empirical Investigation of the Effects of Brain Drain on Developing Countries since 21st Century: A case of Afghanistan**....48
Mujeeb Ur Rehman Rahimi

Chapter 7 **Innovation and R&D Activities in China's Biotechnology and Pharmaceutical Sectors**....63
Tao Zeng

Chapter 8 **Explain the Relationship between Personality and Organizational Commitment in the Office Staff of the National Logistics Company South Oil**....68
Naimi EA and Ghafeli A

Chapter 9 **Reciprocity based Concept of Nonprofit Marketing**....72
Novatorov EV

Chapter 10 **Determination of Youth Migration-The case of Tsegedie Wereda**....82
Abrha FW

Chapter 11 **An Empirical Analysis of Liquidity, Profitability and Solvency of Bangladeshi Banks**....90
Abdullah M

Chapter 12 **Relationship between Spot and Futures Markets of Selected Agricultural Commodities in India: An Efficiency and Causation Analysis**....102
Raghavendra RH, Velmurugan PS and Saravanan A

Chapter 13 **Economic Analysis of Cotton Production in the Gezira Scheme: 1970-2004**.......110
Bushara MOA and Ahmed AMM

Chapter 14 **A Note on the Interrelation of Volatility Puzzle, Equity Premium Puzzle, and Mean Reversion through State Dependent Preferences**.......122
Sung-Sup C and Giannikos IC

Chapter 15 **Impact of Macro Variables on Karachi Stock Exchange**.......126
Rabia N and Khakan N

Chapter 16 **Characteristics of International Acquisitions based on Evidence in Southeast Asia**.......132
Khaliq IH, Naeem B, Abbas Q and Khalid S

Chapter 17 **Measuring the Performance of the Kuwaiti Banking Sector before and after the Recent Financial Crisis**.......138
Atyeh MH, Yasin J and Khatib AM

Chapter 18 **The Effect of the Global Financial Crisis on Earning Management in Tehran Stock Exchange (Evidence from of the Products of Petroleum and Chemical Industry)**.......141
Rezaei M and Neghabi ZH

Chapter 19 **Sources of Public Funds and Economic Prosperity: The Nigerian case**.......147
Onyele KO and Nwokoacha EB

Chapter 20 **Multifractal Detrended Cross-correlation Analysis of Gold and WTI Crude Oil Price Time Series**.......158
Burugupalli S

Chapter 21 **Personalized Temporal Trading Functionalities Engaged in Calendar Market Anomalies: Empirical Evidences from the 2007 and 2009 Financial Crises**.......163
Vasiliki A Basdekidou

Chapter 22 **The Simple Long Volatility Trade**.......173
Chaturvedi V

Chapter 23 **Relationship between FDI and GDP: A case Study of South Asian Countries**.......177
Baig MM, Kiran S and Bilal M

Chapter 24 **The Impact of External Environment on Export Performance**.......181
Jamshidi H and Moazemi M

Chapter 25 **The Influences of Macro-Economic Factors on Capital Market Performance in Pakistan**.......187
Kabeer MA, Iqbal A, Najaf K and Najaf R

Chapter 26 **Sharing Economy and Healthcare Today: ICT, Knowledge, Skills, Projects, Practical Experience in Improving Clinical and Economic Outcomes**.......193
Luisetto M

Chapter 27 **Islamic Calendar Effect on Market Risk and Return Evidence from Islamic Countries** **196**
Akhter A, Sandhu A and Butt S

Permissions

List of Contributors

Index

Preface

The field of finance is concerned with the distribution and investment of assets and liabilities. It can broadly be divided into personal, public and corporate finance. The efficient and effective management of money for an organization to achieve the desired objective is referred to as financial management. The major objectives of financial management are profit maximization, wealth maximization, maintenance of proper cash flow and minimization on capital cost among many others. The applications of this discipline are in the estimation of requirement of funds, determination of the capital structure as well as in investment fund. This book traces the progress of this field and highlights some of its key concepts and applications. The topics included herein on financial management are of utmost significance and bound to provide incredible insights to readers. This book will serve as a reference to a broad spectrum of readers.

This book is a result of research of several months to collate the most relevant data in the field.

When I was approached with the idea of this book and the proposal to edit it, I was overwhelmed. It gave me an opportunity to reach out to all those who share a common interest with me in this field. I had 3 main parameters for editing this text:

1. Accuracy – The data and information provided in this book should be up-to-date and valuable to the readers.
2. Structure – The data must be presented in a structured format for easy understanding and better grasping of the readers.
3. Universal Approach – This book not only targets students but also experts and innovators in the field, thus my aim was to present topics which are of use to all.

Thus, it took me a couple of months to finish the editing of this book.

I would like to make a special mention of my publisher who considered me worthy of this opportunity and also supported me throughout the editing process. I would also like to thank the editing team at the back-end who extended their help whenever required.

Editor

Abnormal Returns to Shareholders of M&A Participating Firms: Evidence from the Kuwaiti Stock Market

Mohammed Tarabay[1]* and Jamil Hammoud[2]

[1]American College of the Middle East, Kuwait City, Kuwait
[2]Rafik Hariri University, Mechref, Lebanon

Abstract

Mergers and Acquisitions (M&A) continue to occur in the world of business, albeit in waves similar to cycles. As such, M&A have remained a research interest for academics as well as practitioners.

While there is convergence among researchers toward finding positive abnormal returns accrued to target firm shareholders, returns to shareholders of acquiring firms remain a question of debate and conflicting evidence. This study attempts to examine the wealth effects of acquisitions in the Kuwaiti economy for the shareholders of both, acquiring and target firms, during the period of 2004-2009. The event study methodology is used to examine whether there were positive or negative returns accruing to the shareholders of the participating firms around the announcement of the acquisition in the cases of 43 acquiring firms and 30 target firms.

Keywords: Mergers and acquisitions; Abnormal returns; M&A; Finance; Kuwait; Event study methodology

Introduction

The number of mergers and acquisitions is rapidly growing worldwide, in part due to their value as a growth strategy for companies. Moreover, companies seek M&A to diversify their activities or in hopes of realizing economies of scale and economies of scope. Greater efficiency in the face of mounting pressures to cut costs has always been a key promise of M&A incidences.

Regardless of the reasons, managers have to sell M&A deals to their shareholders, in order to move forward. Consequently, returns to shareholders resulting from M&A deals have been subject to extensive practical and academic research and studies. In one dimension of the issue, interest revolves around the creation of shareholder wealth resulting abnormal returns associated with M&A.

Need for the study and research issue

Companies have been seeking M&A in various countries, markets, and industries for a number of reasons, chief among which are growth strategy, economies of scale, economies of scope and diversification. One important aspect of any M&A incidence is return to shareholders of both acquiring and target firms.

While research converge around the conclusion that positive abnormal returns accrue to shareholders of target firms, returns to shareholders of acquiring firms is still subject to question and conflicting evidence. Consequently, this warrants further research, in hopes that advancing our knowledge of this issue influences the business case of M&A.

Accordingly, the primary issue of this study is to examine M&A returns for the shareholders of participating firms, in the context of the Kuwaiti economy, during the period 2004-2009. It is noteworthy here that Kuwait is a single-source developing economy, and as such, it is contextually different from other economies already studied.

Literature Review

Our review of research and literature on M&A allows for categorization of studies done along three lines: wealth creation, returns to shareholders of target firms and returns to shareholders of acquiring firms.

Wealth creation

Research about the impact of M&A on the wealth creation of participating firms is plenty. Rani et al. [1] studied a sample of 623 Indian incidences between 2003 and 2008 and found significant short-term wealth creation impact. Subeniotis et al. [2] studies M&A wealth effects in the US stock market during 2005 and found 10% abnormal returns for target firms and insignificant returns for acquiring firms. Jensen and Ruback reviewed some of the major scientific evidence in the field of mergers and acquisitions and concluded that acquirers earned zero or negative returns as opposed to targets that earned significant positive returns. Consistent with Jensen and Ruback study, were those of Rhoades and Mueller [3,4]. Rhoades concluded that efficiency gains eluded the newly integrated firms despite the pre-merger efficiency, and Mueller observed that the anticipated profitability from the merger did not materialize.

Target firms

Most studies conducted on the returns of target firms show positive abnormal returns on the day of the announcement of the event. Langetieg [5] found that target firms earn significantly positive abnormal returns averaging 10.7% over the time interval t_{-6} through t_{-1}. Dodd [6] analyzed 151 merger proposals that took place between 1970-1977. Using a market model, the researcher reported large positive abnormal returns accruing to target firm shareholders on the day of the merger, and the day before. Dodd and Ruback [7] found that target firm shareholders earn statistically significant positive abnormal returns in the month of the first announcement. These abnormal returns averaged 20.58% for successful mergers and 18.96% for unsuccessful

***Corresponding author:** Mohammed Tarabay, Assistant Professor, American College of the Middle East, Kuwait City, Kuwait
E-mail: mohtarabay@hotmail.com

merger proposals. Consistent with the reported previous measures and Using 399 takeovers that occurred in the United States from 1975 to 1984, Frank et al. [8] reported that targets experience announcement gains up to 28%.

Acquiring firms

While there is convergence in the field that target firm shareholders earn statistically positive abnormal returns during the period around the announcement, returns to shareholders of acquiring firms remain debatable.

Chaudary and Sarwar [9] examined returns to shareholders of acquiring firms in the US pharmaceutical industry during the period 2003-2008 and found no significant abnormal returns. Another study done by Karamanos et al. [10] on Greek bank M&A during the period 1996-2013 reveals insignificant abnormal returns for the shareholders of acquiring firms and 7.44% positive abnormal returns for target firm's shareholders. Yet the results of a study on Indian M&A during the period 2003-2008 "indicate that M&A generate statistically significant abnormal returns on the announcement as well as higher post M&A returns for shareholders of the acquiring firms" [11]. In their study of 10 emerging markets, Ma et al. [12] report that stock markets expected cumulative positive abnormal returns for acquiring firm's shareholders in three different event windows: a two-day (0,1) window, a three-day (-1,+1) window, and a five-day (-2,+2) window. Tsai [13] also reported, "Cumulative abnormal announcement returns of the bidders are significantly positive for mergers where the target is a private firm and cash is used as the exchange medium."

As we go back to earlier research, we observe that conflicting evidence continue to prevail. Dodd and Ruback [7] found significant positive abnormal returns to acquiring firm shareholders in the twelve months prior to the tender offer. Langetieg [5] found cumulative excess returns over the time interval t_{-72} through t_{-7}; however, the researcher reported that the post-merger performance is not statistically significant from that of a control group. Frank et al. [8] suggested negative post-merger abnormal returns using equally weighted index, but positive post-merger performance using a value-weighted index. Jensen and Ruback found positive abnormal returns to successful tender offers, and negative abnormal returns to unsuccessful mergers and tender offers. Using data from 1955 to 1987 and a model adjusted for firm size effect and beta risk, Agrawal et al. [14] found that stockholders of acquiring firms suffer statistically significant negative returns of -10%. Loughran and Vijh [15] found evidence suggesting that mergers underperform matching firms, whereas tender offers outperform merging firms. The average return difference between mergers and matching firms was -15.9% with -2.36 t statistics, while the average mean difference between tender offers and matching firms was 40.3% with t statistics of 1.67.

M&A in the context of the Kuwaiti economy

As the literature review above reflects on the results of studies done in different countries and markets, one has to bear in mind that we cannot generalize the results due to differences in regulatory frameworks and characteristics of financial systems. In Kuwait for instance, mergers and acquisitions are a last resort to avoid due to the ownership structures of companies, and the nature of the managerial boards. However, the global financial crisis is changing these practices. The central bank is forcing companies to consider restructuring through mergers and acquisitions. In a statement issued by the central bank of Kuwait (2008), Governor Sheikh Salem Abdul-Aziz Al-Sabah regarded mergers and acquisitions "a choice that is becoming increasingly necessary, given the challenges that have emerged with the global economic crisis and its impact on companies, not only in Kuwait, but also at the regional and international efforts."

The Kuwaiti economy represents an interesting case to study due to its special characteristics as a developing country. The economy is mainly a one-source economy in which oil revenues constitute 90 percent of state revenues. This in return led to structural imbalances in which the public sector highly dominated the private sector. With government owning half of the countries shareholding companies' investors had no choice but to invest their surplus funds in the local real estate market or abroad [16]. However, with financial liberalization and privatization, the private sector grew larger and began to play a bigger role. In 1970, the government formed a committee to regulate the stock market, and the number of listed companies and in turn trading volume increased rapidly. Due to speculative trading and the wide spread growth of new companies by the use of posted dated checks; Kuwait witnessed its first stock market crash [16]. In response to the crisis, the government banned the establishment of new shareholding companies, and highly restricted the use of postdated checks. In addition, the government also compensated losing traders by buying their shares. This act on behalf of the government, and the announcement that it will protect shareholders' rights and safeguard the financial position of companies in Kuwait led to a prevailing impression on the part of the private sector that the government would support the sector in times of need. As this impression persists, business firms developed a moral hazard behavior to exploit the situation. Business firms engage in aggressive growth strategies, hold a lot of debt, engage in risky transactions and expect the government to support them in difficult times. The recent financial crisis intensified the prevailing intuition, as the credit and liquidity crisis continued, and to safeguard the financial system, the parliament approved in 2009 to buy all consumer credit from business firms. Previous literature in the fields of merger and acquisitions confirmed that acquirers perceive targets with high level of equity as attractive, and are willing to pay higher premium to obtain equity. This study, however, proposes that acquirers, acting as risk takers and expecting to free ride credit crisis at the expense of the government, will engage in mergers and acquisitions with targets that finance their aggressive growth strategies with debt as an exceptional case of the Modigliani and Miller propositions that firms with less leverage are more susceptible to acquisition.

As a response to the recurrent crisis in the Kuwaiti economy, such as the stock market crash, the Iran-Iraq war, followed by the Iraqi invasion of Kuwait and the recent financial crisis, the central bank of Kuwait has been pursuing a strategy of encouraging mergers and acquisitions since 1989, advising Kuwaiti companies to seriously look at available opportunities for restructuring through mergers and acquisitions. However, several factors caused weakness in Kuwait's mergers. For instance, as local investments were limited, local firms and banks succeeded in pursuing international and regional acquisitions. Consequently, authorities amended legislation to allow companies to merge and restructure before resorting to liquidation or bankruptcy, as well as legislation regulating the privatization of many public services. The most prominent factor remains the fact that owners and top stakeholders still view this matter negatively and find that it deprives them of certain incentives. As shareholders continue to view mergers and acquisitions as value destroying investment that decreases their wealth, we should expect merger and acquisition activities taken by management of Kuwaiti firms associated with negative revaluation of acquiring firm shares, and consequently, negative abnormal rates of returns.

Research Methodology

The study employed three statistical techniques: The Event Study Methodology, the Pearson correlation test, and multiple regression analysis to test the following two hypotheses:

1. Null Hypothesis: There are no abnormal returns for acquiring firm shareholders in the event of a merger or acquisition

2. Null Hypothesis: There are no abnormal returns for target firm shareholders in the event of a merger or acquisition

The event study methodology

First adopted by Fama et al. [17], the event study methodology is a widely recognized statistical technique, which aims at investigating the impact of an event on stock returns. The process of applications of the event study methodology starts by defining the date on which the information event happened, then observing actual stock returns for a previously defined period around the event date. The third step involves calculating the expected rates of return for the impacted firm over the period of study, followed by measuring the excess or abnormal returns for the firm as the difference between actual returns and expected returns [18].

More specifically, we are using this methodology in our study as prescribed below.

1. The study used the official announcement of the merger or acquisition plan as an event date.

2. The event windows were divided into two 20-day periods: the 20-day before and 20-day after the event.

3. The logarithmic normal function was used to compute the daily actual rate of return for each stock as follows:

$$\mathbf{K_t = LN\,(P_t/Pt_{-1})*100}$$

Where

K_t=the daily stock return in percentage

P_t=the stock price on day t

$P_{t-1=}$the stock price on day t_{-1}

4. The market model was applied to estimate the expected return for each company as follows:

$$\mathbf{K_{jt} = \alpha_j + \beta_j K_{mt} + \varepsilon_{jt}}$$

Where

$K_{jt=}$the rate of return on security j for date t

K_{mt}=the rate of return on the market index, the Kuwait stock exchange all market index was used for the study

α_j and β_j=estimated parameters that vary from one security to another. This study estimated the parameters utilizing a 200-day estimation period, which ranges from days -220 to -21 relative to the event date

ε_{jt}=the stochastic error term of security j in period t, which meets the assumption of the linear regression model

5. Once the parameters were obtained, the expected return for each firm was calculated using the following equation:

$$\mathbf{\hat{K}_{jt=} \hat{\alpha} + \hat{\beta} K_{mt}}$$

For each company, we calculated the expected return for two 20-day event windows. The first period covered the 20-days before the event window ranging from day -21 through one day (-1) prior to the event date. The second period covered the 20-days after the event window ranging from day +1 through day +21 or 21 days after the event date.

6. The abnormal returns (AK) were generated as follows:

$$\mathbf{AK_{jt=} K_{jt} - \hat{K}_{jt}}$$

Where

AK_{jt}=the abnormal return for firm j, date t

K_{jt}=the actual return on firm j, date t

$\hat{K}_{jt}$=the expected return derived from the market model on firm j, date t

7. The average abnormal for the whole sample on day t, was derived using the following equation:

$$\mathbf{AK_t = \frac{1}{n} \sum_{j=1}^{n} AK_{jt}}$$

Where

$AK_{t=}$the average abnormal return for the sample, date t

$AK_{jt=}$the abnormal return derived from the market model on firm j, date t

N=the number of acquiring firms in the sample group

8. The cumulative abnormal returns (CAK) were obtained from the following equation:

$$\mathbf{CAK_t = \sum_{t=-20}^{+20} AK_t}$$

Where

CAK_t is the summation of the average abnormal return for the sample over the event time, day t_{-20} through day t_{+20}

9. Finally, the student t-test was used to examine whether AK_t and CAK_t were significantly different from zero during the t_{-20} days through t_{+20} day period. Since the population standard deviation is not 100% known, and that the distribution in relatively large (n>30) with a tendency to be normally distributed, the t statistic is an appropriate test to be used. The shape of the sampling distribution is essentially influenced by (n-1) degrees of freedom.

Data selection and description

The study analyzed acquiring and target firms listed on the Kuwaiti stock exchange during the period 2004 through 2009. The final sample consisted of 43 acquiring firms, and 30 targets. A firm or a merger case was excluded from the research if the available data was insufficient or not reliable. In addition, if the same company participated in several acquisitions, or was termed as a "frequent acquirer" the firm was counted separately for each merger case. However, if a firm was involved in more than one merger or acquisition in a year, only the first case was utilized because the second one would be highly affected by the effects of the first case, which might exacerbate the returns and deviate the actual effect of the event.

Data sources included Alcara database, Noor financial fund database, public newspapers, and annual reports. The announcement date for firm mergers and acquisitions that fit the criteria for this study was cross-referenced with the four data sources and these data sources were found to be consistent. Figures on daily stock returns and market price movements were extracted from the Kuwaiti stock exchange database. The Kuwait stock market index prices were referenced as the basis for determining abnormal returns. To meet the criteria of firms to be included in this study, the business firms would have had to possess the following set of characteristics:

1. Be headquartered in Kuwait, or belonging to a Kuwaiti holding company.
2. Listed on the Kuwait stock exchange
3. The merger or the acquisition must have been officially announced in the newspaper or some other official publication.
4. Contained a minimum of 150 observations of daily stock prices for estimation purposes.
5. Only mergers and acquisitions that took place between 2004 and 2009 were included in the sampling frame.

Findings

Abnormal returns for acquiring firm's shareholders

Hypothesis 1 is formulated to test the effect of mergers and acquisitions on wealth creation of acquiring firm shareholders. The null hypothesis 1 states that there are no abnormal returns for acquiring firm shareholders in the event of a merger or acquisition. To test this hypothesis, the event study methodology was utilized to examine whether shareholders of acquiring firms realized any abnormal returns or cumulative abnormal returns around the announcement of the acquisition or merger.

Table 1 illustrates daily average abnormal returns (AAAK) for 43 acquirers during the period t_{-20} through t_{+20} relative to the event date ($t_{=0}$), the date on which the acquiring firm officially announced the merger or acquisition t-statistic and P-value for each day were also calculated and presented. The results revealed that acquiring firm shareholders experienced significant (0.05 level) positive abnormal returns of 0.6682% with a t-statistic of 2.067 on the event date. In the pre-event period from t_{-20} through t_{-1}, acquiring firm shareholders experienced significant (0.01 level) negative abnormal returns on day t_{-7} of -0.9808 % with a t-statistic of -2.954, and significant negative abnormal return on days t_{-19} (0.1 level) and t_{-4} (0.05 level) with t statistics of -1.759 and -2.382 respectively. In the post event period, ranging from t_{+1} through t_{+20}, acquiring firm shareholders witnessed significant (0.05 level) negative abnormal returns of -0.5217 % with a t-statistic of -2.107 on day t_{+7}.

Table 2 contains the cumulative abnormal returns (ACAK) for the acquiring firm shareholders associated with the t-statistic and P-values for each day during the event window period. The results point to the fact that acquiring firm shareholders consistently realized negative cumulative abnormal returns over the entire event window. These cumulative abnormal returns ranged from positive +0.0117% at the beginning of the study period to negative -3.0013% percent on day t_{+20}. The cumulative abnormal return for the entire event window, day t_{-20} through day t_{+20} was -3.0013% with a t-statistic of -1.652.

There is considerable evidence that acquiring firms realize negative abnormal returns around the official announcement date, as can be seen from the frequency of negative abnormal returns shown in Tables 1 and 2. Wherever t-statistics are negative and significant at the 5% level, the event affected returns in a negative manner. Around the official announcement date of t_{-1}, t_0 and t_{+1}, positive excess returns averaged around statistically insignificant 0.1738% (0.467), 0.6682% (2.067) with a 5% significance level, and statistically insignificant -0.0104% (-0.030). t -statistics are given in the accompanying brackets. In addition, Table 2 reveals that average cumulative abnormal returns for acquirers for the days around the merger announcement period reported consistently significant negative abnormal period for the entire week before the announcement period. On the day of announcement, cumulative abnormal returns reported negative -1.7168% with a t-statistic of -1.408. clearly and consistent with other research findings in the field of mergers and acquisitions literature, acquirers do not earn positive abnormal returns, and as this study shown, may even realize negative abnormal returns.

Days	AAK	t-Statistic	p-Value
-20	0.0117	0.034	0.973
-19	-0.5867	-1.759	0.086*
-18	-0.5407	-1.575	0.123
-17	0.093	0.241	0.81
-16	0.1671	0.445	0.659
-15	-0.055	-0.195	0.847
-14	0.1769	0.586	0.561
-13	0.1858	0.515	0.609
-12	0.32	1.012	0.317
-11	0.32	1.103	0.276
-10	-0.0295	-0.114	0.91
-9	0.1471	0.507	0.615
-8	0.1486	0.427	0.671
-7	-0.9808	-2.954	0.005***
-6	-0.1826	-0.561	0.578
-5	-0.3677	-1.154	0.255
-4	-1.0952	-2.382	0.022**
-3	-0.0235	-0.056	0.956
-2	-0.2673	-0.774	0.443
-1	0.1738	0.467	0.643
0	0.6682	2.067	0.045**
1	-0.0104	-0.03	0.976
2	0.2337	0.66	0.513
3	-0.1157	-0.321	0.75
4	-0.5271	-1.497	0.142
5	-0.0452	-0.103	0.918
6	0.1186	0.348	0.729
7	-0.5217	-2.107	0.041**
8	0.1498	0.512	0.611
9	-0.008	-0.033	0.974
10	-0.044	-0.148	0.883
11	0.111	0.369	0.714
12	-0.0989	-0.323	0.749
13	0.4184	1.274	0.21
14	-0.078	-0.273	0.787
15	-0.213	-0.866	0.391
16	-0.119	-0.367	0.716
17	0.2971	1.053	0.298
18	-0.179	-0.625	0.535
19	-0.4772	-1.476	0.148
20	-0.1761	-0.613	0.543

*, **, *** Indicates 10, 5, and 1 %, levels of significance, respectively.

Table 1: Average abnormal returns for acquiring firm's shareholders (AAAK).

Figures 1 and 2 provide a graphical representation of the movements of average abnormal returns and cumulative average abnormal return

Days	CAAK	t-Statistic	p-Value
-20	0.0117	0.034	0.973
-19	-0.5749	-1.375	0.176
-18	-1.1157	-2.743	0.009***
-17	-1.0226	-1.943	0.059*
-16	-0.8556	-1.544	0.13
-15	-0.9105	-1.592	0.119
-14	-0.7337	-1.186	0.242
-13	-0.5478	-0.945	0.35
-12	-0.2278	-0.372	0.711
-11	0.0921	0.133	0.895
-10	0.0626	0.09	0.929
-9	0.2097	0.277	0.783
-8	0.3583	0.455	0.651
-7	-0.6225	-0.832	0.41
-6	-0.8051	-0.916	0.365
-5	-1.1728	-1.141	0.26
-4	-2.268	-1.993	0.053*
-3	-2.2915	-1.793	0.080*
-2	-2.5587	-1.781	0.082*
-1	-2.3849	-1.764	0.085*
0	-1.7168	-1.408	0.167
1	-1.7272	-1.426	0.161
2	-1.4935	-1.136	0.262
3	-1.6091	-1.246	0.22
4	-2.1362	-1.487	0.144
5	-2.1814	-1.432	0.16
6	-2.0627	-1.363	0.18
7	-2.5844	-1.72	0.093*
8	-2.4347	-1.658	0.105
9	-2.4427	-1.684	0.1
10	-2.4867	-1.668	0.103
11	-2.3757	-1.524	0.135
12	-2.4745	-1.521	0.136
13	-2.0562	-1.238	0.222
14	-2.1341	-1.325	0.192
15	-2.3471	-1.426	0.161
16	-2.4661	-1.569	0.124
17	-2.169	-1.302	0.2
18	-2.348	-1.387	0.173
19	-2.8252	-1.622	0.112
20	-3.0013	-1.652	0.106

*, **, *** Indicates 10, 5, and 1 %, levels of significance, respectively.

Table 2: Cumulative Abnormal Returns for Acquiring Firm's Shareholders (ACAK).

of acquirers over the 41-day event window. A cursory look at Figures 1 and 2 reveals an initial period of increasing returns, which declines sharply a few days before the official announcement event day. Such a downward trend is particularly indicative in the week preceding the merger or acquisition announcement. This swift downward shift in average and cumulative average abnormal returns over the events measurement period suggests that the market did not reward the acquirer shareholders in mergers and acquisitions. In reality, it could be argued that acquirers as a group lost economic value as reflected by the average cumulative abnormal returns (ACAK) which was negative at the beginning of the period, then increasing until it was positive during the period t_{-11} through t_{-7}, to take negative values again for the rest of the entire test period.

Figure 1 reveals that the average abnormal returns fluctuated around zero for the entire event window, particularly interesting was the sharp decline in returns during the week previous to the event day (t_{-7} throughout t_{-2}), it is believed that this is the period in which the announcement of the merger or acquisition started to leak into the market. Another noticeable observation is the positive reaction of the market on announcement date. Thus, Figure 1 does not give a clear indication that acquirers realize significant negative abnormal returns around the official announcement date.

Table 3 shows that 37.2% of the firms reported negative returns on event date and around 62.8% of the acquirers realize abnormal returns between below 1%. Although there is a slight positive market reaction on the day of the announcement, the analysis of the entire study period emanating from this data indicates that the null hypothesis can be supported, which predicts that acquirers in case of a merger or acquisition do not realize any excess returns. The results of this study is consistent with the recent research findings of other research efforts in the field of merger and acquisitions reporting similar results that acquirers, realize significant negative abnormal returns or insignificant slight positive abnormal returns in best case scenario.

Abnormal returns for target firm's shareholders

Hypothesis 2 is formulated to test the effect of mergers and acquisitions on wealth creation of target firm shareholders. The null hypothesis 2 states that there are no abnormal returns for target firm shareholders in the event of a merger or acquisition. To test this hypothesis, the event study methodology was utilized to examine whether shareholders of target firms realized any abnormal returns or cumulative abnormal returns around the announcement of the acquisition or merger.

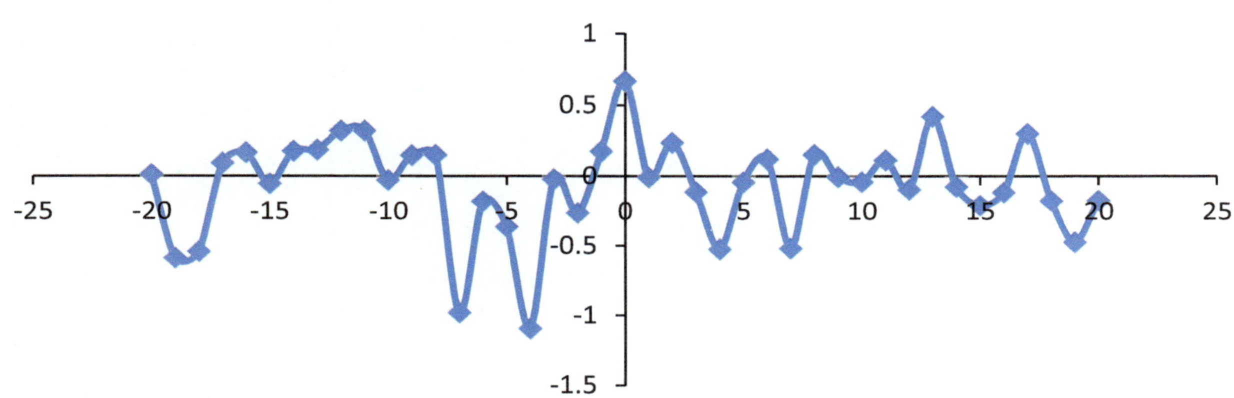

Figure 1: Average abnormal returns for acquiring firm shareholders (AAAK).

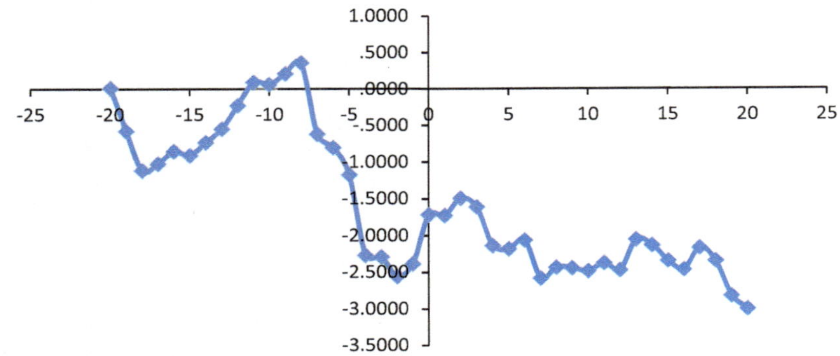

Figure 2: Cumulative abnormal returns for acquiring firm shareholders (ACAK).

Classes	Frequency	Frequency %	Cumulative frequency	Cumulative %
(-4, -3)	1	2.33	1	2.3
(-3, -2)	1	2.33	2	4.7
(-2, -1)	8	18.6	10	23.3
(-1, 0)	6	13.95	16	37.2
(0, 1)	11	25.58	27	62.8
(1, 2)	8	18.6	35	81.4
(2, 3)	2	4.65	37	86
(3, 4)	2	4.65	39	90.7
(4, 5)	1	2.33	40	93
(5, 6)	2	4.65	42	97.7
(6 ,7)	1	2.33	43	100

Table 3: Event day abnormal returns frequency distribution of acquirers.

Table 4 illustrates daily average abnormal returns (TAAK) for 30 targets during the period t_{-20} through t_{+20} relative to the event date ($t_{=0}$), the official announcement date of the merger or acquisition t-statistic and P-value for each day were also calculated and presented. On the event day, target firm shareholders gained statistically significant (1% level) abnormal returns of 1.5912% with a t-statistic of 3.598. For the 20-day-period before the event day, average abnormal returns reported statistically significant (5% level) positive 1.1272% on day t_{-15} with a t-statistic of 2.639. Moreover, during this pre-event period, target firm shareholders reported 5 negative values of average abnormal returns with only one value being statistically significant at the 10% level on day t_{-5} with an average of -0.673% and a t-statistic -1.751. All other negative average abnormal returns for target firm shareholders were small and statistically insignificant.

For the 20-day-period after the event date, the average abnormal returns for target firms reported only statistically significant (5% level) negative value of -1.726% on day t_{+4} with a t-statistic of -2.524. Worth noting at this level is that none of the average abnormal returns during this period were statistically significant and different from zero.

Table 5 contains the cumulative abnormal returns (TCAK) for the target firm shareholders associated with the t-statistic and P-values for each day during the event window period. The Table shows that target firm shareholders earned positive cumulative abnormal returns (1% and 5 % level) starting of t_{-15} throughout day t_{+3}. The event day return reported significant positive cumulative average positive return of 4.7525% with a t-statistic of 3.044 (0.01 significance level). The highest level of cumulative positive abnormal return occurred on day t_{+1} of 4.8286% with a t-statistic of 2.974 (1% significance level). There was no reported negative cumulative abnormal return. The cumulative

Days	TAAK	t-Statistic	p-Value
-20	0.033	0.124	0.903
-19	0.5666	1.069	0.294
-18	0.4861	1.39	0.175
-17	0.363	0.863	0.395
-16	0.1691	0.402	0.69
-15	1.1272	2.639	0.013**
-14	0.1226	0.322	0.75
-13	0.4181	0.974	0.338
-12	0.4428	0.922	0.364
-11	0.191	0.481	0.634
-10	-0.5047	-1.464	0.154
-9	0.589	1.542	0.134
-8	0.1293	0.252	0.803
-7	0.1312	0.305	0.763
-6	0.2259	0.572	0.572
-5	-0.673	-1.751	0.091*
-4	-0.2094	-0.562	0.579
-3	-0.3973	-1.101	0.28
-2	0.4915	1.193	0.243
-1	-0.5406	-1.097	0.282
0	1.5912	3.598	0.001***
1	0.076	0.174	0.863
2	-0.5202	-1.292	0.206
3	-0.32	-0.647	0.523
4	-1.726	-2.524	0.017**
5	-0.9773	-1.285	0.209
6	0.205	0.424	0.675
7	0.3984	0.96	0.345
8	0.0667	0.159	0.875
9	-0.5077	-1.19	0.244
10	0.2231	0.611	0.546
11	0.2612	0.64	0.527
12	-0.1223	-0.251	0.803
13	0.2927	0.711	0.483
14	-0.1778	-0.468	0.643
15	-0.71	-1.662	0.107
16	-0.1801	-0.585	0.563
17	-0.2015	-0.678	0.503
18	-0.0041	-0.01	0.992
19	0.4501	1.299	0.204
20	-0.4356	-0.979	0.336

*, **, *** Indicates 10, 5, and 1 %, levels of significance, respectively.

Table 4: Average abnormal returns for Target Firm Shareholders (TAAK).

abnormal return for the entire event window, day t_{-20} through day t_{+20}, was statistically insignificant 0.8431% with a t-statistic of 0.286.

Days	TAAK	t-Statistic	p-Value
-20	0.033	0.124	0.903
-19	0.5996	1.082	0.288
-18	1.0858	1.656	0.108
-17	1.4487	1.73	0.094*
-16	1.6179	1.684	0.103
-15	2.745	2.99	0.006***
-14	2.8677	3.132	0.004***
-13	3.2858	3.515	0.001***
-12	3.7286	3.386	0.002***
-11	3.9195	3.882	0.001***
-10	3.4148	3.441	0.002***
-9	4.0038	3.641	0.001***
-8	4.1331	3.661	0.001***
-7	4.2643	3.622	0.001***
-6	4.4902	3.722	0.001***
-5	3.8172	3.014	0.005***
-4	3.6077	2.945	0.006***
-3	3.2104	2.535	0.017**
-2	3.7019	2.804	0.009***
-1	3.1613	2.152	0.040**
0	4.7525	3.044	0.005***
1	4.8286	2.974	0.006***
2	4.3084	2.536	0.017**
3	3.9884	2.198	0.036**
4	2.2625	1.083	0.288
5	1.2852	0.536	0.596
6	1.4902	0.663	0.513
7	1.8886	0.894	0.378
8	1.9553	0.9	0.375
9	1.4475	0.614	0.544
10	1.6706	0.675	0.505
11	1.9318	0.724	0.475
12	1.8095	0.623	0.538
13	2.1022	0.694	0.493
14	1.9244	0.666	0.511
15	1.2144	0.441	0.662
16	1.0343	0.375	0.71
17	0.8327	0.3	0.766
18	0.8286	0.294	0.771
19	1.2787	0.453	0.654
20	0.8431	0.286	0.777

*, **, *** Indicates 10, 5, and 1%, levels of significance, respectively.

Table 5: Cumulative Abnormal Returns for Target Firm Shareholders (TCAK).

Figure 3 provides the graph of average abnormal returns of the 30 target firms for day t_{-20} through day t_{+20} relative to the event day. Similar to that of acquiring firms, the movement of average abnormal returns of target firms was up and down around zero. The largest average abnormal return was 1.5912% on the event day, and the smallest average abnormal return was -0.673% on day t_{+5}.

Figure 4 presents the daily movements of the cumulative average abnormal returns of target firm shareholders. As illustrated in the graph, there is a swift upward drift of cumulative abnormal returns during the pre-event period. However, the cumulative abnormal returns decline rapidly on the post event week to stabilize by the end of the event window. Consistent with other research efforts on returns of target firm shareholders, evident in this study, the premium paid to target firm shareholders increases the abnormal returns which then declines again and disappears towards the end of the study period.

Table 6 presents the frequency distribution of event day abnormal returns of target firms. Event day returns which ranges from around -4% to 7% were divided into 11 equal intervals. The cumulative frequency distribution reports that only 30% of the firms reported negative abnormal returns on the event day while the remaining 70% reported positive values. Clearly, it can be seen that target firm shareholders have earned cumulative positive abnormal returns on the days leading to the event date, however earned statistically insignificant abnormal returns over the entire test period.

Internal validity analysis

The researchers were vigilant about internal validity threats of the model being tested, and statistical methods were employed to ensure that errors were kept at a minimum.

Non-normalcy condition

Non-normalcy condition suggests that the distribution of the data points do not reveal the typical bell shaped distribution curve. Figures 5 and 6 present a graphical representation of the scatter and shape of the data points for the sample of mergers and acquisitions adopted in the study.

Figures 5a and 5b plot the frequency distribution of the data points representing event day abnormal returns for acquirers and targets in the study sample. The histogram drawn represents the number of occurrences for given demarcated values for the given sample distribution. The coordinates plotted in Figures 5a and 5b tended towards a fairly and seemingly normally distributed set of data points for acquirers and targets.

The cumulative frequency distribution plots the frequencies in

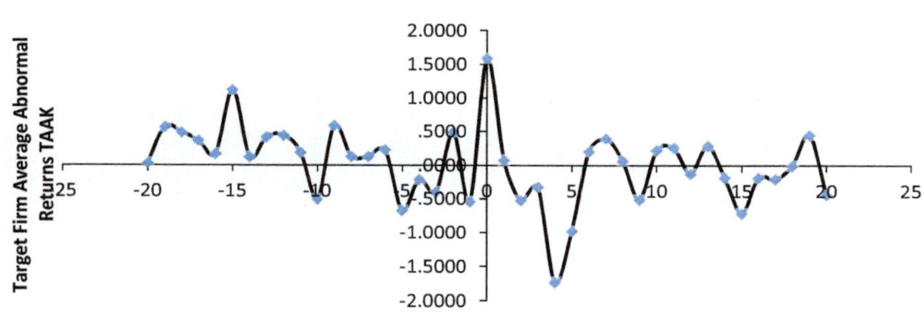

Figure 3: Average abnormal returns for target firm shareholders (TAAK).

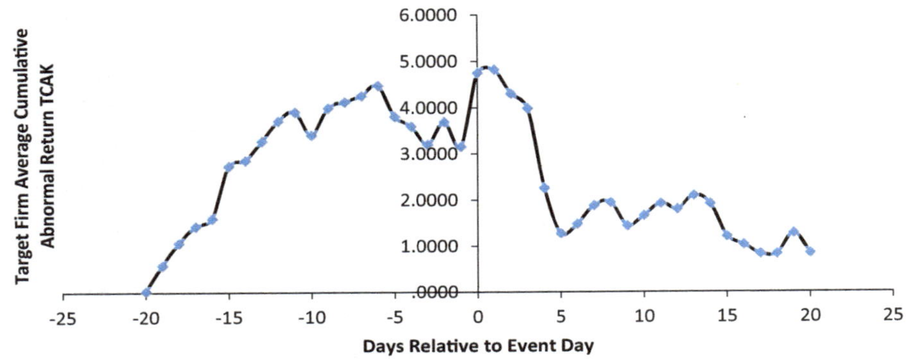

Figure 4: Cumulative abnormal returns for target firm shareholders (TCAK).

Classes	Frequency	Frequency %	Cumulative Frequency	Cumulative %
(-4, -3)	1	3.33	1	3.33
(-3, -2)	2	6.67	3	10
(-2, -1)	2	6.67	5	16.67
(-1, 0)	2	6.67	7	23.33
(0, 1)	2	6.67	9	30
(1, 2)	8	26.67	17	56.67
(2, 3)	6	20	23	76.67
(3, 4)	2	6.67	25	83.33
(4, 5)	3	10	28	93.33
(5, 6)	1	3.33	29	96.67
(6, 7)	1	3.33	30	100

Table 6: Event day abnormal returns frequency distribution of targets.

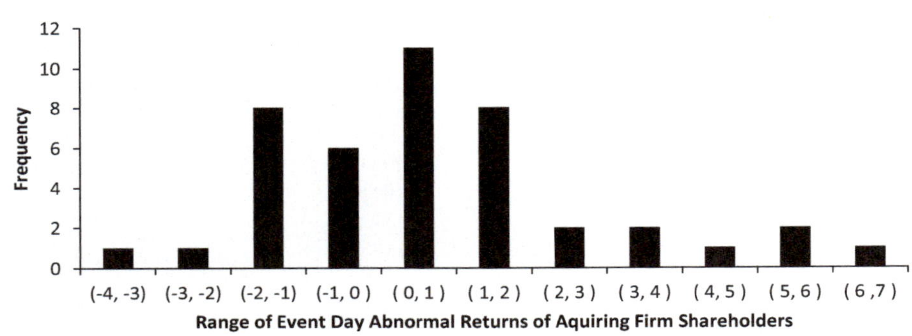

Figure 5a: Bar chart of frequency distribution of event day abnormal returns of acquiring firm shareholders.

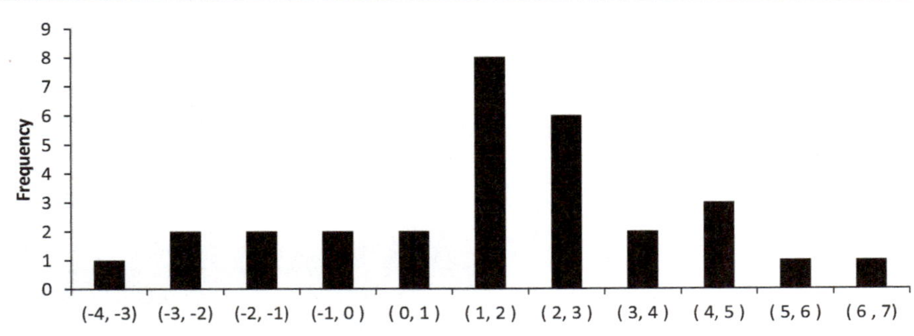

Figure 5b: Bar chart of frequency distribution of event day abnormal returns of target firm shareholders.

progressive fashion for the number of occurrences of given values in the data set. The cumulative frequency distribution captures the percentage of scores between the lowest bound and the given bound being examined. The cumulative frequency curve plotted in Figures 6a and 6b

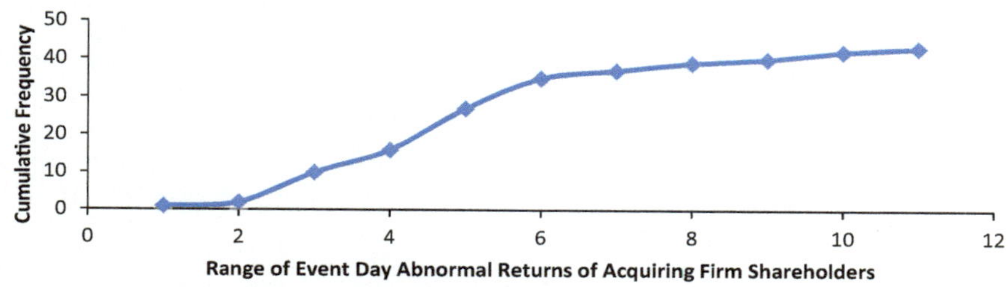

Figure 6a: Graph of cumulative frequency distribution of event day abnormal returns of acquiring firm shareholders.

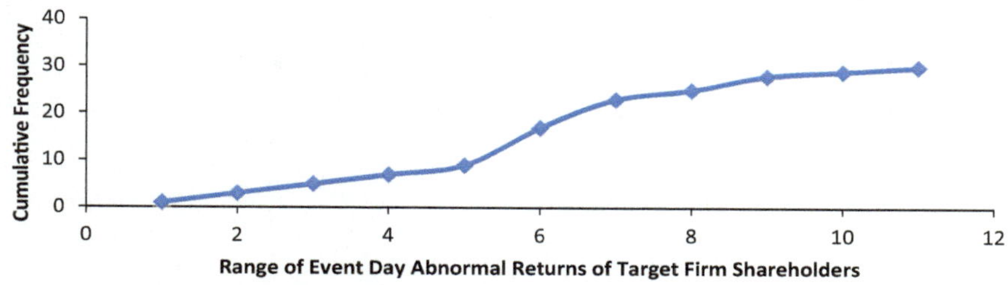

Figure 6b: Graph of cumulative frequency distribution of event day abnormal returns of target firm shareholders.

approximates that of a normally distributed set of data points.

Sequencing of variables

This study hypothesized that the official announcement of a merger or acquisition triggers a response in the stock prices of the acquiring or target firm resulting in positive or negative abnormal returns. Such a conjectured relationship rests on the premises that the event, or the official announcement of the merger, is directly associated with the dependent variable, abnormal returns. Granger posits that the future is affected by the present, or the past. Accordingly, this study postulated, that since the independent variable, or the official announcement of the event, preceded that the dependent variable, abnormal stock returns, it stands to reason that the dependent could not have caused the independent variable. It is more realistic to state that the independent variable preceded and caused or influenced, the latter event, abnormal stock returns.

Rival explanation

Occurrences of major events in the acquiring and target firms may significantly affect abnormal returns. Major events such as earning announcements, business risk behavior shifts, or restructuring might be competitors to merger and acquisition announcements in analyzing the abnormal return in a given period. For the 43 merger and acquisition cases in the acquiring firm study samples, and 30 cases of targets, none of the elements in the set of data points recorded an event significant enough to rival the merger or acquisition announcement in the explanation of the hypothesis being tested. Some of the merger cases in both samples were excluded due to unavailable or unreliable dataset.

The researchers did a careful search for possible rival explanations that could have contributed to the event of abnormal stock price reactions during the period around the announcement of the merger and specifically in day's t_{-1}, t_0, and t_{+1}. The groups of firms that composed the sample study of this research effort did not appear to have any significant major event that could rival the announcement of the merger or acquisition in explaining the stock price changes over the 41-day event window.

Conclusion

This study examined the effect of M&A on returns to shareholders of participating firms, in the Kuwaiti economy, during the period 2004-2009. A brief summary of the research findings from the statistical analysis conducted in this study are:

1– During the event period, which ranged from 20 days before the announcement date to 20 days after the event or announcement date, the shareholders of acquiring firms obtained statistically significant negative abnormal returns from the acquisition despite the noticeable positive reaction of the market on the event date.

2– During the event window period, which ranged from 20 days before the event date, through 20 days after the event date, the shareholders of target firms obtained statistically significant positive cumulative abnormal returns in the period preceding the event date through few days in the post event period, but declined afterwards.

The empirical evidence of this study lends support and extends the literature available in mergers and acquisitions. The practical and theoretical implications of this study are consistent with previous integration debates suggesting that target firm shareholders earn significant abnormal returns, while bidders realize negative rates of return. Despite the overwhelming evidence that mergers and acquisitions are not value creating, the ongoing process of mergers worldwide presents a conundrum to academics, regulators, and financial analysts.

References

1. Rani N, Yadav SS, Jain PK (2013) Market response to the announcement of mergers and acquisitions: An empirical study from India. Vision 17: 1-16.
2. Subeniotis DN, Kroustalis IG, Tampakoudis IA, Poulios M (2011) Empirical examination of wealth effects of mergers and acquisitions: The US economy in Perspective. Journal of Financial Management & Analysis 24: 30-38.
3. Rhoades SA (1993) The Efficiency Effects of Horizontal Bank Mergers. Journal of Banking and Finance 17: 411-422.
4. Mueller DC (1995) Mergers: Theory and Evidence. In: Mergers, Markets and Public Policy. Giuliano Mussati (ed.), Kluwer Academic Publishers, Dordrecht, pp: 9-43.

5. Langetieg TC (1978) An application of a three-factor performance index to measure stockholder gains from merger. Journal of Financial Economics 6: 365-383.
6. Dodd P (1980) Merger proposals, management discretion and stockholder wealth. Journal of Financial Economics 8: 105-137.
7. Dodd PR, Ruback R (1977) Tender offers and stockholders returns: An empirical analysis. Journal of Financial Economics 5: 351-374.
8. Frank J, Harris R, Titman S (1991) The post-merger equity-price performance of acquiring firms. Journal of Financial Economics 29: 81-96.
9. Chaudary S, Sarwar A (2015) Returns to shareholders in acquisitions into the U.S. pharmaceutical companies. International Journal of Health and Economic Development 1: 14-27.
10. Karamanos A, Bakatselos G, Roena A (2015) Abnormal stock market returns to announcements of M&A banking deals in Greece 1996-2013. Management Dynamics in the Knowledge Economy 3: 317-338.
11. Rani N, Yadav SS, Jain PK (2012) Impact of mergers and acquisitions on returns to shareholders of acquiring firms: Indian economy in perspective. Journal of Financial Management & Analysis 25: 1-24.
12. Ma J, Pagán JA, Chu Y (2009) Abnormal returns to mergers and acquisitions in ten Asian stock markets. International Journal of Business 14: 235-250.
13. Tsai C (2008) The cumulative abnormal returns of acquiring companies: Evidence from mergers. Journal of Accounting, Finance & Management Strategy 4: 23-43.
14. Agrawal A, Jaffe J, Mandelker G (1992) The post-merger performance of acquiring firms: A re-examination of an anomaly. Journal of Finance 47: 1605-1622.
15. Loughran T, Vijh AM (1997) Do long-term shareholders benefit from corporate acquisitions? Journal of Finance 52: 1765-1790.
16. Elimam A, Girgis M, Kotob S (1997) A Solution to Post Crash Debt Entanglements in Kuwait's Al-Manakh Stock Market. Interfaces 27: 89-106.
17. Fama EF, Fisher L, Jensen M, Roll R (1969) The adjustment of stock prices to new information. International Economic Review 10: 1-21.
18. John MD, Cox SH, MacMinn RD (1988) The Theory of Finance: Evidence and Applications. The Dryden Press, New York, pp: 202-2012.

Pension Fund Management: The Case of Ethiopian Social Security Agency

Kokobe Seyoum Alemu*

Lecturer and Researcher, Ambo University, Ethiopia

Abstract

The research study evaluated pension fund management of Ethiopian social security agency. To attain these objectives, eleven years' financial statements were used as a secondary data and different ratio analysis was carried out to examine the status of fund management of Ethiopian social security agency. Those ratios shows that the organization current assets is very much large when compared with its current liabilities which shows the organization is in the best position to pay off all of its current liability. Again, the finding displays the asset turnover has been decreasing from time to time which shows under utilization of companies asset. In addition to this, large percentage of the asset of social security is financed by equity and small percentage is financed by debt. Lastly, the analysis puts that the organization is absorbent up to 50% of its income. That means up to 50% of them is consumed by its expenses.

Keywords: Pension; Management; Social security; Social security fund; Ethiopia

Introduction

A huge increase in life expectancy is one of the great achievements of the human race over the past two centuries [1]. Despite this fact, inability to work is beyond control of the individuals. Injury or other sickness may occur despite precaution and the weakness resulting from old age is a natural event. Hence, a person may lose his means of income when he is unable to work. During this time the dependents will face harsh living conditions since their means of survival has come to an end. This problem brings the origin of social security. It is with this purpose that Ethiopian social security agency was established in 1963.

Apart from this, the social securities are part of the financial sector of the economy and play a significant role in economic building. In performing financial intermediation function of asset transformation, pensions funds are generally intended to fulfill and provide the public with two primary functions: to furnish a saving mechanism and to alleviate poverty among old through provision of income payments on retirement so as to make consumption flow.

Regardless of this immense contribution to the society, like many other developing countries of the world, a pension system is not adequately developed in Ethiopia. Until recently, the Ministry of Finance had been collecting the contributions made by the employees of the public servants and the military. Recently, this execution is transferred to the right authority, i.e., Social Security Authority. This shows the age-old problem of fund administration in the field. Like other financial institutions, Pension system is one of the strategically important areas in the state policy, and therefore requires ongoing control through an authorized body to ensure their soundness and safeguard the interest of affiliate workers. Such a body shall be responsible for regulation and control over the activities of the pension funds, including investment activity. According to Urwin [2], there is increasing evidence to support a link between superior investment performance and an institutional investor's strong management. He added that, many pension funds are beginning to realize that their management arrangement should be a top priority, not only through responsibility to literally billions of individuals, but also because it creates an opportunity for wealth creation. The management of pension fund should include all the receipt and payments including investment and return from investment. This needs proper management and much coordination among the concerned parties. But those things are not an easy task in developing countries like Ethiopia which easily can be seen from current Ethiopian situation.

For a long time Ethiopian social security agency has an aim to collect and accumulate money to effect a payment for old age and invests the left over in appropriate investment options. Regardless of this intention, funds have been simply gotten without adequately generating additional income and to keep it in their bank account. This less development of pension fund in Ethiopia is exacerbated by an increase in inflation, coupled with poor management of pension funds, which has slashed the funding ratio of Ethiopian pension funds. The pension funds now face significant funding gaps and are forced to increase premiums (as witnessed currently) and if the funding ratio does not recover in time, they may have to cut a pension right which is not possible in reality.

Evidently, the improper management has profound implications and raised questions as to the quality and sophistication of pension fund management [3].

The purpose of this paper was to investigate the pension fund management of Ethiopian social security by properly looking at the management's efficiency in properly undertaking its activities, in improving organizational earning and in selection of the best investment opportunities so that the best fund administration of the pension scheme have been applied by the management.

Thorough investigations of Ethiopian social security pension fund management practices do have an immense utility in helping the institution and government to build up on their strengths and to take measures on their weakness. In addition to this, the finding can provide guide lines for strategy and policy formulation aimed at improving the

***Corresponding author:** Kokobe Seyoum Alemu, Lecturer and Researcher, Ambo University, Ethiopia, E-mail: kokseyoum@yahoo.com

operational conditions of pension fund management. Again this paper adds to the existing literature in several ways in that it is only recently that attention paid to pension fund management in Ethiopia. Last but not least, the knowledge of the pension fund management can be a base for those who have currently expected to apply the system of pension for their employees like NGO's and private.

Literature

Pension fund management

Pension fund management requires the investment of assets to achieve the long-term provision of funding for retirement [2]. Institutional social security, in some measures or other, exists in almost all countries today. However, there is much variation between countries with regard to the levels of protection, scope, coverage and effectiveness of the system in place. As a group, the developed countries have the most advanced social security and pension fund management systems. With very few exceptions, institutionalized social security and pension fund management in the developing world is of relatively recent origin having appeared only after the Second World War, following the emergence of several independent states at the end of the colonial era [4].

Pension fund management in advanced economies

According to Preqin Special Report [5] Public pension funds are important and experienced investors in alternatives and on average allocate 5.5% of their capital to private equity, with significant commitments also existing to hedge funds, private real estate and infrastructure. He examined the financial statements of over 150 public pension funds from North America, Europe and the UK to ascertain how well their investments across various asset classes were performing. His data shows that the 20 largest public pension funds have a total of $224 billion allocated to private equity, and their high levels of assets under management make fund managers keen to attract this type of investor. The long term, high risk nature of alternatives are well matched to long term liabilities of pension plans, providing diversity to investment portfolios, and giving potential to yield high returns [6].

Practice of pension fund management in emerging economies

According to Ventura [7], Brazilian pension funds are minority shareholders with no direct involvement in the operations of their investee companies. Thus, they must invest in transparent companies, ones that treat their shareholders fairly and whose management is responsible and renders full account of its administration. This shows that a good quality Corporate Governance contributes to improved company management. China has National social security fund (NSSF). According to Impavido [8], Fund management has also been centralized ("pooled" in Chinese terminology) as a way to improve standards. The central government's fiscal transfers to nine of these thirteen provinces are managed by the national social security on behalf of the provinces for a period of at least five years and for a guaranteed rate of return. The provinces do not need to pay NSSF the management fee, which is covered by Ministry of Finance (MOF) budget. When we come to India, Government employees are covered under provident fund and pension fund with a pay as you go system. Pension Funds are managed by Pension Fund Administrators and they are responsible for taking investment decisions but in some jurisdictions, pension fund management can be by asset management and insurance companies and some management decisions may be the responsibility of Boards of Trustees in some corporate organizations. Pension Fund Custodians are those who keep custody of pension funds [9].

Practice of pension fund in developing countries

According to Catala [4] in the last two decades, many developing countries implemented pension reforms from publicly managed pay-as-you-go defined benefit systems to privately managed fully funded defined contribution schemes. One of the potential macroeconomic benefits typically associated with such pension reforms is the development of domestic financial markets. In fully funded pension systems, the argument goes the rapid accumulation of domestic financial assets by pension funds bolsters the domestic bond and stock markets. More developed domestic financial markets, in turn, lead to more efficient allocations of both domestic and foreign savings to productive investments in the domestic economy, which spurs productivity and growth. Pension funds could trade frequently, increasing the liquidity of the domestic stock markets, and thus crowding in savings and new investors. Similarly, the intense trading of stock by pension funds and their large size may induce them to seek the introduction of innovations and new financial instruments to lower transaction costs, again attracting additional savings and new market participants [4].

Social security agency's investment policy, guidelines and practices in Ethiopia

The prevailing type of security system in Ethiopia is the government sponsored Social Security system. The history of the formal social security system in Ethiopia dates back to the formulation of the Pension and Social Security Authority (PSSA) in 1963(Pubic Service Pension, Proclamation N. 209/1963). This decree covered only the military and civil service workers. For these groups, the pension scheme was funded by a mandatory contribution. Since only government employees are covered by the pension scheme, large portion of the eligible age population is used to be excluded. Given this limited coverage, broad-based reduction of old age poverty is not possible. Moreover, the implied saving mobilization role of such financial institution cannot be realized. When we examine the structure of the labor force in Ethiopia, the majority of the employed population works for either the informal sector , the private sector or is self-employed [3]. These employees fail to have access to pension services and thus are vulnerable for income instability especially in their old age.

Private organizations' and NGO's provide their employees with provident fund which is paid in lamp sum amount at their employment termination. But, as a result of the low interest rates and the rising inflation at the time the lump sum benefits due to retiring beneficiaries were meaningless [3]. For this and other reasons, the government of Ethiopia currently included all employees in pension fund net. Conversion of the Provident Fund into a pension payment introduced some element of adequacy into the retirement package for the workers. But, the existence of pension fund by itself is meaningless unless it is properly managed. According to Guidelines for the investment of social security funds [10], the investment policy of a social security scheme should be based on prudent-person principles and appropriate quantitative restrictions. It should take into account risk management; diversification and dispersion; matching assets and liabilities, including considerations of duration and maturity; currency matching; and performance measurement and monitoring [11].

Whatever principles the investing institution may adopt, there have to be competent and honest managers to apply them.

It is, therefore, essential to ensure the competence and integrity of managers. The governing body of the social security scheme or of the investing institution should adopt criteria concerning the expertise that is required of investment managers and other advisers on investment policy and strategy and their implementation.

Methodology

This research has been conducted on a longitudinal base in which data collection for the research was made across time. To analyze those data concerned with pension fund management, different period data were collected and compared. Both primary and secondary data was used in this study by giving high attention to secondary data as longitudinal data is the most important for this analysis. Primary data was collected through unstructured interview made with employees and management of the organization. This will enrich the secondary data obtained from records of the organization and help to understand the research problem more. Secondary data, which is the most important component for this study, were obtained by examining various years' financial statements of the organization under study. The researcher use eleven years (1999-2011) consecutive data from the financial statements of the organization for the analysis. To analyze the data collected from eleven consecutive years of financial statements of Ethiopian social security agency, time series analysis was applied. From this ratio, percentage, table and graph were used. Proper pension fund management can be analyzed by using different financial ratios that provide information about five areas of financial performance like Short-term solvency, activity, financial leverage and profitability. Financial statements cannot provide the answers to the preceding five measures of performance. However, management must constantly evaluate how well the firm is doing, and financial statements provide useful information [12,13].

Data Analysis and Discussion

This part is devoted to the presentation and analysis of the data collected as per the purpose and the objective of the study. In order to have relevant information about the pension fund management of Ethiopian social security, relevant documents are used as data sources. The Ethiopian pension authority, administers four pension schemes namely: old age pension, invalidity pension, sickness benefits/pension and work injury pension. In this scheme, normal retirement age is 60 years for both males and females and the scheme is applicable on any type of work. Minimum years of service to qualify for pension entitlement are 10 years. During this period the funds generated from the contributions were invested in different areas of investment like government Treasury bill, time deposit and stock. This investment need proper management in applying cost benefits analysis in the selection of investment areas. Unavailability of proper management of such programs can lead to increased incidence of poverty.

Short-term solvency

Current ratio: Too low current ratio may suggest that a firm may face difficulty in paying its short term liabilities. Too high ratio indicates that too much capital is tied up in current assets and the firm may be sacrificing some returns possibilities. For this organization, the items included in the current assets are: receivables, cash and treasury bills. So as can be easily understood from the table below, the organization is very much liquid in paying back its current liability. It's very much large when compared even with standard of 2.0 birr. This shows that there are idle resource investment in current asset and this resources could have been invested somewhere else that it can get return. For the organization it is better to invest those resources for better return. Even for your surprise, this organization does not have long term liability till 2009. That means the organization have only current liability which should be paid within one year [14]. The main reason for this is lack of financial market that makes investment very much illiquid. Because, in Ethiopia due to lack of financial market; investors should wait until maturity if they invest their money in long term asset which makes investment in long term asset boring. As a result investor does not have a willingness to borrow long term debt and invest. Due to this illiquidity nature of investment much of the organization asset are tied up in the current assets (Table 1 and Figure 1).

Activity

Ratios of activity are constructed to measure how effectively the firm's assets are being managed. The level of a firm's investment in assets depends on many factors.

Total asset turnover: This ratio show how many birr of sales are supported by one dollar of the assets. The table shows that the organization gets that amount of birr in sales from the investment of 1 birr in fixed assets. The organization is better at the beginning that it is getting more than its investment. But, the amount of sales per one birr invested in fixed asset has decreased continuously which may be caused by different factors as fall in revenue or large investment in fixed assets. However, as the table attached at the end shows, the revenue amount is increasing from time to time. But the increase in fixed asset is very much larger than the increase in revenue that results in the fall of the ratio. We cannot say the organization is underutilizing its asset as we don't have industry average. But we conclude that the organization is not performing as it did before. The ratio of past year can be used to judge the organization performance. So it is better for the organization to increase the amount of its revenue or decrease investment in fixed asset. Nevertheless, that can only be advised if we are sure that the

	1999	2000	2001	2002	2003	2004	2005	2006	2007	2008	2009
Current ratio	15.75	12.15	30.84	8385.26	0	66499.8	81626.8	87796.61	103745.05	141807.95	207528.47

Table 1: Current ratio or quick ratio.

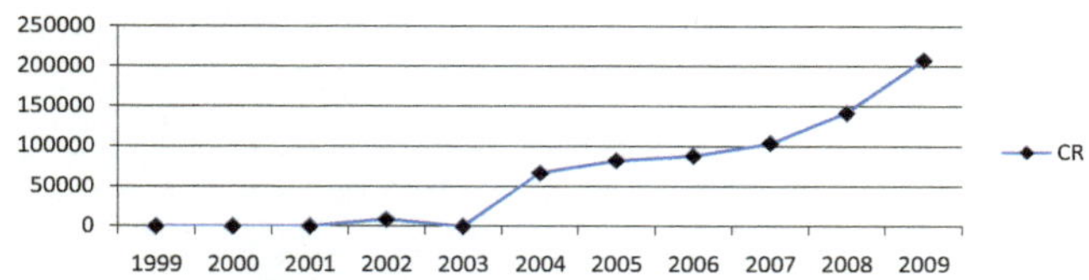

Figure 1: Current ratio (CR) or acid taste ratio.

	1999	2000	2001	2002	2003	2004	2005	2006	2007	2008	2009
ratios	1.15	1.57	0.97	0.34	0.28	0.3	0.29	0.29	0.3	0.34	0.32

Table 2: Assets turn over.

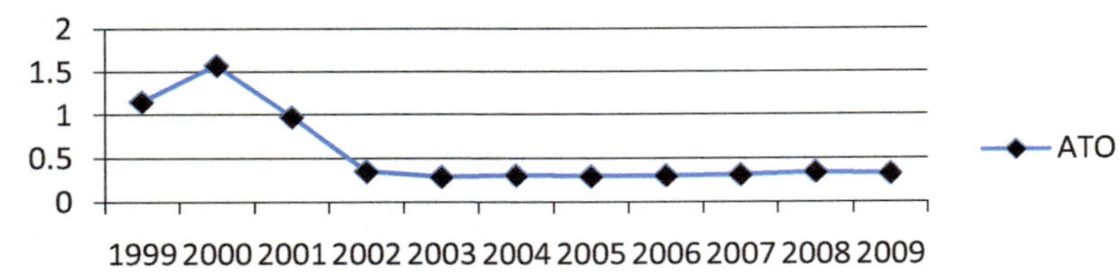

Figure 2: Asset turnover ratio (ATO).

	1999	2000	2001	2002	2003	2004	2005	2006	2007	2008	2009
RTO	1.44	8.12	1136.04	32.29	7.88	6.86	6.59	7.99	8.47	8.77	10.31
ACP	253.05	44.93	0.321	11.3	46.26	53.2	55.38	45.63	43.04	41.58	35.4

Table 3: Receivable turn over and average collection period.

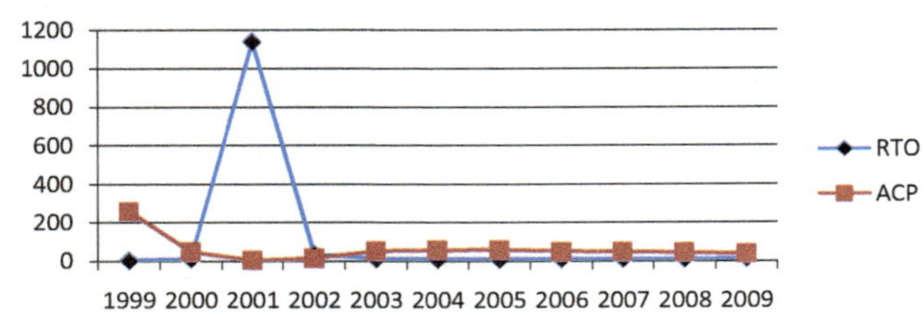

Figure 3: Receivable turnover (RTO) and average collection period (ACP).

organization is performing below industry average (Table 2 and Figure 2).

Receivables turnover and average collection period (days' sales outstanding): Measures the liquidity of a firm's accounts receivable. It indicates how many times or how rapidly accounts receivable are converted in to cash during a year. The receivables turnover ratio and the average collection period provide some information on the success of the firm in managing its investment in accounts receivable. A ratio substantially lower than the average for the industry may suggest that a firm has more liberal credit policy and there is inadequate collection efforts. Again a ratio substantially higher than the industry average may suggest that a firm has more restrictive credit policy and more rigorous collection effort [15].

The receivable turnover section which is labeled as (RTO) shows how many times the receivable of the organization is changed in to cash. The organization is showing the better position in changing it receivable to cash from time to time. This value is more meaning full if it is explained in terms of average collection period. Again on this part the organization is continuously improving its performance in collecting its receivable from time to time. However, still we do not have industry average to compare it against and to judge whether the organization is better in collecting its receivable or not. But we can conclude that the organization is improving its performance from time to time (Table 3 and Figure 3).

Financial leverage

Financial leverage is related to the extent to which a firm relies on debt financing rather than equity. Measures of financial leverage are tools in determining the probability that the firm will default on its debt contracts. The more debt a firm has, the more likely it is that the firm will become unable to fulfill its contractual obligations. In other words, too much debt can lead to a higher probability of insolvency and financial distress.

On the positive side, debt is an important form of financing, and provides a significant tax advantage because interest payments are tax deductible. If a firm uses debt, creditors and equity investors may have conflicts of interest.

Debt ratio, debt-equity ratio and equity multiplier: Debt to equity ratio measures the proportion of total assets financed by the firm's creditors. Debt ratios provide information about protection of creditors from insolvency and the ability of firms to obtain additional financing for potentially attractive investment opportunities. Equity multiplier is a way of examining how a company uses debt to finance its assets. In other words, this ratio shows a company's total assets per dollar of stockholders' equity. As we can see from the table below large part of the organization's asset is financed by equity. The organization is less dependent on debt. As has been said before, the organization is very much reluctant in borrowing funds from outside because of the lack of financial market. This impede the organization from borrowing funds from outside and invest which in turn makes the organizations' underutilization if its capacity. Only small proportion of the organizations asset is financed by outsiders. So it is better for the organization to use its capacity by borrowing funds from outside.

The intention of those all ratios are to check the level of gearing with in this organization and it shows that large percentage of the asset of the organization is financed by equity. That means the level of liability with in this organization is very much small especially long term debt. Even if this decrease the financial distress for this organization, it is using below its debt capacity. It is better for the organization to include its debt within the organization and invest in income generating activities. Having less debt ratio makes the organization to get debt easily with less cost as its default probability is less. By using this capacity the organization can borrow funds and invest in income generating activities.

The debt to equity ratio also shows the amount of debt for every one birr invested in equity. As can be seen from the table the organization has less than one birr debt for every one birr invested in the organization.

Again the equity multiplier section of the table shows the amount of the total asset of the organization available for every one dollar invested in the equity. The table shows that all the items on this section are near to one birr which shows much of the asset is invested by equity (Table 4 and Figure 4).

Profitability

One of the most difficult attributes of a firm to conceptualize and to measure is profitability. In a general sense, accounting profits are the difference between revenues and costs. Unfortunately, there is no completely unambiguous way to know when a firm is profitable. At best, a financial analyst can measure current or past accounting profitability. Many business opportunities, however, involve sacrificing current profits for future profits. In general, a firm is profitable in the economic sense only if its profitability is greater than investors can achieve on their own in the capital markets. One of the measures of profitability is profit margin.

Profit margin: The most important margin is the net profit margin. In general, profit margins reflect the firm's ability to produce a product or service at a low cost or a high price. The net profit shows the amount left over after all expenses are deducted. So the net profit margin shows from the amount of revenue gained by the organization what percentage is left after the whole expenses are deducted. For the organization to be better, getting revenue by itself do not have any value. If the whole gained revenues are expensed, it will become the mere establishment for the organization. As result the organization should manage its expense and decrease it to the minimum degree. As can be seen from the above table, the organization is retaining up to 50% and more of its revenue. Actually as we don't have the standard to compare with we cannot say it is good or bad. But, we can generalize from its past performance that the organization performance have decreased a little bit and now become better than the year before (Table 5 and Figure 5).

Conclusion

Social Security is a public program designed to protect individuals and their families from income loses due to unemployment, old age, sickness or death; and to improve their welfare through public services like medical care and economic assistance. In this study, an attempt has been made to assess the extent of the management of pension fund in Ethiopia. To answer this different period data were compared against each other by taking different ratios. This is to analyses different capacity of the organization starting from short term debt paying ability of the organization to its profitability.

Under this different ratios are applied in understanding the organizations performance like Short-term solvency which shows the ability of the firm to meet its short-term obligations. In this the Ethiopian social security agency is very much liquid. That means the amounts of current asset when compared with current liabilities are very much large and the organization can easily pay back its short term liability. But this large investment in current asset is not free of cost that the organization could have invested some of those assets somewhere else in order to generate income.

The second variable that has been included under this study is Activity. That is the ability of the firm to control its investment in assets. Under this asset turn over, receivable turn over and average collection period of the organization was analyzed. With this context we cannot say it is good or bad due to the lack of industry average. However, by looking the past experience of the organization we can say that the asset turnover has been decreased from time to time even if the amount of revenues generated is increasing. So it is advisable for the organization

	1999	2000	2001	2002	2003	2004	2005	2006	2007	2008	2009
debt ratio	0.0634654	0.0819065	0.0115531	6.64E-05	0	9.19E-06	8.26E-06	8.39E-06	7.01E-06	5.64E-06	0.0054125
Debt to equity ratio	0.0677662	0.0892137	0.0116881	6.64E-05	0	9.19E-06	8.26E-06	8.39E-06	7.01E-06	5.64E-06	0.005442
Equity multiplier	1.0677662	1.0892137	1.0116881	1.0000664	1	1.0000092	1.0000083	1.0000084	1.000007	1.0000056	1.005442

Table 4: Financial leverage (debt ratio, debt to equity and equity multiplier).

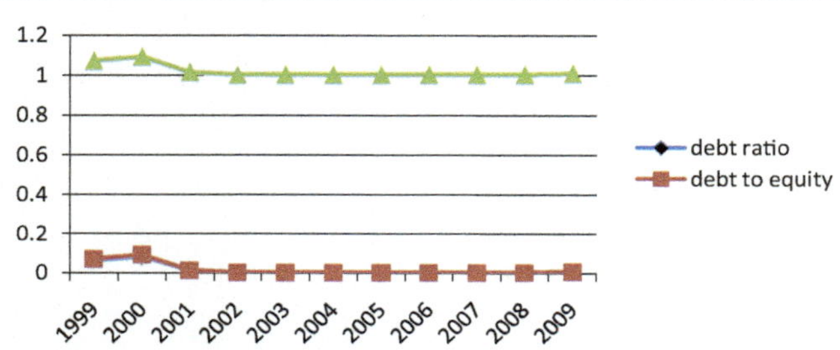

Figure 4: Financial leverage (debt ratio, debt to equity and equity multiplier).

	1999	2000	2001	2002	2003	2004	2005	2006	2007	2008	2009
NPM	0.5	0.37	0.31	0.53	0.44	0.49	0.46	0.51	0.59	0.62	0.63

Table 5: Net profit margin (NPM).

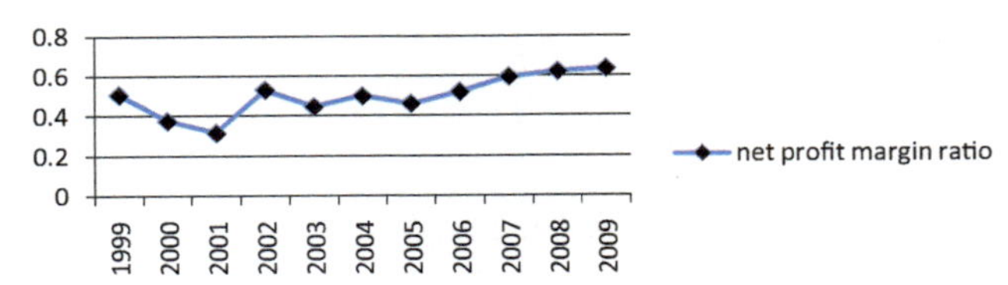

Figure 5: Net profit margin.

either to decrease investment in asset or increase revenue. To talk about receivables turnover is a little bit difficult because of industry average and the Ethiopian social security has a mix in performance that it moves ups and downs.

The third variable that has been included in this study is financial leverage which shows the extent to which a firm relies on debt financing. This part demonstrates that, the Ethiopian social security agency is very much averse in financing its asset by outsiders. The amount of debt is very much small when compared with its equity. The organization did not use its capacity for debt. This idle capacity could generate income for the organization and it is better for the organization to use its capacity by borrowing and investing the money in income generating activities. The main reason for this is lack financial market that the organization should hold the investment in long term assets until maturity even if it need money due to the lack of this market.

The fourth and the last but not the least variable that have been included is Profitability which is used to measure the extent to which a firm is profitable. The profitability of the organization is a function of many variables. Even if revenue is the major item in profitability it is not the only because, profit is the difference between revenues and expenses. So for the organization to be profitable it is better to control its expense. This activity is measured by using profitability ratios. The profit margin of the organization shows that the Ethiopian social security agency saves up to 50% of its income from being expensed. But as has been stated above we cannot say it is good or bad due to the lack of industry average. The organization profitability is increasing during the last few years. However the organization can use all of its debt capacity and control its expenses to get more profit.

Recommendations

In view of the findings and the conclusion of the study, the following recommendations are suggested in the hope that it would help for policy interferences.

1. Since Government is responsible for Social Security, it is better for the government to make and analyze the investment area that it will benefit not only social security agency but also other member of the society.

2. Idle resources that are kept in current assets should be invested somewhere else to generate income. Those resources have a cost and it should be invested. Holding only small percentage of those resources that help us to pay current liabilities are enough.

3. Again it is better for the organization if it borrows and invests in long term income generating activities that the organization can benefit from it. The organization is underutilizing its capacity. That means it can borrow large amount of money with little cost that make it the debt to be easy for the organization.

4. The government should facilitate the establishment of financial market that it will benefit the organization and other part of the society.

References

1. Truell (2011) How to Manage Pension Costs by Edmund Q Finance.
2. Urwin R (2012) Best practice in investment governance for pension funds.
3. Asaminew E (2010) Adopting Private Pension System in Ethiopia 10: 1.
4. Catala NM (2004) Pension Funds and Corporate Govern, Developing Countries: What do We Need to Know?
5. Preqin (2011) Special Report Public Pension Plans and Alternative Assets.
6. Philip DE (2002) The European Pension Management Industry.
7. Ventura LC (2001) Corporate Governance and its application in Pension Fund Management.
8. Impavido G, Hu YW, Li X (2009) Governance and Fund Management in the Chinese Pension System.
9. Imam A (2011) Pension fund management in India: government role and Regulatory issues.
10. (2004) Guidelines for the investment of social security funds, ISSA 28th General Assembly, Beijing 12-18.
11. Exley J, Mehta S, Smith A (2003) Pension Funds-A Company Manager's View.
12. Public Pension Fund Management in India (2001) Conference on Public Pension Fund Management.
13. Yin R (1989) Case Study Research Design and Methods: Applied Social Research Methods, 5, Sage publications.
14. (2011) Proclamation No. 209-1963 Public servants pension.
15. (2004) Guidelines for the investment of social security funds in Ethiopia.

Customer Metrics and How Store Performance is Related to Them

Bjorn P[1]* and Matteo A[2]

[1]Department of Int. Management and Economics, Copenhagen Business School, Denmark
[2]School of Business Society and Engineering, Malardalen University, Sweden

Abstract

This paper aims to give the reader an overview of the latest available metrics to track customer behavior in physical retail stores. This presentation is mainly based on a literature review and leads in the next step to the question about how useful are such metrics and how can they used. Therefore, a representative study in Sweden was conducted to measure which factors have an impact on customer performance and which not. Based on statistical analysis the paper finds out that there is a significant relation between the usage of metrics and the profitability of the store.

Keywords: Marketing; Tracking; Customer metrics; Customer behavior; Physical retail stores

Introduction

Business and marketing management studies show that maintaining transactions with customers is essential for a sustainable growth [1]. However, the more the business grows, the more data and information needs to be collected and interpreted. This fact can be critical for physical stores, often referred as "offline store" or "brick and mortar store" [2]. Brick and mortar means in this context that the customer can has a physical interaction with goods in the store (Ibid). The thesis aims to give the reader an overview of different metrics (e.g. retention rate, turnover per customer) that can be used to track customers in physical stores. The term metrics is defined in this paper that metrics are any type of measurement used to quantify data in a corporate environment [3]. This study will focus only on marketing metrics that are related to physical retail stores. In addition, this study shows which metrics are used by profitable stores.

In the 1980s, the science of shopping and with that the tracking of customers in stores became popular. Underhill describes that these studies were mostly carried out in the form of research projects and due to that the measurement of the customer was not constant and the metrics were not standardized [4]. At the time, data was collected only once a year, allowing stores to have less than once a year insights of how the customer acts. Advisory firms who also created the metrics later did the interpretation of the data.

Later on, graphical driven user interfaces were improved and led to the development of the internet and with that the possibility of online retailing [5], changing the way of how retailing can be carried out [6]. The risks and potentials derived from this development forced the stores to use metrics in order to measure and control their performance more effectively (Ibid). The metrics that were developed for this purpose gave companies the opportunity to track their activities and to improve their knowledge about the customer constantly [7].

Afterwards, a large number of online stores arose, which used modern technology to track and measure consumers [5]. The metrics used nowadays by online shops are highly standardized and contain measures like visits, queries, click-through and conversion rates [7]. In online stores the metrics are well connected, which allows the store manager to analyze how changes in the store influence the way customers act (Ibid). This can also be done frequently and in real time (Ibid). However, traditional physical stores might suffer from the inadequacy of their personnel capabilities and their information system (e.g. customer relationship system) to develop and use similar powerful metrics as online stores [5]. Accordingly physical stores lack in the possibility to carry out experiments in order to find ways to become more profitable (Ibid).

Problem statement

The background shows that physical stores have a deficit when it comes to the application of certain metrics. Shankar et al. states that when it comes to shopper marketing, there is a lack in standardized metrics for the physical store [7]. However, in the past years there was an increase in marketing metrics, which aims to give the user more insight into the performance of the marketing activity and the way customers act [8]. The usage of metrics in marketing helps to increase the accountability of the firm, justifying spending and the selection of marketing actions in general [9]. When the store is able to use metrics in order to identify drivers of customer behavior, the managers can use that knowledge to maximize profits of the store [10].

According to Shankar et al., traditional metrics to track customers and measure their performance are insufficient [7]. The term performance is defined in this paper as how a customer contributes to the profitability of the company. This means that a customer with high performance buys more products on a more regular basis from the same store than one with a lower performance. Therefore, they need to be augmented and new metrics have to be tested [7]. Especially metrics that measure attention and reflection of customers could be interesting and would provide useful information for the shop manager for example cross buying metrics (Ibid). It might be possible that the data collection can be automated in order to calculate this metrics. The metrics can then be constantly calculated and analyzed on a day-to-day base. The resulting insights that the manager get from the metrics need to be implemented into applications in order to make the interpretation easy to understand for people at different management levels [7].

Academic research explored in the past years a wide range of metrics that are able to track the customer and their shopping cycle in more detail [7]. Most of these metrics that appear to be efficient

***Corresponding author:** Bjorn P, Department of Int. Management and Economics, Copenhagen Business School, Denmark, E-mail: bp.int@cbs.dk

in theory tend to be hard or too complex to track within a physical store [8]. In the physical world, store managers and personnel might not understand how to use such metrics. More commonly, they do not have access to proper tools to measure the metrics that can lead to a wrong usage and interpretation of the metrics [7]. Furthermore, it could be the case that the interpretation of some of the metrics is too complicated and would require too much time [11]. This would lead to inefficiency because of the complexity of the data or the lack of proper tools, especially for small businesses (Ibid). Based on that it can be necessary to define specific metrics related to the level of management (e.g. store manager, worker) where they are used [7]. Doing so, would lead to the fact that each level would get access to the required metric to carry out the job.

Research Questions and Hypotheses

The purpose of this study is to investigate to which extend metrics, that are discussed in current research publications, are used in physical retail stores. Through these questions, the reader gains more understanding of metrics that can be used in order to track customers effectively and efficiently. Furthermore, the study examines which metric groups are used by profitable stores and whether there are differences between physical retail stores which can be clustered by using attributes for example size, profitability and type of business. This leads to the following research questions:

RQ1: What ways are there to measure customers' performance in physical retail stores?

RQ2: How do the profitability of the store and the usage of specific metrics correlate?

RQ3: Which role plays the complexity in how store managers see the usability and usefulness of the metric groups?

Based on these research questions and the prior problem statement, the four hypotheses are stated and further tested in this study.

The variety of metrics can range from those that are easy to use and implement like the sales figure [8], to more complex such as cross buying metrics which are forecasting and probability metrics that are based on statistical calculations and requires constant data collection in order to make reliable predictions [12]. Current research has shown that companies tend to use only single metrics although it states that some metrics cannot be used alone [13]. The complexity of some of the metrics requires knowledge and special training for the operating personnel as well as a complex IT system [14]. Furthermore, the operationalization is for various metrics not easy and requires knowledge about this and the resources for testing the metrics [8]. For this study we assume that knowledge for dealing with the metrics is linked to the education. Based on this the following hypothesis can be stated:

H1: The usage of metrics depends on managers' education.

According to Shankar et al. [7], big retail chains have the possibility to use technology and knowledge to analyze and influence customer decisions within the store. They grow according to Reinarz et al. and dominate the market place [7,13]. From a management point of view, this can be seen as complex which requires a standardized metric system [7]. Furthermore, bigger companies have more IT capabilities that can be used in order to collect and analyze data [10].

H2: Stores that belong to a retail chain use more metrics.

Kumar et al. stated that specific metrics require special knowledge that can lead to a lower usability of the metrics [14]. The way of how easy the metric is seen, influence the way how useful participants of the survey see metrics due to a lack of understanding them [8]. This leads to the following hypotheses H3a and H3b.

H3a: The individual preferences of the usefulness of metrics are related with the usability.

H3b: Profitable stores rank the usability and the usefulness higher.

Getting to know the customer and understand its behavior is crucial for the success and profitability of the company [1]. Stores get through specific metrics more insights about how customers act in the store [9]. Based on this the following hypothesis can be drawn:

H4: Stores that use more metrics are more profitable.

In order to answer the research questions and to test the hypotheses, a review of customer metrics in current research will be shown to give an overview of common metrics that are stated by the recent literature.

Review of Customer Metrics in Current Research

In the past, metrics were used by marketers and managers to justify spending in marketing [8]. Latest development, however, has shown that there is an increase in marketing metrics, which increment the accountability of the firm [8,9]. Nowadays, metrics can measure various facts about how a customer acts in a store, from retention of customers to clicks on specific websites e.g. see Farris et al. The next part will present four groups in which the metrics for customer performance can be divided [15].

Customer value

Current research has developed multiple metrics to measure customer value, both on individual (e.g. customer lifetime value) and aggregate level (e.g. customer equity) [8]. Customer Value is seen in this case as the perceived value that a customer has towards a product and how he contributes with that to the sales of the store [16]. This group of metrics, according to current research, can be used by marketers to measure customer selections and the outcome of marketing campaigns [8]. By using this metrics, the manager can lead marketing efforts to those customers who can appreciate and collect the message that the firm develops and delivers [9]. The result of these marketing campaigns can be analyzed and measured with customer value metrics, which can help to draw future patterns for the return on marketing (Ibid). According to Venkatesan and Kumar, there are specific demographic drivers of customer value [17]. Based on these findings, it is possible to generate strategies to allocate resources more efficiently. The calculation is also from an overall firm perspective useful since there are linkages between the value of customers and the overall value of the firm [18]. However, many metrics of this group such as Customer's Lifetime Value (CLV) are difficult to implement in a physical retail store according to Petersen et al. [8]. The importance of customer value as a system of measurement, lead to the development of specific metrics: for this study, 12 customer value metrics have been collected from current researches.

The first important metric that is possible to analyze in this group is the Customer's Lifetime Value (CLV); this metric helps to predict possible future customer patterns by analyzing previous purchasing data [17]. In order to draw such pattern through the usage of sophisticated statistical models, the marketer needs to investigate the present value of the customer such as his or her contribution margin and the cost of marketing the firm is spending in order to reach the customer (Ibid). The data collected by the marketer comes from each transaction the customer makes in a period of time which is usually not more than one month (Ibid).

A related metric to CLV is the Past Customer Value (PCV), which is used just to measure the past profit of each customer [8]. This metric is calculated based on the same information as the CLV through the customer transactions within the last month [17]. However this metric focuses on the value that the customer had in the past instead of the value over the whole lifetime which include assumptions about the future value [8,11].

More complex to measure is the Customer's Referral Value (CRV) [8]. This metric considers the number of attempts that a marketing campaign needs to be run before the customer reacts and addresses his or her behavior to the company [11]. The complexity of this metric derives from the amount of data necessary to build the statistical model and the range of time, usually between three to six months, depending on the industry (Ibid).

Based on databases, marketers can measure the Share of Wallet, focusing on how the customer spends his or her budget within the same business area. This metric can be used to calculate the share of the budget a customer spent in the store, compared to the spending's in stores of competitors. For this metric external data about the size of the wallet and competitors is needed [8]. The results can direct the firm's marketing efforts towards certain customers in order to increase their designated Share of Wallet and profitability (Ibid). Furthermore, it is stated that the share of wallet and the CLV are linked in the way that the share of wallet influences the CLV (Ibid).

A common metric, easy to recognize, is the Basket Size, which represents the quantity of products a customer buys in a single shopping session [19]. According to current research, customers with a smaller Basket Size tend to pay a higher price because they are pushed by an unplanned consumption need (Ibid). At the opposite, customers with larger basket size planned the shopping session and will stick with certain brands (Ibid). Both this opposite sizes indicate a relationship development between the customers and firm (Ibid). Customers with intermediate Basket Size seek for the lowest price which limits the development of relationships with the firm [20]. Analyzing this metric allows marketers and store managers to make certain adjustments in order to lead intermediate Basket Size customer to switch to a larger or smaller Basket Size (Ibid).

Another important metric is the Level of Price Discounts. Discounts are perceived by customers as a gain because the price they pay is less than the normal price [21]. Because of this benefit, the customer is more prone to develop a relationship and be loyal to the firm (Ibid). The level of price discount leads the customer to make a decision, whether to buy an item or more from the same firm faster because of a motivation by discounts [19].

Store managers often deal with issues like the return of items purchased by customers. This can be measured with a metric called Proportion of Returns, which shows how often a customer brings items back to the store [19]. If this number is high, it means that the quality of the product or the specifics are below standards and the level of customer satisfaction is low (Ibid). Store managers must put great efforts in order to deal with these situations because there is a threshold beneath where customers cut down the relationship with the firm (Ibid). The faster and more effective the responses are, the higher is the customer happiness which can lead to retain of loyalty and processes like positive word of mouth (Ibid).

Part of the customer value metrics analyze the level of interaction between customers and a specific firm [19]. Such metrics measure the frequency of these interactions whereby a high ratio creates a feeling of familiarity and trust (Ibid), which contributes to increase the firm's profit. The most common frequency related metric is the Purchase Frequency, used by marketers to measure how many times a customer purchases from the same store (Ibid). The higher the Purchase Frequency is, the higher is the familiarity and the possibility that the customer returns in the future to buy again (Ibid). According to Morgan and Hunt [22], a high purchase frequency produces satisfaction and trust, while other authors observed that a higher ratio of this metric leads customers to develop positive impressions and engages benefits derived from the interaction itself [23].

Communications allow firms to inform and establish interaction with the customers, for this reason the Frequency of Marketing Communication is a critical issue to measure because it is able to influence customers' choice [24]. According to Fournier [25], this metric is important in order to calculate the real range and effectiveness of the communication and the different thresholds that the message sent by the firm can reach. Upon a certain threshold, the customer perceives the communication as a way to develop a mutual beneficial relationship with the firm but when the frequency of marketing communication is too high and exceeds this threshold, the effect is the opposite (Ibid). Beyond this threshold in fact, the customer feels that the firm does not understand his or her needs but only pushing its products for profit's sake (Ibid). The right balance for this metric should be in between, where the frequency is not too low nor too high (Ibid).

When the customer purchases, he or she can decide to use different stores (offline or online), services or firms [26]. Each one of these have different characteristics that can ease the purchase and usage of a specific channel instead of others (Ibid). A critical factor when talking about mortar and bricks stores is the distance between the stores and the customer; such issue can be measured through the Travel Cost Proportion. This metric calculates the sum of all travels the customer does in order to reach a specific store (Ibid). According to Bell et al. [27], customers tend to buy in stores near their residence as a result of low travel costs. Physical distance influences the development of relationships with the customer; if a customer establish the same level of relationship with two different stores or firms, he or she will be inclined to purchase in the closest store [19]. Travel Cost Proportion is a metric that can be only used for physical stores, in fact it is not applicable for online stores which do not have to deal with this issue [19].

Another discriminating factor between offline and online stores is the Immediate Product Availability (IPA). When the purchase is made in offline stores, the customer has the possibility to consume the product right after the product was bought [27]. Such experience and interaction with the product cannot be provided by online stores because of the range of time between the process of purchasing and the collection of the item (Ibid). The proper metric to measure this factor is the IPA. This metric measures the cost related to the customer when he or she can experience the immediate consumption of the product or has to wait for a specific period of time (Ibid). The lower this proportion the shorter will be the process of adoption of a store or firm for the customer (Ibid).

The Net Promoter Score as the last metric in this group describes the ratio of promoters (someone who promotes the shop by giving positive comments to third parties) to detractors (someone who spreads critics over a certain store) of the store [8]. According to Reichheld [28], this metric can be used to calculate and analyze customer loyalty. The data can be collected by using surveys. Furthermore, it will be possible to use this metric in order to analyze competitors' customers and use them as a benchmark, if external data is available (Ibid).

Cross buying

According to Venkatesan et al. [19], cross buying is the process of purchasing products that belong to different categories during a single shopping session. Within this behavior, the customer, instead of buying different categories of products in multiple stores, prefers to make the whole purchase in the same round choosing only one store. The first important aspect of such behavior is the direct association between cross buying and customer satisfaction (Ibid). The reason for this is that the individual feels more comfortable making the purchase in one specific store (Ibid). Petersen et al. showed that cross buying consumers increase the revenue and with that the profit of the store [8]. One reason that can make the cross buying a challenge for physical stores is that it requires a more complex marketing strategy (Ibid). The combination of customer, product and message must be chosen wisely in order to get the right effects (Ibid). For the process of identifying the right customers, there are different drivers available (Ibid). Most important is, when it comes to cross buying, to target the right customers with the right products at the right time [8]. According to Kumar et al. [11], there is a difficulty when it comes to the usability and usefulness of this metrics. This is especially the case when drawing conclusions for strategies in order to increase cross buying behavior [11].

The first metric in this group is the Next Product to Buy Model (NPTB). The model is based on a forecasting equation that predicts which product a particular customer is most likely to buy at a specific time [12]. In order to perform this process, different statistical methods can be used. The most common and from various scholars advised is the logistic regression (Ibid). The reason for using this method above others is easy implementation which makes the NPTB model more easy to use [12]. Furthermore Stevens states that logistic regression is the most common used model when it comes to a violation of the normality assumption which is in consumer data often the case. In his research Knott et al. showed that the application of NPTB models help stores to generate more cross selling profits then other common heuristic methods which are not based on statistics [12]. Also if the logistic regression method is the best one, there can be other statistical models be used in order to create NPTB models (Ibid). However, according to Knott et al. [12], the statistical method that is used by the model has not a high influence on the possibility of predictions made by the model about the buying behavior of customers.

Likelihood of Purchase is another metric that can be used in order to get knowledge about the cross buying behavior of the customer [14]. In order to market a product better, it is important to be able to predict what products a customer will buy in the future (Ibid). This is often done in a probability cube where different customers or groups of customers will be shown on the y-axis (Ibid). The products or product groups will be displayed on the x-axis and the time on the z-axis (Ibid). The probabilities are estimated by the marketers (Ibid). First, which probability is there to purchase a certain product? After that the marketer has to assume a probability of when the products will be bought [14]. In order to overcome the inaccuracy of estimations of the marketer, another method was developed (Ibid). It uses the so called Bayesian estimation (Ibid). This is a mathematical and statistical method to specify the range of a weighting factor that could have produced the actual data which was collected during operating the store (Ibid). The improvement compared to the classical way is that this method uses not a single weighting factor like a traditional regression analysis (Ibid). A major problem most companies might face with this metric is, beside the complexity, that they might have a lack of enough data on all their customers to estimate relationships between drivers of purchases that are meaningful (Ibid). In addition, another problem could be that the number of data sets is just too big for computers (Ibid).

The third metric that this study wants to present in this category is the Past Purchase Frequency. With this metric the frequency of the past purchase of a customer is measured [8]. From the measurement of the frequency of the purchases of customers, the metric predicts future purchases of the customer (Ibid). The problem that current research predicts is that customers might not follow the same frequencies over time (Ibid). This holds especially for a non-contractual setting which can be found in a retail business to consumer market (Ibid).

The Inter Purchase Time can be seen as an improvement of the Past Purchase Frequency [17]. This metric measures the time between purchases of a customer. Base for this are data sets from the past which were collected while operating a particular store. To analyze the data, the model uses a generalized gamma distribution [8]. The assumption on which this method is based is that a customer is likely to reduce the frequency of purchase before ending a relationship [29].

The last metric of this group is the Likelihood of Staying Active (LSA). As input variables it uses the time of purchases and the total number of purchases of a particular customer [30].

$$\text{LSA} = \left(\frac{\text{Average Inter Purchase Time}}{\Delta t} \right)^{\text{Number of Total Purchases}} \quad (1)$$

Delta t is the period of time between the first purchase of a customer and the current purchase.

The higher the number, the higher is the likelihood of staying active. This measure was introduced by Schmittlein et al. and used later by Kumar et al. [30,31]. Past research has shown that the likelihood of staying active increases with the channels that a customer uses for transactions [30].

Customer acquisition

It is crucial for the success of marketing that there is a high Customer Retention and a constant acquisition of new customers [8]. This leads to the need of measuring Customer Acquisition and retention (Ibid). It is important to not decide about acquiring customers in an isolated way [32]. According to Thomas [32], retention and acquiring are linked so that a focus on only one of them would lead to not long lasting customers. The goal should also in this case be to increase the CLV (Ibid). Reinartz et al. shows that the likelihood of acquiring new customers, relationship duration and profitability of the customer are linked [13]. However, it is therefore important to have trade-offs between acquisition, retention and profitability in order to maximize the profitability of the firm (Ibid). Verhoef mentions that direct marketing campaigns and/or loyalty programs can increase the purchase behavior of customers [33].

The first metric is the Cost of Acquisition. This metric shows the cost for acquiring a new customer [8]. The measure gives the manager or marketer a guidance which customers should be acquired and which not (Ibid). Previous research has shown that it is not the best to just focus on acquiring the least expensive customers [13]. Profitable customers can be expensive to acquire (Ibid). Therefore this metric should not be used alone since it would not lead to more value creation. It leads just to a reduction of the cost of acquisition (Ibid).

In the same context the metric Cost of Retention can be recalled. This metric describes the cost related to customer retention [8]. Also, this metric needs to be combined with others. Otherwise it leads to the same problems, as stated before, for the cost of acquisition (Ibid).

The next two metrics focus, instead of the cost, on the profit. The first metric is the Acquisition Profit. This metric shows the profit gained through the acquisition of a new customer [8]. Also this metric should be not maximized in isolation. Managers need to focus both on acquisition and retention [13].

The Retention Profit describes the profits gained through the retention of a customer [8]. The same points as for the acquisition profit are for this metric important (Ibid).

The last measure in this group is the Product Return Rate. This metric calculates the number of purchased products that are returned by the customer [8]. Product returns are according to Petersen et al. also key drivers of the CLV. The return of products gets often interpreted in a negative way and has an impact on customer value [34]. However, current research has shown that customers who return 5-10 % of their total purchases, are willing to purchase more in the future [8].

Transaction with customers

This group of transaction-related metrics is the most applied on store level [8]. All metrics of this group are combinable in a model that describes how the metrics influence each other (Ibid). An investigation from Schlesinger showed that conversion percentage and units purchased per transaction are important to monitor [35]. The end result of Schlesinger's study was that these two metrics could be tied directly to future total store sales (Ibid) [35].

The Sales figure is a traditional number from accounting which can also be used to classify customers [35]. This figure fits also to the model developed by Atkinson where he stated that stores need to look at the connections between orders, revenue and visits and should not just focus on one of them [36]. However, sales are a highly aggregated figure so that the user does not get so much detailed insights.

Number of Transactions counts the numbers of transactions in a store [8]. Which can also give an overview of how successful the store is (Ibid). This can directly linked to sales according to the model presented by Schlesinger [35].

Traffic describes the number of visitors of the store in a particular time frame [8]. The next metric that needs to be mentioned is the Conversion Rate. This metric shows in percentage how many of the shopping people actually buy in the store [8]. A problem that occurs when just focusing on this figure is that managers could miss to look on average order size [36]. Just focusing on the Conversion Rate can also mean that the score rises and implies a good development (Ibid). This could be a deception because the value of the metric will also rise, if more shoppers buy but just for a low value [8].

The Average Order Size describes the average value of an order in a store [36]. The metric is the sum of the value of all products that were bought at an average transaction [8,36]. It is hereby important to see the metric in combination with the conversion rate [36].

The metric Average Units per Transaction shows the average number of purchased goods per transaction in the store. Current research has found out that this metric and also the conversion rate correlate strongly with future store sales [8]. According to Schlesinger, average units per transaction should be also a key metric in brick and mortar stores [35].

The Average Unit Price is defined as the price that a purchased good in a store costs in average [8].

To the model of Schlesinger [35], the metric Revenue per Visit can be added. This metric is, according to Petersen et al. [9], the average revenue per visit of a shopper in the store. The metric is also linked to the framework of Atkinson and represents a mixture of conversion rate, number of transactions and sales. However, it is not included in the original framework [36].

Conceptual framework

The following section presents the established framework based on the literature presented in the literature review. This framework contains the four groups of metrics that were used to structure the literature review. Each group contains various metrics that deliver specific information to the manager in order to track and measure the performance of the customer in the store. When looking at customers in a physical retail stores, different metrics can be measured in order to understand how they act in the store [8]. The business needs to understand all four groups of metrics in order to have a complete picture of the customer (Ibid). A full perception of these groups allows managers to gather the appropriate information combining metrics from different groups (Ibid). Because of this, stores have to perform in all metrics to be profitable (Ibid).

Stores need to acquire customers and retain those [13]. This leads to a stable customer base that is necessary for the future success of the store. Transactions with the customers are important since they lead to sales which are the basis for profit. Based on the transactions, the store can detect which customers contribute more to the overall sales and to the profit. Cross buying customers are, according to current research, more profitable than those who do not. Therefore, stores are advised to make the customer to cross buy and/or attract customers who are willing to cross buy. Finally, these actions of the customer and the company have to result in high customer value. This previous metrics have also an influence on the value that a customer has for the firm. With customer value metrics the store manager can measure the value and is able to direct its marketing activity better to the right customers. The following table presents the summary of the metric groups, these contain as well as the related literature and the core concepts of the group (Table 1).

This conceptual framework summarizes the main concepts stated by current research. It will further be used together with the method in order to analyze the results of the survey.

Method

Selection of method and data collection

As Shankar et al. state, it is important to find standardized metrics that measure customer performance in physical stores in the same manner as online stores [7]. Thus, this study aims to explore through current research which metrics, from a theoretical point of view, can be considered as useful and further to understand how such metrics are applied in physical retail stores.

The theoretical concepts about consumer metrics used in this study were collected and have been connected with each other within the literature review. The goal hereby was to see what current research has studied in connection to the research topic. The chosen concepts have been selected by reading scientific articles found in the data bases like Google Scholar, Web of Science, Elsevier. The keywords used to search such articles were: metric, marketing, customer, consumer,

Group	Contained metrics	Core concept	Complexity	Sources
Customer Value	CLV, PVC, CRV, Share of Wallet, Basket Size, Level of Price Discounts, Proportion of Returns, Purchase Frequency, Frequency of Marketing Communication, Travel Cost, Immediate Product Availability, Net Promoter Score	Measuring of Customer Value on individual and aggregate level. Future patterns for the return of marketing can be drawn.	Complex	(Petersen et al., [8]) Venkatesan and Kumar, [17]) Grupta et al., 2004)
Cross Buying	NPTB model, Likelihood of Purchase, Past Purchase Frequency, Inter Purchase Time, LSA	Process of purchasing of products from different categories in one shopping session. Cross buying customers are more profitable, however it requires a complex marketing strategy.	Complex	(Venkatesan et al., [19]) Petersen et al., [8]) Knott et al., [12]) Kumar et al., [14])
Acquisition	Cost of Acquisition, Cost of Retention, Retention Profit, Acquisition Profit, Product Return Rate,	Customer Retention and Acquisition is important to have stable profits. Trade-off between acquisition and retention are needed in order to increase profit of the firm.	Not complex	(Petersen et al., [8]) Tomas, 2001) Reinarz et al., 2005) Verhoef, [33])
Transaction	Conversion Rate, Average Purchase per Transaction, Traffic, Average Unit Price, Number of Transactions, Average Order Size, Sales, Revenue per Visit	These metrics are mostly at store level applied. Schlesinger's research (2008) shows that these metrics have a direct connection to future sales.	Not complex	(Schlesinger, [35]) Petersen et al., [8]) Atkinson, [36])

Table 1: Framework based on the literature review (own illustration).

measurement, tracking, KPI, performance, store, retail. All these keywords were used in a separate and conjoint way in order to get more results from the search.

A quantitative survey has been designed in order to collect the data (see appendix 2). In order to answer the research questions and to test the hypotheses in this study, the method of a quantitative survey is seen as more fitting then a case study since the chosen method allows it to generalize and gives an overview on how methods are used in a variety of physical retail stores [37]. The possibility of getting deep into a specific case contributed not to the answering of the research questions.

For a more efficient collection, the survey had two versions: an online version sent via email or through LinkedIn and an offline variant, where the authors met the managers inside the stores which contributes to 83% of the collected data and was the main channel of data collection [37]. All in all 61 data sets were collected from the on- and offline survey. Thus, through these tools the data was collected within two weeks. This section presents the method behind this process of data collection.

The survey had the goal to collect primary data about how companies deal with metrics for measuring customer performance in physical retail stores. Primary data is according to Stevens et al. data that was collected for the first time [38]. This data was collected specifically for the project in order to have a strong matching between the purpose, theoretical framework and the data of the study.

Choice of scale: When deciding which scale suited the research best, it was important to make sure that both the respondents and the researchers have no difficulties in interpreting the scale and the result of the survey. Zander stated further that a scale with the options "sometimes", "often", etc. can lead to misunderstandings when asking people with different cultural- or knowledge backgrounds [39]. Therefore this study used the Likert Scale, when it comes to a differentiated statement for example "How useful are transaction metrics?" [37]. For other questions like "Do you know transaction metrics?" the options for the answers were given in a binary form with "Yes" and "No" (Ibid). This made the statements clear and with only these two options the respondent needed to decide (Ibid). In order to keep the answers of the study more structured the answers for the fix measurements were also given (e.g. industry, profit margin).

Development of the Questionnaire: The survey consisted of 27 questions. Seven of these were fixed questions to classify the store and the owner/manager. The survey had in total 61 respondents. Table 2 shows the questions used in the survey and the connection to the theories as well as the answer options.

Simplicity and clearness are the factors that were chosen for the development of the questionnaire in order to make it easy for the respondents to understand the questions. For this reason, the survey was divided in sections for each group of metrics, providing a short description on what kind of metrics are included. This partition in groups is important in order to limit confusion or possible misunderstandings. This led to multiple "yes" and "no" questions instead of one question that asks for the used metric group. Based on this structure, it was easy for the respondent to recognize and focus on different groups for which they might have knowledge under different terminology. The structure of the questionnaire by metric group made it possible for the respondents to focus on one metric group by answering the related question and to ask if there was a lack in knowledge about this metric group and the contained metrics.

The questions were developed after constructing the theoretical framework for this thesis. Hereby it was important to collect information that helped to answer the research questions. The questions asked for information regarding the classification of the company (fix measurement), how store managers use metrics and how they see it in the future, as well as to the profitability of the store, this is illustrated in Figure 1.

At the end of the questionnaire, seven questions for fix measurement about the store and the manager were asked. Asking personal questions at the end is according to Fisher the best way to get the respondent answering all asked questions [40]. This is especially crucial for getting as much complete responses as possible when conducting an online survey. The questions can with that be divided into three groups that are presented in the following figure and that structure the analysis. The data for the group “Using metrics” was collected for each of the metric groups (e.g. Customer Value, Cross Buying, etc.)

Operationalization: The operationalization shows the asked questions and the connection of these to the theory to get an understanding why this questions were asked and how the answers will be connected to the theory when it comes to the analysis. Furtherm-ore the options for answers are shown in the table below (Table 2).

Distribution of the Questionnaire: In order to embrace a wide share of brick and mortar stores, the questionnaires were delivered in two ways. The most efficient way, in terms of number of answers, was to visit the stores and ask for the store manager to answer the

Theory	Questions	Answer Options
Customer value metrics	Do you know metrics to calculate customer value?	Yes or No
	Do you use metrics to calculate customer value?	Yes or No
	How useful are metrics for customer value?	Scale from 1 "Not useful" to 5 "very useful"
	How do you see the usability of this metrics?	Scale from 1 "Very difficult" to 5 "Very easy"
	Would you consider to use customer value metrics in the future?	Yes or No
Cross Buying metrics	Do you know metrics to measure cross buying behavior?	Yes or No
	Do you use metrics to calculate cross buying behavior?	Yes or No
	How useful are metrics for cross buying behavior?	Scale from 1 "Not useful" to 5 "very useful"
	How do you see the usability of this metrics?	Scale from 1 "Very difficult" to 5 "Very easy"
	Would you consider to use cross buying metrics in the future?	Yes or No
Customer acquisition metrics	Do you know metrics to measure acquisition?	Yes or No
	Do you use metrics to calculate acquisition?	Yes or No
	How useful are metrics for acquisition?	Scale from 1 "Not useful" to 5 "very useful"
	How do you see the usability of this metrics?	Scale from 1 "Very difficult" to 5 "Very easy"
	Would you consider to use acquisition metrics in the future?	Yes or No
Customer transaction metrics	Do you know metrics to measure transactions?	Yes or No
	Do you use metrics to calculate transactions?	Yes or No
	How useful are metrics for transactions?	Scale from 1 "Not useful" to 5 "very useful"
	How do you see the usability of this metrics?	Scale from 1 "Very difficult" to 5 "Very easy"
	Would you consider to use transactions metrics in the future?	Yes or No
Fix measure	Level of education	University; High School; Non academic
	Relevant work experience	Open Answer
	Profitability of store	Open answer
	Country	Open answer
	Type of business	Franchise; Retail chain; Independent store
	Type of Industry	Beauty care; Books; Electronics; Fashion; Food; Furniture; Jewelry; Others; Pharmacy; Shoes; Sport
	Usage of IT systems (e.g. ERP, CRM)	Yes or No

Table 2: Operationalization of questionnaire.

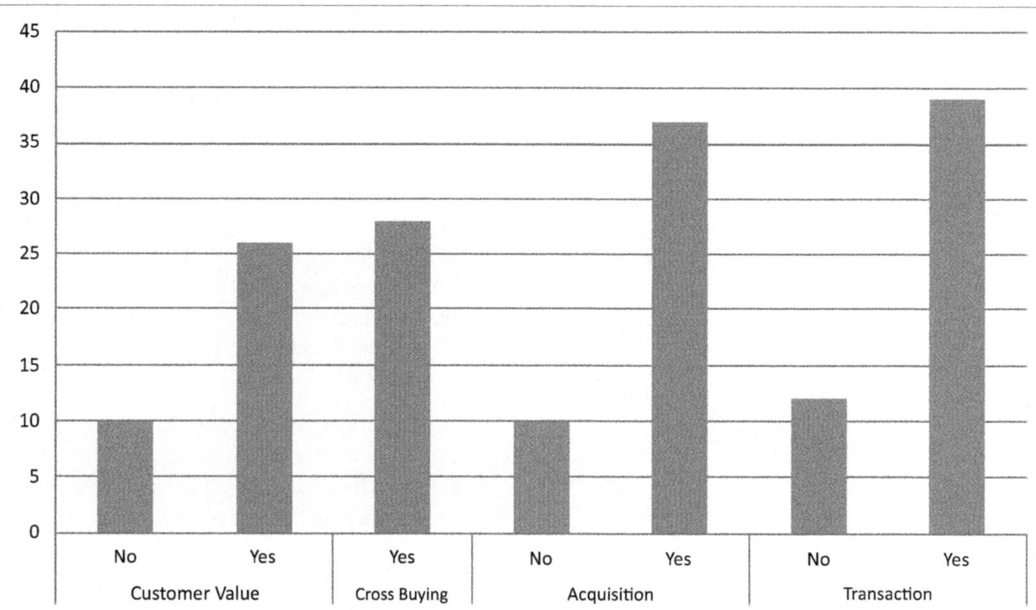

Figure 1: Usage of metrics at stores with or without IT system.

questionnaire. In some stores, where the manager was not present, a letter was sent to the manager in order to inform him about the research and to ask if there is the possibility to get the questions answered. (See the information letter and flyer in appendix 1.) When asking the questions, the groups of metrics were presented by using examples, this was also explained in the online version. If questions regarding the understandability arose during the questioning process, these questions were clarified by explaining which metrics are in the groups or not.

Aside from personal handling, the collection of data was made through an online survey, designed with the same questions [37]. This design is shown in appendix 2. The link to the online form was provided to the managers by email or within a letter using a QR code. Furthermore, the link was shared through private store managers groups at the platforms LinkedIn and Google+, with permission of the group managers.

The main part of the responses (83%) came from the personal visiting of the stores. Only 17% of the responses came from the online survey tool. The stores in this survey were chosen randomly due to the time limit. However, all stores that participated in this survey fulfilled the criteria that they were physical and retail stores. The criteria to choose the respondents were limited in order to get a variety of different retail stores and with that be able to see patterns in the data that could state something about what influences the way metrics are used. This variety of physical retail stores helped to explore the reasons for using metrics and hence the development of concepts and constructs in this study.

Analysis method

Statistical techniques: The correlation analysis aims to measure the correlation between variables by using the Spearman's rank correlation, for which, normality cannot be assumed [41]. Furthermore, this method focuses on the relative difference between specific metrics and business groups. In this study, the correlation analysis was used to check whether there is a correlation between the profitability and the usage of specific metric groups. In addition, the respondents with no knowledge about the metrics were not included into this part of the analysis:.

In order to get more insights in how stores use metrics, the technique of regression analysis was applied and profitability became the dependent variable [41]. This method was chosen to gain a deeper knowledge for whether there is significance between an independent variable and the profitability. Thus, the beta value out of this analysis can give then additional information on how high is the impact: the higher the number, the higher the impact. Furthermore, the regression analysis in SPSS created an analysis of variance (ANOVA) table that gave information regarding the significance by presenting the p-value for each regression test. With this information it was possible to evaluate whether the regression model is useful in order to predict the relationship between the independent variables and the dependent variable.

The third major analysis in this paper was done by using the Wilcoxon-Signed-Rank-Test [41]. It was chosen in order to analyze the answers about the usefulness and usability. The data in this case is ordinal, which is not possible to analyze with higher statistical methods like regression, thus, this non-parametric test was chosen. The test itself compares the respondent's answers, contrasting each time two variables and with that analyzing two metric groups at the same time. This resulted in a total of six comparisons for the four metric groups, comparing each variable. Once the analysis was done it was possible to rank the metric groups based on the individual usefulness and values of usability of the respondents.

Furthermore, the results of the survey were also graphically presented, using descriptive statistical analysis (see for a list of descriptive statistics Argyrous) [41]. These methods were used mainly to show relationships between the fix measures and the way stores evaluate the different metric groups. An overview of the factors that influence the implementation of the metrics can be seen in the analysis.

Reliability, Validity and Generalization: Reliability of the questionnaire depends on whether the study can be reproduced and repeated several times [37]. The method used for this study is quantitative; therefore it is crucial to think about reliability. Thus, in order to get high reliability it is necessary that tools and techniques used to gather the data ensure the possibility of repeating the research. According to Bryman and Bell, a study can be considered reliable when future researches result into similar outcome using a comparable process [37].

To get accurate information; only specific stores were targeted for this survey. The stores needed to be physical and needed to have retail operations. Furthermore, the survey was addressed only to owners and/or managers of the store in order to get reliable information about the metrics used by the store. Alongside, an online version of the survey (Google forms) was delivered, allowing to answer the questions freely and accurately. Through this process it was possible to ensure that the gathered data was reliable. Afterwards, the collected data was elaborated in excel files and further with SPSS system in order to apply statistical analysis. The statistical tools used to analyze this study are presented in the heading before.

Validity is also important for the sake of the study and it can be achieved by using theories and concepts in the questionnaire [37]. This was achieved by designing the survey along the literature review. Terms like customer value, cross-buying or transaction metrics were mentioned in the questionnaire and the theories were incorporated to answer the research question. The cause and effect relation, on which this study is based, was tested by using the statistical software SPSS from IBM. This cause and effect relationships are according to Fisher a way to reflect internal validity [40].

The range for which the result of this study is included can be generalized because such range depends on the sample size. In the correlation analysis the result had a meaningful difference to support the hypothesis. Also, the significance in the regression analysis was high enough with the given sample size to draw a meaningful conclusions out of the collected data [42-45].

Limitations

The first point that limits the following analysis is that the data was collected by a survey. The researchers were willing to keep the influence as low as possible to get answers that are representing the truth and are not influenced by third parties. However, it might be the case that for example the answers regarding the profitability might vary a bit from the true numbers because the managers wanted to make their store look more profitable.

Furthermore, due to a limited time frame that was given to conducting this research, the number of surveyed store is 61 respondents is limited which might result in slightly different results in future research. Also the type of industry that was surveyed might have an impact on the outcome of the study. In this case the fashion industry makes 41% of the responses followed by other with 26% and on third place electronic stores with ca. 8% of responses.

Results and Analysis

The analysis shows the empirical data on customer performance metrics based on the 61 collected data sets. The analysis gives a descriptive overview of the results and factors that influence the usage of metrics. After that it presents the connection between the usefulness and usability of metrics and the profitability. The second in depth look will be on the fact whether there is an individual preference of metrics. The last in-depth analysis will focus on the question whether there is a correlation between the profitability of the store and the usage of metrics. The analysis will focus at relations between the data of the three groups presented in Figure 1 above. First it will look at the relations between the fix measures and whether they have an effect on how metrics are used and implemented (the second group). After that the analysis looks on whether there is a relationship between the usage of metrics in stores and the performance of the store which was measured by using the profit margin.

Circumstances that effect the implementation of metrics

The first factor that influences whether a store uses a metric group or not is the type of business which can be an independent store or a store that belongs to a retail chain (Figure 2).

In combination with the following table it can be seen that stores that belong to a retail chain use much more often metrics than independent stores. Circa 75% of the stores that belong to retail chains use metrics but only ca. 50% of the independent stores use metrics. This fact verifies the hypothesis H2 that stated that stores belonging to a retail chain might use more metrics then independent stores (Table 3).

This fact can be due to the complexity of metrics and with-the requirements in special educated personal and IT systems. This can be seen in the next figure where the usage of metrics divided by the metric group and the implementation of an IT system, for example an Enterprise Resource Planning (ERP) system or a Customer Relationship Management (CRM) system, is shown. The y-axis shows the number of stores that use the metric group. The figure presents only the respondents that use the specific metric and splits the answers up in using an IT system and not using an IT system (Figure 1).

The stores with an IT system are over all metrics groups more likely to use metrics. Often the data collection of metrics and the later analysis requires information technology to handle the big amount of data as it is especially for the cross buying metrics the case (e.g. Likelihood of Purchase) were only stores with an complex IT system use the metrics. Stores that are member of a retail chain also rank higher in the usefulness of metrics.

Furthermore, analysis shows that an education with a more theoretical base (High School and University) has an influence in the way how useful store managers see metrics. The results are in average 34% higher as with a non-academic (e.g. training on the job) background. This is backed up by the fact that ca. 80% of the managers form stores that belong to a retail chain have a university degree or at least a high school diploma. At the independent stores only slightly above 60% of the asked managers have a high school diploma or a university education. Connected to this analysis part is the first hypothesis that stated:

H1: There might be a difference in the usage of metrics depending on the education

Analysis has shown that there is a difference in the usage of metrics depending (on) the variables education and the usage or IT systems like ERP or CRM systems. It turned out that stores with more educated personnel (high school or university degree) used more metric groups then stores where the personal only had a non-academic education like training on the job. The following figure shows the average scores for the usefulness by independent stores and retail chains (Figure 3).

They gave on average a score of 4.35 and this is ca. 17% higher as the average value of 3.73 that were given by the independent stores over all metric groups. The reason for this is that stores that belong to a retail chain have better IT systems which can be seen in the following figure about the implementation of ERP and similar systems. This allows the stores to calculate complex metrics which increases the view on the usefulness of the metrics by the store manager. Furthermore, this requires more educated personal to run the system as well as to interpret the results (Figure 4).

The second factor that influences this result is the way that education of the personal is required in order to gain knowledge out of more complex metrics. The usage of metrics, moreover, is affected by the degree of implementation of the IT system. As a result, stores with such a system tend to use significantly more metric groups then those who did not. This influence between the usage of metric groups and the implementation of IT systems leads to the next hypothesis:

H2: Stores that belong to a retail chain use more metrics.

This hypothesis was confirmed by the analysis as shown above in Figure 3. The data shows that stores belonging to a retail chain tend to

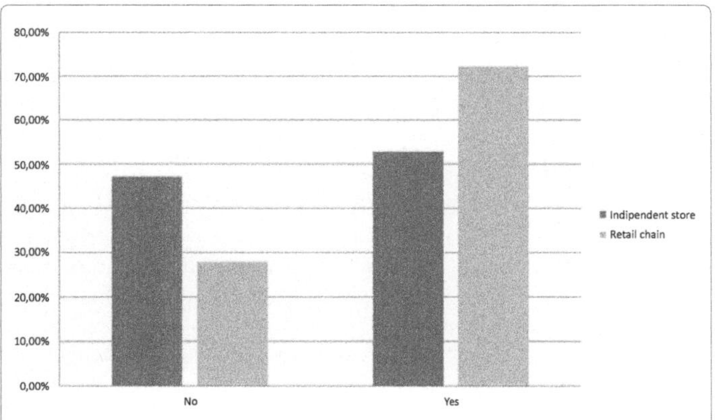

Figure 2: Usage of metrics by business type.

Usage of metrics per store type			
	Independent store	Retail chain	Grand Total
No	47.22%	27.91%	33.61%
Yes	52.78%	72.09%	66.39%
Grand Total	100.00%	100.00%	100.00%

Table 3: Usage of metrics per business type.

Figure 3: Score of usefulness divided by business type.

use more metrics rather than independent stores. A possible reason to explain such trend can be connected to the previous hypothesis (H1), where education and data complexity are possible discriminant factors that limit the usage of metrics. Observing the degree of usability and usefulness reported within the survey, it is possible to draw a regular pattern where store managers tend to understand and use more simple metrics above those which are considered to be more complex and require a deeper knowledge.

Before analyzing the relationship between the usage of metrics and the profitability of the store, it can be useful to see whether there is an individual preference of metrics so that a ranking of metrics can be created. When looking at the ranking of the metrics depending on the evaluation of the usefulness of the metrics, the analysis shows these results (Table 4).

The result of this analysis shows that Acquisition metrics and Transaction metrics score always above the Cross Buying and Customer Value metrics. A ranking of the metrics can be created based on whether the group scores above all other with the positive ranks or not. For the usefulness this results in the following ranking of the metrics were Cross Buying and Customer Value are at the same rank (Table 5).

This shows that Transaction and Acquisition metrics are the once who get according to the data on individual basis the highest scores in usefulness. One reason for this can be that, as current research showed, these are the metrics that are easy to understand and also most widely used in practice. Thus, the results support prior research.

When looking at the usability, the results of the Wilcoxon test looked like follows (Table 6).

When comparing the pairs of metric groups presented in Table 6 and how they rank against each other, this results in the following ranking of the metric groups. The metric group that scores above

Figure 4: Implementation of an IT system by business type.

all other in the pair comparisons is on rank one (in this case the Transaction metrics) (Table 7).

Also, in this ranking the metric groups that are based on current research are easy to understand rank higher in usability then the more difficult groups [8]. This can be explained by the fact that the metrics from these groups are easier to measure. Transaction metrics are for example to a high grade measurable based on the information collected by the cashier register. Interesting is that cross buying scores are at the last position which can be due to the reason that the metrics out of this group are the most complex once. The view on this individual preference shows that the hypothesis H3a can be verified:

H3a: The individual preferences of the usefulness of metrics go in hand with the usability.

This hypothesis H3a can be verified since data showed that for both the usefulness and the usability, Transaction and Acquisition metrics ranked first and second based on an individual preference.

Contribution of metric groups to the profitability of the store

The graphical analysis has shown that the profitability is in average higher for those stores who valued the usefulness and the usability higher compared to those stores who saw not so much usefulness. In the two following figures the colors indicate the usability and usefulness score given by the managers. A darker color was given for a low score (1) of usability and usefulness, while a lighter colors expresses a high score (5). The x-axis describes the average profitability of the stores that gave the scores (Figures 5 and 6).

This correlation shown in the last two figures, which describes the average profitability for each metric group divided by the score given for usefulness and usability, lead to the estimation that the profitability of the store can be explained by the view of usefulness of the metrics. Based on that the data was used to prove how the observed data looks in relation to the linear model of regression between the usefulness as independent variable and the profitability as dependent variable. This was done for all metrics and is presented in the following Table 8.

The plots presents that the average of the observed value lies close to the linear function. However the scattering of the data is huge. The correlation analysis shows that there is a non-random association between the variables profitability and the value of usefulness of the different metric groups. In order to quantify how strong the relationship between the variables is, the R Square needs to be taken into consideration. In this case the R Square indicates that 17% (Transaction) up to 42% (Cross Buying) of its variation is accountable for the relationship with one another. With looking on the ANOVA (F, df1, df2, and Significance) it has to be evaluated whether the regression model is better in predicting value then using the mean of the values. Most interesting for this is the Significance, presented as the p-value. It ranges in this case from <0,001 (Customer Value, Cross Buying, Acquisition) to 0,001 (Transaction) and shows the probability of

Pairs	Negative Ranks	Positive Ranks	Difference
Usefulness_Acquisition-Usefulness_Cross_Buying	13	18	5
Usefulness_Acquisition-Usefulness_Customer_Value	12	17	5
Usefulness_Cross_Busing-Usefulness_Customer_Value	16	16	0
Usefulness_Transaction-Usefulness_Acquisition	12	15	3
Usefulness_Transaction-Usefulness_Cross_Buying	8	20	12
Usefulness_Transaction-Usefulness_Customer_Value	7	19	12
Grand Total	68	105	37

Table 4: Result Wilcoxon signed rank test usefulness.

Usefulness ranking	
Transaction	#1
Acquisition	#2
Customer Value	#3
Cross Buying	#4

Table 5: Ranking of metric groups based on usefulness value.

Pairs	Negative Ranks	Positive Ranks	Difference
Usability_Acquisition-Usability_Cross_Buying	13	16	3
Usability_Acquisition-Usability_Customer_Value	13	21	8
Usability_Cross_Busing-Usability_Customer_Value	16	14	-2
Usability_Transaction-Usability_Acquisition	4	21	17
Usability_Transaction-Usability_Cross_Buying	4	27	23
Usability_Transaction-Usability_Customer_Value	3	26	23
Grand Total	**53**	**125**	**72**

Table 6: Result Wilcoxon signed rank test usability.

Usability ranking	
Transaction	#1
Acquisition	#2
Customer Value	#3
Cross Buying	#4

Table 7: Ranking of metric groups based on usability.

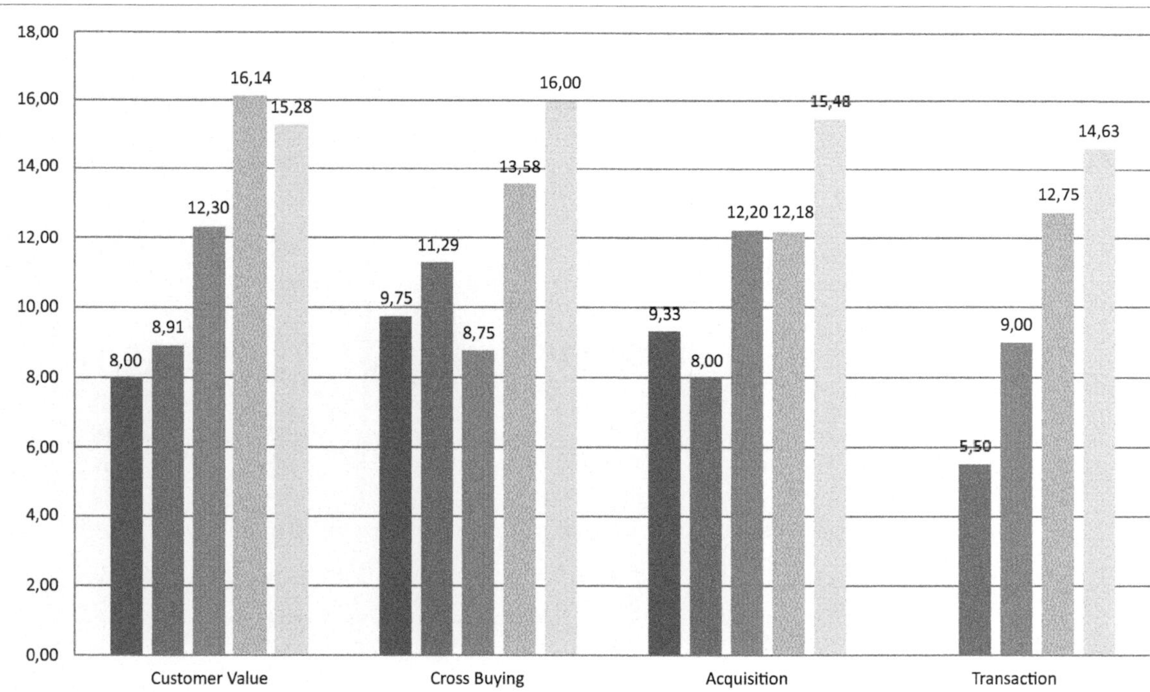

Figure 5: Average profit by usability of metric groups.

getting the F value. In this case it is lower than 0,05 so it indicates that the regression line is significant better than the prediction of values by using the mean. The value of the beta (b1) describes the slope of the regression line. It turns out that an increase of 1 value in how the usefulness is seen, relates to an increase of 1,8 (Customer Value) to 3,1 (Cross Buying) percent points in profitability (Figure 7).

The reason for this might be that also stores, who do not use the metrics, still see the usefulness as high. The results of this analysis come close to the answer of the first research question. Beside the usefulness, the usability is a critical factor. This determines how stores evaluate the possibility of using metrics to track consumers. A lack in knowledge and or in technology might be factors that lead to low ranks in the usability of metric groups. In the usability it can be seen that there are the same patterns like with the answers for the usefulness (Table 9).

The profitability is in average higher at those stores who saw the usability as more easy (higher rank). By looking at the R square value for the usability of the metric groups as independent variable, it can be seen that 17% (Acquisition) to 23% (Customer Value) are accountable for the shown relationship between the usability of specific metric groups and the profitability of the store. Looking at the ANOVA, the

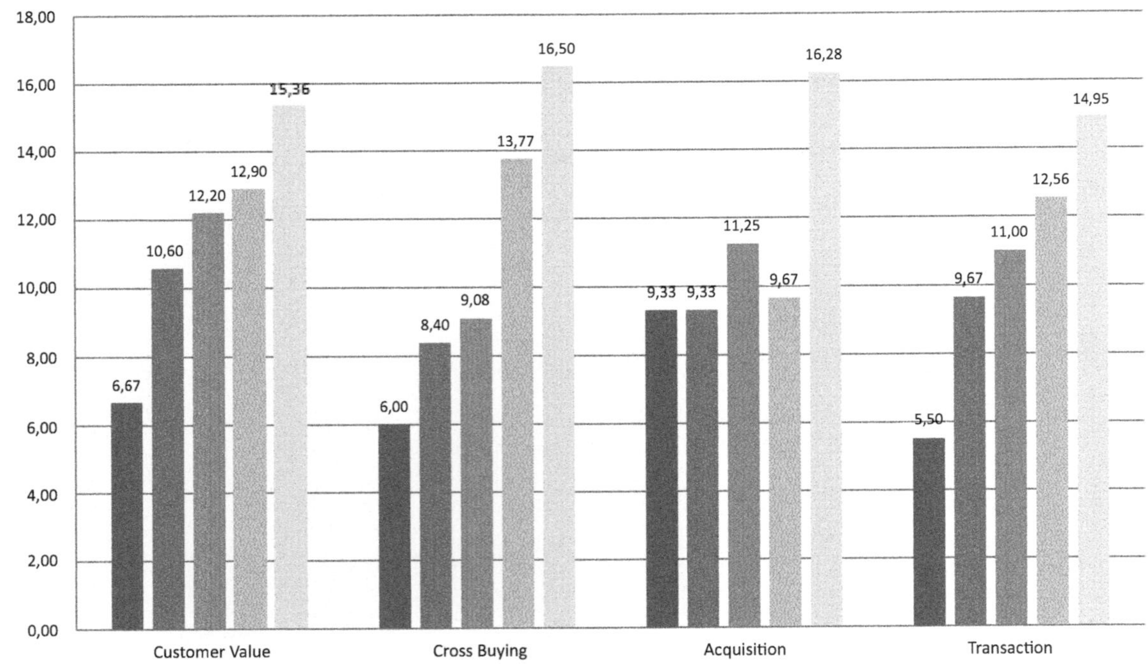

Figure 6: Average profitability by usefulness of metric groups.

	Equation	R Square	Model Summary			Parameter Estimates		
			F	dfl	df2	Sig.	Constant	bl
Customer Value	Linear	0.191	13.914	1	59	0.000	6.170	1.833
Cross Buying	Linear	0.418	42.337	1	59	0.000	1.139	3.058
Acquisition	Linear	0.261	20.826	1	59	0.000	5.435	1.982
Transaction	Linear	0.171	12.199	1	59	0.001	4.333	2.115

Table 8: Model summary and parameter estimates usefulness/profitability.

	Equation	R Square	Model Summary			Parameter Estimates		
			F	dfl	df2	Sig.	Constant	bl
Customer Value	Linear	0.233	17.919	1	59	0.000	5.839	1.970
Cross Buying	Linear	0.223	16.966	1	59	0.000	6.295	1.863
Acquisition	Linear	0.169	12.001	1	59	0.001	7.033	1.627
Transaction	Linear	0.180	12.943	1	59	0.001	0.776	2.789

Table 9: Model summary and parameter estimates usability/profitability.

significance is between <0,001 (Customer Value and Cross Buying) up to 0,001 (Acquisition and Transaction) with that it can be said that also in this case, the regression model is significant better in predicting values than the mean. The amount of increase in percentage points of the profitability that is explained by the increase of valuing the usability higher or lower ranges from 1,6 (Acquisition) to 2,8 (Transaction) (Figure 8).

To conclude, this regression analysis part it is important to clarify that these kind of relations represent a piece of the complete picture and that there is a difference in correlation and causation also if the significance is high (p<0,05). This leads to the verification of the hypothesis H3b:

H3b: Profitable stores rank the usability and the usefulness higher.

For all metric groups there was a correlation between the usability/usefulness and the profitability. In all cases the linear regression model was a better fit to explain the relation then the calculation of the mean that already indicated a correlation. A critical point could be that the fact that more profitable stores have a more complex structure and defined reporting if they are part of a retail chain so that the managers have to collect more data so that the reason for the increase in profitability is not only the different view on the usefulness and usability. This could lead to future research.

	Profit class			
Average number of used metric groups	0-5%	6-10%	11-15%	16+%
	1.75	2.08	2.88	3.21

Table 10: Used metric groups by profitability class.

With the view on the usage of metrics based on profit classes, the Hypothesis H4 can be verified. Stores who are more profitable use in average more metrics then those who are not so profitable (Table 10).

This leads already to the answer of the research question RQ2, where it was questioned if stores which use metrics are more profitable.

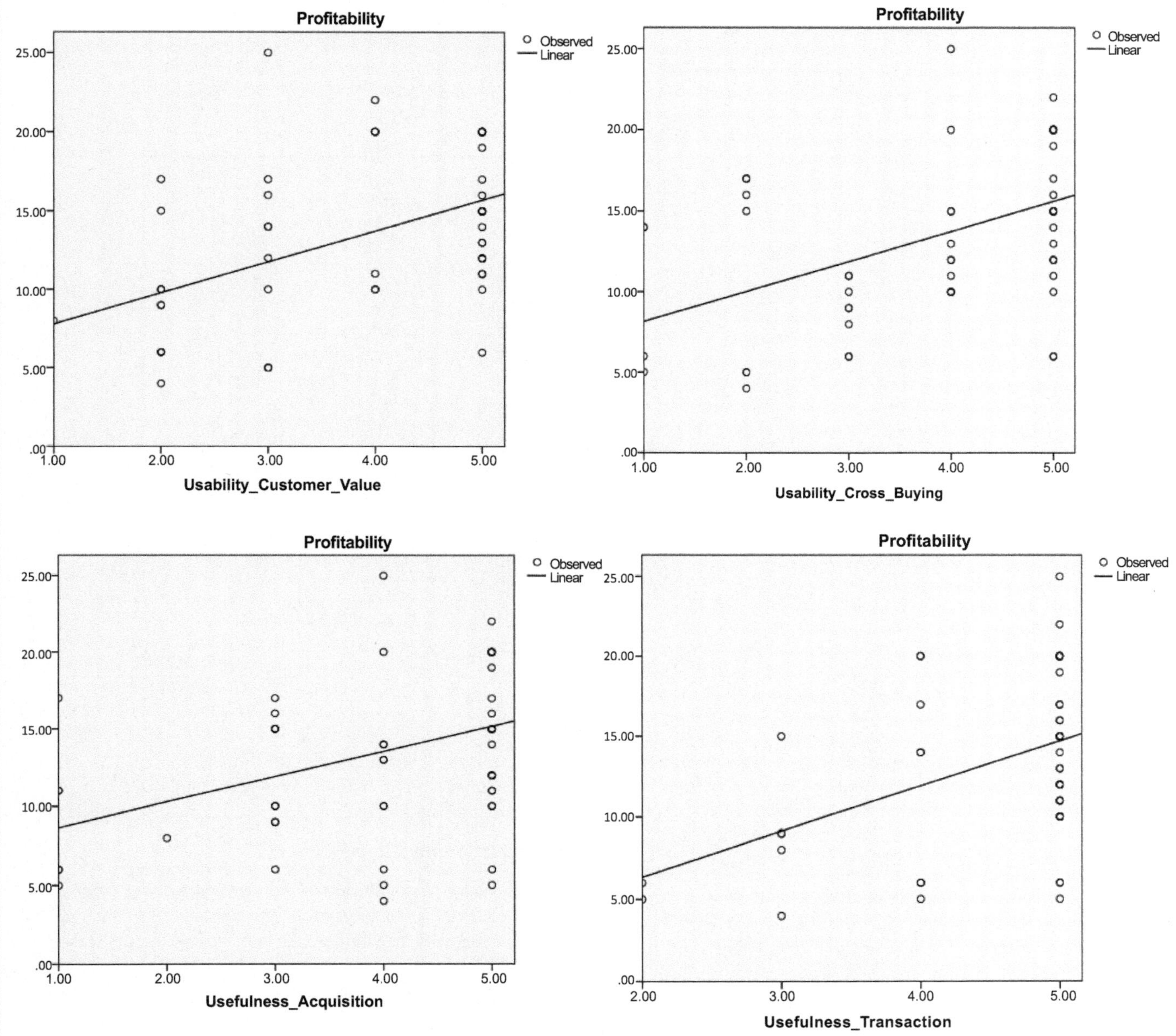

Figure 7: Plots of linear regression: usefulness/profitability for each metric group.

And hypothesis H4 can be verified:

H4: Stores that use more metrics are more profitable.

The analysis has shown that stores in the lowest profit class (0-5% profit margin) tend to use 1.75 metric groups in average compared to stores from the highest group (16+% profit margin) who used 3.21 metrics in average.

In order to answer the research question RQ2 that asked whether stores that use metrics to track customers are more profitable, a correlation analysis was performed. The result is shown in the next figure (Figure 8).

The result shows clearly that there is a correlation between the usage of metrics and the profitability of the store the analysis showed an increase in the profitability of stores who use metrics compared to the once who did not used the metrics of specific groups. This holds for all of the four metric groups. Furthermore, it can be seen that there is the biggest difference between using Cross Buying metrics or not. The increase in profitability is above 5%, whereby the usage of transaction metrics does not affect the profitability of the store so much. This indicated that Cross Buying metrics have a bigger impact on the profitability and with that gives that store managers more insights in order to run the store more profitable.

Conclusions

This study aimed to investigate the usage of metrics to track customer performance in physical retail stores. The initial literature review provides an overview of metrics that are, based on current research, the main metrics that can be used to track customers in physical retail stores. The metrics were divided into four groups: Customer Value,

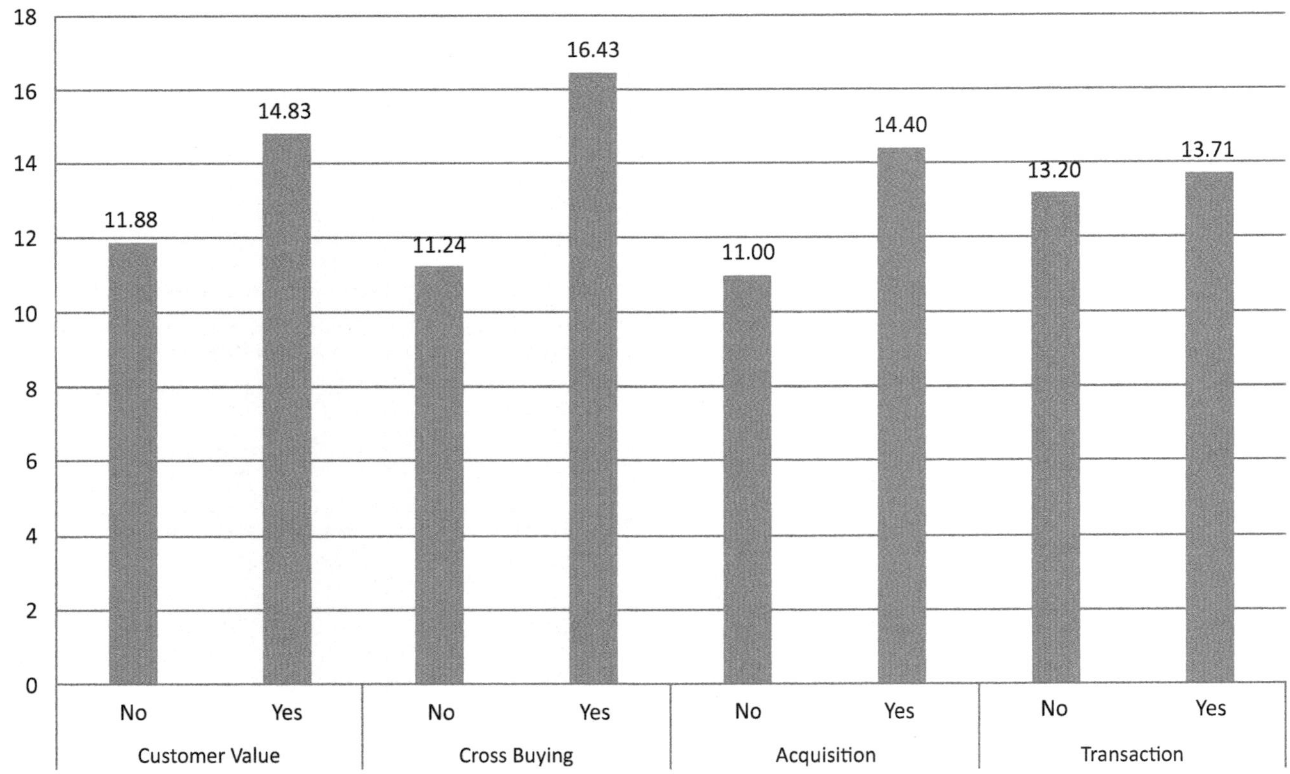

Figure 8: Correlation of profitability and the usage of metrics.

Cross Buying, Acquisition and Transaction. Extant literature showed that the metrics from the Customer Value and Cross Buying groups were more complex when it comes to collecting, storing and analyzing the data. Therefore they require, more IT resources, while the other two groups were less complex and thus easier to implement and use [11].

The fact that the metric groups differed in the outcome as well as in the complexity, led to the research question number two which asked whether there is a correlation between the profitability of the store and the usage of specific metrics. The study's result and analysis shows that there is a correlation between the usage of specific metrics and the store profitability. Basically stores, who use more metrics, are more profitable. This correlation is the highest in the group of Cross Buying metrics which are, according to current research as well as the findings, considered to be more complex to understand, use and to implement. However, it is important to state that correlation is not equal to causation. A resulting correlation does not necessarily means that this factor is the only reason for higher profitability. There might be more factors that play a role and might be linked to the usage of metrics e.g. how much control a store manager wants to have or whether the store has also an online store.

The fact that metric groups differ in complexity and that elaborated metric groups have a higher positive correlation with the profitability of the store is followed by the question, which role the complexity plays when it comes to how a store manager sees the usability and usefulness of specific metric groups. Research has shown that metrics that are easier to use, rank in the individual preferences for usability and usefulness higher than those groups with more complex metrics (e.g. Cross Buying). The requirement of IT systems as well high educated personnel makes, according to the analysis, the use of this metrics more difficult. However, companies who used this kind of metrics showed a significant increase in profitability which indicated that the investment in educated personnel as well as IT infrastructure is a success factor.

Managerial implications

The research in this study showed that manager's get through the usage of metrics from specific metric groups more insights into their business. Groups of metrics that are more complex, according to the analysis, showed a higher correlation with the store profitability. This leads to the advice that managers should implement more elaborated metrics in order to get useful insights into their business. Thus, that holds also true for the store level in retail business. This helps the management of the store to get more detailed information and supports decision making right on time.

The research showed that the number of used metrics is crucial: more profitable stores use more metric groups. The increased number of metrics give store managers a more complete overview of the business and reduce the risk of focusing only on the increase of single measurements. However, it is necessary to mention that, according to current research, too many metrics would make decision making more difficult. Therefore, managers of physical retail stores should select metrics in a way that they add value to each other.

As stated before, the complexity of metrics leads to more valuable insights that influence the profitability of the stores. Managers are advised to also use the more complex metric groups and not just rely on the metrics that are easier to implement and to analyze. This fact leads to the implication that the IT system in the store should be enough developed to handle these metrics and deals with the amount of data used by calculating such metrics. In particular, this is the case when it comes to Cross Buying metrics, where investments in a modern scalable IT system improve the way metrics can be calculated and analyzed.

Future Research

The study of customer performance becomes more and more elaborate. This complexity derives from the necessity of collecting new kind of data in order to improve the knowledge about the customer behavior.

The term "brick and mortar stores" seems to be not contemporary. Therefore, there could be a spill-over of knowledge from online operations to offline operations this leads to the development of the term "click and mortar stores" which are a combination of retail and online stores. In connection to this, future research should observe how online operations have an influence on how stores use offline metrics. It can be assumed that the online operations have a much higher impact on the knowledge about metrics then what the level of education has.

Nowadays, the market offers innovative technologies and software (e.g. 3D camera scanning) so that companies are able to track the customer's pattern and analyze it, combining a multitude of factors and variables. The goal for these technologies is to reduce the gap between offline and online store in terms of customer tracking systems. For this reason such innovations are leading to an implementation of ways to track the customer inside the brick and mortar store, where more and more the customer is observed and analyzed in real time in order to allow the managers to have a quick response. This new technology and the effect on the tracking of customers can be a topic for future research.

Major technological companies like Google and IBM are leaders in this field, offering business solutions and improved software that allow other companies and managers to collect and analyze such data. However, the demand for such technology is growing fast which will lead soon to a possible overall cost reduction, allowing more businesses to use and implement their data collection process. A possible trend for this fast growing market is the opportunity to simplify the user experience through, for example, an improved usage of graphic tools, in order to make the data interpretation easier and accessible also for those mangers who have lower education. These developments and which factor determine a better usability of such software for less educated managers could be answered by future research.

Furthermore, in the future it is plausible to believe that more companies will develop a deeper integration between online and offline store, leading to combination and mutation of already existing metric groups and the development of new hybrid metrics, able to track customer performance for both channels at the same time. This could lead, according to the authors of the thesis, to an advancement in Cross Buying analysis and would give more insights on the way customers behave. Future research has to look therefore on factors that determine the development of solution and the implementation in stores.

References

1. Wind Y, Mahajan V (2002) Convergence marketing. Journal of Interactive Marketing 16: 64-79.
2. Rajamma RK, Paswan AK (2007) Services purchased at brick and mortar versus online stores, and shopping motivation. Journal of Services Marketing 21: 200-212.
3. Rouse M (2015) Tech Target. Hamtat fran Business Metric Definition.
4. Underhill P (2009) Why we buy: The science of shopping. Simon and Schuster.
5. Griffin MP, White DS, Shea TP (2008) Applied e-commerce metrics for small-to medium-sized enterprises. International Journal of Business Information Systems 3: 374-390.
6. Graham PG (1999) Small business participation in the global economy. European Journal of Marketing 33: 88-102.
7. Shankar V, Inman JJ, Mantrala M, Kelley JE, Rizley R (2011) Innovations in shopper marketing: current insights and future research issues. Journal of Retailing 87: 29-42.
8. Petersen JA, McAlister L, Reibstein DJ, Winer RS, Kumar V, et al. (2009) Choosing the right metrics to maximize profitability and shareholder value. Journal of Retailing 85: 95-111.
9. Rust RT, Lemon KN, Zeithaml VA (2004) Return on marketing: Using customer equity to focus marketing strategy. Journal of Marketing 68: 109-127.
10. Kumar V, Shah D (2009) Expanding the role of marketing: From customer equity to market capitalization. Journal of Marketing 73: 119-136.
11. Kumar V, Petersen AJ, Robert PL (2008) How Valuable is Word of mouth. Harvard Business Review 85: 139-146.
12. Knott A, Hayes A, Neslin SA (2002) Next-product-to-buy models for cross-selling applications. Journal of Interactive Marketing 16: 59-75.
13. Reinartz W, Thomas JS, Kumar V (2005) Balancing acquisition and retention resources to maximize customer profitability. Journal of Marketing 69: 63-79.
14. Kumar V, Venkatesan R, Reinartz W (2006) Knowing what to sell, when, and to whom. Harvard Business Review 84: 131-137.
15. Farris PW, Bendle NT, Pfeifer PE, Reibstein DJ (2006) Marketing metrics: 50+ metrics every executive should master. Pearson Education.
16. Keiningham TL, Cooil B, Aksoy L, Andreassen TW, Weiner J (2007) The value of different customer satisfaction and loyalty metrics in predicting customer retention, recommendation, and share-of-wallet. Managing Service Quality: An International Journal 17: 361-384.
17. Venkatesan R, Kumar V (2004) A customer lifetime value framework for customer selection and resource allocation strategy. Journal of Marketing 68: 106-125.
18. Gupta S, Lehmann DR, Stuart JA (2004) Valuing customers. Journal of marketing research 41: 7-18.
19. Venkatesan R, Kumar V, Ravishanker N (2007) Multichannel shopping: causes and consequences. Journal of Marketing 71: 114-132.
20. Mazumdar T, Papatla P (1995) Effects of shopping basket size on price and promotion responses. Prcing Strategy and Practics 3: 16-24.
21. Kalyanaram G, Winer RS (1995) Empirical generalizations from reference price research. Marketing Science 14: G161-G169.
22. Morgan RM, Hunt SD (1994) The commitment-trust theory of relationship marketing. Journal of Marketing 58: 20-38.
23. Hinde RA, Tajfel H (1979) Towards understanding relationships. Academic Press, London 7: 275-280.
24. Ansari A, Mela CF, Neslin SA (2008) Customer channel migration. Journal of Marketing Reserach 45: 60-76.
25. Fournier S (1998) Consumers and their brands: Developing relationship theory in consumer research. Journal of Consumer Research 24: 343-353.
26. Ward MR (2001) Will online shopping compete more with traditional retailing or catalog shopping? Netnomics 3: 103-117.
27. Bell DR, Ho TH, Tang CS (1998) Determining where to shop: Fixed and variable costs of shopping. Journal of Marketing Research 25: 352-369.
28. Reichheld FF (2003) The one number you need to grow. Harvard Business Review 81: 46-55.
29. Jap SD (2001) The strategic role of the salesforce in developing customer satisfaction across the relationship lifecycle. Journal of Personal Selling & Sales Management 21: 95-108.
30. Kumar V, Venkatesan R (2005) Who are the multichannel shoppers and how do they perform?: Correlates of multichannel shopping behavior. Journal of Interactive Marketing 19: 44-62.
31. Schmittlein DC, Morrison DG, Colombo R (1987) Counting Your Customers: Who-Are They and What Will They Do Next? Management science 33: 1-24.

32. Thomas JS (2001) A methodology for linking customer acquisition to customer retention. Journal of Marketing Research 38: 262-268.

33. Verhoef PC (2003) Understanding the effect of customer relationship management efforts on customer retention and customer share development. Journal of Marketing 67: 30-45.

34. Blanchard D (2007) Supply Chains Also Work in Reverse. Industry Week 1: 48-49.

35. Schlesinger L (2008) The Limited's Model. Conference on Customer Experience Management in Retailing at Babson College. Babson College 85: 1-14.

36. Atkinson G (2008) Overstock's web analytical triangle. Conference on Consumer experience Management in Retailing at Babson College. Babson College.

37. Bryman A, Bell E (2011) Business research Methods. (3rd edn), Oxford University Press, Oxford.

38. Stevens RE, Ruddick ME, Wrenn B, Sherwood PK (1997) The marketing research guide. (2nd edn), Routledge Mental Hea, New York.

39. Zander L (1997) The licence to lead An 18 country study of the relationship between employees' preferences regarding interpersonal leadership and national culture. Stockholm University, Stockholm.

40. Fisher CM, Buglear J (2010) Researching and writing a dissertation: an essential guide for business students. Pearson Education.

41. Argyrous G (2011) Statistics for research: with a guide to SPSS. Sage publications.

42. Fournier S, Dobscha S, Micck DG (1998) Preventing the Premature Death of Relationship Marketing. Harvard Business Review 76: 42-51.

43. Pauwels K, Ambler T, Clark B, LaPointe P, Reibstein DJ, et al. (2008) Dashboards&Marketing: Why, What, How and Which Research is Needed? Marketing Science Institute, Cambridge MA.

44. Roberts J, Ambler T (2006) Beware the Silver Metric: Marketing Performance Measurement Has to Be Multidimensional. Marketing Science Institute, Cambridge MA.

45. Stevens JP (2012) Applied multivariate statistics for the social sciences. Routledge.

4

Equity Prices and Real Output: Evidence from a Structural VAR for the MINT Economies

Onikola HO*

ALBA Graduate Business School at the American College of Greece, Athens

Abstract

This paper presents a bivariate structural VAR model which investigates the interrelationships between the stock market indexes of the MINT economies - Mexico, Indonesia, Nigeria and Turkey; and a significant macro-economy proxy measured by the growth rate of industrial production using monthly data from 2000:1 to 2014:12 obtained from DataStream International, World bank, IMF and stock exchange sites of each countries where available. Improving on previous studies, we employed the Bai and Perron test to determine the significant break period and the Coefficient covariance matrix was specified by employing the HAC (Newey-West) method and allowing error distributions to differ across breaks which identified a common break (pre and post crisis) period for all the MINT economies corresponding to respective economic activity of the countries. Examining possible relationship between the variables, our Granger/Block exogeneity test reveals that, the null hypothesis will not be rejected in all cases, except the hypothesis that stock returns has a lead-lag effect on industrial production for the case of Mexico during the pre-crisis period but reverse is not the case. Our VAR estimation revealed that real activity shocks only explain a small fraction of the variability in real stock prices during the pre-crisis period than the post-crisis period in the case of Indonesia, Nigeria and Turkey excluding Mexico which explained larger variation in the pre-crisis than the post-crisis period for both the stock return and real activity. The results also reveals smaller variation of each variable on one another for variation of real activities due to innovations from stock returns for Nigeria and Indonesia alone while Mexico ant Turkey depicts the opposite. Thus, the study provides additional evidence for the absence of the direct linkage between real stock returns and real economic activities measured by industrial production which shows that the market is inefficient and perhaps not derived or guided by fundamentals, more so, the impact of the global financial crisis is also revealed and policy recommendation provided.

Keywords: MINT economies; Stock prices; Industrial production; SVAR; Structural breaks; Causality; Bai and Perron

Introduction

Over the recent periods, modeling and forecasting stock market volatility has been the subject of vast empirical and theoretical investigation by academics and practitioners alike. There are a number of motivations for this line of inquiry; perhaps, volatility is one of the most important and widely used concepts in the whole of finance. Notwithstanding, attention to the relationship between the share market and the rest of the economy has been on the increase by finance specialist, economist and other stakeholders. Furthermore, the severe market decline in 2008 resulting from the subprime lending in US has reawakened research on this topic. Traditionally, stock markets play an important role in the economy; by enhancing the growth of commerce and expanding the capital formation required for the development of industries and building capacities. In the economy, the financial sector is expected to serve as the driver and catalyst to achieving full diversification of the economy. The idea is to strengthen the domestic financial market by developing competence and skills for financial services industry which will in turn have an impact on the industrial productivity of the country by improve access to finance and build an integrated infrastructure for the financial industry and other growth driven industry of the economy. Indicatively, the stock exchange provides long-term capital for major sectors of the economy including businesses and the government and its indexes are often used as an indicator of economic health.

At any phase of an economy, a number of sectors of the economy need long-term capital to grow. The stock exchange is an essential establishment in the capital market that ensures the efficient re-distribution of resources for economic activities. Economic development requires commitment to long-term investment. The path to economic recovery and growth may require increasing production inputs - land, labor, capital and technology - and or increasing their productivity. From past trend, countries that have found themselves in a recession phase have revived their economies through several productivity enhancement schemes. For instance, Japan from the end of the World War II and the United States of America from the 1970's have made high productivity the center point of their economic planning and the results have been resounding. Also, middle income countries like Hong Kong, South Korea, Singapore, and the Philippines have embraced boosting productivity schemes as an integral part of their national planning and today they have made significant in-roads into the world industrial. Intuitively, we can argue that productivity is essential in boosting economic growth and the standards of living of the people – using per capita income; hence, its measurement cannot but be of importance to both policy makers and researchers.

Nonetheless, concerns about the inability of the stock market movements to be explained by economic fundamentals during the recent decades have been on its rise. These concern surfaces not only for the advanced economies; the US' stock market, European and Asian markets but also the perceived emerging market economies. This is well apparent in the advanced economies when their stock markets witnessed unprecedented highs in the mid-1990s but were sharply

***Corresponding author:** Onikola HO, ALBA Graduate Business School at The American College of Greece, Athens, E-mail: hamonikola@gmail.com

reversed in the early and late 2000s as a result of excessive speculation. Studies have revealed that most of the rise in equity prices during the second part of the 1990s in the US was not due to fundamental values such as projected earnings growth or dividends but to exogenous shocks and/or market irrational behavior. This is similar to the conclusion of other researchers who reported that fundamental variables themselves such as discount rates, earnings, dividends, industrial production etc. did not help explain stock price movements.

Motivated by the above, we observed that such explanations did not exist for emerging markets economies owing to the specificity and difference in the market conditions along development line. It is in this initiative we consider to examine the MINT economies which could not be explained by the class of models according to which the stock market may be a leading indicator of real economic activity considering the unambiguous results established by studies that real activity explained only a small fraction of the variation in real stock returns. More importantly, understanding the macroeconomic variables that could impact the stock market index, with the recent data of the MINT economies can be useful for investors, traders as well as the policy makers. As a distinguish factor from the conclusions of result above, the MINT countries face a number of economic and political challenges. For instance, Nigeria is the only member of MINT running a current Account surplus - US$5,016 million in the second quarter of 2013 [1]. There are leadership and economic challenges in Indonesia and political issues in Turkey while Nigeria has been grappling with serious security and terrorism challenges since 2009. Although MINT countries share some features in common, they also diverge in several respects. In terms of wealth for instance, Mexico and Turkey are at approximately the same level, earning annually about US$10,000 per capita. This compares with US$3,500 per head in Indonesia and US$1,500 per capita in Nigeria [2].

Literature Review

Several studies exist in the finance literature that examines the linkages between macroeconomic fundamentals and stock returns. For instance, the result of the study of equity prices and macroeconomic fundamentals of developed economies revealed different sensitivities in the way stock prices reacted to changes in the fundamentals suggesting that stock markets appeared to move independently of them in the long run, especially in the post-euro period while Fama, Barro, Schwert found that there exists a strong short-run correlation between stock returns and macroeconomic fundamentals for the United States (US) and between these magnitudes and other financial variables [3-5]. Lee, Groenewold, Laopodis, Rapach made contributions in this field by estimating SVAR models including stock prices and measures of real activity for several developed countries [6-9]. Furthermore, several studies exist in literature that examine the relation between stock returns and the growth rates of real activity). Allen and Yang estimates SVAR model including prices and dividends and/or earnings of several countries which is similar to the work of bhargava which examined the relationship between P/E ratios, dividend yields, and stock prices in the BRIC nations using monthly data (1999-2009) [11-14]. Chen et al. explored a set of macroeconomic variables as systematic influence on stock market returns by modeling equity return as a function of macro variables and non-equity assets returns for US. They empirically found that the macroeconomic variables such as industrial production anticipated and unanticipated inflation, yield spread between the long and short term government bond were significantly explained the stock returns.

Researching on developed countries, Laopodis examined the dynamic linkages among stock prices, interest rates, inflation, and economic activity for the United States since the 1970s and also reported that there was no consistent, dynamic relationship between real activity and stock prices across different monetary regimes during the last thirty years [8]. Binswanger [15], developed a bivariate structural VAR model which includes growth rates of industrial production and stock prices for US, Japan and an aggregate European economy between the periods of 1960 to 1999 and found that real activity shocks only explain a small fraction of the variability in real stock prices whereas some authors have also argued that the recent stock price movements cannot be explained by fundamental factors and that they are the result of speculative bubbles [16]. According to regression results presented, it suggests a breakdown between stock returns and real economic activity in the US in the early 1980s; which traditionally; have strong relationship. Such a breakdown indicates the development of new sources of variation in stock returns especially during the stock market boom over the 1980s and 1990s. However, this breakdown are not explained by the traditional discounted cash flow valuation model which forms the basis to which stock prices should lead measures of real activity [3].

Similarly, the results of the dynamic relationships between stock prices and economic fundamentals for the period 1990-2009 for France, Germany, Italy, the UK and the US using the rolling-sample co-integration technique and VAR specifications carried out by revealed different sensitivities in the way stock prices reacted to changes in the fundamentals which suggests that stock markets appeared to move independently of them in the long run of the post-Euro period i.e. there was no consistent, dynamic relationship between real activity and stock prices across different monetary regimes during the last thirty years. Nevertheless, economy concluded that not only has the share market increased relative to the real economy but it appears that the inter-relationship between them has also strengthened [7,17]. From the foregoing, we could infer that the share market reflects to some extent the activities and performances in the economy, however, we cannot also rule out the possibility of the influence in opposite direction. This has generated widespread recognition in recent time even though stock market and economic performances interrelationship of countries differs. In Nigeria for example, comparing recent indices from 2005 to 2012; the value of Market Capitalization increased by 191% from $19,356 to $56,389 contrary to the ratio of share-market capitalization to GDP (% of GDP) which declined from 17.2% in 2005 to 12.2% in 2012; however, other countries Mexico, Indonesia and Turkey increases significantly in market capitalization from $239,128, $81,428, and $161,537 in 2005 to $525,057, $396,772 and $308,775 in 2012 which also translates to an increase in (%GDP) 16.6%, 14.7% and 5.7% respectively.

In view of the above conflicting evidence and more significantly, 'developed-economies-dominated' studies, this paper sets out to re-examine the nature of the relationship between the aggregate stock market and general economic activity of the MINT economies which to the best of the our knowledge does not previously exist. The 'MINT' is an acronym coined by the major investment firm Fidelity in 2011 (popularized by Jim O'Neil) for a group of four countries-Mexico, Indonesia, Nigeria and Turkey-that are expected to show strong growth and provide high returns for investors over the coming decade. These countries have been grouped together because of their large populations, favorable demographics and emerging economies. Although, these countries have smaller economies than the BRICs-Brazil, Russia, India and China which is a group of emerging-market economies that enjoyed strong growth for a number of years; however, the BRICs' have started to witness slowed-growth (with the exception of China), investors have started to turned their attention to MINTs, which analysts expected to be the next big thing.

An understanding of the MINT economies reveals that they share some common features: first, the countries have relatively large and growing young populations when compared to the ageing and shrinking populations in many developed countries (including China); second, these countries are geographically well placed to take advantage of large markets nearby. For example, Indonesia is close to China, Turkey being neighboring to the European Union, Mexico is also on America's doorstep, while Nigeria has the potential to serve as economic hub of Africa. Of the four MINT economies, only Nigeria is not yet a member of the G20 group of developed and developing countries; but has huge endowment of natural resource, especially oil and gas. Foreign Direct Investment (FDI) to the BRICS and MINT increased by 349% from US$113.6billion to US$510.4 Billion between the period of 2001 and 2012 [18]. Besides, BRICS and MINT attracted 30% of global FDI, contributed 19% to global GDP, and accounted for 51% of the global population in 2011(World Bank, 2013). For developmental purpose, BRICS and MINT have fundamental policies to promote FDI inflows to their respective countries (especially to sectors that have significant multiplier effects in respect of employment and output, promote technology transfer, or local innovation).

Leveraging on the work of who addresses the dynamic linkages between stock prices and economic fundamentals of developed economies (France, Germany, Italy, the UK and the USA) for the period of 1990-2009, this study empirically analyzes the relationship between stock prices and economic fundamentals of the MINT economies; proxied by industrial production growth rate starting with determining a common break for all the economies using a statistical approach. Also, other works such as Binswanger carried out a related study using developed countries like US, Japan and an aggregated of European countries using data from 1960 to 1999 presented with a bivariate structural VAR model would be a good framework to start with. There are several motivations for this study and approach [15]; examining the relationship of these variables in the MINT economies will give us a broader understanding of the theory and an advantage to compare with the result of previous researchers in the developing economies. Another significant part of this study is to ascertain if similar conclusion will be reached in our study and more importantly if there exist fundamental different between the break periods identified i.e. the pre and post financial crises period for each of the countries.

The rest of the paper is organized as follows. The next section presents a brief description of the data, some summary statistics, and the methodological design for the study. Furthermore, the next sections contains the results from the preliminary statistical investigation regarding correlations and unit root tests, and the main empirical findings from Granger causality analyses, impulse responses and forecast error variance decomposition. This section also contains a discussion of the empirical findings. The final section summarizes the study and concludes with some general policy recommendation.

Research Method

In this section, we approached our empirical investigation chronologically by describing the data and variable construction, outlining the theoretical methodology design; which entails SVAR modeling and Granger causality analyses and then we proceeding with a preliminary statistical analysis which is followed by the main empirical findings of the study.

Data and theoretical methodology

The data used for this study are sourced from the DataStream International for all the MINT economies and additionally from Central bank of Nigeria (CBN) statistical Bulletin where applicable. The data set consists of monthly observations over the period of 2000:01-2014:12 for Mexico, Indonesia, Nigeria and Turkey for each of the countries stock index (SI), industrial production (IND), as well consumer price indices (CPI). Real industrial production (IP) is calculated by dividing the industrial production index by the consumer price index, while its growth rate IPG or y_{1t} is calculated as the first difference of real IP. Real stock prices (SP) are calculated by dividing nominal stock prices by the CPI while real stock returns SR or y_{2t} are calculated as the first difference of real stock prices. All variables are presented in natural logarithms.

In addition to the above, the VAR model is also used for structural inference and policy analysis. In structural analysis, certain assumptions about the causal structure of the data under investigation are imposed, and the resulting causal impacts of unexpected shocks or innovations to specified variables on the variables in the model are summarized. These causal impacts are usually summarized with impulse response functions and forecast error variance decompositions. In a bid to capture the effect of these innovation and the periods of occurrence, we carried out a structural break test by employed the break test. More importantly, our inability to automatically detect a common break for all the MINT economy intuitively justifies our need to carry out the structural break test. The tests of structural break aid our detection of a common break period.

The structural VAR model, shock decompositions and lag length selection: The Vector Autoregressive (VAR) analysis is used in finance for the simulation of the effects on the endogenous variables of shocks to equation error terms. For purpose of simplicity, a VAR is a systems regression model which has more than one dependent variable that can be considered a kind of hybrid between the univariate time series models and the simultaneous equations models. The estimation method has often been advocated as an alternative to large-scale simultaneous equations structural models, however, given the non-theoretical nature of the model, the interpretation of generated shocks may be difficult to interpret. Therefore, an extension of the VAR model (the structural VAR or SVAR) which imposes theory-based restriction on the VAR to enable the identification of the errors terms will be adopted in this paper. Variant of the SVAR model have been extensively used in macroeconomics and finance, such as who use their model to decompose movements in real output and the rate of unemployment into those driven by aggregate demand and supply shocks.

The model adopted in this paper is similar to the SVAR model estimated by who analysis the important of fundamentals - evidence from a SVAR model for the stock markets in the US, Japan and Europe [15]. Similar model was also employed by who analyses the relation between growth rates of real GDP and growth rates of the stock market in Australia [7]. Our motivation has also been drawn of from the works of who concluded that forecasts for some fundamental variables are produced more accurately using VARs than from several different structural specifications. Hence, since this paper also requires the use of variables mentioned, we considered it more appropriate to adopt the method [19].

From the forgoing, the simplest case of VAR model is the bivariate VAR (adopted in this study), where there are only two variables, y_{1t} and y_{2t}, each of whose current values depend on different combinations of the previous k values of both variables, and error terms as specified below:

$$y_{1t} = \beta_{10} + \beta_{11}y_{1t-1} + \ldots + \beta_{1k}y_{1t-k} + \alpha_{11}y_{2t-1} + \ldots + \alpha_{1k}y_{2t-k} + u_{1t}$$
$$y_{2t} = \beta_{20} + \beta_{21}y_{2t-1} + \ldots + \beta_{2k}y_{2t-k} + \alpha_{21}y_{1t-1} + \ldots + \alpha_{2k}y_{1t-k} + u_{2t}$$

Where u_{it} is a white noise disturbance term with? $E(u_{it}) = 0$, (i = 1,2), $E(u_{1t}u_{2t}) = 0$

We estimate a two-variable model that consists of the first differenced log of real share index (ASI) denoted as y_{1t}, and the first differenced log of industrial production (IND), y_{2t} Given the importance of industrial production or real GDP as a measure of real economic activities especially by previous studies, we decided to follow this tradition in this paper because the relation between stock returns and growth rates of industrial production appears to be more significant than the relation between stock returns and growth rates of real GDP.

The reduced form of the VAR model is represented by the bivariate system

$$y_{1t} = \beta_{10} + \beta_{11}y_{1t-1} + \alpha_{11}y_{2t-1} + u_{1t}$$
$$y_{2t} = \beta_{10} + \beta_{21}y_{2t-1} + \alpha_{21}y_{1t-1} + u_{1t}$$

Or

$$\Delta Z_t = \begin{bmatrix} \Delta y_{1t} \\ \Delta y_{2t} \end{bmatrix} = \begin{bmatrix} \beta_{10} \\ \beta_{20} \end{bmatrix} + \begin{bmatrix} \beta_{11}(L) & \alpha_{12}(L) \\ \alpha_{21}(L) & \alpha_{22}(L) \end{bmatrix} \begin{bmatrix} \Delta y_{1t-1} \\ \Delta y_{2t-1} \end{bmatrix} + \begin{bmatrix} u_{1t} \\ u_{2t} \end{bmatrix}$$

Where

y_{1t} and y_{2t} = Endogenous variables

α_{i0} = Parameter representing intercept

L = Lagged operator (selection criteria explained below)

u_{1t}, u_{2t} = the observed error terms of the reduced VAR model (reduced form residuals or reduced form shocks). The error terms u_{1t}, u_{2t} are white noise disturbances which, however, will usually be correlated unless there are no contemporaneous effects between Δy_{1t} and Δy_{2t}. Ignoring intercept terms, we can write equation (1) in a more compact notation as

$$\Delta Z_t = \beta(L) L \Delta Z_t + u_t$$

Given the fact that the series y_{1t} and y_{2t} are both covariance stationary and assuming that β(L) is invertible, we can write:

$$\Delta Z_t = \left[I - \beta(L)L\right]^{-1} u_t$$

Which is the bivariate infinite order average representation (BMA) of (1)?

As the residual u_{1t}, u_{2t} are usually correlated, they cannot be structural innovations which are supposed to be uncorrelated with each other. The unobserved structural innovations come from a VAR representation of the structural form (SVAR), which we suppose can be written as

$$B(L)\Delta Z_t = u$$

Where B(L) a matrix of structural parameters is derived by identifying restrictions and u^t is a vector of the uncorrelated white noise disturbances u_{1t}, u_{2t} which are the structural shocks or structural innovations.

If the matrix polynomial $\left[I - \beta(L)L\right]$ is invertible, so is the matrix polynomial and the SVAR can also be expressed as BMA

$$\Delta Z_t = \left[\beta(L)\right]^{-1} u_t = \delta(L) u_t$$

Or

$$\begin{bmatrix} \Delta y_{1t} \\ \Delta y_{2t} \end{bmatrix} = \begin{bmatrix} \lambda_{11}(L) & \lambda_{12}(L) \\ \lambda_{21}(L) & \lambda_{22}(L) \end{bmatrix} \begin{bmatrix} u_{1t} \\ u_{2t} \end{bmatrix}$$

Where $\lambda_{ij}(L)$ are the infinite polynomials in the lag operator L

Lag length selection: The lag length for the VAR(p) model was determined by using model selection criteria. The general approach is to fit VAR(p) models with orders p = 0,…, p_{max} and choose the value of p which minimizes some model selection criteria. Model selection criteria for VAR(p) models have the form:

$$IC(p) = \ln|\bar{\Sigma}(p)| + c_T \cdot \varphi(n,p)$$

Where $\bar{\Sigma}(p) = T^{-1}\sum_{t=1}^{T} \varepsilon_t \varepsilon_t'$ is the residual covariance matrix without a degree of freedom correction from a VAR(p) model, c_T is a sequence indexed by the sample size T, and $\varphi(n,p)$ is a penalty function which penalizes large VAR(p) models. The three most common information criteria are the Akaike (AIC), Schwarz-Bayesian (SIC) and Hannan-Quinn (HQ):

$$AIC(p) = \ln|\bar{\Sigma}(p)| + \frac{2}{T} pn^2$$

$$SIC(p) = \ln|\bar{\Sigma}(p)| + \frac{\ln T}{T} pn^2$$

$$HQ(p) = \ln|\bar{\Sigma}(p)| + \frac{2\ln\ln T}{T} pn^2$$

All criteria add a penalty to the one-step ahead MSE which depends on the sample size T, the number of variables m and the number of lags q. While for large T penalty differences are unimportant, this is not the case when T is small.

In general, for T ≥ 20 SWC and HQC will always choose smaller models than AIC. The three criteria have different asymptotic properties. AIC is inconsistent (in fact, it overestimates the true order with positive probability) while HQC and SWC are consistent and when m > 1, they are both strongly consistent (i.e. they will choose the correct model almost surely). Intuitively, AIC is inconsistent because the penalty function used does not simultaneously goes to infinity as T → ∞ and to zero when scaled by T. Consistency however; it is not the only yardstick to use since consistent methods may have poor small sample properties. Extensively study the small sample properties of these three criteria using a variety of data generating processes and data frequencies and found that HQC is best for quarterly and monthly data, both when y_t is covariance stationary and when it is a near-unit root process [19].

The AIC criterion asymptotically overestimates the order with positive probability, whereas the SIC and HQ criteria estimate the order consistently under fairly general conditions if the true order p is less than or equal to p_{max}. In general, we prefer to use a simple bivariate model instead of a VAR due to its ability to accommodate further fundamental variables, thus; we only need to impose one additional identifying restriction, which does not require a strong a priori assumption based on a specific economic theory. After the VARs model has been estimated, we will thereafter impose an additional restriction in order to identify the structural shocks.

Preliminary statistical results

Our initial descriptive result reveals that the hypothesis of normality for Jarque-Bera statistics is rejected for all variables. The distributions of stock returns and real IPG are negatively skewed and leptokurtic relative to the normal distribution (Table 1). The descriptive statistics of real stock price returns and growth of industrial production for the break period identified (Table 2).

We evaluated the effect of stationarity in the series using the ADF and KPSS method (Table 3); and observed that a variety of alternative unit root tests provides evidence of non-stationarity for the stock prices and the industrial production (result are presented in later sections) with the exception of only Nigeria which has its stock price stationary at level. Accordingly, real stock returns and real IP growth rate appear to be stationary for all observed series. Given that real stock returns and the real IP growth rate are stationary, and that there is no cointegration, a VAR model for real stock returns and real IP growth rate is thereby considered for our analysis.

The graphs in Figure 1 show the development of the log levels of real stock prices and industrial production from 2000:01 to 2014:12. Real stock prices have a similar trend of an initial decline from 2000 before starting to increase around 2003 until the 2007 crises period for Mexico, Indonesia and Turkey; while for the Nigeria's case there has been an initial steady increase until a slight decline in 2008 half way due to the capital market re-capitalization followed by the decline in caused by the financial crises originated from the US. However, since the 2003 the actual patterns of real stock price development vary similarly among the MINT economies swinging steady upward. The boom is most prevalent during the period of 2003 to 2007 in Mexico, followed by Indonesia, then Turkey and Nigeria. As the booming comes to an end; witnessing the financial crises, it also appears that all the MINT economies have a similar share of the loss in terms of the trend. However, it becomes obvious that Nigeria has a more prevalent period during the crises as it took the longest time to recover as compared to others. Out of the countries; Indonesia recovered faster followed by Mexico, Turkey and worst felt is Nigeria.

In a similar fashion, we observed several structural breaks for all the market at different point in time of the markets. Significant among these breaks is the financial crises in 2008 which was common among all market. We observed that the impact was more severe in the Nigeria capital than other markets. The markets of Mexico, Indonesia and Turkey increase steadily after the financial crisis while in the case of Nigeria; no increase in share price was noticed. From the foregoing; we identified a common structural break period between the periods of 2007 to 2009 which was as a result of the crisis 2). We also discover a similar recovery period of 2000:02, 2009:01, 2009:03 and 2009:02 for the Mexico, Indonesia, Nigeria and Turkey capital market respectively as reflected in their share prices. We therefore identified the period 2000:01–2009:03 associated with the re-boom of the market as a structural break period for this study as further explained by Figure 2.

	Mean	Standard deviation	Skewness	Kurtosis	Jarque-Bera	pr.
2000:01-2014:12						
Mex return	0.006797	0.055708	-0.568579	4.012922	17.29691	0
Mex ipg	0.001084	0.008401	-0.179224	4.166856	11.1132	0.00382
Indo ret	0.005609	0.069612	-1.091788	7.457595	183.75	0
Indo ipg	0.004821	0.063188	-0.916941	9.857151	375.77	0
Nig. return	0.000386	0.072183	-0.34646	8.539174	232.42	0
Nig. ipg	0.001052	0.064249	-0.10273	4.872632	26.46935	0
Turk return	-0.002325	0.109709	-0.550691	4.734227	31.47851	0
Turk ipg	0.003676	0.055238	-0.543497	4.924529	36.43671	0

Table 1: Preliminary descriptive.

	Mean	Standard deviation	Skewness	Kurtosis	Jarque-Bera	pr.
2000:01-2009:03						
Mex return	0.005895	0.064445	-0.627889	3.385314	7.908299	0.019175
Mex ipg	0.000547	0.009496	-0.050659	3.669583	2.101947	0.349597
Indo ret	0.000297	0.078274	-1.180658	6.730879	89.35333	0
Indo ipg	0.005134	0.076108	-0.854053	7.575195	109.3127	0
Nig. return	0.000908	0.072507	-1.451366	8.459756	175.2428	0
Nig. ipg	0.00134	0.073624	-0.187246	4.320866	8.639275	0.013305
Turk return	-0.010857	0.126364	-0.457688	4.038731	8.785682	0.012366
Turk ipg	0.002251	0.054149	-0.850187	5.926414	52.50286	0
2009:04-2014:12						
Mex return	0.008235	0.038245	0.419185	3.176303	2.110094	0.348176
Mex ipg	0.001939	0.006245	-0.314127	4.219438	5.409984	0.066871
Indo ret	0.014077	0.052395	0.199667	4.240889	4.885409	0.086925
Indo ipg	0.004321	0.034151	-0.254937	4.524938	7.433043	0.024318
Nig. return	-0.000447	0.072184	1.452825	8.807343	121.2331	0
Nig. Ipg	0.000592	0.046003	0.450283	3.326325	2.637831	0.267425
Turk return	0.011277	0.074866	0.000811	2.642711	0.367016	0.832345
Turk ipg	0.005947	0.057259	-0.139455	3.517771	0.994397	0.608232

Table 2: Structural break descriptive.

Augmented Dickey-Fuller Test [ADF]						
	Real stock prices			Industrial Production		
Country	Log Level	Log difference	Comment	Log Level	Log difference	Comment
Mexico	-0.862579	-12.18113[a]	I(1)	-0.57315	-15.81547[a]	I(1)
Indonesia	-0.7113	-10.63546[a]	I(1)	0.994704	-7.204279[a]	I(1)
Nigeria	-1.534423	-11.01869[a]	I(1)	-4.178927[a]	-	I(0)
Turkey	-2.34311	-15.21201[a]	I(1)	-0.919655	-14.52331[a]	I(1)
Kwiatkowski-Phillips-Schmidt-Shin Test [KPSS]						
	Real stock prices			Industrial Production		
Country	Log Level	Log difference	Comment	Log Level	Log difference	Comment
Mexico	1.518578	0.12143[a]	I(1)	1.469732	0.055696[a]	I(1)
Indonesia	1.557214	0.121791[a]	I(1)	1.708427	0.194179[a]	I(1)
Nigeria	0.374571	0.195799[a]	I(1)	1.163066[a]	-	I(0)
Turkey	0.618685	0.254862[a]	I(1)	1.590569	0.050471[a]	I(1)

Table 3: Unit root test (ADF and KPSS).

[a]Rejection of the null hypothesis of non-stationarity at the 5% level. For the ADF tests, we used the Schwarz Info Criterion. The KPSS bandwidth was automatic selected using Newey-West Bandwidth and the lag truncation for the Bartlett kernel is set to 4.

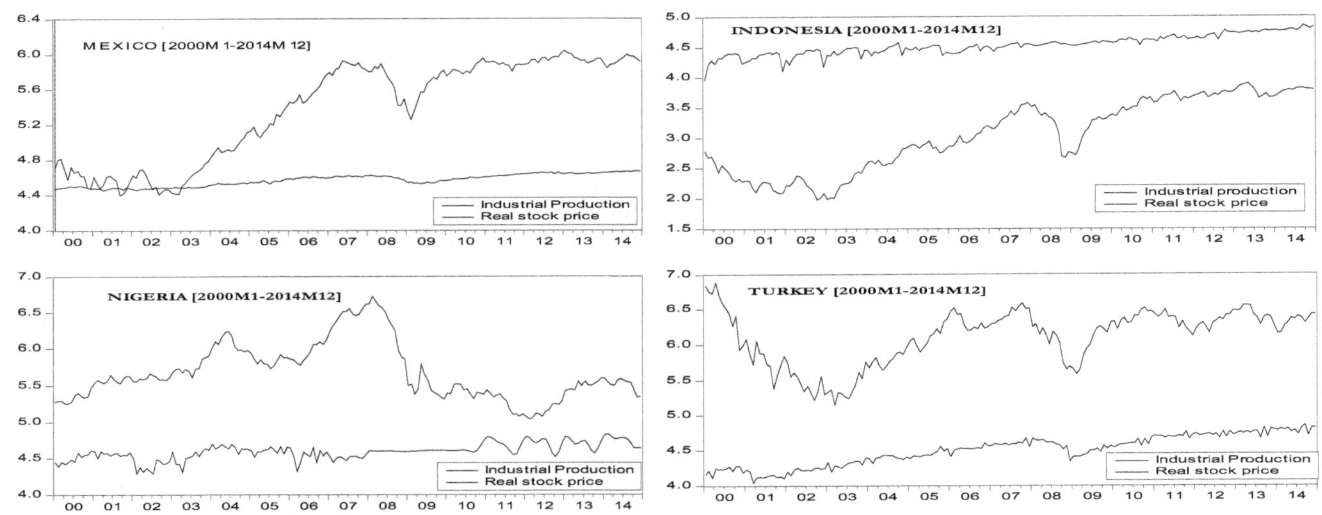

Figure 1: Log levels of real stock prices and industrial production.

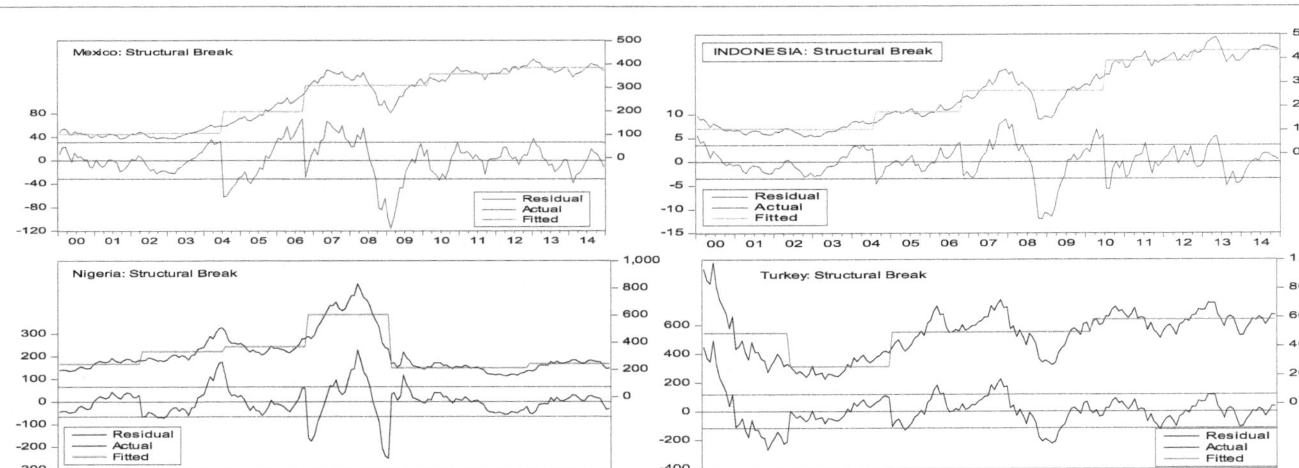

Figure 2: Prices level structural break of stock market shocks.

According to the results of the augmented Dickey–Fuller unit (ADF) root test, as well as of the Kwiatkowski-Phillips-Schmidt-Shin Test (KPSS), all variables (log levels) are I(1) and, therefore, non-stationary at their levels but stationary at their first differences except the time series for the Nigerian industrial production that is I(0) and, therefore stationary at level. However, when we test the presence of unit root in the same series during the break periods 2001:01-2009:03 and 2009:04-2014:12, we observed that the Nigeria industrial production series has unit roots in the post crisis period (2009:04-2014:12) and marginally shows the absence of unit roots before the crisis period (the full results from all tests and periods are available upon request).

Thus, it is concluded that each series is not stationary and thus needs to become stationary by being differenced once except for the Nigeria industrial production variable that is already stationary at level; hence, requires no differencing. Consequently, the new test values are 0.2830, 0.3423 and 0.0914, respectively (the full results from all tests are available upon request). In general, it was found that each variable is non-stationary in its raw form but becomes stationary when expressed in first differences. This holds true for all countries' series and both sub-periods. In addition, when using the 2001 instead of 1999, there was not qualitative difference in our results.

After determining the stationarity level of the series, we estimated the VAR model by including the growth rate of the two variables as well as a constant parameter. Firstly, we set the lag length. The lag length for the VAR(p) model was determined by using model selection criteria. The general approach is to fit VAR(p) models with orders p=0,..., p_{max} and choose the value of p which minimizes some model selection criteria. We use four different lag length criteria (final prediction error (FPE), Akaike information criterion (AIC), Schwarz information criterion (SIC), Hannan–Quinn information criterion (HQ)) and estimate the model for lag lengths of 0–12. The optimal lag length for each model was chosen by applying the Akaike Information Criterion on the un-differenced VAR models; however, for our series observed in the post crisis period with 67 observations, we chose the Hannan-Quinn Criterion (HQ) which appears to be the most accurate criterion [20] with the exception of sample sizes smaller than 120, for which the Schwarz Information Criterion (SIC) is more accurate. In case of the presence or absence of a long-run relationship, the possibility of a short-run relationship between the fundamental ratios and the stock indexes may still exist, we thereby carried out causality test employing the Granger causality/Block Exogeneity Wald test with an error correction term (if co-integration exists) or without an error correction term (if co-integration does not exist) to investigate this issue.

The FPE and the AIC advised the inclusion of more lags than the SC and HQ criterion in both the pre and post crisis period. For the pre-crisis period with more observation, we employed the AIC criteria which suggest two lag criteria in the case of Indonesia and Turkey while eight and four lag criteria for the case of Mexico and Nigeria respectively while the HQ criteria employed for the post crisis period; suggests different lag criteria for each of the countries; Mexico (two), Indonesia (four). Nigeria (six) and Turkey (three) to explain the current level of the growth rate of industrial production in the VAR. We thereby set our lag criteria for the VAR models as given in Table 4 and Appendix 1 and 2.

	FPE	AIC	SC	HQ
2000:01-2009:03				
Mexico	8	**8***	1	1
Indonesia	2	**2***	1	1
Nigeria	4	**4***	1	2
Turkey	2	**2***	2	2
2009:04-2014:12				
Mexico	3	12	2	**2***
Indonesia	12	12	1	**4***
Nigeria	10	10	4	**6***
Turkey	3	10	2	**3***
*lag length chosen				

Table 4: Optimal lag length selection.

	Summary Block Exogeneity/ Granger Causality Test
2000:01-2009:03	
Mexico	Uni-directional causality from IPG to SP return
Indonesia	No causality between SR and IP growth
Nigeria	No causality between SR and IP growth
Turkey	No causality between SR and IP growth
2009:04-2014:14	
Mexico	No causality between SR and IP growth
Indonesia	No causality between SR and IP growth
Nigeria	No causality between SR and IP growth
Turkey	No causality between SR and IP growth
SR - Stock price return	
IP- Industrial Production	

Table 5: Block exogeneity/granger causality test.

Main empirical results

Table 5 presents the Granger-causality test results which show that, the null hypothesis will not be rejected in all cases, except the hypothesis that Mexico SR has a lead-lag relationship with IPG but not vice versa during the pre-crises period. That means there is a unidirectional causality running from SR to IPG. We proceed with the observation and analysis of the impulse response shocks from and to each variable for all the MINT nations. The figures at the appendix reveals some selected impulse response graphs for stock returns (SR) and industrial production growth rate (IPG) for both the pre and post structural breaks identified.

The results of the responses of stock return and industrial production growth of all the countries for both periods under investigation is presented in Figure 3. Several conclusions can be inferred; firstly, during the pre-crisis period for the case of Mexico, we observed a more turbulent alternating response from growth in industrial production to stock return which did not to be absorbed even after a year period; which is in contrast to the reaction in the other countries. During this period, an initial negative reaction in stock return is observed due to shocks in industrial production for the case of Indonesia; while Nigeria and Turkey depicts an alternating between positive and negative response before the shock is finally absorbed in periods 4, 7 and respectively. This could be as result of unexpected rise in stock prices that is not caused by real activity shocks which tends to induce investors to move funds into the stock market from the interest paying bond market; the length of period observed however, seems enough for this effect to take place. This is similar to the negative effect found in the four-variable SVAR model for the US estimated by previous researchers, therefore, it does not seem to be a statistical objective of our bivariate SVAR model [8]. For the reaction of the growth of industrial production due from stock return; it is evidenced that shocks in the Mexico stock return has an exerted positive response

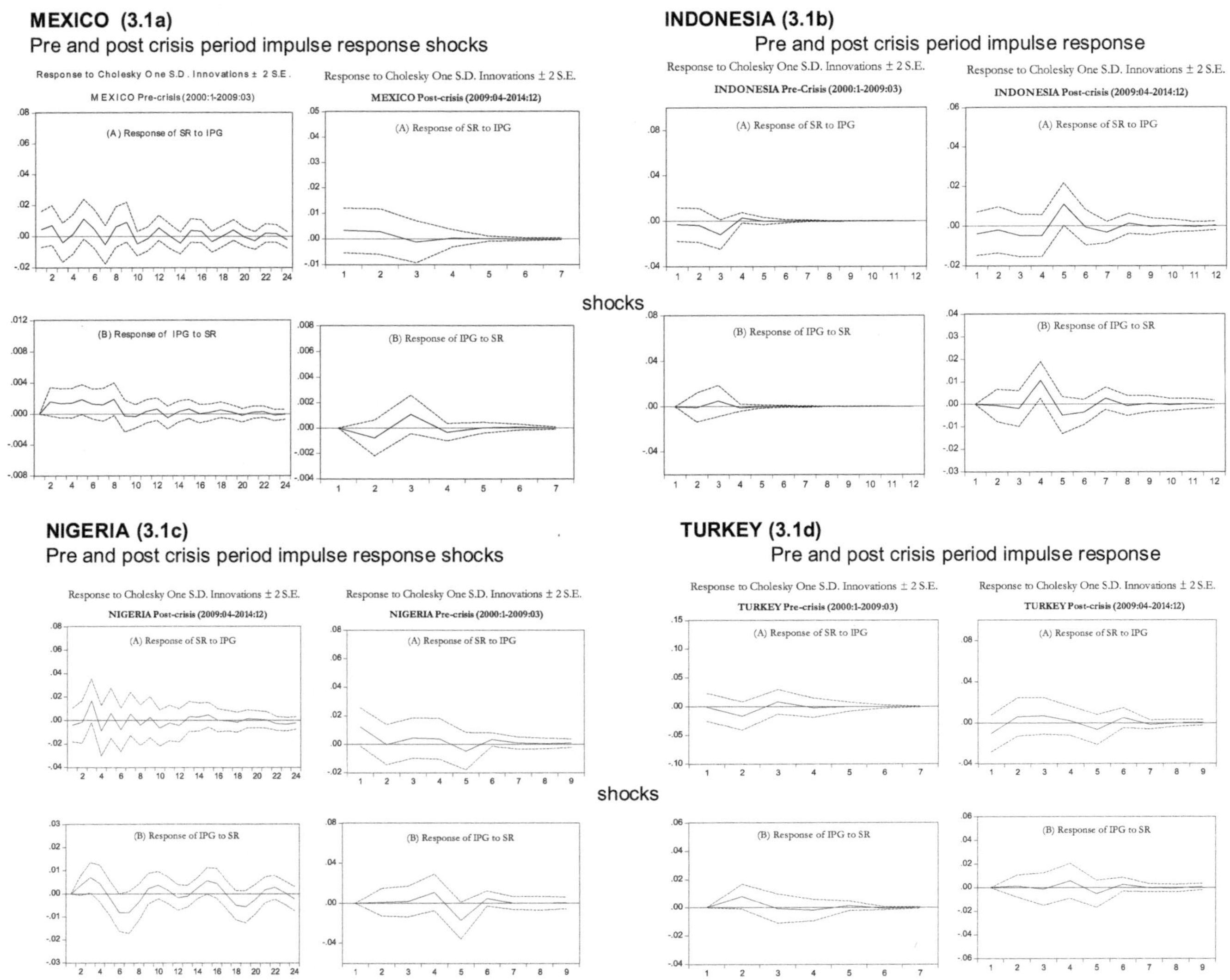

Figure 3: Impulse responses shock for pre and post crisis period.

in industrial production growth rate for a long period; same is true in the case of Indonesia, however, the influence was felt slightly and for a very short period. Conversely, for the case of Nigeria and Turkey, there is an alternating reaction positively and negatively before the shocks were fully absorbed.

For the period after the crisis 2009:03-2014:12, the picture is quite different in the sense that both stock return and industrial production growth 'behave well' to shocks from one another except for the case of Nigeria. For the responses of stock return in Mexico, Indonesia and Turkey; the behavior is relatively stable for shocks in industrial production than the reverse. Also, they get absorbed faster after periods of three, seven and seven months respectively. On the contrary, the Nigeria's story is different in terms of the signs, length of time and responses of the variables on each other. For the case of stock returns; an innovation in the industrial production growth takes a very long time to account for the sign and the shape of the responses in the former. Similarly, during this period, the behavior of the shocks of stock returns to industrial production behaved unstable continuously and persistently for a very long period. This is evidenced in the variance decomposition results where for the case of stock returns where almost 17% of the error forecasting variance of due from industrial production whereas 82% is due to own shock whereas the instability in the signs and response of industrial production due to shocks from stock returns is too long to imagine a possible absorption of the shock of the later.

Furthermore, an effort to analyze the forecast error variance decompositions reveals two interesting observations. On the first part, it provides clear evidence of the fundamental differences in the periods under consideration; and on the other part it reveals different how the each of the countries responded to the changes over the periods. As depicted in Table 6, the shock in industrial production for all the countries explains a small proportion of the variability in the stock returns during the pre-crisis period 2000:01-2009:03 while this proportion becomes larger in the model estimated for the period 2009:03-2014:12 except for the case of only Mexico which has the reverse as her case. For instance, the Mexico's industrial production shocks explained about 9.63% of the variability in stock returns at longer horizon over the pre-crisis period while only about 1.57% is observed for the same length of horizon. In contrast, for the cases of Indonesia, Nigeria and Turkey; innovations in the industrial production resulted in about 2.71, 3.53 and 2.03% the variability in stock returns during

Stock price forecast error variance decompositions for different periods				
	2000:01-2009:03		2009:03-2014:12	
	variance attributed to:		variance attributed to:	
Period	Own shock	IPG rate	own shock	IPG rate
Mexico				
1	99.39467	0.605331	99.13196	0.86803
2	98.00684	1.993163	98.50715	1.49284
3	97.60157	2.398426	98.40768	1.59231
4	97.56401	2.435991	98.40208	1.59792
5	94.42554	5.574459	98.40128	1.59872
10	90.78156	9.218441	98.40072	1.59928
11	90.81805	9.181947	98.40072	1.59928
12	90.36423	9.635769	98.40072	1.59928
Indonesia				
1	99.83807	0.161929	99.22126	0.778739
2	99.61283	0.38717	99.02712	0.972883
3	97.41012	2.58988	97.89296	2.107045
4	97.28355	2.716452	96.84618	3.153816
5	97.28406	2.715945	91.70566	8.294344
10	97.28253	2.717466	91.2677	8.732297
11	97.28253	2.717467	91.26534	8.734663
12	97.28253	2.717467	91.26463	8.735372
Nigeria				
1	97.01704	2.982965	99.49871	0.501285
2	97.13698	2.863025	99.44785	0.55215
3	96.89593	3.10407	91.59557	8.404434
4	96.85703	3.142972	89.81294	10.18706
5	96.52762	3.472376	89.00123	10.99877
10	96.45861	3.541399	85.49513	14.50487
11	96.46086	3.539137	85.38961	14.61039
12	96.46229	3.537803	85.02481	14.97519
Turkey				
1	99.99122	0.00878	98.00443	1.995572
2	98.40252	1.597483	97.38739	2.612611
3	97.98562	2.014376	96.62049	3.379508
4	97.96473	2.035272	96.56558	3.434417
5	97.96479	2.035214	95.81582	4.184183
10	97.96432	2.035698	95.33542	4.664581
11	97.96432	2.035698	95.33393	4.66607
12	97.96432	2.035698	95.33394	4.666056

Industrial Production growth forecast error variance decompositions for different periods				
	2000:01-2009:03		2009:03-2014:12	
	variance attributed to:		variance attributed to:	
Period	Own shock	Stock return	Own shock	Stock return
Mexico				
1	100	-	100	-
2	97.14649	2.853514	98.44535	1.554653
3	95.12809	4.871909	95.68613	4.313867
4	93.15534	6.844658	95.42686	4.573137
5	90.35379	9.646208	95.42992	4.570076
10	85.05036	14.94964	95.4216	4.578404
11	85.0539	14.9461	95.4216	4.578404
12	84.78054	15.21946	95.4216	4.578404
Indonesia				
1	100	-	100	-
2	99.98793	0.012074	99.97598	0.024019
3	99.53615	0.463846	99.66505	0.334952
4	99.51474	0.485258	90.73146	9.26854
5	99.51502	0.484983	89.33677	10.66323
10	99.51463	0.485365	88.25713	11.74287
11	99.51463	0.485365	88.25527	11.74473
12	99.51463	0.485365	88.25601	11.74399
Nigeria				
1	100	-	100	-
2	99.98045	0.01955	97.67057	2.329427
3	99.92587	0.074129	92.85788	7.142118
4	97.89383	2.106174	90.75016	9.249843
5	93.06253	6.937468	91.55512	8.444877
10	92.74547	7.254526	82.97347	17.02653
11	92.74571	7.254291	83.17712	16.82288
12	92.74229	7.257711	83.09575	16.90425
Turkey				
1	100	-	100	-
2	97.82732	2.172678	99.94435	0.055653
3	97.87488	2.125119	99.9026	0.097402
4	97.7676	2.232399	99.01775	0.982255
5	97.71592	2.284076	98.23106	1.768941
10	97.70803	2.291968	98.02541	1.974589
11	97.70803	2.291968	98.02567	1.974327
12	97.70803	2.291968	98.0252	1.974804

Table 6: Impulse responses shock for pre and post crisis period.

the period before the crisis while this become larger after the crisis period over a longer horizon to 8.73, 14.97 and 4.66% respectively. In Indonesia, the explained proportion only increased by 2.03% to 4.66% while for Nigeria, an increased from 3.53% to 14.97% is observed.

It is worth mentioning that the result above is similar for the case of Indonesia and Nigeria when measuring the variability of industrial production due to the shocks in stock returns with the exception of Mexico and Turkey. In Mexico and Turkey, the explained proportion drops from 15.21 and 2.29% to 4.5 and 1.97% respectively for the different periods while for the case of Indonesia and Nigeria, the explained proportion becomes larger from 0.48 and 7.25 to 11.74 and 16.04 for the different periods under consideration respectively. Although, there are relatively close result in the causality test for both periods, however, results from the impulse responses and variance decomposition suggests the non-existence of link between the industrial production and stock market index for both the periods in the MINT during the period under study. This is in line with the study of [12,15].

Conclusions

This paper presents a structural vector autoregressive (SVAR) model which includes the growth rates of stock prices and industrial production of MINT economies using recent data (monthly) between the periods of 2000 to 2014. We statistically identified two common structural break periods for all the economies coincidentally at their recovery stages from the massive global financial crisis induced by the subprime market in the US. We used a bivariate - variable model to distinguish between two categories of structural shocks – the first being the stock market shock and the second is the macroeconomic shock. Following the work of who assumed that the stock market shock has only a temporary effect on real output although it may have a permanent effect on real share price whereas the macro shock has a potentially permanent effect on the economy and real share prices [15]. Motivations for this study steam from examining whether the variables dynamic interaction differs during the identified pre and post crisis; and more importantly, to examine the impact and interaction of the duo on the economy; as well as provide relevant policy measures to achieve the perceived objectives for the coined word 'MINT'.

Evidence from our causality test reveals zero dynamic linkages between the economic performance and stock market growth for both identified period with the exception of Mexico; which shows that stock market have some linkages with the industrial production of the economy during the pre-crisis period. Of course, trend shows that Mexico has a substantial manufacturing sector which is becoming integrated into US supply chains (geographical advantage) and is producing increasingly sophisticated products; however, this is not justifiable during the post-crises period. This feature casts some reservation of the data and on our model specification which imply that the difference between the two series is driven by a stochastic trend which is independent of that underlying real output and fundamental share prices. Accordingly, manufacturing in Turkey is still concentrated towards the lower end of the value chain and its prospects are closely tied to its neighboring country - Europe's. Similarly, manufacturing in Indonesia and Nigeria is still relatively underdeveloped and oil production is far more important in these countries but hindering the development of the industrial sector as a result of resources mismanagement.

Furthermore, our estimated model assesses the effects of the two types of shocks for each of the two variables in the model. In general, it was found that the effects of both shocks appear to be unstable and not well behave especially for Nigeria in the post crisis period and Mexico in the pre-crisis period. Also, for the case of Indonesia and Turkey, the shocks seem to dies out quite quickly - most of the action was over after about four and six periods. This implies that in addition to the market size and strategic geographical location of MINT, these countries need to ensure that the existing legal framework for investment protects investors and creates a level field for competition in the domestic market. Another factor worth mentioning is the need for the MINT economies to ensure political stability in their countries as this will reduce investment risk. For the case of Mexico whose prospects are closely tied to USA's, it should create an enabling platform should be made to improve production capacity as it has the tendency to pick up significantly from this in the long run.

More importantly, there seems to be different priority of development of certain sector/infrastructure for each of the MINT; for instance, Nigeria and Turkey facing political crises coupled with relative underdeveloped production capacity requires urgent platform in order to keep up in the MINT-family this is because financial markets tend to overreact to political events. Furthermore, MINT need to invest more in their human capital to ensure FDI inflow result in sustainable long-term economic growth The governments of countries with relatively low level or inefficient infrastructure, especially transportation and energy (e.g. Indonesia and Nigeria) need to investment more in these sectors.

References

1. Waterman T (2014) MINT nations: The economies of Nigeria and Turkey at a glance, Punters gallery.
2. BBC (2014) The Mint countries: Next economic giants?
3. Fama EK (1990) Stock returns, expected returns, and real activity. Journal of Finance 45: 1089-1108.
4. Barro RJ (1990) The stock market and investments. Review of Financial Studies 3: 115-131.
5. Schwert GW (1990) Stock returns and real activity: A century of evidence. Journal of Finance 45: 1237-1257.
6. Lee BS (1995) Fundamentals and bubbles in asset prices: evidence from the US and Japanese asset prices. Financial Engineering and Japanese Financial Markets 2: 69-122.
7. Groenewold N (2000) Fundamental share prices and Aggregate Real Output. University of Western Australia, Department of Economics Discussion Paper.
8. Laopodis NT (2006) Dynamic interactions among the stock market, federal funds rate, inflation and economic activity. The Financial Review 41: 513-545.
9. Rapach DE (2001) Macro shocks and real stock prices. Journal of Economics and Business 53: 5-26.
10. Lee BS (1998) Permanent, temporary and non-fundamental components of stock prices. Journal of Financial and Quantitative Analysis 33: 1-32.
11. Chung H, Lee BS (1998) Fundamental and non-fundamental components in stock prices of Pacific-Rim countries. Pacific-Basin Journal of Finance 6: 321-346.
12. Allen DE, Yang W (2003) Do UK stock prices deviate from fundamentals? Mathematics and Computers in Simulation in press.
13. Bhargava V, Dania A, Malhotra DK (2006) The Relationship between Price-Earnings Ratios, Dividend Yield and Stock Prices: Evidence from BRIC countries. Journal of Emerging Market.
14. Binswanger M (2004) How important are fundamentals? Evidence from a structural VAR model for the stock markets in the US Japan and Europe. Journal of International Financial Markets, Institutions and Money 14: 185-201.
15. Shiller RJ (2005) Irrational Exuberance. Princeton University Press.
16. Balke N, Wohar M (2001) Explaining Stock price movements: Is there a case for fundamentals? Federal Reserve Bank of Dallas Economic Review.
17. WDI (2015) Standard and Poor's Global Stock Markets Fact book and supplemental S&P data. The World Bank.
18. Laopodis NT (2010) Equity prices and macroeconomic fundamentals: International evidence. Journal of International Financial Markets. Institutions and Money 21: 247-276.
19. Ivanov, Kilian (2005) A Practitioner's Guide to Lag Order Selection for VAR Impulse Response Analysis. Studies in Nonlinear Dynamics and Econometrics.

Granger Causality between Growth in the Education Sector and Social Economic Services in Nigeria

Oluwapelumi A* and Olaride OB

Department of Mathematics and Statistics, Rufus Giwa Polytechnic, Owo, Ondo State, Nigeria

Abstract

The relationship between two variables has been mush studied using the concepts of Granger causality. In this study, Nigeria economic data from 1981 to 2015 is used to investigate the causal relationship between education sector growth and socio-economic services (education, health, road & construction and transport & communication), employing unit root test, Johansen co-integration and Granger causality approaches. The result of the study showed that there is long run Granger causality between the education growth and the recurrent expenditure on socio-economic services.

Keywords: Health growth; Socio-economic; Granger causality; Johansen co-integration

Introduction

The relationship between two variables has been mush studied using the concepts of Granger causality. Granger causality is a term for a specific notion of causality in time-series analysis. The idea of Granger causality is a pretty simple one: A variable *X Granger-causes Y* if *Y* can be better predicted using the histories of both *X* and *Y* than it can using the history of *Y* alone.

Granger introduced the concept of Granger causality in 1969 and it has been widely used in econometric studies to test availability and the direction of the causality. Furthermore, Johansen's cointegration analysis is employed to determine any long-term relationship between the variables before the causality test. The first step in time series analysis is to investigate the stationarity of variables, also called the unit root test. Accordingly, the existence of a unit root at frequency zero would imply that the stochastic trend is non-stationary [1]. Gujarati and Porter [2] point out that it is so often to meet non-stationary time series and the estimates of non-stationary variables will lead to spurious regression. Thus, their economic interpretation will not be meaningful. Furthermore, unrelated time series may appear to be related using conventional testing applications such as ordinary least squares regression. To this end, we utilise the Augmented Dickey–Fuller test (ADF), and the Phillips–Perron test (PP) to examine whether the data are non-stationary [3,4]. The augmented Dickey–Fuller (ADF) unit root test is one of the most accepted and widely used tests to investigate the stationarity of series [5].

Regression analysis based on time series data implicitly assumes that the underlying data is stationary [2] and it is usually the case that time series variables of macro economy are non-stationary. Alternatively, cointegration analysis allows for spurious results to be avoided by using non-stationary data, but all those series have to be integrated into the same order. Despite the range of different cointegration tests in the literature, the Engle–Granger and Johansen [6,7] tests are widely used. In this study, the Johansen cointegration test is employed to test the existence of a long-run equilibrium relationship among the variables and employed Granger causality analysis to determine the direction of causality between education sector growth and socio-economic services.

The adequacy of socio-economic service determines a country's success in education and another; failure to improve quality and efficiency of the entire education system, coping with population growth reducing poverty, or improving environmental conditions. A good socio-economic service in a country reduces outbound education, provide access at all levels of education and improve the quality and efficiency of the entire education system.

Relevant literature on Granger causality formulate econometric models in continuous time offers several advantages in the context of causality testing: they can take account of the interaction among variables during the unit observation period; they can be represented as a causal chain where each of the variables responds directly to the stimulus of only a proper subset of the other variables while there is interaction between all the variables during the observation period; they allow a clear distinction to be made between stock and flow variables; and their form does not depend on the unit observation period. Considered from a continuous time perspective, the problem that spurious Granger causality relationships can arise due to temporal aggregation.

Ashipala and Haimbodi look at the relationship between public investment and economic growth in South Africa, Botswana and Namibia using the VECM methodology. They find that the effect of public investment on growth is not significant however, it has the correct sign. On the other hand, private investment is shown to have a long run growth impact in South Africa and Namibia. However, they find evidence indicating a reverse causality from GDP growth to public investment. The causality is negative in the case of Botswana suggesting that as the economy grows investment in public goods declines, which contradicts the Keynesian theory and Wagner's law.

Loizides and Vamvoukas [8] employed the trivariate causality test to examine the relationship between government expenditure and economic growth, using data set on Greece, United Kingdom and Ireland. The authors found that government size granger causes

***Corresponding author:** Alabi Oluwapelumi, Department of Mathematics and Statistics, Rufus Giwa Polytechnic, Owo, Ondo State, Nigeria
E-mail: oluwapelumialabi@yahoo.com

economic growth in all the countries they studied. The finding was true for Ireland and the United Kingdom both in the long run and short run. The results also indicated that economic growth granger causes public expenditure for Greece and United Kingdom, when inflation is included. McCories and Chambers [9] formulating models in continuous time offers a basis for correcting for the effects of temporal aggregation in observed discrete data through a discrete time analogue, in a way that does not rely on our positing a definite time unit in which the data are generated. In an empirical application, they showed that imposing these restrictions, and precisely, matters in testing for Granger causality. Their results complement those in the fixed-interval time aggregation literature, especially those recently obtained by Marcellino [10] and Breitung and Swanson [11].

Lean and Smyth [12] employed annual data for Malaysia from 1970 to 2008 to examine the causal relationship between economic growth, electricity generation, exports and prices in a multivariate model. Their first major finding of the study is that there is unidirectional Granger causality running from economic growth to electricity generation. The second major result is that neither the export-led nor handmaiden theories of trade are supported. The third main finding is that there is no causal relationship between prices and economic growth.

Nurudeen and Usman applied cointegration and error correction methods to determine the relationship between government expenditure and economic growth in Nigeria. Their results show that government total capital expenditure, total recurrent expenditures, and government expenditure on education have negative influence on economic growth. On the contrary, increasing government expenditure on transport and communication results to an increase in economic growth. Pradhan explores the nexus between transport infrastructure (road and rail), energy consumption and economic growth in India over the period 1970-2007. He finds evidence of unidirectional causality from transport infrastructure to economic growth.

Siyan carry out co-integration test to determine the long run relationship between economic growth and road transportation in Nigeria. Their result show that road transportation has an impact in the economic development in Nigeria. From the result economic growth in Nigeria depended on the level of good and accessible road transportation and the level of road transport infrastructures that will complete the business activities and facilitate trade of Small and Medium scale Enterprises in Nigeria. A recent work, Harun examine the effect of health and social service sector growth on the flow of inbound health tourism between 2004:Q1 and 2015:Q4 by employing Granger causality and Johansen cointegration approaches. Their findings suggested that there is a long-run Granger causality from domestic health and social work expenditures to health tourism income whereas this is non-existence in the opposite direction.

Materials and Methods

The study is based on time series data obtained from National Bureau of Statistics bulletin Republic of Nigeria that covers the period from 1981 to 2015. The GDP_t of education (EGDP) is used as a proxy variable for economic growth of the education sector, which is reported in current basic prices. And the recurrent expenditure on socio-economic services i.e., health ($HEXP_t$), education ($EEXP_t$), road and construction ($RCEXP_t$) and transport and communication ($TCEXP_t$). The remaining variable is real exchange rate (RER_t) and it is used a proxy variable in order to test the effects of relative price changes. All variables are expressed in logarithm forms and seasonally adjusted.

The following model was used to investigate the relationship between education sector growth and socio-economic services.

The model formulation of rooted in the theoretical framework as postulated by Bloch and Tang (2003), the model was specified as follows:

$$EGDP_t=f(HEXP_t, EEXP_t, RCEXP_t, TCEXP_t,\beta_i)+u_t$$

Where $EGDP_t$ is the amount of the gross national product in education, $HEXP_t$ is the recurrent expenditure on health, $RCEXP_t$ is recurrent expenditure on road & construction, $TCEXP_t$ is transport and communication, β_i is the parameter to be estimated and u_t is the error term.

Unit root test

For the purpose of this study, Augmented Dickey–Fuller test (ADF), and the Phillips–Perron test (PP) are used to examine the stationarity of the data [3,4].

i. Augmented Dickey–Fuller test (ADF): The ADF test here consists of estimating the following regression [2]:

$$\Delta Y_t = \beta_1 + \beta_2 t + \delta Y_{t-1} + \sum_{i=1}^{m} \alpha_i \Delta Y_{t-i} + \varepsilon_t$$

where Δ is the first difference operator, *t* is the time trend, *k* denotes the number of lags used, and ε_t is the error term. βi, δ and α_i are parameters. The null hypothesis that series Y_t is non-stationary can be rejected it δ is statistically significant with negative sign. In addition, *m* shows the optimal lag order, which is chosen carefully using the Schwarz criterion (AIC) in empirical method.

ii. The Phillips–Perron test (PP): this is a complementary feature of the ADF unit root test Phillips and Perron use nonparametric statistical methods to take care of the serial correlation in the error terms without adding lagged difference terms. Since the asymptotic distribution of the PP test is the same as the ADF test statistic [2].

Now that we know the problems associated with non-stationary time series, the practical question is what to do. To avoid the spurious regression problem that may arise from regressing a non-stationary time series on one or more non-stationary time series, we have to transform non-stationary time series to make them stationary. Alternatively, to avoid spurious results co-integration analysis could be adopted, using non-stationary data, but all series have to be integrated to the same order. For the purpose of the study Johansen co-integration test would be used.

$$EGDP_t=\beta_0+\beta_1 HEXP_{t\text{-}}\beta_2 EEXP_{t+}\beta_3 RCEXP_t+\beta_4 TCEXP_t)+u_t$$

Ganger causality

Granger causality test can be assessing by regressing each variable on lagged values of it and the other and it can be implemented as follow:

$$EGDP_t = \alpha_1 + \sum_{h=1}^{n} \beta_{1h}'' EGDP_{t\text{-}h} \sum_{i=1}^{p} \beta_{2i} HEXP_{t\text{-}i} +$$
$$\sum_{j=1}^{q} \beta_{3j} EEXP_{t\text{-}j} + \sum_{k=1}^{r} \beta_{4k} RCEXP_{t\text{-}k} + \sum_{l=1}^{s} \beta_{5l} TCEXP_{t\text{-}l} + u_{1t}$$

$$HEXP_t = \alpha_2 + \sum_{h=1}^{n} \gamma_{1h} HEXP_{t-h} \sum_{i=1}^{p} \gamma_{2i} EGDP_{t-i} +$$
$$\sum_{j=1}^{q} \gamma_{3j} EEXP_{t-j} + \sum_{k=1}^{r} \gamma_{4k} RCEXP_{t-k} + \sum_{l=1}^{s} \gamma_{5l} TCEXP_{t-l} + u_{2t}$$

$$EEXP_t = \alpha_3 + \sum_{h=1}^{n} \delta_{1h} EEXP_{t-h} \sum_{i=1}^{p} \delta_{2i} HEXP_{t-i} +$$
$$\sum_{j=1}^{q} \delta_{3j} EGDP_{t-j} + \sum_{k=1}^{r} \delta_{4k} RCEXP_{t-k} + \sum_{l=1}^{s} \delta_{5l} TCEXP_{t-l} + u_{3t}$$

$$RCEXP_t = \alpha_4 + \sum_{h=1}^{n} \lambda_{1h} RCEXP_{t-h} \sum_{i=1}^{p} \lambda_{2i} EEXP_{t-i} +$$
$$\sum_{j=1}^{q} \lambda_{3j} HEXP_{t-j} + \sum_{k=1}^{r} \lambda_{4k} EGDP_{t-k} + \sum_{l=1}^{s} \lambda_{5l} TCEXP_{t-l} + u_{4t}$$

$$TCEXP_t = \alpha_5 + \sum_{h=1}^{n} \phi_{1h} TCEXP_{t-h} \sum_{i=1}^{p} \phi_{2i} RCEXP_{t-i} +$$
$$\sum_{j=1}^{q} \phi_{3j} EEXP_{t-j} + \sum_{k=1}^{r} \phi_{4k} HEXP_{t-k} + \sum_{l=1}^{s} \phi_{5l} EGDP_{t-l} + u_{5t}$$

where *n, p, q, r, s* denote the number of lagged variables, ε_{it} are error terms that are assumed to be normally distributed and white noise.

Interpretation of results

Time series plots for all variables employed in the study are provided in Figure 1. It display the amount of GDP in education (HGDP), recurrent expenditure on education (EEXP), health (HEXP), road and construction (RCEXP), and transport and communication (TCEXP). All the variables show an upward fluctuating movement especially after 1998. There is a significant drop in 2010 except HGDP that show upward trend [13-15].

From the analysis, the unit root test was conducted to ascertain the stationarity of the data using both the Augmented Dickey Fuller (ADF) and the Philips-Perron (PP). The results of the test in Table 1 show that all the variables in the model are stationary at 0.05 significant level. Knowing the unit-root properties of the variables, co-integration test was conducted to ascertain the long-run relationship between education sector growth and socio-economic services (education, health, road and construction and transport and communication). The Johansen co-integration test result in Tables 2a and 2b reveal the empirical reality of four (4) co-integrating equations at 0.05 significant level. The hypothesis which states there is no long-run relationship between growth in education and socio-economic services is rejected at 0.05 significance level. Therefore, there is a long-run relationship between growth in growth in education sector and socio-economic services in Nigeria.

The empirical analysis from Table 3 shows the estimation results of the equation used in the study, the R-squared of 0.96 is the coefficient

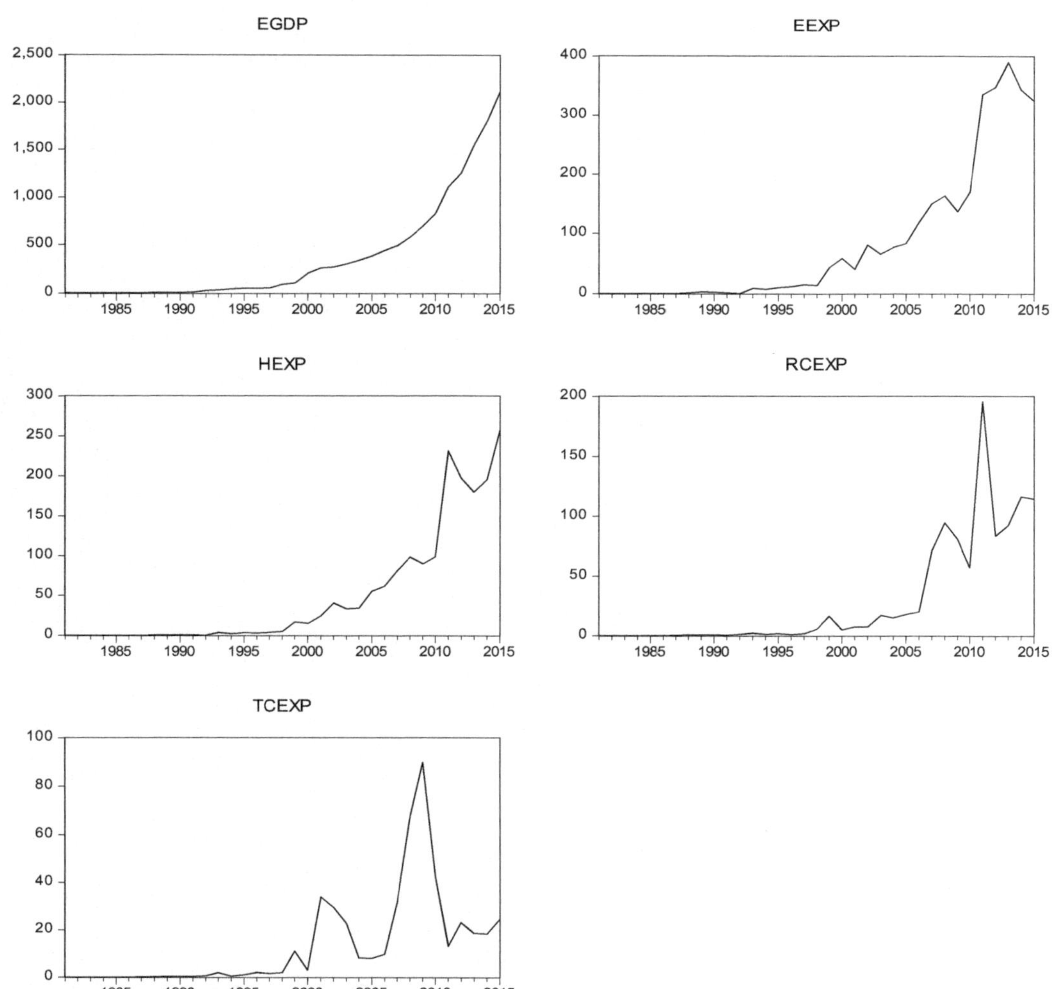

Figure 1: Time series plot for the amount of original value (in billion naira).

Variables	Augmented Dikey-Fuller (ADF)			Philips-Perron (PP)		
	t-Statistics	P-value	Order of integration	t-Statistics	P-value	Order of integration
EGDP	14.31696	0.0000	Stationary at level.	14.31696	0.0000	Stationary at first diff.
EEXP	4.850758	0.0001	Stationary at level.	-5.087712	0.0000	Stationary at first diff.
HEXP	2.181846	0.0444	Stationary at level.	-6.075018	0.0000	Stationary at first diff.
RCEXP	2.710985	0.0154	Stationary at level.	-9.896061	0.0000	Stationary at first diff.
TCEXP	-2.797766	0.0089	Stationary at level.	-2.142164	0.0399	Stationary at level.

Table 1: Stationarity (Unit root) test.

Hypothesized No. of CE(s)	Eigenvalue	Trace Statistic	0.05 Critical Value	Prob.
None*	0.939774	212.4471	69.81889	0.0000
At most 1*	0.891897	119.7287	47.85613	0.0000
At most 2*	0.603026	46.31450	29.79707	0.0003
At most 3*	0.380868	15.82634	15.49471	0.0446
At most 4	0.000150	0.004952	3.841466	0.9429

Trace statistics indicates 4 co-integrating equations at 0.05 level* denotes the rejection of the hypothesis at 0.05.

Table 2a: Johansen co-integration rank test (trace statistic).

Hypothesized No. of CE(s)	Eigenvalue	Trace Statistic	0.05 Critical Value	Prob.
None*	0.939774	92.71837	33.87687	0.0000
At most 1*	0.891897	73.41420	27.58434	0.0000
At most 2*	0.603026	30.48816	21.13162	0.0018
At most 3*	0.380868	15.82139	14.26460	0.0281
At most 4	0.000150	0.004952	3.841466	0.9429

Maximum eigenvalue indicates 4 co-integrating equations at 0.05 level* denotes the rejection of the hypothesis at 0.05.

Table 2b: Johansen co-integration rank test (Maximum Eigenvalue statistic).

Variable	Coefficient	Std. Error	t-Statistic	Prob.
HEXP	8.898184	0.812444	10.95237	0
RCEXP	-5.330769	0.683506	-7.799155	0
TCEXP	1.293628	0.636589	2.032126	0.0514
C	9.69139	14.36278	0.674757	0.5052
R-squared	0.959226	Mean dependent var		386.5712
Adjusted R-squared	0.953602	S.D. dependent var		560.3538
S.E. of regression	120.7013	Sum squared resid		422495.3
Durbin-Watson stat	1.33218	Long-run variance		4031.503

Table 3: Long Run Regression.

of determination indicates that 96% variation in education growth can be explain by the socio-economic services. The Adjusted R-squared is a standardized measure which controls the effect of any differences that may due to chance. The adjusted R-square of 95% suggests that the model in used is fit in explanation the variation in amount GDP in education sector put in consideration the losses of degree of freedom cause by the number of independent variables (education, health, road and construction, transport and communication), that is the independent variables are statistically significant in determining the total variation in education sector growth in Nigeria. The t-statistic suggests that each parameter in the model employed in the study is statistically significant at 0.1 level of significant.

$$EGDP_t=9.7+0.81EEXP_{t+}8.9HEXP_t+-5.3RCEXP_t+1.3TCEXP_t$$

From the model of the study it can be observed that the government recurrent expenditure on education, health and transportation & communication contribute positively to the education sector growth in Nigeria, given its coefficient (0.81, 8.9 and 1.3 respectively) of the equation it is statistically significant at 0.1 level of significant and it

Lag	LogL	LR	FPE	AIC	SC	HQ
0	-828.3894	NA	5.93e+15	50.50845	50.73519	50.58474
1	-659.9343	275.6539	1.01e+12	41.81420	43.17466	42.27195
2	-569.4489	120.6471*	2.14e+10*	37.84539*	40.33957*	38.68460*

LR sequential modified likelihood ratio (LR) test statistic (each test at 5 % level), *FPE* final prediction error, *AIC* Akaike information criterion, *SC* Schwarz information criterion, *HQ* Hannan–Quinn information criterion* indicates lag order selected by the criterion.

Table 4: VAR Lag Order Selection Criteria.

is capable of determining the variation in education sector growth in Nigeria. This implies a unit change in EEXP, HEXP and TCEXP will cause 0.81, 8.9 and 1.3 unit change in amount of Gross Domestic Product in education (EGDP) in Nigeria. The recurrent expenditure on road and construction from the model can be seen to have a negative relationship on amount of Gross Domestic Product in education in Nigeria and statistically significant in determining the variation in education sector growth, given its coefficient (-5.3) which is less than 0.1 level of significant. This implies that a unit change in RCEXP will cause 5.3 unit decrease change in amount of Gross Domestic Product in education (EGDP) in Nigeria.

Having considered the unit root test, co-integration test and the long run relationship regression. VAR Granger causality test was applied to investigate the direction of causality among variables and the results are shown on Table 4. Several hypothesis concerning Granger causality relationship between HGDP and EEXP, HGDP and HEXP, HGDP and RCEXP, EGDP and TCEXP, EEXP and HEXP, EEXP and RCEXP, EEXP and TCEXP, HEXP and RCEXP, HEXP and TCEXP, RCEXP and TCEXP were considered. According to the findings, the χ^2 statistics test rejects the null hypothesis of no Granger causality from HEXP and RCEGDP to EGDP, from EEXP and HEXP to RCEXP and from EEXP to EGDP, which indicate that there is bidirectional Granger causality from recurrent expenditure on health and road & construction to education sector growth, also that there is unidirectional Granger causality from recurrent expenditure on education and health to recurrent expenditure on transport & communication, and from recurrent expenditure on education to education sector growth, at 0.05 level of significance (Table 5).

Conclusion

Granger pointed out that if co-integration exists in a pair of I(1) series, there must be causation in at least one direction. The study investigates the relationship between education sector growth and socio-economic services, and to identify any possible direction of causality between them. The main result of the study shows that socio-economic service has much to contribute to education sector growth. Furthermore, it sends an important message to policymakers about the developments of socio-economic sectors in providing potential as a service sector. Another finding of the study is that there are both bidirectional and unidirectional causality from education sector growth to recurrent expenditure on some socio-economic services in Nigeria. This can be explained by the economic contribution of education sector

Effect Cause					
	EGDP	EEXP	HEXP	RCEXP	TCEXP
EGDP	-	2.67 (0.2636)	10.55*(0.0051)	7.33* (0.0256)	3.78 (0.1508)
EEXP	12.76* (0.0017)	-	2.83 (0.2434)	6.02 (0.0493)	10.04* (0.0066)
HEXP	17.89* (0.0001)	1.59 (0.4517)	-	5.78 (0.0557)	6.29* (0.0431)
RCEXP	27.11* (0.0000)	1.75 (0.4169)	2.19 (0.3354)	-	1.11 (0.5740)
TCEXP	2.92 (0.2317)	2.76 (0.2514)	1.42 (0.4918)	1.410.4939)	-

*denotes statistical significance at 5% level. Figures in parenthesis are p-values.

Table 5: VAR Granger causality/block exogeneity Wald tests (χ^2 statistics).

growth to the whole sector, which is still limited. However, the revenue collected through fees constitutes an insignificant proportion of the revenue of the institutions, using the fund allocated for socio-economic service appropriately may improve quality of education, education sector growth such that outbound education may also be reduce to minimum in Nigeria.

References

1. Torraleja FAG, Vázquez AM, Franco MJB (2009) Flows into tourist areas: an econometric approach. Int J Tour Res 11: 1-15.
2. Gujarati DN, Porter DC (2009) Basic econometrics. (5th edn.), McGraw-Hill, New York.
3. Dickey DA, Fuller WA (1979) Distribution of the estimators for autoregressive time series with a unit root. Econometrica 74: 427-431.
4. Phillips P, Perron P (1988) Testing for a unitroot in time series regression. Biometrica 75: 335-346.
5. Park S, Lee J, Song W (2016) Short-term forecasting of Japanese tourist inflow to South Korea using Google trends data. J Travel Tour Mark.
6. Johansen S (1988) Statistical analysis of cointegration vectors. J Econ Dyn Control 12: 231-234.
7. Johansen S (1991) Estimation and hypothesis testing of cointegration vectors in Gaussian vector autoregressive models. Econometrica 55: 1551-1580.
8. Loizides J, Vamvoukas G (2005) Government Expenditure and Economic Growth: Evidence from Trivariate Causality Testing. Journal of Applied Economics 8: 125-152.
9. McCrorie JR, Chambers MJ (2006) Granger causality and the sampling of economic processes. Journal of Econometrics 132: 311-336.
10. Marcellino M (1999) Some consequences of temporal aggregation in empirical analysis. Journal of Business and Economic Statistics 17: 129-136.
11. Breitung J, Swanson NR (2002) Temporal aggregation and spurious instantaneous causality in multiple time series models. Journal of Time Series Analysis 23: 651-665.
12. Lean HH, Smyth R (2010) Multivariate Granger causality between electricity generation, exports, prices and GDP in Malaysia. Energy 35: 364-3648.
13. Laudau D (1986) Government and Economic Growth in LDCs: An Empirical Study. Economic Development and Cultural Change 35: 35-75.
14. Barro RJ (1991) Economic Growth in Cross-Section of Countries. Quarterly Journal of Economics 106: 407-443.
15. Engen EM, Skinner J (1992) Fiscal Policy and Economic Growth. Taxation and Economic Growth 50: 617-642.

6

An Empirical Investigation of the Effects of Brain Drain on Developing Countries since 21st Century: A Case of Afghanistan

Mujeeb Ur Rehman Rahimi*

Graduate School of Economics and Management, Ural Federal University Yekaterinburg, Russia

Abstract

The purpose of this study is to find out the factors behind the flood of Afghan migrants the world witnessed during the past couple of years. After the withdrawal of some portion of US and NATO forces in 2014, people of Afghanistan suffered mainly from continued security concerns which ultimately stimulated migration of young minds at large but this is not the only factor we analyzed during the process. The push factors such as cost of weddings in some parts of Afghanistan is a profound problem and it was observed from the investigation of the sample population as a stimulus for youth to go abroad to work and save money for getting married. We investigated the unemployment factor on brain drain from Afghanistan on a large scale. This factor clearly proved to be the major driver of migration based on the results obtained in this empirical study. Furthermore, each year thousands of students leave Afghanistan to study in different parts of the world on scholarship. We investigated the role of educational scholarships on motivating youth to leave Afghanistan and their probability to return back to their homeland. It was demonstrated through the analysis of sample data that mostly those students who travel abroad for study purposes do not return back to Afghanistan, thereby creating a vacuum in terms of productive young minds. In addition, Social pressure is a common influence on people's behavior within the different communities in Afghanistan. We analyzed the relationship between people adopting the path of migration with social pressures from society. The analysis of the data showed a positive relationship of the societal pressures on the youth leaving country.

The nature of research for my study is based on quantitative methodology. This research targeted mainly the Afghan population living overseas because these are the people who are most affected one way or the other by some internal factors that's why they migrated. We have also included citizen's views that live within Afghanistan in order to understand prospects of migration from the participants. However, a convenience sampling method was used in this study as specific people were targeted that we believe would take part in the survey. Social Media such as Facebook and Vkontakte was used to deliver the questionnaires to the respondents. The Statistical Package for Social Sciences (SPSS) statistical models such as Chi square test, binomial probability test, and a one sample test were used to test the hypotheses statements. A pairwise test was used to rank the factors in terms of major influence on migration.

Keywords: Brain drain; Afghanistan; Weddings; Cronback alpha; Social pressure

Introduction

Brain drain definition: It is the phenomenon in which skilled labor of a country flees to another country in order to earn better living.

This tendency of talented and competent people leaving their native land is a big issue for some countries, since these people has expertise in certain disciplines such as medical, engineering, motor repairing etcetera, whose capabilities can be utilized to boost a country's economy and helps in administrative affairs. The countries which are unable to contain their educated people will certainly experience economic loses.

Every year many developed countries has a policy in which they announce education scholarships to attract competent students from under developed countries which latter can become an asset for the guest country [1].

Migration: National and International Aspects

Policy of states regarding immigration

Iranian government policy towards Afghans: Iran has been one of the biggest stake holders after Pakistan for retaining Afghan refugees. Iran ministry of interior is responsible for the affairs of foreign nationals in cooperation with the Ministry of Foreign affairs and the ministry of labor.

Refugee matters are handled by the Ministry's Bureau of Aliens and Foreign Immigrant Affairs (BAFIA), established in the early 1980s.

In 1976, Iran approved the 1951 UN Refugee Convention and its 1967 Protocol with reservations regarding Articles 17 (wage earning employment), 23 (public relief), 24 (labor legislation and social security), and 26 (freedom of movement). The provisions in the Refugee Convention regarding the above Articles are meant to ensure in large measure the equality of treatment of refugees with nationals. For instance, Article 24 is meant to ensure that the refugees are covered by national labor law and also entitled to social security on par with nationals [2].

German immigration policy: German is most desired country for migrants after United States. In January 2005, Germany introduced an immigration policy through which scientists and professionals from different walk of life can be attracted to the German labor market.

In April 2012, European blue card legislation was implemented in Germany which allows highly skilled professionals from non-European

***Corresponding author:** Mujeeb URR, Graduate School of Economics and Management, Ural Federal University Yekaterinburg, Russia
E-mail: mujeebrn@yahoo.com

countries after fulfilling certain conditions easily find job and live in the Germany [3]. As for as refugees are concern, Germany recognizes the rights of those people as a refugee who faces a serious life threat in their country or has a fear of prosecution due to their religion or nationality. According to article 39 on citizenship treaty on European Union, people from all European Union member countries have the right to obtain job in Germany free from discrimination.

People from Non-European countries can only migrate to Germany if they are skilled.

Germany has three types of immigration titles:

1) 90 days' temporary visa
2) Residence permits
3) Settlement permits.

Demographics of Germany according to Federal Statistical Office of Germany as per the year 2015, Afghanistan ranks in 20th (Table 1).

France immigration policy: France has been one of the friendly immigrant countries in Europe. The ministry of foreign affairs of France controls the flow of immigrants. In comparison with the other European countries, France has a strict policy regarding residence permit. The residence permit in France is called the carte de séjour. If you are a non-EU citizen, in order to stay in France for more than 3 months, people need a temporary residence permit, skills and talents residence card or retired residence permit [4].

France gives asylum to those people who fears of persecution in their country due to the race, religion or person belong to a political group.

Application for asylum status is processed by the French office for protection of refugees and expatriates. After the OFPRA (French Office for the Protection of Refugees and Stateless Persons) issues a certificate of deposit of the request, the petitioner must go to the place where he/she lives, which will issue a receipt of request for asylum which is valid for three months [5].

Britain immigration policy: Immigrants adopt different ways to arrive to Britain such as;

- Family of person already obtained nationality status, can invite other members of the family to Britain.
- Stay in Britain for long term work.
- Students who have received scholarship to study in Britain or want to study on self-finance basses.
- Temporary workers or people coming to Britain for the purpose of recreation.

Asylum is awarded to those people with some expertise in a selected area. Simply a young applicant with a doctorate and proof of high earnings will have more chances of acceptance than someone who is less skilled - and therefore find it's easier for them to come to the UK (Figure 1).

Since 2001 the world witnessed continues increase in migration. Afghanistan is 2nd to Syria in terms people leaving their homes for Europe or other countries [6] (Table 2).

Afghanistan in brief

Afghanistan is geographically land locked country within south and central Asia. The population of Afghanistan is approximately 33 million. It ranks 42 in terms of most populous country in the world. It has about 2430 km border with Pakistan making it the biggest border with its neighbors. Afghanistan has a border with Pakistan in the south and east; on its western side is Iran. On north the border is connected with Turkmenistan, Uzbekistan and Tajikistan, china is located in the Fareast border with Afghanistan. It covers an area of 652860 square km. It ranks 41, in terms of largest countries in the world.

Rank	Countries	Population
1	Turkey	1,506,113
2	Poland	740,962
3	Italy	596,127
4	Romania	452,718
5	Syria	366,556
6	Greece	339,931
7	Croatia	297,895
8	Serbia	260.212
9	Russia	230,994
10	Bulgaria	226,926
11	Kosovo	208,619
12	Austria	181,756
13	Hungry	178,221
14	Bosnia and Herzegovina	167,975
15	Spain	155,918
16	Netherlands	147,322
17	Iraq	136,399
18	Portugal	133,929
19	Ukraine	133,774
20	Afghanistan	131,454

Table 1: Ranking of countries on Migration (2015).

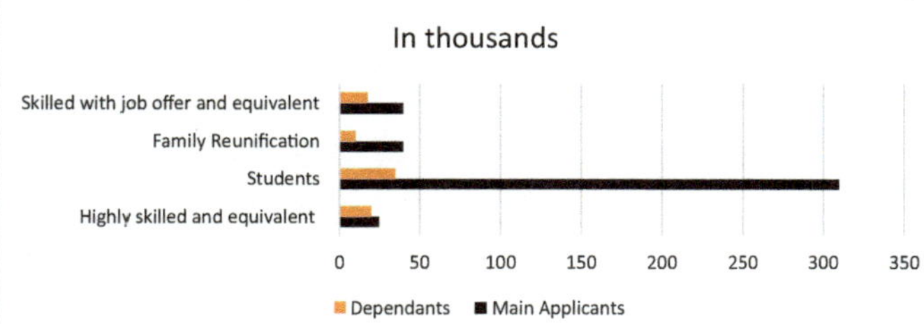

Figure 1: Changes in Systematic Risk following the Terrorist Attacks in France.

Area (km²), 2015	6,52,860
Population (millions), 2015	33
Population density (people per sq.km), 2015	49.82
Population ages 0-14 (% of total), 2015	44
Population ages 15-64 (% of total), 2015	53.5
Employment to population ratio, 15+ (%), 2016	43.3
GDP per capita ($), 2015	619.8
GNI PPP per capita ($), 2009	860
Economic Growth (%), 2013	3.9
Unemployment (%), 2015	40
Population living in less than a dollar per day (millions)	9
People living under national poverty line (%), 2007/8	36
Literacy rate	38.2
Annual number of school graduate, 2013	2,66,000
University graduates, 2016	6,56,257
Net migration rate out of 1000 (2016 estimated)	1.2

Table 2: Population Statistics [7].

As per 2015 statistics 2.7 million Afghans are still living as refugees in Pakistan and Iran. 2013 statistics shows that 46% of the Afghan population are under the age of 15 and 74% of the population in the rural population. The average birth rate for a single woman is 5 during her life.

Afghanistan is diverse country based on ethnicity, linguistically and religiously. Pashtun is largest and politically strongest ethnic group in Afghanistan. It makes up 42% of the population of Afghanistan. The other major ethnic groups are Tajik, Uzbek, Hazara, Aimaq, Baloch and others.

Pashto and Dari are the two official languages of Afghanistan. Afghanistan is divided into 34 provinces administratively and every province has its own capital and provincial administration. Several decades of war and its complexities within different ethnics has made Afghanistan one of the poorest countries in the world. Until 2014, the country's GDP was $60.58 billion. As per 2012, the total exports were $2.7 billion. The unemployment rate was 35% reported in 2008. According to a report in 2009, around 42% of the population lives on less than a dollar per day. The external debt for Afghanistan totals $1.5. Due to the inclusion of remittances from Afghan expats from abroad and international aid has grown 10% annually since last decade. Agriculture is the back-bone of the nation's economy. Da Afghanistan bank is the central bank of Afghanistan and Afghani is used as nation's currency.

One of the forces which brought improvement in the economy was over 5 million Afghan expatriates who brought with them energy, education entrepreneurship skills and the capital needed to start business. As per the human development index, Afghanistan is 5th least developed country in the world. For both male and female, the average life expectancy is estimated to be around 60 years.

The literacy rate of Afghanistan has been very low but since numerous schools are been made throughout Afghanistan, it is increasing. Education is one of the tools which can bring development and economic revival in Afghanistan [7].

Greater enrollments in education determines the degree of societal stability which is a dream that yet to be accomplished. 40% of Afghan children does not go to school as per the UNICEF report [8].

Research objectives

It has been more than 4 decades that Afghanistan is confronted to devastations mostly due to internal conflicts which has resulted in human flight in millions in many sections of the world.

Afghanistan government has taken some steps to stop this phenomenon in recent past. Social media and electronic media were used as a tool to disseminate Afghan Government's Campaign to curb brain drain.

This research is conducted to understand the reasons for Afghans that has caused them to flee to other countries [9].

The aim of this study concerns the following objectives:

- To find out the dominant factors that caused brain drain.
- To know, is there any role of unemployment in losing the trained people (brain drain).
- To explore how much part is played by social pressure in pushing people to leave country.
- To understand uncertainty factors causing brain drain.
- To explore wedding constraints as a push factor on brain drain.
- To recognize Educational scholarships part in brain drain.
- To analyze the role of job opportunities from abroad or job attractions on people departing from country.
- To understand the Demographics of the population sample.

Origin of migration from Afghanistan

Migration before 1979: Movement of large number of people from Afghanistan is not a recent history. Records show that Afghans has been migrating to Pakistan and Iran since centuries. As a result of the natural disasters in 1850s, thousands of people from Northern Areas of Afghanistan migrated to Iran aimed taking shelter. In Area of Torbat-e-Jam Iran, it is known that some 15,000 migrants from Afghanistan have been settled between 1880 and 1903 [10].

In the last centuries, Afghanistan has not been under good economic prosperity. For the reason that, there was not enough industries built in the country which caused widespread unemployment in Afghanistan.

As a result of Oil boom large labor market from Afghanistan were compelled to move to Iran, Pakistan and other Middle Eastern Countries in 1973 for work [11].

When large number of Pashtuns in the currently named KPK area of Pakistan migrated to Oil rich gulf countries, this provided a good opportunity for Afghans labors to work in Pakistan [12].

In the same time, high wages in the Islamic republic of Iran and increase in taxes in Afghanistan, labors were induced to move to Iran. As a result of that, before soviet Occupation of Afghanistan thousands of Afghan migrants were present in Iran [13].

Labors from Afghanistan migrated to Iran and Pakistan were welcomed because they migrated legally and also provided them with the cheap labor. The Afghans in Iran were mostly working in bricks industry and construction and were receiving very low remuneration as compared to Iranian citizens.

This indicates that instead of devoting their capabilities that these migrants exhibited, were unfortunately wasted because of many reasons whatsoever [14].

Migration at the time of Soviet Union invasion (1979): The first large migration from Afghanistan happened in 1979 at the time of soviet invasion. In the following 10 years, because of resistance against Soviet Forces on the side of Mujahedeen, masses on large number from Afghanistan flee to Pakistan and to the Islamic Republic of Iran [13].

Due to their culture and language similarity and because of common boundaries with the Islamic Republic of Iran and Pakistan, these refugees had nowhere to go but to these countries [14]. Refugees were mostly from villages where people had to escape because of bombings and targeted killings [15].

During the years of war 1979 and 1989, approximately 2.6 million people escaped to Iran to take shelter where they were welcomed by the Iran Authorities and were given "blue card" which reminded them of the refugee and gave them the right to get education, healthcare and food. They were also given the permission to work on a low wage. They were called "Mohajerin" which means involuntary religious migrant. The people migrated to Iran were belonged to Hazara community mostly who are Shia sect largely which is also the official religion of

Iran. It was considered the duty of every Iranian to help their religious brothers and sisters. Out of 2.6 million migrated to Iran because of soviet invasion, only 5-10% were contained in Refugee camps and the remaining were settled in cities and villages of eastern part of country [16].

The intensity of war after the soviet invasion also effected Pakistan where according to one statistics between 1979 and 1989, 1.5 million people crossed the border to Pakistan.

The Pashtun tribes living on both sides of the border has strong ties. These tribes share religious, culture, language and some family relationship in which one brother is living across the border in Pakistan and other brother's family is living Afghanistan.

The war between the rival parties between 1981 and 1985 were heightened which compelled large population to leave the country and take shelter in Pakistan. The people migrated to Pakistan were mostly living in Refugee camps as compared with the refugees fled to Iran. Government of Pakistan at that time used these refugee camps as a base to train and brain wash the people to fight against the Soviet Union forces.

During the Soviet occupation between 1980 and 1985 the net migration rate of Afghanistan's population was -56.7/1000 persons [17].

The government of Pakistan were happy because they were receiving extensive amount of financial assistance from international community for these refugees. That's why they were kept in the refugee camps with the miserable lives to portray their condition. The United States were also involved in this game and was in search to find ways to defeat his rival mighty Soviet Union forces to establish an Islamic government in Afghanistan that can be controlled.

In 1989 Soviet Union withdrew their forces from Afghanistan. After that, the war of control over Kabul started between Mujahedeen. As a result of that again huge population migrated to Pakistan.

More than 6 million Afghans migrated to Pakistan in 1990 due to bombing and combat especially in rural areas of Afghanistan.

By that time, Afghans were the biggest group of displaced people thorough out the world, almost half of the total population in Afghanistan [18].

Migration at the Time of Taliban Rule (1992): Pakistan back Taliban in1992 took control of the government in Kabul. This was the time when 2nd biggest migration of the history of Afghans took place. The middle class and considerably educated people fled to Pakistan and Iran.

Compare to the first migration in these countries, they were not welcomed by the government of Pakistan and Iran. This time Pakistan and Iran governments were not able to attract good financial assistance from International Community. At the same time, international community didn't give their attention to the issues in Afghanistan [13].

In 1990, the first voluntary repatriation program in Pakistan was established. In 1992, under tripartite agreement between Iran, Afghanistan and UNHCR, the first repatriation of Afghan refugees started [18].

During 1993 and onwards, the government of Iran provided temporary cards to the newly and undocumented migrated refugees. This time they were not given those rights which they were obliged in the first migration at the time of soviet regime invasion in Afghanistan. They were named "panadehandegan" which carried lower status as compared to the past [16].

In 1994, Taliban intensified their combat against the Northern allies which resulted once again the flow of people to Pakistan and the Islamic republic of Iran and continued till 2000. Between 1991 and 2000, over 300,000 Afghan refugees migrated to Pakistan. These events helped to explain the negative net migration of -6.5/1000 persons [16]. However, this time UNHCR stopped their food assistance to these refugees which compelled them to look for work in rural areas [17].

Migration at the end rule of Taliban regime (2001): During the invasion of US on Afghanistan to end the Talban regime in 2001, the 3rd largest scale of migration of people from Afghanistan occurred. The 9/11 attacks in America caused much attention of international community towards Afghanistan.

Despite of worse security situation in Afghanistan, Iran and Pakistan tried to decrease the number of refugees living in their countries. In addition, Islamic Republic of Iran tried to implement a policy on their citizens which did not allow them to hire the Afghan Refugees [18].

Pakistan also put some solid steps and closed many refugee camps. Force deportation of these refugees started during this period. Although the intensity of deportation in Iran was high than Pakistan [13].

In 2002, UNHCR started their assisted voluntary return program for Afghan refugee living in the Islamic of Iran and Pakistan [19]. Due the UNHCR efforts more than 1.5 million refugee returned from Pakistan and 250,000 from the Islamic Republic of Iran concurrently. The UNHCR also extended their assistance where returnees were given cash support to cover transport cost.

Currently 1.3 million registered and about 2.6 million unregistered Afghan refugees living in Pakistan. While this number in Iran ranges from 0.9 million registered and about 2 million unregistered refugees [20].

Major occupation of afghan refugees in Iran

Almost the entire refugees fled to Iran without any formal migration system in order to safeguard their family. According to one research conducted by the Afghanistan Research and Evaluation Unit (AREU) which pinpoints the irregular behavior towards the Afghan migrants in both countries Iran and Pakistan. Iran showed reservations on protocol of 1951convention of refugees which restricted the refugees to a low-income occupation. Thus, the right of living as a refugee in Iran was given to a very few number of people. Those people who lived in Iran for 20 or odd years were given a temporary permission to stay in Iran. Therefore, it created an environment which had an impact on both the Afghan workers and the local employees [21].

The sample data from the afghan refugee population indicated high activity for the male population of age between 10 and above was 64%, the female population which constitute 41% of the total migrated people out of which only 8.2% was employed [21] (Figure 2 and Table 3).

Approximately 80% of the total Afghan population in Iran was working in three sectors, manufacturing, construction and trade and commerce. Less 10% of the population was working in agriculture sector.

In contrast to Iranians who would work in public sector, the Afghan labor use to work for long hours, without insurance and regulations and relatively on low wages.

The working tendency of Afghans in Iran which was distributed into three sectors indicates that the Afghans are less involved in Agriculture sector and more in manufacturing which is about 30% of the sampled population. The construction sector which requires less skill is a source of income for major population (Table 4).

The average hours per week for Afghan labors in Iran 51.3% for men and 30 hours for women and the total hours in a week is 49 hours (Figure 3).

The distribution of Afghan employees according to employment status shows that regular worker (39%), casual worker (28%) and self-employed (23%) (Table 5).

The average income of Afghan men employees is 37 USD per week and women earns about 12 USD per week. This big difference of income between men and women is due to difference in working hours and the type of work they do. Men are generally lined to have good level of education which is associated to higher income as compared to women.

Considering the percentage of women took part in the survey is much lower in contrast to men, therefore the analysis of female wages should be considered with caution.

The net earnings of women per week for Afghan women employees are approximately 7.8 USD in the industry sector and 29 USD in the agriculture sector.

Women are put under discrimination as shown by men/women wage ratio which is above 200 [21] (Table 6).

The numbers in parentheses above refer to the number of persons in the particular Branch of economic activity.

Migration of Afghans to Europe

As per the reports of the "international organization for migration" from January 2015 to 27 January 2016, a number of around 1.1 million people arrived to Europe by land and see routes. Afghans are next to Syrians in terms of migrants chose Europe as destiny.

According to European Union statistics 942,400 migrants from Afghanistan have applied for Asylum in different European countries. Similarly, the afghan ministry of Refugees and repatriation said that the number of Afghans applied for Asylum in 44 different European countries exceeds to 250,000 out of which 150,000 are in Germany.

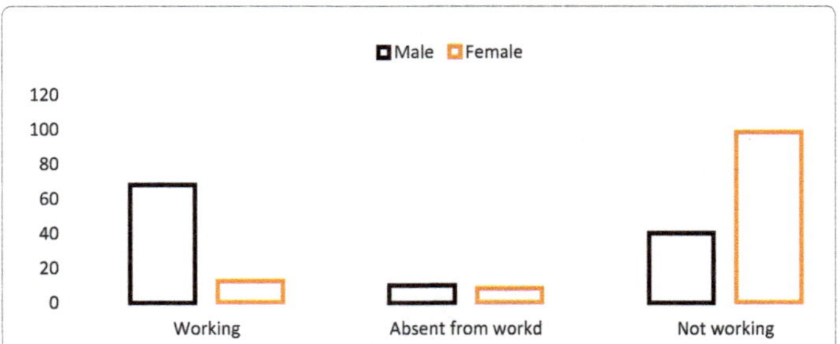

Figure 2: Afghan Population working activity [21].

Activity	Male	Female	Total
Employed	2191	253	2444
Unemployed	90	69	159
Total	2281	322	2603

Table 3: Afghan Labor Force by Sex [21].

Branch of economic activity	Male	Female	Total
Agriculture	9.9	5.9	9.5
Manufacturing	26.2	58.9	29.6
Construction	28.6	1.2	25.8
Wholesale, retail and trade	25.1	2.8	22.8
Transport and communication	2.9	0	2.6
Other services	7.2	31.2	9.5
Total %	100	100	100
Total Number	2191	253	2444

Table 4: Afghans Currently Employed by Sex and Branch of Economic Activity (%) [21].

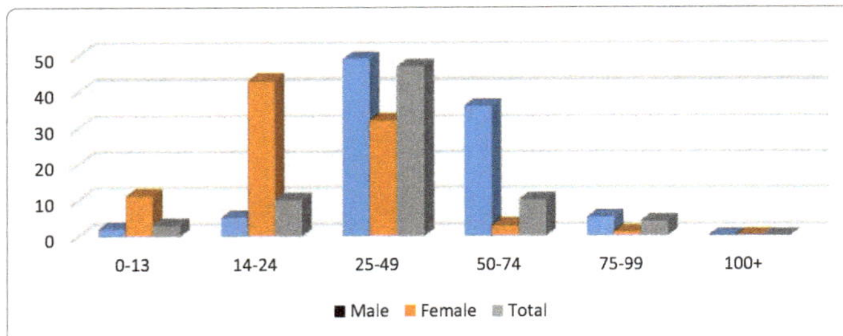

Figure 3: Hours per week [21].

Employment status	Male	Female	Total
Employer	1.7	0	1.5
Self Employed	23.1	15.4	22.3
Unpaid family worker	3.4	7.5	3.8
Private regular worker	39	38.7	39
Seasonal worker	4.7	4.3	4.7
Private casual worker	28.1	34	28.7
Total %	100	100	100
Total number	2191	253	2444

Table 5: Afghans Currently Employed by Sex and Employment Status (%of Total) [21].

Branch of economic activity	Male	Female	Total	M/F ratio
Agriculture	34.75 (217)	28.64 (15)	34.36	121.3
Manufacturing	39.95 (574)	7.64 (149)	33.25	522.7
Construction	38.22 (626)	18.88 (4)	38.16	202.4
Wholesale, retail and trade	34.98 (551)	15.71 (7)	34.73	222.7
Transport and communication	34.11 (64)	-	34.11	-
Domestic servants	50.96 (4)	-	50.96	-
Other services	33.38 (154)	16.01 (79)	27.56	208.5
Total	37.10 (2190)	11.74 (254)	34.45	315.9

Table 6: Average Earnings of Afghan Employed Per Week (US$) by Sex and Branch of Economic Activity [21].

If someone goes to understand the number of Afghans travelled illegally to Europe, they will be surprised to see how this number has mounted in recent couple of years. Study conducted by the European Union which shows that almost 26,215 Afghans claimed Asylum in different European countries in 2013, this number increased to 41,370 and in 2015 it raised to 250,000.

These refugees suffered from numerous difficulties while striving to reach Europe in which many of them gave their lives on their way to Europe. Afghan Ministry of Refugees and Repatriations stated that more than 800 migrants sunk in the Mediterranean Sea while trying to cross it on boats to get to Europe.

Due to worse security situation in Afghanistan and other countries in 2015 resulted refugee crisis in Europe. Consequently, many of the European countries strengthen their policy regarding refugees and has tried to send back some of the refugee to their home countries.

Some European countries such as Germany count the Afghan refugees as the economic migrants. Therefore, the German Chancellor Angela Merkel had said that they have started "serious talks" with the Afghan government about the repatriation of the Afghan refugees whose asylum applications were rejected by the German government.

German interior minister on a visit to Kabul said that we have come to an agreement with the Afghan Government according to which the Afghans whose applications for Asylum has been rejected will be sent back to Afghanistan. He further stated that we do not consider Afghans as refugee but we take them as migrants because the security situation in Afghanistan is now better [22].

According to a statement released by the Ministry of Refugees and repatriation, they have welcomed 135 people after rejection of their application for Asylum in Germany. Stated further, rising unemployment is the main reason for leaving Afghanistan and more young people are willing to migrate to other countries because of the poverty and uncertain future [23]. Afghanistan counts in 2nd in terms of rank of countries people migrated from [24] (Figure 4).

According to the same report Hungry comes second in terms of migrants moved their applications for Asylum. It had 177,130 applications by the end of December 2015 (Table 7).

Research Methodology Theory and Hypothesis of Brian Drain

Weddings in Afghanistan

Getting marriage in Afghanistan has become a serious problem for youth in Afghanistan. Huge money is involved in booking weddings halls, lavish meals and for bride payment. The groom's family pay the bride price to her family which varies in different parts of Afghanistan. It is all controversial tradition and doesn't have basses in Islam. In some sections of society, people mixes tradition with dowry which is has to be paid to bride when her husband dies or gives her divorce. The huge money that has to be paid to bride becomes the cause for groom to own money from people and ultimately he has to either travel to neighbouring countries or far distant countries in order to save money for his debt payments.

Usually, the groom's family has to initiate the proposal of marriage to bride family and it is up to bride family to reject or to accept. The father of bride or some elder in her family set price to be paid for bride. The amount of money depends on family background, education, age, reputation of the girl. For example the price tag for wedding, especially in Kabul, the common price for wedding is 10,000$.

Examples of bride prices in some provinces are given below (Table 8).

The high prices for getting in marriage relationship has forced large number of youth to go to Iran, Pakistan, Gulf or European countries to find work in order to pay for their bride price and for their wedding. The effects is on both sides where men has to work for long years sometime and women have to stay awaited till their men come and wed them [25].

According to a survey in Herat and Balkh provinces the range of dowries range between 400$ to 11,000$, the minimum cost on engagement is from 500$ to 2000$, marriage celebration costs people $4,000 to $15,000, the precelebration of marriage costs them $1,500 to $5,000. The total minimum average marriage cost in Herat and Mazar is $10,000 and the maximum average is $33,000 [26].

Overseas jobs

Working abroad is always a dream for professionals. It provides an opportunity for people to explore different cultures and living lifestyles. Working abroad provide them with the experience of meeting new people, learning their language and also earn money that is hard for them to earn in their country [27].

On other side, Afghanistan receives huge amount of money as a remittances from abroad. Although Afghanistan does not share data regarding remittances to IMF. According to the World Bank estimate, 15% of households in Afghanistan receives remittances from abroad.

As per report released by the international fund for Agriculture development, the remittances for Afghanistan in 2006 was 2.5$ which is 30% of the total GDP at that time.

The value of remittances by Afghans from USA and Canada is approximately 75 million dollars which is very significant amount. From Netherland amount $85,085 is sent to Afghanistan in 2008. Afghans living in Germany sent EUR 22 million in 2004. However, this data does not confirm the reliability of the statistics as it is only an indication [28,29].

The World Bank provides data between 2008 and 2013. The table of the summary is given below (Table 9).

Fragile government and neighbouring country's interventions

Since the start of 21st century, security in Afghanistan is a big challenge for the forces in Power. At the same time, unfortunately Afghans couldn't witness serious steps on behalf of US government to end the war in Afghanistan because of their own hidden agendas. Besides, there are number of threats that Afghan Government is dealing with.

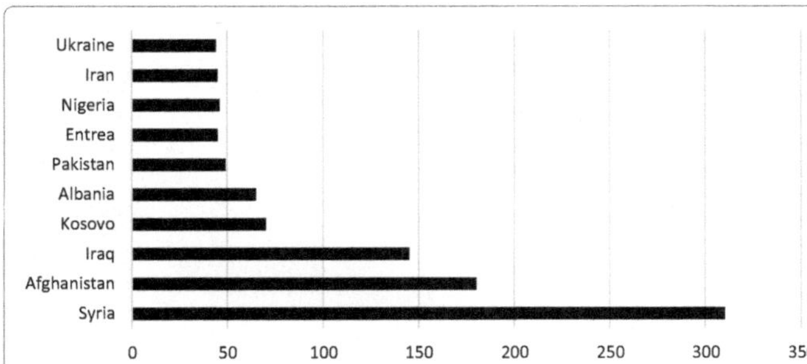

Figure 4: Top 10 origins of people applying for asylum in the EU.

Germany	Sweden	Italy	France	Netherlands	UK
140,910	32,215	29,615	20,630	16,450	13,905

Table 7: Countries with most asylum acceptance.

Province	Min. AFN	Max. AFN	Min. USD	Max. USD
Maidan Wardak	400,000	800,000	5,900	11,800
Nangarhar	100,000	500,000	1,450	7,245
Loye Paktia (khost, Paktika and paktia)	1,000,000	1,200,000	14,500	17,390
Farah	800,000	1,500,000	11,800	21,733
Faryab	66,000	135,000	1,000	2,000

Table 8: Bride prices in some provinces.

Internal threats: Without looking to the serious problems in Afghanistan, government is busy in making rivals that may post threat to the existence of the Government. In fact, it is sign of failed states which are unable to control insurgency in their countries. The economic development has been effected by the weak corruption, bad governance and failure in handling internal divisions.

Threats from extremists: Almost all insurgencies in Afghanistan are backed by the extremist followers. Still several extremist groups such as Taliban and others are posing serious threat to the government of Afghanistan.

USA role in counter terrorism: There is a history of repeated mistakes made by US government due to their poor strategy in Afghanistan. Still Afghanistan is looking toward current USA government which has promised that they will change their policy towards Afghanistan. There was strict silence from the current president of the United States in his election campaign which has caused Afghan officials anxious.

Trumps cabinet seemed to show little interest in ending Afghan war. It is still uncertain whether he will continue spending billions of dollars funding in Afghanistan or we see a different roadmap.

Neighbours interventions: There is a long history of interference from Pakistan in destabilizing peace in Afghanistan. Pakistan has an obvious reason for that. There is a long 2600 km controversial border issue between Pakistan and Afghanistan.

Pakistan is compelled to not allow Afghanistan a developed country because at the end Afghanistan can claim their territory. Apart from Pakistan, other neighbouring countries have its own interests in Afghanistan as well which all together make the scenarios more tense and uncertain [30].

Youth unemployment

After the past continued several decades of war, has caused Afghanistan among the poorest countries in the world. The international community has been keenly participating in re-construction process of Afghanistan but still the future of Afghanistan economy is uncertain. Each year more than 400,000 students are getting their degrees from universities within and outside Afghanistan and looks for the opportunities in the job market. As per the report of the National Risk and Vulnerability Assessment (NRVA) 2007/2008 report, the unemployment rate for men was 10% and 15% for women which were significantly higher than the national unemployment rate which was 7.1%.

Due to lack of limited opportunities in the market youth hunts for the jobs in neighboring countries like Pakistan, Iran and Tajikistan. These Afghans usually become migrant workers as attractive employment option as they can gain good money and learn skills needed in the market.

National statistics

- Youth under the age of 25 show a high rate of unemployment than the population overall (7%): 10% for men and 15% for women.
- This figure rises to 45% if the inactive population under taken into account.
- 75% of employed women work as unpaid family worker (Figure 5).

The unemployment index shows variations in unemployment from 2006 to 2016. We can witness a steady movement in unemployment rate from 2006 to 2008 which is around 8% till 2013 but we see a high jump in unemployment rate in 2014 to 25% and then get maximum increase of 40% in 2015. According to a participatory youth survey conducted to understand employment market in Afghanistan, it was found that the labor market is unable to provide job opportunities for graduated youths. As per the survey, only 28.7% of the youth had jobs in hand. The worst effected among the provinces was Badakhshan and Kunduz which had unemployment rates of 88% and 85%, respectively.

According to below table, Afghanistan is the 4th country with highest unemployment rate in the world (Table 10).

Country-Wise Distribution of Afghan-Immigrants in some parts of the World Between 2000 to 2010 (Table 11).

Distribution of Afghan Immigrants by Education Level: Distribution of Afghan Immigrants by education level in different years starting from 2000 to 2015 in regular 5 intervals (Table 12).

Research methodology

It is important to note, when we intent to make decision about how we should design our research, it is vital to understand the importance of relationship between variables. Generalizing to larger groups of individuals than those actually forming part of the investigation I used convenience sampling research method which is a type of non-probability sampling collected from population members who are conveniently available to participate in the survey.

My design of research was based on self-completion questionnaires, which a type of quantitative data collection method in which a series

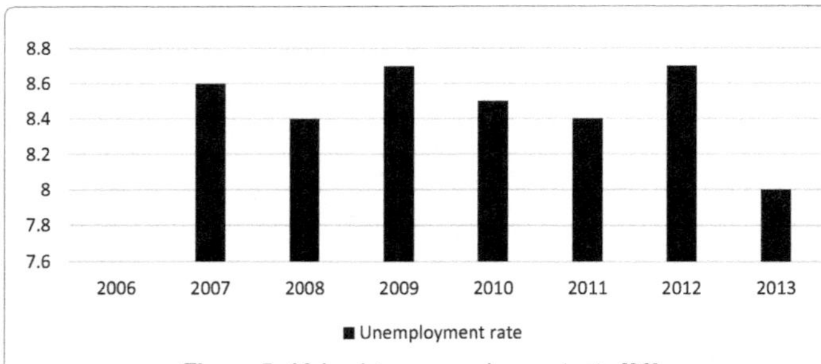

Figure 5: Afghanistan unemployment rate [32].

Annual migrant remittance inflows- Afghanistan (US$ Million)						
2008	2009	2010	2011	2012	2013	Remittance as share of GDP (%)
104	228	460	460	460	543	*

Table 9: Remittances [29].

Country	Last		Previous	Highest	Lowest	
Djibouti	54	Dec.2010	59.5	59.5	43.5	% Yearly
Congo	46.10	Dec, 2013	49.1	66.9	45.4	
Bosnia and Herzegovina	40.58	Jan, 2017	40.87	46.1	39.03	
Afghanistan	40.00	Dec, 2015	25	40	8	
Kenya	40.00	Dec, 2011	12.7	40	12.7	
Kosovo	32.90	Dec, 2015	35.3	57	30	
Gambia	29.80	Dec, 2013	22	29.8	6	
Yemen	29.00	Dec, 2011	17.8	29	13.7	

Table 10: Unemployment rate in the world.

Australia								
2000			2005			2010		
Total	M-Total	F-Total	Total	M-Total	F-Total	Total	M-Total	F-Total
11296	6776	4520	16751	9097	7654	18184	9788	8396
	60%	40%		54%	46%		54%	46%
Canada								
2000			2005			2010		
Total	M-Total	F-Total	Total	M-Total	F-Total	Total	M-Total	F-Total
22605	11685	10920	36990	18810	18180	42251	21397	20854
	52%	48%		51%	49%		51%	49%
Switzerland								
2000			2005			2010		
Total	M-Total	F-Total	Total	M-Total	F-Total	Total	M-Total	F-Total
1980	1167	813	2104	1240	864	2234	1317	917
	59%	41%		59%	41%		59%	41%
Germany								
2000			2005			2010		
Total	M-Total	F-Total	Total	M-Total	F-Total	Total	M-Total	F-Total
72199	40107	32092	55111	29353	25758	48752	25615	23137
	56%	44%		53%	47%		53%	47%
Denmark								
2000			2005			2010		
Total	M-Total	F-Total	Total	M-Total	F-Total	Total	M-Total	F-Total
1482	839	643	4385	2302	2083	5366	2796	2570
	57%	43%		53%	47%		53%	47%
France								
2000			2005			2010		
Total	M-Total	F-Total	Total	M-Total	F-Total	Total	M-Total	F-Total
2444	1384	1060	2520	1421	1099	4189	2529	1660
	57%	43%		56%	44%		60%	40%
Britain								
2000			2005			2010		
Total	M-Total	F-Total	Total	M-Total	F-Total	Total	M-Total	F-Total
14873	9740	5133	16034	9740	6294	19940	12942	6998
	65%	35%		61%	39%		65%	35%
Netherlands								
2000			2005			2010		
Total	M-Total	F-Total	Total	M-Total	F-Total	Total	M-Total	F-Total
19836	11337	8499	32409	18174	14235	32409	18174	14235
	57%	43%		56%	44%		56%	44%
United States								
2000			2005			2010		
Total	M-Total	F-Total	Total	M-Total	F-Total	Total	M-Total	F-Total
36413	18746	17667	50772	24764	26008	57542	27278	30264
	51%	49%		49%	51%		47%	53%

Table 11: Country-Wise Distribution of Afghan-Immigrants in some parts of the World Between to 2000 to 2010 [33].

2000				**2005**				**2010**			
Total	Low	Medium	High	Total	Low	Medium	High	Total	Low	Medium	High
1.59%	1.26%	1.16%	4.14%	1.82%	1.34%	1.31%	4.96%	1.91%	1.40%	1.29%	5.31%

Table 12: Distribution of Afghan Immigrants by Education Level [33].

of questions are presented to the respondents and they choose from options available. Questions are made simple, clear and not very long.

I used two types of data collection techniques, primary and secondary in order to explore the factors causing brain drain.

For primary data I created questionnaire to get a sample of data from target population that live in Afghanistan and another questionnaire was created to find reasons about people leaves the country from those Afghans who lives abroad.

Data collection was started in the beginning of February and finished the data gathering process until 15 February. Distinct types of questions were used for both questionnaires. A sample number of 71 participants contributed their responses by those who live abroad and 87 participants that live in Afghanistan. Each participant who lives in Afghanistan was presented with 6 questions and 29 questions were included in form intended for the participants who lives abroad.

Before launching my hunt for data collection I made several constructs with many items scales. 5 Likert scale (Strongly disagree, disagree, undecided, agree, strongly agree) were used for each item scale. The main target for my constructs was those Afghan citizens who live overseas, as their opinions are more valuable than those live within Afghanistan and can be considered true actors for my Research.

During the data collection process I come across through numerous challenges and limitations. The 1st challenge was to explain the form to each and every respondents. Some of them would understand with little instruction but a lot of them were related to people who had low education level and needed a lot more time to explain the contents within form. Another challenge was to find people whose relatives or friends are living abroad. Most of the time it would happened that participants would not respond due to sensitivity of the topic for them because of the reason that their asylum application were in progress. So, they would hesitate in filling and submitting the form.

In current world of communication technology, internet and Facebook messengers are giving us opportunity and possibility to get access to a large population in the world.

Social media was used to communicate my questionnaire to the target population. However, more emphasize was given to Facebook Messenger and less to others like VK, Whatsup, Viber etc. The reason for not using Emails was to get immediate response from audiences.

I used social networks to collect data, for example my friends in Facebook, VK and my friends' friends. Whenever I received a response from a friend I would request to send the questionnaire to others in their friend list.

Research hypothesis

Hypothesis is essentially a 'tentative proposition which is subject to verification through Subsequent investigation'. In several occasions the researcher tries to detect the relationship between scale items and subject. It therefore can be stated that hypothesis is declaration of relationships between its variables and give support to the researcher of how the original hunch might be tested.

Following are some of the hypothesis that will be tested in my analysis.

H1: There is a relationship between Brain drain and unemployment perception in Afghanistan.

H2: The foreign job opportunities have a positive influence on brain drain.

H3: Social pressure is a factor for brain drain in Afghanistan.

H4: The uncertainty about Afghanistan's future will influence brain drain.

H5: The expensive weddings in Afghanistan do not affect brain drain.

H6: Educational scholarships have a positive influence on brain drain from Afghanistan.

Hypothesis Testing and Findings

In this chapter, the analysis of data collected will be carried out. It will be demonstrated that how participants responded to various questions presented to them. I will also try to find whether my hypothesis is proved when pass through some scientific patterns and also I will find powerful push factors from all the variables mentioned in my research constructs. Meanwhile, the demographic characteristics of the sample population will also be analyzed.

In 6.1, we will analyze questionnaire that is collected from participants living in Afghanistan.

In 6.2 and 6.3, the data which are collected from Afghans living abroad will be put under scrutiny.

Demographic profile of Afghans population living in Afghanistan

Section 1: This section was aimed to find out whether people in Afghanistan are willing to go abroad if they were given a chance. For this purpose I did a binomial proportion test, the result shows that people are not happy with the current situation in Afghanistan. Out of 87 participants who took part in the survey, 65 people was on the view that looking to the overall condition of Afghanistan, if they have a chance in hand to leave Afghanistan to go abroad, they will avail the chance. On the other hand 22 participants were satisfied from the current condition of Afghanistan and they had opinion if they were given chance they will reject and will prefer to stay in Afghanistan. Maybe because they belong to a wealthy financial background or due to their high paid jobs (Table 13).

Section 2: In this section those participants were asked whose answer was affirmative to the question if they were given chance to go abroad, where they will prefer to go. Five choices were presented to them Asia, Europe, Gulf, North America and other. Out 87 of participants 45 gave their choice for Europe if they were given chance, 23 selected other choice, 8 North America, 7 of them chose Asia and 4 Gulf.

Looking to the current flow of immigrants we saw that Europe was the 1st destiny for migration.

We witnessed a lot of Afghans travelled to Germany, some to France, Finland and others.

Section 3: In 3rd section of questionnaire, the participants who answered positive to 1st question were asked about their duration of stay. From total of 87 participants 32 chose forever, 19 of them selected ten or more years while 18 of them was happy to stay for the duration of two or five years if they were given chance.

From above observations we come to know that mostly people are happy to choose life time stay duration if chance for migration was given to them.

Section 4: In this section, participants were asked about their opinion to choose reasons from the choices given in the questionnaire. We witnessed a more diverse opinion from the participants, each choice were looked to be equally important for participants.

From 86 participants 27 chose reason for their immigration to pursue higher education, 22 gave their opinion for political instability, 20 blamed low number of opportunities in Afghanistan and 11 participants were of the opinion to choose comfortable life styles in foreign countries.

Section 5: In this section participants are asked to state their point of views regarding whether Afghanistan is affected from brain drain.

Section 1	If given chance, would you leave your home country and live abroad?		
	Category	**Figure**	**Observed Prop.**
	YES	65	75%
	NO	22	25%
Section 2	If you said yes to the 1st question, where would you go?		
	Category	**Figure**	**Observed Prop.**
	Asia	7	8%
	Europe	45	52%
	Gulf	4	5%
	North America	8	9%
	Other	23	27%
Section 3	If you answered yes to 1st question, how long would you stay abroad?		
	Category	**Figure**	**Observed Prop.**
	Five years	18	20%
	Forever	32	38%
	Ten or more years	19	22%
	Two years	18	20%
Section 4	In your opinion why people prefer to migrate?		
	Category	**Figure**	**Observed Prop.**
	Low number of opportunities	20	23%
	Political Instability	22	25%
	Pressure from society	7	8%
	They feel more comfortable with the lifestyle abroad	11	13%
	To pursue higher education	2700%	31%
Section 5	Do you believe that your country suffers from immigration of highly skilled and educated people?		
	Category	**Figure**	**Observed Prop.**
	YES	68	78%
	NO	19	22%
Section 6	Can brain drain be turned into positive force for development?		
	Category	**Figure**	**Observed Prop.**
	YES	73	84%
	NO	14	16%

Table 13: Demographic profile of Afghans population living in Afghanistan.

We realized that majority of the participants agreed from the statement that Afghanistan is under influence of brain drain like of most of the countries in the world. 78% agreed with the opinion and 22% were included in the rejecters as shown by the binomial proportion test.

Section 6: In this last section of the questionnaire conducted from people living in Afghanistan, participants were asked; can brain drain be transformed into positive force for Afghanistan?

It is observed from their responses that the highest percentage of participants gave their response that Afghanistan can gain from this wave of human flight.

84% of the participants give their opinion in the favor of "Yes" while only 16% was against this idea. This is might be because of the reason that prevailing economy of Afghanistan is in a very fragile condition and cannot give employment to skilled and educated youth, so it suites them to migrate rather to waste their life. Afghanistan can gain benefits in a way that, it can encourage remittance inflows and reduces international transaction cost.

Demographic profile and hypothesis testing of the Afghan respondents living abroad

Section 1: In this section Ages of participants took part in the survey are put under analysis. Countries are effected most when brain drain of youth take place which is also the issue of concern for Afghanistan. The survey revealed that maximum number of participants participated in the survey was youth in our sample of the population. In total of 71 participants 47% are between 21 to 25 years, 26% between 26 30, 17% are between 15 to 20 years old (Table 14).

Section 2: In this section, respondents were asked about their hometowns or provinces they belong to in Afghanistan. It is revealed that majority of participants took part in the survey belonged to Herat province which constitute 33% of the sample population. The next comes Kabul and Laghman which is 11% respectively in our sample of population.

Section 3: During the last few years we saw a wave of refugee crisis due to deteriorating internal civil wars in Afghanistan Syria and others. European countries were mostly effected by this wave. Some of the respondents in our sample of population represent students that travelled abroad for getting higher education. Our goal was to understand the demographics of the population by the years they departed from Afghanistan.

After analysis of the sample population we come to know that 28% (20) of the respondents travelled abroad in 2015. Then during the year 2016, 25% (17) of the respondents departed the country. After that comes 2013 and 2014 in which 15% (11), respectively, our respondents took its journey to abroad either for getting higher education or owing to worsen security circumstances.

Section 4: As it is said in the previous section that European countries especially Germany were mostly hit by this refugee crisis which is apparent in the analysis.

Since my data are based on convenience sampling, therefore I could receive responses easily from the participants who were under my reach.

As I am currently based in Russia, hence it will be found that Afghans participants who contributed their responses are mostly from Russia.

25% of the contributions in my survey have been made by Afghans living in Russia. The 2nd most contributors were from Germany which is 15%, then 8% France, after that UK, Kuwait, USA, Thailand and Turkey respectively constitute 6% of the sample population. A small portion (4%) of the responses contributed by Afghans living in Sweden, Saudi Arabia, Malaysia, India and UAE, respectively.

Section 5: In this section, participants were asked to state their opinion about the trend in which majority of Afghans either leaving or have desire to make their journey to other countries will affect Afghanistan in some ways.

81% of the respondents recorded their perspectives affirmative towards the statement which says that Afghanistan will be affected if this trend continues while 19% was against this argument.

Section 6: Millions of Afghans living through the world are engaged either in earning money or for study purposes. The Table below shows that 64% of our sample population belongs to the student fraternity, 9% of them operate some of kind businesses and 16% belongs to those groups that have employment in different organizations.

Section 7: The fundamental purpose of my study is to collect data about the population sample that have some educational background one way or the other.

Table below shows statistics of the population in terms of their education. The maximum number of respondents in my population sample holds Bachelor degree which is 45%. The next to bachelor degree comes Master's degree which is 23%. 15% of population have high school certificate, then comes the respondents with College certificate which is 13% and 4% of the population possess 4% have doctoral degree.

Section 8: In this section participants are explained in terms of their Professions. Respondents are asked to state their Professional background. After analysis of the population sample we understood that Engineering is on top in terms of majority in numbers which is 23%. 21% had economics background, 15% of them was either graduated or studying Bachelor of Administration and so on. In some part of Afghanistan, they lack proper doctors like in Paktika province we have only doctor throughout the province. In Afghanistan, we are short of professionals for example, we recruit engineers from neighbor countries.

Section 9: Each and every year billions of dollars are sent by migrant workers to their home countries. According to KNOEMA statistics Afghanistan received 445.22 million US dollar as remittance in 2012. So this can be considered a positive side of brain drain. The main purpose of my latest question was to understand whether the respondents of my survey are sending money to their family in Afghanistan. Out of 71 respondents 32 said they send money to their family and 39 said they don't send money to their families in Afghanistan.

Section 10: In this section my goal was to know how much of my population sample has citizenship rights in the countries they are living. In view of the fact that we can sense some of respondents have the probability to return to their home country.

Section 11: Afghanistan is a multiethnic society. The population of the country is divided into a wide variety of ethno linguistic groups. Our purpose for this section was to find out the dominant ethnicities who left Afghanistan for different reasons. Our survey statistics shows Tajik is on lead to all other ethnicities which comprises 38% of my sample population. Pashtuns was 2nd in number to Tajik who departed from Afghanistan which encompasses 32% then comes Uzbek which covers 11% of my sample population and so on.

Hypothesis Testing

As stated previously that my main focus in the research is on those people who are living abroad. In my opinion, some people who are living in Afghanistan may reject the probability that they will live in Afghanistan even if they had chance to settle abroad. So, most of the people who are living abroad, have gone through some sufferings, that's why they preferred to leave country. So, for this purpose the opinions of the participants who live abroad are more valuable in this respect than the participants who live in the original country (Table 15).

Factor-wise Cronback alpha

In Table 16, a test is conducted to check the reliability of data and also to see that whether random error is causing inconsistency. Additionally, to find whether lower reliability is at manageable level through running Reliability test. From the table above it is clear that the acceptable level of Cronback alpha has been obtained which is 0.873. This indicates that the data has satisfactory internal consistency reliability.

Hypothesis 1

a) There are thousands of people graduating each year from the universities in Afghanistan and abroad which makes it difficult for the people to find jobs.

b) Nepotism is one of the reasons for unemployment.

c) Afghanistan's government doesn't have the resources to employ graduates.

d) 0 cells (0.0%) have expected frequencies less than 5. The minimum expected cell frequency is 14.2.

0 cells (0.0%) have expected frequencies less than 5. The minimum expected cell frequency is 17.8.

It was hypothesized that there is a relationship between the Brain Drain and unemployment perception in Afghanistan. When Chi Square Test was applied on the data, I came to understand that there is strong relationship between Unemployment and Brain drain.

As the observed P-value is less than α value (0.05), so it can be concluded that alternate H1 is accepted and we can say unemployment factors has great influence on people leaving Afghanistan.

Hypothesis 2

Employment opportunities abroad: It was hypothesized that overseas employment opportunities encourages People in Afghanistan to migrate to other countries.

In order to test the hypothesis, one sample T-test was applied on the data. We obtained high T-value of 14.674 and our α-value is also less than 0.05 which indicates that H2 is accepted.

Section 1	Age		
	Category	**Figure**	**Observed Prop.**
	Between 15 to 20	12	17%
	Between 21 to 25	33	47%
	Between 26 to 30	19	26%
	Between 31 to 35	4	6%
	Between 36 to 45	3	4%
Section 2	Name of province you belong to in Afghanistan?		
	Category	**Figure**	**Observed Prop.**
	Paktika	5	7%
	Parwan	5	8%
	Panjsher	7	10%
	Nangarhar	8	11%
	Balkh	3	4%
	Farah	4	5%
	Laghman	8	11%
	Kabul	8	11%
	Herat	23	33%
Section 3	Which year did you depart from your country?		
	Category	**Figure**	**Observed Prop.**
	2016	17	25%
	2015	20	28%
	2014	11	15%
	2013	11	15%
	2011	1	2%
	2010	4	6%
	2009	5	8%
	2005	1	2%
Section 4	Name of country you currently live in?		
	Category	**Figure**	**Observed Prop.**
	Canada	5	7%
	France	5	8%
	Germany	11	15%
	U.S.A	4	6%
	UK	4	6%
	UAE	3	4%
	Russia	18	25%
	India	3	4%
	Kuwait	4	6%
	Malaysia	1	2%
	Saudi Arabia	3	4%
	Sweden	3	4%
	Thailand	4	6%
	Turkey	4	6%
Section 5	Do you think this tendency of people leaving Afghanistan has some impact on it?		
	Category	**Figure**	**Observed Prop.**
	YES	58	81%
	NO	13	19%
Section 6	What defines you?		
	Category	**Figure**	**Observed Prop.**
	Student	46	64%
	Business Owner	9	13%
	Employee	16	23%
Section 7	What is your level of Education?		
	Category	**Figure**	**Observed Prop.**
	Bachelor	32	45%
	College	**9**	13%
	Doctoral	3	4%
	High School	11	15%
	Masters	16	23%
Section 8	What is your academic discipline?		
	Category	**Figure**	**Observed Prop.**
	Advance Material sciences	1	2%
	Business Administration	11	15%
	Computer Science	5	8%
	Economics	15	21%
	Engineering	16	23%
	General Studies	7	9%
	Medical	7	9%
	Political Science	9	13%
Section 9	Do you support financially your relatives living in Afghanistan?		
	Category	**Figure**	**Observed Prop.**
	YES	32	45%
	NO	39	55%
Section 10	Is this country your permanent residence?		
	Category	**Figure**	**Observed Prop.**
	YES	30	42%
	NO	41	58%
Section 11	What is your ethnic background?		
	Category	**Figure**	**Observed Prop.**
	Arab	5	8%
	Hazara	7	9%
	Pashtun	23	32%
	Tajik	27	38%
	Turkmen	1	2%
	Uzbek	8	11%

Table 14: Demographic profile and hypothesis testing of the Afghan respondents living abroad.

Overall Cronback Alpha	Number of items
0.873	18

Table 15: Reliability Statistics.

So, it is concluded that factors related to job opportunities abroad such as the job attractions itself, their attractive salaries and the greed to earn more which in the people's view can be achieved when they travel and get job in foreign countries.

Hypothesis 3

Our 3rd hypothesis was about social pressure factors causing brain drain in Afghanistan. Binomial test was used on data which indicates that 94% of the sample population believe that a Social pressure factor motivates people in Afghanistan to leave for foreign countries. The P-value is less than α value of (0.05) so, H3 is accepted.

From the data analysis it was found that social pressures elements such as jealousy from their relatives who lives abroad and the pressure to earn more money to match the society status has powerful inspiration for the people to travel abroad.

Hypothesis 4

It was hypothesized in this part that prevailing Uncertainty in Afghanistan does not cause human flight (Brain Drain) from Afghanistan.

Constructs	Variables	α
Unemployment	➢ There are thousands of students graduating each year from the universities in Afghanistan and abroad which makes difficult for them to find job. ➢ Nepotism is one of the reason for unemployment ➢ Afghanistan's government doesn't have resources to employee graduates.	0.868
Job opportunities abroad	➢ Top talent is leaving the country because they are attracted to job offers abroad. ➢ Attractive salaries abroad are one of the reasons for the human capital flight to some extent. ➢ High socioeconomic growth abroad is also an influential factor which motivates youngsters to depart from the country.	0.864
Social Pressure	➢ Social pressure has a strong influence on people to flee from country. ➢ People some feel jealous of their relatives that live overseas, which forces them to go abroad for greener pastures. ➢ The pressure to earn more money makes young people to leave the country for abroad.	0.868
Uncertainty	➢ People are under immense anxiety due to overall uncertainty which encourages educated youth to leave the country. ➢ Future plans of current USA and NATO forces for Afghanistan are ambiguous. ➢ Neighboring countries' interventions are the main the cause of uncertainty in the country.	0.874
Expensive weddings	➢ A greater expenditure burden lies on male side of the weddings which become the catalyst for them to leave country because of their inability to meet their marriage expenses. ➢ High dowries makes difficult for the people to get married, so they are compelled to flee to other country in order to save money for marriage. ➢ Unwanted societal traditions and customs is one of the reasons for making marriages expensive.	0.860
Educational Scholarships	➢ Educational Scholarships available internationally makes many talented youth to leave the country for abroad and some of them are unlikely to return back. ➢ An agreement should exist between Afghanistan and host countries to counter this phenomenon. ➢ The government of Afghanistan's failure to provide scholarship opportunities to intelligent students will force them to look for opportunities abroad.	0.858

Table 16: Factor-wise Cronback Alpha.

		Mean	N	Std. Deviation	Std.Error Mean
Pair 1	Unemployment	12.8	71	1.849	0.219
	Job opportunities Abroad	11.87	71	2.329	0.276
Pair 2	Social. Pressure	13.13	71	1.748	0.207
	Uncertainty	13.55	71	1.285	0.152
Pair 3	Expensive. Weddings	10.72	71	2.958	0.351
	Educational. Scholarships	12.14	71	2.565	0.304

Table 17: Paired samples statistics.

We used one sample T-test to analyze the hypothesis, the high mean value (4.5) of variables from the sample of population suggest that there is a strong bond between prevailing Uncertainty and Brain drain from Afghanistan.

The P-value of tested data confirms that H4 is rejected and Null Hypothesis is accepted and we can say that the factors that is mentioned in the variables such as ambiguous future plans of NATO forces and USA which currently Afghanistan is fully dependent on, makes the security situation of Afghanistan uncertain which in turn pushes most of the educated Youth of Afghanistan to leave the country for better futures.

Hypothesis 5

a) A greater expenditure burden lies on the male side of the weddings which become the catalyst for them to leave country because of their inability to meet their marriage expenses.

b) High Dowries makes difficult for the people to get married, so they are compelled to flee to other country in order to save money for marriage.

c) Unwanted societal traditions and customs is one of the reasons for making marriages expensive.

d) 0 cells (0.0%) have expected frequencies less than 5. The minimum expected cell frequency is 14.2. It was hypothesized in the section that the expensive weddings in Afghanistan does not influence Brain drain from Afghanistan.

Chi square test is used to test the data I found that, the elements mentioned above i.e., greater expenditure burden on Male side of weddings, unnecessary societal traditions and customs and high dowries in marriages has greater impact on brain drain phenomenon. The P-value implies that H5 is rejected and null hypothesis is accepted.

Hypothesis 6

Descriptive statistics: It was hypothesized that Educational Scholarships abroad has a positive influence on brain drain from Afghanistan. After analysis of the data from given sample of population it is clear that the factors related to Educational scholarships to Afghans from abroad such as Government's failure to provide quality education to Afghans and their less probability to return back takes away talented youth from Afghanistan.

It evident from P-value which is less than α value of 0.5 and also from the high mean value of 4.05, Null hypothesis is rejected and on this basis H6 is accepted.

Dominant Factors Effecting Brain Drain from Afghanistan

We put all the six Constructs under investigation in our research. As we know that the more less is the Standard Error Mean and on the other hand the greater is the Mean of the construct, the stronger is the factor (Table 17).

We saw in the above table that Uncertainty proves to be the stronger factor in all constructs which forces Afghan Youth to leave the country. When we rank the stronger factors affecting the brain drain we find that Uncertainty comes first, the 2nd factor is Social Pressure, the 3rd is unemployment, the 4th is educational scholarships, 5th factor in rank is job opportunities abroad and the least strong factor is Expensive weddings.

Conclusion

At a time when we see large of number of youth taking their path towards European countries, the government of Afghanistan is putting some steps in stopping this tendency. However, this phenomenon can also bring benefit to both countries. The source country receives remittances and the migrated country can use the skill of youth in their economic development. In this part of our study, we will discuss the various factors that influences the youth to leave the country and take reside in different parts of the world. Further we will also discuss their demographics and their opinions regarding the questions that we put forward to them.

In this context, the flow of human capital can be determined through several socioeconomic and political factors. For example Nganga has stated some of the factors like high fees, shortage of lecturers and insufficient facilities becomes a push factor for Kenyans to work and study abroad. Moreover, according to Glennie and Chappell (2010) which found 5 causes that makes the skilled and educated youth to leave the country. It consists of wages, employment, professional development, and socioeconomic political conditions and networks.

The research objectives in my survey had somewhat the same type of factors that had to be analyzed behind the flow of youth heading towards European and some other countries on such a large scale. As mentioned in chapter 2 about the high wedding costs that become the reason of social conflict and family disputes in Afghanistan. There are some incidences of youth that has commit suicide or has left the country to earn money in order to cover marriage expenses. The participants in my survey has considered this as a prominent issue for youth and high dowries and others extra societal traditions makes the marriage tough for the youth of Afghanistan. Although Afghan government has passed a bill which has restricted the marriages expenses to $3,500 but still people are waiting for government's action in this regard. We put our questions under test to check the relationship between the unemployment items and brain drain from Afghanistan we found that the maximum number of respondents had opinions about the factors such as nepotism, lack of government resources and large number of graduates each year from Universities, play positive role for young Afghans to leave the country. Constitution of Afghanistan allows every citizen of Afghanistan to get equal access to job opportunities. However, there is high scale of nepotism in different ministries of Afghanistan in job hiring and promotions.

In order to stop skilled worker from migration government has to put serious steps to curb this constraints and make sure the constitutional right of every Afghan to have job. To the role of high level of uncertainty in Afghanistan in pushing youths to take a decision about leaving the country, the respondents in the survey favored the notion that uncertainty is one of the cause along with other factors like unwillingness of big powers such as USA and NATO in bringing peace in Afghanistan is a push factor for some Afghans to depart from country. The political elite along with other big figures has to unite and try to convince the stack holders that it is beneficial for every country to be peace in Afghanistan. Otherwise world will witness this flood of refugees more intense in coming years. Since the past several decades Pakistan has involvement in destabilization and has its own vested interests in Afghanistan. Hence, it is important for the world specially USA to take note of Pakistan supporting insurgency which raising uncertainty in Afghanistan.

Having job abroad has become a question of identity for people. It is considered a status symbol. Some think if they go abroad, the future life of their children will be secured. Today's youth are much fantasied by the lavish style of livings in the west and they imagine as if they depart from Afghanistan, they will easily find employment and will become rich. In our survey it was hypothesized that there is a connection between young generations going for migration and the job opportunities abroad. The respondents accepted the idea of foreign job opportunities effect on youth leaving the country. It has been understood from some Afghan immigrants living in different countries that they did not have the same privileges that they were entitled to in Afghanistan. Most often they cannot pick jobs according to their professions.

In most of the remote villages of Afghanistan, pressure from the community members whose relatives are abroad are so high that they push the other people within the society to go abroad. To understand this phenomenon we tried to find relationship between rate of migration and social pressures. The respondents' views did not differ from the idea that social pressure has a role in encouraging people to leave the country. In reaching to these objective families sometime sell their properties in order to send their loved ones abroad. To avoid such incidents of putting the children's lives at risk, government has a responsibility to educate them about the dangers that their children my encounter when once they go on a travel to Europe or other country.

It is a good move for students to get scholarships and go for higher education because some of them are not in a position to afford higher education in Afghanistan due to lack of funds or poverty. The problem arises when these students get their degrees abroad and decide not to return to Afghanistan. For this purpose, we asked our respondents to state their opinions regarding students going abroad for getting higher education and their unlikeliness to return to Afghanistan, majority of the participants agreed that students after graduation choose to live permanently and does not return back to Afghanistan. It is important to mention that Administrative office of the president of Afghanistan has started a program with the name of Tashweeq 2016 which encourages young graduates studied from universities in different parts of the world to take part in nation building process by applying for one of the jobs online. The process is very transparent and based strictly on merit. Additionally, it is worth mentioning that Afghanistan should sign a memorandum of understanding (MOU) with the countries where Afghan graduates should be sent back to Afghanistan after graduation. We have some stories of Afghans who went on scholarship program to western countries and didn't return to Afghanistan after graduation.

Looking to the different aspects of Afghanistan, the employment crisis, the security situation and the future uncertainty factor hanging over Afghanistan, the importance of people adopting migration as an alternative cannot be neglected. As it is known that brain drain is a problem but at the same time this move have some advantages to countries as well.

First, brain drain can bring remittances from abroad. According to World Bank report developing countries received $25 billion dollars as remittance in 2010. Tajikistan was one of the leading countries which received more than 3rd of its GDP through remittances. In 2015, Afghanistan received more $300 million as remittance from abroad. So, it looks lucrative business. At same time Afghanistan need some energetic youth who can take control of country's vital affairs.

To conclude Afghans can only be stopped from migration if Government initiate programs where every Afghan feel they can earn a dignified life in Afghanistan. The first priority of the government should be to bring peace in Afghanistan because the solutions of the major problems are linked with the security. Moreover, it has been observed that within the ministries of Afghanistan jobs are mostly given on ethnic bases. In some ministries there is rule of Tajiks while in others jobs are distributed on being Pashtun or Hazara. Also there is nepotism barrier for majority of Afghans when they go to hunt for jobs. All afore mentioned factors create frustrations within the young members of the society which compels Afghan youth to see for other alternatives in which one of them is migration.

Acknowledgement

Foremost, I would like to express my sincere gratitude to my Supervisor Professor Dmitry Berg for the continuous support of my Thesis study and research. His guidance helped me in all the time of research and writing of this thesis.

Besides my supervisor, I also thank my fellow classmates Mr. Ismaila Bojang, Najibullah Loodin and Rashid Abban for the encouragement, useful comments and support.

Last but not the least, I would like to thank my family: my parents for giving birth to me at the first place and supporting me spiritually throughout my life.

References

1. What is Brain Drain in Economics? - Definition, Causes, Effects & Examples.
2. Piyasiri W (2006) ILO-UNHCR Cooperation Towards Comprehensive Solutions for Afghan Displacement – Research Phase, Afghan Households in Iran.
3. Immigration to Germany, Wikipedia.
4. Baltic Legal immigration Services, Immigration to France.
5. French Property Law in France (2017) The French law resource, Visa and immigration law in France.
6. Casciani D (2011) BBC News home affairs correspondent. How does the British immigration system currently work?
7. Brief history of Afghanistan (2017) Razia's Ray of Hope Foundation.
8. Catherine P (2016) The Diplomat: Measuring Afghanistan's Education Problem.
9. Frud B (2015) Radio free radio, Afghanistan Tries to Stem Tide of Migration 'Brain Drain'.
10. Abbasi-Shavazi MJ, Glazebrook D, Jamshidiha G, Mahmoudian H, Sadegh R (2005) RETURN TO AFGHANISTAN? A Study of Afghans Living in Zahedan, Islamic Republic of Iran, Afghans in Iran. Kronenfeld DA (2008) Afghan refugees in Pakistan: Not all refugees, not alwaysin Pakistan, not necessarily Afghan? Journal of Refugee Studies 21: 43-63.
11. International Crisis Group (2009) Afghanistan: What now for refugees? Asia Report.
12. Stigter E (2006) Afghan migratory strategies - An assessment of repatriation and sustainable return in response to the convention plus. Refugee Survey Quarterly 25: 109-122.
13. Ashrafi A, Moghissi H (2002) Afghans in Iran: Asylum fatigue overshadows Islamic brotherhood. Global Dialogue 4: 89-99.
14. Monsutti A (2006) Afghan Transnational Networks: Looking Beyond Repatriation. Synthesis Paper Series, Afghanistan Research and Evaluation Unit, Kabul.
15. Abbasi-Shavazi M (2005) Return to Afghanistan? A Study of Afghans Living in Tehran. AREU Case Study Series, Afghanistan Research and Evaluation Unit, Kabul.
16. UNHCR (2005) Government of Pakistan and United Nations High Commissioner for Refugees Census of Afghans in Pakistan.
17. Turton D, Marsden P (2002) Taking Refugees for a Ride? The Politics of Refugee Return to Afghanistan. AREU Issues Paper Series, Afghanistan Research and Evaluation Unit, Kabul.
18. Lumpp K (2004) Voluntary repatriation to Afghanistan - Key features. Refugee, Survey Quarterly 23: 149-173.
19. Progress Report on the Solutions Strategy for Afghan Refugees.
20. Wickramasekara P, Sehgal J, Mehran F, Noroozi L, Eisazadeh S (2006) Afghan households in Iran: Profile and impact, ILO-UNHCR Cooperation Towards Comprehensive Solutions for Afghan Displacement – Research Phase.
21. Center for strategic and Regional Studies (CSRS) (2016) The crisis of Afghan migrants in Europe and neighboring countries. Afghan migrants toward Europe in 2015.
22. Ministry of Refugees and Repatriation (2016) Afghanistan welcomed the voluntary repatriation of refugees from Germany.
23. BBC News (2016) Migrant crisis: Migration to Europe explained in seven charts.
24. Fazal M (2016) Afghan analysis Network, context and culture, the bride price, The Afghan tradition of paying for wives.
25. Khalid R (2017) Transconflict, the effects of wedding costs on the peace process in Afghanistan.
26. How to find work overseas (2017) Working overseas, guides community resources.
27. Cordesman AH (2016) Afghanistan: The Uncertain Impact of a Year of Transition.
28. Youth Employment Policy Brief: Afghanistan (2013) International Labor Organization.
29. Afghanistan Unemployment Rate.
30. Institute for employment research (IAB), Data set of Afghans in few European and other countries.

Innovation and R&D Activities in China's Biotechnology and Pharmaceutical Sectors

Tao Zeng*

School of Business and Economics, Wilfrid Laurier University, Waterloo, Ontario, Canada

Abstract

This paper examines innovation and R&D expenditures in China's biotechnology and pharmaceutical sectors. We found that R&D spending for these industries was much lower than spending in operating activities, which suggests a suboptimal allocation of resources. We also found that the proportion of intangible assets to total assets (including patents, trademarks and licenses) were also much lower than those in industrialized countries such as Canada and the U.S. We also examined other factors that were associated with R&D spending in these sectors. Using the China Stock Market Financial Statement Database and the SINA financial database, it was found that Chinese biotechnology and pharmaceutical firms' expenditures in R&D activities are positively associated with ownership structure, but negatively associated with firm size, and with investments in other assets including inventory and fixed assets.

Keywords: Intangible assets; R & D activities; Biotech and pharmaceutical firms; Ownership

Introduction

Innovation has been a central theme for the growth and development of firms in nearly all developed and developing economies. The question of why some firms spend large amounts on R&D while others do not is one that interests both policy-makers and academics. This study examines innovation and R&D expenditures among biotechnology and pharmaceutical firms in China.

China is one of the world's largest investors in research and development. According to the OECD, Chinese spending on R&D increased 19% per year between 1995 and 2005, reaching US$30 billion in 2005 and ranking China sixth in the world in R&D spending. When we adjust this spending on the basis of purchasing power parity between different countries, China would actually rank third in the world behind only the U.S. and Japan. However, in terms of GDP per capita, R&D spending in China is quite low, far lower than the OECD average [1]. Many researchers have suggested that R&D expenditures are not used efficiently in China and point to the low output of internationally-valuable patents. According to Oxford Analytical, while United States Patent Office (USPTO) patents issued to Chinese companies increased twenty-fold over the last 15 years, China still ranked only 12th in USPTO patents received in 2008. But it was actually foreign firms, rather than domestic firms, that lead this innovation activity. From 2003 to 2007, multi-national corporations generated 1,125 USPTO patents where the lead inventor on the patent was located in China. In contrast, Chinese domestic firms and institutes created only 244 lead inventor patents [2].

This study is motivated by the lack of research on R&D investment in China. A large body of literature exists that focuses on innovative activities in the U.S., Japan and other industrialized countries [3-6]. For example, Falk [7] investigated the determinants of business-sector R&D intensity using a panel of OECD countries and found that tax incentives for R&D have a significant and positive impact on business R&D spending. Griffiths and Webster [8] traced the innovation pathways of new creations from R & D activity and found that R&D activity is a highly path-dependent process that relies heavily on firm specific effects such as managerial style, use of incentive schemes for employees, debt ratio etc.

A few studies have shown that while managers have a tendency to under-invest in R&D, institutional investor ownership influences firms to increase investment in R&D [9-13].

One current study examines the impact of environmental uncertainty (such market, technological, or competitive uncertainty) on a firm's investment in R & D [14]. Using a survey study of Chinese firms, it found that market uncertainty, as well as technological and operations capability, had positive influences, while competitive intensity and marketing capability had negative effects on R&D investments.

This paper is the first of its kind for China. It is also the first study to compare intellectual property between China and Canada. Using the China Stock Market Financial Statement Database (CSMAR) and the SINA financial database (www.sina.com), we found that spending in R&D activities is much lower than spending in other activities such as advertising, entertainment, conferences, and the like, which suggests a suboptimal allocation of resources in R&D. When compared with industrial countries such as Canada, we found that the proportion of intangible assets to total assets, including patents, trademarks and licenses, is much lower among companies in China.

Also, while the top 10 Canadian biotechnology and pharmaceutical firms have an average of 30% of their intangibles assets situated in Canada and the top 10 American biotechnology and pharmaceutical firms have an average of 23% of their intangibles assets situated in the U.S., the top 10 Chinese biotechnology and pharmaceutical firms have an average of only 0.8% of their intangible assets situated in China. Further analysis showed that in China, expenditures by biotechnology and pharmaceutical firms in R&D are positively associated with ownership structure, but negatively associated with firm size, and with investments in other assets, including inventory and fixed assets.

In the next section, we discuss data collection and present results.

***Corresponding author:** Tao Zeng, Associate Professor, School of Business and Economics, Wilfrid Laurier University, Waterloo, Ontario, Canada, E-mail: tzeng@wlu.ca

Data Collection and Preliminary Results

Financial data was collected from the China Stock Market Financial Statement Database (CSMAR). We also collected corporate ownership information and preferential tax rates from the SINA finance database. The SINA finance database covers accounting and economic data of listed Chinese firms, such as financial statements and footnotes, financial analysis, ownership structure, top ten shareholders, etc. The firms selected for this study were all involved in the biotechnology or pharmaceutical sectors.

We selected the 10 largest Chinese biotechnology and pharmaceutical firms (according to total assets) in 2009. We then calculated the ratio of intangible assets over total assets; original cost and net balance for intangible assets were obtained from balance sheets; intangible assets included innovation-related assets and non-innovation-related assets; innovation-related assets included patents, trademarks, and licenses; non-innovation-related assets included the rights to use land and building. We excluded non-innovation-related assets from intangible assets.

Part I of Table 1 shows the intangible asset ratio. It shows that on average, the cost of intangible assets is 0.8% of total assets and that the net balance of intangible assets are 0.3% of total assets. The maximum intangible cost ratio is 3.6% and the intangible net value is 1.2% while the minimum intangible cost ratio is 0.3% and the intangible net value is 0.

We also selected the 10 largest Canadian and the 10 largest American, biotechnology and pharmaceutical firms (according to total assets) in 2009 and calculated the ratio of intangible assets over total assets. Part II of Table 1 presents the intangible asset ratio. It shows that on average, the cost of intangible assets are 32% and 23% respectively of total assets in Canada and the U.S., while the net balance of intangible assets are 21% and 17% respectively of total assets in Canada and in the U.S. The maximum intangible cost ratio is 87% and the intangible net value is 65% while the minimum intangible cost ratio is 0.6% and the intangible net value is 0. Table 1 indicates that the intangible asset ratio is much lower in Chinese firms than in Canadian and American firms.

Next, we examined the allocation of funds among R&D activities and other business activities. We collected cash outflows related to other operating activities from the footnotes of financial statements in 2009; cash outflows include spending on advertising, promotion, travel expenses, conference expenses, office expenses, utilities, rent, entertainment, transportation, R&D, etc.

We were able to find cash outflow information on 42 firms accounting for about one-third of all firms in the biotechnology and pharmaceutical sectors. Table 2 sets out the proportion of cash outflows in advertisement and promotion, conferences, entertainment and R&D spending. It shows that in 2009, there was more spending in advertising, promotion, conferences or entertainment than in R&D. On average, R&D spending was about 5% of total cash outflow of other operating activities and about one-third of firms did not spend any money on R&D. This suggests that although firms complained of a shortage of public funding, they did not an optimally allocate their internal resources. Firms preferred to spend on advertising, entertainment and conferences, rather than on innovation.

To determine what is associated with a firm's R&D spending in the biotechnology and pharmaceutical sectors, we designed the following regression model, whereby we regressed intangible assets on firm ownership structure (including ownership concentration, state ownership and inside ownership), firm characteristics (including size, leverage, profitability, inventory intensity, fixed asset intensity), and government tax and subsidies. This is consistent with the methodology of previous studies [15-22].

$$R\&D_t = \alpha_0 + \alpha_1 OWN_t + \alpha_2 STA_t + \alpha_3 INS_t + \alpha_4 SIZ_t + \alpha_5 LEV + \alpha_6 ROA + \alpha_7 INV + \alpha_8 TAX + \alpha_9 FIX + \alpha_0\ SUB + \varepsilon_t$$

Where:

$R\&D_{it}$: intangible assets (including patents, trademarks and licenses) measured as intangible assets net of the right to use land, divided by total assets, for firm i in year t.

OWN_{it}: Ownership concentration, measured as the percentage of shares held by the 5 largest shareholders for firm i in year t.

STA_{it}: State ownership, measured as the number of shares owned by the state over the total number of outstanding shares, for firm i in year t.

INS_{it}: Equal to 1 when there are shares held by management, and 0 otherwise, for firm i in year t.

SIZ_{it}: Firm size, measured as a log of total assets, for firm i in year t.

LEV_{it}: leverage, measured as the sum of short- and long-term debts over total assets, for firm i in year t.

ROA_{it}: return on assets, measured as profit over total assets, for firm i in year t.

INV_{it}: inventory intensity (being the ratio of inventory to total assets) for firm i in year t.

FIX_{it}: Capital intensity (being the ratio of fixed assets to total assets) for firm i in year t.

TAX_{it}: Statutory tax rate for firm i in year t.

SUB_{it}: government subsidies, measured as other cash inflows relating to operating activities, reduced by total assets, for firm i in year t.

α_0 is the intercept, α_1 and α_{10} to are coefficients of the explanatory variables.

The ownership concentration variable is defined as the percentage of shareholdings by the top 5 shareholders. The state ownership variable is defined as the percentage of shares held by the state over the total number of outstanding shares. T he inside ownership variable is a dummy variable, taking 1 if some of the firm's shares are held by key officers, senior managers, etc, and 0 otherwise.

Firm's statutory tax rates (*TAX*) can be equal to the nominal tax rate of 33% (25% since 2008), or lower if a preferential tax rate is applied. Preferential tax rates can be granted to firms in specific regions (e.g., special economic zones), or to firms from specific industries (e.g., farming or high-technology). Preferential rates can be as low as 24%, 18%, 15%, or even 7.5%. Statutory tax rates are disclosed in the income statement footnotes.

For the regression model we used data for the years of 2001-2005 because footnotes to financial statements are available in the SINA financial database only after 2000, while ownership structure and any changes thereto, are disclosed in the SINA financial database only up to 2005. After 2005, shares are merely described as tradable or non-tradable.

Part 1	(Million Yuans)	(Million Yuans)	(Million Yuans)		
Chinese firms	**Total asset**	**Intangible asset (cost)**	**Intangible asset (net)**	**Intangible cost/TA (%)**	**Intangible net/TA (%)**
Shanghai Fosun	11527	32	18	0.28	0.16
Harbin Pharma	10007	80	17	0.80	0.17
North China Pharma	7301	98	67	1.34	0.92
Jilin Aodong	7162	36	14	0.50	0.20
Chongqing Taiji	6523	68	10	1.04	0.15
Guangdong Kangmei	6217	11	0	0.18	0
Joincare Pharma	6146	221	72	3.60	1.17
Northeast Pharma	6079	14	7	0.23	0.12
Yunnan Baiyao	6005	18	0.6	0.30	0.01
SinoPharma	5465	3	3	0.05	0.05
Average				0.83	0.29
Part II	**(Million Cnd$)**	**(Million Cnd$)**	**(Million Cnd$)**		
Canadian firms	**Total asset**	**Intangible asset (cost)**	**Intangible asset (net)**	**Intangible cost/TA (%)**	**Intangible net/TA (%)**
Valeant Pharma	2067	1805	1335	87.32	64.59
Patheon Inc.	791	5	3	0.63	0.38
Atrium Innovations	634	187	186	29.50	29.34
QLT Inc.	420	0	0	0	0
Angiotech Pharma	370	204	131	55.14	35.41
Cangene Co.	345	53	42	15.36	12.17
Paladin Labs	235	106	43	45.11	18.30
GLG Life Tech	230	25	23	10.87	10
Aeterna Zentaris	86	42	17	48.84	19.77
Cardiome Pharm	71	22	16	30.99	22.54
Average				32.37	21.25
Part III	**(Million US$)**	**(Million US$)**	**(Million US$)**		
US firms	**Total asset**	**Intangible asset (cost)**	**Intangible asset (net)**	**Intangible cost/TA (%)**	**Intangible net/TA (%)**
Pfizer	212949	90196	68015	42.36	31.94
Merck & Co.	112090	50481	47656	45.04	42.52
Johnson & Johnson	94684	21180	16323	22.37	17.24
Abbott Laboratories	52417	10800	6292	20.60	12.00
Amgen	39629	5301	2567	13.38	6.48
Bristol-Myers	31008	4839	2865	15.61	9.24
Eli Lilly	27461	4369	3700	15.91	13.47
Baxter International	17354	1029	513	5.93	2.96
Genzyme	10061	3689	2313	36.67	22.99
Gilead Sciences	9699	1112	1062	11.47	10.95
Average				22.93	16.98

Data Source: EDGAR database, SEDAR database, SINA financial database – www.edgar.com; www.sedar.com; www.sina.com

Table 1: Intangible Property/Total Assets in Biotechnology and Pharmaceutical Firms: Canada, China and the United States.

Table 3 reports results from the regression model. It shows that state ownership (*STA*) is positively related to R&D, which suggests that firms owned by the state invest more in R&D. This result is consistent with arguments that state ownership provides an incentive for government shareholders to closely monitor management to pursue long-term goals; and in so doing, reduce agency costs. Hence state ownership has positive effects on R&D spending [18,23]. It may also suggest that a good reputation for heavy investment in R&D activities benefits management such that these managers are more likely to receive a promotion and a promising political career. This result is consistent with the criticism that state-owned firms account for a large share of R&D spending while there is a shortage of R&D spending in private firms.

Table 3 also shows that the coefficient of *SIZE* is negative and significant, which does not provide support for economies of scale in R&D investment. Further, the coefficients in *INV* and *FIX* are negative and significant, which suggests that inventory-intensive and capital-intensive firms spend less on R&D; it implies that *INV* or *FIX* is a substitute for R&D. Other variables, such as ownership concentration, inside ownership, return on assets, government subsidy, applied tax rates, and debt-asset ratio were not found to be significant.

Conclusion and Summary

In this study, we found that Chinese firms spend more on activities such as advertising, entertainment, or conferences than they do in R&D, which suggests a suboptimal allocation of resources for R&D. When compared with industrial countries such as Canada and the U.S., we

Stock code	Advertisement/Cash (%)	Conference/Cash (%)	Entertainment/Cash (%)	R&D/Cash (%)
000513	2.13	3.04	68.17	3.81
000518	13.67	0	9.24	10.6
000538	22.87	0.15	1.43	1.29
000566	28.06	0	4.8	4.63
000597	20.74	26.64	2.38	0
000606	8.6	5.2	1.43	0
000661	0.47	0	0.71	2.46
000739	26.58	0	6.82	15.46
000750	0.08	0	1.44	0
000915	2.59	0.81	1.33	0.70
000990	2.38	0	7.92	3.89
002030	0.91	1.45	3.55	0
002038	0	2.48	2.48	52.49
002252	0	3.32	5.18	0
002275	50.15	11.1	3.09	2.3
002287	38.91	12.88	7.56	4.99
002349	0	0	0.97	5.83
300009	6.25	14.76	3.11	9.04
300026	8.74	17.1	8.17	13.1
300049	0	0	0	0.08
600161	20.85	12.65	9.66	5.03
600196	3.1	18.58	5.58	11.06
600329	16.88	29.78	2.03	5.14
600351	32.09	15.56	1.82	0
600380	51.31	2.32	1.86	2.6
600385	0	6.6	6.1	0
600422	6.68	30.28	2.17	2.14
600488	2.81	0	1.76	11.22
600521	2.71	7.56	4.79	34.58
600530	40.79	0	1.54	4.18
600535	13.28	16.2	7.87	0
600594	3.96	14.4	1.33	1.21
600613	0	0	5.04	0
600664	39.45	17.99	0.6	1.31
600671	16.67	19.69	2.27	0
600706	2.01	0	16.5	0
600771	0	0	4.57	0
600781	0	0	8.21	0
600789	10.93	12.88	7.98	6.43
600829	4.1	3.55	2.13	0.26
600869	0.27	7.17	3.34	0
600976	51.22	0	0	3.58
Average	13.15	7.48	5.64	5.22
Total # of firms	42			
%firms with zero R&D	33.3			
% firms with AD greater than R&D	64.3			
%firms with conference greater than R&D	52.4			
%firms with entertainment greater than R&D	61.9			

Table 2: Cash Flow Related to Operations: Chinese Biotechnological and Pharmaceutical Firms.

found that the proportion of intangible assets to total assets (including patents, trademarks and licenses) are much lower among Chinese firms. While the top 10 Canadian biotechnology and pharmaceutical firms have an average of 30% of their intangibles assets situated in Canada, the top 10 Chinese biotechnology and pharmaceutical firms have an average of only 1% of their intangible assets situated in China.

The reason why Chinese firms have minimal innovation and R&D investment, as explain by Wiki, the free encyclopedia, is that these firms lack the autonomic intellectual property and financial resources to develop their own brand products, and they rely on a repetitive production of low-value added or imitation drugs [24].

Further analysis showed that in China, biotechnology and pharmaceutical firms' expenditures in R&D are positively associated with ownership structure; but negatively associated with firm size and with investments in other assets such as inventory and fixed assets. However, ownership concentration, inside ownership, tax rate, government subsidy, profitability, and leverage are not significantly associated with R&D spending.

Parameter	Est value	St dev	t student	Prob(>|t|)
Intercept	0.24	0.06	4.00***	0.00
OWN	-0.02	0.02	-0.86	0.39
STA	0.01	0.01	2.10**	0.04
INS	-0.01	0.01	-1.38	0.17
SIZE	-0.02	0.01	-3.11***	0.00
LEV	-0.02	0.02	-0.98	0.33
ROA	0.01	0.00	1.48	0.14
INV	-0.11	0.04	-2.94***	0.00
TAX	0.01	0.03	0.32	0.75
FIX	-0.07	0.02	-3.23***	0.00
SUB	-0.04	0.03	-1.59	0.11
R2	0.18			
R2(adj)	0.14			

*** significant at 0.01 level; ** significant at 0.05 level; * significant at 0.1 level based on two-tail t-test

OWN: ownership concentration, measured as the percentage of shares held by the 5 largest shareholders
STA: state ownership, measured as the number of shares owned by the state over the total number of outstanding shares
INS: equal to 1 when there are shares held by management, and 0 otherwise
SIZE: firm size, measured as a log of total assets
LEV: leverage, measured as the sum of short- and long-term debts over total assets
ROA: return on assets, measured as profit over total assets
INV: inventory intensity, measured as the ratio of inventory over total assets
FIX: capital intensity, measured as fixed assets over total assets
TAX: statutory tax rate
SUB: government subsidies, measured as other cash inflows relating to operating activities, reduced by total assets

Table 3: Regression Results: The dependent variable is R&D, intangible assets (including patents, trademarks and licenses) measured as intangible assets net of the right to use land, divided by total assets

These findings are interesting and important. But they should also be treated with some caution as they are not robust to changes in the measurement, the sample, and the time period covered by this study. Future studies may collect more updated data and include both national and multi-national firms in China.

This study is of interest to policy-makers, corporate management and academics who wish to examine corporate R&D and innovation activities to determine what motivates firms to spend on R&D. Future studies should examine if government subsidies are efficiently used to encourage R&D and examine what role tax policy can play in encouraging firms to spend more on R&D.

Acknowledgements

The author gratefully acknowledges the financial support she received for this research from the CA/Laurier Research Centre. The author thanks participants at the 2013 International Conference of Academic Disciplines for their helpful comments. The author also thanks the anonymous reviewers for their insight comments.

Authors' Biography

Tao Zeng is an Associate Professor and CGA. She obtained her PhD degree at Queen's University in 2001. She has many publications in academic journals including Accounting Perspectives, Canadian Journal of Administrative Sciences, Chinese Management Studies, Canadian Tax Journal, Asian Review of Accounting, etc. She is an Associate Editor of British Journal of Economics, Management & Trade, on Editorial Board of Journal of Financial Studies and Research and Journal of Business and Financial Affairs. Her teaching interest is taxation. Her research interests are capital market and international business and tax.

References

1. OECD observer (2007) Chinese innovation: China can rekindle its great innovative past, though some reforms may be needed first. Science & Technology Section: 263.
2. http://www.researchrecap.com/index.php/2010/03/18/.
3. Stemberg R, Amdt O (2001) The Firm or the Region: What Determines the Innovation Behavior of European Firms? Economic Geography 77: 364-382.
4. Dushnitsky G, Lenox MJ (2005) When Do Firms Undertake R&D by Investing in New Ventures? Strategic Management Journal 26: 947-965.
5. David P, O'Brien JP, Yoshikawa T (2008) The Implications of Debt Heterogeneity for R&D Investment and Firm Performance. Academy of Management Journal 51: 165-181.
6. Hall BH, Lotti F, Mairesse J (2012) Evidence on the Impact of R&D and ICT Investment on Innovation and Productivity in Italian Firms. Economics of Innovation and New Technology 22: 300-328.
7. Falk M (2009) What Drives Business Research and Development (R&D) Intensity Across Organisation for Economic Co-Operation and Development (OECD) Countries? Applied Economics 38: 533-547.
8. Griffiths WE, Webster EM (2004) The Determinants of Research and Development and Intellectual Property Usage among Australian Companies, 1989 to 2002. CIES, Innovation Systems and Industrial Organisation Program, University of Adelaide, Adelaide, Australia, Discussion paper no. 0415
9. Baysinger BD, Kosnik RD, Turk TA (1991) Effects of Board and Ownership Structure on Corporate R&D Strategy. Academy of Management Journal 34: 205-214.
10. Hansen GS, Hill CWL (1991) Are Institutional Investors Myopic? A Time-series Study of Four Technology-driven Industries. Strategy Management Journal 12: 1-16.
11. Kochhar R, David P (1995) Institutional Investors and Firm Innovation: A Test of Competing Hypotheses. Strategic Management Journal 17: 73-84.
12. Franko LG (1989) Global Corporate Competition: Who's Winning, Who's Losing and the R&D Factor as a Reason Why. Strategic Management Journal 10: 449-474.
13. Zahra SA (1996) Goverance, Ownership, and Corporate Entrepreneurship: The Moderating Impact of Industry Technological Opportunities. The Academy of Management Journal 39: 1713-1735.
14. Su Z, Xie E, Peng J (2010) Impacts of Environmental Uncertainty and Firm's Capabilities on R&D Investment: Evidence from China. Innovation: Management, policy and Practice 12: 269-282.
15. Kelm KM, Narayanan VK, Pinches GE (1995) Shareholder Value Creation during R&D Innovation and Commercialization Stages. Academy of Management Journal 38: 770-787.
16. Hitt MA, Hoskisson RE, Johnson RA, Moesel DD (1996) The Market for Corporate Control and Firm Innovation. Academy of Management Journal 39: 1084-1119.
17. Hundley G, Jacobson CK, Park SH (1996) Effects of Profitability and Liquidity on R&D Intensity: Japanese and U.S. Companies Compared. Academy of Management Journal 39: 1659-1674.
18. Hess K, Gnuasekarge A, Hovey M (2008) State Dominant and Non-state Dominant Ownership Concentration and Firm Performance: Evidence from China. Working Paper, University of Waikato, New Zealand.
19. Lin H-C, Zeng T (2011) Ownership structure and R&D spending: evidence from China's listed firms. Chinese Management Studies 5: 82-93.
20. Kato T, Long C (2006) Executive Turnover and Firm Performance in China. The American Economic Review 96: 363-367.
21. Li H, Zhou L-A (2005) Political Turnover and Economic Performance: the Incentive Role of Personnel Control in China. Journal of Public Economics 89: 1743-1762.
22. Innovation Lags in China despite R&D Investment Growth. Guest Post by Oxford Analytical.
23. Bos D (1991) Privatization: A Theoretical Treatment. Clarendon Press, Oxford, UK.
24. Pharmaceutical Industry in China. Wikipedia: The Free Encyclopedia.

Explain the Relationship between Personality and Organizational Commitment in the Office Staff of the National Logistics Company South Oil

Naimi EA and Ghafeli A*

Management Department, Islamic Azad University, The International Center for Persian Gulf, Iran

Abstract

This article aims to explain the relationship between personality type and organizational commitment in the Office staff of the National Oil Company supplies the south. This study is the research methodology and decision-oriented applied research (the objective) and survey (in terms of data collection). The Statistical population included the Office staff of National South Oil Company supplies that their number is 472 and with random sampling method using a sample of 147 of them as the sample was selected. The results show that among all the component elements of character and commitment, there is a significant relation and this relationship is negative correlation between neuroticism component and the rest are positive. The intensity of this relationship is the association between the components of emotional commitment and loyalty is highest.

Keywords: Personality; Commitment; National company; South oil

Introduction

Today, most managers agree that human resources are the most important capital [1]. Having committed employees aware of and loyal is the most important organization's success factor. The priority of every company needs to attract and keep qualified staff is committed and the failure to achieve this means a loss of efficiency, lack of growth and the loss of business. Success in the competitive world belongs to the companies that are committed and loyal employees knowing self-greatest asset [2]. The concept of commitment is at the psychological literature has been widely discussed. Organizational commitment is willing to continue working with an organization [3]. Organizational commitment has three dimensions, namely: a) Identify accepted goals and values of the organization: b) Efforts; strong desire for a big effort in order to achieve organizational goals c) Loyalty: an affinity and interest as part of the organization [4]. Organizational commitment to the same extent that the implications, both individual and organizational cause. Therefore, researchers and managers in order to promote this important variable and influenced by a variety of methods to test and explore a variety of factors to the success of the organization and consequently the development of society. Based on this thinking, the researcher in this study deals with one of the individual variables as the type of personality. In the 21st century, one of the most crucial issues in the study of organizational behavior influences the diversity of the workforce, such as personality, organizational performance [5]. Personality characteristics and processes that combine a set of relatively stable behavior in response to people, objects and ideas established in the environment [6]. Character has five dimensions that are extraversion, neuroticism or relationship between the diversity of the workforce, such as personality and in private businesses studied enough and documentary-making, especially in developed countries, but it is in the public sector, especially in developing countries, are is not considered appropriate [5]. Organizations tend to have a workforce with high commitment; the results suggest that organizational commitment to important outcomes such as reduced employee turnover, higher motivation and organizational citizenship behavior leads. A number of studies have shown that people with five characteristics compared to those higher goals set for themselves and to achieve their goals are more committed. Rasouli and eslami in their study entitled "The Relationship between personality traits and mental health staff job satisfaction and Army" with cross-sectional study was conducted among all commandos hillock, to the conclusion that the correlation between personality types and mental health as well as between job satisfaction and mental health existed. Personality type (B) and job satisfaction had a greater share in predicting mental health. Gerami and colleagues in a research study entitled "Comparison of personality characteristics of speed and overtaking unauthorized drivers with non-offending drivers in Tabriz," a descriptive science comparative method, concluded that between personality type drivers offending and non-offending there is a significant difference. The results achieved show that between sensation seeking, seeking experience, diversity, adventure, boredom and lack of inhibition, there is a significant relationship between drivers and non-offending. Sadat Kazemi et al. in their study entitled "The relationship between value and personality of talent management, citizen engagement and organizational alienation of traditional bureaucratic organizations" in the 2970 survey by the research director of the traditional industries, concluded that bureaucratic organizations more humanistic nature. Moghimi and colleagues in their study entitled "The relationship between personality type A & B-style management" of managers-of Education and Agriculture Organization of Qom, concluded between certain types of styles and character there is significant relationship management effectiveness. Vndchgyny and Amin Roodposhti in a research study entitled "The relationship between gender and organizational commitment with respect to age," the executive Gilan with analytical and descriptive methods were found between gender and commitment organizational commitment and normative commitment, there is no significant

***Corresponding author:** Abdollah Ghafeli, Management Department, Islamic Azad University, The International Center for Persian Gulf, Iran
E-mail: abdollah87.ghafeli@gmail.com

relationship, but there relationship between gender and emotional commitment. Khanifar et al. in a research study entitled "The Role of communication, effective listening and commitment" in Social Security and Agriculture Organization of Qom to the conclusion that among the components of effective listening and organizational commitment, positive relationship and there is significant [7]. Similarly, effective listening and affective commitment, continuous norm and there is a positive significant relationship. -Test performed on the data, the relationship between effective listening and commitment components of commitment and emotional commitment in the first place and second place was normative.

Research Methodology

This study examines the relationship between personality types and explain the research that organizational commitment, today. Overall, this research method can be according to two criteria for the purpose of research and data collections are divided. Segmentation based on objective, this research can be applied to both. Also because the aim of finding an answer to the problem and as a result can immediately be used in decision-making, it can be used as a research-oriented decision. This means that the aim of the researchers find answers to a problem that the result can be immediately used in decision-making. In terms of data collection, for the purpose of describing the phenomenon studied and to better understand the terms and conditions and helping in the decision-making process except research and data collection; the required data with two objectives (formulating hypotheses, and testing hypotheses) and to certain methods (library and field) will be collected. In the first phase of collecting information in order to formulate hypotheses of library methods and the means of receipt, in the second round of questionnaires to collect information (questionnaire, organizational commitment and character) is used. The population of this research unit National Oil Company supplies the south and the unit of analysis is the individual. To describe the variables of descriptive statistics such as frequency, percentage, mean, median, drawing diagrams, and etc., will be used. Also to ensure the internal consistency of Cronbach's alpha coefficient of the questionnaire and to ensure the normal distribution Kolmogorov-Smirnov test data and to assess the correlation between variables according to the normality or non-normality of the distribution of the Pearson correlation test or Spearman will become.

Demographic variables

Table 1 reviews the distribution of personality factors, organizational

Gender of workers		
Percent	**Number**	
61.2	90	**Male**
38.8	57	**Female**
100.0	147	**Total**
Levels of education		
8.8	13	Diploma
32.0	47	AS
26.5	39	BA
21.8	32	Master
10.9	16	Dr
100.0	147	Total
Marriage		
38.1	56	Single
61.9	91	Married
100.0	147	Total

Table 1: Characterized by cognitive variables.

Significant level	Kolmogorov-Smirnov	Variables
0.09	1.29	Openness to experience
0.17	1.30	Loyalty
0.09	1.25	Extroversion
0.17	1.39	Compatibility
0.10	1.22	OCD
0.09	1.19	Affective commitment
0.16	1.34	Commitment
0.10	1.22	Normative
0.18	1.36	Organizational commitment

Table 2: Kolmogorov-Smirnov normality review for variables.

Maximum	Minimum	Standard deviation	The average	Personality factors
4.67	2.67	0.42	3.23	Openness to experience
5.00	2.00	0.59	3.63	Deontology
4.67	2.33	0.50	3.46	Extroversion
5.00	3.00	0.45	3.85	Compatibility
4.17	1.73	0.44	2.71	Neuroticism

Table 3: Mean and standard deviation of personality.

Maximum	Minimum	Standard deviation	The average	Variables
4.43	2.86	0.36	3.49	Affective commitment
4.60	3.00	0.35	3.82	Continuous commitment
4.80	3.00	0.37	4.03	Normative commitment
4.61	3.09	0.26	3.78	Organizational commitment

Table 4: The mean and standard deviation organizational commitment and its components.

commitment and its components to investigate the distribution of personal and Organizational commitment factors and components of the Kolmogorov-Smirnov was used. Results were shown in Table 2.

If Kolmogorov-Smirnov test results of above tables show the results showed that personality factors and organizational commitment and its components normally have been distributed. ($p<0.05$ significant level of personality factors and organizational commitment and its components more than 05/0 respectively). So to describe the variables of mean and standard deviation and to respond to hypotheses used parametric tests.

Describes the personality factors: If results of table and the graph above shows, the average personality factors from 2.71 to 3.85, respectively (2.71 to 3.85 for neuroticism and agreeableness). That since questions of character, on 5-item Likert scale "strongly disagree = 1 to very agree = 5", respectively (Table 3). In fact, the number 3 will be above the middle of the spectrum. Neuroticism was lower than the middle, but was higher than the average of the rest of staff of mediocrity. Describes the organizational commitment and its components (Table 4).

The main hypothesis of this study: The main hypothesis: the personality traits of staff and their organizational commitment in the logistics unit of the National South Oil Company have an effect. The null hypothesis: the personality traits of staff and their organizational commitment in the logistics unit of the National South Oil Company have an effect. To answer this hypothesis, because the variables are small and there was no violation of the normality of the data, the multiple regression analysis was used. Solidarity linear combination of personality characteristics and organizational commitment in the staff was 0.587. In fact, the effect of personality characteristics and organizational commitment among employees is 34.5 of that; this is a significant correlation (Table 5).

Total squares regression analysis of variance shown in Table 6.

Because the sum of squares in the regression analysis 001/0 P<, 948/3=(141, 5) F, so relation personality traits and organizational commitment of staff is significant (significance level of less than 05/0 respectively). Table 7 illustrates the regression analysis.

Secondary research hypotheses: Pearson correlation results show that:

a) Organizational commitment extroversion with the staff was positive and statistically significant relationship. P<0.05, r=0.319 level was less significant for the ratio of 0.05. The null hypothesis is rejected and the hypothesis is confirmed. I.e., between extroversion and Organizational commitment employees per unit of National South Oil Company supplies a significant relationship.

b) The relationship between extroversion and emotional commitment with the staff was positive and statistically significant relationship (P<0.05, r=0.184) level was less significant for this ratio of 0.05. The null hypothesis is rejected and the hypothesis is confirmed. Ie between extroversion and emotional commitment of employees per unit of National South Oil Company supplies a significant relationship.

c) The relationship Continuous commitment to consistency in staff was positive and statistically significant relationship (P<0.05, r=0.530) level was less significant for this ratio of 0.05. So assuming 0 refute and hypotheses research confirms, that means the adaptability of employees and continuous commitment of National South Oil Company supplies a significant relationship.

d) The relationship between Normative commitment and consistency in staff was positive and statistically significant relationship (P<0.05, r=0.207) level was less significant for the factor of 0.05. So assuming 0 is rejected and confirmed the hypothesis that means between compatibility and staff per unit of National South Oil Company supplies a significant relationship.

Significance level	Correlation Square	Correlation
0.001	0.345	0.587

Table 5: The mean and standard deviation organizational commitment and its components.

Level of significance	Mean square	Degrees of freedom	Total squares	Effects
.001	0.764	5	11.461	Regression
	0.259	141	21.775	Residuals
		99	33.236	Total

Table 6: Analysis of variance sum of squares of regression.

Significance level	t	Beta	Std. Error	B	Variable
.001	11.016		0.154	1.701	Fixed
.001	5.571	0.331	0.026	0.146	Openness to experience
.002	3.156	0.188	0.031	0.097	Deontology
.001	4.462	0.303	0.039	0.175	Extroversion
.001	3.980	0.253	0.038	0.150	Compatibility
.182	-.410	-0.024	0.036	-0.075	Neuroticism

Table 7: Regression analysis for the effects of the personality traits of organizational commitment among employees.

Conclusion

At a confidence level of 99% based on Correlation of test results we can say:

a) The main hypothesis given that, it was claimed, personality traits influence employees' Organizational commitments to them, the results confirm this effect. In other words, the relationship between personality traits and organizational commitment rejected. In similar researches like vatan ara and khaefollahi et al. the relationship between the components of organizational commitment and personality traits confirmed.

b) In hypothesis 1 considering that, it was claimed, the personality trait of extroversion and organizational commitment and its components there are, the results confirm this effect, in other words the relationship between extroversion and organizational commitment and components rejected it. In this same vatan ara and Khaefollahi et al. The relationship between the components of organizational commitment and character features confirmed.

c) In the hypothesis 2 considering that, it was claimed, compatibility between the character traits and organizational commitment and its components there are, the results confirm this effect, in other words the relationship between compliance and commitment and components rejected it. In research same vatan Ara and Khaefollahi et al. The relationship between the components of organizational commitment and character features confirmed.

d) In hypothesis 3 considering that, it was claimed, the personality trait openness to experience and organizational commitment and its components there are, the results confirm this effect, in other words the relationship between openness to experience and commitment enterprise and its components declined. In the researchs same vatan-Ara and Khaefollahi et al. The relationship between the components of organizational commitment and character features confirmed.

According to the organization's documentation and interviews with executives and experts of the company the following suggestions offered:

a) Managers can enhance organizational commitment through extroversion features, to strengthen the relationship between staff and provide conditions for dialogue, joy, boost morale and personnel necessary to provide energy and determination to grow in spite of the isolation conditions seeking personnel away from the workplace.

b) Managers to enhance organizational commitment by strengthening the compatibility can, with training and education, and awareness of the negative consequences of denunciation of cooperation and conflict with their polite behavior, they will be in a direction other than cavil, conflicts with colleagues and behaviors non polite conduct and informing staff about the positive consequences of usefulness, reliability, cooperation and kindness and help them to learn the behaviors necessary to take action.

c) Managers to enhance organizational commitment, openness to create the conditions through features that boost the IQ of employees, develop new ideas, inventive and varied activities, take the necessary steps to take.

Managers to enhance organizational commitment by strengthening loyalty can to help employees do their job fully, be careful in their work, are reliable, effective things to do, avoid confusion and develop their own work plans.

References

1. Alireza AK, Azam AA (1389) Factors affecting organizational commitment. Journal of Business Management 7.
2. Dadnya, Akram (1388) The impact of job satisfaction in organizational success. The Islamic Republic Ayran.
3. Muhammad AH, Yan J, Nazar H, Zafar ZA (2014) Factirs Affecting Organizational Commitment Among Bank Officer In Pakistan. Journal of Business and Management 16: 18-24.
4. Morrow PC (1993) The theory and measurement of work commitment. Greenwich: JAI Press 15: 171-188.
5. Davis M, Damary S (2012) The Influence of personality Dimensions on Organizational Performance. International Journal of Humanities and Social Science 2: 184-194.
6. Mustafa A, khoshi A, Hussein HZ (1389) The relationship between commitment and character in a military organization: A case Study of a military unit in Tehran. Military Psychology Quarterly.
7. Moghimi SM, Hussein K, Mahla AK (1387) A study of relationship between personality style and the effectiveness in public organizations managers. Journal of Public Administration 1: 87-104.

9

Reciprocity Based Concept of Nonprofit Marketing

Novatorov EV*

Department of Management, Higher School of Economics, National Research University, Russia

Abstract

The author deconstructs the prevailing conceptualization of nonprofit marketing and concludes it rests on three principles: voluntary exchange, an open system organization, and self-interest motivation. A review of the genesis of these principles revealed that alternative principles were ignored in the social science literature. Based on a qualitative analysis and critical hermeneutic approach a revised conceptualization of nonprofit marketing was suggested which incorporated the principles of reciprocity, the features of a contingency-choice system model of formal organizations, and collectivistic interest motivation. A revised definition of nonprofit marketing is offered based on these principles.

Keywords: Nonprofit marketing; Reciprocity; Substantivist economic anthropology; Public interest; Nonprofit sector; Collectivist sociology

Introduction

Interest among nonprofit administrators in the application of marketing tools to nonprofit sector services emerged from the tax revolt of the late 1970s and early 1980s in the US. With theshrinkage and withdrawal of grants from federal and state governments, municipalities and nonprofit organizations were confronted with the issue of how to satisfy the growing expectations of taxpayers in a milieu of reduced financial resourses. During this period of financial scarcity, the public administrationabd nonprofit literature witnessed an attempt to rethink the nature of public and nonprofit sectors management through theactive importation and borrowing of private sector techniques. Several commentators labeled thisprocess of importation as integration of public and private sector management or in briefer terms "managerialism" [1-3]. Marketing in the public sector was part of the managerialism movement [4,5]. From the beginning, the concept of marketing in the nonprofit and public sectors was criticized in the marketing literature as confusing [6,7]. Nevertheless eventually, it became widely embraced by marketing scholars and consultants [8]. In 1978, Lovelock and Weinberg noted that by the end of the 1970s there was no longer any serious controversy among marketing scholars about the appropriateness of the concept for the public and nonprofit sectors [9]. However, despite this apparent agreement among marketing academics, public administrators and academics in public administration and nonprofit areas have not unanimously embraced the utility of the concept of non-profit and public sector marketing [4,5,10-12]. During the subsequent three decades the "marketing to nonmarketers" problem in thecontext of the public sector, has split public administrators into two camps comprised of its supporters and opponents. Roberto [12], an active proponent of marketing, observed: "Marketing's recent and growing participation in public sector management has received a bipolar love-hate evaluation." Supportive commentators refer to public sector marketing as "a comprehensive strategy for effecting social change" with "unique concepts and techniques" which are "coming of age" and are merely "misunderstood" [9,11-13]. Critical commentators do partially recognize the need of public administrators to adopt new management techniques to deal with the prevailing environment of «less-government-more- user-fees». However, they refer to the application of marketing principles within the nonprofit and public administration fields as "confusion compounded", "an inappropriate model", "intellectualization", "absurd", "the megalomaniac marketing supremacy syndrome", and "a dramatic imitation" of social relationships [14-17]. Ironically, the ultimate goal of proponents and opponents was essentially the same—to increase the effectiveness and responsiveness of public organizations in a changed financial environment. The essence of the difference in opinions appears to relate to the means by which this commonly recognized goal should be achieved. The "marketing to nonmarketers" issue has wide geographic and disciplinary scope. It can be found in such diverse disciplines as political science, arts and culture, health promotion, fundraising, and nutrition education. The geography of the debates ranges from the Republics of the former Soviet Union, across Europe and Scandinavia, through North America, to New Zealand and Australia. The problem was perhaps best articulated by Walsh [3] who suggested the need to redefine public marketing "...if it is to be specifically public service marketing rather a pale imitation of a private sector approach within the public sector." The intent of this paper is to deconstruct the prevailing conceptualization of public sector marketing into a set of underlying principles, contrast these principles with alternative principles, and use the alternative principles as a basis for developing a superior conceptualization of public sector marketing.

Method

To pursue the objectives the study employed a critical hermeneutic approach that focused on deconstruction, understanding, and interpretation [18]. The major tool employed to attack the problem was negative case analysis. Kidder [19] compares procedures of negative case analysis with statistical tests of significance. A goal of both methods is "to handle error variance." During negative case analysis all existing propositions, null hypotheses, or assumptions underlying theories or concepts, are tested and refined against alternative explanations until no or a minimum possible number of alternative explanations are left. Kidder [19] notes: "negative case analysis requires that the researcher look for disconfirming data in both past and future observations. A single negative case is enough to require the investigator to revise a hypothesis." This method is consistent with the Hegelian method of dialectic, which suggests that any proposed thesis should be countered

***Corresponding author:** Novatorov EV, Professor, Department of Management, Higher School of Economics, National Research University, Russia
E-mail: enova@mail.ru

by an antithetical proposition in order to achieve synthesis. Application of negative case analysis in this study included two major elements. The first element dealt with results of the investigative research and included a search for alternative concepts or disconfirming data. For example, if investigative research found that some concepts from the social science disciplines were borrowed to develop the public sector marketing concept (e. g. the concept of formal organizations from organizational theory, or the concept of social exchange from sociology), then these concepts (the concepts of formal organization and social exchange in our example) were analyzed and the existence of alternative conceptualizations was investigated in the organizational theory or sociological literatures. If alternative conceptualizations were found then they were studied and analyzed in the context of their usefulness for the public sector marketing discussion. The second step in negative case analyses was to investigate the potential for conceptual consistency among and between the existing and the revealed alternative concepts. For example, if alternative conceptualizations of both social exchange theory and formal organizations were found, they could be compared with each other looking for possible consistency, connections, or links among them. The negative case analysis attempts to find out if researchers who developed the concept of public sector marketing suppressed evidence. Kahane [20] contends that such actions can occur when a researcher "conceals evidence unfavorable to his own position." It does not necessarily means that a researcher on purpose hid or omitted evidence or al ternative concepts. As suggested by Douglas [21] a researcher may have a diversity of reasons for suppressing evidence. Negative case analysis assists in avoiding the suppression of evidence by checking if alternative conceptualizations were considered and consequentially incorporated. Maxwell [22] noted that: "the most serious threat to the theoretical validity of an account is not collecting or paying attention to discrepant data, or not considering alternative explanations or understandings of the phenomena you are studying." The conceptualization of public sector marketing cannot be generic and universal if its originators purposefully or mistakenly ignored alternative explanations. The issue is analogous to public hearings and legal proceedings, where both offensive and defensive parties are given the right to be heard. In order to be fair, the negative case analysis focused on the evidence available and reported prior to, and not after, development of the concept of public sector marketing.

Prevailing Conceptualization of Public Sector Marketing

Kotler and Murray [23] suggested one of the earliest and most influential conceptualizations of public sector marketing. It was elaborated upon in a text published in the same year [24]. Kotler adopted [25,26] definition, and Blau and Scott's [27] classification, of formal organizations. In Kotler's [24] interpretation, a formal organization is "a purposeful coalescence of people, materials, and facilities seeking to accomplish some purpose in the outside world." Different purposes determine different types of formal organizations: business concerns seek to benefit their owners: service organizations seek to benefit their clients; mutual benefit organizations seek to benefit their members; and commonweal organizations seek to benefit the public at large. In spite of differences in goals, Kotler contended that all formal organizations were involved in exchange relationships with various categories of publics. However, the concept of voluntary exchange is only one of several possible philosophical alternatives for explaining the relationships between formal organizations and their publics. Other options include: the love system, characterized by the underlying motive of benevolence on one side without any necessary reciprocation by the other; and the threat system characterized by an underlying motive of malevolence on one side. Thus, in Kotler's interpretation, a church and its members, a police department and citizens, a charity and its donors, and so on: are all engaged in exchange transactions that involve taxes, services, money, contributions, feelings of well-being, or other tangible and intangible benefits. If an organization is willing to exchange resources with an identified public, then this category of public becomes the organization's market or "distinct group of people and/or organizations that have resources which they want to exchange, or might conceivable exchange, for distinct benefits" . Having introduced the notions of organization, public, market and exchange, Kotler explained the differences between marketing and a sales orientation. The marketing concept involves continuously adjusting the firm's offerings to the targeted customers' needs. In contrast, a sales orientation involves continuous adjustment of buyers' needs to the firm's offerings. He asserts that a sales orientation is likely to be characteristic of an unresponsive organization, while a marketing orientation is likely to result in a highly responsive organization. Kotler [24] favors the latter and defines marketing as being applicable for all types of formal organizations: The analysis, planning, implementation, and control of carefully formulated programs designed to bring about voluntary exchanges of values with target markets for achieving organizational objectives. It relies heavily on designing the organization's offering in terms of the target market's needs and desires, and on using effective pricing, communication, and distribution to inform, motivate, and service the markets.

Assumptions of the prevailing conceptualization of public sector marketing

Advocates of the prevailing conceptualization of public sector marketing believe that public administrators should be interested in "understanding what the organization exchanges with each public; i.e., what each party gives and gets... [and what are]...the motivations underlying their transactions and satisfactions received" [28]. Three major principles underling this conceptualization of public sector marketing are: (1) An open-system model of formal organizations, borrowed from organizational theory [29]; (2) the concept of social exchange, adapted from individualistic sociology [30]; and (3) Self-interest motivation, advocated by formalist's economic anthropologists [31]. These principles and their origins are discussed in the follow sub-sections.

An open-system model of public agencies

This principle assumes that an organization is "a purposeful coalescence of people, materials, and facilities seeking to accomplish some purpose in the outside world" [28]. The primary functions of such an organization are: (1) Input—attraction of sufficient resources; (2) Throughput—conversion of these resources into various products; and (3) Output—distribution of these throughputs to the public. This conceptualization of a formal organization as a resource conversion machine is consistent with the precepts of an open-system model of organizations, designed to respond to external and internal pressures.

Self-interest motivation

The doctrine contends that pursuit of personal self-interest is the essential motivation for exchange between any organization and their publics. Although Kotler [28] avoided the term "self-interest," Bagozzi [32], who acknowledged Kotler's influence and advice, openly recognized the central role of self-interest motivation in the context of public sector marketing: " many individuals, groups, and firms pursue their own self-interest. This is what Adam Smith meant by his reference to an "invisible hand, the pursuit of self-interest can be the foundation for the web of kinship, economic, and social institutions". Adam Smith [33] described the quid pro quo principle that underlies his philosophy of the invisible hand in the following terms: "whoever offers to another a bargain of any kind, proposes to do this: give me that what I want and you shall have this which you want". Shapiro [34] similarly believed that this central role of self-interest in the context of public and nonprofit marketing was sufficiently self-evident that there was no need to discuss it: "I shall not bother discussing theconcept of self-interest; it can be taken for granted."

Voluntary exchange and public agencies

A central assumption underlying this principle is that all organizations seek to attain their goals through the voluntary exchange mechanism. They perceive voluntary exchange to be the only viable mechanism through which formal organizations can attract, convert, and distribute resources [28]. Kotler argues that voluntary exchanges are not limited to such conventional resources as: goods, services, and money [but] include other resources such as time, energy, and feelings" [26]. He believes that voluntary exchange in all of its resource forms should be conceptualized as a transaction, and that it is the central tenet underpinning the notion that marketing is generic. Such exchanges require the existence of at least two conditions: (1) The availability of two parties, and (2) That each party possesses some resource that is valued by another party [28].

Limitations of the prevailing conceptualization of public sector marketing

Some negative comments towards applying the marketing philosophy and techniques in the public sector have emerged in the public administration literature. Opponents of marketing in the public administration field felt uncomfortable with Kotler's generic transactional conceptualization of public marketing, which suggests no differences between public and private management; public, private and the nonprofit sectors; and the role and application of marketing in these different sectors. Rainey, Backoff, and Levine [35] contested Kotler and Murray's and Murray's [2,23] positions that there were only limited differences between formal organizations and between managing public and private entities; that their trends converged; and that as a result, marketing was appropriate in the public sector. In contrast, Rainey et al. [35] postulated that there are crucial differences between the two sectors and, thus, in the role of marketing in public agencies. Drawing from the literature existing at that time and organizing their data into three major categories (environmental factors, organization-environment transactions, and internal structure and processes), Rainey et al. [35] contended that a public organization: works in an environment with less market exposure; has more legal and formal constraints on its procedures and spheres of operation; relies more on the "coercive" and "monopolistic" nature of many government activities; and has less decision-making autonomy. Allison and Walsh [3,36] reached similar conclusions. These analyses challenged the notions of the appropriateness of both the marketing philosophy and voluntary exchange in the delivery of public services services. Differences between the public and private sectors were at least partially recognized in subsequent literature on public sector marketing. Crompton and Lamb [37] argued that government organizations are committed to allocate resources equitably, while private sector organizations direct resources only at the most responsive target markets. Equity principles require public organizations to deliver services to all citizens on a fair basis. In contrast, commercial organizations selectively serve only responsive customers. Although differences were recognized and incorporated into some conceptualizations of public sector marketing, the controversy remained salient. Crompton and Lamb, Mokwa and Permut, and Coffman, who all accepted the distinctive positions of commentators on both sides of the debate, demonstrated the centrality of controversy [37-39]. They recognized Rainey et al.'s [35] crucial differences between public and private organizations, but they accepted the Kotlerian conceptualization of marketing based on the voluntary exchange paradigm as the basis of their conceptual frameworks. Doubts were raised that the conceptualization of public sector marketing authentically reflected the public realm [3]. Walsh and Loveday argued that public sector marketing as it is operationalized has little in common with the public realm. According to Walsh, marketing has not developed in a fashion that is specific to the context of government. He believes that the current conceptualization of marketing reflects a simple semantic adjustment of commercial marketing definitions, for example, by dropping the notion of profit without substantive adaptations to the political context of the public realm. Loveday questions whether public sector marketing is in any way innovative. He argues that "what the marketers claim as their own has been developed by a lot of other people as well; marketers have made a distinctive contribution in thinking it through in the context of selling products, first tangibles and more recently intangibles, to a mass market" (p. 174). Both authors support Walsh's conclusion that there needs to be a rethinking and re-examination of public sector marketing in order to develop its new politically informed form. Empirical studies seem to support these critical voices. Contrary to Lamb and Crompton's [37] findings about the growing acceptance of marketing philosophy in public agencies, Graham [1] found that after 10 years of attempting to implement it in public sector organizations, most agencies still were not customer-oriented as defined by the generic marketing concept. Smith's [40] study found that marketing was viewed only as a promotion technique concerned with specific problems such as an AIDS campaign. Marketing continued to be perceived by many public administrators as unethical, goal distorting, and as an inappropriate model and framework for public service delivery [17,41-43]. It appears that public sector marketing should undergo further modifications to address the concerns of those public administrators who remain skeptical towards it.

Results of negative case analysis

Negative case analysis found that alternative assumptions (negative cases) were available to those who introduced the public sector marketing concept. A search for negative cases and rival hypothesis revealed that those available were : (1) open-system and closed-system perspectives on formal organizations that could be operationalized using microeconomic or political system paradigms; (2) individualistic and collectivistic versions of social exchange theory; and (3) "formalist" and "substantivist" perspectives in economic anthropology with distinct views on the history of marketing exchange and types of economic analysis. The following subsections discuss the overlooked concepts in more detail.

A Closed-system Model of Formal Organizations

A search for rival hypotheses in the organizational theory literature suggests that formal organizations can be conceptualized not only from an open-system model perspective but also from a closed-system model perspective. Hall [44] summarized major differences between these two approaches: The closed-system model views organizations as instruments designed for the pursuit of clearly specified goals, and thus directing organizational arrangements and decisions toward goal achievement and toward making the organization more and more rational in the pursuit of its goal. The open-system model views organizations as not only concerned with goals, but also responding to external and internal pressures. In some cases, the open perspective virtually ignores the issue of goals. The closed-system conceptualization of organizations is an older perspective that stems from Weber's classical analysis of bureaucracy. Weber [45] defined an organization as "a system of continuous purposive activity of a specified kind." This perspective suggests that an organization has a clear and explicit goal that determines its internal structure and the tasks undertaken to achieve this goal. Tasks are divided among members of the organization so that each member has responsibility for an area of activity that matches his/herc ompetence. Decision-making in a closed-system organization is based on an established normative order and is manifested by clearly specified rules and a chain of command. Selection of members is based on an individual's skills and technical competence. The person's membership with the organization is documented in the form of a written contract that delineates the individual's duties and level of remuneration [45]. The open-ended or "natural-system" perspective on organizations emanates from a critique of the closed-ended system [29] and is based on the conventional microeconomic paradigm. This perspective puts lesser emphasis on an organization's concern with goals and greater emphasis on its responsiveness to external pressures: The major misconception [of the closed-system model] is the failure to recognize fully that the organization is continually dependent upon inputs from the environment and that the inflow of materials and human energy is not constant. This perspective is based on assumption of scarce energy and resources. The main goal of the organization is perceived to be survival in a competitive surrounding environment that consists of other organizations that compete for the same resources. A need to survive, forces the organization to adapt to both controllable internal and non-controllable external forces. Therefore, it is conceptualized as a "natural system" which imports energy in the form of people and materials (input) from its external environment, alters it in some way (the throughput), and distributes it back to the environment (output). Survival dictates a "broadening of organizational goals" because the organization is dependent on what is imported to it, how it transforms inputs, and how the environment accepts the organization's output. Finally, there has been an attempt in the organizational literature to develop a balanced model of formal organizations that encompasses elements of the both the open-system and closed-system perspectives. The major assumption of this perspective is that organizations have multiple conflicting goals and thus have to make strategic choices in response to internal and external threats. This perspective tries to control three major factors: individuals within an organization; the environment of the organization; and form of the organization. Individuals within the organization are seen as the mechanism through which environmental and organizational characteristics are shaped. The environment is considered as being unstable and varying from predictable to non-predictable. By choosing the best strategic choice-response to a changed environment, the organization attempts to fit itself to the changed environment and accordingly changes its form. That is why contingency and choice are major elements of this perspective [44]. The negative case analysis suggests that the open-system definition of an organization, in contrast to the closed-system definition, invites an organization-environment approach, which implies that an organization is engaged in xchange relationships with the competitive environment [46]. In such an approach, differences between the goals of formal organizations become less apparent since all types of organizations are concerned with the issue of survival through efficiently attracting and distributing scarce and valued resources, and ensuring there is a difference between accrued revenues and expenditures. An open-system model interpretation of the four types of formal organizations classified by Blau and Scott [27] suggests the generic nature of operational goals [29], management functions [23], and marketing applications [47] for both public and private types of organizations. The alternative Weberian closed-system definition of organizations emphasizes the critical role of clearly specified organizational goals that will result in different, not generic, operational tasks; management functions; and internal and external arrangements of organizations. From the Weberian perspective it is important to distinguish between profit organizations concerning with goal of survival and budget organizations concerning with bureaucratic goals. For example, a goal to maximize profit institutionalizes the existence of business organizations that are concerned with profit management. In the internal arrangements, subparts or units are accountable for the success or failure to attain this goal as well the whole organization. Therefore, management and accountability are decentralized, and responsibility is divided among the organization's parts without jeopardizing the unity of the total operation's achievement of the profit goal. Subordinates are empowered and have discretion to amend rules or regulations in order to keep their operations profitable [48]. In the external arrangements, the profit goal directs decision-making relating to selection of the most profitable market segments for an organization. However, similar to the Weberian separation of profit and bureaucratic organizations Von Mises notes that: "There are areas of man's activities in which there cannot be any questions of profit management and where bureaucratic management must prevail." Bureaucratic management is bound by law and budget and concerned with those areas where profit management cannot operate. Bureaucratic management means management in strict accordance with the law and budget, so bureaucratic organizations do what the law and the budget order them to do. Accordingly, as Von Mises notes [48]: "bureaucratic management is bound to comply with detailed rules and regulations fixed by the authority of a superior body. The task of a bureaucrat is to perform what these rules and regulations order him to do. His discretion to act according to his own best conviction is seriously restricted by them." Bureaucratic management requires very rigid internal and external arrangements. Internally, it implies detailed discretion based on bureaucratic procedures and codes of ethics such as, for example, the American Society for Public Administration (ASPA) Code of Ethics [49]. Externally, the law and budget requires bureaucratic managers to serve members of the community equally, and without showing preference to one client over another. The open-system model assumption about formal organizations fits well with the activities of business agencies and profit management. Business concerns are encouraged to compete for scarce financial resources with other business concerns in a competitive environment that is boosted by this economic development. However, the social exchange school by ignoring the closed-system model of formal organizations fails to acknowledge the difference between profit oriented and bureaucratic oriented management. Profit and bureaucratic organizations are situated in different economic and political environments. Public agencies often enjoy the status of monopolists with no need to compete and with relatively stable funding in the form of tax-support from the public-at-large who own these organizations. Von Mises [48] noted: "In public administration there is no connection between revenue and expenditure. The public services are spending money only; the insignificant income derived from special sources is more or less accidental." The main general goal common to most public agencies is effective implementation of the tasks established by the public at large, based on rigid compliance with detailed rules and regulations established by the authority or superior body that politically represents the public at large. However, the open-system interpretation of public agencies distorts the pursuit of such a goal and inevitably arouses conflict between the requirement to comply with detailed regulations and the need to generate revenue. Negative case analysis suggests that the term "bureaucracy" does not necessarily have negative connotations, and the term "overbureaucratized" when used to characterize an organization does not necessarily imply an unresponsive organization as was suggested by the social exchange school [24]. Blau and Scott [27] in an introduction to their classification of formal organizations cautioned about this fallacy: Note also that the criticism that an organization is "overbureaucratized" means quite different things in the four types of organizations. In the case of mutual-benefit associations, such as unions, overbureaucratization implies centralization of power in the hands of officials. Here it does not refer to inefficiency; indeed, bureaucratized unions are often ruthlessly efficient. But in the case of business concerns overbureaucratizion implies an elaboration of rules and procedures that impairs operation efficiency, and here the term is not used in reference to the power of management officials to decide on policies, since such managerial direction is expected and legitimate. In other words, if business concerns are bureaucratized it means that they are unresponsive and there is an authentic need to move towards a de-bureaucratization process and higher responsiveness through application of the marketing concept, as the social exchange school suggests. However, if commonweal organizations are bureaucratized it does not necessarily mean that they are unresponsive and that there is an urgent need to implement the marketing concept. On the contrary, Blau and Scott [27] argue that "the maintenance of efficient bureaucratic mechanisms that effectively implement the objectives of the community" is the major task of commonweal organizations. According to Blau and Scott [27], the de-bureaucratization of commonweal organizations (or Kotler's suggestion to apply the marketing concept to make them more responsive) may lead to commonweal organizations jeopardizing their ability to effectively implement community objectives. Public Interest and "Coercion Mutually Agreed Upon Negative case analysis revealed the existence of alternative conceptualizations of motivation. Hardin [50] formulated the limitation of self-interest motivation in the context of commonly held resources (commons) in his essay "The Tragedy of Commons." Hardin [50] illustrated the tragedy of the commons by using the example with of a pasture fixed in size that is accessible to all the residents of a village. Motivated by self-interest all the villagers sought to maximize their own use of the pasture by grazing as many cattle as possible and expanding the size of their own herds. Since each villager followed the same logic, the tragedy occurs. Receiving personal benefits, villagers fail to recognize that all villagers will share the costs of the increased grazing. In other words, they fail to recognize that in the end the cumulative effect of their short run independent pursuit of self-interest will harm their collective interest. Without adequate and timely collective measures, the pasture will be destroyed. The example demonstrated that increasing demand on limited resources and a philosophy of unlimited access to commonly held resources eventually might lead to mutual destruction and harm. Hardin argued that education efforts to prevent the tragedy of commons are not enough since there can be free riders who will take advantage of others' voluntary self-restrained actions. The solution suggested by Hardin to this type of problem is "mutually agreed upon coercion," a coercion agreed upon by a majority of the people affected through democratic voting procedures. Mutually agreed upon coercion may take the form of a law, rule, regulation, fine, or a graduated tax. Such an approach, however, requires people and agencies that will be responsible for enforcement of these procedures: that is, bureaus and bureaucrats. The limits of self-interest motivation in different non-economic contexts have been articulated conceptually and supported empirically in the social science literature. For example, the sociological literature introduced game The Prisoners Dilemma when two captured suspects are confronted with several alternatives for confession/non-confession and different types of punishments. A usual result of this game suggests that both suspects could receive minimum punishment if they co-operate with each other. However, each of them by following personal self-interest to minimize personal punishment inevitably harms each other's' personal self-interest. Nevertheless, Hardin's position was debated by libertarians who associate the word "coercion" with the word "anathema" and by representatives of the public choice solution in the public administration literature. Representatives of this school questioned if "the mutually agreed upon coercion" is democratic and voluntarily agreed upon by a majority of citizens. Representatives of the public choice solution coined the term "free rider," arguing that there would be members of a community who would prefer to use common resources while others ere paying for them. Public choice school advocates of the "user pays system" and "vouchers" seek to increase the discretion of individuals by compelling them to "vote with their feet" for levels of taxation and a need government services. The social science literature seems to give a balanced consideration of the self-interest and the coercion perspectives. The self-interest motivation was recognized in sociology, anthropology, and social psychology [30,51,52]. The "coercion mutually agreed upon" perspective was also recognized by many as a legitimate principle for doing things appropriate for a democratic country. Writers, whose studies were cited by the social exchange school, characterized it either as a "visible hand," "quid pro without quo," "pure gift," "one-way transfer," "grant economy," "bureaucratic management" or simply "government" and "public administration." For example, the philosopher Berdyaev [53] distinguished two motivational principles in regard to economic life: "One of them says: In economic life follow up your own personal interest and this will promote the economic development of the whole, it will be good for the community, for the nation, for the state. The other principle says: In economic life serve others, serve the whole community and then you will receive everything which you need for your life." Similarly, the economist Von Mises referred to the same distinction as "two contrary methods of doing things" in a democratic society: "the private citizens' way and the way in which the offices of the government and the municipalities are operated." Von Mises termed them, "profit management" and "bureaucratic management." Another economist Boulding [54], adapting from the philosopher Sorokin [55] the distinction between compulsory and familistic types of social relationships, discussed the malevolence and benevolence types of motivation that underlie the threat and love integrative forces. The anthropologist Sahlins [56] distinguished between altruistically motivated transaction and subordination to central authority, as did Polanyi and Dalton [57,58] who differentiated between politically or socially defined obligations and self-interest motivation. Finally, one of the definitions of government articulated by Abraham Lincoln recognized the limits of invisible hand and a need for bureaucratic management: "a legitimate object of government, to do for a community of people, whatever they need to have done, but cannot do, at all, or cannot, so well do, for themselves-in their separate, and individual capacities" [59]. Negative case analysis suggests that self-interest motivation fits well with the activities of business organizations or profit management. However, negative case analysis also suggests that there is a contradiction in the social exchange school's conceptualization of public sector marketing between self-interest motivation and the code of ethic practiced by public administrators. Contrary to the social exchange school interpretations, Blau and Scott [27] argued that self-interest plays a limited role in the governance of nonbusiness formal organizations such as mutual-benefit associations, service organizations, and commonweal organizations. They contended that in the case, for example, of a mutual benefit association such as a labor union, self-interest condemns the organization: "If union leaders usurp the role of prime beneficiary and run the union as if they owned it for their personal benefit, the oganization is condemned for no longer serving the proper functions of a labor union". Service organizations are in a similar case. In service organizations, such as social work agencies, hospitals, schools and universities, the welfare of clients, participants, patients, and students is presumed to be the chief concern. This concern usually is cemented in codes of ethics adopted by professions as, for example, oaths, rules, or codes of ethic in the medical, military, law enforcement, and jurisprudence professions. These regulations are based on an assumption that while customers are able to look after their own self-interest in a store, the same customers often do not know what will best serve their own interest in relationships with professional service organizations.

For example, patients in a hospital may or may not want surgery intervention in their bodies. However, it is a doctor or medical professional who determines and decides for patients what is in their best interest and what is the best treatment for a particular health problem based on professional and ethical considerations. Similarly, clients who pay lawyers for legal advice may guess what is good in their case, but it is the lawyers who decide what is in the client's best legal interest on the basis of professional and ethical standards, and not considerations of personal gain at the expense of the client. Lawyers who personally gain at the expense of client interests are usually condemned by the bar association and deprived of their practice. Finally, in the example of a university used by Kotler [24], Blau and Scott argue: "students are best served when professional educators determine what and how they are to be taught and not when students themselves decide what and how they need to study". Blau and Scott [27] identified clear differences between the motivations of business and public decision-makers: while the businessman's decisions are expected to be governed by his self-interest--as epitomized in the phrase "caveat emptor"--the professional's decisions are expected to be governed not by his own self-interest but by his judgment of what will serve the client's interest best. The professions are institutionalized to assure, in the ideal case that the practitioner's self-interest suffers if he seeks to promote it at the expense of optimum service to clients.

In the Code of Ethics developed by the American Society for Public Administration (ASPA) employees of public sector organizations are seen to "serve the public interest beyond serving oneself [49]. The ASPA's guidelines are consistent with contention that public servants must "abstain from exchange relationships" with clients and serve the public interest in "detached manner" with personal "disinterest." The presence of self-interest in the relation of clients with commonweal organizations inevitably leads to ethical and even legal conflicts. For example, Locke and Woicenshyn [60] argue that the cynical egoism code that is commonly taught in business schools as the subjective expected utility (SEU) model is inappropriate for the character of social service because it advocates dishonesty ", if one feels like it, if it helps gratify one's immediate desires, and if the cost (likelihood of getting caught) is low" (p. 406). In the like vein, Blau and Scott [27] note: Commonweal organizations, in sharp contrast, are not expected to be oriented to the interests of their "clients," that is, those persons with whom they are in direct contact. A police department, for example, that enters into collusion with racketeers fails to discharge its responsibility to the public-at-large and is no longer the protective organization it is assumed to be. Likewise, if policemen solicit bribes instead of enforcing the law, or the police commissioner runs the department to further his political ambitions, the public's position as prime beneficiary of the organization suffers.

Redistribution and Reciprocity Arrangements

Negative case analysis suggests that arrangement of formal organizations with environments can be explained from not only an exchange perspective, as suggested by the social exchange school, but also from the redistribution or reciprocity perspectives. The concept of redistribution, as well as the concept of reciprocity, was developed by those adapting a substantivist perspective in economic anthropology [56-58,61]. This perspective attempts to analyze economic life in primitive and modern societies from three different approaches: reciprocal arrangements based on the symmetry principle; redistributive arrangements based on the centricity principle; and marketing exchange arrangements based on price-making markets.

Reciprocity implies a symmetrical sequence (AB/ BA) between just two partners or (AB/BC/CA/AC) between more than two fixed partners. Redistribution is centripetal movement of resources among many actors within a group upon one central figure followed by the action of that central figure upon the actors within the group in unison and repartition (BA/CA/DA/ and then A/BCD). Finally, marketing exchange is chaotic movements (A/BCD, B/ACD, and C/ABD) [61]. This "sunbstantivist" perspective is different from the "formalist" perspective that recognizes only marketing exchange arrangements [31]. Substantivists theorize that redistribution is payment to, and disbursement by, a central political authority. It implies a hierarchically structured group and that there is a center of the group. The primary mechanism of redistribution is sharing. Members of a group pool their resources at a center, and this pooled or common resource is then shared among the group members according to commonly accepted distributive rule. The tax systems of industrial countries or payments to the chief in primitive societies are typical examples of redistributive arrangements. Sahlins [56] referred to redistribution as "pooling." Pooling is "centralized movements: collection from members of a group, often under one hand, and redivision within this group. This is "pooling" or "redistribution" ... pooling is socially a within relation, the collective action of a group." The most important principles that characterize redistribution arrangements are centricity and the group membership rules. While Sahlins believed that it was wise to separate the array of economic transactions in the ethnographic record into two types (reciprocity and redistribution) because their social organizations are very different, Ekeh [62], whose study was adopted by the social exchange marketing school to develop public sector marketing concept, used a different approach. Referring to Levi-Strauss's [63] studies of kinship, Ekeh [62] distinguished between direct reciprocity and generalized reciprocity. Direct reciprocity characterizes relationships where actor A expects to be benefited directly by actor B, whenever A benefits B. Ekeh refers to this type of reciprocity as restricted exchange and notes that restricted exchange can take two major forms. Given only two parties, A and B, restricted exchange has the form A→B, and this is referred to as exclusive restricted exchange. Given several parties, for example, three individuals A, B, and C, restricted exchange has the form A→B→C and this is referred to as inclusive restricted exchange.

Both types of restricted exchange based on direct reciprocity are characterized by the notion of quid-pro-quo, emotional load, attempts to maintain equality, tensions, distrust, frequent conflicts over fairness, instability, mechanical solidarity, and brittle relationships [62,64-66]. Restricted or dyadic exchange is traditional economical exchange motivated by self-interest motivation and profit considerations. This exchange is characterized by Adam Smith's quid-pro-quo notion: "whoever offers to another a bargain of any kind, proposes to do this: give me that what I want, and you shall have this which you want" [33]. Univocal reciprocity characterizes relationships that involve at least three actors and where actors do not benefit each other directly, but only indirectly. Ekeh refers to this type of relationship as generalized exchange that also has two forms. Chain generalized exchange has the form A→B→C→A, where, "→" signifies "gives to." It is operated by chain univocal reciprocity when actors in the system are so positioned that they operate a chain of univocal reciprocations to each other as individual units. Net generalized exchange operated by net univocal reciprocity. Net univocal reciprocity denotes empirically observed situations where relationships can be individual-focused or group-focused. In individual-focused exchange relationships, the group as a whole benefits each member consecutively until all members have each received the same amount of benefits and attention (ABC→D; ABD→C; ACD→B; BDC→A). In a group-focused exchange, individuals give to the group as a unit and then gain back as part of the group from each of the unit members (A→BCD; B→ACD; C→ABD; D→ABC). Generalized exchange produces a high degree of social solidarity among parties, and establishes trust and commitment. Ekeh believed that generalized exchange and univocal reciprocity generate collective rights and lead to concepts such as "payment of taxes" and "citizenship".

This negative case analysis suggests that interpreting of a formal organization's interaction with its environment as a voluntary exchange of values, fits well with business organizations and the profit management philosophy. Business and marketing scholars have commonly accepted this law of exchange. However, negative case analysis and a review of original sources used by the social exchange school [23,24] suggests some contradictions in the interpreting public agencies' interaction with their environment in terms of voluntary exchange. For example, contrary to the assertions of the social exchange marketing school that adopted the Blau and Scott taxonomy of organizations, Blau denied that voluntary exchange was applicable to public organizations. The reason for his denial was the inherent conflict between bureaucratic rules of conduct and exchange relationships in these types of organizations. For example, when discussing service organizations, Blau noted: Professionals are expected to be governed in their work exclusively by professional standards of performance and conduct and not by considerations of exchange with clients. Although free professionals depend on fees from clients for their livelihood, the professional code of ethics demands that they do not let this fact influence their decisions and that these economic transactions do not affect the social interaction in which professional services are rendered to clients. The professional must refrain from engaging in reciprocal social exchange with clients lest his decisions be influenced by the exchange instead of being based only on his best judgment in terms of professional standards.

Discussing commonweal organizations, Blau noted the existence of the same conflict between bureaucratic rules and exchange transactions citing the empirical studies that he and Scott used in their work on classification of formal organizations in 1962: The situation of bureaucratic officials who provide services to clients is similar to that of professionals. Officials in a bureaucracy are expected to treat clients in a detached manner in accordance with official rules, and this requires that officials abstain from exchange relationships with clients, because exchange transactions would make them obligated to and dependent for rewards on clients. Even if it is only the gratitude and approval of clients an official wants to earn, his concern with doing so can hardly fail to influence his decisions and lead him to depart from official procedures. If officials become dependent on clients either for rewards they personally seek or for services of clients the oganization needs, they must enter into exchange transactions with clients, which means that they cannot strictly follow bureaucratic procedures in their relations with client.

The absence of direct exchange relationships between nonbusiness organizations and their clients based on the quid pro quo notion was a principal argument used by Luck [6,7] against acceptance of the broadened marketing proposition and the social marketing concept. Luck noted the existence of exchange relations of public organizations with their clients as a process of "corruptly committing illegal acts," which is consistent with Blau's position of a "departure from official procedures." In response to its critics, the social exchange marketing school attempted to use the notion of an indirect quid pro quo and to introduce concepts of indirect, restricted, generalized, and complex exchanges [32,47]. However, a closer analysis of these concepts revealed that this school still relies heavily on an exchange paradigm that ignores the "absence of exchange relations with clients" requirement as a fundamental condition in the functioning of public agencies. The results of negative case analysis suggest that consciously or unconsciously the social exchange school of marketing overlooked the main condition for governing the functioning of public organizations suggested by Blau: An essential element of professional and bureaucratic detachment is the absence of exchange relations with clients. Exchange transactions create obligations that make it impossible to conform undeviatingly to professional or bureaucratic standards.

Thus, the complex exchange concept has limited adequacy for conceptualization and explanation of public agencies' interaction with their environment. It appears that the concept of redistribution might be superior conceptual constructs for operationalizing and accounting for such interactions, because it recognizes the "absence of exchange relations with clients" requirement to be crucial for bureaucratic management. Development of the redistribution conceptualization of public sector marketing . The redistribution conceptualization of public sector marketing is based on a closed-system model of formal organizations; "coercion mutually agreed upon" motivation; and a redistribution arrangement mode. This perspective attempts to view a public agency as a bureaucratic organization. The agency is viewed as a substantively constrained subsystem of a larger political system having relatively little freedom for responsive action without approval from a dominant political center that governs the system. A public agency is subject to tight central control enforced by the city manager's office and/or by a city council. Almost all decisions have to "go through channels" and be authorized by the central authorities before actions can be taken. This perspective stresses pursuit of clearly specified goals and procedures, and a pyramidal hierarchy of positions and regulations. They are designed in accordance with the philosophy that says, "If this is the goal, then these are the most rational procedures for achieving it." The tasks, sphere of activities, and authority to make deci sions are clearly delineated, tightly defined and proscribed. They are assigned to members of the agency based on their position in the hierarchical pyramid. All decisions are centralized and employees in the middle and lower echelons of the pyramid have very limited discrete decision-making authority. This perspective implies that a public agency achieves its goals through the notion of redistribution. Redistribution entails obligatory payments of money objects (taxes) by community members to a democratically elected government. The government uses the receipts for its own maintenance, as emergency stock in case of individual or community disaster, and for the provision of needed different community services. Redistribution payments (taxes) to a government (socially recognized center) are an expression of politically and democratically defined obligations, and redistribution disbursements (public services) by government are determined democratically by political, legislative decisions, and voting procedures. This perspective postulates that the collective needs are best met when the managers and it employees of a public agency serve the public interest rather than their own self-interest. From this perspective, a public agency's interaction with its interest groups diagrammatically can be represented as: C ← AB, then C → BA, where: "←" signifies "redistributive payments"; "→" signifies "redistribution disbursements;" and "C" is a city council or the city manager's office with a subservient agency, and "B" and "A" are groups of citizens.

Redistribution Marketing

The data and results of the study suggest that the marketing-like activities of public organizations could be descriptively termed as "redistribution marketing." The historical root of redistribution marketing is administered trade. Under administered trade "prices, as well as all other terms, had been negotiated with the king before any transactions could take place" [67]. Historical records document that under the system of administered trade the king "fixes the price of every sort." After "the terms were agreed upon and the king's customs paid" the merchant had "full liberty to trade, which is proclaimed throughout the country by the king's cryer" [67]. Although records of administered trade stem from the eighteenth century, they seem to aptly describe the modern regulation policies of local government regarding collection of taxes and the approval of fee structures for some government services. Redistribution is the central concept underlying redistribution marketing. A city council, as an elected and commonly recognized political authority collects property and sale taxes from citizens and deposit them into the general fund. After taxes have been collected, they are distributed among the different services delivered to the community. Government establishes the agency, finances it, determines its goals, mission, and rules, and authorizes it to provide services for the community including some that require fees. An agency is a bureaucratic closed-system organization with a clearly defined mission, moral principles, hierarchical structure, and internal arrangements designed to effectively implement the mission. A professional administrative marketer is someone who seeks to understand, plan, and manage redistributive arrangements. She or he would not be expected to focus upon selling the agency's services and generating revenue, but to look at the agency, its mission, and its problems in a rational manner: identifying objectives; discovering the recreational needs of citizens through research; weighing the opportunities and constraints; determining the resources available to the agency and exploring alternative sources of resources; examining the various ways, in which client requirements can be met and the amount of human resources and type work that needs to be done. Additionally, an administrative marketer would be concerned with the resources, efforts, and time that citizens, donors, and partners are willing to contribute; location of the agency's facilities and scheduling of times when these services are offered; behavior of employees in accordance with established moral standards and, finally, control mechanisms which help to determine if the agency is functioning as planned, or whether changes and adjustments are required in response to new citizen demands. All of this is embraced in the following definition of administered marketing:

Redistribution marketing is the analysis, planning, implementation, and control of programs designed to facilitate redistributive arrangements within a community for achieving established objectives.

Conclusion

The concept of redistribution marketing developed in this study differs from existing conceptualizations in several important ways. Conceptualizations of nonprofit marketing can be characterized as a continuum. On one side would be located perspectives that consider marketing as a set of tools for managing exchanges [9,24,38,39,68,69]. Marketing is perceived as being concerned with satisfying clientele needs and, hence, the marketing is defined as identifying and fulfilling people' needs through the integrated use of marketing tools with the goal of creating consumer satisfaction, which is the organization's primary goal [24]. At the other end of the continuum are perspectives that do not consider marketing to be defined by with exchange processes. These perspectives discard both the voluntary exchange of values and marketing concept as means for meeting visitors' needs. According to these conceptualizations, marketing is a set of tools designed to induce behavior change. From this premise, the marketing concept is defined as inducing changes in existing patterns of behavior. Persuasive communications and adapting to existing patterns of behavior are seen as marketing's two primary characteristics. This perspective distinguishes between a core area of mission and an augmented mission and argues that tools of persuasion are central to achieving the core area of mission, while marketing and sales orientations are appropriate for the augmented mission activities [15,70,71]. Between the continuum extremes, there are conceptualizations that incorporate elements of both extremes. For example, Dixon does not accept the conceptualization of marketing as a management technology, arguing that marketing is a social activity and a social science concerned with study of such market activities as buying and selling. A similar conceptualization but with different nuances is offered by Pandya and Dholakia [72] who positioned their approach in the political economy paradigm developed in the marketing literature by Arndt [73]. Their perspective advocates conceptualization of social marketing based on both exchange, redistribution and reciprocity arrangements, although the authors mistakenly perceive the later two arrangements as other forms of exchange.

Redistribution marketing is a synergetic concept. It accepts the premise of supporters of exchange conceptualizations that marketing is a management technology [74-78]. However, it rejects the concept of voluntary exchange as being universal and as underlying all of marketing activities. Instead, it recognizes the concept of redistribution, but does not accept that it is merely another form of exchange. Economic anthropologists and historians derive it from the classic notion of redistribution with all the rules and premises that comprise this system that have been developed and documented.

References

1. Graham P (1995) Are public sector organizations becoming customer centered? Marketing Intelligence and Planning, 13: 35-47.
2. Murray MA (1975) Comparing public and private management: An exploratory essay, Public Administration Review 35: 364-371.
3. Walsh K (1994) Marketing and public sector management, Euro J Market 28: 63-71.

4. Mansfield H (2011) Social Media for Social Good: A How-to Guide for Nonprofits, McGraw-Hill.
5. Miller KL (2013) Content Marketing for Nonprofits: A Communications Map for Engaging Your Community, Becoming a Favorite Cause, and Raising More Money. The Jossey-Bass Nonprofit Guidebook Series. San Francisco, CA: Jossey-Bass. Mokwa MP, Dawson WM, EA Prieve (1980), Marketing the arts. New York: Praeger Publishers.
6. Luck D (1969) Broadening the concept of marketing-Too Far. Journal of Marketing 33: 53-55.
7. Luck D (1974) Social marketing: Confusion compounded, J Market 38: 70-72.
8. Nickels WG (1974) Conceptual conflicts in marketing, J Eco Busines 27: 140-3.
9. Lovelock CH, Weinberg CB (1978) Public and nonprofit marketing comes of age. In G. Zaltman and T. Bonoma (Eds.), Review of Marketing, 413-452. Chicago, IL: American Marketing Association.
10. Adreasen AR (1995) Marketing social change: Changing behaviour to promote health, social development, and the environment, San Francisco, CA: Jossey-Bass Publishers.
11. Hastings G, Haywood A (1991) Social marketing and communication in health promotion, Health Promotion International 6: 135-145.
12. Roberto E (1991) Applying a marketing model in the public sector, In O'Fairchellaigh C, Graham P, Warburton J (1991) Service delivery and public sector marketing (112-134), Sydney: Macmillan & Co.
13. Leathar DS, Hastings GB (1987) Social marketing and health education, J Service Market 1: 49-52.
14. Arndt J (1978) How broad should the marketing concept be? J Market 42: 101-103.
15. Capon N, Mauser G (1982) A review of nonprofit marketing texts. J Market 46: 125-128.
16. Monieson DD (1988) Intellectualization in macromarketing: A world disenchanted, J Macromarketing 8: 24-36.
17. Vanden Heede A, Pelican S (1995) Reflections on marketing as an appropriate model for nutrition education, J Nutrition Education 27: 141-150.
18. Bleicher J (1980) Contemporary hermeneutics, London: Routlege and Kegan Paul.
19. Kidder LH (1981) Qualitative research and quasi-experimental frameworks. In MB Brewer, BE Collins (Eds.), Scientific inquiry and the social sciences (123-145). San Francisco, CA: Jossey-Bass.
20. Kahane H (1973) Logic and philosophy, (2d ed.) Wadsworth, CA: Belmont.
21. Douglas JD (1976) Investigative social research, Beverly Hills, CA: Sage Publications.
22. Maxwell P (1996) Qualitative research design: An interactive approach. London: Sage Publications 27.
23. Kotler P, Murray M (1975) Third sector management: The role of marketing. Public Administration Review, 35: 467-72.
24. Kotler P (1975a) Marketing for nonprofit organizations, Englewood Cliffs, NJ: Prentice Hall.
25. Kotler P, Levy SJ (1969a) Broadening the concept of marketing, J Market 33: 10-15.
26. Kotler P (1972) A generic concept of marketing. Journal of Marketing 36: 46-54.
27. Blau P, Scott D (1962) Formal organizations. San Francisco, CA: Chandler Publishing Co.
28. Kotler P (1975b) Overview of political candidate marketing, Advances in Consumer Research 2: 761-769.
29. Katz D, Kahn RL (1966) The social psychology of organizations. New York: John Wiley & Sons.
30. Homans GC (1969) Social behavior: Its elementary forms, New York: Harcourt, Brace, and World.
31. Belshaw CS (1965) Traditional exchange and modern markets. Englewood Cliffs, NJ: Prentice-Hall.
32. Bagozzi RP (1975) Marketing as exchange, J Market 39: 32-39.
33. Smith A (1850) An Inquiry into the Nature and Causes of the Wealth of Nations, Edinburgh: Black.
34. Shapiro B (1973) Marketing for nonprofit organizations, Harvard Business Review 51: 123-132.
35. Rainey HG, Backoff RW, CH Levine (1976) Comparing Public and private Organizations, Public Administration Review 36: 233-244.
36. Allison GT (1992) Public and private management: Are they fundamentally alike in all unimportant respects? In JM Shafritz, Hyde AC (Eds.) Classics of public administration. Pacific Grove, CA: Brooks/Cole Publishing Company.
37. Lamb C, Crompton JL (1981) The status of the concept in public recreation and park agencies, Journal of the Academy of Marketing Science 9: 1-14.
38. Mokwa MP, Permut SE (1981) Government marketing: Theory and practice. New York: Praeger Publishers.
39. Coffman LI (1986) Public sector marketing: A guide for practitioners, New York: John Wiley and Sons. 25
40. Smith G (1988) Applying marketing to the public sector: The case of local authority leisure centers, Int J Public Sector Management 1: 36-45.
41. Buchanan DR, Reddy S, Hossain Z (1994) Social marketing: a critical appraisal, Health Promotion International 9: 49-57.
42. Ehling WP, White J, Grunig JE (1992) Public relations and marketing practices, In J.E. Grunig (Ed.), Excellence in public relations and communication management, Hillsdale, N J:Lawrence Erlbaum Associates.
43. O'Fairchellaigh C, Graham P, Warburton J (1991) Service delivery and public sector marketing, Sydney: Macmillan & Co.
44. Hall RH (1972) Organizations: Structure and process. Englewood Cliffs, NJ: Prentice-Hall.
45. Weber M (1946) Bureaucracy. In M. Weber. Essays in Sociology 23-34, Edited and translated by Gerth HH, Wright Mills C, Oxford University Press 8: 63-71.
46. Yuchtman E, Seashore SE (1967) A resource approach to organizational effectiveness, American Sociological Review 32: 891-903.
47. Kotler P, Levy SJ (1969b) A new form of marketing myopia: Rejoinder to professor Luck, J Market 33: 55-57.
48. Von Mises (1944) Bureaucracy. New Haven: Yale University Press.
49. Van Wart M (1996) The sources of ethical decision making for individuals in public sector, Public Administration Review 56: 525-533.
50. Hardin G (1968) The tragedy of commons, Science 1245-1248.
51. Belshaw CS (1976) jkhkh, NewYork: Pergamon Press Inc.
52. Thibaut JW, Kelley HH (1959) The social psychology of groups, New York: Wiley.
53. Berdyaev NA (1948) The origin of Russian communism. Glasgow: Geoffrey Bles, The University Press.
54. Boulding K (1970) A primer on social dynamic, NewYork: Free Press.
55. Sorokin PA (1964) Basic trends of our times. New Heaven, CT: College & University Press Publishing 28.
56. Sahlins MD (1965) On the sociology of primitive exchange, In M Banton (Ed.) The relevance of models for social anthropology (139-236) London: Tavistock Publications.
57. Polanyi K (1944) The great transformation, Boston: Beacon Press.
58. Dalton G (1971) Primitive, archaic, and modern economies, In G. Dalton (Ed.) Economic anthropology and development New York: Basic Books.
59. Shafritz JM, Russell EW (1997) Introducing public administration, New York: Longman.
60. Locke EA, Woiceshyn J (1995) Why businessman should be honest: The argument from rational egoism, J Organizational Behavior 16: 405-414.
61. Polanyi K, Arensberg CM, Pearson HW (1957) Trade and market in early empires. New York: The Free Press.
62. Ekeh PP (1974) Social exchange theory: The two traditions. Cambridge, Mass:

Harvard University Press. Frazer J (1919) Folklore in the Old Testament Vol. II. London: Macmillan & Co.

63. Levi-Strauss C (1969) The elementary structures of kinship, Boston: Beacon Press. English translation of Claude Levi-Strauss, Les Structuresa Elementares de la Parenete. 1967, Revised Edition.
64. Gillmore MR (1987) Implications of general versus restricted exchange, In K. Cook, (Ed.) Social exchange theory, 27-34, Beverly Hills, CA: Sage Publications.
65. Uehara E (1990) Dual exchange theory, social networks, and informal social support, American Journal of Sociology 96: 521-57.
66. Yamagishi T, Cook KS (1993) Generalized exchange and social dilemmas, Social Psychology Quarterly 56: 235-248.
67. Arnold R (1957) A port of trade: Whydah on the guinea coast. In Polanyi, Arensberg KCM, Pearson HW (Eds) Trade and market in early empires, 145-174 New York: The Free Press.
68. Manoff RK (1985) Social marketing: New imperative for public health, New York: Praeger Publishers.
69. McCort DJ (1994) A framework for evaluating the relational extent of a relationship marketing strategy: The case of nonprofit organizations, J Direct Marketing 8: 53-59.
70. Lauffer A (1984) Strategic marketing for not-for-profit organizations, New York: The Free Press.
71. Rados DL (1981) Marketing for nonprofit organizations, Boston, MA: Auburn House.
72. Pandya A, Dholakia N (1992) An institutional theory of exchange in marketing, Euro J Market 26: 19-41.
73. Arndt J (1981) The political economy of marketing systems: Reviving the institutional approach, J Macro market 1: 36-47.
74. Arndt J (1985) On making marketing science more scientific: The role of orientations, paradigms, metaphors, and puzzle solving, J Market 49: 11-23.
75. Arnold MJ, Fischer JE (1996) Counterculture, criticism, and crisis: Assessing the effect of the sixties on marketing thought, J Macro market 16: 118-133.
76. Crompton JL, Lamb CH (1986) Marketing government and social services. NewYork: John Wiley and Sons.
77. Kotler P (1979) Strategies for introducing marketing into nonprofit organizations, Journal of Marketing 43: 37-44.
78. Kotler P, Roberto E (1989) Social marketing: Strategies for changing public behaviour, New York: The Free Press.

10

Determination of Youth Migration-The Case of Tsegedie Wereda

Abrha FW*

Aksum University, Aksum, Tigray, Ethiopia

Abstract

The study is conducted in Tsegede wereda found in the western zone of Tigray having the objective of assessing the determinants of youth migration in the wereda. The deal with the study, questionnaires and interview data gathering instruments were applied to collect data from the primary. The collected data were presented, analyzed and interpreted though both qualitative and quantitative methods of data analyzing. The data's are presented and discussed in tabulations using numbers and percentages beside to the description of finding from the interview. Most of the adults in the study area have good knowledge on migration simply but they do not have enough knowledge on the overall impacts of migration. This is to mean that have no enough knowledge on migration. According to the data, the most frequently migrated part of the society are the adults, the most reproductive one. In the area under the study the adults are migrating because of different reasons like shortage of income, absence of good work opportunity, lack of land of plough to be a modern farmer, the desire to be rich in a short period of time because of some people get rich with such kind of opportunities, and lack of awareness on the social, political, economic and academic and psychological consequences of migration. The adults only show what is there in terms of money but not consider what is there in relation to the above mentioned problems.

Keywords: Youth migration; Tsegede wereda; Western zone; IOM

Introduction

Background of the study

Migration is the movement of people from one place to another place. This type of migration can be permanent, temporary, volunteer or forced. People can move from one place to another place outside its country, like moving from Asia to Germany, like moving from Ethiopia to Libya and inside its country, like Aksum to Addis Ababa and from shire to Humera immigration.

Permanent migration is when someone moves from one to another and has no plan to return his/her original home. Temporary migration is limited by time. This could be for seasonal employment. Forced migration involves the migration having no choice while voluntary migration is done by self-need without force [1].

People migrate from place to place for different reasons. As it is expressed by the International Organization for Migration (IOM), the main reasons for migration of people from one place to another place are: economic, social, political and environmental. As this organization justified it, the economical migration is related with moving to another place to find work or peruse a particular career. Social migration is to be closer for families or friends for a better quality of life while political migration is moving to another place to escape war or political persuasion and environmental migration occurs as a result of nature disasters like earth quake [2].

Thus, this research focuses on the type of migration that people made to seek job or to find work to the western countries to have better life that they are or as a result of the economic problem they face.

The youth employment crisis pushes millions of people, especially youth women and men towards the decision to migrate with the purpose of seeking alternatives to improve their job prospects. Many of them migrate to urban areas and big cities within their countries or seek new opportunities in foreign countries. According to the statistics of IOM (2009), roughly 27 million leave their countries of birth to seek employment aboard as international migration [2]. International migration can bring new opportunities, in terms of employment and training but youth workers, especially youth men and women and those in irregular situations face certain challenges and vulnerabilities in the migration. The labor migration experiences can end up representing either an opportunity or a risky to youth people and can lead them to decent work or it's very opposite, depending on policies and measures supporting them such as provision of better knowledge to the world of work, more and better social protection, education and training for employment, entrepreneurship development, social inclusion and an effective institutional frame work [2].

The Ethiopian youth are also migrating to aboard, especially to the western countries through facing so many problems and challenges from every corner of the countries. As the student researcher observes and listens to mass Medias, especially TV and radio, the Ethiopian youth who migrate to Arab countries are facing very difficult challenges and even up to life lose.

This study tries to figure out the determinant factors of youth migration to western countries, especially the youth of Tsegede wereda.

Statement of the problem

People migrate from place to place not for the sake of migrating of moving but they have their own reasons and aims. There are different determinant factors that make people migrate. For instance, it is expressed by the International Organization for Migration (IOM), the main reasons for migration of people from one place to another place are: economic, social, political and environmental. Besides, one of the major pulls for migration of people was the prospect of freedom in various areas of life. For example, religious freedom may be important to a migrant who cannot openly practice his religious in his home country.

***Corresponding author:** Fitsum Weldu Abrha, MA, Aksum University, Aksum, Tigray, Ethiopia, E-mail: abrha.fitsum@yahoo.com

But, the degree of migration differs in terms of educational background, level of skills they have, legality and numbers. Youth migrants from poorer economic backgrounds and with fewer skills and educational attainment were seen as more and more likely to migrate irregularly. Under circumstance that put their health or lives at risk and to end up in indecent working conditions.

And this is why we see and hear that people from countries like Ethiopia, (poor country) and the like are migrating to western countries like Kuwait, Dubai (reach countries).

In the current situation, there are a lot of words that people can work; there is a relatively good access of education and scientific way of agricultural production in Ethiopia but still there is migration especially to western countries. So why do people made migration is not known and that is why the student researcher initiated to conduct a research on the determinants of youth migration to western countries. Hence, the main aim of this research was to figure out the determinant factors of youth in Tsegede wereda.

Research questions

This research was conducted to investigate and answer the following main research questions.

1. What are determinants factors for youth migration in wereda Tsegede.
2. What is the impact of migration of youth for the youth themselves and the study area?

Objectives of the study

This research paper has both general and specific objectives.

General objectives: The overall objective of this study was to investigate the determinants of youth migration in wereda Tsegede.

Specific objectives: The specific objectives of this study are:

1. To assess the determinant factors of youth migration in the study area.
2. To explain the socio-economic impacts of migration in the area under the study.
3. To create positive attitude towards migration on youth in the study area.
4. To help for the creation of awareness on migration

Significance of the study

This research paper may help in the following aspects. This study tried to identify the determinant factors of youth migration. As a result, it helps youths to have good awareness on the impact of migration or avoids the negative attitude towards migration and reinforces them to work in their home land. Besides, it will also help for other researchers as a reference for further researches.

Scope of the study

This study was meaningful if it were being zonal or regional, because as the sample size increases, the reliability of the study increases. But, because of the constraints of shortage of access, time and money and to manage the study in a meaningful way, the research paper was delimited in three preparatory schools of wereda Tsegede.

Limitation of the study

In doing this research, the researcher had faced the following limitations

1. There was lack of experiences in conducting the senior essay on how to deal with it.
2. There was also lack of accesses due to the fact that the researcher was being serving in very remote areas that have no accesses.
3. Because of the too long distance between the researcher and the advisor, there was a very big problem in getting updated comments from the respected advisor. However, for the successful accomplishment of the paper the researcher exerted the necessary efforts.

Organization of the study

This study has five chapters. Chapter one, is about introduction part. Chapter two is about review of the related literature. Chapter three deals with the methodology part which consists of data sources, instruments to collect data, sample size and sampling technique and methods of data analysis. The fourth chapter was presenting, discussing, interpreting of data and the last chapter is about summary and recommendation.

Review of Related Literature

Migration

Migration is the movement of people from one place to another place. This type of migration can be permanent, temporary, volunteer or forced. People can move from one place to another place outside its country, like moving from Asia to Germany, and from Ethiopia to Libya and inside its country, like the movement of people from Aksum to Addis Ababa and from shire to Humera are migration. Permanent migration is when someone moves from one to another and has no plan to return his/her original home. Temporary migration is limited by time. This could be for seasonal employment. Forced migration involves the migration having no choice while volunteer migration is done by self-need without force [1].

Migration refers to the movement of people from one geographic area to another geographic area in order to establish a new residence. Before people actually migrate, they usually compare relative opportunities offered by the present and anticipated habit [3].

Permanent migration is when someone moves from one place to another and has no plans to return to their original home. Temporary migration is limited by time. This could be for seasonal employment. Forced migration involves the migrant having no choice but to move. Voluntary migration is the opposite of this. International migration is when a person moves from one country to another country. For example people moves from the UK to the USA. Internal migration is when people migrate within the same country or region. An example of this would be someone migrating from Manchester to London migration is defined as a permanent or semi-permanent change of residence of an individual or group of people, usually for more than one year. Migration changes continually and is affected by changes in the political circumstances of a country the social and economic circumstances, and the physical geography [4].

Migration is the periodic departure and turn of a population. It is best developed in insects like the butterflies, dragonflies, fishes like eels, and in several birds and mammals. Migration movements are controlled by circadian, lunar and tidal rhythms as well as season`s variations [5].

Root causes of migration

Migration is a complex process and has been a feature of human societies for many centuries. There are many reasons why people choose to migrate, including; poverty armed conflict social strife political turmoil economic hardships [6]. People have moved from their home countries, for all sorts of reasons. Some are drawn to new places by `pull` factors, others find it difficult to remain where they are and migrate because of `push` factors. These have contributed to the recent movement of people here but are also the reason why people from here have emigrant to other countries. Historically some were transported or sold into slavery or left because of poverty, hunger, persecution, discrimination, civil war, unemployment and, more recently, simply for education and better jobs [7].

There are a number of "pull" factors that draw people towards countries like the United States to seek a better life. Aging populations and low fertility rates in industrialized countries have resulted in a decline in "replacement workers" entering the work force, while also creating greater demand for service-sector jobs and low-skills employment. Developed countries like US have come to rely on immigrant labor to fulfill their labor needs and will need to so even more in the future as the country faces a mass retirement of body boomers. In the absence of a livable wage, access to credit, insurance, or social welfare benefits, the value of migration is greater than its hardship or potential for exploitation (Ibid).

Types of migration

There are various types of migration classification these are internal and international migration, voluntary and forced migration and permanent and temporary migration. Furthermore the phenomenon of migration has often been classified in to various types on the basic motivation, distance and time. Because of motivation migration depend up on factors that make the migrants move.

Voluntary migration: The major reason for voluntary migration is economic. Almost all studies confirm that most of the migrants (excluding forced and sequential migration) have moved in search of better economic opportunities. Hence "migration is normally viewed as an economic phenomenon. Though noneconomic factors obviously have some bearing, most studies concur those migrants leave their area of origin primarily because of lack of economic opportunities, in the hope of finding better opportunities elsewhere" (Ibid).

Voluntary migration may be temporary or permanent. One is a temporary migration either because he is unwilling to settle down permanently in the host country or because the circumstances in the host country do not permit him to a permanent immigrant. Many migrants to the Middle East, for example, have no inclination to settle down permanently. They would rather prefer to work therefore some time and a large number of immigrants in different countries, including in the Middle East countries, who cannot extend their stay even if they would like to do so. Immigrant works that are recruited on contact basis will have to return once the contact periods over unless they succeed in getting another job and are permitted to extend their stay. Same countries hire labor from other countries for agriculture opportunities. Many of them may be regular migrants. Many countries admit temporary migrant labor on a systematic basis. Throughout history, there has been movement of people across national bounders for setting down in new places. However, the nineteenth and early twenty centuries witnessed permanent inter-continental migration on a precedent scale (Ibid).

Forced Migration: This is a type of migration occurring when people are forced by the states or some other political or military power. Forced migration is produced by power that one individual or group possess over another individuals, Example, slave trade have gone to Africa for countries, take people by force and making them live in another countries and repatriations and feeling of people due to political or religious persecution (Ibid).

Push and pull factors of migration

Pull factors: Migrations are drawn increasingly to countries by the following factors; Developed countries, or industrialized city areas within countries, draw labor from countries or areas where incomes are lower. International transport has never been easier to access information. Falling birth rates in developed countries contribute to labor shortages and skills gaps. Extra people are required when there is rapid economic expansion. People are drawn to stable democracies where human rights and religious freedoms are more likely to be respected. Many people in other parts of the world speak English. Youth people move in order to get better jobs or improve their qualifications, including their language skills.

Push factors: Negative factors at home add to the reasons why people feel compelled to move. Lack of prospects for career advancement, poverty and low income, high unemployment rates, persecution and poor human rights, internal conflict and war, natural disasters, climate change and famine are the main push factors. Other push factors include primitive conditions, natural disasters, poor medical care, as well as slavery and political fear. Push factors come in many forms. Sometimes these factors leave people with no choice but to leave their country of origin. Below are three examples of push factors that drive people to emigrate from their home countries.

Lack of jobs/ poverty; economic factors provide the main motivation behind migration. In fact, according to the International Labor Organization, approximately half of the total population of current international migrants, or about 100 million migrant workers, have left home to find better job and lifestyle opportunities for their families aboard (International Labor Office of the Director-General, 2008). In some countries jobs simply do not exist for a great deal of the population. In other instances, the income gap between sending and receiving countries is great enough to warrant a move.

Civil strife /war/ political and religious persecution; some migrants are impelled to cross national borders by war or persecution at home. These immigrants may be considered refugees or asylum seekers in receiving countries. According to the next put forth by the convention, a refugee is "someone who is unable or unwilling to return to their country of origin owing to a wee-founded fear of being persecuted for reasons of race, religion, nationality, membership of a particular social group, or political opinion".

Environmental problems; environmental problems and natural disasters often cause the loss of money, homes, and jobs [4].

Consequence of migration

Migration may impact on development in various and complex way. Migration affects a migrant`s home country in different directions; in particular, shocks related for migrate processes include in labor supply as well as changes in productivity. Migration process includes endogenous behavior or policy responses as sending countries affect labor resources availability and productivity. Consequence of migration viewed from two directions. On one hand causes urbanization, unemployment, income inequality, ecological stress and population mal-distribution whereas on the other hand migration is necessary part of economic growth, equilibrating tendencies, facilitating industrialization, improving income distribution, and introducing technological change in agriculture, generalize that migration is the human right ensuring choosing ones destination to improve welfare and economic benefit [8].

At its best, migration can be a rewarding experience that is made in the interest of the house hold welfare, but in most cases moving to another countries and being separated from ones immediate family takes place at considerable emotional cost. Especially temporary circular migration increases the risk for family breakdown, fragmentation of social network and psycho social stress [7]. The emotional impact is not just limited to the migrant themselves, but also to the family cannot afford to emigrate together, they emigrate one member at a time resulting in eroded family structure and relationships (Ibid).

Advantage of migration

Brain drain however has some beneficial effects too. The sending countries benefit from the emigrant remittances. Farther same of the professionals and other skilled personnel may return home with better knowledge and experience which could contribute to national development [9]. In countries like India, though brain drain has caused shortage of certain categories of personnel, many doctors, engineers, and other skilled personnel find it difficult to find a suitable job. The substantial increases in the seats courses, like medical science, engineering, etc are increases in the supply of such human resources at rates faster than their absorption in the employment sector. Hence, it would be prudent for the government to device policies that would facilitate the better utilization of, human resources for natural development. Measures should also be taken to ensure the emigrant will pay the nation the public expenditure incurred for his education and will make same farther contribution (Ibid).

Apart from monetary factors, discouragement and disillusion in the professional field are also responsible for brain drain. As the UNESCO succinctly point out brain drain or the migration of educated and talented people, is part of the wider issue of development and differences in levels of development between countries. For this reason, brain drain cannot be treated realistically as a subject on its own. The means of responding to the problem are for the large part associated with aspects of national activities of which immigration is by no means always the first concern education planning, human resources assessment, bringing about the conditions conductive to creative scientific work or even ensuring a favorable social and political climate (Ibid).

Migration in ethiopia

Ethiopia is one of the countries with large number of migrants in North America, Europe, and the Middle East. According to Tefer and Beruk, by the end of 2005, more than one million Ethiopians migrated to the rest of the world. Looking for better education, employment opportunities, and political stabilities are considered major causes for migration. Political migration was intensified in Ethiopia during 1970-1990 due to political instability at the time.

Although the stock of migration is decreasing since 1990, migration is still important and a hot issue in the current day Ethiopia. According to the population and housing census conducted in 2007, Ethiopia's population grew by about 2 million people. At the same time, close to 120 thousands Ethiopian left their country very year.

Political and economic reasons accounted for the increase of Ethiopian migrants since the 1970s. But, these are by no means those only reasons. According to Abye, some migrants come from a well to do family who can afford the travel and living expenses aboard [10]. Those who are facing hard ship at home are not those who migrants because the poor cannot afford to travel. Hence, it can be argued that although the initial reason of migration is political instability, the recent migration trend can be accounted for by the desire to acquire Western culture and enjoy better standard of living. This, however, does not include those who migrant to the Middle East whose case is mostly economic.

Methodology of the Study

Research area and nature of the study

This research paper was conducted in Western zone of Tigray region, in wereda Tsegede at three preparatory schools and the nature of the research is primarily quantitative and in some way qualitative with descriptive type of research design.

Data sources

To attain the aim of this study, both primary and secondary data sources were used. Primary data sources; the primary data sources to the study were students and teachers from three preparatory schools of wereda Tsegede and those who return home from migration (immigrants). Secondary data sources; the main sources for secondary data were related literatures articles, journals, reports of the office and documents [11].

Sample size and sampling techniques

The total population of this research paper was all students and teachers of preparatory schools which currently exist in three schools in Tsegede wereda and are 348 and 28 in number respectively. Out of the total population 348 (Male=206 and Female=142), from these 102 students and 8 teachers were taken using sample random sampling method, especially the lottery method. This sampling method was selected since it avoids biasness and errors of sampling. Besides, five individuals from the migrants were included as sample respondents purposively.

Methods of data collection

The instruments used to gather data from the sample respondents were questionnaire and interview. The questionnaires contained both close and opened ended formats and were prepare for students and teacher respondents. This tool was selected because it helps to gather data with minimum cost faster than any other tool. In addition to this, interview wade made with five respondents. This is because, it helps to get some facts related to the issue under the study in a more clear way.

Methods of data analysis

The researcher had used both qualitative and quantitative methods of data analyze to analyze the data that was collected from different tools. Data from the questionnaire was analyzed quantitatively using tables, and percentages and data from interview was analyzed through qualitative method in terms of description the fact findings.

Analysis and Interpretation of Data

This chapter deals with the analysis and interpretation of data collected from different respondents through questionnaire, and interview.

For the study, 8 questionnaires were distributed to all the selected teachers and students from the school. The responses are arranged in two ways. The close ended questions are arranged in table forms. Under each table, analysis and interpretation were made. The open ended and interview questions are analyzed and interpreted using qualitative methods by bringing similar ideas together.

Characteristics of respondents

In this sub topic the researcher tried to list overall characteristics of the selected respondents like sex, age educational qualification and work experiences of the respondents who participate in the questionnaire. The characteristics of the respondents (their demographic) are listed under here in table form (Table 1).

As it can be seen in the above Table 1, item 1, regarding the student respondents, 62 (60.8%) of them are male and 40 (39.2%) are female respondents and from the teacher respondents, 75% are male and the rest 25% are females.

Regarding the age of respondents 12 (11.5%) of them are found at the age of 13-14 years and the rest 38 (37.2%) are found 15-20 years. 47 (46.1%) from the total respondents are also found at the age between 21-30 and the rest are found 31-40years.

Concerning the age of teacher respondents, 3 (17.6%) from the total respondents are found in the age range of 21-30 years. 11 (64.7%) respondents found in the age of between 30-40 years and the rest 3 (17.6%) are above 40 years.

Regarding the educational status of the selected respondents, all the student respondents are grade eleven and twelve students. From the teacher respondents, all are degree holders.

In case of the work experience of the teacher respondents, 5 (62.5%) respondents have 1-10 years of work experience, 3 (37.5%) are having work experiences of 11-20years.

Analyzing questionnaires

This sub section deals with the presenting analyzing and interpreting of the data gathered by questionnaire from the respondents (Table 2).

As we can see from Table 2 in the above, 64.7% of the student respondents said that Yes, but the rest 33.3% student respondent said No. concerning the teacher respondents all of them said that Yes. This shows that the majority of the respondents have enough information on migration. According to most of respondents, there people especially adults who migrate to aboard particularly to Saudi Arabia (Table 3).

As it was seen from the above table, from total student respondents 84 (82.3%) have replied that they have never been migrated to other countries. But 18 (17.6%) are migrated to Saudi Arab. In connection to this as the data from the wereda office showed, 231 adults migrate per a years in average.

What we can conclude that there is high rate of migration of adults in the wereda.

With regard to item 2 of the same table, all of the respondents were worked on labor force before their migration to aboard. In item 3, almost all (88.9%) of the respondents were earned below 100 Birr per a month.

So working on labor force works and shortage of monthly income can be the determinant factors for their migration (Table 4).

As it was indicated in Table 4 of the above, the majority who account 71.6% from the total student respondents replied that the main course for migration of adults in the area under the study are absence of work, low income, lack of land for agriculture. Other who constitute 7.8%, 11.77 and 8.8% from the student respondents responded that absence of work, low income and lack of land respectively are the

No	Items	Respondents			
		Students		Teachers	
		No	%	No	%
1	Sex				
	• Male	62	60.8	6	75
	• Female	40	39.2	2	25
	Total	102	100	8	100
2	Age 11-12 years	—	—	—	—
	• 13-14 years	12	11.8	—	—
	• 15-20 years	38	37.2	—	—
	• 21-30 years	47	46.1	7	87.50%
	• 30-40 years	5	4.9	1	12.50%
	• Above 40 years	—	—	—	—
	Total	102	100	8	100%
3	Grade eleven and grade twelve	102	100	—	—
	• Diploma	—	—	—	—
	• Degree	—	—	8	100%
	Total	102	100	8	100%
4	Work experiences of teachers				
	• 1-10 years	—	—	5	62.5
	• 11-20 years	—	—	3	37.5
	• 21-30 years	—	—	—	—
	• Above 30 years	—	—	—	—
	Total	—	—	8	100

Source: Field survey of 2016.

Table 1: Personal information of respondents.

No	Items	Alternatives	Respondents			
			Students		Teachers	
			NO	%	No	%
1	Do you have any information about migration?	Yes	66	64.7	8	100
		No	36	35.3	—	—
		Total	102	100	8	100

Table 2: Respondents know-how on migration.

No	Items	Alternatives	Respondents			
			Students		Teachers	
			No	%	No	%
1	Have you ever been migrated outside your country?	Yes	18	17.6	—	—
		No	84	82.3	—	—
		Total	102	100	—	—
2	If your answer is Yes, in what job did you participate before your migration?	Government	—	—	—	—
		In my own job	—	—	—	—
		Labor force	18	18	—	—
		If other	—	—	—	—
		total	18	18	—	—
3	Your monthly income before your migration?	Below 100 Birr	16	88.9	—	—
		101-200 Birr	2	11.1	—	—
		201-400 Birr	—	—	—	—
		More than 400	—	—	—	—
		Total	18	100	—	—

Table 3: Number of migrants.

No	Items	Alternatives	Respondents			
			Students		Teachers	
			No	%	No	%
1	What do you think the causes for migration were?	Absence of work	8	7.8	—	—
		Low income	12	11.7	—	—
		Lack of land to plough	9	8.8	—	—
		Unsuitable social life	—	—	—	—
		All	73	71.6	8	100
		Other(if)	—	—	—	—
		Total	102	100	8	100

Table 4: Cause of migration.

No	Items	Alternatives	Respondents			
			Students		Teachers	
			NO	%	No	%
1	What do you think the negative impact of migration?	Social isolation	13	12.7	—	—
		Health problem	3	2.9	—	—
		Economic problem	11	10.7	—	—
		Psychological problem	7	6.8	—	—
		Death	8	7.8	8	100
		All	60	58.8	8	100
		Total	102	100	8	100

Table 5: Impacts of migration.

causes of migration and all of the teacher respondents replied that all what are mentioned earlier. In addition to these, the respondents added that to be rich in short period of time, lack of awareness on the causes of migration, lack of good word work opportunities and the like are the main cause of migration in the study area. In connection with this, research finding indicated that lack of prospects for career advancement, poverty and low income, high unemployment rates, persecution and poor human rights, internal conflict and war, natural disaster, climate change and famine are the main push factors. Other pushes factors include primitive conditions, natural disasters, poor medical care, as well as slavery and political fear. Push factors come in many forms. Sometimes these factors leave people with no choice but to leave their country of origin.

So what someone can infer from this idea is that, the main determinants factors to adults in Tsegede wereda are more or less economic problems like low income, absence of good and valuable work, shortage of land that can be ploughed, the desire to get rich in short period of time, and the experiences they observe from their parents, and neighbors that they get rich from migration (Table 5).

As it stated in the table above, most of the student respondents replied that social isolation, health problem, economic problem, psychological problem and death are the impacts of migration. On the other hand, all of the teacher respondents replied the same response as their students. In addition to these, the respondents said that loss of productive citizen, the adult one, toss of very qualified person what we call brain drain, loss of cultural belies and traditions. Moreover migration leads to be illiterate instead of being educated. It lowered the self-esteem and confidence of those who migrate in every aspects of the community participation. With regard to the consequences of migration, scholar indicted that migration process includes endogenous behavior or policy response as sending countries affect labor resources availability and productivity. Consequences of migration viewed from two directions. On one hand causes urbanization, unemployment, income inequality, ecological stress and population mal-distribution [8]. At its best, migration can be a rewarding experience that is made in the interest of the house hold welfare, but in most cases moving to another countries and being separated from ones immediate family takes place at considerable emotional cost. Especially temporary circular migration increases the risk for family breakdown, fragmentation of social network and psycho social stress [7]. The emotional impact is not just limited to the migrant themselves, but also to the family left behind. Especially in poorer households where the whole family cannot afford to emigrate together, they emigrate one member at a time resulting in eroded family structure and relationships (Ibid).

From the above idea, we can understand that the impact of migration is very wider it ranges from the personal up to the family. People loss their children because of death at the migration journey, they loss their identities, deny their human right, they became infected by different diseases, loss of educated people and the like (Table 6).

Regarding the advantage of migration, all of the teacher respondents and most of the student respondents said yes. But 24 (23.5%) out of the total student respondents replied migration have no an advantage. As most of the respondents replied it, migration can have an advantage. When they justify this, through migration, you can avoid poverty; can help your family, can help the nation by currency exchange and the like. In line with this researches indicated that brain drain however has some beneficial effects too. The sending counties benefit from the emigrant remittances. Farther same of the professional and other skilled personnel may return home with better knowledge and experience which could contribute to national development (Table 7) [9].

As the above table shows, 90 (88.2%) of the respondents responded that there is illegal way of migration in their local areas and the rest 12 (11.76%) of the respondents said there is legal way of migration. In addition to this, 8 (100%) of the teacher respondents replied, as there is illegal way of migration in their surrounding or town. Therefore, we can understand that, there is illegal way of migration in Tsegede wereda which suffers a lot of individuals.

With regard to the role of the government to reduce migration in the area, almost all of the respondents have similar idea. They said that the government should teach its citizen on the impact of migration, it should have to create a behavioral change through awareness creation programs, there should be good work opportunity for the adults that satisfy its hunger of economy, it should support financial for those who have nothing and send the citizen by legal forms. Moreover, the people should also say no to migration.

Analyses of data which was gathered from interview

An interview was made with five returned migrants in order to strengthen the data gathered from questionnaire. Accordingly five questions were raised to them. The first question raised was do you have any information about the cause of migration? Or why do people especially the youth migrate to Arab countries?

As interview was made with the concerned body, they said there are various causes for migration of individuals from their mother land to other countries especially to Arab countries. To get money, to be rich, to have better life etc. are the factors that pulls individuals from their home land. On the other hand low income level relative to consumption, poor life condition poor living standards are the pushing factors for individuals.

What do you think are the social, economic, cultural and psychological impacts of migration? For this question the interviewee said that migration has social, cultural, economic and psychological impacts. Social impact means it results in social isolation. That is since the migrants are new for the place which they are going, they live isolated from their family or former society up until they can to speak the language of that place they reach in. economically, there would loss of money if they return out of tasks. At this time they lost more money especially transportation cost for outgoing and in going. Psychologically, migration results feeling as the migrated individuals faces such suffer, pain and even loss of their life it results in psychological feeling for the mass as it has blood relation.

Since migration has the above listed impacts, the government supports for the returned migrants who migrates illegally starting from providing free transportation service by taking from that evil condition to reach their home up to giving money which help them to engage in different activity that makes them productive and successful.

No	Items	Alternatives	Respondents			
			Students		Teachers	
			No	%	No	%
1	Do you think migration has an advantage? If your answer is Yes, how?	Yes	78	76.5	8	100
		No	24	23.5	__	__
		Total	102	100	8	100

Table 6: Advantage of migration.

No	Items	Alternatives	Respondents			
			Students		Teachers	
			NO	%	No	%
1	What kind of migration do you apply in your town mostly?	Illegal	90	88.24	8	100
		Legal	12	11.76	__	__
		Total	102	100	8	100

Table 7: Forms of migration.

What kind of solution do you think to stop migration? There are a number of solutions to stop migration following its negative impacts. Giving advice to the people how much migration is dangerous, starting from the health of individual level up to the national level (i.e. decreasing of the economy of that country as the productive work forces are migrated).

Conclusion and Recommendation

This chapter focuses on the conclusion based on the finding and recommending some possible suggestions.

Conclusion

The study conducted in Tsegede wereda found in the western zone of Tigray having the objective of assessing the determinants of youth migration in the migration wereda. To deal with the study, questionnaires and interviews data gathering instruments were applied to collect data from the primary. The collected data were presented, analyzed and interpreted through both qualitative and quantitative methods of data analyzing. The data are presented and discussed in tabulations using numbers and percentages beside to the description of finding from the interview. Based on the analysis discussions made in chapter four the following conclusions are drowned.

1. Most of the adults in the study area have good knowledge on migration simple but they do not have enough knowledge on the overall impacts of migration. This is to mean that have no enough knowledge on migration.
2. According to the data, the most frequently migrated part of the society are the adults, the most reproductive one.
3. In the area under the study the adults are migrating because of different reasons like shortage of income, absence of good work opportunity, lack of land to plough to be a modern farmer, the desire to be rich in a short period of time because of some people get rich with such kind of opportunities, and lack of awareness on the social, political, economic and academic and psychological consequences of migration. The adults only show what is there in terms of money but not consider what is there in relation to the above mentioned problems.

The analysis also realizes the main determinants factors for adults' migration are better opportunity at destination areas encouragement by the experience of previous migrants relative and friends who have been able to secure improved livelihood in receiving countries and able to send remittance to families. Migrants also motivated by non-economic factors like need for modern life, administrative and security issues.

The adults are migrating to aboard illegally through the help of illegal brokers and they face tremendous problems like beating, paralyzed migrants physically, sexual harassment, death confiscation money and the like. The researchers also investigate the socio-economic and political consequence of migration. Economically, migration has both positive and negative impacts on the economy of the country. Migrants send remittance to their families and reduce the level of poverty of their families, but there is also losing of capable and productive youth adults that are necessary for the wellbeing of the country.

Recommendations

Considering the above conclusions, the researcher has forwarded the following recommendations.

There should be a sanction on migration by the government official on the condition of mass adult migration. Because, migration consume the young adult and productive capabilities full adults as well as educated citizens migration has its own advantage.

Government official of that particular community should also give special training expiring on job innovation, specialization and equal access for adults engaged in local and domestic employment.

The wereda should also provide special awareness to the adults about the challenges and consequences of migration both at destination and during the time of journeys.

The government official of the wereda should eliminate the push factors in the kebelle by creating high employment opportunity, wage increments and advancement of other workers benefits for the adults labor force.

Migrants should identify very well about their destination and the route ways of migration before starting journey in order to reduce the challenges and problems of migration.

Even though it is advisable not to migrate from the nation, migrants should follow the legal process of migration through legal government or private employees and employ agency in order to control the illegal employees from brokers.

With regarding to the minimizing solutions, the government should teach its citizen on the impact of migration, it should have to create a behavioral change through awareness creation programs, there should be good work opportunity for the adults that satisfy its hunger of economy, it should support financially for those who have nothing and send the citizen by legal forms. Moreover, the people should also say no to migration.

References

1. Kerlinger (1995) The migration experiences in Africa Stockholm. Nordiska Africa institute.
2. International Organization for Migration (2005) Results of the survey engaging Diasporas as agent for development.
3. Zanden JWV (1990) The social experience: An introduction to social sociology. (2ndedn), the hole state university, McGraw pp: 1-680.
4. Daniels (2002) Failed Trade Policy & Immigration: Cause and Effect. Public citizen pp. 1-5.
5. Rana (2009) Essential of ecology and environmental science. (5thedn) PHL learning private limited, Ecology.
6. United Nations (2006) International migration report 2006: A Global Assessment. Department economics and social Affairs, Population Division.
7. Benda P (2002) Global Migrants, Global refugees: problems and solutions. Journal of Refugee studies 15: 325-326.
8. Copper D (1992) Urban Refuges: Ethiopian and Eritrean in Cairo: American University in Cairo press.
9. Schmeidl S (2001) Conflict and Forced Migration: A Quantitative review, 1964-1995. Berghahn Books, oxford, Newyork pp. 62-94.
10. Zelberg A (2012) Root Causes of Migration. Maryland Catholic Conference.
11. Moqueninte T, Asmelash B (2009) Remittance inflows in ethiopia and country experiences: The practice and the potential for improvement. Proceeding of the sixth international conference on the Ethiopian economy, Ethiopian Economy Association.

An Empirical Analysis of Liquidity, Profitability and Solvency of Bangladeshi Banks

Abdullah M*

Assistant Professor, Independent University, Dhaka, Bangladesh

Abstract

The financial sector of Bangladesh is small and underdevelopment and this sector resides of banking and an emerging capital market. The banking sector in the country comparatively more developed than the equity market, even though both are developing in international benchmark. In light of recent events that have taken place in the Bangladesh, the importance of knowing the financial position of banks is imperative for investors. Most investor use balance sheet, income statement, change in equity and statement of cash flow to calculate different ratios for technical analysis. Investor uses this ratio and trend analysis to invest in capital market. In this research I take 29 banks as sample size and calculate their different ratios. For examining the applicability of Altman's Z-Score model to forecasting banking failures. The emphasis of this research is to endorse the cogency of Altman's Z-Score model as a predictor of Bangladeshi bank failures. I after analyzing the all sample banks Z-Score I found that 7 banks are in healthy financial position and 22 banks are in insolvent during the time period of FY 2009-2014. Islamic or Sariah follower banks are doing better than conventional banks. Sate owned banks are doing better than before. This research indorses that those banks are in insolvent zone for their published financial review or trend statement. This supplementary material is probable to intensification stockholder assurance by their ability to make more conversant decisions.

Keywords: Financial performance; Liquidity; Bankruptcy; Bangladesh; Bank; Credit risk; Z-score; Bank profitability

Introduction

For bankruptcy companies in general and public shareholding will suffer financial distress. Not only owners are affected, but also other financial statements users, such as investors, creditors, and the economy in general will also be affected. Consequently, an early warning of bankruptcy could be taken as a precaution to be established to lower the risk and danger levels of company bankruptcy or distress. The motivation for this study arises from the arguments made by several authors who identified financial ratios and financial indicators that are used as a yardstick for bankruptcy prediction. It is based on where he compared a number of financial ratios of group of companies for the five years prior to bankruptcy period with another group of companies that are not bankrupt [1]. Then Altman [2,3], developed a model (Altmanz-score) which was the most renowned model in predicting company bankruptcy using financial ratios. Mr. Mahtab [4] has done another study and that was focused on Bangladeshi two groups of Banks, Conventional and Islamic Banks. So I focused my study on the performance evaluation of Bangladeshi Banks. I discuss about many ratios and performance indicator and compare their efficiency and effectiveness of operations of Banks in term of their return on investment, return on asset, return on equity and other company performance indicator. The research was based on secondary data and they are collected from five banks published annual reports. These data were analysed to test the financial performance of the banks by using ratio analysis which were selected by Altman Z score model. Those ratios are liquidity, profitability, efficiency and financial leverage. Working capital shows the position of a company's liquidity, efficiency, and overall health and it includes cash, inventory, accounts receivable, accounts payable and the portion of debt due within one year. Positive working capital generally indicates that a company is able to pay off its short-term liabilities almost immediately. Negative working capital generally indicates a company is unable to do so. The retained earnings of a company are the percentage of net income this is not paid out as dividends to its shareholders and it is retained to reinvest or to pay down debt that is accumulated over the year. The lower the outcome of ratio, the more a company is funding assets by borrowing or through retained earnings which again increases the risk of bankruptcy if the firm cannot meet its debt obligations. Companies with low profit margins tend to have high asset turnover, while those with high profit margins have low asset turnover. Companies in the retail industry tend to have a very high turnover ratio due mainly to cutthroat and competitive pricing. The measure of a company's financial leverage Debt-equity ratio relates the amount of a firms' debt financing with the amount of equity financing. CI Staff [5], indicator such as Earnings before Interest & Taxes to Total Assets is a variation on return on assets, and that show the efficiency of a company. This ratio assesses a firm's ability to generate profits from its assets before deducting interest and taxes. It Measures operating efficiency apart from tax and leveraging factors. It recognizes operating earnings as being important to long-term viability of banks and indicates a percentage of customer deposits; customer deposits as a percentage of total liabilities, and total equity as a percentage of total assets were computed to compare banks financial performance.

Problem Statement

The focus of my study is to apply an evolved model of Altman's Z score namely the 'Z" Score model [6] to failed banks. This model overcomes the manufacturing limitation of Altman's pioneering model and can be used on financial institutions. The main objective is to verify if the Z" Score is a true indicator of financial failure for a financial institution. The recent global crisis has demonstrated the importance

***Corresponding author:** Abdullah M, Assistant Professor, Independent University, Dhaka, Bangladesh, E-mail: htasfiq@gmail.com

of banks both at national and international levels. Business failures are a natural phenomenon in Bangladeshi economic system with firms entering and exiting as a function of overall business activity and expectations [7].

Corporate failure is the sequential conclusion due to systematic and non-systematic factors. Financial and accounting literature has over and over again renewed the confidence in ratio analysis as a proficient predictor of corporate failure. Nevertheless, more attention should be focused on the prediction of banking failures [8].

Financial performance is a subjective measure of how well a firm can use assets from its primary mode of business and generate revenues. The financial performance is also used as a general measure of overall financial health performance over the period. There are many different ways to measure financial performance. As far as ratios are concerned, there are numbers of ratios existing to evaluate the financial performance of a firm. These ratios can be classified into several categories such as liquidity ratios, profitability ratios, solvency ratios etc. Another effective indication of corporate performance in predicting financial solvency of a firm is Altman's Z-score. This is nothing but a combination of financial ratios to form an index of profitability. The ratios used to calculate Z-score are working capital to total assets, retained earnings to total assets, EBIT to total assets, market value of equity to total liabilities and sales to total assets [4].

In Bangladesh the Z score does not apply to every situation. It can only be used for forecasting if the company being analysed can be compared to the database. The Z-score formula for predicting bankruptcy was developed in 1968 by Edward I. Altman, a financial economist and professor at the Leonard N. Stern School of Business at New York University. The Z-score is a multivariate formula for a measurement of the financial health of a company and a powerful diagnostic tool that forecasts the probability of a company entering bankruptcy within a 2 year period. A good way to measure the possibility of bankruptcy is to use Z score model [2]. Therefore many companies in Bangladesh are suffering from financial distress risk due to very poor management capability and operating inefficiency although its reflection to the stock price is absent from the market in many instances. The Altman Z score, model though may not be fully applicable for companies in Bangladesh, yet proves its strong validity and correctness in predicting financial status of the Z category companies [9].

The Problem Statement of this research is to "Measure the financial performance of the banking sector in Bangladesh by using various standard of ratio as current ratio, Retained earnings to total assets ratio, return on assets ratio, book value of equity to total liabilities ratio and linking all of them together to find out the impact on profitability through the use of Altman Z Score".

Purpose of the Study

1. To measure the financial performance of Bangladesh Banking Sector using Altman's Z-score test and ratio analysis.
2. To test the correlations of five ratios with Z-score.
3. To measure the short-term financial position between five banks through liquidity ratios.
4. To analyse the short-term profitability position between five banks through profitability ratios.
5. To analyse the efficiency between five banks through efficiency ratios.
6. To analyse the leverage of five banks through financial leverage ratios

Literature Review

Altman's Z-score

The Altman Z-Score (Named on Edward Altman, New York University professor) is a combination of five financial ratios to estimate the financial position of a company and also a toll for predict corporate bankruptcy. Though Altman planned to invent the Z-Score in the 1960s, the concept of trying to predict which companies would bankrupt was new in that time. Altman use a statistical analysis called multivariate analysis to investigate some traditional ratio-analysis. These give him a concept that not only the effects of several ratios on the "performance of company" bankruptcy model, but to consider how those ratios affected each other's in this model. Edward I. Altman [2], after evaluating 66 companies Altman developed Z-Score model, half of them was filed for bankruptcy between 1946 and 1965. He started investigating his model with 22 ratio, then he classified them into five categories. They are:

1. Liquidity Ratio
2. Profitability Ratio
3. Leverage Ratio
4. Solvency Ratio
5. Activity Ratio

Edward I. Altman [2], Altman model is 90% accurate in classifying the bankrupt firms and 80% accurate in speculating the next financial situation. In 2009, Morgan Stanley strategy analyst, Graham Secker, used the Z-score to rank a basket of European companies. He found that the companies with weaker balance sheets underperformed the market more than two thirds of the time. Morgan Stanley also found that a company with an Altman Z-score of less than 1 tended to underperform the wider market by more than 4%. The Altman model has been used in air transport to successfully predict carrier failures as early as the 1980s where it correctly presaged the bankruptcy filings of both Braniff and Continental [10], and in subsequent years to track airline financial performance. Because of the significant increase in the use of leasing to finance assets in this industry, that model has become less reliable over time. Jhon Aiyabei [11], analyze the financial performance of small business firms based on MDA for the measurement and significance of financial distress. Lin Lin and Jenifarpisse [12], used Conditional probability analysis (CPA) model to determine merger acquisitions to prediction of the corporate failure.

The Z-Score model was based on 66 sample of manufacturing company; half of them were same pair groups. The formula for the Z-Score is:

$$Z = 6.56T1 + 3.26T2 + 6.72T3 + 1.05T4$$

T1 = (Current Assets-Current Liabilities) / Total Assets

T2 = Retained Earnings / Total Assets

T3 = Earnings before Interest and Taxes / Total Assets

T4 = Book Value of Equity / Total Liabilities

This equation gives a coefficient from the result of step by step multiple discriminate analysis or MDA regression (Table 1). Richard D [13], there is a reverse situation for ratios value. High ratios increase the Z score and minimize the risk of failure, on the other hand low ratios increase the risk of failure. The values were derived from the

Situation	Z-Score	Indicator	Remarks
1	Less than 1.1	Insolvent	The score indicates a high probability of distress within this time period.
2	Among 1.1 and 2.66	Healthy	There is a good chance of the company going bankrupt within the next 2 years of operations
3	2.6 and above	Secure	The company is considered 'Safe' based on the financial figures only.

Table 1: Z-Score and survivability indicators.

intercept of Z score. Altman [2], found that the values of the Z were 1.1 and 2.66. Firms with scores of <1.1 fit a bankruptcy profile, while firms with scores>2. 6 fit the solvency profile. Scores between the two values lie in what Altman [2] called the "gray zone" where profiling is more difficult. If the analyst wanted one key score in place of the "gray zone, " he argued for a 2.6 cut off because that zone contained.

T1 working capital / total asset

Working capital is needed for day-to-day operations. Working capital is a common measure of a company's liquidity, efficiency, and overall health. It includes cash, inventory, accounts receivable, accounts payable and the portion of debt due within one year.

Positive working capital generally indicates that a company is able to pay off its short-term liabilities almost immediately. Negative working capital generally indicates a company is unable to do so.

The formula of Working Capital to Total Asset is:

$$Working\ Capital\ to\ Total\ Asset\ Ratio = \frac{Working\ Capital}{Total\ Asset}$$

There are several ways to evaluate a company's working capital. Such as, by calculating the inventory-turnover ratio, the receivable ratio, the payable ratio, the current ratio and the quick ratio.

Working capital management is a very important factor, which has a direct positive effect on profitability as well as liquidity of the company. Liquidity and profitability are both the two different sides of same coin. Optimum level of liquidity guarantees a firm to meet their short term debts and the proper management of flow can be promised by a profitable business. The most important items inside determination of working capital are inventories of the corporation, its accounts receivables and payables [14]. The management of working capital frequently considered a tool to maintaining competence of the business inside their operations. Working capital is often assessed by lenders to judge the financial short term paying back ability in difficult financial period [15].

There is a strong linear relationship between profitability of the firm and its working capital efficiency. The ability of the company to earn profit can be referred to as the profitability of that company. Profit is determined by deducting expenses from the revenue incurred in generating that revenue. The amount of profit can be a good measure of the performance of a company, so I can use profitability as a measure of the financial performance of a company. Proper Working capital management ensures that the company increased its profitability. Effective working capital management is very important due to its significant effect on profitability of company and thus the existence of company in the market. Efficient working capital management involves planning and controlling current assets and current liabilities in a manner that eliminates the risk of inability to meet due short term obligations on the one hand and avoid excessive investment in these assets on the other hand [14,16].

Mobeen Ur Rehman and Naveed Anjum [15], empirically examine the effects of working capital management on the profitability of Pakistan cement industry. Secondary Data was collected from Annual Reports and the sample size is 10 consisting of Pakistan cement Companies listed in KSE from 2003-2008. The relationship between working capital management and profitability is examined using statistical tools. The result accepts the hypothesis that there is a positive relationship between working capital management and profitability on the cement sector of Pakistan. Deloof [14,17], discussed that most firms had a large amount of cash invested in working capital. It can therefore be expected that the way in which working capital is managed will have a significant impact on profitability of those firms. Using correlation and regression tests he found a significant negative relationship between gross operating income and the number of days accounts receivable, inventories and accounts payable of Belgian firms. On basis of these results he suggested that managers could create value for their shareholders by reducing the number of days' accounts receivable and inventories to a reasonable minimum. The negative relationship between accounts payable and profitability is consistent with the view that less profitable firms wait longer to pay their bills.

T2 retained earnings / total assets

The retained earnings of a company are the percentage of net income this is not paid out as dividends to its shareholders and it is retained to reinvest or to pay down debt that is accumulated over the year. The retained earnings to total asset ratio is calculated as follows:

$$Retained\ Earnings\ to\ Total\ Assetsratio = \frac{Retained\ Earnings}{Total\ Asset}$$

Total assets refer to the total amount of assets that is owned by an organization. And the assets must have the economic value that is expended over time to yield a benefit for the owner. Assets are also classified on the balance sheet as either current assets or long term assets. A current asset, such as an account receivable is expected to be liquidated within one year. A long-term asset, such as a fixed asset, is expected to be liquidated in more than one year.

Through retained earnings to Total Assets I measure the extent to which a company relies on debt or leverage on that particular year. The lower the outcome of ratio, the more a company is funding assets by borrowing instead of through retained earnings which again increases the risk of bankruptcy if the firm cannot meet its debt obligations

Retained Earnings/Total Assets indicates how much assets will be financed from retained earnings. The increase in retained earnings will give capital adequacy to the firm and which indicates favorable impact on debt to equity ratio [18].

Retained Earnings to Total Assets measures the amount of reinvested earnings or losses, which reflects the extent of the company's leverage. Companies that have low RE/TA are financing capital expenditure through borrowings rather than through retained earnings. Companies which have high RE/TA suggest a history of profitability and the ability to stand up to a bad year of losses [19].

Retained earnings is the account which reports the total amount of reinvested earnings or losses of a firm over time. The account is also referred to as earned surplus. It should note that the retained earnings account is subject to manipulations. In addition the RE\TA ratio measures the leverage of a firm. those Firms with high RE. Relative to low RE, financed their assets through retention of profits and have not utilized as much debt [2].

Retained earnings to total assets are an indicator of the "cumulative profitability" of the firm overtime which indicates the efficiency of management in manufacturing, Sales, Administration and other activities [20].

Retained earnings to total assets measures profitability that reflects the company's age and earning power [21].

Retained earnings represent the accumulation of earnings that have remained within the entity. Retained earnings can be affected by reorganizations and stock dividend declarations, if so, consideration should be given to readjusting retained earnings. To increase retained earnings a company must generates profits either through operations or the profitable sell-off of assets or division or the forgiveness of the debt [22].

The ratio indicates the ability of a firm to earn profit and thereby securing retained earnings. Normally a firm has higher retained earnings, a firm will not starve for liquidity crunch and also the firm can reinvest in the appropriate venture at cheaper cost [23].

T3 Operating earnings / total assets

CI Staff [5] this is a variation on return on assets, which is net income divided by total assets. This ratio assesses a firm's ability to generate profits from its assets before deducting interest and taxes. It Measures operating efficiency apart from tax and leveraging factors. It recognizes operating earnings as being important to long-term viability.

Earnings before interest and tax (EBIT) to total assets ratio indicates a proportion between the measure that shows company's profitability and company's assets [8]. It measures the productivity of the firm's assets notwithstanding any tax or leverage factors. "Since a firm's ultimate existence is based on the earning power of its assets, this ratio appears to be particularly appropriate for studies dealing with corporate failure" [2]. In short, it represents general profitability of the company's assets. EBITDA would not be a very accurate measure of a bank's financial position as it takes into account depreciation and amortization which would not be applicable to the nature of a bank's operations.

This ratio is calculated by dividing the total assets of a firm into its earnings before interest and tax reductions. Vineet Chouhan, Bibhas Chandra and Shubham Goswami [24], Predicting financial stability of select BSE companies revisiting Altman Z score In essence, it is a measure of the true productivity of the firm's assets, abstracting from any tax or leverage factors. Since a firm's ultimate existence is based on the earning power of its assets, this ratio appears to be particularly appropriate for studies dealing with corporate failure. Furthermore, insolvency in a bankruptcy sense occurs when the total liabilities exceed a fair valuation of the firm's assets with value determined by the earning power of the assets. (EBIT/TA) is a version of return on assets (ROA), an effective way of assessing a firm's ability to squeeze profits before factors like interest and tax are deducted.

This ratio is used to evaluate the company's ability to generate operating profit with existing asset. When the company has high profit with low asset, it has a relatively low chance of getting default. It is due to the dollar of asset that is able to generate a larger amount of operating profit. On the other way, lower income might not be enough to cover company's daily expenses (Thai, 2014)Earnings before interest and tax (EBIT) to total assets ratio indicates a proportion between the measure that shows company's profitability and company's assets [25]. In short, it represents general profitability of the company's assets. Data to calculate this ratio is collected from the income statement and balance sheet.

There are no general norms for this ratio. It is recommended to compare this ratio to those of the companies, working within the same industry.

$$EBIT\ to\ Total\ Asset\ Ratio = \frac{EBIT}{Total\ Asset}$$

Earnings before interest and taxes (EBIT) equal net income, plus interest expense, plus taxes. Assets (Total assets) - a balance sheet item, representing what a company owns

T4 Market value of equity / book value of total liabilities

This is a measure of a company's financial leverage. It is reciprocal of the familiar debt-equity ratio. Debt-equity ratio relates the amount of a firms' debt financing with the amount of equity financing. Market Value of Equity is the total current market value of all common and preferred shares on the other side Book Value of Total Liabilities is the sum of all current and long-term liabilities of a firms' balance sheet. If a company has no debt that is unlevered firm, there is some sort of benefit with debt. By acquiring debt financing firm get extra money for investment and make a tax shield from the debt [26]. That is the leverage and debt-equity ratio show the picture how a firm using the debt to maximizing profit. What is considered a "high" debt-to-equity ratio differs depending upon the industry, because some industries tend to utilize more debt financing than others. There is no single value above which would be deemed a high debt-to-equity ratio. For calculation of debt-equity ratio I have to divide firm's equity with the total amount of debt.

$$Equity\ to\ Debtratio = \frac{Market\ Value\ of\ Equity}{Book\ Value\ of\ Total\ Liabilities}$$

VikasTyagi, describes that a higher debt-equity ratio generally means that a company has been aggressive in financing its growth with debt [27]. This can result in unpredictable earnings as a result of the additional interest expense. If a lot of debt is used to finance increased operation, the company could potentially generate more earnings than it would have without this outside financing. If this were to increase earnings by a greater amount than the debt cost, then the shareholders benefit as more earnings are being spread among the same amount of shareholders. However, the cost of this debt financing may outweigh the return that the company generates on the debt through investment and business activities and become too much for the company to handle. This can lead to bankruptcy, which would leave shareholders with nothing.

The debt-equity ratio also depends on the industry in which the company operates. If capital intensive industries as auto manufacturing tend to have a debt-equity ratio above 2, while personal computer companies have a debt-equity of under 0.5 [28]. The financial industry, for example, typically has a higher debt-to-equity ratio. This is for the fact that banks and other financial institutions borrow money to lend money, which results in a higher debt-equity ratio. There are more sectors that have high capital structure so they have higher debt-equity ratios, such as services, utilities and the industrial goods sector. As a result, investors must look at a company's historical debt-to-equity ratio figures to determine if there have been significant changes that could indicate a red flag. In addition, investors must also make comparisons between other similar companies and the industry as a whole to determine if a particular firm has what could be considered a high debt-to-equity ratio.

Optimal debt-equity ratio is considered to be about liabilities = equity, but the ratio is very industry has this type ratio because it depends on the proportion of current and non-current assets. The more non-current the assets and equity is required to finance these long term investments [29]. A higher total debt-to-equity ratio indicates that the sector has been increasing the relative share of debt in external financing, whereas a lower debt-to-equity ratio indicates that the sector is financing a decreasing proportion of its activities through debt as compared to financing through their equity. Variations in the market value of equity can also cause changes in the ratio. Therefore, if a financial corporation's ratio is 3.5 it means that the liability outstanding is 3. 5 times larger than their shareholder's equity. Higher debt can result in volatile earnings due to additional interest expense as well as increased vulnerability to business solvency [29]. However, opposing to what many believe, debt is not necessarily a bad thing, it can be positive, provided it is used for productive purposes such as purchasing assets and improving processes to increase net profits. Also, the debt-to-equity ratio is more significant when relate over a period of time. Non-consolidated debt data gives important info about the total liability of the financial corporation's sector. For these reason Edward I. Altman [2] us this ratio as a variable for his Z-Score model for a better concept of a firms' financial performance.

Research Framework

$Z = 6.56T1 + 3.26T2 + 6.72T3 + 1.05T4$

T1 = (Current Assets - Current Liabilities) / Total Assets

T2 = Retained Earnings / Total Assets

T3 = Earnings before Interest and Taxes / Total Assets

T4 = Book Value of Equity / Total Liabilities

Research Questions

Q_1: What is the relationship between Working Capital to Total Assets and Z-score?

Q_2: What is the relationship between Retained Earnings to Total Assets and Z-score?

Q_3: What is the relationship between EBIT to Total Assets and Z-score?

Q_4: What is the relationship between Market Value of Equity to Total Liabilities Z-score?

Hypothesis

Ho_1: There is a negative relationship between Working Capital to Total Assets and Z-score.

Ha_1: There is a positive relationship between Working Capital to Total Assets and Z-score.

Ho_2: There is a negative relationship between Retained Earnings to Total Assets and Z-score.

Ha_2: There is a positive relationship between Retained Earnings to Total Assets and Z-score.

Ho_3: There is a negative relationship between EBIT to Total Assets and Z-score.

Ha_3: There is a positive relationship between EBIT to Total Assets and Z-score.

Ho_4: There is a negative relationship between Market Value of Equity to Total Liabilities and Z-score.

Ha_4: There is a positive relationship between Market Value of Equity to Total Liabilities and Z-score.

Research Design

Research design is crucial as it acts as a blueprint for the collection, measurement and analysis of data. In this study, I have selected ex post facto design, because this study required structured and précised way to show the relationship among different variables and to test hypotheses.

The method of data collection

Under the method of data collection, I have selected secondary data through annual report. Because I wanted to communicate with different employees of banks by asking them many questions.

Researcher control of variables

In ex post facto research I uses historical data that cannot be manipulated by researchers. In my research my dependent variable is financial performance and that cannot be changed by me. My research could be stated as ex post facto design.

Degree of research question crystallization

My study was Formal study as I tried to explain the relationship among different variables.

Purpose of the study

My study was designed for testing hypotheses quantitatively which required a good number of samples which reflected the investor.

The time dimension

I focused on longitudinal study. I have studied on 29 different banks of Bangladesh as samples for and they did not need to be studied again for the same study. I have analyzed6 years annual repot data.

The topical scope

The topical scope for my research is statistical study. I used statistical analysis to collect quantitative information because it is designed for breadth instead of depth.

The research environment

My research occurred in actual environment conditions. My research environment could be specified as stimulation. This option was chosen because I had to receive information from historical data and relationships in variables of my study were required.

Sampling

In Bangladesh, the total number of banks is 64 where state-owned banks are 4, private commercial banks are 32, Islamic commercial banks are 8, foreign banks are 09 and specialized banks are 11. So, this is not possible to take all the banks as a research data for the research and it is also not possible to evaluate all the banks financial performance. For this reason to obtain a probable result, a sampling procedure has been conducted.

Sample unit: For doing the research, I have taken private commercial banks and state-owned banks as a sample unit to evaluate the financial performance and to find out what effects will occur on profitability.

Sample size: For getting a better result, I have taken different level of private commercial banks as a sample size and those are Bank Asia

Limited, AB Bank Limited, Brac Bank Limited, Dautch Bangla bank Limited, Dhaka Bank Limited, Agrani Bank Limited, Basic Bank Limited, Easter Bank Limited, IFIC Bank, Janata Bank, Mercantile Bank Limited, Mutual Trust Bank Limited, One bank Limited, Premier Bank Limited, Prime Bank Limited, Pubali Bank Limited, Rupali Bank Limited, Shahjala Bank Limited, Social Islami Bank Limited, Standard Bank Limited, South East Bank Limited, Trust Bnak Limited, The City Bank, United Commercial bank Limited, Islami Bank Limited, Exim Bank Limited, ICB Islamic Bank Limited, Fist Security Islami Bank Limited, Uttara Bank Limited and it will help me to complete my research. The total sample size for the research is 29.

Sample procedure: The most important step for sampling is that how I do my research and collect data for getting the proper information. It is not sure that the providing information after the research is accurate because the research is based on secondary data and the total sample size is only 29. For that reason, this sample procedure will be probability sample procedure.

Data Analysis

In 2009, Z-Score of Bank Asia Limitedis1.829080966 so that bank was performing good as this is greater than 1.1 so bank's financial position was healthy up to 2011. From 2011 to 2014, Bank Asia Limited's performance was below 1.1 and that is declining trend of performance. On an average Z-Score value is 0.946211502, this is also stating the fact that the Bank Asia was insolvent. From Table 2, we can see that Bank Asia Limited's overall financial position is insolvent and trend shows that performance is getting worse.

In 2009, Z-Score of AB Bank Limited are 5.555341493 so that bank was performing good as this is greater than 2.6 so bank's financial position was secure. In 2010 AB Bank Limited was healthy. From 2011 to 2014, AB Bank Limited's performance was below 1.1 and that is declining trend of performance. On an average Z-Score value is 1.658249831, this is also stating the fact that the AB Bank Limited was insolvent. From Table 3, we can see that AB Bank Limited's overall financial position is Healthy and trend shows that performance is getting worse.

In 2009, Z-Score of Brac Limited is -0.045822189 so that bank was performing poorly as this is less than 1.1 so bank's financial position was insolvent. From 2010 to 2014, Brac Bank Limited's performance was below 1.1. On an average Z-Score value is 0. 021480171, this is also stating the fact that the Brac Bank Limited was insolvent. From Table 4, we can see that Brac Bank Limited's overall financial position is insolvent and trend shows that performance is getting better.

In 2009, Z-Score of Dautch Bangla Bank Limited is 1.005247418 so that bank was performing poorly as this is less than 1.1 bank's financial position was insolvent. From 2010 to 2014, Dautch Bangla Bank Limited's performance was below 1.1. On an average Z-Score value is 0.812640457, this is also stating the fact that the Dautch Bangla Bank Limited was insolvent. From Table 5, we can see that Dautch Bangla Bank Limited's overall financial position is insolvent and trend shows that Z-score volatility is too high.

In 2009, Z-Score of Dhaka Bank Limited is 1.224478092 so that bank was performing good as this is greater than 1.1 so bank's financial position was healthy. From 2011 to 2014, Dhaka Bank Limited's performance was below 1.1 and that is declining trend of performance. On an average Z-Score value is 1.041098355, this is also stating the fact that the Dhaka Bank Limited was insolvent. From Table 6, we can see that Dhaka Bank Limited's overall financial position is insolvent.

In 2009, Z-Score of Agrani Bank Limited 0.003339096 so that bank was performing poorly as this is less than 1.1 so bank's financial position was Insolvent. From 2010 to 2014, Agrani Bank Limited's performance was below 1.1 and that is declining trend of performance. On an average Z-Score value is 0.084776014, this is also stating the fact that the Agrani Bank Limited was insolvent. From Table 7, we can see

Year	Z-Score	Indicator	Average
2009	1.829080966	Healthy	
2010	1.268538299	Healthy	
2011	1.451911972	Healthy	
2012	0.530534185	Insolvent	0.946211502
2013	0.360403495	Insolvent	
2014	0.236800094	Insolvent	Insolvent

Table 2: Data analysis of Bank Asia..

Year	Z-Score	Indicator	Average
2009	5.555341493	Secure	
2010	1.052672451	Healthy	
2011	0.967978315	Insolvent	
2012	1.018492668	Insolvent	1.658249831
2013	0.759504208	Insolvent	
2014	0.595509853	Insolvent	Healthy

Table 3: Data analysis of AB Bank limited..

Year	Z-Score	Indicator	Average
2009	-0.045822189	Insolvent	
2010	-0.286252537	Insolvent	
2011	-0.106734377	Insolvent	
2012	-0.113000077	Insolvent	0.021480171
2013	0.039942471	Insolvent	
2014	0.640747732	Insolvent	Insolvent

Table 4: Data analysis Brac Bank limited.

Year	Z-Score	Indicator	Average
2009	1.005247418	Insolvent	
2010	0.455119337	Insolvent	
2011	0.679372597	Insolvent	
2012	1.000651292	Insolvent	0.812640457
2013	0.92297793	Insolvent	
2014	0.812474169	Insolvent	Insolvent

Table 5: Data analysis of Dautch Bangla Bank limited.

Year	Z-Score	Indicator	Average
2009	1.224478092	Healthy	
2010	0.986605678	Insolvent	
2011	1.003653894	Insolvent	
2012	1.046265571	Insolvent	1.041098355
2013	0.985375779	Insolvent	
2014	1.000211114	Insolvent	Insolvent

Table 6: Data analysis of Dhaka Bank limited.

Year	Z-Score	Indicator	Average
2009	0.003339096	Insolvent	
2010	-0.162509365	Insolvent	
2011	-0.002784539	Insolvent	
2012	-0.38602878	Insolvent	0.084776014
2013	0.532524765	Insolvent	
2014	0.524114909	Insolvent	Insolvent

Table 7: Data analysis of Agrani Bank limited.

that Agrani Bank Limited's overall financial position is insolvent and trend shows that performance is getting better.

In 2009, Z-Score of Basic Bank Limited is 5.824081263 so that bank was performing good as this is greater than 2.6 so bank's financial position was secure. From 2010 to 2013, Basic Bank Limited's performance was more than 1.1 and that indicate that bank was in healthy financial position. In 2014 Basic Bank Limited was insolvent. On an average Z-Score value is 2.29114436, this is also stating the fact that the Basic Bank Limited was healthy. From Table 8, we can see that AB Basic Bank Limited's overall financial position is Healthy and trend shows that performance is getting worse.

In 2009, Z-Score of Eastern Bank Limited is 1.153197804 so that bank was performing good as this is greater than 1.1 so bank's financial position was healthy. In 2010, Eastern Bank Limited's financial position was insolvent. On an average Z-Score value is 2.329345782, this is also stating the fact that the Eastern Bank Limited was healthy. From Table 9, we can see that Eastern Bank Limited's overall financial position is Healthy.

In 2009, Z-Score of IFIC Bank Limited is 1.153197804 so that bank was performing good as this is greater than 1.1 so bank's financial position was healthy. In 2010 IFIC Bank Limited was insolvent. From 2011 to 2014, IFIC Bank Limited's performance was below 1.1 and that is declining trend of performance. On an average Z-score value is 2. 29345782, this is also stating the fact that the IFIC Bank limited was Healthy. From Table 10, we can see that IFIC Bank Limited's overall financial position is Healthy and trend shows that performance is getting better.

In 2009, Z-Score of Janata Bank Limited is 0.853929515 so that bank was performing poorly as this is less than 1.1 so bank's financial position was insolvent. In 2010, Janata Bank Limited's financial positionwas insolvent. From 2011 to 2014, Janata Bank Limited's performance was below 1.1 and that is declining trend of performance. On an average Z-Score value is 0.364374669, this is also stating the fact that the Janata Bank Limited was insolvent. From Table 11, we can see that Janata Bank Limited's overall financial position is insolvent and trend shows that performance is getting worse.

In 2009, Z-Score of Mercantile Bank Limited is 0.633749043 so that bank was performing poorly as this is less than 1.1 so bank's financial position was secure. From 2010 to 2014, Mercantile Bank Limited's performance was below 1.1 and that is declining trend of performance. On an average Z-Score value is 0.284227138, this is also stating the fact that the Mercantile Bank Limited was insolvent. From Table 12, we can see that Mercantile Bank Limited's overall financial position is insolvent and trend shows that performance is getting worse.

In 2009, Z-Score of Mutual Trust Bank limited is 0. 857734615 so that bank was performing poorly as this is less than 1.1 so bank's financial position was insolvent. From 2010 to 2014, Mutual Trust Bank Limited's performance was below 1.1 and that is declining trend of performance. On an average Z-Score value is 0.434647794, this is also stating the fact that the Mutual Trust Bank Limited was insolvent. From Table 13, we can see that Mutual Trust Bank Limited's overall financial position is insolvent and trend shows that performance is getting worse.

In 2009, Z-Score of One Bank Limited is 0.786361994 so that bank was performing poorly as this is less than 1.1 so bank's financial position was insolvent. From 2010 to 2014, One Bank Limited's performance was below 1.1 and that is declining trend of performance. On an average Z-Score value is 1.658249831, this is also stating the fact that the One Bank Limited was insolvent. From Table 14, we can see that One Bank Limited's overall financial position is insolvent and trend shows that performance is getting worse.

In 2009, Z-Score of Premier Bank Limited is 0.566145952 so that bank was performing poorly as this is less than 1.1 so bank's financial

Year	Z-Score	Indicator	Average
2009	5.824081263	Secure	
2010	1.68190398	Healthy	
2011	2.065936981	Healthy	
2012	1.887564213	Healthy	**2.29114436**
2013	1.251097364	Healthy	
2014	1.03628236	Insolvent	**Healthy**

Table 8: Data analysis of Basic Bank limited.

Year	Z-Score	Indicator	Average
2009	1.153197804	Healthy	
2010	0.790681447	Insolvent	
2011	0.974474574	Insolvent	
2012	1.613475164	Healthy	**2.329345782**
2013	7.303866779	Secure	
2014	2.140378925	Healthy	**Healthy**

Table 9: Data analysis of Eastern Bank limited.

Year	Z-Score	Indicator	Average
2009	1.300918718	Healthy	
2010	0.294460975	Insolvent	
2011	0.48758785	Insolvent	
2012	0.776261564	Insolvent	**0.788318078**
2013	0.944799603	Insolvent	
2014	0.925879757	Insolvent	**Insolvent**

Table 10: Data analysis of IFIC Bank limited.

Year	Z-Score	Indicator	Average
2009	0.853929515	Insolvent	
2010	-0.038248682	Insolvent	
2011	0.332854105	Insolvent	
2012	-0.018923182	Insolvent	**0.364374669**
2013	0.613824369	Insolvent	
2014	0.442811891	Insolvent	**Insolvent**

Table 11: Data analysis of Janata Bank limited.

Year	Z-Score	Indicator	Average
2009	0.633749043	Insolvent	
2010	-0.04099097	Insolvent	
2011	0.295482843	Insolvent	
2012	0.228788627	Insolvent	**0.284227138**
2013	0.366022244	Insolvent	
2014	0.22231104	Insolvent	**Insolvent**

Table 12: Data analysis of Mercantile Bank limited.

Year	Z-Score	Indicator	Average
2009	0.857734615	Insolvent	
2010	0.405209564	Insolvent	
2011	0.221274934	Insolvent	
2012	0.391701809	Insolvent	**0.434647794**
2013	0.496142395	Insolvent	
2014	0.235823448	Insolvent	**Insolvent**

Table 13: Data analysis of Mutual Trust Bank limited.

position was insolvent. From 2010 to 2014, Premier Bank Limited's performance was below 1.1 and that is declining trend of performance. On an average Z-Score value is 0.239339886, this is also stating the fact that the Premier Bank Limited was insolvent. From Table 15, we can see that Premier Bank Limited's overall financial position is insolvent and trend shows that performance is getting worse.

In 2009, Z-Score of Prime Bank Limited is 0.706791386 so that bank was performing poorly as this is less than 1.1 so bank's financial position was insolvent. From 2010 to 2014, Prime Bank Limited's performance was below 1.1 and that is declining trend of performance. On an average Z-Score value is 0.434565403, this is also stating the fact that the Prime Bank Limited was insolvent. From Table 16, we can see that Prime Bank Limited's overall financial position is insolvent and trend shows that performance is getting worse.

In 2009, Z-Score of Pubali Bank Limited is 0.640405829 so that bank was performing poorly as this is less than 1.1 so bank's financial position was insolvent. From 2010 to 2014, Pubali Bank Limited's performance was below 1.1 and that is declining trend of performance. On an average Z-Score value is 0.630899433, this is also stating the fact that the Pubali Bank Limited was insolvent. From Table 17, we can see that Pubali Bank Limited's overall financial position is insolvent and trend shows that performance is getting worse.

Year	Z-Score	Indicator	Average
2009	0.786361994	Insolvent	
2010	0.763556365	Insolvent	
2011	0.804434889	Insolvent	
2012	0.755744723	Insolvent	**0.636124015**
2013	0.333915303	Insolvent	
2014	0.372730818	Insolvent	**Insolvent**

Table 14: Data analysis of One Bank limited.

Year	Z-Score	Indicator	Average
2009	0.566145952	Insolvent	
2010	0.372788267	Insolvent	
2011	0.225097445	Insolvent	
2012	0.226028772	Insolvent	**0.239339886**
2013	0.028946429	Insolvent	
2014	0.017032451	Insolvent	**Insolvent**

Table 15: Data analysis of Premier Bank limited.

Year	Z-Score	Indicator	Average
2009	0.706791386	Insolvent	
2010	0.214538365	Insolvent	
2011	0.419962411	Insolvent	
2012	0.436021111	Insolvent	**0.434565403**
2013	0.461624627	Insolvent	
2014	0.36845452	Insolvent	**Insolvent**

Table 16: Data analysis of Prime Bank limited.

Year	Z-Score	Indicator	Average
2009	0.640405829	Insolvent	
2010	0.760551291	Insolvent	
2011	0.506470636	Insolvent	
2012	0.692683577	Insolvent	**0.630899433**
2013	0.62797331	Insolvent	
2014	0.557311955	Insolvent	**Insolvent**

Table 17: Data analysis of Pubali Bank limited.

In 2009, Z-Score of Rupali Bank Limited is 0.058272868 so that bank was performing poorly as this is less than 1.1 so bank's financial position was insolvent. In 2014, Rupali Bank Limited's financial position was healthy. From 2010 to 2013, Rupali Bank Limited's performance was below 1.1. On an average Z-Score value is 0.599435625, this is also stating the fact that the Rupali Bank Limited was insolvent. From Table 18, we can see that Rupali Bank Limited's overall financial position is insolvent and trend shows that performance is getting better.

In 2009, Z-Score of ShahjalaIslami Bank Limited is 1.749143504 so that bank was performing good as this is greater than 1.1 so bank's financial position was healthy. From 2010 to 2014, ShahjalaIslami Bank Limited's performance was greater than 1.1. On an average Z-Score value is 11.412860203, this is also stating the fact that the ShahjalaIslami Bank Limited was healthy. From Table 19, we can see that ShahjalaIslami Bank Limited's overall financial position is healthy.

In 2009, Z-Score of Social Islami Bank Limited is 1.590300694 so that bank was performing good as this is greater than 1.1 so bank's financial position was healthy. In 2010, Social Islami Bank Limited's financial position was insolvent. On an average Z-Score value is 1.199321565, this is also stating the fact that the financial position of Social Islami Bank Limited was healthy. From Table 20, we can see that Social Islami Bank Limited's overall financial position is healthy.

In 2009, Z-Score of Standard Bank Limited is 1.796279978 so that bank was performing good as this is greater than 1.1 so bank's financial position was healthy. In 2010, Standard Bank Limited's financial position was insolvent. From 2011 to 2014, Standard Bank Limited's performance was below 1.1 and that is declining trend of performance. On an average Z-Score value is 0.88747442, this is also stating the fact that the Standard Bank Limited was insolvent. From Table 21, we can see that Standard Bank Limited's overall financial position is insolvent and trend shows that performance is getting worse.

In 2009, Z-Score of South East Bank Limited is 1.090556628 so that

Year	Z-Score	Indicator	Average
2009	0.058272868	Insolvent	
2010	0.275236565	Insolvent	
2011	0.384638674	Insolvent	
2012	0.848787637	Insolvent	**0.599435625**
2013	0.91508542	Insolvent	
2014	1.11459259	Healthy	**Insolvent**

Table 18: Data analysis of Rupali Bank limited.

Year	Z-Score	Indicator	Average
2009	1.749143504	Healthy	
2010	1.366876664	Healthy	
2011	1.327528111	Healthy	
2012	1.550718232	Healthy	**1.412860203**
2013	1.34577502	Healthy	
2014	1.137119685	Healthy	**Healthy**

Table 19: Data analysis of Shahjala Islami Bank limited.

Year	Z-Score	Indicator	Average
2009	1.590300694	Healthy	
2010	1.073512152	Insolvent	
2011	1.272193784	Healthy	
2012	1.260119769	Healthy	**1.199321565**
2013	0.998814661	Insolvent	
2014	1.000988327	Healthy	**Healthy**

Table 20: Data analysis of Social Islami Bank limited.

bank was performing good as this is greater than 1.1 so bank's financial position was healthy. In 2010, South East Bank Limited's financial position was insolvent. From 2011 to 2014, South East Bank Limited's performance was below 1.1 and that is declining trend of performance. On an average Z-Score value is 10.889008076, this is also stating the fact that the South East Bank Limited was insolvent. From Table 22, we can see that South East Bank Limited's overall financial position is insolvent and trend shows that performance is getting worse.

In 2009, Z-Score of Trust Bank Limited is 1.48206737 so that bank was performing good as this is greater than 1.1 so bank's financial position was healthy. In 2010, Trust Bank Limited's financial position was insolvent. From 2013 to 2014, Trust Bank Limited's performance was below 1.1 and that is declining trend of performance. On an average Z-Score value is 0.916365639, this is also stating the fact that the Trust Bank Limited was insolvent. From Table 23, we can see that Trust Bank Limited's overall financial position is insolvent.

In 2009, Z-Score of The City Bank Limited is 2. 220814453 so that bank was performing good as this is greater than 1.1 so bank's financial position was healthy. In 2010, The City Bank Limited's financial position was insolvent. From 2011 to 2014, The City Bank Limited's performance was below 1.1 and that is declining trend of performance. On an average Z-Score value is 0.87299446, this is also stating the fact that the financial position of The City Bank Limited was insolvent. From Table 24, we can see that The City Bank Limited's overall financial position is insolvent and trend shows that performance is getting worse.

In 2009, Z-Score of United Commercial Bank Limited is 0.781932915 so that bank was performing poorly as this is less than 1.1 so bank's financial position was insolvent. In 2010 United Commercial Bank Limited's financial position was insolvent. From 2011 to 2014, United Commercial Bank Limited's performance was below 1.1 and that is declining trend of performance. On an average Z-Score value is 0. 685883956, this is also stating the fact that the financial position of United Commercial Bank Limited was insolvent. From Table 25, we can see that United Commercial Bank Limited's overall financial position is insolvent and trend shows that performance is getting worse.

In 2009, Z-Score of Islami Bank Limited is 7.129397337 so that bank was performing good as this is greater than 2.6 so bank's financial position was Secure. In 2010, Islami Bank Limited's financial position was insolvent. From 2011 to 2014 Islami Bank Limited's performance was below 1.1 and that is declining trend of performance. On an average Z-Score value is 1.800897889, this is also stating the fact that the financial position of Islami Bank Limited was healthy. From Table 26, we can see that Islami Bank Limited's overall financial position is healthy and trend shows that performance is getting worse.

In 2009, Z-Score of EXIM Bank Limited is 1.164116124 so that bank was performing good as this is greater than 1.1 so bank's financial position was healthy. In 2011, EXIM Bank Limited's financial position was secure. On an average Z-Score value is 1.793443355, this is also stating the fact that the financial position of EXIM Bank Limited was healthy. From Table 27, we can see that EXIM Bank Limited's overall financial position is healthy.

In 2009, Z-Score of ICB Islami Bank Limited is -0. 0075826 so that bank was performing poorly as this is less than 1.1 so bank's financial position was insolvent. In 2010, ICB Islami Bank Limited's financial position was insolvent. From 2011 to 2014 ICB ISLAMI Bank Limited's

Year	Z-Score	Indicator	Average
2009	1.796279978	Healthy	
2010	0.592112559	Insolvent	
2011	0.732562673	Insolvent	
2012	0.884250629	Insolvent	
2013	0.782236726	Insolvent	0.88747442
2014	0.537403958	Insolvent	Insolvent

Table 21: Data analysis of Standard Bank limited.

Year	Z-Score	Indicator	Average
2009	1.090556628	Healthy	
2010	0.849597337	Insolvent	
2011	0.672516914	Insolvent	0.889008076
2012	0.981172769	Insolvent	
2013	0.881130829	Insolvent	Insolvent
2014	0.859073981	Insolvent	

Table 22: Data analysis of South East Bank limited.

Year	Z-Score	Indicator	Average
2009	1.48206737	Healthy	
2010	0.634523868	Insolvent	
2011	1.097505114	Insolvent	
2012	1.324424294	Healthy	0.916365639
2013	0.570335631	Insolvent	
2014	0.389337558	Insolvent	Insolvent

Table 23: Data analysis of Trust Bank limited.

Year	Z-Score	Indicator	Average
2009	2.220814453	Healthy	
2010	0.205350775	Insolvent	
2011	0.708555943	Insolvent	
2012	0.514108175	Insolvent	0.87299446
2013	0.86043952	Insolvent	
2014	0.728697891		Insolvent

Table 24: Data analysis of The City Bank limited.

Year	Z-Score	Indicator	Average
2009	0.781932915	Insolvent	
2010	0.296402526	Insolvent	
2011	0.843486952	Insolvent	0.685883956
2012	0.946095679	Insolvent	Insolvent
2013	0.790134743	Insolvent	
2014	0.457250922	Insolvent	

Table 25: Data analysis of United Commercial Bank limited.

Year	Z-Score	Indicator	Average
2009	7.129397337	Secure	
2010	0.712007674	Insolvent	
2011	0.842267254	Insolvent	
2012	0.820851464	Insolvent	1.800897889
2013	0.632854304	Insolvent	
2014	0.668009303	Insolvent	Healthy

Table 26: Data analysis of Islami Bank limited.

Year	Z-Score	Indicator	Average
2009	1.164116124	Healthy	
2010	0.750045444	Insolvent	
2011	5.181350825	Secure	
2012	1.404541155	Healthy	1.793443355
2013	1.288380016	Healthy	
2014	0.972226567	Insolvent	Healthy

Table 27: Data analysis of Exim Bank limited.

performance was below 1.1 and that is declining trend of performance. On an average Z-Score value is -1.126189731, this is also stating the fact that the financial position of ICB Islami Bank Limited was insolvent. From Table 28, we can see that ICB Islami Bank Limited's overall financial position is insolvent also negative and trend shows that performance is getting worse.

In 2009, Z-Score of First Security Islami Bank Limited is 0.989124679 so that bank was performing poorly as this is less than 1.1 so bank's financial position was insolvent. In 2010, First Security Islami Bank Limited's financial position was insolvent. On an average Z-Score value is 0.997654317, this is also stating the fact that the financial position of First Security Islami Bank Limited was insolvent. From Table 29, we can see that First Security Islami Bank Limited's overall financial position is insolvent and trend shows that performance is getting worse.

In 2009, Z-Score of Uttara Bank Limited is -0.599078531 so that bank was performing poorly as this is less than 1.1 so bank's financial position was insolvent. In 2010, Uttara Bank Limited's financial position was insolvent. On an average Z-Score value is -0.751652157, this is also stating the fact that the financial position of Uttara Bank Limited was insolvent. From Table 29, we can see that Uttara Bank Limited's overall financial position is insolvent and trend shows that performance is getting worse.

The failure in Gray area, bankruptcy cannot easily be predicted so all year data shows that all banks are insolvent. The score indicates a high probability of distress within this time period. From Figure 1, we can see that on average Basic Bank, Eastern Bank, Islami Bank and EXIM Bank Limited's performance comparatively better than other banks. As all banks use their fixed Liability (Fixed Deposit) as working capital most of them have negative working capital. Uttara Bank and ICB Islami Bank have negative financial performance.

Based on the level of mean, the condition of banks is not good because here highest mean is T2 between T1-T4. Median is affective to protect bankruptcy because the level of median is 0.757624466 that is lower number then proper number of standard. Minimum Z score is -3.353078608 and average Z-Score is 0.79913588 and it shows that all sample banks are insolvent during the time period. Standard Deviation of Z-score is comparatively higher than T1, T2, T3 and T4 (Table 30).

Correlation of T1 with Z is 0.688157 and it is positive hence the null hypothesis is rejected and alternate hypothesis is accepted. Also correlation of T2 with Z, T3 with Z and T4 with Z are positive so null hypothesis is rejected and alternate hypothesis is accepted (Figure 2). So all null hypothesis will be rejected and all alternate hypothesis will be accepted (Table 31).

From Table 32, it can be found that coefficient of T1=6.56, T2=3.26, T3=6.72 and T4=1.05 and Constant C=-5.75E-10. As R^2=100%, all independent variable together explain the dependent variable. As a result all alternate hypothesis will be accepted and all null hypothesis will be rejected. Here, Significance level is 0.01 and our Probability (F-Statistics) is 0 (Table 33). So Significance level is 0.01 greater than

Year	Z-Score	Indicator	Average
2009	-0.0075826	Insolvent	
2010	-2.258630792	Insolvent	
2011	-3.008525749	Insolvent	
2012	-3.353078608	Insolvent	-1.126189731
2013	0.944799603	Insolvent	
2014	0.925879757	Insolvent	Insolvent

Table 28: Data analysis of ICB Islami Bank limited.

Year	Z-Score	Indicator	Average
2009	0.989124679	Insolvent	
2010	0.4542641	Insolvent	
2011	1.002467048	Insolvent	
2012	1.296142167	Healthy	0.997654317
2013	1.381026755	Healthy	
2014	0.862901154	Insolvent	Insolvent

Table 29: Data analysis of First Security Islami Bank limited.

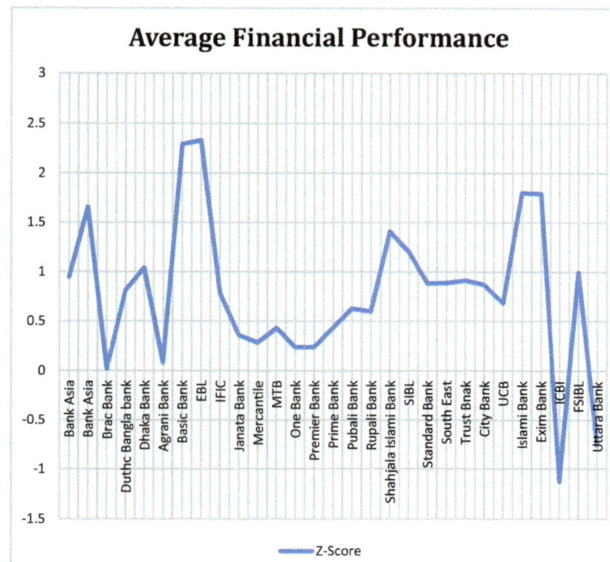

Figure 1: Average financial performance.

Year	Z-Score	Indicator	Average
2009	-0.599078531	Insolvent	
2010	-0.782417352	Insolvent	
2011	-0.327403766	Insolvent	
2012	-0.721857246	Insolvent	-0.751652157
2013	-1.028852892	Insolvent	
2014	-1.050303155	Insolvent	Insolvent

Table 30: Data analysis of Uttara Bank limited.

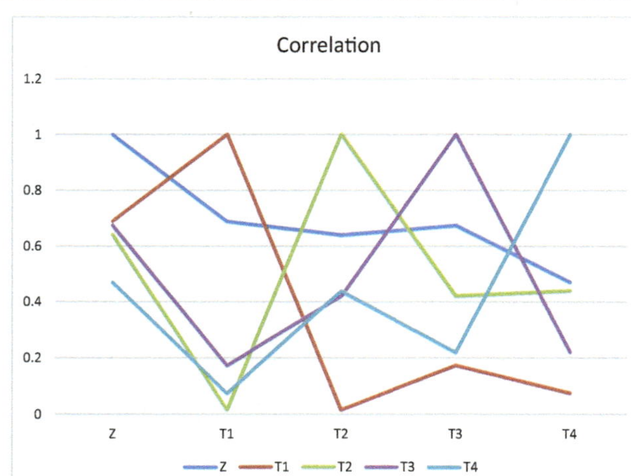

Figure 2: Correlation.

	Z	T1	T2	T3	T4
Mean	0.79913588	0.011474992	0.01186953	0.083804399	0.116190192
Median	0.757624466	0.007265134	0.00964133	0.079863541	0.089687656
Maximum	7.303866779	0.999496369	1	0.667849565	1.13207154
Minimum	-3.353078608	-0.249722417	-1.05443415	-0.080724046	-0.364242531
Std. Dev.	1.187709592	0.109992254	0.147218575	0.064100823	0.191040839

Table 31: Descriptive Statistics.

	Z	T1	T2	T3	T4
Z	1	0.688157	0.638977	0.673559	0.470427
T1	0.688157	1	0.014205	0.171937	0.074284
T2	0.638977	0.014205	1	0.419615	0.438622
T3	0.673559	0.171937	0.419615	1	0.218286
T4	0.470427	0.074284	0.438622	0.218286	1

Table 32: Correlation.

Variable	Coefficient	Std. Error	t-Statistic	Prob.
C	-5.75E-10	3.78E-10	-1.52114	0.130094
T1	6.56	1.92E-09	3.42E+09	0
T2	3.26	1.69E-09	1.93E+09	0
T3	6.72	3.61E-09	1.86E+09	0
T4	1.05	1.21E-09	8.69E+08	0

Table 33: Regression.

the Probability (F-Statistics), as a result all alternate hypothesis will be accepted and all null hypothesis will be rejected. And the model is good fit (Table 34).

Significance of the Study

The aim of this research was to analyse the financial performance of Bangladeshi banks using statistical analysis of summary financial information and selected financial ratios. Here are some significant finding of this research:

- Here, R2=100%, all independent variable together explain the dependent variable. As a result all alternate hypothesis will be accepted and all null hypothesis will be rejected.
- Significance level is 0.01 greater than the Probability (F-Statistics), as a result all alternate hypothesis will be accepted and all null hypothesis will be rejected.
- Correlations of T1, T2, T3 and T4 with Z are positive so null hypothesis is rejected and alternate hypothesis is accepted.
- Based on the level of mean, the condition of banks is not good because here highest mean is T2 between T1- T4.
- Median is affective to protect bankruptcy because the level of median is lower number then proper number of standard.
- Based on minimum Z score and average Z-Score they show that financial position of 22 banks are insolvent and 7 banks are healthy during the time period.
- Standard Deviation of Z-score is comparatively higher than T1, T2, T3 and T4.
- Some banks have negative working capital, so they cannot liquidate day to day business. But banks cover that liquidity by using long-term Liability (Fixed Deposited).
- Most of banks have low equity than liability. Because they are taking more deposit than loans.

R-squared	1	Mean dependent var	0.799136
Adjusted R-squared	1	S.D. dependent var	1.18771
S.E. of regression	2.72E-09	**Log likelihood**	3187.484
Sum squared resid	1.25E-15	**F-statistic**	8.26E+18
Prob(F-statistic)	0		

Table 34: Alternate Hypothesis.

In all testes all the null hypothesis are rejected, so we can say that there is a relationship between the independent variables and the dependent variable.

Conclusion

The financial sector of Bangladesh is mostly small and developing. This sector resides of banking and an emerging capital market. The banking sector in the country comparatively more developed than the equity market, even though both are developing in international benchmark (Table 34). The basic reasons of the Bangladeshi financial sector barriers are lack of market discipline due to lack of rivalry in the banking industry. Excessive government involvement and political influences, economic and political corruptions, operational and managerial disorganization and incompetence result vicious cycle. For this reasons we are far away from economic development, industrialization, and social progress [30]. From this research it is found that most of Islamic Banks are doing well than other banks. Their Z-Score is better comparing to standard. Most of the state-owned bank used to follow the traditional working procedures few years ago. But our state owned banks are now doing better than before for adopting of IT. By managing working capital and credit risk all Banks will do better in Future. Those banks that have negative Z-Score they should take some immediate steps to reduce doubt about their going concern. So after this research with sample size of 29 banks, it can be easily understand that on an average all rivalry banks are doing better and soon they will overcome their existing problems.

References

1. Beaver WH (1966) Financial Ratios as Predictors of Failure, J Account Res: Empirical Research in Accounting: Selected Studies 4: 71-111.
2. Altman EI (1968) Financial Ratios, Discriminant Analysis and Prediction of Corporate. J Fin 23: 589-609.
3. Altman EI (1994) Corporate Distress Diagnosis: Comparisons Using Linear Discriminant Analysis and Neural Networks (the Italian Experience). J Banking Financ 18: 505-529.
4. Mahtab N (2013) Financial Performance of Conventional and Islamic Banks in Bangladesh: An Analysis Based on Rati.
5. Staff C (2012) The Altman Z-Score. American Association of Individual Investors.
6. Altman EI (1995) Emerging Markets Corporate Bonds: A Scoring System. Salomon Brothers Inc, New York, USA.
7. Lawrence EC, Robert M (1986) Corporate Bankruptcy Prediction and the Impact of Leases. J Bus Financ Account 13: 571-585.
8. Chieng JR (2013) Verifying the Validity of Altman's Z" Score as a Predictor of Bank Failures in the Case of the Eurozone. National College of Ireland, Ireland.
9. Chowdhury A (2009) Rationalities of Z-Category shares in Dhaka Stock Exchange: Are they in financial distress risk? BRAC University Journal 1: 45-58.
10. Gritta R (1982) Bankruptcy Risks Facing the Major U.S. Airlines. Journal of Air Law & Commerce 36: 83-108.
11. Aiyabei J (2002) Financial Distress: Theory, Measurement and Consequence. The Eastern Africa Journal of Humanities and Sciences.
12. Piesse LL (2003) Financial risk assessment in takeover: The effect of bidder firm shareholders wealth. International Journal of Risk Assessment and Management 4: 332-347.
13. Richard D, Bahram A. (2008) An Update on Airline Financial Condition and Insolvency Prospects Using the Altman Z Score Model, Transportation Research Forum 47: 133-138.
14. Agha H (2014) Impact of Working Capital management on profitability. European Scientfic Journal.
15. Rehman MU, N Anjum (2013) Determination of the impact of working capital management on profitability.
16. Eljelly A (2004) Liquidity-Profitability Tradeoff: An empirical Investigation in an Emerging Market. Int J Commerce Management 8: 48-61.
17. Deloof M (2003) Does Working Capital Management Affects Profitability of Belgian Firms? Journal of Business Finance & Accounting 10: 573-587.
18. Kasilingam DG (2012) Profitability and solvency analysis of a manufacturing company using dupont and Altman model.
19. Mamo AQ (1968) Applicability of Altman model in predicting financial distress of commercial banks in Kenya.
20. Muthukumar G, Sekar M (2014) Fiscal Fitness of Select Automobile Companies in India: Application of Z-score and Springate Models.
21. Sasivimol M, Polwat L (2014) Applying Emerging Market Z-Score Model to Predict Bankruptcy: A Case Study of Listed Companies in the Stock Exchange of Thailand.
22. Lucarelli A (2013) Using the Z- scores as a turnaround tools.
23. Parvez A (2014) Evaluating the financial Health of Steel authority of India limited using Altman's Z Score Model.
24. Chouhan V, Chandra B (2014) Predicting financial stability of select BSE companies revisiting Altman Z score. International Letters of Social and Humanistic Sciences 26: 92-105.
25. Thai GA (2014) A Revisited of Altman Z-Score Model for Companies Listed in Bursa Malaysia. International Journal of Business and Social Science 5: 197-206.
26. Miller MA (1963) Corporate income taxes and the cost of capital: A correction. American Economic Review 53: 433-443.
27. Tyagi V (2014) A Study to Measures the Financial Health of Selected Firms with Special Reference to Indian Logistic Industry: An Application Of Altman's Z Score. Industrial Engineering Letters 4: 43-51.
28. David PLL (2012) Bankruptcy and Financial Standing Models Application for SMEs. The Seventh International Conference on Software Engineering Advances.
29. OECD (2013) Financial Balance Sheets. National Accounts of OECD Countries.
30. Abdullah M (2015) In Industry Wise Contribution to Bangladeshi Gross Domestic Product: In Which industry we should emphasize more.

Relationship between Spot and Futures Markets of Selected Agricultural Commodities in India: An Efficiency and Causation Analysis

Raghavendra RH*, Velmurugan PS and Saravanan A

Department of Commerce, School of Management, Pondicherry University (A Central University), Pondicherry, 605 014, India

Abstract

This study empirically examines the market which reacts first in India by assessing the relationship between spot and future prices of agricultural commodities such as Soya bean, Chana, Maize, Jeera and Turmeric for a period from January 2010 to March 2015 traded in NCDEX, Empirical results suggest the existence of long-run equilibrium relationships between futures and spot prices for all the 5 agricultural commodities that were taken for this study. Regression model pertaining to Lead-Lag relationship between Spot and Future markets suggests that for the commodities Maize, Jeera and Turmeric, both the spot and future markets price plays the leading role in the price discovery process and said to be informationally efficient and reacts more quickly to each other.

Keywords: Agriculture; Price discovery; Regression model; Futures; Cointegration

Introduction

The agricultural production system in India has undergone profound changes over the decades due to adoption of green revolution technologies coupled with price support policy of the government [1]. After independence, various policy initiatives undertaken for protecting agriculture sector affected the growth in agricultural commodities markets adversely. The Essential Commodities Act 1955 envisaged price and movement protection applicable to various agricultural commodities, particularly food grains such as paddy, wheat, coarse grains and pulses to protect the interests of producers as well as of consumers. During the process of economic liberalization, it was felt that there is a need to reorient policies and regulations in agricultural commodities. The Khusro Committee recommended reintroduction of futures trading in most of the major commodities [2]. The Government of India constituted another committee headed by Professor K.N. Kabra in June 1993 on Forward Markets [3], which also emphasized the need for introduction of futures trading in 17 commodity groups covering a wide range of agricultural commodities. It also recommended strengthening of the Forward Markets Commission (FMC) and various amendments in Forward Contracts (Regulation) Act 1952 to bring fairness and efficiency in futures trading operations.

The National Agriculture Policy announced in July 2000 envisaged external and domestic market reforms by putting in place a mechanism of futures trade/market and dismantling of all control and regulations in agricultural commodity market [4]. As a result, the Government of India issued notifications on April 1, 2003 and permitted futures trading (except options trading) for a wide range of agricultural commodities.

Distress sale of agricultural commodities immediately after harvesting due to lack of farmers' capacity to wait for opportune time for getting remunerative prices and also because of the uncertainty involved in possible future prices has always been one of the major concerns for producers as well as consumers [4-6]. Futures contracts help in performing two important management functions, i.e. price discovery and price risk management for the specific commodity [4,7,8]. Price discovery is the process of revealing information about future spot prices through the future markets. It is useful for producers as they get a fair idea about the prices likely to prevail at a future point of time and hence, can allocate their limited available resources among various competing commodities for optimizing their profits. It also provides food processors and consumers an idea about prices at which the specific commodity would be available at a future point of time. Although futures trading in a large number of agricultural commodities were re-introduced in India in the year 2003, government is always skeptical about its efficiency and likely impact on the price movement of agricultural commodities. The ban on futures trading of some major agricultural commodities in February 2007 makes it imperative to explore whether the futures market has really been able to achieve its above-stated objectives of price discovery and risk management or not. Thus, understanding the influence of one market on the other and role of each market segment in price discovery is the central question in market microstructure design and has become an increasingly important research issue among academicians, regulators and practitioners alike as it provides an idea about the market efficiency, volatility, hedging effectiveness and arbitrage opportunities, if any.

The essence of the price discovery function hinges on whether new information is reflected first in changes of future prices or changes of spot prices. Hence, there exists lead-lag relationship between spot and futures market by information dissemination. All the information available in the market place is immediately incorporated in the prices of assets in an efficient market. So, new information disseminating into the market should be reflected immediately in spot and futures prices simultaneously. This will lead to perfect positive contemporaneous co movement between the prices of those markets and there will be no systematic lagged response and therefore no arbitrage opportunity.

***Corresponding author:** Raghavendra RH, Research Scholar, Department of Commerce, School of Management, Pondicherry University (A Central University), Pondicherry-605 014, India, E-mail: raghavpondiuni@gmail.com

This prediction arises directly from the Cost of Carry (COC) model of future pricing which postulates that

$$Ft = S_t e^{(r-y)(T-t)} \quad (1)$$

where, Ft is the futures price of the commodity at time t, St is the spot price of the commodity at time t, r is the interest rate foregone while carrying the underlying commodity, y is the price fluctuation on the commodity and T-t is the remaining life of the futures contract. Equation (1) is justified by a "no-arbitrage" assumption, since Ft > Ste (r-y) (T-t) would enable traders/ farmers to profit by selling futures and buying at spot, while Ste (r-y) (T-t) > Ft would allow profits by buying futures and short selling at spot. The assumptions that underlie these arguments are that future and spot markets are perfectly efficient, and that transaction costs are zero. This simple version of the model also assumes that the interest rate and addition to price are constant over the life of the futures contract, although in practice they will vary, as will r – y, the net cost of carry of the underlying commodity. Most importantly, in the real world, the existence of market frictions such as transaction costs, margin requirements, short-sale constraints, liquidity differences and non-synchronous trading effects may induce lead-lag relationship between the futures contract and its underlying spot market. In addition, if there are economic incentives for traders to use one market over the other, a price discovery process between the two markets is likely to happen [9]. This implies that futures and spot market prices are inter-related and can be traced under different market frictions through price discovery mechanism.

Accordingly, there exist diversified theoretical arguments pertaining to the causal relationship between spot and futures markets by information dissemination. The main arguments in favor of futures market leads spot market are mainly due to the advantages provided by the futures market includes higher liquidity, lower transaction costs, lower margins, ease leverage positions, rapid execution and greater flexibility for short positions. Such advantages attract larger informed farmers/ traders and make the futures market to react first when market- wide information or major stock-specific information arrives. Thus, the future prices lead the spot market prices. In addition, the low cost contingent strategies and high degree of leverage benefits in futures market attracts larger speculative traders from a spot market to a more regulated futures market segments, leading to reduction in informational asymmetries of the spot market through reducing the amount of noise trading, helping price discovery, improving the overall market depth, enhancing market efficiency, and increase market liquidity.

In such a situation, the spot market will react first when market-wide information or major stock- specific information arrives. Hence, spot market leads the futures market. Besides, there exists a bidirectional relationship between the futures and spot markets through price discovery process [10-14], where both the spot and future markets are said to be informationally efficient and reacts more quickly to each other. However, frictions in markets, in terms of transaction costs and information asymmetry, may lead to return and volatility spillovers between spot and futures markets. Besides being of academic interest, understanding information flow across markets is also important for hedgers for hedging and devising cross-market investment strategies. This paper analyzes the issue of price on futures and spot markets which is of interest to traders, financial economists and analysts. Although futures and spot markets react to the same information, the major question is which market reacts first in agricultural commodity markets in India by assessing the relationship between the spot and future prices of Soya bean, Chana, Maize, Jeera and Turmeric commodities traded in NCDEX for the period from January 2010 to March, 2015 (Table 1).

Review of Literature

This section outlines both theoretical as well as empirical literature related to analyzing the theoretical arguments on the major question that which market price reacts first whether (a) futures prices tend to influence spot prices or (b) spot prices tend to lead futures prices or (c) a bidirectional feedback relationship exists between spot and futures prices.

Jian Yang and David J Leatham examined the price discovery function for three U.S. wheat futures markets, the Chicago Board of

Symbol	Soya bean	Turmeric	Jeera	Chana	Maize
Description	SYBEANIDR	TMCFGRNZM	JEERAUNJHA	CHILLI	MAIZEKHRF
Trading system	NCDEX Trading System	NCDEX Trading System	NCDEX Trading System	NCDEX Trading System	NCDEX Trading System
Hours of Trading	Mondays through Fridays : 10:00 AM to 05:00 PM	Mondays through Fridays : 10:00 AM to 05:00 PM Saturdays : 10.00 AM to 2.00 PM	Mondays through Fridays : 10:00 AM to 05:00 PM	Mondays through Fridays : 10:00 AM to 05:00 PM	Mondays through Fridays: 10:00 a.m. to 11.30 p.m./ 11.55 p.m
Trading unit	10 MT	5 MT	3 MT	5 MT	10 MT
Quot/BaseVal	Rs per Quintal	Rs. Per Quintal	Rs per Quintal	Rs. Per Quintal	Rs. Per Quintal
Tick size	Rs. 1/-	Rs. 2	Rs 5	Rs. 2	Re. 1
Max order size	500 MT	250 MT	150 MT	150 MT	500 MT
Delivery center	Indore	Nizamabad	Unjha	Khammam	Gulabbagh
Initial margin	5%	5%	5%	5%	5%
Opening of contracts	Trading in any contract month will open on the 10th of the month. If the 10th day happens to be a non-trading day, contracts would open on the next trading day	Trading in any contract month will open on the 1st day of the month. If 1st happens to be a non-trading day, contracts would open on the next trading day	-do-	-do-	-do-
Final Settlement Price	The Final Settlement Price (FSP) shall be arrived at by taking the simple average of the last polled spot prices of the last three trading days,	The FSP shall be arrived at by taking the simple average of the last polled spot prices of the last three trading days	-do-	-do-	-do-

Source: Contract specification, NCDEX, India

Table 1: Future contract specifications of selected agricultural commodities traded in NCDEX

Trade, Kansas City Board of Trade, and Minneapolis Grain Exchange. The maintained hypothesis is that futures markets search more for information than spot markets to find an equilibrium price, thus greatly improving the price discovery function. The tests reveal the existence of one equilibrium price across the three futures markets in the long run, but no cointegration among prices in the three represent active spot markets.

Silvapulle and Moosa investigated the relationship between futures and spot prices for the WTI crude oil, using daily observations during the period from 1985 to 1996. Linear causality tests revealed that futures prices lead spot prices, while nonlinear causality tests showed that bidirectional causality between the two markets exists. In particular, they detected feedback from spot prices to futures prices and also that both the futures and the spot market react to new information at the same time. However, they indicated that this lead lag relationship varies significantly over different time periods. Summarizing, it should be pointed out that even if the futures market holds the dominant role to the price discovery procedure, the spot market plays an essential role for its function as well [15].

Fabio Mattos, Philip Garcia investigates the relationship between spot and futures prices in the Brazilian agricultural market, focusing on the effects of trading activity on the price discovery mechanism of futures markets. The results are mixed, but several points begin to emerge. In general, higher trading activity is linked to the presence of long-run equilibrium relationships between spot and futures prices. In these cases, futures prices appear to play a more dominant role in the pricing process. In more lightly traded markets, neither long run relationships nor short-run leads and lags can be found.

Kumar and Sunil investigated the price discovery in six Indian commodity exchanges for five commodities. For their study they have used the daily futures and spot price and also engaged the ratio of standard deviations of spot and future rates for empirical testing of ability of futures markets to incorporate information efficiently. Besides, the study has empirically analyzed the efficiency of spot and future markets by employing the Johansen cointegration technique. They found that inability of future market to fully incorporate information and confirmed inefficiency of future market. However, the authors concluded that the Indian agricultural commodities future markets are not yet mature and efficient [16].

Zapata, Fortenbery and Armstrong examined the relationship between 11 future prices traded in New York and the World spot prices for exported sugar by considering the observation from January 1990 to January 1995. They found that the future market for sugar leads the cash market in price discovery. However, they also found unidirectional causality from future price to spot but not vice versa. The finding of cointegration between futures and cash prices suggests that sugar future contract is a useful vehicle for reducing overall market price risk faced by spot market participants selling at the world price.

Kedarnath discussed the significance of price discovery and risk management by commodity futures for the development of commodity spot market in India. The result of interdependence between commodity future and spot market in agricultural commodities also supported the relevance of commodity future trading in Indian commodity market.

Jabir Ali, Kriti Bardhan Gupta analyzed the efficiency of agricultural commodity markets by assessing the relationships between futures prices and spot market prices of major agricultural commodities in India. The efficiency of the futures market for 12 agricultural commodities for the period of 2004 to 2007, traded at one of the largest commodity exchanges of India, i.e., National Commodity and Derivatives Exchange Ltd, has been explored by using Johansen's cointegration analysis and Granger causality tests. Unit root test procedures such as Augmented Dickey-Fuller and non-parametric Phillips-Perron were initially applied to examine whether futures and spot prices are stationary or not. Results show that cointegration exists significantly in futures and spot prices for all the selected agricultural commodities except for wheat and rice. This suggest that there is a long-term relationship between futures and spot prices for most of the agricultural commodities like maize, chickpea, black lentil, pepper, castor seed, soybean and sugar. The causality test further distinguishes and categorizes the commodities based on direction of relationship between futures and spot prices. The analysis of short-term relationship by causality test indicates that futures markets have stronger ability to predict subsequent spot prices for chickpea, castor seed, soybean and sugar as compared to maize, black lentil and pepper, where bi-directional relationships exist in the short run.

Given the above background, it should be pointed out that the above existing literatures pertaining to lead-lag relationship between price changes in international and domestic futures and spot markets are well established by information dissemination. They are related to different countries and consequently with different commodity market structure and macroeconomic fundamentals. Further, samples are drawn at different time periods and employed different models with different assumptions and obviously their results are mixed. Further, there is no specific study on these 5 agricultural commodities based on NCDEX data during the post global economic crisis period.

Hence based on the research gap, the present study attempts to investigate which market price reacts first between spot and futures prices of selected agricultural commodities traded in NCDEX, using ADF and PP test, Cointegration and Regression Model pertaining to Lead-Lag relationship between Spot and Future Markets.

Data Source and Methodology

Data and tools used

We used daily data of spot and future price of Soya bean, Chana, Maize, Jeera, and Turmeric for the period from January 2010 to March 2015 collected from National Commodity and Derivative Exchange (NCDEX). Rationale behind selecting these five agricultural commodities is that currently these five commodities' contracts are the most active trading contracts in NCDEX. In this study, the techniques used for analysis are panel unit root test which is Augmented Dickey-Fuller (ADF) test or Phillips-Perron (PP) test, Johansen Co-integration test and Regression Model pertaining to analyzing the Lead-Lag relationship between Spot and Future Markets.

Johansen's Cointegration and Regression model were employed to examine the lead-lag relationship between spot and futures markets of the selected agricultural commodities. Augmented Dickey-Fuller and Phillips-Perron tests were employed to verify the stationarity of the data series. Further, the necessary lag length of the data series was selected on the basis of Schwarz Information Criterion (SC). Johansen's Cointegration test is employed to examine long-run relationship among the variables after they are integrated in an identical order.

After identifying cointegration between spot and future prices of the selected agricultural commodities, the regression model was employed to examine the lead-lag relationship between the two and it is presented below:

$$\Delta SPOT_t = C_1 + \sum_{k=1}^{n} \alpha_{1i} \Delta SPOT_{t-k} + \sum_{k=1}^{n} \beta_{2i} \Delta FUT_{t-k} + u_{1t}$$

$$\Delta FUT = C_2 + \sum_{k=1}^{n} \beta_{1i} \Delta FUT_{t-k} + \sum_{k=1}^{n} \alpha_{2i} \Delta SPOT_{t-k} + u_{2t}$$

Where, SPOTt and FUTt are spot and future market prices of individual agricultural prices at time t, u_{1t} and u_{2t} are white noise disturbance terms. The analysis of unit root, co-integration and causality tests for different commodities were performed using econometric software Eviews Version 6.

Results and Discussion

Figures 1-5 plot the daily spot and future price movement of five Indian agricultural commodities viz., Soya bean, Chana, Maize, Jeera and Turmeric.

While observing the above graphs we can come to a conclusion that the futures price of agricultural commodity and the underlying spot market are moving into same direction. So there may be a chance to have an influence by the price of futures on the commodity spot market. In the coming part of the paper, examining the interrelation between spot and futures prices of selected agricultural commodities traded in NCDEX.

Descriptive statistics

Table 2 presents descriptive statistics for 5 spice agricultural commodities Chilli, Coriander, Jeera, Pepper and Turmeric traded in NCDEX India, from Januray 2010 - March 2015. The mean spot prices are Rs 3050.80, Rs. 3330.85, Rs. 1244.22, Rs.13702.00 and Rs.7712.95 for Soya bean, Chana, Maize, Jeera and Turmeric respectively. Similarly, the mean futures prices are Rs.3020.63, Rs.3316.57, Rs.1226.92, Rs.13930.47 and Rs.7358.54 for Soya bean, Chana, Maize, Jeera and Turermic respectively.

The mean spot prices Soya bean, Chana, Maize and Turmeric are more than their mean future prices, except Jeera. Standard deviation, which is a tool for measuring volatility shows that the spot price of Soya bean, Chana and Turmeric are more volatile compared to their future prices. Whereas in the case of Jeera and Maize, the future prices are more volatile than the spot prices. Normality is tested using Jarque-

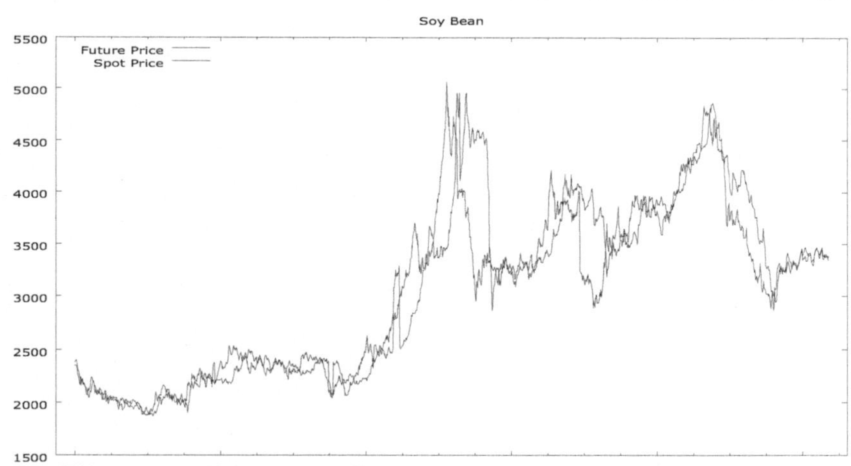

Figure 1: Yearly plotting of spot and future price movements of soyabean.

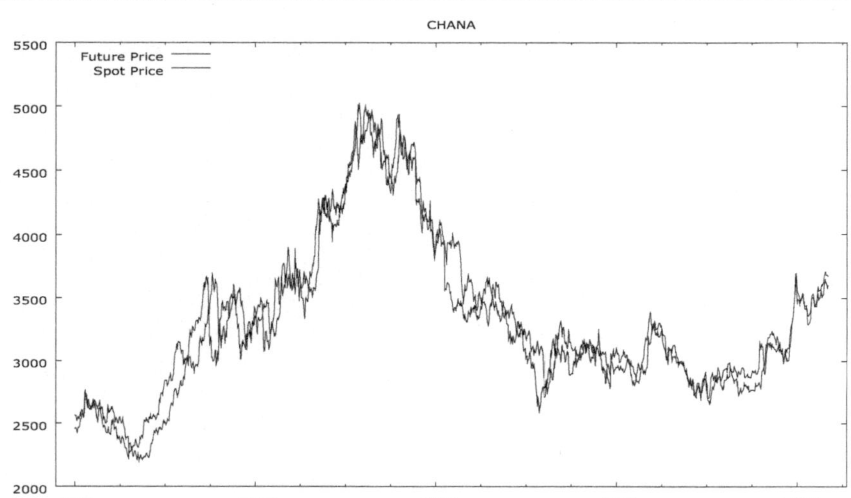

Figure 2: Yearly plotting of spot and future price movements of chana.

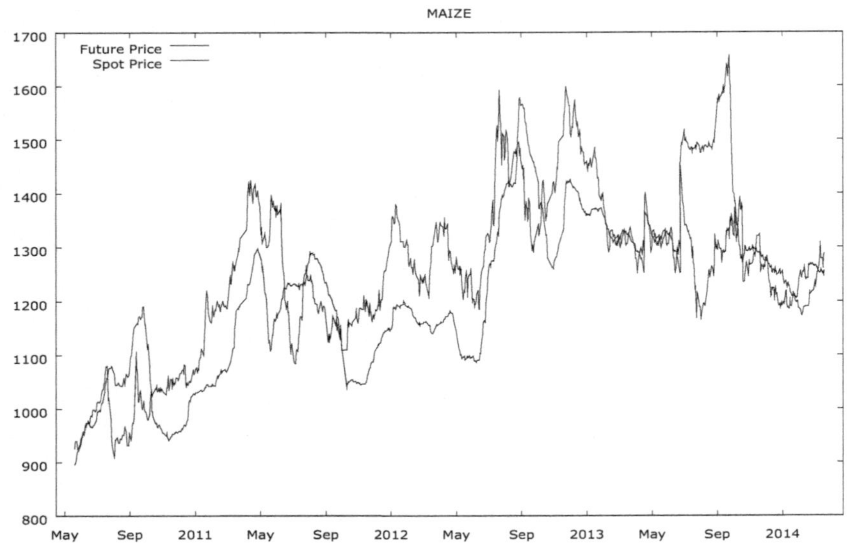

Figure 3: Yearly plotting of spot and future price movements of maize.

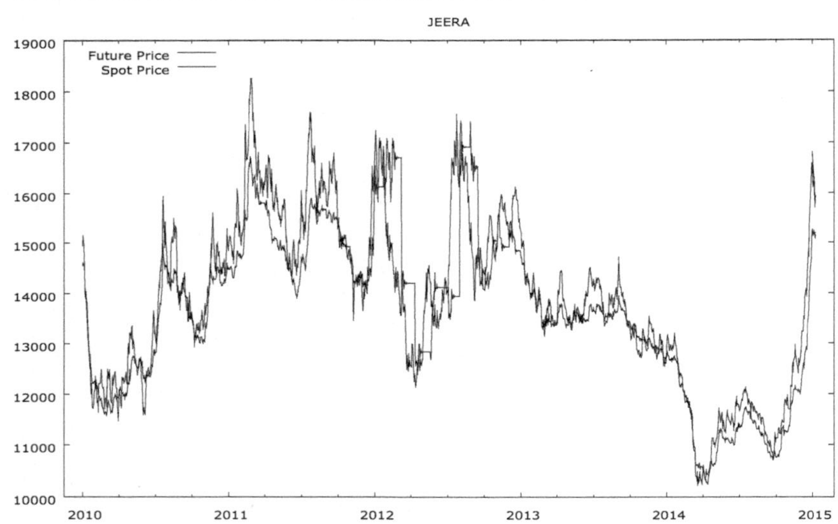

Figure 4: Yearly plotting of spot and future price movements of jeera.

		Mean	Std. Dev.	Skewness	Kurtosis	Jarque-Bera	Probability
Soy Bean	Spot	3050.8060	837.6233	0.2612	1.7829	111.9836	0.0000
	Future	3020.6360	767.9924	0.2783	1.9711	87.3511	0.0000
Chana	Spot	3330.8530	633.9555	0.7454	3.0603	114.5549	0.0000
	Future	3316.5680	616.6130	0.8213	3.0841	139.2204	0.0000
Maize	Spot	1244.2240	141.2040	-0.2368	2.8247	10.9058	0.0043
	Future	1226.9210	157.7985	0.1975	2.5725	14.4829	0.0007
Jeera	Spot	13702.0100	1542.3830	-0.0690	2.5067	16.5198	0.0003
	Future	13930.4700	1634.3680	0.0305	2.4297	20.7128	0.0000
Turmeric	Spot	7712.9580	3720.3760	1.1642	2.9688	337.7515	0.0000
	Future	7358.5490	2718.7310	1.2149	3.7900	406.6315	0.0000

Note: * 1% level significant

Sources: Calculated by the authors' using Eviews

Table 2: Descriptive statistics of different agricultural products.

Bera test, where it is found the data attained normality at 1% level. Kurtosis of the normal distribution is 3 for Chana spot and future and Turmeric futures. For all other commodities it is below 3. Finally, regarding the asymmetry of the distribution of the series around their

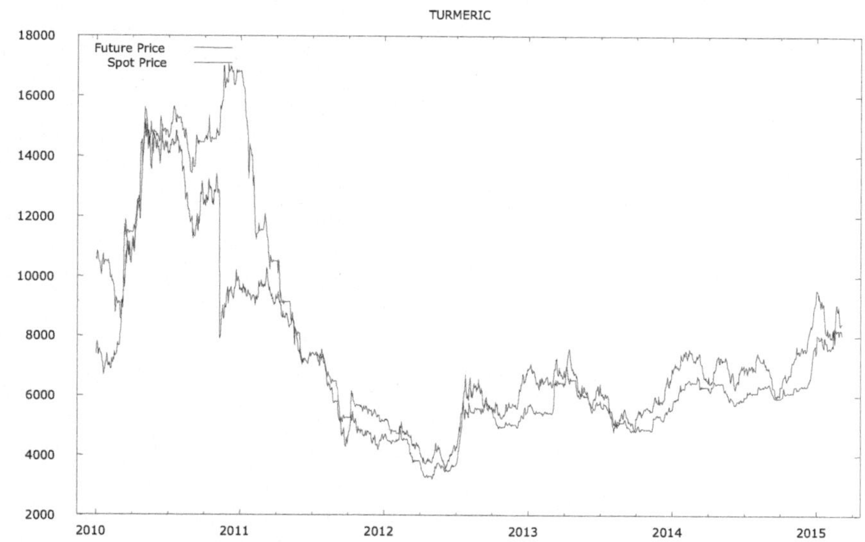

Figure 5: Yearly plotting of spot and future price movements of turmeric.

		ADF Test			PP Test		
		Intercept	Intercept and Trend	No Intercept or Trend	Intercept	Intercept and Trend	No Intercept or Trend
Panel A: Level							
Soy Bean	Spot	-1.5361	-2.3245	0.0071	-1.5834	-2.4034	-0.0151
	Future	-1.6856	-1.6711	0.0038	-1.7309	-1.7204	-0.0412
Chana	Spot	1.3042	-1.2536	2.5519	1.2841	-1.2692	2.5240
	Future	0.1086	-1.9616	1.4679	0.1351	-1.9266	1.5171
Maize	Spot	-1.9639	-1.8611	-0.1262	-2.3141	-2.2742	-0.1716
	Future	-2.3389	-2.2527	-0.1494	-2.5774	-2.5311	-0.1757
Jeera	Spot	-1.5495	-0.6471	1.1911	-1.5125	-0.9080	1.0570
	Future	-1.5911	-1.2498	0.7440	-1.5853	-1.0966	0.8441
Turmeric	Spot	-1.0445	-0.6875	-0.8123	-1.1253	-0.8398	-0.8272
	Future	-1.2428	-1.1759	-0.1910	-1.3293	-1.2957	-0.2300
Panel B: First-difference							
Soy Bean	Spot	-26.3648*	-26.3540*	-26.3732*	-25.8837*	-25.8720*	-25.8949*
	Future	-29.5034*	-29.4928*	-29.5102*	-29.7074*	-29.6967*	-29.7155*
Chana	Spot	-37.4737*	-37.5825*	-37.3700*	-37.4637*	-37.5625*	-37.3873*
	Future	-35.0390*	-35.0673*	-34.9870	-35.0200	-35.0787*	-34.99621
Maize	Spot	-37.5966*	-37.5943*	-37.6089*	-37.9334*	-37.9271*	-37.9447*
	Future	-37.1192*	-37.1183*	-37.1313*	-37.1695*	-37.1670*	-37.1814*
Jeera	Spot	-15.8670*	-15.9375*	-15.7552*	-30.9909*	-30.8946*	-31.0035*
	Future	-28.1958*	-28.2217*	-28.1607*	-28.1945*	-28.2193*	-28.1607*
Turmeric	Spot	-32.1049*	-32.1108*	-32.1115*	-32.6203*	-32.6107*	-32.6307*
	Future	-36.3570*	-36.3511*	-36.3681*	-36.3504*	-36.3437*	-36.3617*

*1% and **5% level significant

Sources: Calculated by the authors' using Eviews

Table 3: ADF test and PP test results.

mean, we found negative skewness for spot price of Maize and Jeera. For all other remaining price series is Soya bean, Chana and Turmeric there is positive skewness during the period of study.

Unit root test

In order to examine the cointegration of spot and futures prices of the selected commodity price series, it is customary to first examine the level of integration in each of the given commodity price series. This can be done by examining the unit root properties in each commodity price series. In this paper, we use the augmented Dickey-Fuller (ADF) test and the Phillips-Perron (PP) test to examine whether the sample commodity price series are stationary. Both tests are based on the null hypothesis that the series is unit root. Both tests are used without intercept and trend, with intercept and with intercept and trend. The ADF test assumes homogeneity in the disturbance term. However, the heterogeneity and temporary dependence in the disturbance term is accounted by the PP test.

Table 3 presents the results of ADF and PP tests for spot and future price of agricultural commodities Soya bean, Coriander, Jeera, Pepper and Turmeric traded in NCDEX India, from Januray 2010 - December 2015. Panel A in Table 3 presents the results of unit root tests in level series. Results show the non-rejection of the null hypothesis of the ADF and PP test for the selected agricultural commodity price series indicating that all the commodity price series under study are non-stationary series. Panel B in Table 3 reports the results of unit root tests in the first difference series. Results indicate that all commodity price series are I (1), that is, all the series become stationary after first difference. Hence, we can go forward to test the cointegration among them using Johansen cointegration test.

Johansen co-integration test

After testing the precondition of non-stationary time series (i.e. the series were stationary at their first difference) Johansen and Juselius cointegration test has been carried out to determine the existence of a long-run relationship between the selected agricultural commodities traded in NCDEX. Johansen Co-integration Test for agricultural commodities spot and future price in five groups was tested and displayed in Table 4. The results show that all the above 5 group of selected agricultural commodities, there is evidence of co-integrating vector(s) according to the Trace statistic. That is between (a) Soya bean spot price and future price, (b) Chana spot price and future price (c) Maize spot price and future price (d) Jeera spot price and future price (e) Turmeric spot price and future price.

The co-integration results indicate that the H_0 of zero can be rejected using the 95% critical value. This implies that the selected commodities spot and future prices are co-integrated with one co-integrating vector. The existence of cointegration between the spot and futures prices confirms the first necessary condition for long-term market relationship. Based on the cointegration test, we find that there is a long-market relationship in all the above 5 agricultural commodities traded in India (Soya bean, Chana, Maize, Jeera and Turmeric).

Regression model for ascertaining lead-lag relationship

The above Table 5 results of regression model reveal mixed findings. There is one-way causal linkage from future market to spot market prices for two agricultural commodities, viz., Soya bean and Chana. This indicates that information gets reflected first in the future prices and then it transmitted to spot market prices in the above two agricultural commodities. Further, the table result also confirms the

Name of the Commodity	Ho: vector (r)	Trace statistic	p-value	Max-Eigen Statistics	p-value
Soy Bean	r = 0	57.47021	0.0000*	54.90166	0.0000*
	r ≤ 1	2.568548	0.1090	2.568548	0.1090
Chana	r = 0	80.73057	0.0000*	81.73057	0.0000*
	r ≤ 1	2.382425	0.1081	2.582425	0.1081
Maize	r = 0	22.85695	0.0033*	15.72411	0.0292**
	r ≤ 1	7.132841	0.0076*	7.132841	0.0076*
Jeera	r = 0	72.44795	0.0000*	65.51446	0.0000*
	r ≤ 1	6.933486	0.0085*	6.933486	0.0085*
Turmeric	r = 0	20.39199	0.0084*	19.30953	0.0073*
	r ≤ 1	1.082463	0.2981	1.082463	0.2981

*1% and **5% level significant

Sources: Calculated by the authors' using Eviews

Table 4: Johansen co-integration test results.

	Regression Equation	C	$\Delta SPOT_{t-1}$	$\Delta SPOT_{t-2}$	ΔFUT_{t-1}	ΔFUT_{t-2}	Log Likelihood	Inference
Soy Bean	ΔF on ΔS	7.9441	-0.0371	0.0314	1.0498	-0.0465	-8152.103	F→S
		(0.1279)	(0.1329)	(0.1959)	(0.0000)*	(0.0240)**		
	ΔS on ΔF	-6.0926	1.1228	-0.1489	0.0725	0.0168	-8189.723	
		(0.2545)	(0.0000)*	(0.0000)*	(0.0035)*	(0.5279)		
Chana	ΔF on ΔS	14.5649	0.0167	-0.0127	1.0255	-0.0337	-6618.622	F→S
		(0.0747)	(0.6195)	(0.6964)	(0.0000)*	(0.2558)		
	ΔS on ΔF	-0.8166	1.0748	-0.1386	0.0674	-0.0029	-6411.629	
		(0.9059)	(0.0000)*	(0.0000)*	(0.0055)*	(0.9079)		
Maize	ΔF on ΔS	13.3268	-0.0259	0.0257	1.0226	-0.0328	-4394.794	F↔S
		(0.0091)*	(0.5968)	(0.5981)*	(0.0000)*	(0.3028)		
	ΔS on ΔF	1.055101	1.1942	-0.2063	7.91E-06	0.9625	-3926.328	
		(0.7438)	(0.0000)*	(0.0000)*	(0.9997)	(0.0000)*		
Jeera	ΔF on ΔS	117.8588	0.1480	-0.1449	1.0215	-0.0330	-10159.98	F↔S
		(0.0134)**	(0.0000)*	(0.0000)*	(0.0000)*	(0.2155)		
	ΔS on ΔF	31.3169	0.9694	-0.0174	0.0803	-0.0353	-9767.564	
		(0.3934)	(0.0000)*	(0.4948)	(0.0001)*	(0.0852)		
Turmeric	ΔF on ΔS	24.0386	1.0055	0.0096	1.0589	-0.0664	-9928.237	F↔S
		(0.0994)	(0.0000)*	(0.7797)	(0.0000)*	(0.0110)**		
	ΔS on ΔF	-20.1513	1.1715	-0.1801	0.0713	0.0077	-9478.873	
		(0.0620)	(0.0000)*	(0.0000)*	(0.0043)*	(0.6900)		

Notes: Parenthesis shows t-statistics *1% and **5% level significant

Sources: Calculated by the authors' using Eviews

Table 5: Regression model.

bidirectional relationship between commodity futures and spot market for three selected agricultural commodities viz., Maize, Jeera and Turmeric. This reveals that both the spot and future markets price of these three agricultural commodities plays the leading role in the price discovery process and said to be informationally efficient and reacts more quickly to each other.

Conclusion

The future markets of agricultural commodity depends on the transparency and efficiency of its functioning in terms of price risk management, price discovery, flexible contact specification, controlling unfair speculation, commodity delivery system, coverage, infrastructural support, etc. Empirically the study of this research examines the market which reacts first in agricultural commodity markets in India by assessing the relationship between the spot and future prices of Soya bean, Chana, Maize, Jeera and Turmeric traded in NCDEX, using Johansen's cointegration approach. Empirical results suggest the existence of long-run equilibrium relationships between futures and spot prices for 5 agricultural commodities viz., Soya bean, Chana, Maize, Jeera and Turmeric that were taken under this study. The relationship direction of future price and spot price are in general, where there is one-way causal linkage from future market to spot market prices for two agricultural commodities, viz., Soya bean and Chana. Further, the table result also confirms the presence of bidirectional relationship between commodity futures and spot market for three selected agricultural commodities viz., Maize, Jeera and Turmeric.

References

1. Chand R (2003) Government intervention in food grain market in new context. Policy Paper 19, National Centre for Agricultural Economics and Policy Research (NCAP), New Delhi, India.
2. Khusro Committee (1980) Report of the Committee on Forward Markets, Ministry of Civil Supplies, Government of India, New Delhi, India.
3. Kabra KN (2007) Commodity futures in India. Economic and Political Weekly 42: 1163-1170.
4. Sahadevan KG (2002) The sagging agricultural commodity exchanges: Growth, constrains and revival of policy options. Economic and Political Weekly 37: 3153-3160.
5. Singh JP (2001) Strategy for effective agricultural marketing extension to meet the challenges in 21st century. Manage Extension Research Review.
6. Acharya SS (2001) Domestic agricultural marketing policies, incentives and integration, in Acharya SS, Choudhri DP (edn.), Indian Agricultural Policy at the Crossroads, Rawat Publications, Jaipur, India.
7. Kolamkar DS (2003) Regulation and policy issues for commodity derivatives in India. In Thomas S (eds.), Derivatives Market in India, OUP, New Delhi, India.
8. Ahuja NL (2006) Commodity derivatives market in India: development, regulation and futures prospects. International Research Journal of Finance and Economics 2: 153-162.
9. Zou L, Pinfold J (2001) Price functions between NZSE 10 index, index futures and TeNZ: A Co-integration approach and error correction model. Working Paper Series Department of commerce, Massey University, Auckland.
10. Turkington J, David W (1999) Price Discovery and Causality in the Australian Share Price Index Futures Market. Australian Journal of Management 24: 97-113.
11. Chris B, Alistar GR, Stuart R (2001) A trading strategy based on the lead-lag relationship between the spot index and futures contract for the FTSE 100. International Journal of Forecasting 17: 31-44.
12. Hyun-Jung R, Graham S (2004) The impact of stock index futures on the Korean stock market. Applied Financial Economics 14: 243-251.
13. Kenourgios D (2004) Price Discovery in the Athens Derivatives Exchange: Evidence for the FTSE/ASE-20 Futures Market. Economic and Business Review 6: 229-243.
14. Chang CC, Lee YH (2008) Asymmetric Causal Relationship between Spot and Futures in Taiwan. International Research Journal Finance and Economics 14: 113-121.
15. Silvapulle P, Moosa I (1999) The relationship between the spot and futures prices: evidence from the crude oil market. Journal of Futures Markets 19: 175-193.
16. Kumar S, Sunil B (2004) Price Discovery and Market Efficiency: Evidence from Agricultural Futures Contract. J South Asian Management 11.

13

Economic Analysis of Cotton Production in the Gezira Scheme: 1970-2004

Bushara MOA* and Ahmed AMM

Department of Agricultural Economics, University of Gezira, Wad Medani, Gezira, Sudan

Abstract

The Gezira Scheme contributes more than 50% of cotton produced in the Sudan. During the seventies up to late eighties cotton alone contributed between 45 and 65% of the total foreign currency earning. Fluctuation in area, production, average yield and, benefits started from the begging of nineties in addition to high cost of production year after year and Government agricultural policies.

Therefore this study was an attempt to evaluate economic indicators (net present worth (NPW) and benefit cost ratio B/C ratio) of cotton production in the Gezira Scheme for the period (1970/71-2003/2004), also to compare three different periods of cotton production in Gezira (joint account system 1970/71-1980/81), (individual account system1981/82-1991/92), and (liberalization 192/93-2002/03) with respect to: Economic indicators (net present worth (NPW), benefit cost ratio B/C ratio), area, production and average yield. To identify some policy measures that may help to improve the production of cotton in the Gezira Scheme. The study mainly based on analysis of secondary data of cotton crop in Gezira Scheme. The methods of analysis used including the measurements of economic evaluation, descriptive statistics, simple mathematics, tabular analysis to describe the different periods.

The study proved that the economic evaluation during the periods (1970/71-2003/2004), (1970/1971-1980/1981), (1981/1982-1991/1992) and (1992/1993-2003/2004) were feasible and positive, fluctuation in the benefits, costs, and net benefits related to the Government agricultural policy. It's recommended that the Government agricultural policies should be proper and subsidized to agriculture particularly increasing the area of cotton crop, and reducing the cost of production are more important, downstream cotton processing for added value, up stream of cotton inputs processing for import substitutions and improving of cotton productivity through research development and extension is necessary.

Keywords: Project analysis; Cotton Gezira scheme; Sudan; Net present worth; Economic indicators

Introduction

Background

Sudan is the largest country in Africa, the area of the Sudan is about one million square miles (2.5 million square kilometers). It is characterized with a variety of climates zones from the desert in the North to tropical zone in the South. This gives it favourable environments for all agricultural activities as well as integrated investment in industries.

The country forms a wide basin sloping gently down towards the North, with high land on the other three sides. The Red Sea Hills and the Ethiopian Highlands on the Eastern side, Jabel Marra range on the western side and the Imatong range in the far South [1].

The Nile system is the main feature in the country, starting in Lake Victoria and running through the country for two and a half thousand miles. Agricultural sector is the most important sector in terms of its contribution to both Growth Domestic product (GDP) and employment. In 2001 agriculture directly accounted for 45.6% of the GDP (Bank of Sudan, 2001). The sector also provides about 80% of the country's exports (excluding petroleum) and contributes to livelihood of 80% of its population. The agricultural sector is the source of raw martial for processing factories in the country including textiles, sugar, vegetable oil, soap factories, grain mills, dairies, etc., which contribute 17% of the GDP and sum 20% of foreign exchange earnings [2].

Agriculture in the Sudan depends on two principal sources of water: direct rainfall and irrigation principally, from the Nile and its tributaries. There are also flood irrigation schemes fed by seasonal rivers in the east of the country in the Gash and Tokar deltas. There are five distinct sub-sectors of the Sudanese agriculture, modern irrigated farming, mechanized rain fed crop production, traditional rain fed farming, livestock and forestry.

The irrigated sub-sectors consist of four million (feddan=0.42 hectare) of cultivated land. The major components of these sub-sectors are large-scale schemes, which are Gezira, Rahad and New Halfa. Among the main agricultural sectors, the irrigation sector contributes 27% of agricultural

GDP and it produces most of the cotton, sugarcane, legumes and orchard crops grown in the Sudan.

The population of the Sudan is about 32.2 million of which 75% are rural according to 2004 population projection, with annual growth rate of 2.8%.

The cotton varieties are: Barakat variety (Extra-long stable cotton) cultivated in Gezira scheme and

Tokar Delta. Barac 67 (Aaka) (Medium stable cotton): It was cultivated in Elgezira, Elrahad, and Elsuki. New Halfa, Blue Nile and White Nile schemes. Albar 12/57 (Short stable cotton): It was cultivated in Nuba Mountain Corporation.

***Corresponding author:** Mohamed OA Bushara, Department of Agricultural Economics, University of Gezira, Wad Medani, Gezira, Sudan
E-mail: mosman@uofg.edu.sd

The importance of cotton for the Sudanese economy: Now cotton is cultivated in both the rain fed and irrigated sectors and has a great competitive force. Cotton is not perishable commodity and can be transported for long distances and stored for long periods of time without losing its competitive qualities. Cotton is one of the most important hard currency earning crops; it contributes between 25-60% of the Sudanese national income. More than 13% of the total population depends on cotton cultivation and its subsequent activities before export. Cotton is a permanent source of income for farmers. Most of the industries in the Sudan depend on it for example spinning, textile, oil, soap and paper industries. After harvest, cotton cultivated lands provides a rich posture for livestock. Cotton stalks are used as a source of energy to meet the various needs of the Gezira population [3]. This study is to investigate cotton production at the different phase of its history to update information and evaluate economic aspects of the cotton production in the Gezira scheme.

Problem statement

In the Sudan cotton has been the most important cash crop and foreign-currency earner. Sudan was traditionally one of the world's largest producers of long-stable cotton and medium producer of medium-stable cotton. All cotton in the Sudan is produced under state management, and about 90% of cotton is irrigated, while the remaining 10% is cultivated under rain-fed and flood irrigated conditions [4].

The Gezira Scheme contributes more than 50% of cotton produced in the Sudan. During the seventies up to late eighties cotton alone contributed between 45 and 65% of the total foreign currency earning [5]. In addition cotton is considered as a main source of income for about 13% of the labour-force.

Fluctuation in area, production, average yield, prices and high cost year after year, and in addition Government policies affect cotton's benefits, farmer's net return and farmer motivation. The Scheme contributes about 58% of cotton produced in Sudan, there for the economic evaluation of cotton production in the Gezira Scheme would be very important.

Objectives of the study

The main objective of this study is the economic evaluation of cotton production in the Gezira Scheme.

The specific objectives of the study are:

1. To calculate economic indicators, net present worth (NPW) and benefits cost ratio (B/C) of cotton in the Gezira scheme for the period (1970/71-2003/2004).
2. To compare indicators (NPW) and (B/C) for three different periods (1970/19711980/1981), (1981/1982-1991/1992) and (1992/1993-2003/2004).
3. To identify some policy measures that may help improve the production of cotton in the Gezira Scheme.

Research questions

This study answers the main Research questions of economic indicators and the proper basis for comparison of cotton production in the Gezira scheme.

1. What are the main factors affect cotton benefits and farmer's net return?
2. What are the values of economic indicators (NPW and B/C ratio)?
3. What methods appropriate to engage farmers within the three different approaches (joint, individual account and liberalization)?

Historical Background

The Gezira scheme

The name EL-Gezira, that is "the island" was originally applied to all the Gezira scheme which is the largest, oldest, and most important agricultural and also the largest farm in the world under one management, lying between the Blue Nile and the White Nile, without any defined limit to the south. For practical purpose, now it includes only the triangle lying North of Sennar, Kosti railway, a gross area of some 5 million feddan [3].

The Gezira is a gently sloping plain of black clay soil of about 5 million of feddan lying South of Khartoum between the Blue Nile and White Nile. Rainfall was uncertain and before irrigation only shifting cultivation and nomadic grazing was possible. After an initial pilot scheme for cotton at Tayba, in the heart of the Gezira plain, the Sennar Dam was constructed on the Blue Nile in 1925.

The main Gezira area is about 1.2 million feddans lying adjacent to the blue Nile, and the Managil extension developed between the year 1957/58 and 1962/63 covering on area of about 0.88 million feddan lying to the south west of Gezira scheme [6].

The map in Figure 1 Illustrates the Gezira and Managil irrigated area by groups and blocks. Topography of the Gezira is related to the characteristic of the two rivers. The Blue Nile comes from mountains catchments (Ethiopia plateau) and flows at a relatively steep slope (1/10,000). The seasonal variation of its discharge ranges is as follows: In the low season from January to June, the mean total discharge of the main river below Khartoum is some 13.8 Billions of cubic meter (1 Billions=1,000 million) cubic meters, of which the White Nile contributes 10 Billion and the Blue Nile 3.8 Billion. The Atbra River is dry for practically the whole of this period. From the beginning of July, the main river rises rapidly until the peak of the flood is reached about the end of August (discharge is 76 Billions, of which 16 Billion came from the white Nile 48 Billion from the blue Nile and 12 Billion from the Atbara considering the year as a whole. The surface of soil of the Gezira with high clay content. Soils are in general very good.

The climatic conditions of the Gezira area differ from one zone to another. The annual average rainfall is apparently 400-500 millimeters (mm) in the south, and this average drops gradually towards the North (average 200-300 mm). Climate differences are also observed in the average temperature and relative humidity.

Administration: The Gezira and Managil scheme, has been divided into 18 (eighteen) groups, 10 (ten) in the Gezira and 8 (eight) in the Managil extension. Each group divided into 7-10 blocks with block inspector on top of each, assisted by a number of inspectors. To facilitate the flow of information from the management to the farmers, a production council was set up in each block inspector, which includes some farmers as members. The entomologist, and agricultural extensionist, the agricultural engineer, the auditor, and accountant inspector are also members in the group council. The function of this council is to discuss and settle all problems facing the agricultural program.

Cotton in the Gezira Scheme: Cotton crop was introduced in the Sudan at prehistoric periods and was found barred with deeds since empire 50 years Before Christ (B.C). It seemed that its cultivation

Figure 1: Map illustrates the Gezira and Managil irrigated area by groups. Source: (Sudan Gezira Board) Statistical Information unit [7].

was transferred from India to west Asia to Africa. In the 19th century Mumtaz Basha the Turkish Governor of Sawakin tried growing cotton in Delta Tokar in 1850. A half a century later Sir Reginald Wingate, the Governor General of the Sudan invited an American businessman to invest in the Sudan [3]. An area of 10,000 feddans was allotted on lease hold to him at Zeidab in the Northern Province in 1903.

In 1906, the first pump was installed and Egyptian cotton was grown. In 1907 the area was increased to 800 feddans of cotton the Zeidab farm was later managed by the Sudan plantation syndicate using direct labour which later was substituted with land rent after the interference of the Sudan Government at that time, in 1908 the company had put the system into real practice. In 1911 the experiment was introduced into the Gezira plains. A pump was installed and the syndicate was asked to manage an area of 600 feddan at Tayba village 250 feddan were grown with cotton and 350 with other crops. The success of the experiment resulted, into an extension of area to 2000 feddans. Another increase was of 1000 feddans was made in 1914. The syndicate at its own cost established another pilot pumping station to irrigate 2000 feddans at Barakat and additional pumps followed at Hag Abdalla, and Wad EL nor south of Barakat. In 1925 Sennar Dam was built and the Gezira Scheme came into being. The Gezira area was leased from its owners for 25 years and was distributed to these owners on leasing bases.

The cotton area increased from 80031 feddans in 1925/26 to 206274 feddans in 1938/39. The average yield per feddan was about 4.5 kentars. However in 1931/32 up to 1934/35 the cotton was seriously affected by diseases and the yield dropped to 1.4-2.3 kentars. The year 1950/51 was a time mark in the scheme history of the Gezira Scheme. It is the year when was nationalized and the management was entrusted to the Sudan Gezira Board which substituted the Sudan plantation syndicate, the area was 207433 feddans and the average yield per feddans about 6.78 kentars. the share were settled at 49% to tenants, 36% to Government, 10% to administration and 5% to social services and local Government calculated after covering the joint account.

Another point mark in the Gezira scheme history is that of Managil Extension which increase the Gezira scheme area from less than one million feddans to 2.1 million feddans in (1958/62).

The joint system gave way in 1981/82 to tenant individual account system. The later system made the tenants accountable to all costs relative to the production of their crops. Government and administration shares during the joint account system were transferred into land rent and water charges imposed on the cultivated areas and are revised each year. This system gave efficient tenants the reaps of their efforts since each tenant is considered individually.

Important development in the Gezira scheme: Cotton production is the production relations these relations were based on the cotton crop and were revised several times to change sharing Percentage of farmers relative to that of the Government which maintaining the share of administration at 10%, in 1980/81.

The cotton marketing: The marketing of cotton at the time the Sudan syndicate, after nationalization of cotton trade during the May regime when solutions took over the marketing for cotton and later in 1985 when Sudan Cotton Corporation was transferred in to the Sudan Cotton Company Limited (Public company). In 1993 under privatization policies shifting the ownership of Sudan Cotton Company limited from the state to the tenants (Figure 1).

Development stages of cotton production in the Gezira scheme (1970/1971-2003/2004)

The development stages of cotton production included the area, production, average yield, for the years 1970/1971–2003/2004 production relations in the Gezira Scheme for the same period (Table 1).

The Table 1 indicates the area grown with cotton was decreased gradually from the first period (1970/1971-1980/1981) to second period (1981/1982-1991/1992) and third period (1992/19932003/2004).

The above Table 1 indicates fluctuation of cotton production over those 34 years and also the average yield of cotton crop.

Cotton cultivated area, production, average yield had been decreased. The decrease was attributed to many factors among them were the following:

1. Shortage in machinery and spare parts needed for land preparation and the cultivation of cotton.
2. Lack of required inputs at the right time. Moreover, it has been found that some of these inputs were not in accordance with scientific specification.
3. Seasonal labour problems and failure to harvest the crop in right time.
4. Dependence of cost of production of other crops on income from cotton.
5. Fluctuation in prices, high cost of production and direct and indirect taxes might have negatively affected farmer motivation.
6. Agricultural government policies. (Pricing, Taxes, Finance, etc.)
7. Administrative technical and political factors (Table 2).
   - Report at archives section (annual report 1970/71-198081)
   - Information and Financial Analysis Unit (report of cotton accounting (1981/82-199/2000)
   - Accounting section (2000/2001-2003/2004)

Production relations in the sudan gezira board (SGB)

The production relations in Gezira scheme is based on the partnership agreement between the tenants, the board of directors and the government, which was mainly directed towards the promotion of cotton production neglecting to some extent the production of other crops which were the responsibility of the tenants themselves.

Season	Areas (Fed.)	Production	Average Yield Kentar/Fed.
1970/1971	5,88,371	31,83,087	5.41
1971/1972	5,89,387	29,17,466	4.95
1972/1973	5,89,387	24,04,699	4.08
1973/1974	6,04,420	30,52,321	5.05
1974/1975	6,03,364	27,75,474	4.6
1975/1976	3,95,637	10,68,220	2.7
1976/1977	4,99,434	18,22,934	3.65
1977/1978	5,18,607	22,24,824	4.29
1978/1979	4,98,023	16,28,535	3.27
1979/1980	5,40,890	14,38,767	2.66
1980/1981	5,01,202	11,52,765	2.3
1981/1982	4,35,314	16,89,018	3.88
1982/1983	4,84,315	22,71,437	4.69
1983/1984	4,97,729	24,48,827	4.92
1984/1985	4,64,792	24,26,214	5.22
1985/1986	4,00,528	14,17,869	3.54
1986/1987	4,15,074	20,46,315	4.93
1987/1988	3,83,037	17,50,479	4.57
1988/1989	4,04,505	20,99,381	5.19
1989/1990	3,57,984	14,78,474	4.13
1990/1991	2,51,048	9,31,388	3.71
1991/1992	2,15,506	12,11,144	5.62
1992/1993	1,74,703	7,25,017	4.15
1993/1994	1,49,603	5,74,476	3.84
1994/1995	2,53,147	9,84,742	3.89
1995/1996	3,01,245	12,47,154	4.14
1996/1997	3,31,047	12,74,531	3.85
1997/1998	2,46,220	10,88,292	4.42
1998/1999	1,53,924	6,80,344	4.42
1999/2000	2,59,495	5,83,864	2.25
2000/2001	2,00,000	9,00,000	4.5
2001/2002	2,00,000	9,40,000	4.7
2002/2003	2,50,000	13,75,000	5.5
2003/2004	2,44,900	12,46,661	5.09
Average	3,82,436	16,19,404	4.24
Source: Sudan Gezira Board [7,8].			

Table 1: Areas grown with cotton and quantities produced over 34 years, from 1970/19712003/2004, Source: Sudan Gezira Board [7].

The partnership agreement regulated the duties and rights of each partner. The board of directors was assigned to the managerial tasks in a way that made the scheme operated efficiently. It was required to act on behalf of the joint undertaking [7]. Their responsibilities included: Formulating policies to allocate economic resources available to the most productive uses. Planning for acquiring and utilizing funds. Controlling and implementation of the policy formulated. The tenant's duty under the terms of the joint undertaking was to do all a labour needed for agricultural operations of cotton (e.g. sowing, irrigating, weeding, thinning, fertilizer scattering, harvesting, and delivering the produced to the local collecting stations in the area).The Government provides land and water resources [8].

Joint account system: Joint account system was a production relationship system proposed to recover from the tenants all the costs of inputs and services provided by the scheme and other party [9]. since in effect all costs were assumed to be volume related, these costs were

Season	Gross Benefits (in cash flow)	Gross cost (out cash flow)	Net (Return)
70/71	12,83,38,566	5,61,10,277	7,22,28,289
71/72	11,43,68,309	5,85,31,331	5,58,36,977
72/73	12,43,56,485	5,70,44,798	6,73,11,688
73/74	11,98,88,345	6,01,70,303	5,97,18,043
74/75	11,66,73,785	7,77,91,363	3,88,82,423
75/76	8,05,49,390	7,13,53,680	91,95,710
76/77	14,48,08,750	9,35,99,203	5,12,09,548
77/78	21,25,16,160	10,66,57,178	10,58,58,983
78/79	21,25,69,053	10,63,74,345	10,61,94,708
79/80	15,25,73,654	11,67,56,042	3,58,17,612
80/81	8,71,70,714	7,52,56,134	1,19,14,580
Total	1,49,38,13,210	87,96,44,653	61,41,68,558
Average	13,58,01,201	7,99,67,696	5,58,33,505
81/82	11,32,55,438	9,43,49,577	2,49,60,646
82/83	14,85,35,008	11,39,87,246	4,56,14,108
83/84	19,45,32,077	15,53,14,246	6,22,70,477
84/85	12,66,30,156	9,33,22,248	4,92,54,360
85/86	12,40,09,900	8,70,28,580	4,72,40,104
86/87	11,15,62,753	7,09,41,042	4,56,47,638
87/88	10,62,29,271	6,29,30,158	4,97,18,889
88/89	24,46,21,798	11,84,34,809	12,99,16,598
89/90	22,17,06,127	11,61,89,464	10,96,47,989
90/91	2,56,67,545	2,06,48,998	72,24,670
91/92	2,01,97,769	1,51,06,504	61,53,801
Total	1,43,69,47,842	94,82,52,873	57,76,49,279
Average	13,06,31,622	8,62,04,807	5,25,13,571
92/93	1,93,56,109	2,05,82,544	37,92,871
93/94	2,13,75,787	1,32,26,608	88,99,925
94/95	6,44,30,075	2,94,14,303	3,57,52,892
95/96	7,67,41,306	3,71,60,701	4,05,38,824
96/97	7,69,86,383	6,13,57,120	2,10,84,884
97/98	5,58,37,243	4,55,82,451	1,55,15,204
98/99	2,76,18,695	2,69,79,799	65,43,946
99/2000	3,15,66,751	3,53,98,611	59,52,063
2000/2001	5,61,82,707	3,93,75,767	1,91,91,599
2001/2002	6,52,95,008	3,68,32,320	2,96,97,609
2002/2003	8,37,03,764	4,67,15,314	3,83,67,992
Total	57,90,93,827	39,26,25,539	22,53,37,810
Average	5,26,44,893	3,56,93,231	2,04,85,255

Table 2: The development stages of cotton benefits, costs, and net return of cotton for three periods (1970/71-1980/81), (1981/82-1991/92), (1992/93-2002/2003) in US dollar.

deducted from cotton crop sales value, all the proceeds over and above the total cost were divided among them.

The individual account system: The individual account system and the land water charges have been introduced in the Gezira scheme in 1981/1982 season to replace the joint account system, this system was proposed to recover from each individual tenant the cost of inputs and services provided for him by the scheme and other party, all proceeds over and above the total accrue. The tenant individual account were to be debited with advances, interest on debit, services contracted on an individual basis, material draw on an individual basis and per feddan land and water charges. The in cash and in kind loans provided for cotton were deducted from the tenant' cotton proceeds. Cotton is the only crop sold through the Sudan Gezira Board [8,10], so it was loaded by the debits of the other crops. Its account was charged with various deductions and costs which do not related to cotton.

The economic liberalization policy: Beginning from the season 1990/1991, the financing of cotton operations from the central bank was cancelled and substituted for commercial financing through "The Banks Consortium Fund" which is a number of commercial banks assigned to finance the production of cotton and wheat crops. In February 1992, a number of economic procedures were declared which were directly reflected on the Gezira Scheme, included complete liberalization of the price of the Sudanese pound and equal liberalization of foreign currency transactions. It also included of almost prices of goods and services and remarkable deduction in Government subsidies and other procedures meant to liberalization the Sudanese economy to be in consistence with world economic and financial interactions (Table 3).

Introduction

Cotton average yield in the Sudan is low compared to other cotton producing countries, best practice average yield and average yield achievable in research stations. Cotton average yield in Sudan is only 53, 47, 35 and 61% of the cotton average yield in Egypt, China, Australia and Pakistan, respectively [8].

The World Bank (2000) stated that cotton average yield in the Gezira scheme is only 37.5, 35.8 and 30.5% of the achievable levels in field research for extra-long, medium and short stable cotton, respectively.

It was a challenged for everyone working in the field of production research to find ways and means to improve yields. Such efforts have to be different from traditional approaches aimed at developing high yielding varieties, agronomic management practices and insect pest control. Improvements in traditional cultivation practices would affect yields positively, but a sustained increase in yields requires a non-traditional technological innovation. It is a challenge for researchers to develop such a technology.

The adoption rate for GE technology is the highest for any new technology in the agriculture industry. But, the technology is still new and implications are not fully understood. The technology must be used without compromising the environment sustainability, farmers' interest and mishandling of the cotton genome. The challenges of GE technology include acceptability to the public, employment of the technology for creating non-existing combinations and improving yield [11].

According to Ginger gross accrual revenues for cotton production have been on a downward trend from 1996 to 2002 averaging $195.98 per acre [11]. Total enterprise costs averaged $190.48 on a per acre basis and $0.84 on a per pound basis from 1996 to 2002. Additionally, producers, on average, received positive net incomes in 1996 through 1998 and negative net incomes from 1999 through 2002. The average net income for producers from 1996 through 2002 was $5.50 per acre. Furthermore, producers had an average enterprise cost of production of $0.53 per pound from 1996 through 2002. The enterprise cost of production represents the cotton lint price necessary to break-even after accounting for all non-primary product income.

Gross accrual revenues for irrigated cotton production from 1996 to 2002 averaged $297.45 per acre. Total enterprise costs averaged $250.87 on a per acre basis and $0.63 on a per pound basis from 1996 to 2002. Additionally, producers, on average, received positive net incomes in all years evaluated in this study with the exception of 2000. The average net income for producers in the Texas High Plains (THP) (1999) from 1996 through 2002 was $46.58 per acre. Furthermore, producers had an average enterprise cost of production of $0.43 per pound from 1996 through 2002.

From Table 4 gross revenues foe irrigated cotton production in

Season	Government Share%	Tenants Share%	Administration Share %	Local government Share %	Social development Share %	Reserve Fund%
1950/51-1956/57	40	40	20	-	-	-
1957/58-1962/63	42	42	10	2	2	2
1963/64-1964/65	40	44	10	2	2	2
1965/66-1968/69	36	48	10	2	2	2
1969/70-1970/71	36	47	10	2	3	2
1972/73-1975/76	36	47	10	2	3	2
1976/77-1980/81	36	47	10	2	3	2

Source: PSERU (Planning And Socio-Economic Research Unit) (1950/51-1980/81) Literature Review [8]

Table 3: The development of profits share for the three partners during the joint account system.

Periods	Average gross revenues per feddan	Average gross cost revenues per feddan	Average net incomes per feddan
1970/71-1980/81	251.96	148.37	103.59
1981/82-1991/92	333.41	220.02	113.39
1992/93-2002/2003	229.86	155.84	74.02

Table 4: Profitability of cotton production in The Gezira Scheme for the period (1970/711980/81), (1981/82-1991/92) and (1992/93-2002/2003) per dollar.

Gezira Scheme during the period (1970/71-1980/81) averaged 251.96 dollar per feddan. Total gross cost averaged 148.37 dollar per feddan. The average net income for producers in Gezira Scheme from (1970/71-1980/81) was 103.59 dollar per feddan. In (1981/82-1991/92), revenues averaged 333.41 dollar per feddan. Total gross cost averaged 220.02 dollar per feddan. The average net incomes (net benefits) was 113.39 dollar per feddan. In (1992/93-2002/2003), gross revenues averaged 229.86 dollar per feddan. Total gross cost averaged 155.84 dollar per feddan. The average net incomes were 74.02 dollar per feddan (Table 4) [8].

Data and Methodology

The theoretical frame work of the model

In the economic analysis of an agricultural project, the changing value of money over time must be considered. If the project extends over several accounting periods, the values of the cost and benefits streams must be standardized to provide a proper basis for comparison. This can be done by reducing the values to their "present worth" also referred to as present value or discounted value. The process of calculating the present value of a sum of money due sometime in the future is called discounting. It calculates the present value of future cash flows. Discounting looks backward from the future to the present [12,13].

Discount factor

The rate for discounting is called the discount factor. The difference in the value of the same sum of money in two different periods is determined by the discount factor. This is affected by the length of time and by the discount factor used. At any given discount factor the value of the sum of money becomes less and less far in the future it is to be received. For instance, $100 today is more value than $100 to be received one year later. Also the greater the discount rate, the greater the difference will be between the value of a sum of money in two different periods. For purposes of discounting Gittinger assumes that both costs and benefits fall on the last day of each project year, including the first year, and so all costs and benefits in the first year are discounted as though they arose at the end of the year. Given the discount rate, the present worth of an amount due in any year in the future can be found by multiplying that amount by the discount factor shown in the tables for corresponding year [12].

Discounted measures of project worth: Two important measures of project worth incorporate the principle of discounted measures: a. Benefit/cost ratio.

b. Net present worth, also called net present value.

Benefit/cost ratio: The benefit cost ratio compares the present worth of the benefits and cost of a project and express their relation as a ratio. The discount rate used is usually the opportunity cost of capital. The method of discounted gross benefits divided by the total discounted gross costs.

Net present worth: The net present worth is the difference between the present worth of the benefits and costs of a project. As in the case of the benefits/cost ratio, the rate used for discounting is usually the opportunity cost of capital. The simple decision rule is to accept projects for which the net present worth is positive. Unlike benefit/cost ratio, it's not affected by the different methods used in calculating it [13].

Decision formulas criteria

- NPW (net present worth) or (net present value)

$$NPW = \sum_{n}^{t} \frac{(B_t + C_t)}{(1+r)^t} \qquad (1)$$

B=Benefits t=year C_t=cost

r=rate of interest (discount factor)

$(1+r)^t$=defined as present worth factor

Decision rule of this formula: - Accept IF NPW>0 Reject IF NPW<0

Benefit/Cost Ratio

$$B/C = \frac{\sum_{t=1}^{n} \frac{B_t}{(1+r)^t}}{\sum_{t=1}^{n} \frac{C_t}{(1+r)^t}} \qquad (2)$$

Decision rule: - If B/C>1.0 accept IF B/C<1.0 reject.

Periods of analysis

The proper basis for comparing three different periods of cotton production in the Gezira scheme (joint account system 1970/71-1980/81), (individual account system 1981/82-1991/92), and (liberalization 192/93-2002/03) with respect to:

Source of data: This study mainly based on analysis of secondary data of cotton crop such as area, production, average yield, benefits, costs, return, net return. The most important sources of secondary data includes: Agriculture Administration, Statistical Information Unit, Financial Administration (Accounting Section), Report and Papers relating to cotton production at the Archives Section (annual report and statement of accounts for the years ended 30th June, Information and Financial Analysis Unit (report of cotton accounting 1981/82-1999/2000), Planning And Socio-Economic Research Administration "PSERA", Informal And Private Institutions (Bank of the Sudan, Sudan cotton company etc.).

Results and Discussion

It was found that the mean cotton area decreases from 538,975 Feddan in the first period and to 391,803 feddan in second period and to 229,035 feddan in the third period respectively and it has been found that the mean production in the same period decreases from 2,151,736 Kentar in the first period to 1,797,322 Kentar in the second period and to 943,038 in the third period respectively while cotton average yield during the same periods increases from 3.99 in the first period to 4.59 K/f in the second period and decreases to 4.12 k/f in the third period. That means the cotton cultivated area had been decreases steadily from first period to the second period and third period respectively and also production decreases steadily from 2,151,736 Kentar to 1,797,322 Kentar and to 943,038 Kentar. That means the major factor affecting cotton production was the area allocated for cotton. Cotton average yield increases from 3.99 to 4.59 and decrease to 4.12 that means the best period is the second one (individual account system) that means the Government policies affecting cotton average yield because that period has many advantages (Figures 2-4).

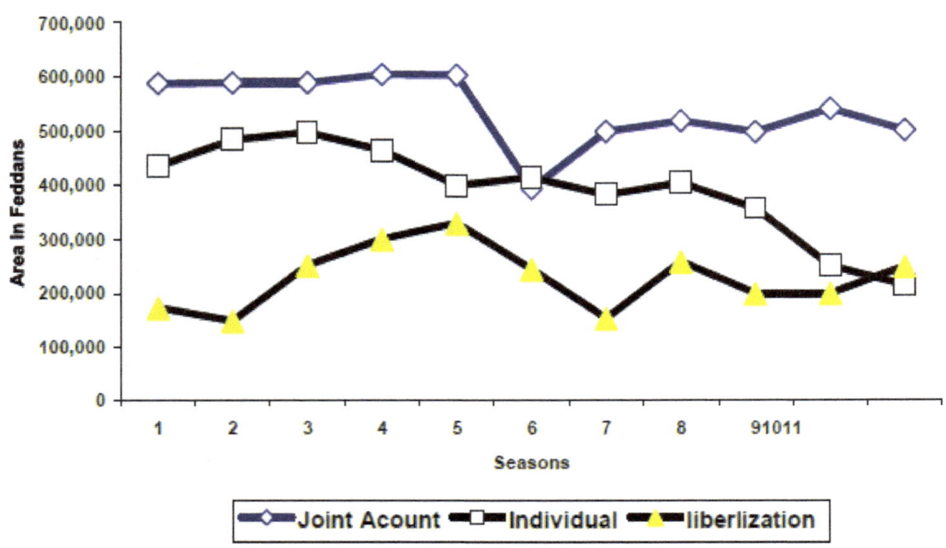

Figure 2: Cultivated Areas During (JAS), (IAS), (LIB) systems.

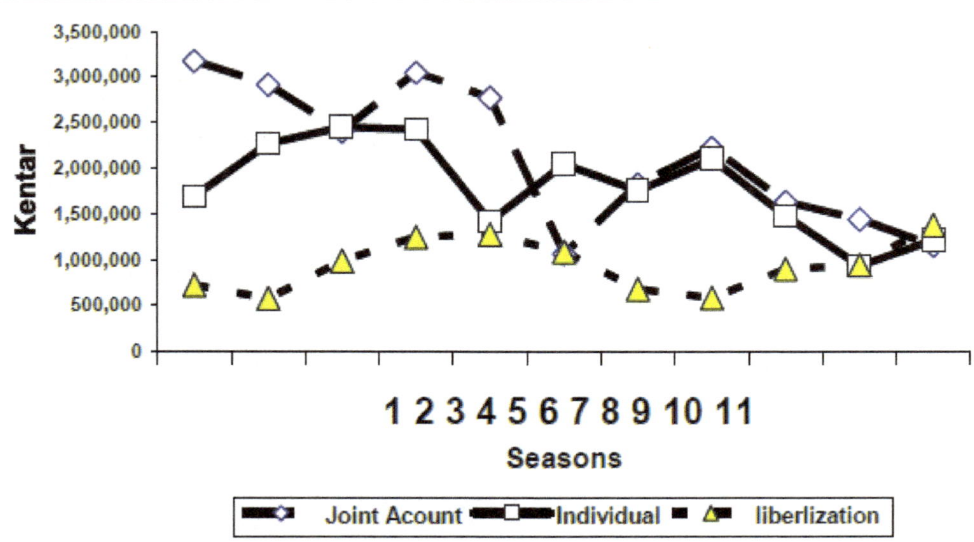

Figure 3: Cotton Production During (JAS), (IAS), (LIB) systems.

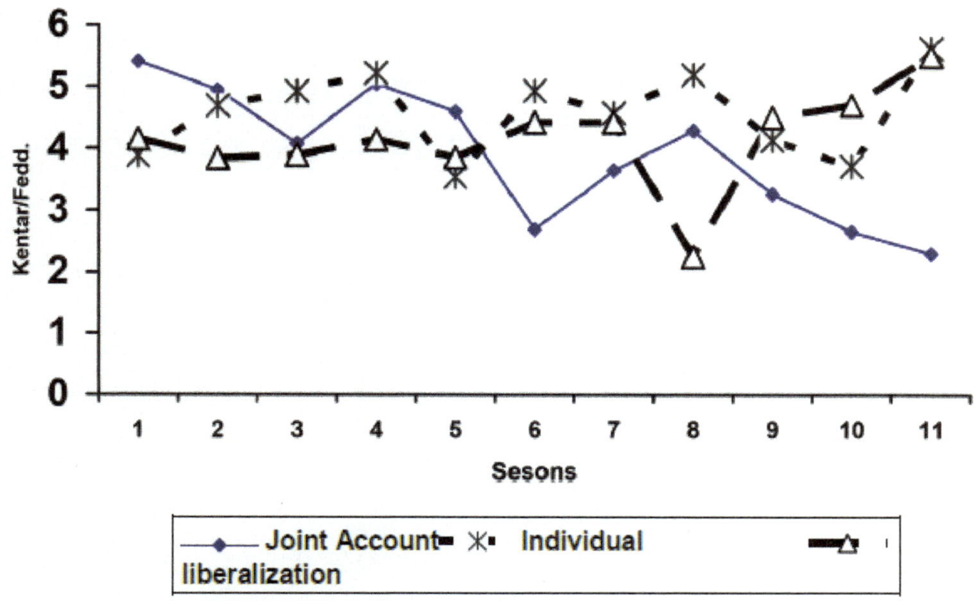

Figure 4: Cotton Average yield During (JAS), (IAS), (LIB) systems.

Three periods' joint account, individual account and liberalization:

1. **First period (1970/71-1980/81)**

It was found that the mean area allocated in this period for cotton production 538,975 Feddan, the mean production amounted to 2,151,736 Kentar, average yield 3.99 kentar/Feddan.

2. **Second period (1981/82-1991/92)**

It found that the mean area allocated in this period for cotton production 391,803 Feddan, mean production amounted to 1,797,322 Kentar, average yield 4.59 Kentar/Feddan.

3. **Third period (1992/93-2002/03)**

It found that the mean area allocated in this period for cotton production 229,035 Feddan, mean production amounted to 943,038 Kentar, average yield 4.12 Kentar/Feddan (Table 5).

It was clear that the coefficient of variation for the three period differ significantly from one period to another, ranging from 11.96% for JAS to 22.81 for IAS and 25.63 for LIB that means the variation in cultivated area is low during JAS period compared to IAS and LIB respectively, while the variation in production and average yield were high during the JAS than LIB and IAS respectively this result is consistent with the results (Table 6).

E B/C at 12%=1.68.

ENPW at 12%=$ 438,890,074.

From the above Table 6 the calculation of economic benefit/cost ratio and net present worth of Gezira cotton (Dollars) for years (1970/1971-2003/2004) were those:

- present worth of gross benefits at 12%=1,039,679,541.
- present worth of gross cost at 12%=618,837,857 - present worth of gross return at 12%=438,890,074.
- the E B/C=1,039,679,541/618,837,857=1.68.

	Area	production	Average yield
Joint account system	11.96%	35.94%	27.31%
Individual account system	22.81%	28.10%	14.87%
Liberalization	25.63%	29.90%	19.06%

Table 5: Coefficient of Variation for the three periods.

The economic benefit cost ratio (EB/C ratio)=1.68 that means the project is economically feasible because the simple decision rule is to accept the project if the benefit/cost ratio is greater than one and to reject it if the ratio is less than one and the economic net present worth (ENPW)=438,890,074$ that means the economic net present worth is positive. (The simple decision rule is to accept the project).

E B/C at 12%=1.78 (JAS). (ENPW) at 12%=340,819,877$ (JAS).

E B/C at 12%=1.44 (IAS). (ENPW) at12%=87,124,036$ (IAS).

E B/C at 12%=1.49 (LIB). (ENPW) at 12%=10,086,706$(LIB)

The above Table 7 shows that the calculation of economic benefit/cost ratio and economic net present worth of Gezira cotton (Dollar) in different periods (1970/1971- 1980/1981), (1981/19821991/1992), (1992/1993-2002/2003), joint account, individual account, liberalization respectively at 12% were those:

First periods (1970/1971-1980/1981), joint account

- present worth of gross benefits at 12%=779,735,486$.
- present worth of gross cost at 12%=438,915,609$-present worth of gross return at 12%=340,819,877$.
- the E B/C=779,735,486/438,915,609=1.78.

Second periods (1981/1982-1991/1992), individual account

- present worth of gross benefits at 12%=231,982,202$.
- present worth of gross cost at 12%=160,988,623$.
- present worth of gross return at 12%=87,124,036$.
- the E B/C=231,982,202/160,988,623=1.44.

Season	Present worth of gross. benefits at 12%	Present worth of gross cost. At 12%	Present worth of return at 12%
70/71	114,606,339	50,106,477	64,499,862
71/72	91,151,542	46,649,471	44,502,071
72/73	88,541,817	40,615,896	47,925,922
73/74	76,248,987	38,268,312	37,980,675
74/75	66,154,036	44,107,703	22,046,334
75/76	40,838,541	36,176,316	4,662,225
76/77	65,453,555	42,306,840	23,146,715
77/78	85,856,529	43,089,500	42,767,029
78/79	76,737,428	38,401,139	38,336,289
79/80	49,128,717	37,595,446	11,533,271
80/81	25,017,995	21,598,511	3,419,484
81/82	29,106,648	24,247,841	6,414,886
82/83	34,014,517	26,103,079	10,445,631
83/84	39,879,076	31,839,420	12,765,448
84/85	23,173,319	17,077,971	9,013,548
85/86	20,213,614	14,185,659	7,700,137
86/87	16,288,162	10,357,392	6,664,555
87/88	13,809,805	8,180,921	6,463,456
88/89	28,376,129	13,738,438	15,070,325
89/90	23,057,437	12,083,704	11,403,391
90/91	2,387,082	1,920,357	671,894
91/92	1,676,415	1,253,840	510,765
92/93	1,432,352	1,523,108	280,672
93/94	1,410,802	872,956	587,395
94/95	3,801,374	1,735,444	2,109,421
95/96	4,067,289	1,969,517	2,148,558
96/97	3,618,360	2,883,785	990,990
97/98	2,345,164	1,914,463	651,639
98/99	1,021,892	998,253	242,126
99/2000	1,041,703	1,168,154	196,418
2000/2001	1,854,029	1,299,400	633,323
2001/2002	2,154,735	1,215,467	980,021
2002/2003	2,762,224	1,541,605	1,266,144
2003/2004	2,451,928	1,811,473	859,455
Total	1,039,679,541	618,837,857	438,890,074

Table 6: The economic present worth of the gross benefits, gross costs and return for years (1970/1971-2003/2004) per Dollars at discount factor 12%.

Season	Present worth of Gross Benefits At 12%	Present worth of Gross Cost At 12%	Present worth of Returns at 12%
70/71	11,46,06,339	5,01,06,477	6,44,99,862
71/72	9,11,51,542	4,66,49,471	4,45,02,071
72/73	8,85,41,817	4,06,15,896	4,79,25,922
73/74	7,62,48,987	3,82,68,312	3,79,80,675
74/75	6,61,54,036	4,41,07,703	2,20,46,334
75/76	4,08,38,541	3,61,76,316	46,62,225
76/77	6,54,53,555	4,23,06,840	2,31,46,715
77/78	8,58,56,529	4,30,89,500	4,27,67,029
78/79	7,67,37,428	3,84,01,139	3,83,36,289
79/80	4,91,28,717	3,75,95,446	1,15,33,271
80/81	2,50,17,995	2,15,98,511	34,19,484
Total	*77,97,35,486*	*43,89,15,609*	*34,08,19,877*
81/82	2,91,06,648	2,42,47,841	64,14,886
82/83	3,40,14,517	2,61,03,079	1,04,45,631
83/84	3,98,79,076	3,18,39,420	1,27,65,448
84/85	2,31,73,319	1,70,77,971	90,13,548
85/86	2,02,13,614	1,41,85,659	77,00,137
86/87	1,62,88,162	1,03,57,392	66,64,555
87/88	1,38,09,805	81,80,921	64,63,456
88/89	2,83,76,129	1,37,38,438	1,50,70,325
89/90	2,30,57,437	1,20,83,704	1,14,03,391

90/91	23,87,082	19,20,357	6,71,894
91/92	16,76,415	12,53,840	5,10,765
Total	*23,19,82,202*	*16,09,88,623*	*8,71,24,036*
92/93	14,32,352	15,23,108	2,80,672
93/94	14,10,802	8,72,956	5,87,395
94/95	38,01,374	17,35,444	21,09,421
95/96	40,67,289	19,69,517	21,48,558
96/97	36,18,360	28,83,785	9,90,990
97/98	23,45,164	19,14,463	6,51,639
98/99	10,21,892	9,98,253	2,42,126
99/2000	10,41,703	11,68,154	1,96,418
2000/2001	18,54,029	12,99,400	6,33,323
2001/2002	21,54,735	12,15,467	9,80,021
2002/2003	27,62,224	15,41,605	12,66,144
Total	*2,55,09,925*	*1,71,22,152*	*1,00,86,706*
2003/2004	24,51,928	18,11,473	8,59,455
Total	*24,51,928*	*18,11,473*	*8,59,455*

Table 7: The economic present worth of the gross benefits, gross costs and return in different periods (1970/1971-1980/1981), (1981/1982-1991/1992), (1992/1993-2002/2003), joint account, individual account, liberalization respectively per Dollars at discount factor 12%.

Third periods (1992/1993-2002/2003), liberalization account

- present worth of gross benefits at 12%=25,509,925$.

- present worth of gross cost at 12%=17,122,152$ - present worth of gross return at 12%=10,086,706$.

- the E B/C=25,509,925/17,122,152=1.49.

In these three periods, it was found that the E B/C ratio decreases from 1.78 to 1.44 in the second period and increases to 1.49 in the third period.

It has also been found that the economic net present worth decreases from 340,819,877$ to 87,124,036$ and to 10,086,706$ in the third period respectively (Figures 5 and 6).

In the Sudan cotton is the most important cash crop and foreign-currency earner. It was found that the big fluctuations in cotton area, production, decreases of benefits and increasing of production cost during the seventies, eighties up to the season 2003/2004. Combinations of factors were negatively affecting cotton area and production during the different periods. These were due to insufficient and timely finance Government agricultural policy improper implementation of intended crop rotation, centralized decision of area allocated by management and difficulties in irrigating areas.

From Tables 6 and 7 it was found that the calculation of the economic benefit/cost ratio (EB/C ratio) of the cotton production in the Gezira Scheme to the period (1970/71-2003/2004) has improved that the ratio is greater than one, that means accepted also the economic net present worth has improved that the calculation for the same period (1970/1971-2003/2004) was positive.

The comparison between the three periods (joint account system 1970/1971-1980/81), (individual account system 1981/82-1991/92) and (liberalization 1992/93-2002/2003) with respect to the (EB/C) and (ENPW), area, production, average yield, cost of finance and inflation resulted in Tables 8 and 9 below:

Summary, Conclusion and Recommendation

Introduction

In this section the conclusions are summarized below:

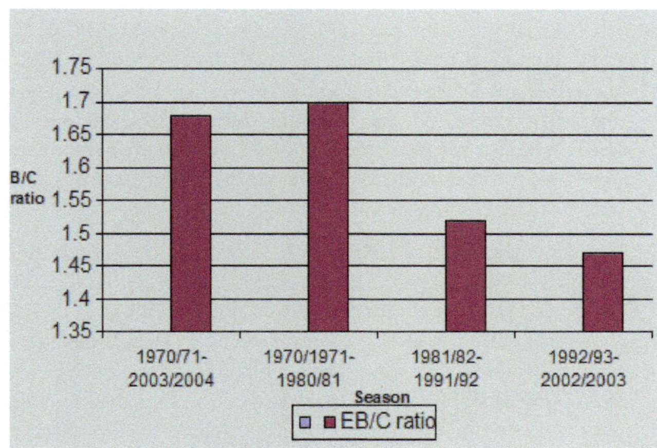

Figure 5: Economic Benefits Cost Ratio.

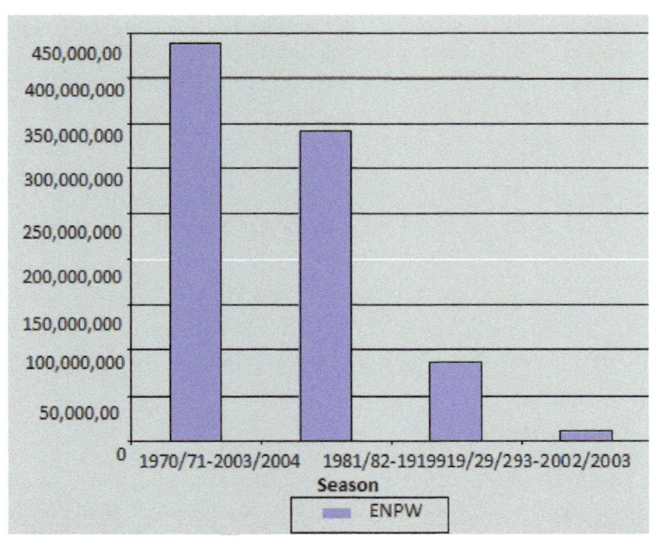

Figure 6: Economic Net Present Worth.

	Joint AC	Individual AC	Liberalization
Area (mean) feddan	5,38,975	3,91,803	2,29,035
Mean production	21,51,736	17,97,322	9,43,038
Average yield	3.99	4.59	4.12
Source of finance	Bank of Sudan	Bank of the Sudan The banks consortium fund	The banks consortium fund
Cost of finance	7%	9%	12-45%
General inflation	0.97-33.91	22.56-122.52	8.02-130.44
Gross benefit (dollar)	1,49,38,13,210	1,43,69,47,842	57,90,93,827
Gross cost (dollar)	87,96,44,653	94,82,52,873	39,26,25,539
Return (dollar)	61,41,68,558	57,76,49,279	22,53,37,810
Discounts (dollar)	0	16,87,53,813	5,14,01,286
Net return (dollar)	61,41,68,558	40,88,95,466	17,39,36,524
Discount factor	12%	12%	12%
Present worth of gross benefit at 12% (dollar)	77,97,35,486	23,19,82,202	2,55,09,925
Present worth of gross cost at 12% (dollar)	43,89,15,609	16,09,88,623	1,71,22,152
Present worth of return at 12% (dollar)	34,08,19,877	8,71,24,036	1,00,86,706
Present worth of net return at 12% (dollar)	34,08,19,877	6,03,12,716	76,74,729
EB/C ratio	1.78	1.44	1.49
Economic net present worth (dollar)	34,08,19,877	8,71,24,036	1,00,86,706

Table 8: Comparison between three periods (1970/71-1980/81), (1981/82-1991/92), (1992/93-2002/2003).

1. The calculation of the economic benefit/cost ratio (EB/C ratio), and economic net present worth (ENPW) of cotton production in the Gezira Scheme for the period (1970/712003/2004) was that: EB/C ratio=1.68, and economic NPW=438,890,074 dollar. The B/C ratio is accepted and the net NPW is positive that means the economic evaluation of cotton production in Gezira Scheme were positive and feasible.

2. The summary of the comparison between the three periods (1970/71-1980/81), (1981/821991/92), (1992/93-2002/2003) - JAS, IAS and LIB with respect to EB/C ratio, and ENPW area, production and the average yield. It found that EB/C ratio=1.78, 1.44, 1.49 respectively and the ENPW=$340,819,877-$87,124,036-$10,086,706 respectively that means the EB/C ratio is better in the joint account system than liberalization and individual account system respectively. The economic net present worth (ENPW) also is better in the joint account system (JAS) than the individual account system (IAS) and liberalization (LIB) respectively. On other hand the (JAS), (IAS), (LIB) compared with respect to area, production and average yield, it was found that the mean total area allocated for cotton=538,975-391,803-229,035 feddan respectively is better under the (JAS) than the (IAS) and (LIB) respectively and also the mean production=2,151,736-1,797,322-943,038 Kentar respectively but the average yield=3.99-4.59-4.12 kentars/feddan respectively which is better under the (IAS), (LIB) and (JAS) respectively because the (IAS) aimed at motivation the tenants to increase cotton crop production.

3. It have been improved that the increasing and decreasing of the EB/C ratio and ENPW through the different periods (JAS, IAS and LIB) related to the agricultural policy of the Government (Figure 7).

Season	Akaka	Barakat
1993/94	74	121
1994/95	80	94
1995/96	72	124
1996/97	78	103
1997/98	83	120
1998/99	46.05	70.95
1999/2000	46.28	75.58
2000/2001	33.36	75
2001/2002	33	58
2002/2003	48.34	65.61
2003/2004	63.7	81
2004/2005	46.2	71

Table 9: Prices of the cotton lint per dollar for the period 1993/94-2004/2005.

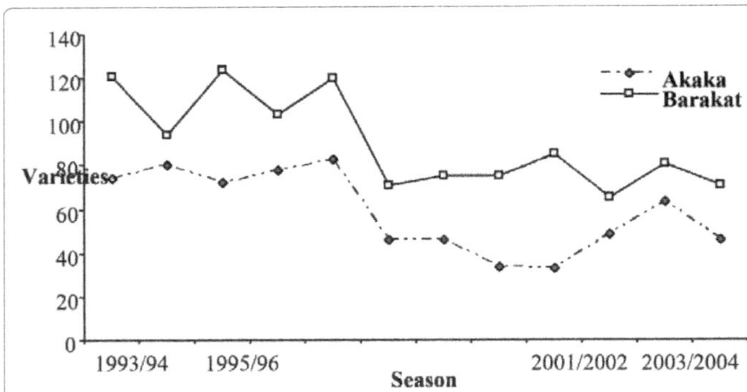

Figure 7: Prices of the cotton lint per dollar for the period 1993/94-2004/2005.

Recommendations

The result of economic evaluation of cotton production in the Gezira Scheme is accepted but it needs revision of Government policies and more incentives to the producers and part of the petroleum revenues should be devoted to agriculture particularly to the cotton production to increase the farmer's net return. It's recommended that the agricultural Government policies should be proper and subsidized to agriculture particularly increasing the area of cotton crop, yields and reducing the cost of production are more important, downstream cotton processing for added value, up stream of cotton inputs processing for import substitutions, and improving of cotton productivity through research development and extension is necessary.

References

1. El-Hassan AM (1967) Structure of the Sudan Economy. In El-Hassan AM (Ed) An Introduction to the Sudan Economy. Khartoum University Press.

2. Sudan A (2002) Large Irrigated Agricultural Scheme.

3. Yousif GM (1997) The Gezira Scheme the Greatest on Earth. Africa University House, Sudan pp: 321.

4. Company1 SC (1993) Country Statement of the Sudan delegation to 52 plenary meeting New Delhi.

5. Company2 SC (1993) Sudan Cotton Facts and Figures. Khartoum-Sudan.

6. Taha TE (1973) The Development of Managil South Western Extension to the Gezira Scheme: A case study. Barakat 14: 240-250.

7. Board SG (2004) Statistical Section and Information Unit Agriculture Administration) Area, Production, Average yield 1970/71-1999-2002.

8. Unit PSER (2004) Sudan Reports and papers relating to cotton production at the Archives Sections (1911/12-1970/71), for different periods

9. Abdalla AK (1993) Production Responsibility Centre and Average Yield Information.

10. Board SG (2004) Report of Cotton Accounting (2000-2004).

11. Blackshear J, Johnson P (2004) Profitability of Cotton Production in the Texas High Plains 1996-2002. Texas Tech University, USA.

12. Gittinger JP (1982) Economic Analysis of Agricultural Projects. Johans Hopkins University Press, Baltimore, USA.

13. Gittinger JP (1973) Compounding and discounting Tables for project Analysis. Johans Hopkins University Press, Baltimore, USA.

A Note on the Interrelation of Volatility Puzzle, Equity Premium Puzzle, and Mean Reversion through State Dependent Preferences

Sung-Sup C[1] **and Giannikos IC**[2*]

[1]*Graduate School of Business Administration, Gachon University, Seongnam-daero, Korea*

[2]*Department of Economics and Finance, Zicklin School of Business, Baruch College, City University of New York ,USA*

Abstract

According to empirical studies, there is a systematic pattern in the temporal behavior of asset returns and this is related to the business cycle. We propose a simple model that captures this behavior. This model is built around a state dependent preference structure where the state dependency is related to the business cycle. In this setting the volatility puzzle, the equity premium puzzle and mean-reversion appear to be indeed interrelated phenomena. A necessary condition for the three puzzles to be explained is that the state variable is negatively correlated with the market portfolio cum business cycle.

Keywords: Volatility puzzle; Equity premium puzzle; Mean reversion

Introduction

In the standard utility-based asset-pricing model [1], a rational agent maximizes expected utility where preferences are assumed to be time-separable and state independent. It is a well-known fact that this model exhibits lack of volatility. It is indeed obvious that, in the absence of exogenous stochastic shocks, the system tends to a fixed point, which implies low volatility. Even in the case of exogenous shocks the resulting dynamics are more stable than empirical evidence suggests as Mehra and Prescott [2] have, among the first, demonstrated within the framework of an elegantly simple model. Among the various empirical studies that have verified the above Shiller [3], Hansen and Singleton [4] and Grossman, et al. [5] are quite prominent.

Thus, an improved asset-pricing model needs an ingredient, which can counteract the smoothing mechanism inherent in the classic model. Several approaches have been presented in attempting to construct models, which can overcome this deficiency. One approach by De Long et al. [6] can be viewed as an attempt to introduce some sort of irrationality. The form of irrationality chosen in this particular model requires the agent to be shortsighted and then more variability results. Another approach, by Epstein and Zin [7], has the agent more concerned about the timing of the resolution of uncertainty. This frustrates the intertemporal arbitrage operation, and thus distorts the smoothing mechanism. Yet another modeling approach, used initially by Constantinides [8], uses the idea of habit formation on the time domain. A positive feedback loop arises from this formulation, which uses a modified preference structure. This approach was extended by a series of papers including Campbell and Cochrane [9], who presented a precisely calibrated model that is broadly consistent with the stylized facts of the financial markets. In all of these different attempts, the common theme is to be able to disable the smoothing mechanism inherent in the dynamic structure of the standard model.

There have been a number of empirical studies though, which have been pointing out towards a different research route. For instance, Ferson and Merrick [10] found that the failure of the standard model is associated with the business cycle. By controlling this cyclical effect, they found less evidence against the standard model in non-recessionary periods but more evidence in recessionary periods. Schwert [11] related stock market volatility to some macro-economic variables, found correlations, and also revealed that both macro-economic variables and the stock market are more volatile in recessionary periods. Others have found that mean reversion in asset returns is related to stock market volatility Campbell and Shiller [12], for instance, claim that the mean reversion and volatility puzzle are interrelated phenomena), and the effect seems more significant in recessionary periods Schwert [11].

Overall there seems to be a cyclical pattern, related to the business cycle, in the observed temporal behavior of asset returns. Thus one could argue that the temporal behavior of asset returns is state dependent, where the state dependency arises from, and is related to, the business cycle. But the temporal behavior of asset returns should be explained within an asset-pricing model. This suggests that the inclusion of some state variable, which is correlated with the business cycle, should be a part of an alternative asset-pricing model.

We propose a simple model, which captures this idea. In this model, the investor's preference structure, which includes a state variable, is correlated with the business cycle. Since the proposed preference is state dependent, the resulting dynamics will be more volatile and will blunt the smoothing mechanism inherent in the classical model. In addition to offering insights with regard to the volatility puzzle, the correlation structure in this model becomes a driving force that resolves both the equity premium puzzle and explains the mean reversion of asset prices. An interesting finding is that all three puzzles are, in this model, driven by the same correlation structure, which seems to suggest that the three are in fact interrelated phenomena.

The state dependent preferences recent literature includes Mehra and Sah [13], Kraus and Sagi [14], Melino and Yang [15] and Danthine et al. [16]. Mehra and Sah [13] derive the partial equilibrium effects of small fluctuations in agent's subjective discount rate and risk aversion on the volatility of asset prices. The other three papers undertake different variations of state-dependent risk aversion. Kraus and Sagi [14] analyze

***Corresponding author:** Christos I Giannikos, Department of Economics and Finance, Zicklin School of Business, Baruch College/CUNY, One Baruch Way, Box B10-225, New York, USA, E-mail: christos.giannikos@baruch.cuny.edu

a complex multi agent model in continuous time where agents exhibit randomly changing risk aversion. Danthine et al. [16] employ the simplest variant of the standard model towards state dependency by allowing the representative agent's coefficient of relative risk aversion to vary with the underlying economy's growth rate. They demonstrate that for very low coefficients of relative risk aversion, the equilibrium risk free and risky security returns are demonstrated to have volatilities and an associated equity premium that substantially exceed what is found in data. Melino and Yang [15] undertake a similar exercise using Epstein-Zin/Weil preferences where the Coefficient of Relative Risk Aversion (CRRA) and the Elasticity of Intertemporal Substitution (EIS) can be specified independently. With state dependence in both CRRA and EIS, they are able to match perfectly the first two moments of equity and risk free returns. Finally Gordon and St-Amour [17] present a model of time varying risk aversion and estimate the implied process on risk aversion arising from consumption and financial data. They find that risk aversion is strongly countercyclical, rising during recessions and falling during expansions.

The outline of this paper is as follows: Section 2 presents the model and basic results, section 3 discusses the implications of the results and section 4 concludes.

The Model

This is a representative agent type of an exchange economy and can be thought of as an economy populated by many identical agents. There exists a single consumption good and two financial assets, a risky stock and a risk-free bond. It is an exchange economy and production and technology are not modeled here.

The rate of return of the risky asset follows the Ito process,

$$\frac{dP}{P} = \alpha\, dt + \sigma\, dz \tag{1}$$

with expected return α, volatility σP2P, and dz is a Wiener process.

The rate of return of the risk-free asset is r.

The equity, or risk, premium is naturally defined as,

$$\pi = \alpha - r \tag{2}$$

The instantaneous direct utility function of the representative agent is u(c, x) where c is consumption and x is a state variable that follows an Ito process with mean f and standard deviation g,

$$dx = f\,dt + g\,dw \tag{3}$$

where f and g are positive constants and w is a Wiener process.

If W is the wealth of the agent and ωis the fraction invested in the risky asset then

$$y = \omega W$$

is the amount of wealth invested in the risky asset.

Finally the correlation between the two Wiener processes dz and dw is given by,

$$\phi\, dt = E[dz\, dw] \tag{5}$$

Following is the optimization problem that the representative agent faces,

$$\underset{c,y}{Max}\,\{E_t \int_t^{\infty} e^{-\rho(\tau - t)} u(c,x)\, d\tau\} \tag{6}$$

subject to (3) and the following additional budget constraint:

$$dW = (rW + \pi y - c)dt + \sigma y\, dz \tag{7}$$

Applying the Hamilton/Jacobi/Bellman equation and Ito's lemma, the indirect utility function V (W, x) will satisfy the following equation,

$$\rho V(W,x) = Max\{u(c,x) + V_W(rW + \pi y - c) + \tfrac{1}{2}V_{WW}\sigma^2 y^2 + V_x f + \tfrac{1}{2}V_{xx}g^2 + V_{Wx}\sigma y g\phi\} \tag{8}$$

where subscripts denote partial derivatives with respect to corresponding variables.

The first order conditions are,

$$-V_W(W,x) + u_c(c,x) = 0 \tag{9}$$

$$\pi V_W + \sigma^2 y V_{WW} + \sigma g \phi V_{Wx} = 0 \tag{10}$$

In equilibrium, an investor holds all of his wealth in the risky asset, and net borrowing will be zero. Thus the equilibrium condition is,

$$y(W,x) = W \tag{11}$$

In order to get a closed form solution we need one more refinement: to specify the instantaneous utility function. We assume that,

$$u(c,x) = e^{-\lambda x}\frac{c^{1-\delta}}{1-\delta} \tag{12}$$

where δ is the coefficient of the relative risk aversion (CRRA) and λ is a constant.

Under the above assumptions the value function should be of the following form:

$$V(W,x) = e^{-\theta x}\frac{W^{1-\delta}}{1-\delta} \tag{13}$$

With equation (12), equation (9) becomes,

$$c^* = e^{\frac{\theta-\lambda}{\delta}x}\, W \tag{14}$$

From the above follows that,

$$Var(\frac{dc}{c}) = \sigma^2 + [(\frac{\theta-\lambda}{\delta})g]^2 + 2(\frac{\theta-\lambda}{\delta})\phi\sigma g \tag{15}$$

Where σP2 P= Var (dW/W), and φσg=Cov (dW/W, dx).

In equation (15), the first two terms of the consumption volatility are always positive. For the volatility of consumption to be less than that of wealth, the covariance (last) term has to be negative and must exceed the second term in absolute value. This requires, φ, the correlation between dx and dW, to be negative, assuming θ>λ. In other words, the negative correlation structure between dx and dW is a necessary condition for solving the volatility puzzle. In addition, if -2σφ>[(θ-λ)/δ] g and θ>xλ, the volatility of consumption is less than that of wealth.

Given equation (12), the portfolio choice equation (10) along with equilibrium condition (11) becomes,

$$\omega^* = 1 = \frac{\pi}{\delta\sigma^2} + \frac{\theta}{\delta\sigma^2}\phi\sigma g \tag{16}$$

where φσg=Cov (dW/W, x). In order for a high equity premium to be consistent with low RRA, the covariance term on the right-hand-side of equation (16) has to be negative. This requires the correlation between x and W to be negative, assuming θ>0. A solution to the equity premium puzzle, therefore, must satisfy φ<0, where θ>0. The reason for this is obvious since the equivalent equation for the standard model is missing the second term on the right-hand-side i.e. it is

$$\omega^* = 1 = \frac{\pi}{\delta\sigma^2} \quad (17)$$

With equation (12) and equation (13), we have

$$V_W = e^{-\theta x} W^{-\delta}$$

$$V_{WW} = -\delta e^{-\theta x} W^{-\delta-1}$$

$$V_x = -\theta e^{-\theta x} \frac{W^{1-\delta}}{1-\delta}$$

$$V_{xx} = \theta^2 e^{-\theta x} \frac{W^{1-\delta}}{1-\delta} \quad (18)$$

$$V_{Wx} = -\theta e^{-\theta x} W^{-\delta}$$

$$c^* = e^{\frac{\theta-\lambda}{\delta}x} W$$

$$u(c^*, x) = e^{-\lambda x} \left(\frac{1}{1-\delta}\right) W^{1-\delta} e^{(\theta-\lambda)\frac{(1-\delta)}{\delta}x}$$

Substituting (9), (10) and (11) into (8) yields,

$$\rho V = u(c^*, x) + V_W W(r + \tfrac{1}{2}\pi) - V_W c^* + V_x f + \tfrac{1}{2} V_{xx} g^2 + \tfrac{1}{2} V_{Wx} W \sigma \phi \quad (19)$$

Substituting (18) into (19), we get,

$$(r + \tfrac{1}{2}\pi) - \tfrac{1}{2}\theta\sigma g\phi + \left(\frac{\delta}{1-\delta}\right) e^{\frac{\theta-\lambda}{\delta}x} - \frac{\rho}{1-\delta} - \frac{\theta f}{1-\delta} + \frac{1}{2}\frac{\theta^2 g^2}{1-\delta} = 0 \quad (20)$$

Differentiating equation (20) with respect to x, we have the following,

$$\pi_x - \sigma_x \theta g\phi + 2r_x = 2\left(\frac{\delta}{\delta-1}\right)\left(\frac{\theta-\lambda}{\delta}\right) e^{\frac{\theta-\lambda}{\delta}x} \quad (21)$$

We assume here that σBxB and rBxB are both equal to zero. The justification for this is the following. In regards to the interest rate derivative this is a direct consequence of the interest rate been easier to measure than the premium. Thus investors will respond more to interest rate changes than to premium changes. Their responses, in turn, will dampen the interest rate changes more than the risk premium changes and hence rBxB=0. Concerning the derivative of the volatility, there exist some stylized facts that suggest that it might not be equal to zero. For example, it is argued that the volatility is known as conditionally heteroskedastic, and unconditionally leptokurtic. The discrete time (G)ARCH model fits well in this case because it creates simulated data series that exhibit persistence and busting. But, these facts are associated with high frequency data (e.g. daily data). Mean reversion, on the other hand, is a long horizon phenomenon, which tends to follow the business cycle frequency. In investigating the long run behavior of asset prices, therefore, we can assume that σBxB=0.

With σBxB and rBxB being equal to zero then, (21) directly implies

$$\pi_x = 2\left(\frac{\theta-\lambda}{\delta-1}\right) e^{\frac{\theta-\lambda}{\delta}x} \quad (22)$$

From the above we can conclude that mean reversion can also be justified in the context of this model if δ>1, (φ<0) and θ>λ.

So we have arrived at the following proposition:

UProposition: UIn the context of the above model there exist parameter values, which are compatible with resolving the volatility puzzle, the equity premium puzzle and mean reversion simultaneously.

The Implications of the Model

Empirical studies (Ferson and Merrick [10], Schwert [11], Ferson and Harvey [18], Fama and French [19], and Kandel and Stambaugh [20] among others) have established that there exists a cyclical pattern in the temporal behavior of asset returns, the cyclicality being related to the business cycle. We therefore proposed here a model where investors behave cyclically. This is captured by a state dependent preference structure where a state variable is correlated with the market portfolio cum business cycle. In these circumstances, we prove that a negative correlation structure becomes instrumental towards explaining the three major puzzles. A negative correlation structure clearly implies that people are more relaxed in making economic decisions when the economy is booming but become more desperate when the economy is in recession. Of course with any concave utility function, the marginal utility is low in a boom and high in recession. But with the negative correlation structure we propose this effect becomes magnified.

Obviously, when agents exhibit such a cyclical preference structure, the temporal behavior of asset returns becomes cyclical.

It is possible to offer an intuitive explanation to the above inter-related phenomena. Consider investors at the thought of the business cycle expecting a rise. Since rises are highly persistent, the investor would expect the bull market to last for some time. One would also expect the marginal utility of consumption to fall and the demand for securities to rise along with security prices. Contrast this with investors at the peak anticipating a fall in the economic activity. One would expect that marginal utility of consumption would rise causing a shift away from securities and thus price declines. The point is that this cyclical change in the attitude should magnify swings in stock returns over the business cycle. The ultimate roots of swings in stock returns relate back to swings in economic activity in general. Hence mean reversion.

We also have high volatility in the stock market, not necessarily because the market is crowded with noise traders, but because investors have cyclically volatile preferences. In the face of a linear budget constraint and a concave, with respect to consumption, preference structure, investors still want to smooth out their consumption stream. But with the proposed preference structure, they will be affected by a cyclically volatile state variable. The correlation structure in our model allows this kind of transformation of the state variable volatility into the stock market volatility. In other words, a volatile state variable in the utility function becomes absorbed into the stock market and makes it volatile. Since the state variable in the preferences co-varies with the stock market, the consumption process does not have to move together with the stock market; consumption becomes smoother, and the stock market becomes more volatile.

The high equity premium is also justified within our model. When the stock market becomes more volatile (i.e., stock becomes more risky), the risk-free asset becomes more valuable since the safe asset provides a hedging service. When the safe asset becomes more valuable, the real interest rate becomes lower. The observed high equity premium can now be explained through this low real interest rate as data also confirms.

Conclusion

We have introduced a model that is built around a state dependent preference structure where the state dependency is related to the business cycle. In this setting the volatility puzzle, the equity premium puzzle and mean-reversion appear to be interrelated phenomena.

We have also identified the state variable in the preference structure in terms of its correlation structure with the market portfolio (business cycle). So investors behave cyclically in our model. But how can we interpret this state variable in the preference structure? We argue below that it is due to a liquidity-related imperfection.

Many economists have argued that liquidity-related imperfections follow the business cycle, and that the failure of the standard model comes from this liquidity-related imperfection [21]. Moreover, Mehra and Prescott [2] argue that an alternative preference structure must be shown useful for organizing and interpreting not only behaviors in the financial markets but also those in other markets. If we interpret this alternative preference structure as something related to liquidity, then the extension to other markets follows easily. Liquidity-related imperfections are well recognized in terms of other markets, and many economists argue that economic phenomena can be better explained by incorporating this liquidity-related imperfection (for an earlier survey of the literature see Hayashi [22]).

Indeed the state dependency of our model can be thought of as a Lucas [23] taste shock to the utility function, which could, in turn, approximate a decision problem in the face of liquidity constraints. Liquidity constraints are difficult to deal with since they imply multi-linear or non-linear budget constraints. According to the Household Production Approach [23] though, we can effectively deal with state dependent preference structure with a single linear budget constraint, by interpreting the state variable as something related to liquidity, say, a liquidity need. Our model, therefore, can be thought of as an attempt to capture the flavor of liquidity constraints, and yet avoid the analytical intractability of modeling them directly while working within the context of the standard model. The question of empirically testing the proposed model is left to future research.

Acknowledgements

The authors are grateful to William Brock, George Constantinides, Duffie [24], Bong-Soo Lee, Howard Thompson and John B. Donaldson for comments while they retain responsibility for any remaining errors. Christos Giannikos wishes to acknowledge a summer research grant from the Wasserman Department of Economics and Finance, Zicklin School of Business, Baruch College, CUNY.

References

1. Lucas R Jr (1978) An Equilibrium Model of the Business Cycle. Econometrica 46: 1429-1445.
2. Mehra R and Prescott E (1985) The Equity Premium: A Puzzle. Journal of Monetary Economics, 15: 145-161.
3. Shiller R (1981) Do Stock Prices Move Too Much To Be Justified By Subsequent Changes in Dividends. American Economic Review 71: 71-87.
4. Hansen LP and Singleton KJ (1983) Stochastic Consumption, Risk Aversion, and the Temporal Behavior of Asset Returns. The Journal of Political Economy 91: 249-265.
5. Grossman SJ, Melino A and Shiller RJ (1987) Estimating the Continuous-Time Consumption-Based Asset Pricing Model. Journal of Business and Economic Statistics 5: 315-327.
6. De Long JB, Shleifer A, Summers L, and Waldman R (1990) Noise Trader Risk in Financial Markets. The Journal of Political Economy 98: 703-738.
7. Epstein L and Zin S (1989) Substitution, Risk Aversion and the Temporal Behavior of Consumption and Asset Returns. Econometrica, 57: 937-969.
8. Constantinides G (1990) Habit Formation: A Resolution of the Equity Premium Puzzle. The Journal of Political Economy 98: 519-543.
9. Campbell J and Cochrane J (1999) By Force of Habit: A Consumption Based Explanation of Aggregate Stock Market Behavior. The Journal of Political Economy 107: 205-251.
10. Ferson W and Merrick J (1987) Non-Stationarity and State-of-the-Business-Cycle Effects in Consumption Based Asset pricing Model. Journal of Financial Economics 18: 127-146.
11. Schwert G W (1989) Why Does Stock Market Volatility Change Over Time? The Journal of Finance 44: 1115-1153.
12. Campbell JY and Shiller RJ (1988) Stock Prices, Earnings and Expected Dividends. The Journal of Finance 43: 661-676.
13. Mehra R and Sah R (2002) Mood Fluctuations, Projection Bias, and Volatility of Equity Prices. Journal of Economic Dynamics and Control 26: 869-887.
14. Kraus A and Sagi J (2000) Aggregation of State Dependent Preferences When Markets are Incomplete. Mimeo, Haas School of Business, University of California, Berkeley, USA.
15. Melino A and Yang A (2003) State Dependent Preferences Can Explain the Equity Premium Puzzle. Review of Economic Dynamics 6: 806-830.
16. Danthine JP, Donaldson JB, Giannikos C and Guirguis H (2003) On the Consequences of State Dependent Preferences for the Pricing of Financial Assets, Mimeo, Columbia University.
17. Gordon S and St-Amour P (2003) Asset Returns and State Dependent Preferences. Mimeo, Universite Laval.
18. Ferson W and Harvey C (1991) Variation of Economic Risk Premiums. The Journal of Political Economy 99: 385-415.
19. Fama E and French K (1988) Permanent and Temporary Components of Stock Prices. The Journal of Political Economy 96: 246-273.
20. Kandel S and Stambaugh R (1990) Expectations and Volatility of Consumption and Asset Returns. Review of Financial Studies 3: 207-232.
21. Zeldes SP (1989) Consumption and Liquidity Constraints: An Empirical Investigation. The Journal of Political Economy 97: 305-346.
22. Hayashi F (1985) The Effect of Liquidity Constraints on Consumption: A Cross-Sectional Analysis. The Quarterly Journal of Economics 100: 183-206.
23. Lucas R (1975) An Equilibrium Model of the Business Cycle. The Journal of Political Economy 83:1113-1144.
24. Duffie D and Singleton K (1993) Simulated Moments Estimation of Markeov Models and Asset Prices. Econometrica 61: 929-952.

Impact of Macro Variables on Karachi Stock Exchange

Rabia N* and Khakan N

University of Lahore, Lahore, Pakistan

Abstract

In this paper we have studied that impact of macro variables on Karachi stock exchange. Karachi stock exchange is very interesting topic for the discussion. Karachi stock exchange is known as one of the oldest stock exchange of Asia. Karachi stock exchange is the largest stock exchange of Pakistan. Karachi stock exchange is the dependent variables and inflation, interest rate and exchange rate and GDP are the independent variables. We have taken the data from period 1992 to 2012. We have found that there is 80 %variation. Therefore we can say there is a strong relationship among the variables. While other variables have shown that GDP, interest rate and inflation has strong relationship with kse stock index while interest rate have negative relationship with Karachi stock exchange. The increase and decrease the stock prices will affect the performance of the economy. In this paper researcher want to found out the fundamental marc variables which have impact on stock exchange and also want to found out that what are the impact of these variables on the government policies like monetary and facial policy. Fundamental macro variables are export, money, supply, interest rate.

Keywords: Facial policy; Monetary policy; Asia; GDP; interest rate; Inflation

Introduction

Karachi stock exchange is very interesting topic for the discussion. In this paper we have find out impact of macro variables on Karachi stock exchange. Karachi stock exchange is known as oldest stock exchange of Asia Karachi stock exchange is the largest stock exchange of Pakistan. Stock market means the prices of securities which are traded in stock exchange. Stock exchange has a vital role for the fostering capital formation. Stock exchange has a main role for the healthy economy of any country. Stock exchange is work as a channel between stock investors and stock borrowers. In the words simple stock market is place where we can trade securities. According to different approaches statues that stock market contain two types of investors. One approaches says that investors use their different techniques to overcome the stock market prices and market is insufficient there. The second approaches says that all the investors have the same information ad cannot beat the stock prices. Koh says that share price depends upon the effect of macro variables. Khenet et al. analysis that stock market performances are affected because macroeconomic variables are flotation in nature [1-4]. Lee and Wang in Thailand stock exchange and stock return have positive relationship. Mohamed et al. analyzed that impact of different variables on stock return. Bollersley investors are very attractive towards the profits. With the help of determination of value of demand and supply we can know prices of securities which are traded in stock market as daily basis. The fluctuation in stock market due to different factors like economic and political behavior of country. Karachi stock exchange also reacts due to these factors. In simple words during business hours buyers and sellers exchange their holdings. Stock exchange is the place where investors seek reward in the shape of capital gain. Exchange investment projects are useful to mobilize the nation's saving. Stock market is the channel between savings and borrower's. According to leading stocks of world reported that negative growth ranging from Pakistan 50.8% and china 2.7% during the facial year. Since the last decade the Pakistani stock market was highly disturbed due to financial crises. In March 2005 stock market was crashed in year 2005. The second collage was observed in year 2006. The biggest crash in the may 2008 to January 2009 it was the worst crash in the history of Pakistan. Karachi stock exchange was dropped more than 12 thousand points. There are many reasons due to which prices of demand and supply increases and decrease and have impact on market behavior. According to different researches increase in inflation will increase in the income of demand and supply. The main reason for inflation of any country is there is inverse relationship between demand and supply. According to different economist view that increase in prices of things will indicate the inflation. In other words inflation means expansion of money supply. Many researchers have proved that the rate on inflation has impact on the stock market volatility. Commonly we can say inflation has two main parts 1) expected inflation 2) unexpected inflation. Expected inflation rate is plan one year to year between economists and consumer. Unexpected inflation means that what we can expect between economic and consumers. In this study has shown that main effect of unexpected inflation is due to redistribution of wealth. After the world war 2 in USA the inflation rate is between 3% to 6% for many years which has impact On the performance of the stock market inflation created natural bias. Due to inflation in the world every country has worst stock market. In this paper also explores that if government could not control the inflation then worst stock market ratio will increase. In the high inflation many assets failed to keep up. Government should control it soon otherwise stock will be collapse over 95%. Morever, many studies has shown that in the period of high inflation dividend will increase in consumer prices. For the policy point of review stock prices and inflation has relationship. According to famar stock market are reflect from the macroeconomic variable therefore it is efficient. Chakravarity shows that stock market and inflation relationship. Mukherjee has shown there is two way causation between stock market performance and inflation. Inflation is due to increase rate and volatility. Inflation has very huge impact on the economic competitiveness. This study has shown that how there is relationship between interest rate and inflation rate. According to

***Corresponding author:** Rabia N, University of Lahore, Lahore, Pakistan
E-mail: rabianajaf@hotmail.com

different hypothesis high inflation shows high uncertainty. According to Li henggua inflation and stock prices has multiple relationships [5]. According to Zhaorang shows that we cannot consider impact of inflation on stock prices a single factor. Modern economy has common feature is called stock market. Stock market is famous for the development of the economy. After the stock market failure government has enable of raise financing for new projects. The status of investment in stock market is long term. Any variable which has impact on economy also impact of stock exchange [6]. According to different economist's inflation is one of the factors which have negative impact of stock exchange. We can measure stock market performance with the help of market capitalization. In this paper we discuss the following issue like 1) what is correlation between stock market and inflation 2) how much correlation between stock market liquidity and inflation. In all the countries inflation caused by monetary authorizes. Therefore, we can say impact of inflation on the stock market has implications on policy market. All the studies shown that stock market performance has effect on the economy [7-9]. The basic characteristics of this Indian economy that it has strong economic growth. A unique feature of this economy is that it has become second faster economy of the world. In the financial year 2008, 2010 the GDP growth has average near about 6.8% [10]. The target growth rate is 8% and the growth of Indian s service sector was 9.5% in 2008-2009. The best feature of Indian economy that it has high growth. In recent years Asian economy was facing crisis and Indian economy has proven its strength. According to different research foreign exchange reserves has record level in June [11-15]. In June 2009, the foreign exchange reserves were reaching a record level of \$300. In May 2002, the Indian rupees were in strength as compared to dollar \$1=rs 43.51. In 2004, the inflation rate contained at 5.5% in 2006 the inflation rate was at 6% and slow down at the beginning of the year 2009 was 9% (Figures 1-4 and Table 1).

Scope of Study

The scope of this study is find nature and strength of relation between stock return and inflation, and interest rate.

Objectives

1) What are the relationship between stock market and inflation?

2) What are the relationship between stock market and interest rate?

3) What are the relationship between stock market and exchange rate?

Methodology

The purpose of this study is to measure that affect of marc variables on the stock prices of Karachi. We explained the research model by

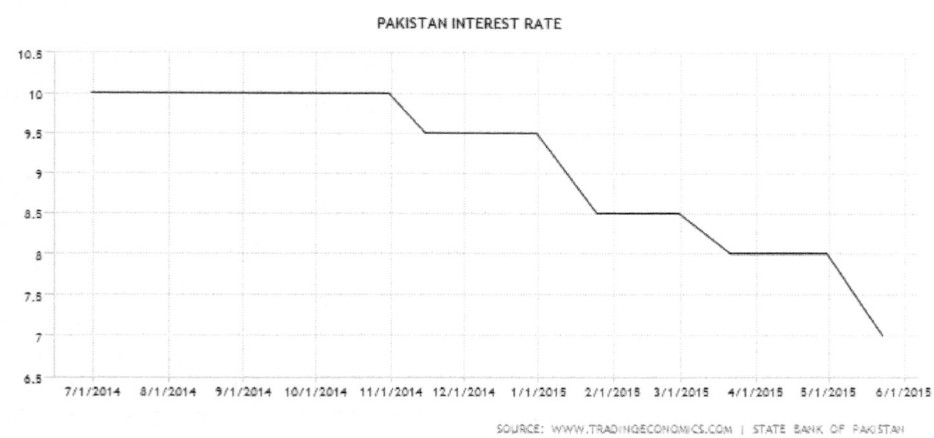

Figure 1: Pakistani interest rate.

Figure 2: Pakistani Growth rate.

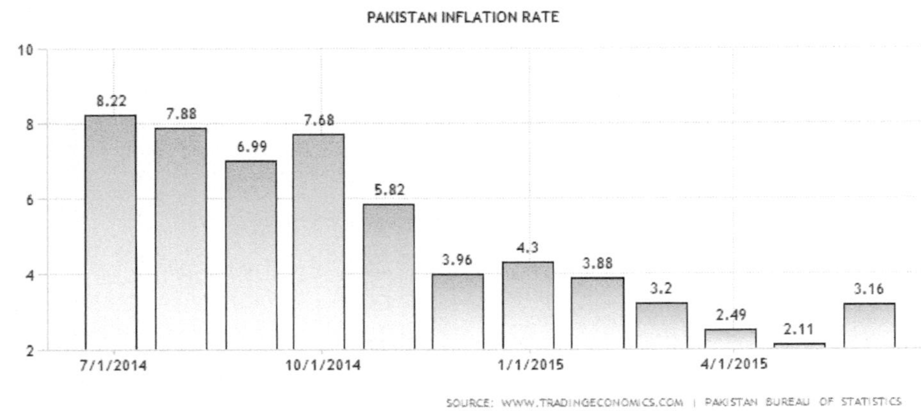

Figure 3: Pakistani inflation rate.

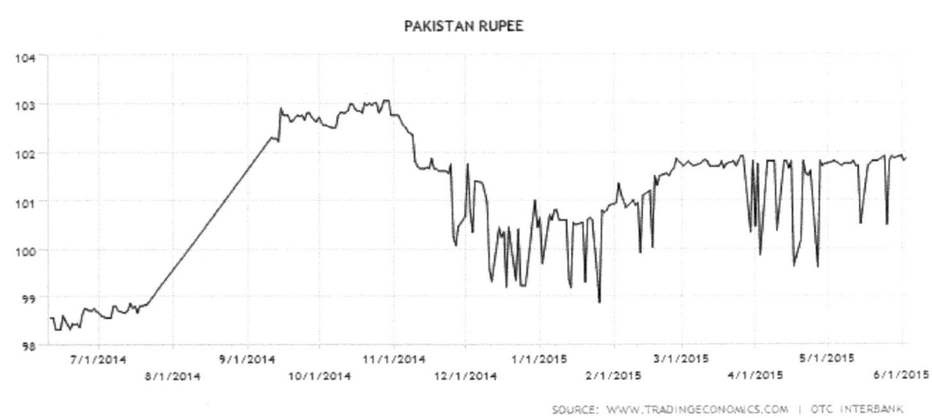

Figure 4: Pakistani rupee.

No.	Market	%
1	United States	47.7
2	Japan	10.3
3	United Kingdom	10.4
4	France	4.3
5	Canada	3.4
6	Germany	2.8
7	Switzerland	2.7
8	Italy	2.2
9	Australia	2.1
10	Netherlands	2.1

Table 1: Top Ten Biggest Stock Markets in the World (% of Total).

using the different variables. In this model Karachi stock exchange is the dependent variables and other are independent variables. We use yearly data from 1992 to 2012 (Figures 5 and 6).

The model:

Y=a+b1(x1)+b2(x2)+b3(x3)+b4(x4)+e

Y=a+b1(Δexc)+b2(Δgdp)+b3(Δinflation)+b4(Δint rate)

Where y =dependent variable

X1=exchange rate

X2=GDP

X3=inflation

X4=interest rate

Statistical tools

For the interpretation of the model we have used Pearson product movement correlation coefficient and multiple regression models. Table 2 shows that there is positive relationship between Karachi stock prices and exchange rate and there is negative relationship between interest rate and Karachi stock prices. At the end 100% change in independent variable will lead to 5.3033% change in stock prices [16]. For the purpose of checking that data is significant or not we use t ratio.

Method

Table 2 shows the relationship between dependent variables and independents variables.

Δkse 100 index=a +b1(Δex)+b2(ΔIR)+b3(Δinf)+b4(ΔGDP)

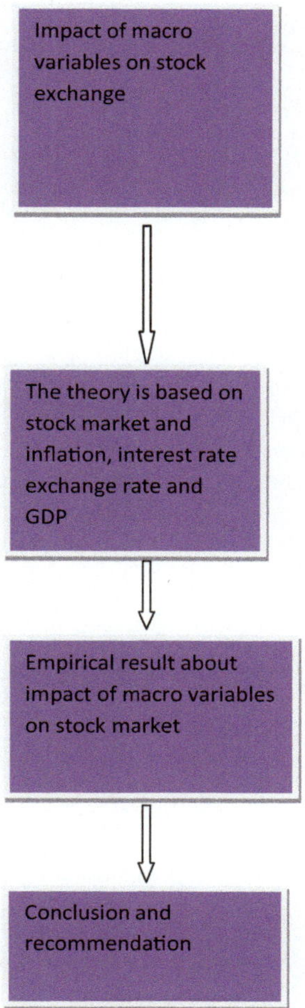

Figure 5: Research Framework.

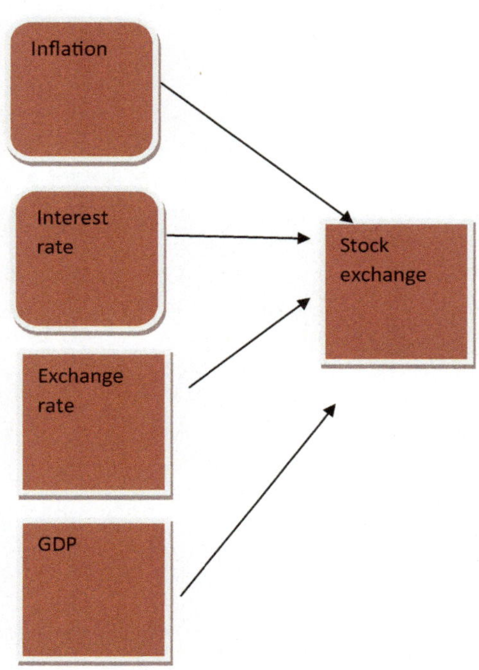

Figure 6: Theoretical framework.

All the data have shown that change in the independent variable will cause change in dependent variable. Table 2 shows that exchange rate, interest rate and gdp has positive and inflation show the negative relationship.

R2

R2 is used to checking that data is fit or not. It ranges normally form 0 to. The value of r2 is 0.8098 which is nearest to 1. It means there is 80% variation and this model is good fit.

Pearson's product movement correlation co efficient:

The purpose of person's product movement correlation is the show the relationship is positive and negative. It is represented by p and denoted by greek letter. It ranges from +1 to -1.

GDP and KSE 100 index

After the evaluation of data in Tables 6 and 10 shows that have not strong relationship. The model suggests that there is 15.5% correlation is present (Table 3-4).

F ratio

The purpose of f ratio is that overall model is significant or not. For this purpose we use a confidence interval. The value of f ratio in Table 4 is 15.9593 which shows that exchange rate and stock prices are the positive relationship.

Sample size	20
Coefficient of determination R^2	0.8098
Readjusted	0.7591
Multiple correlation coefficient	0.8998
Residual standard deviation	21.3378

Table 2: Relationship between dependent variables and independents variables.

Independent variables	Coefficient	Std. Error	Partial	T	P
(Constant)	-65.7771				
Exchange	1.5386	0.3921	0.7119	3.926	0.0015
Interest	-2.3135	2.3151	-0.2499	-0.998	0.3336
Inflation	4.1828	1.3476	0.6255	3.105	0.0074
GDP	5.3033	3.0641	0.4081	1.732	0.1041

Table 3: Relationship between dependent variables and independents variables.

Source	DF	Sum of Squares	Mean Square
Regression	4	29065.1541	7266.2886
Residual	16	6829.5823	455.3056

Table 4: Relationship between dependent variables and independents variables.

F-ratio	15.9593
Significance level	P<0.002

Table 5: Relationship between dependent variables and independents variables.

Variable	R
Exchange	0.7558
Interest	-0.4301
Inflation	0.4649
GDP	0.1538

Table 6: Relationship between dependent variables and independents variables.

Interest rate and kse stock prices:

Tables 5-9 shows that there is negative relationship between stock exchange and interest rate and correlation is insignificant because value of 0.585 is greater than 0.05. The study of nishat and shaheen in 2007 shows that there is negative correlation between interest rate and stock prices. When inflation rates moved to high then government should try to control hyper inflation. Increase the rate of has a bad impact on stock prices [17,18].

Inflation rate and kse 100 index

Tables 10 and 11 shows that there is moderate positive relationship between inflation and stock prices index and the p value is less than 0.05 therefore correlation is significant. For all the tables it has shown that independent variables shows positive and negative and weak correlation [19-21].

Conclusion

We have discussed the brief summary of the paper that changes in the macroeconomic variable have impact on the stock exchange prices in any nation. There are no variables which have impact on the stock prices. There are three types of stock exchange in Pakistani economy. 1) Islamabad stock exchange, 2) Karachi stock exchange, 3) Lahore stock exchange. Karachi stock exchange is one of biggest stock exchange of Pakistan economy and it has capacity to capture 76% of the capital market of Pakistan. Karachi stock exchange is the backbone four economies. In the Table 1 r2 is used to check that model is good or not. Value of r2 shows that model is good. And we used the t test to check that individual significant and f test is used to check that model is significant or not. According to Pearson's correlation model shows that exchange rate and stock prices have positive correlation. There is a moderate positive correlation between inflation and stock exchange. The relationship between interest rate and stock prices is negative. All these relationship has shown that there is not strong correlation among the variables.

		KSE	Exchange
KSE	Correlation Coefficient Significance Level Pn		0.757 0.0002 20
Exchange	Correlation Coefficient Significance Level Pn	0.757 0.0002 20	

Table 7: Relationship between dependent variables and independents variables.

		KSE	Interest
KSE	Correlation Coefficient Significance Level Pn		-0.431 0.0585 20
Interest	Correlation Coefficient Significance Level Pn	-0.431 0.0585 20	

Table 8: Relationship between dependent variables and independents variables.

		KSE	Inflation
KSE	Correlation Coefficient Significance Level Pn		0.466 0.0388 20
Inflation	Correlation Coefficient Significance Level Pn	0.466 0.0388 20	

Table 9: Relationship between dependent variables and independents variables.

		KSE	GDP
KSE	Correlation Coefficient Significance Level Pn		0.155 0.5172 20
GDP	Correlation Coefficient Significance Level Pn	0.155 0.5172 20	

Table 10: Relationship between dependent variables and independents variables.

		Exchange	Interest	Inflation	GDP
Exchange	Correlation Coefficient Significance Level Pn		-0.437 0.0547 20	0.194 0.4158 20	-0.219 0.3567 20
Interest	Correlation Coefficient Significance Level Pn	-0.437 0.0547 20		0.345 0.1382 20	-0.418 0.0657 20
Inflation	Correlation Coefficient Significance Level Pn	0.194 0.4158 20	0.345 0.1382 20		-0.098 0.6788 20
GDP	Correlation Coefficient Significance Level Pn	-0.219 0.3567 20	-0.418 0.0657 20	-0.098 0.6788 20	

Table 11: Relationship between dependent variables and independents variables.

Recommended

1) Practitioners and analysts should try to prediction about the future stock prices.

2) They should find out the stock market movement.

3) Investors should forecast how financial market changes.

References

1. Adrangi (1998) Impact of the Inflation Evidence 20: 63-76.
2. Bakshi (1996) About Inflation, Asset Prices and Interest Rates. Review of Financial Studies 10: 342-277.
3. Caporale (1998) Correlation between Inflation and Stock Prices, 9: 268-269.
4. Charles, Adjasi (2008) What is the Effect of Exchange Rate on the Indian Stock Exchange, Banking and finance Research 3.
5. Chatrath (1999) Relationship between Inflation and growth rate 9: 439-449.
6. Choudhry (1998) Relationship between Inflation and Rates of Return: University of Sadina, Department of Banking.
7. Dicky (1979, 1981) Likelihood Ratio with a Unit Root. Econometric 40: 1059-1074.
8. Engle (1988) Co-integration and estimation and testing. Econometric 57: 253-278.
9. Fama (1982) Relationship between Stock Returns and Money. African Economic Review 73: 547-567.
10. Fama (1978) Relationship Asset Returns and Inflation. J financ 57: 2012323.
11. Fisher (1931) The Theory of Interest.
12. Fraser (2000) Has shown The UK Stock Market's Relationship with and American Stock Markets.
13. Gallagher L (2005) The Stock Return- and Inflation. Economics Letters 77: 149-158.
14. Geetha, et al. (2011) What are The Relationship between Inflation and Stock Market: Evidence from Mal China. Int J Eco financ 1: 1-18.
15. Geske (1981) What is impact of Fiscal and Monetary Linkage between Stock Returns and Inflation? 9-83.

16. Graham (1996) Inflation, Real Stock Returns, and Monetary Policy. Applied Financial Economics 8: 27-37.

17. Granger (1989) Discuses about the different recent developments in a concept of causality. J Eco 37: 199-214.

18. Granger (1997) A bivariate Causality between Stock Prices and Exchange Rates.

19. Greenspan, Allen (1996) What Do Budget Deficits Do? Issues and Options: 139-148.

20. Hamrita (2007) The Multi-Scale Interaction between Interest Rate and inflation.

21. Hardouvelis GA (1988) The predictive power of recent monetary regimes. Journal of banking 44: 339-358.

Characteristics of International Acquisitions Based on Evidence in Southeast Asia

Khaliq IH[1]*, Naeem B[2], Abbas Q[2] and Khalid S[3]

[1]*Pacific Western University (USA), Warid Telecom, Pakistan*
[2]*Department of Management Sciences, COMSATS Institute of Information Technology, Lahore, Pakistan*
[3]*Lecturer, Department of Education, University of Sargodha, Sargodha, Pakistan*

Abstract

This study investigates large cross border deals above USD 1 billion during the 2000 to 2011 time frame to explore whether deal values, valuation multiples and payment modes differ for acquisitions by emerging market firms when compared with acquisitions by developed market acquirers; for diversified acquisitions vis-à-vis non-diversified acquisitions; or during a recessionary phase.

We find that mean deal values differ with the economy of the acquirer and target (emerging market/developed market). Contrary to expectations, valuation multiples are not impacted by either the economy of the acquirer and target or during recession. Bidders pay similar premiums when they make related and unrelated acquisitions. Payment is more likely to be in the form of cash for unrelated acquisitions and in the form of stock for higher deal values. Recession and economy of acquirer and target do not impact the payment method.

There are several research studies which have looked at characteristics of acquirers, targets and market reactions to acquisition announcements. However, understanding emerging market firms' deal characteristics vis-à-vis developed market firm's deals and understanding the impact of recession on deal characteristics raises a significant research question which we explore.

We thank FOBE 2012 organizers at IMT Ghaziabad, India for comments on an earlier version of the paper.

Keywords: Characteristics; International acquisitions; Southeast; Emerging market

Introduction

Markets react differently when developed and emerging market firms make cross border acquisitions depending on whether the acquirer and target is developed or developing [1,2]. The characteristics of acquirers and target have been studied in several research studies. However, given that acquisitions by emerging market firms have grown from a meager 2% of worldwide cross border deal volumes in 1999 to 29% of worldwide cross border deal values in 2010, understanding of emerging market firms' deal characteristics vis-à-vis developed market firm's deals raises a significant research question. This study investigates cross border deals above USD 1 billion during the 2000 to 2011 time frame to explore whether deal values, valuation multiples and payment modes (cash/stock) differ depending on whether the acquirer or target is from a developed market or emerging market. We also examine the impact of related and unrelated acquisitions on deal characteristics. Our data period helps us to cover another question which is whether deal characteristics are impacted by recession during the recession phase of 2001 and 2008-2009.

Figure 1 plots the cross border deal values along with the share of developed and emerging market acquirers. We clearly see that recession has had an impact on the value of cross border Mergers and Acquisitions (M&A) causing it to decline in the years of recession. Hence, we make a hypothesis that recession has an impact on deal value (Figure 1).

Theory and hypothesis

Our research question is motivated by several studies on internationalization. The review of these studies can primarily be divided into several categories. Reasons for going cross border [3-6], characteristics of acquirers and targets [7,8], and value effects of going cross border [1,9,10]. We place our study in the literature for cross border deals where acquirers and targets belong to different kinds of economies and whether these differences in deal characteristics are significant.

Chernykh, Liebenberg and Macias document the growth of acquisitions by emerging market firms during the period 1990 to 2007 [11]. They report a sharp increase in the number and size of

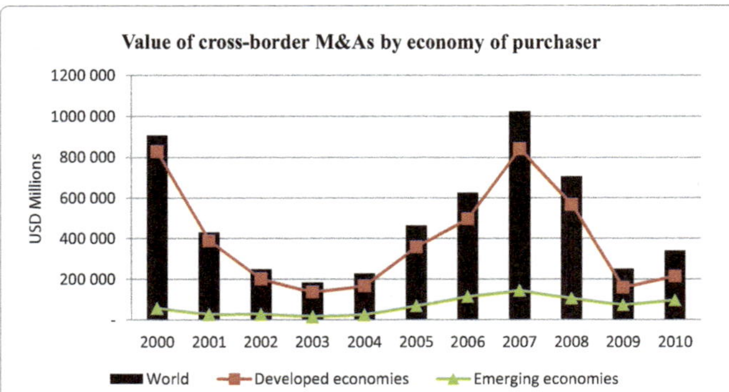

Figure 1: Computed from UNCTAD World Investment Review 2011.

***Corresponding author:** Imran Hameed Khaliq, Pacific Western University (USA), Warid Telecom, Pakistan, E-mail: imranhameedkhaliq@gmail.com

acquisitions by emerging market firms and note specifically the growth of acquisition of developed market targets by emerging market firms. In this study, we analyze cross border deals during the 2000 to 2011 time frame to explore whether deal values, valuation multiples and payment modes (cash/stock) differ depending on whether the acquirer or target is from a developed market or emerging market.

Hypothesis 1: There are differences between deal values, valuation multiples and payment modes between the different Acquirer-Target pairs

Our study also finds its place in literature where major economic events like recession impact the decision to go cross border for an acquisition. Acharya, Shin and Yorulmazer, Aguiar, Mark, and Gopinath have described how assets in an economy undergoing a crisis are sold off at low rates [12,13]. This study tries to explore whether individual deal characteristics are impacted by recession during the recession phase of 2001 and 2008-2009. Aguiar et al. have found that median price to book value ratios declined during the Asian financial crisis for acquisitions of Asian firms. We extend this logic to state that it is likely that worldwide assets are sold off at low valuation multiples during a recession [13].

Hypothesis 2: There are differences between deal values, valuation multiples and payment modes between the different Acquirer-Target pairs before and after recession

Jahera, Hand and Lloyd study various factors that impact acquisition premiums in controlling stake acquisitions and find that diversification has a negative influence on acquisition premium [14]. King, Dalton and Daily in their review of M&A literature found that related acquisitions have a positive impact on performance [15]. On the basis of these studies we test the hypothesis that acquisition of controlling stakes in related industries would involve a higher valuation multiple paid out.

Hypothesis 3: Acquisition of controlling stakes in related industries would involve a higher valuation multiple paid out Faccio and Masulis find that the method of payment cash, stock or combination of payments is influenced by deal characteristics such as shareholding of majority owners; relative size of bidder and target, leverage of bidder; whether the deal is in the same industry or not etc [16]. Facciao and Mausilis report that the probability of a cash financed deal decreases when the bidder and target are in the same industry [16]. Martin studies the impact of various factor that influence the method of payment in a deal including growth opportunities of bidders, managerial stock ownership, cash levels with acquirers, institutional share ownership and business cycles [17]. They find that an increase in stock market values is associated with an increase in stock financed deals. We study the impact of deal characteristics such as deal value, industry of acquirer and bidder, economy of bidder target pairs, percentage ownership sought and recession on the method of payment.

Hypothesis 4: The choice of payment mode might depend on whether the deal is in a diversified or same industry, business cycle, economy of the target and percentage ownership sought.

Data and Methodology

We analyze large value cross-border deals above USD 1 billion listed in the Bloomberg database from 2000 to 2011. Bloomberg lists 2309 cross-border deals for the 2000 to 2011 time frame with deal values above USD 1 billion. The reason we choose 1 billion USD deals is to understand the capital flows between the economies in a more representative way. After dropping deals that are not complete or deals where the acquirer or target nation is not mentioned, we are left with a sample of 1367 observations. Acquiring and Target countries are categorized as Developed (D) or Emerging (E) on the basis of UNCTAD classification. The 1367 deals comprise of 1118 deals by developed market acquirers and 249 deals by emerging market acquirers. We classify deals by acquirer and target country pairs to arrive at 964 deals where both acquirer and target are from developed nations (DD) and 154 deals where the acquirer is developed while the target is from an emerging market. (DE) There are 131 deals where the acquirer is from an emerging county and the target is from a developed country (ED) and 118 deals by an emerging market acquirer in an emerging market target (EE) (Table 1).

This table documents the number of completed deals classified by acquirer and target economies on the basis of Bloomberg data.

We collect data from Bloomberg on various deal particulars such as target and acquirer industry sector, target and acquirer nation, percentage sought, percentage owned before deal, total announced value of deal, deal status and valuation multiples paid for the deal namely book value multiple, revenue multiple, and net income multiple.

Table 2 summarizes the deal characteristics for acquirer and target pairs. We observe that the mean deal value for DD (developed acquirer and developed target) is the highest 3.6 billion USD, followed by ED when Emerging market firms acquire developed market targets at 2.9 billion. The percentage sought in cases where the target is from a Developed country is higher, median value 100% for both DD and ED compared with cases when the target is emerging, median values are 58% for DE and 60% for EE deals. We also observe differences in the valuation multiples paid between different acquirer target pairs (Table 2).

This table summarizes the deal statistics for deal value, percentage sought, book value multiple, revenue multiple and net income multiple.

We observe from Figure 1 that there has been a dip in worldwide acquisition activity during and after recession in 2001 and then again during 2007 to 2009 time frame. We investigate the impact of the recessionary phase on mean deal values, taking the official recession phase as announced by National Bureau of Economic Research (NBER). The 9 month period from March 2001 to November 2001 and 18 month period from December 2007 to June 2009 was identified as a recessionary phase by NBER. Since, it is difficult to determine the duration of the post-recession impact phase; we have ignore that period, and only consider the official recession period for our study. We create an additional variable called recession, coded 1/0 for the recessionary phases as defined by NBER.

Table 3 describes the number of acquisitions in each target industry sector during the period 2000 to 2011 by acquirer and target country pairs. We find that acquisitions during the period in terms of numbers were led by acquisitions in the financial sector for both developed and emerging market acquirers. The next priority for developed market acquirers was consumer non-cyclical firms such as pharmaceuticals

	Target-Developed	Target-Emerging	Total
Acquirer-Developed	DD 964	DE 154	1118
Acquirer-Emerging	ED 131	EE 118	249
Total	1095	272	1367

Table 1: Description of Acquirer-Target Pairs.

Acquirer Target pair	Statistics	Deal Value USD million	% Sought	Book value multiple	Revenue multiple	Net Income multiple
DD	mean	3,615.82	82.28	11.12	10.85	50.77
	median	2,008.77	100.00	3.56	2.35	25.91
	std deviation	4,860.21	29.85	78.15	77.92	144.11
DE	mean	2,512.20	59.29	24.79	21.66	62.37
	median	1,816.00	57.65	3.09	2.56	24.83
	std deviation	2,087.10	36.21	189.11	139.67	139.79
ED	mean	2,929.24	71.38	5.19	3.88	31.48
	median	1,765.00	100.00	3.08	2.06	19.49
	std deviation	2,814.04	38.43	7.57	6.32	35.06
EE	mean	2,086.87	61.69	3.57	3.42	25.54
	median	1,568.87	59.85	2.88	2.45	19.78
	std deviation	1,259.12	35.89	2.71	2.95	27.55

Table 2: Descriptive Statistics.

Target Industry Sector	No. DD	% of DD	No. DE	% of DE	No ED	% of ED	No. EE	% of EE	No. Total	% of Total
Basic Materials	75	8%	20	13%	21	16%	12	10%	128	9%
Communications	125	13%	21	14%	6	5%	29	25%	181	13%
Consumer, Cyclical	80	8%	11	7%	10	8%	3	3%	104	8%
Consumer, Non-cyclical	194	20%	26	17%	18	14%	8	7%	246	18%
Diversified	12	1%	1	1%	3	2%	6	5%	22	2%
Energy	64	7%	14	9%	33	25%	18	15%	129	9%
Financial	192	20%	40	26%	12	9%	31	26%	275	20%
Government		0%	2	1%		0%		0%	2	0%
Industrial	118	12%	7	5%	18	14%	4	3%	147	11%
N.A.	7	1%	2	1%		0%	1	1%	10	1%
Technology	35	4%	3	2%		0%	1	1%	39	3%
Utilities	62	6%	7	5%	10	8%	5	4%	84	6%
	964		154		131		118		1367	

Table 3: Industry wise Description of the Acquirer-Target Pairs.

Target Industry Sector	Bn USD DD	% of DD	Bn USDDE	% of DE	Bn USD ED	% of ED	Bn USD EE	% of EE	Bn USD Total	% of Total
Basic Materials	337	10%	65	17%	76	20%	20	8%	499	11%
Communications	540	15%	50	13%	28	7%	68	28%	685	15%
Consumer, Cyclical	175	5%	22	6%	16	4%	7	3%	220	5%
Consumer, Non-cyclical	843	24%	53	14%	56	15%	16	6%	967	21%
Diversified	22	1%	3	1%	4	1%	8	3%	37	1%
Energy	198	6%	31	8%	96	25%	47	19%	372	8%
Financial	660	19%	101	26%	35	9%	60	24%	857	19%
Government	0	0%	8	2%	0	0%	0	0%	8	0%
Industrial	279	8%	27	7%	51	13%	6	2%	363	8%
N.A.	13	0%	6	2%	0	0%	1	0%	20	0%
Technology	95	3%	4	1%	0	0%	3	1%	102	2%
Utilities	323	9%	16	4%	22	6%	10	4%	372	8%
Total	3486		387		384		246		4503	

Table 4: Deal Values of Acquirer-Target Pairs-Industry wise.

and healthcare firms. While, next to financial sector firms emerging market firms chose to acquire basic material firms such as metals and plastics from developed markets and communications sector firms from emerging markets. Priority of emerging market acquirers seems to be resource seeking when they acquire in the developed world and market seeking when they acquire in the emerging markets (Table 3 and Figure 2).

This table summarizes the number of acquisitions by acquirer target pairs in each target industry sector. It provides the number of deals as well as its percentage of total deals, pair wise and industry wise.

Table 4 summarizes the deals values in each target sector by acquirer target pairs. Interestingly, when we look at the deals in terms of value of deals in a particular industry sector, for all completed deals above USD 1 billion, we find that financial sector does not have the highest number of deals. Consumer non-cyclical deals are of the highest value followed by financial sector deals. When developed acquirers acquired firms in developed markets the highest total deal value was in consumer, non-cyclical sector, while they spent the maximum amount on financial sector targets when they made acquisitions in emerging markets. Acquisitions by emerging market firms in developed markets were resource seeking as they have spent 25% in value terms on energy sector followed by 20% on basic materials. Emerging market acquisitions in other emerging markets were with a view to expand markets as they have made the largest acquisitions in communications sector (Table 4 and Figure 3).

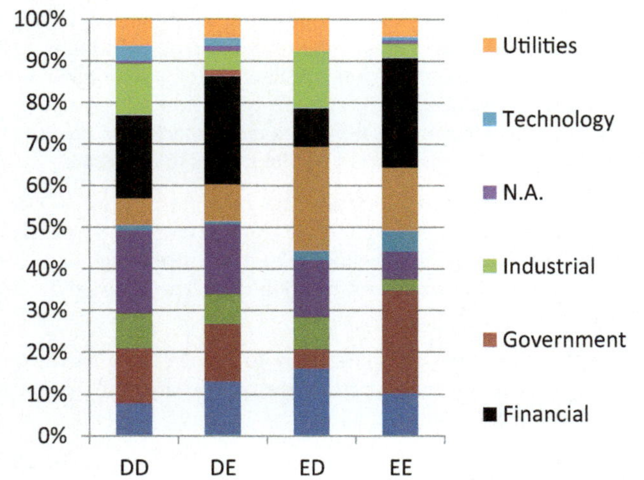

Figure 2: The number of deals in the target industry sectors during the 2000 to 2011.

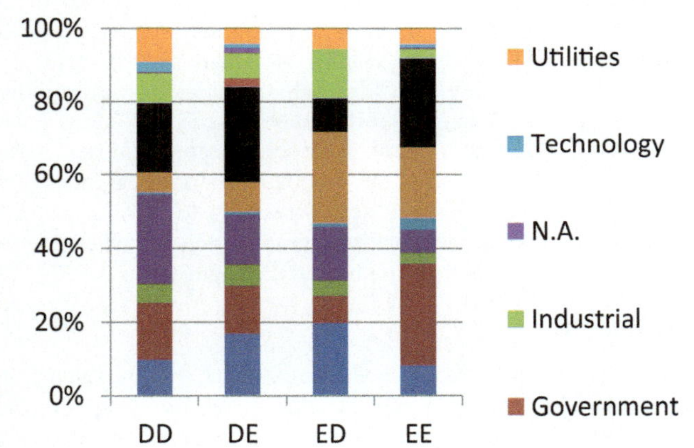

Figure 3: Deals in value terms in target sectors.

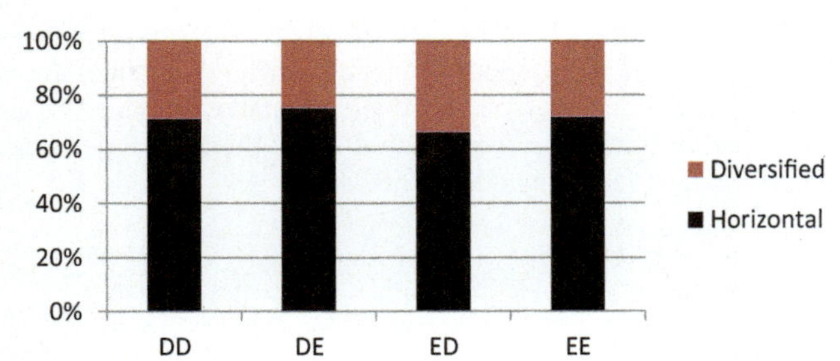

Figure 4: Illustrates the percentage of diverisfied and horizontal deals for acquirer target pairs.

This table summarizes the deal values in billion USD in each target industry sector by acquirer target pairs. It provides the deal values for the industry as well as its percentage of total deals pair wise.

Next, we examine the type of deals (diversified/non-diversified) made by developed and emerging market firms. Figure 4 provides the distribution of diversified and non-diversified deals for each of the acquirer target pair. We observe that the proportion of same industry deals is similar for all acquirer target pairs at around 70% of deals (Figure 4).

Morck, Shleifer and Vishney found that acquiring firms suffered negative abnormal returns when they made diversifying acquisitions. We analyze acquisition multiples paid to test whether they are influenced by whether the deal is diversified or horizontal [18].

For testing the first three Hypothesis, we adopt a multifactor analysis of variance (ANOVA) test. We use the ANOVA test to test the hypothesis that the mean announced deal values, deal multiples do not vary with deal characteristics such as acquirer-target pairs, recession and diversification.

For our fourth Hypothesis, we use a multinomial logistic model. We have three categories of payment modes – stock, cash and combination. Since they are unordered, we can use multinomial logit model. The probability in other categories is compared to the probability of payment in the reference category. In our case, the reference category is payment by cash.

$$Ln\left(\frac{P(payment = stock)}{P(payment = cash)}\right) = \beta_{10} + \beta_{11}(diversified) + \beta_{12}(deal\ value) + \beta_{13}(control) + \beta_{14}(countrypair) + \beta_{15}(recession)$$

$$Ln\left(\frac{P(payment = combination)}{P(payment = cash)}\right) = \beta_{20} + \beta_{21}(diversified) + \beta_{22}(deal\ value) + \beta_{23}(control) + \beta_{24}(countrypair) + \beta_{25}(recession)$$

Results

We test for the analysis of variance in deal characteristics and analyze whether they are influenced by the economy of target and acquirer, by whether the acquisition is diversified or in the same industry sector, and during recession (Table 5).

Deal value is impacted by acquirer target pairs and by whether the deal is diversified or horizontal. However, surprisingly mean deal values are not impacted by recession. Hence we find that though number of deals fell during recession as depicted in Figure 1, the mean deal values for large deals above USD 1 billion were not impacted by recession (Table 6).

We find that there is a significant difference in mean deal values between diversified and non-diversified deals. Mean deal values of horizontal deals during the 2000 to 2011 time frame are 3.6 billion while diversified deals are for 2.4 billion.

Next we study the impact of acquirer target economies, diversification and recession on three valuation multiples – book value

Source	Partial SS	df	MS	F	Prob > F
Model	29.76	5	5.95	11.98	0.00***
pair_no	13.42	3	4.47	9.00	0.00***
diversified	16.53	1	16.53	33.28	0.00***
recession	0.23	1	0.23	0.46	0.50
Residual	676.24	1361	0.50		
Total	705.99	1366	0.52		

(*** $p<0.01$, ** $p<0.05$, * $p<0.1$).

Table 5: Results of a multi factor ANOVA with the log of announced deal value as the dependent variable.

	Mean (USD million)	Std. Dev.	Freq.
Horizontal Deals	3626.028	4677.821	976
Diversified Deals	2464.209	2909.14	391
TTotal	3293.715	4279.098	1367

Table 6: Summary of announced total value.

Source	Partial SS	Df	MS	F	Prob > F
Model	12783.163	5	2556.6	0.59	0.7114
pair no	1900.4206	3	633.47	0.14	0.9329
diversified	8796.5484	1	8796.5	2.01	0.1566
recession	1120.1937	1	1120.2	0.26	0.6129
Residual	1926895.3	441	4369.4		
Total	1939678.4	446	4349.1		

a: Book Value Multiple.

Source	Partial SS	df	MS	F	Prob > F
Model	336.061242	5	67.212	0.33	0.8958
pair no	304.154672	3	101.38	0.5	0.6856
diversified	9.08560265	1	9.0856	0.04	0.8332
recession	18.2361838	1	18.236	0.09	0.7654
Residual	90236.8119	441	204.62		
Total	90572.8731	446	203.07819		

b: Revenue Multiple.

Source	Partial SS	df	MS	F	Prob > F
Model	29764.35	5	5952.9	0.54	0.7459
pair no	23175.186	3	7725.1	0.7	0.5519
diversified	5548.1176	1	5548.1	0.5	0.4784
recession	399.70916	1	399.71	0.04	0.849
Residual	4860024.3	441	11020		
Total	4889788.7	446	10964		

c: Net Income Multiple.

Table 7: Results of a multi factor ANOVA with the deal multiples as the dependent variable.

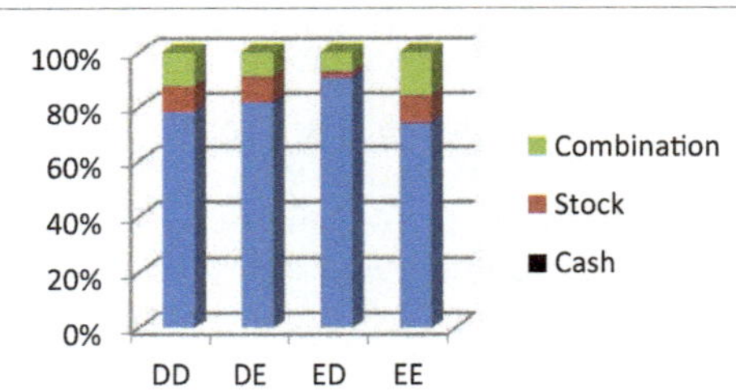

Figure 5: Illustrates the breakup of payment type for acquisition target pairs.

multiple, revenue multiple and net income multiple for controlling stake acquisitions defined as cases where percentage acquisition sought is more than 50%. We also limit our analysis to cases where all three multiples are available for a deal. The analysis of variance results for valuation multiples are tabulated in Table 7. We find that the economy of acquirer and targets, diversification and recession have no impact on valuation of deals. This seems to indicate that emerging market economies stand at par with developed market acquirers in large acquisitions. Similarly the hypothesis that assets may have been sold at fire sale prices during recession is not true in the case of high value asset sales. Also, the sector of the acquirer and target whether same or diversified does not impact deal valuation multiples (Table 7).

Payment Type: Next we investigate whether the payment type (cash/Stock/ combination of stock/cash is influenced by whether the acquirer and target are from developed or emerging countries, deal values, percentage sought and whether the deal is diversified or not.

We code deals with 1 for cash deals, 2 for stock deals and 3 for cash and stock combinations, debt, debt combinations, etc. 117 deals do not have payment data which are excluded from our analysis.

The deals break up by payment type and acquirer target economy is as follows (Figure 5).

We observe that cash is the primary mode of payment in most deals. However, in case of emerging markets acquisition of developed market targets the largest proportion of deals are in cash followed by combination deals. The proportion of stock deals for emerging market acquisitions in developed market targets is very low. This seems to be arising from the reluctance of developed market targets to hold shares in emerging market firms or from regulatory and listing issues

We run a multinomial logit with the base outcome as cash deal, second outcome as stock deal and the third as combination deals to determine the factors that would impact the livelihood of a firm going for a cash or stock or combination deal depending on the deal characteristics.

We find that deals are more likely to involve stock payment if announced deal values and percentage of the target sought to be acquired is higher (Table 8).

This table presents the results from a multi nominal logit test with payment in cash as the base outcome, and payment in stock and combination of cash and stock and other payment modes as the alternate outcome.

We interpret these results to mean that if the deal is diversified then the log odds for a stock deal decrease by 1.429 units and a combination deal decrease by 0.745 units keeping all other deal characteristics constant. While if the log of the deal value is increased by 1 unit then the log odds of the deal being a stock deal increase by 0.295 units and by .497 units for a combination deal. If the percentage sought is increased by 1 unit, then the log odd of the deal being a stock deal increase by 0.0136 units and a combination deal increase by .0123 units. Whether the acquirer and target are developing or emerging and whether there is a worldwide recession does not impact the payment mechanism.

Conclusions

Cross border deals have gained in importance over the last decade, with an exponential growth in acquisition by emerging market firms. Researchers have studied characteristics of acquirers and targets and announcement effect of acquisitions. However, there has been a limited focus on understanding emerging market firm deal characteristics vis-à-vis developed market firms.

Our results indicate that mean deal values differ between acquisition target pairs. As per expectations the highest mean deal values are for developed market acquisitions of developed market targets. We also observe that diversification impacts deal values; horizontal deals have higher mean deal values then diversified deals.

Deal Characteristics	Stock	Combination
diversified	-1.429***	-0.745***
	-0.329	-0.231
log_dealvalue	0.295**	0.497***
	-0.13	-0.111
percent sought	0.0136***	0.0123***
	-0.00405	-0.00343
pair no	-0.0211	0.0163
	-0.0297	-0.0233
recession	-0.155	-0.254
	-0.283	-0.251
Constant	-5.059***	-6.786***
	-1.161	-0.998
Observations	1,250	1,250

Standard errors in parentheses (*** p<0.01, ** p<0.05, * p<0.1)

Table 8: Results from a multi nominal logit test with payment in cash.

It is interesting to note that deal valuation multiples are not significantly impacted by either the economy of the acquirer or target, by whether the deal is diversified of not and whether the deal took place during recession. This seems to indicate that emerging markets are not worse off than developed markets with respect to negotiations on price, and should be explored further.

There has been a dip in acquisitions during recession phases during 2000 to 2010. Research on exploring the impact of recession on mean deal values has been limited. Contrary to expectations, mean deal values during recession are not significantly different from values during a non-recessionary phase. This result needs to be analyzed further as there could be a post-recession impact phase which has been ignored in our study.

Cash has been the primary form of payment for all acquirer target pairs; however the probability for stock payments increases for larger deal values and cases where a higher percentage of ownership is sought. The likelihood of cash payment is higher for diversified acquisitions which are in line with expectations.

Our studies bring out some interesting stylized facts about mergers and acquisitions over the 2000 to 2011 time frame. We address research questions on deal characteristics and raise questions for further research in this area. The way forward could be to look at the universe of all the cross border deals and then test the robustness of our results. In future research we would also like to explore other characteristics of acquirer and target like the different characteristics of the countries and the value created for each kind of pair. The results in this study motivate us to further our study in understanding the regulations of the countries which might be one of the reasons for the payment mode adopted by the firms. However, this study brings forth a new dimension to the cross border deals literature and provides an incremental path in this area for further exploration.

References

1. Chari A, Ouimet PP, Tesar LL (2010) The Value of Control in Emerging Markets. Rev Financ Stud 23: 1741-1770.
2. Gubbi SR, Aulakh PS, Ray S, Sarkar MB, Chitoor R (2010) Do international acquisitions by emerging-economy firms create shareholder value? The case of Indian firms. Journal of International Business Studies 41: 397-418.
3. Dunning JH (1988) The eclectic paradigm of international production: A restatement and some possible extensions. Journal of International Business Studies 19: 1-31.
4. Teece DJ (1985) Multinational Enterprise, Internal Governance, and Industrial Organization. American Economic Review 75: 233-238.
5. Teece DJ (1986) Transaction Cost Economics and the Multinational enterprise. Journal of Economic Behaviour and Organization 7: 21-45.
6. Buckley PJ, Casson M (1976) The future of the multinational enterprise. Macmillan, London.
7. Barkema HG, Vermeulen F (1998) International expansion through start-up or acquisition: A learning perspective. Acad Manage J 41: 7-26.
8. Brouthers KD, Brouthers LE (2000) Acquisition or greenfield start-up? Institutional, cultural and transaction cost influences. Strategic Management Journal 21: 89-97.
9. Jensen MC, Ruback RS (1983) The market for corporate control: The scientific evidence. Journal of Financial Economics 11: 5-50.
10. Andrade G, Mitchell M, Stafford E (2001) New evidence and perspectives on mergers. Journal of Economic Perspectives 15: 103-120.
11. Chernykh L, Liebenberg IA, Macias AJ (2011) Changing Direction: Cross Border Acquisitions by Emerging Market Firms.
12. Acharya V, Shin H, Yorulmazer T (2007) Fire-sale FDI. CEPR Discussion Paper no. 6319. London, Centre for Economic Policy Research.
13. Mark A, Gopinath G (2005) Fire-Sale FDI and Liquidity Crises. The Review of Economics and Statistics 87: 439-542.
14. Jahera JS, Hand J, Lloyd WP (1985) An Empirical Inquiry into the Premiums for Controlling Interests. Quarterly Journal of Business and Economics 24: 67-77.
15. King DR, Dalton DR, Covin JG, Daily CM (2004) Meta-Analyses of Post-Acquisition Performance: Indications of Unidentified Moderators. Strategic Management Journal 25: 187-200.
16. Faccio M, Masulis RW (2005) The Choice of Payment Method in European Mergers & Acquisitions. Journal of Finance 60: 1345-1388.
17. Martin KJ (1996) The Method of Payment in Corporate Acquisitions, Investment Opportunities, and Management Ownership. Journal of Finance 51: 1227-1246.
18. Morck R, Shleifer A, Vishney RW (1990) Do Managerial Objectives Drive Bad Acquisitions. Journal of Finance 45: 31-48.

Measuring the Performance of the Kuwaiti Banking Sector Before and After the Recent Financial Crisis

Atyeh MH[1]*, Yasin J[2] and Khatib AM[1]

[1]*School of Business, Australian College of Kuwait*
[2]*School of Business, Australian College of Kuwait*

Abstract

The objective of this research is to investigate the determinants of the performance of the Kuwaiti banking sector before and after the recent financial crisis over the period of 2006-2012. The data utilized is based on the yearly financial statements of the Kuwaiti banks that are listed on Kuwait Stock Exchange over the same period. There are several methods have been used to identify the determinants which impact the performance of the banking sector. In this research, a ratio analysis technique is considered efficient and more reliable method than other approaches. Other factors such as trend, government regulations and other economic factors are also included. The study found that the overall banking sector performance increased considerably in the first two years of the analysis. A significant change in trend is noticed at the onset of the global financial crisis in September 2008, reaching its peak before the global financial crisis. This resulted in decreasing the profitability, return on equity, assets and capital.

Keywords: Banking sector; Financial performance; Financial ratios; Interest spread rate; Kuwait stock exchange (KSE); Growth ratios; Financial crisis

Introduction

The banking industry in general is an old industry and it is one the major factors behind the development of the countries' economies due to the contribution that it provides to the countries and societies.

In Kuwait the banking sector is different than the banking sectors in other countries. The banking sector in Kuwait is considered one of the major sectors that are contributing to the Kuwaiti economy. The banks in Kuwait are divided into two categories which are the traditional banks and the Islamic banks.

The study will be based on the yearly financial statements of all the Kuwaiti listed banks form (2006-2012) except Warba Bank which will be excluded due to the unavailability of its data since it's a newly established bank.

The performance measurement of the banking sector will include an analysis for some internal factors that have a direct affect on the banking sector performance in Kuwait such as the interest rates and the financial ratios. Other factors will be considered such as external factors will be considered such as the growth rates and the Kuwait stock Exchange (KSE) movements during that period since the banks that are included in this research are all listed on the KSE.

Our main source of data and financial information are the Kuwait Stock Exchange website, banks websites and Zawya research in addition to the available market news and information.

Literature Review

In light of the change in the economic, market conditions and new management needs, banks started to work on improving their capabilities to measure their performance after the recent financial crisis that took place in 2008.

Measuring the performance of the banking sector in general is related to many factors that directly affect this kind of institutions. One of these factors is the cost management which requires a better management. Other factor is about managing the relationship with the clients which requires a deeper relationship, in addition to the pricing decisions and its appropriation to the market.

Many scholars have discussed measuring the performance of the banking sector tools and devices such as Tarawneh et al. [1-5]. Measuring the performance of the banking sector topic has received high attention by the researchers over the previous years [6]. However, little research has been done on measuring the banks performance in the gulf region in general and Kuwait in particular.

Some researchers have discussed the banking institutions performance and focused mainly on the cost efficiency and the key performance indicators. However, Isik et al. and Berger et al. in their study believe that looking on both profit efficiency and cost would lead to a more accurate results than focusing on the cost efficiency only[7,8].

The literature on measuring the banks performance shows that the accounting indicators are the main tools such as the profitability and cost financial ratios [5]. However, other researchers have criticized using these accounting tools to measure the performance and recommended using other approaches such as Berger and Humphrey [9].

Many scholars from many countries have implemented the performance indicators method to measure the banks performance, whilst other researchers suggest that the use of these indicators could lead to incorrect results. Some of the researchers that criticized the previous method are Marginson from Australia, Barnett from the United Kingdom [10,11].

Modell and Vakkuri et al. in their research recommend using the financial performance indicators due to the importance of the results that it would lead to. De Kool and Weick confirm the conclusion of the

***Corresponding author:** Dr. Atyeh MH, Assistant Professor, School of Business, Australian College of Kuwait, E-mail: m.atyeh@ack.edu.kw

previous two studies and add that this measurement tool makes sense and a good management method [12-15].

Samad examined the performance of the banking sector in Bahrain and used the financial ratios of seven commercial banks over the period from 1994 to 2001[16]. The performance of these banks was compared to Bahrain banking sector which was considered as a benchmark. The study results indicate that these commercial banks are less liquid, less profitable with a high credit risk.

Methodology

This paper uses the ratio analysis approach to examine the performance of the banking sector in Kuwait. The study relies on the financial statements of the past seven years from 2006 till 2012 for the banks that are listed on Kuwait stock exchange.

This research paper is different than other studies in in two things they are the methodology and the sample coverage. The methodology used in this research is the ratio analysis method considering the banking industry financials for the period after 2009 financial crisis until 2012 and compared to the period before the financial crisis, 2006 to 2008.

Using the ratio analysis method to measure the performance of the banking industry shows clearly the effect of the recent 2008 subprime breakdown on the banking industry and identifies the banking sector weaknesses and strengths [16].

Data and descriptive statistics

The number of observations for each bank is 7 observations while the total number observations are estimated to be 63 observations are shown in Table 1.

Results and Discussion

Below are the average major financial ratios of the banking sector in Kuwait for the period between 2006 and 2008 (before the financial crisis) and the period between 2009 and 2012 (after the financial crisis) (Table 2).

Financial ratios

Return on Assets (ROA) is an indicator of how profitable the company is relative to its total assets. Moreover, it gives an idea of how the management is using its assets efficiently to generate profits. In our case, the banking sector seems to be having a stable ROA rate of 1% between year 2006- 2008 (before the financial crisis) and 2009- 2012 (after the financial crisis).

Return on Equity (ROE) is the amount of net income returned as a percentage of shareholders equity. In addition, it measures the banking sector profitability by revealing how much profit the bank generates with the money shareholders have invested. The Table above shows that the ROE during the period from 2006 till 2008 (before the financial crisis) was 14% while the period after the financial crisis between 2009 and 2012.

Concerning the Return on Capital (ROC), it measures the returns of the Banking sector as a percentage of its capital. Therefore, ROC in years 2009 till 2012 has witnessed a decrease by 18% if we compare to the period before the financial crisis.

Net Profit Margin (NPM) indicates how the company effectively is controlling the cost and expenses whether it was operating or non-operating expenses. In our case the banking sector profitability seems to be decreased by nearly the half after the recent financial crisis, 23% if we compare to 46% before the financial crisis period.

Spread in Interest Rare (SIR) is the difference between the average of the interest received and interest paid by the banks. The net interest rate spread is a key determinant of the banking sector profitability. I our case, the average SIR decreased after the financial crisis by 1% to become 4% (2009-2012) after it was 5% (2006-2008).

Growth ratios

The table below shows the growth percentages of the major indicators for both periods 2006-2008 (before the financial crisis) and 2009-2012 (after the financial crisis) (Table 3).

It is clear from the figures above that the recent financial crisis has affected the performance of the banking sector in Kuwait negatively. Through looking at the major financial ratios for the two periods mentioned, we conclude that the average growth in total assets was decreased to 7% after it was 20% in the period before the crisis. Regarding the total liabilities, it seems to be decreased as well to 6% after it was 22%. While growth ratio of total equity was increased to 12% after it was 5%. In terms of the net income, and due to the decrease in the banking sector profits that we have seen above, the growth rate I income seems to be decreased by 6% if we compare the income growth rates of the two periods.

The Figure 1 shows that the movement of the Kuwait Stock Exchange (KSE) index over the period tested in the study from year 2006 till 2012. It is clear that the KSE index sharply declined in September 2008 which is the beginning of the financial crisis. Hence,

#	Bank Name	Ticker	Observations
1	National Bank of Kuwait	NBK	7
2	Gulf Bank of Kuwait	GBK	7
3	Commercial Bank of Kuwait	CBK	7
4	Ahli Bank of Kuwait	ABK	7
5	Kuwait International Bank	KIB	7
6	Burgan Bank	BURG	7
7	Kuwait Finance Bank	KFH	7
8	Boubyan Bank	BOUBYAN	7
9	Ahli United Bank	AUB	7
No. of Obs.			**63**

Table 1: Number of Observations for Each Bank.

Ratios	Average 2009-2012	Ratios	Average 2006-2008
Interest Received	5%	Interest Received	8%
Interest Paid	2%	Interest Paid	2%
Spread in Interest Rate	4%	Spread in Interest Rate	5%
Return on Assets	1%	Return on Assets	1%
Return on Equity	5%	Return on Equity	14%
Return on Capital	24%	Return on Capital	42%
Net Profit Margin	23%	Net Profit Margin	46%

Table 2: Average Major Financial Ratios Of The Banking Sector.

Growth Rates	Average 2009-2012	Growth Rates	Average 2006-2007
Total Assets	7%	Total Assets	20%
Total Liabilities	6%	Total Liabilities	22%
Total Equity	12%	Total Equity	5%
Net Income	-16%	Net Income	-22%

Table: 3 Growth percentages of the major Indicators.

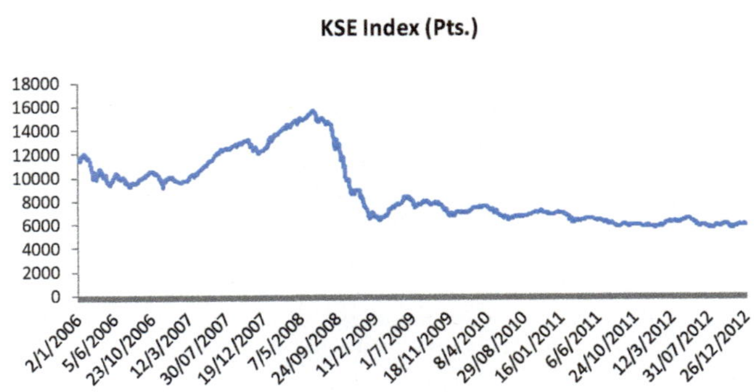

Figure 1: The Movement of The Kuwait Stock Exchange.

we conclude that the Kuwaiti banking sector performance is moving in parallel with the movement of the KSE index which is directly effect by the global market.

Summary and Conclusion

This research paper measured the performance of Kuwait banking sector over the period between year 2006 to 2012 to include the effects of September 2008 financial crisis.

The results indicate that the overall banking sector performance in terms of profitability, capital, equity and assets has been declined since September 2008 up to 2012 as the banks' operating environment deteriorated due to the global financial crisis and a slowing economy.

Despite these alarming features, Kuwaiti banks have managed to continue with their normal day to day business during the global financial crisis. Kuwaiti banks' low leverage and profitability allowed them to remain liquid and well-capitalized; avoiding any need for extraordinary liquidity or government support.

References

1. Tarawneh M (2006) A Comparison of Financial Performance in the Banking Sector: Some Evidence from Omani Commercial Banks. International Research Journal of Finance and Economics 3: 103-112.
2. Halkos G, Salamouris D (2004) Efficiency measurement of the Greek commercial banks with the use of financial ratios: a data envelope analysis approach. Management Accounting Research 15: 201-224.
3. Webb RM (2003) Levels of efficiency in UK retail banks: a DEA window analysis. International Journal of the Economics of Business 10: 305-322.
4. Lacewell SK (2003) Do Efficient Institutions Score Well Using Ratio Analysis? An Examination of Commercial Banks in The 1990s. Journal of Commercial Banking and Finance 2: 17-33.
5. Yeh QJ (1996) The Application of Data Envelopment Analysis in Conjunction with Financial Ratios for Bank Performance Evaluation. Journal of the Operational Research Society 47: 980-988.
6. Seiford LM, Zhu J (1999) Profitability and Marketability of the Top 55 U.S. Commercial Banks Management Science 45: 1270-1288.
7. Isik I, Hassan MK (2002) Cost and Profit Efficiency of the Turkish Banking Industry: An Empirical Investigation. The Financial Review 37: 257-280.
8. Berger AN, Mester LB (1997) Inside the black box: What explains differences in the efficiencies of financial institutions? Journal of Banking and Finance 21: 895-947.
9. Berger AN, Humphrey DB (1997) Efficiency of financial institutions: International survey and directions for future research. European Journal of Operational Research 98: 175-212.
10. Marginson S (1995) Universities and the new perpetual motion. Campus Review 5: 8–9.
11. Barnett R (1992) Improving Higher Education: Total Quality Care. Buckingham: The
12. Society for Research into Higher Education and Open University Press 26: 472-475.
13. Modell S (2004) Performance measurement myths in the public sector: A research note. Financial Accountability and Management 20: 39-55.
14. Vakkuri J, Meklin P (2006) Ambiguity in performance measurement: a theoretical approach to organisational uses of performance measurement. Financial Accountability and Management 22: 235-250.
15. De Kool D (2004) Monitoring and utilization: surveillance, struggle, symbol or source of inspiration, Conference of the European Group of Public Administration. 1-4 September, Ljubljana, Slovenia.
16. Weick KE (1995) Sense making in Organizations. Sage: Thousand Oaks, CA.
17. Samad A (2004) Bahrain Commercial Bank's Performance during 1994-2001. Credit and Financial Management Review 10: 33-40.

The Effect of the Global Financial Crisis on Earning Management in Tehran Stock Exchange (Evidence From of the Products of Petroleum and Chemical Industry)

Rezaei M[1]* and Neghabi ZH[2]

[1]Department of Management, Islamshahr Branch, Islamic Azad University, Islamshahr, Iran
[2]Faculty member of Islamshahr, Azad Islamic University, Islamshahr, Iran

Abstract

The purpose of this study is to investigate the effect of the global financial crisis on earnings management of listed companies in Tehran Stock Exchange and as evidence from of the products of petroleum and chemical industry. The present study is a descriptive-correlation research based on the nature of the data, a quantitative and an applied research based on the goals. Statistical population of this research were active companies in the field of petroleum and chemical listed in Tehran Stock Exchange in the period from 2008 to 2012 and Due to being limited the statistical population, purposive sampling method was used and twenty eight active companies in field of petroleum petrochemicals were selected as sample. In order to illustrate the explanatory power of explanatory variables, the adjusted coefficient of determination was used and in order to examine the significance of variables and the overall adequacy of model, t-statistic and the F-statistic Fisher were used respectively. Also, Statistical analysis was performed using Excel and E-views software's. The results of this study showed that there is a significant relationship between the size of the company and the management of profit in the global financial crisis. There is a significant relationship between profitability index of company and earnings management in the global financial crisis. There is a significant relationship between sale growth and profit management in global financial crises.

Keywords: Financial crisis; Earnings management; Companies size; Sales growth; Profitability

Introduction

Earning management is one of the controversial and attractive issues in accounting researches. Since investors pay attention particularly to amount of profit as one of the most important factors in making decision, this study is important from the behavioral aspect. Studies have shown that low and stable fluctuation of earning is an indication of its quality. As such, investors invest by more confidence, in stocks of companies that their process of profits is more stable. When companies are under increasing pressure and in unfavorable economic conditions, their managers request accounting unit to improve the last line of financial statements (i.e. profit), and thereby alter its information content.

The required data for decision-making is a very complex issue because its diverse range of users, such as investors (since you need to know the profitability and stability of the company before investing in it), managers (need for knowledge of their company's financial situation), banks and funders (the need to inform the company's ability to repay the loan) require various information [1-3]. Of course, one of the main objectives of accounting standards is that users be able to rely on the financial statements related to good and right decisions. Therefore, the accounting profession needs a way of reporting that is desirable and the interests and profits of all users are maintained. On the other hand, in order to achieve certain goals that provide reasonably certain interest groups, managers may report profits in a way that is inconsistent with the purpose of providing general interest users. Auditors have a duty to verify financial statements by evaluating compliance of financial statements with framework outlined in the accounting standards [4,5]. However, the available flexibility in accounting standards is also emphasized on the professional judgment of accountants in some cases for the choice of accounting method. In fact, the problem is derived from that the earnings management, in some cases, leads to financial statements misleading. Whereas these financial statements have no problems from view point of being place in accounting standards framework and auditors cannot criticize financial statements [6]. When companies are under increasing pressure and in unfavorable economic conditions, their managers request accounting unit to improve the last line of financial statements (i.e. profit), and thereby alter its information content [7,8]. Accounting, despite all of its financial flexibility, does not seems to be able to provide useful data for management are in such conditions. The required data for decision-making is a very complex issue because its diverse range of users, such as investors (since you need to know the profitability and stability of the company before investing in it), managers (need for knowledge of their company's financial situation), banks and funders (the need to inform the company's ability to repay the loan) require various information [9,10].

One of the methods that is sometimes used in order to arrangement informing of optimal situation of the company, is Earning management [11]. Earnings management refers to public intervention of the management in the process of determining profit that is often along with desired goals of management. Profit management is the method that is used in order to manipulate data by management [12,13]. For example, smoothing profits to ensure the sustainability of more profits of investments is an example of manipulating data. Such actions may

***Corresponding author:** Mehdi Rezaei, Department of Management, Islamshahr Branch, Islamic Azad University, Islamshahr, Iran
E-mail: rezaiimehdi65@gmail.com

be significantly affected in the financial statements. There are several ways by which the registered office can be misused in order to manage earnings.

At the most time, illicit records are misused in accounting offices in order to cover up the abuse of financial, in other cases; the records can be misused as a tool to manage earnings [14]. While managing earning, management of the company knows clearly that the goal is to protect the interests of company against the owners of even in other cases. Earning management if for getting the allocated reward due to the maintain the company against profit owners [15].

In fact, what we're looking is the impact of the global financial crisis on earnings management of listed companies in Tehran Stock Exchange (our case study is petroleum products and chemical industry).

It seems that the answer to this question can be very effective for managers and outside investors, companies and potential institutional and independent auditors. Because knowing each one of earning management factors" it will be simpler to prevent earning management specially companies managers.

Therefore, according to the importance of earning and its high information content, usually, managers seek to pursue specific purposes, to manipulate amount of reported earnings. The main problem is that why managers want to manipulate earnings, how to manage their benefits and what are consequences of such behavior?

Review of the Literature

Gonzalez and Garcia-Meca examined the impact of corporate governance on earning management in Latin American markets [16].

The aim of this study is to investigate the relationship between internal mechanisms of corporate governance and earning management. In this study, to measure earnings management, discretionary accruals were used [17]. Also, in this study, sample of non-financial companies of Latin America during the period from 2006 to 2009 were used.

The analysis results showed that there is a non-linear relationship between local ownership and discretionary accruals. Also, Improvement of the effectiveness of corporate governance leads to reduced earning management.

Cormieret al. investigated the impact of corporate governance on earnings management in the initial public offering companies [18].

Previous research has proposed that managers should use earnings management in order to predict profit voluntary. In this study, we examine earnings management conducted in the initial public offering Canada and investigate which companies use better corporate governance system of earnings management in order to achieve their earnings forecast.

The analysis results show that companies that have better predictive of corporate governance, pay less attention to voluntarily prediction in the initial public offering.

Iqbal and Strong examined the impact of corporate governance on earning management in England companies. In this study, the effect of the structure of the board of directors, ownership structure, counselor's structure and capital structure on discretionary accruals are measured that are as an indicator of earnings management [19].

According to this study, the analysis results indicate that the higher the debt-to-equity ratio leads to more misuse earning of companies. Companies are more probable to use precautionary Engagement items for income manipulation.

Mahdavi et al. examined the impact of corporate governance on the quality characteristics of the profits anticipated by the management of listed companies in Tehran Stock Exchange's earnings forecast and concluded that its impact on economic decisions of investors is very important. Many studies were conducted on earnings quality expected by management and identify factors affecting on it. In this study, the effect of corporate governance characteristics on the quality of earnings forecast has been reviewed by management [20,21].

Features of the board, institutional shareholders variables and the Audit Committee have been used in order to assess corporate governance. Also, in order to measure the quality of earnings forecast, two variables called accuracy and bias of management in earning predicted were used. Statistical sample was consisted of 100 companies listed in the Stock Exchange during the years 2005 to 2009 [22].

The results of this study show that corporate governance variables have no affect on quality of earnings expected by management of the company accepted in the Tehran Stock Exchange.

Mousavi et al. examined the relationship between earning forecasted errors by management and corporate governance structure in listed companies in Tehran Stock Exchange during 2004 to 2007 [23].

It should be noted that the structure of corporate governance in this study are included: Percentage of ownership of board members, bound board members, and the board of the board risk of director.

Volume of statistical population was consisted of 363 member companies of Tehran Stock Exchange that 146 companies during the period 2004 to 2008 have been selected due to the limitations of the study.

In order to provide the literature of this study, information contained in the financial statements of companies, software Tadbir Pardaz, Library of Exchange organization, and archive of sites of Stock Exchange were used [24]. Pearson correlation coefficient and multiple linear regression model were used in order to test hypothesizes. The results of this study show that there is a positive relationship between the percentage of ownership of board members, board members and members of the board of directors and the accuracy of earnings forecasted. There is a negative relationship between the risk-management earnings and prediction of earning of management. Testing hypothesizes showed that all hypothesizes are confirmed.

Methodology

This study uses retrospective approach. On the other hand, this study is descriptive-correlation research. Based on the nature of the data, the type of this study is quantities'. This study is application one based on objectives. In order to examine hypotheses of our study and according to the nature of information and research data, information is quantities'.

Method and data collecting tools

Information and data required for this study were collected by using two methods:

1. The information related to this study is theoretical one and from various references such as books and magazines that internationally are available online at sites collected.

2. Raw information and data required in order to verify the hypothesis results were collected through innovative software, processor and necessary measure was collected through direct reference of the Company's financial statements as CD by the Stock Exchange Tehran and the website of this organization.
3. Company financial statements, including balance sheet, income statement, and cash flow statement and notes accompanying the financial statements at the end of each financial year is used as a research tool.
4. In this study, in order to estimate the parameters of descriptive statistics and statistical models in research and analysis and statistical inference, E-views and Excel software are used.

The regression model of study

$$\text{Earning Management}_{it} = a_0 + a_1\text{Size}_{it} + a_2\text{Growth}_{it} + a_3\text{Profitable}_{it} + a_4\text{Levearge}_{it} + a_5\text{Industry}_{it} + \varepsilon_{it}$$

Method of analyzing data

Statistics are discussed as descriptive statistics, probability and inferential statistics. Probability and probability theory are essentially outside the scope of our discussion. Also descriptive statistics such as frequency, mean, variance and assumptions were considered [25,26].

In this study, the combined data is used in order to test the hypotheses. In this way, time series data (the years studied) and sectional (companies surveyed) are combined. Combined data are used to increase amount of observations, raise degrees of freedom, decrease heterogeneity of variance and dynamic of the changes.

In order to estimate the effectiveness of a regression model using compound data, one of the common effects models, fixed effects and random effects using appropriate tests are selected.

First, in order to determine whether the time series xt static (agglomeration time zero) or divergent process (Agglomeration time), we use the Lin and Levine test [27,28].

Similar to study on static variables, here, we also require proper methods for combined data. We use the modified Wald test in order to evaluate heterogeneity of group among remaining of fixed effects regression model. Also, we use two tests F-test and Hausman test in order to determine the effect of fixed or random effects.

To illustrate the explanatory power of explanatory variables adjusted coefficient of determination (Adjusted R2) to investigate the significance of variables and t-statistic to assess the overall adequacy of the F-statistic model Fisher were used. The statistical analysis using software, EXCEL and EVIEWS 7 will be carried out.

The study variables

Dependent variable: This is variable that is not measured, manipulated and selected by the researcher, and we attempt to find their relationship with the dependent variable by evaluating each of the independent variables.

In this study, earnings management is the dependent variable.

Independent variable: It is variable that is measured by the researcher manipulated or selected to influence or determine its association with other variables.

In this study, company size, sales growth and profitability indicators are independent variables.

Control variable: Because of all the variables in the study cannot be examined, researcher neutralizes effects of some variables through statistical control or the research control. The variables whose effects are removable by researcher are called control variable. Financial leverage and efficiency of assets are control variables.

Hypothesis testing

First hypothesis testing

H0: there is no significant relationship between firm size and earnings management in the global financial crisis.

H1: there is a significant relationship between firm size and earnings management in the global financial crisis.

• According to Table 1, since the Durbin-Watson test statistic is placed at a distance of 1.5 to 2.5, assuming correlation between errors is not rejected and regression can be used.

Due to the significance of the test F (34.158) at the level of error smaller than 0.01, it can be concluded that the research regression model consisting of independent variables, control and dependent, independent and control variables can set a good model and explain profit management changes. Amount of coefficient of determination is 0.555, indicating that 55.5% of the total variation of the dependent variable, and is dependent to independent and control variables in the model. Impact factor of company size variable on earnings management is 3.559 that means that a direct and positive impact earnings management.

According to the significant level of t-statistic, variable of company size on earning management (0.015), due to being lower than 5% error level, we can reject H0 hypothesis by 95% confidence and state that there is a significant relationship between company size and earnings management during the global financial crisis.

The research model is as follows:

$$\text{Earning Management}_{it} = 0.482 + 3.559\ \text{Size}_{it} + 0.515\ \text{Levearge}_{it} + 0.796\ \text{Industry}_{it} + \varepsilon_{it}$$

Testing second hypothesis

H0: there is no significant relationship between sales growth and earnings management in the global financial crisis.

H1: there is a significant relationship between sales growth and earnings management in the global financial crisis.

According to Table 2, since the Durbin-Watson test statistic is placed at a distance of 1.5 to 2.5, assuming no correlation between errors is not rejected and regression can be used. According to the significance of the test F (43.059) at the level of error smaller than 0.01, it can be concluded that the research regression model consisting

Significance level	t-score	Estimate deviation	Coefficient deviation	Variable
0.021*	3.651	0.132	0.482	Fix
0.015*	4.611	0.772	3.559	Company size
0.026*	3.083	0.167	0.515	Financial leverage
0.019*	3.882	0.205	0.796	Industry type
2.318		Camera-Watson		
34.158		F-score		
0.000**		Significance level		
0.555		Modified coefficient determination		

*5% error and 1% error**

Table 1: Regression and model significance.

Significance level	t-score	Estimate deviation	Coefficient deviation	Variable
0.014*	4.239	0.117	0.496	Fix
0.021*	-3.258	0.236	-0.767	Company's selling growth
0.026*	3.962	0.134	0.531	Financial leverage
0.018*	4.517	0.159	0.718	Industry type
1.714		Camera-Watson		
43.059		F-score		
0.000**		Significance level		
0.667		Modified coefficient determination		

*5% error and 1% error**

Table 2: Regression and model significance test.

Significance level	t-score	Estimate deviation	Coefficient deviation	Variable
0.029*	3.736	0.114	0.426	Fix
0.038*	-3.021	0.186	-0.562	Index of profitability
0.032*	3.324	0.253	0.841	Financial leverage
0.035*	3.242	0.107	0.347	Industry type
1.803		Camera-Watson		
36.492		F-score		
0.000**		Significance level		
0.483		Modified coefficient determination		

*5% error and 1% error**

Table 3: Regression and model significance test.

of independent variables, control and dependent, independent and control variables can set a good model and explain profit management changes.

Amount of coefficient of determination is 0.667, indicating that 66.7% of the total variation of the dependent variable is dependent to independent and control variables in the model. Coefficient of effect of sales growth over the earning management is -0.767, which reflects the negative impact on earnings management sales growth of companies. According to the significance level of the t-statistic of sales growth variable on earnings management (0.021), due to being lower than the 5% error level, H0 hypothesis can be rejected with 95% confidence. It can be said that there is a significant relationship between the growth of sales and earnings management in the global financial crisis.

The research model is as follows:

$$\text{Earning Management}_{it} = 0.496 - 0.767\ \text{Growth}_{it} + 0.531\ \text{Levearge}_{it} + 0.718\ \text{Industry}_{it} + \varepsilon_{it}$$

Testing third hypothesis

H0: there is no significant relationship between indicators of profitability and earnings management in the global financial crisis.

H1: there is a significant relationship between indicators of profitability and earnings management in the global financial crisis.

According to Table 3, since the Durbin-Watson test statistic is placed at a distance of 1.5 to 2.5, there is no correlation between errors is rejected and regression can be used.

Due to the significance of the test F (36.492) at the level of error smaller than 0.01, it can be concluded that the research regression model consisting of independent variables, control and dependent, independent and control variables can set a good model and explain earning management changes.

Amount coefficient of determination is 0.483, indicating that 48.3% of the total variation of the dependent variable is dependent to independent and control variables in the model.

Coefficient of effect of benefits on earnings management is -0.562, which reflects the negative impact on earnings management is profitability index. Due to the significance level of the t-statistic variable sales growth on earnings management (0.038), due to lower than the 5% level H0 hypothesis can be rejected with 95% and it can be said there is a significant relationship between the index of profitability and earnings management during the global financial crisis.

The research model is as follows:

$$\text{Earning Management}_{it} = 0.426 - 0.562\ \text{Profitable}_{it} + 0.841\ \text{Levearge}_{it} + 0.347\ \text{Industry}_{it} + \varepsilon_{it}$$

Results of Study

Earnings management in the accounting literature is related to issues that arise in earning of accounting. This issue was formed in accounting from the beginning of the twentieth century and then several investigations were conducted by experts in the field of accounting. Each of these studies evaluated specific dimensions of this issue. Earnings management, because of the stigma of some companies in recent years, is at the forefront of public attention. Earnings management, because of the stigma of some companies in recent years is at the forefront of public attention and decision making authorities have paid more attention to this issue and have made several changes.

The earning is calculated and recognized based on accrual accounting. That is on the basis of income fulfillment based and expense occurrence identification engagement but not received or payment in cash. Therefore, in the calculation and recognition of profit estimates, projections and allocation accounting are used.

Therefore, use of income as a measure of the performance of companies, is an issue with uncertainty, because of the influence of the estimates and accounting methods. While cash flow from operations due to lower management role in the manipulation of those criteria in evaluating the company's performance is more reliable.

Comparison of the results with other studies

First hypothesis: Result of test Hypothesis showed that there is a significant profit the size of the company and the management of the global financial crisis. This result is no consistent with results Aghaii et al. and in consistent with the results of Akbar et al. [29-33].

So, it can be concluded that bigger companies have more tend to manipulate the profit than other companies within the financial crises.

Second hypothesis: Hypothesis test result showed that there is a significant relationship between the growth in sales and earnings management in the global financial crisis. This result is consistent with other results Mohammad et al. is consistent with the results of Ali et al. [34-39].

For these companies, we can conclude that companies that have higher growth of sales and lower volatility, their earnings management in those is less.

Third hypothesis: Result of testing hypothesis showed that there is a significant relationship between the index of profitability and earnings management during the global financial crisis. This results is not Consisted with the study by some authors [34-38] are consistent and the results does not match [36-39].

Therefore, it can be concluded that the profitability of companies can play a role in reducing the earnings management of Companies and the managers of these companies do not tend to tamper the profit because of the appropriate profitability.

Proposes of this study

Internal proposes: It is proposed to investors, shareholders and other interest groups in their decisions to buy and sell shares of a company, in order to ensure the non-profit company can manipulate the size of the company, sales growth and profitability index case terms of attention, since the results of these factors have a significant impact on earnings management in companies. It is also recommended to pay attention board the Audit Committees. In this way, you can monitor the behavior of their management control.

External Suggestions:

- We recommend evaluating the effect of "ownership structure" in the management of corporate profits paid during the global financial crisis.
- We recommend investigating the effect of "the Board" on the management of corporate profits paid during the global financial crisis.
- We recommend reviewing the impact of the "Audit Committee" on the management of corporate profits paid during the global financial crisis.
- We recommend evaluating evaluate the effect of "liquidity" on the management of corporate profits paid during the global financial crisis.

We recommend evaluating the effect of "risk management" on the management of corporate profits paid during the global financial crisis.

References

1. Adrian T, Colla P, Shin H (2012) Which financial friction? Parsing the evidence from the financial crisis of 2007-2009. Staff report, federal reserve bank of New York pp: 1-55.
2. Francis B, Hasan I, Li L (2014) Abnormal real operations, real earnings management and subsequent crashes in stock price. Bank Finland research, discussion papers.
3. Ardekani A, Younesi N, Hashemjijoo M (2012) Acquisition, earnings management and firm's performance: evidence from Malaysia. Journal of business studies quarterly 4: 91-110.
4. Rial S, Tano C (2014) The impact of the global financial crisis on audit quality. Master Thesis.
5. Chaiporn V (2014) What explains the initial return of initial public offerings after the 1997 Asian financial crisis? Evidence from Thailand.
6. Xu Y, Carsona E, Fargherb N, Jiang L (2013) Responses by Australian auditors to the global financial crisis. Accounting and finance 53: 303-338.
7. Faiq M, Xia X, Ali M, Usman M, Shahid H (2011) How Asian and global economic crisis prevail in Chinese IPO and stock market efficiency. International business research.
8. Fauzi F, Hewa-Wellalage N, Locke S (2012) The global financial crisis' impact on short-term performance of IPO: the case study of New Zealand firms' IPOs. Asian journal of finance and accounting 4: 180-198.
9. Bloom N (2009) The impact of uncertainty shocks. Econometrica 77: 632-685.
10. Andre D, Dimitrious G (2013) European sovereign debt crisis and the performance of Dutch IPOs. SSRN 30: 308-319.
11. Gholamreza EB, Hashem N, Banimahd F, Mirsepassi N (2011) Check conservatism in the global financial crisis. Knowledge of financial securities analysis.
12. Filip A, Raffournier B (2014) Financial crisis and earnings management. The international journal of accounting 49: 455-478.
13. Armstrong C, Foster G, Taylor D (2008) Earnings management around initial public offerings: A Re-examination. SSRN Electronic Journal.
14. Francis J, Lafond R, Olsson R, Schipper K (2005) The market pricing of accruals quality. Journal of accounting and economics 39: 295-327.
15. Gong G, Louis H, Sun A (2008) Earnings management, lawsuits and stock – for-stock acquirers' market performance. Journal of accounting and economics 46: 62-77.
16. Habib A, Adin MB, Islam A (2013) Financial distress, earnings management and market pricing of accruals during the global financial crisis. Managerial Finance 39: 155-180.
17. Ronen J, Yaari V (2008) Earnings management: Emerging insights in theory practice and research. Springer.
18. King E, Banderet L (2014) IPO stock performance and the financial crisis. Stokholm School of economics. Master thesis in finance. SSRN paper.
19. Molik A, Mir M, McLver R, Bepari M (2013) Effects of audit quality on earnings management during the global financial crisis. Proceedings of 9th Asian business research conference pp: 1-27.
20. Kousenidis D, Ladas A, Negakis C (2013) The effects of the European debt crisis on earnings quality. International review of financial analysis 30: 351-362.
21. Razi Z, Gao L, Yu J (2012) Industry peer firms earnings predictably, financial crisis and IPO underpricing. University of Memphis, Memphis pp: 1-55.
22. Richardson S, Sloan R, Soliman M, Tuna I (2005) Accrual reliability, earnings persistence and stock prices. Journal of accounting and economics 39: 437-485.
23. Richardson G, Taylor G, Lanis R (2015) The impact of Financial distress on corporate tax avoidance spanning the global financial crisis: Evidence from Australia. Journal of banking and finance 52: 112-129.
24. Korteweg A (2007) The costs of financial distress across industries.
25. Wai FW (2013) The initial performance of Malaysia IPOs during the financial crisis: evidence from global financial crisis of 2008. Master of business administration, Universiti Tunku Abdul Rahman, Malaysia pp: 1-54.
26. Ahmadpour, Montazeri A, Hadi (2011) Study on type of earnings management and the impact of company size, ownership structure and corporate governance of accounting advance.
27. Arezzo B, Abbas S, Zanganeh M (2012) Study on Earnings Management in the Time of shares of companies listed in Tehran Stock Exchange. The first regional conference on new approaches in accounting and auditing.
28. Omid P, Ali R, Reza G (2013) examination of the impact of the actual management of profit on the investment behavior of listed companies in Tehran Stock Exchange, accounting developments.
29. Zahra P, Mehdi PR (2012) Study on relationship between earnings management and corporate financial capability. Financial knowledge of the securities 5: 77-88.
30. Saied JK, Saied K, Akbar PA (2009) Study on relationship between income smoothing and corporate financial distress. Financial Accounting. 1: 60-80.
31. Mohsen D, Zadeh H, Vali AK, Ali V (2012) Quality of earnings in financial distress companies. Financial accounting research 4: 1-16.
32. Muhammad ZM (2012) Study on accountants and their role in the recent global financial crisis. The first regional conference on new approaches in accounting and auditing.
33. Ali S, Narges H, Hamed R (2013) The relationship between real earnings management activities and future performance of the listed companies in tehran stock exchange. Management accounting 6: 45-58.
34. Motevassel M, Tohidi F (2012) Evaluation of the financial crisis and the role of accounting and auditing. First regional conference on research and new methods of management and accounting.

35. Beata M, Mehrani S, Kaveh M, Creamy GH (2005) Accruals in the management of firms listed in the Tehran Stock Exchange. Review of accounting and auditing 42: 61-74.

36. Ejad N, Sehr S, Karami MN (2005) Study on earnings management in listed companies in Tehran Stock Exchange. Journal of Social Sciences and Humanities.

37. Hashem N, Mahdi T, Hamid AZ (2014) Economic consequences of accounting information quality management with a focus on variable Svd. Accounting stability 7: 1-15.

38. Hashem V, Talebnia G, Ali J (2013) The effect of earnings management on earnings quality companies with the financial crisis. Accounting knowledge 4: 75-103.

39. Frshad H, Vahid Z (2011) Investors' reaction to the news of the financial crisis over Iran's stock market financial Jhany. Dansh securities analysis exchange 4: 75-100.

Sources of Public Funds and Economic Prosperity: The Nigerian Case

Onyele KO* and Nwokoacha EB

Department of Banking and Finance, College of Management Sciences (COLMAS), Michael Okpara University of Agriculture, Nigeria

Abstract

This study examined the various sources of public funds and their resultant effect on economic growth in Nigeria from 1986-2014. The sources of public funds considered in this study were tax revenue, oil revenue, external debt and national savings. Two models were used in this study; one analyzed the effect of these individual sources of public funds on economic growth, while the other model explained the effect of aggregate government revenue on economic growth. The times series data sourced from Central Bank of Nigeria Statistical Bulletin were analyzed using unit root tests, cointegration tests and vector error correction mechanism (VECM). The unit root test revealed that all the variables were stationary at first difference except tax revenue which was significant at level. The cointegration tests (both Johansen and Engle-Granger) showed that a long run relationship existed between the individual sources of public funds and economic growth, as well as aggregate government revenue and economic growth. The results obtained for model one revealed that tax revenue and oil revenue had a positive effect on economic growth, while national savings and external debt exerted a negative effect on economic growth. With respect to total government revenue, economic growth depleted as a result of changes in total government revenue. Finally, it was recommended among other things that government should fulfil her obligations of social and economic welfare to her citizens, so that anyone who enjoys such services will be conscious of tax payment in Nigeria.

Keywords: Total government revenue; Tax revenue; Oil revenue; National savings; External debt; Economic growth

Introduction

Attaining a sustainable economic balance has been a major goal pursued by the government of Nigeria and other countries [1]. This is because the economy is the hub of every nation. The process of growth and development of an economy hinges on the availability of certain infrastructural facilities required to accelerate various economic activities [2]. This plausibly offers an explanation to why government of every country exert her authority towards maintaining a medium or multiple streams of revenue through which adequate funds are made available towards achieving set goals for the nation [3,4]. Consequently, the government of every country (developed, developing, and under-developed) depends on these funds in order to execute its social and economic obligations to the public and these obligations include provision of infrastructures such as roads, hospitals schools and the rest of them. As such, these funds generated by the government to provide goods and services to the general public are termed "public funds." Therefore, literature abound that amidst multiple sources of government funds, tax revenue have been the major source of public funds globally [5-7]. On the other hand, several authors have also identified oil revenue, aid, grants, national savings and debt as prominent sources of public funds [4,8,9].

Indeed, one of the most effective and efficient means of internal revenue generation for government is through the tax system [7]. In support of the benefits attributed to tax revenue, Nzotta asserted that taxes constitute the key sources of finance to the federation account distributed among the three tiers of government [6,10]. Following the definition given by Ogundele as cited in Ayuba, taxation is the process by which residents of a country or community are legally mandated to pay a specified fraction of their income for the purpose of administration and development of the society [7,11]. As such, it have been inferred that tax payment is beneficial to payers and the entire citizenry, since it is used to achieve some economic and social goals of the nation [10,12]. These benefits notwithstanding, aggregate tax revenue in Nigeria have been paltry over the years. This is due to poor tax administration coupled with the high rate of tax evasion and avoidance among tax payers (individuals and corporate bodies) which have led to fiscal deficit and epileptic economic performance [13,14]. Also, this could be attributed to the over-reliance on oil revenue as a major source of public funds.

The emergence of crude oil in Nigeria has significantly dictated the pace of economic, political, social and cultural progress in the country. Over the years, the importance of oil commodity has been made manifest in the economy of Nigeria in several ways. In the 1970s, the petroleum industry dominated the Nigeria economy after agriculture, generating substantial foreign exchange revenue. With emphasis on oil revenue and economic development in Nigeria, it is glaring that there have been positive changes in the economic life of Nigeria over the years. However, with the volatility in oil prices worldwide, the aggregate revenue generated from this source have dwindled and waned significantly [15,16]. Surprisingly, the Nigerian economy still depends to a large extent on crude oil, despite the significant decline in oil revenue over the years. As such, there have been agitations and campaign for proper diversification of the economy, especially towards resuscitating the agricultural sector and the manufacturing sector in Nigeria by encouraging small and medium scale enterprises [17].

The saying that non-oil revenue (such as agricultural revenue) was the mainstay of the Nigerian economy in the 1960s, 1970s and 1980s underscores the emphasis placed on non-oil revenue as the engine of growth in the Nigerian economy [18,19]. According to Reynolds in

***Corresponding author:** Kingsley O Onyele, M.Sc. Student, Department of Banking and Finance, College of Management Sciences (COLMAS), Michael Okpara University of Agriculture, Umudike, Abia State, Nigeria
E-mail: kingsleyonyele@gmail.com

Chukwuka et al. and Gbaiye, et al., in the decades of 1960s and 1970s, the external sector was dominated by agricultural commodity export, which accounted for about 50% of the gross domestic product (GDP), 90% of foreign exchange earnings, employed more than 75% of the labour force and produced over 70% of total food consumption [20-22]. However, following the discovery of crude oil, coupled with the oil boom of 1970s, the significant revenue generated from agriculture declined drastically as the economy relied solely on oil exports. Notwithstanding the enviable position of the oil sector in the Nigerian economy over the past three decades, the agricultural sector is estimated to be the largest contributor to non-oil foreign exchange earnings [19]. This means that agriculture holds abundant potentials for enhancing and sustaining the country's foreign exchange earnings [18,19,22].

Following the decline in tax revenue, oil revenue and other sources of funds available to government, fiscal deficit have been on the increase which have automatically led to external borrowing to fill the gap. Hence, with increase in external debt, the savings accumulated domestically continued to deplete significantly because the cost of servicing these debts are drawn from national savings. As such, a vicious circle of aggregate revenue, external debt and national savings is created. Consequently, the sources of public funds emphasized in this study are tax revenue, oil revenue, national savings and debt finance. Hence, going through the aforementioned sources of public funds, it becomes paramount to investigate if funds generated through these sources have fostered economic prosperity in Nigeria. Therefore, discoveries from this study will reveal the prominent sources of revenue the government of Nigeria should focus on, and also to investigate the particular source or sources that have contributed to economic growth in Nigeria.

Objectives of the Study

The broad objective of this study is aimed at investigating the relationship between public finance and economic prosperity in Nigeria. The specific objectives are.

- To examine the effect of aggregate tax revenue on real gross domestic product in Nigeria.
- To investigate the relationship between oil revenue on real gross domestic product in Nigeria.
- To ascertain the effect of external and domestic debt on real gross domestic product in Nigeria.
- To investigate the effect of aggregate government revenue on real gross domestic product in Nigeria.

Research questions

- How does aggregate tax revenue affect real gross domestic product in Nigeria?
- What is the relationship between oil revenue and real gross domestic product in Nigeria?
- What effect does external and domestic debt have on real gross domestic product in Nigeria?
- In what way does aggregate government revenue affect real gross domestic product in Nigeria.

Hypotheses

Based on the objectives stated above, the following hypotheses were tested.

Ho_1: Aggregate tax revenue have no significant effect on real gross domestic product in Nigeria.

Ho_2: Oil revenue have no significant effect on real gross domestic product in Nigeria.

Ho_3: External and domestic debt have no significant effect on real gross domestic product in Nigeria.

Ho_4: Aggregate government revenue have no significant effect on real gross domestic product in Nigeria.

Conceptual framework

The various terms used with respect to public funds (government revenue) in Nigeria are briefly explained in this section of the study.

Concept of taxation

The concept of taxation has been a concern of global significance as it affects every economy irrespective of national differences. Therefore, taxation is a powerful tool of economic reform and a major player in every economy of the world [6]. By definition, taxation is a compulsory levy by the government through its agent on the profits, income, or consumption of its subjects or citizens [12]. Similarly, Anyanwu defined tax as the compulsory transfer or payment (or occasionally of goods and services) from private individuals, institutions or groups to the government [23]. According to Nzotta, for tax revenue to play its role of amending economic ills for all, the following four important issues must be put to heart [10].

- First, it must be understood that tax is a compulsory contribution that flows from the citizens to the government, and this contribution is for the benefit of all.
- Secondly, tax imposes a general obligation to the tax payer
- Thirdly, there is a presumption that the contribution of the public revenue made by tax payers may not be equal to the benefits enjoyed by the citizens.
- Finally, a tax is not imposed on a citizen by the government as a result of services rendered to the citizens.

The following are federal government collectible taxes are discussed below.

- **Petroleum profit tax:** Petroleum Profits Tax 1990 of Nigeria demands that all firms engaged in extraction and transportation of petroleum to pay tax. This category of tax is levied on the proceeds from the sale of oil and related substances used by the company in its own refineries plus any other income of the company incidental to and arising from its petroleum operations.
- **Companies income tax:** Companies profit tax is levied on the profits made by companies operating in Nigeria, except those companies engaged in petroleum exploration activities [24].
- **Value added tax (VAT):** Value added tax (VAT) was introduced to replace the sales tax. This is a type of consumption tax that is placed on a product whenever value is added at a stage of production and at final sale. The collection of value-added tax (VAT) in Nigeria is regulated by Value-added tax Act, 1993 [24].
- **Personal income tax:** Personal income tax is based on Pay as you Earn (PAYE), that is the tax payable depends on how much is earned by the tax payer. It is a direct tax levied on income of individuals.
- **Custom duties:** Custom duties represents taxes levied on

imports (and, sometimes, on exports) by the customs authorities of a country to raise state revenue, and/or to protect domestic industries from more efficient or predatory competitors from abroad. This is based on the value of goods imported.

❖ **Excise duty:** Excise duties are taxes levied on locally manufactured goods and services.

Concept of public debt

The need for government borrowing is necessitated by the fact that available funds are not sufficient to meet the needs of the society. As such, foreign countries, international financial organizations and other lenders tend to lend their excess funds to capital scarce economies, like Nigeria. According to Imimole et al. debt was derived from the Latin word "debere" meaning to owe [8]. Debt has been conceptualized as resources of money used in an organization which is not contributed by its owners and but other private individuals, organization, or government. It is important to note that two types of debts exist: domestic debt and external debt. According to Imimole et al., public debt is divided into internal (also known as domestic debt) and external debt [8]. Internal or domestic debt entails when a government borrows from surplus units within the country, while external debt is incurred when the government borrows from foreign lenders. However, debt have also been classified as; productive debt and dead weight debt. According to them, when a loan is obtained to enable the state or nation to purchase some sort of assets, the debt is said to be productive e.g. money borrowed for acquiring factories, electricity, refineries etc. However, debt undertaken to finance wars and expenses on current expenditures are termed "dead weight debts."

A debtor country can obtained the loan by importing goods and services to the value of the loan from the country where the agreement was made without having to give anything in exchange immediately [8]. At the time of maturity of the debt, the borrowing country will have to bear the burden of exporting goods and service without receiving any imports in exchange. However, internal loans do not have the type of burden of exchange of goods and services. These two types of debt, however, require that the borrowers' future savings must cover the interest and principal payment (debt servicing).

Concept and evolution of oil exploration in nigeria

Following the definition of petroleum by Obadan in Ujunwa, petroleum is a mixture of hydro carbon oils obtained below the surface which generally occurs at depths below 1,500 meters [25]. According to him, it serves as raw material for productive purposes known as the petroleum industry resolves. It constitutes a major source of energy in the world marked today and has in fact, become the mainstay of man's progress and civilization. By this definition, Obadan further emphasized that petroleum serves as raw material for varieties of chemicals for the production of pharmaceuticals, fertilizers, fibers, for the manufacture of textile and numerous other products required for human existence [26]. More so, petroleum jelly for the body, candles for lightening and bitumen for tarring roads are some of the byproducts of petroleum.

According to Anyanwu, the first commercial discovery of crude oil in Nigeria was in 1957 by shell which started production in 1958 [23]. In 1961, the federal government of Nigeria further issued ten oil prospecting licenses, each license on the continental shelf to five companies, each license covered an area of 2,560 squares kilometers and was subject to the payment of ₦1 million with these generous concession, full scale one – share and off-shore oil exploration began. Oil was found in commercial quantities at Oloibiri in the Niger Delta. Further discoveries at Afam and Boma established the country as an oil producing Nation. As such, by April 1967, oil from Nigeria had reached 2 million barrels per day [23].

Nigeria is the 11th member of the organization of petroleum exporting countries (OPEC). As a member of OPEC, Nigeria jointly with other members determine at what minimum price level various member countries should sell their crude oil OPEC now determines the level of crude oil production for its member countries in order to prevent a collapse in the crude oil price. The price oil is sold for is largely determined by the organization of petroleum exporting countries (OPEC).

The direct involvement by government in oil exploration began on the birth of Nigerian National Petroleum Corporation (NNPC). Consequently, the role of government in the oil industry has gradually progressed from regulatory to direct involvement in all exploration. Initially government interest was only limited to the licensed companies royalties and other dues offered it from the companies and making rudimentary laws to regulate the activities of the oil industry. This was partly due to the fact that oil was very insignificant to the economy before the late sixties and the relative lack of trained personnel and expertise, [26]. However, due to the oil boom of the early 1970s and early 1980s, the government of Nigeria fully depended on oil revenue as the bedrock of the economy, while neglecting other sectors of the economy [21].

Empirical review

Literature abound that government revenue is essential for infrastructural development and economic prosperity in all countries, developed, developing and under developed countries. In what follows, these literatures are reviewed under the following headings.

Tax revenue and economic growth

Ojong, Anthony & Arikpo, examined the impact of tax revenue on the Nigerian economy. Ordinary least square of multiple regression models was used to establish the relationship between dependent and independent variables [12]. The finding revealed that there was a significant relationship between petroleum profit tax and the growth of the Nigeria economy. It showed that there was a significant relationship between non-oil revenue and the growth of the Nigeria economy. The finding also revealed that there is no significant relationship between company income tax and the growth of the Nigeria economy. It was recommended that government should endeavour to provide social amenities to all nooks and crannies of the country.

Ayinde, Kuranga and Lukman, investigated the impact of capital expenditure, recurrent expenditure and various sources of Government revenue on Nigeria's economic growth using secondary data gathered from Central Bank of Nigeria's publication from 1981 to 2011 [27]. The long-run relationship of economic growth (Gross Domestic Product (GDP) on capital expenditure, recurrent expenditure, oil revenue, non-oil revenue, federation account and federal retained revenue revealed the existence of co-integration. The results from the analysis showed a positive impact of capital expenditure, oil revenue, federation account and federal retained revenue on economic growth. Consequently, the study recommended a re-evaluation and re-assessment of direction of recurrent expenditure and non-oil revenue towards Nigerian development to achieve positive influence on economic growth.

Ayuba analyzed the impact of tax revenue on economic growth using times series data from 1993 to 2012 [7]. The data set sourced from secondary sources were analyzed using the ordinary least squares approach. From the results, it was discovered that tax revenue exerted a positive impact on economic growth in Nigeria. It was thus recommended *inter alia* that efforts should be intensified by government at all levels towards increased collection of non-oil taxes.

Onwuchekwa and Aruwa, investigated the impact of value added tax on the economic growth of Nigeria. The results showed that VAT contributed significantly to the total tax revenue of government and by extension the economic growth of Nigeria. They recommended that, to boost tax revenue VAT need to be increased. This can be achieved not necessarily by increasing the VAT rate of 5% but by closing every VAT revenue leakage, sensitizing the managers of companies operating in Nigeria on the need to remit the VAT revenue collection and proper training of the Federal Inland Revenue staff in charge of VAT revenue collection.

Adeniyi evaluated the effect of tax administration on revenue generation to the Enugu state government [14]. The studied incorporated both primary and secondary data which was analyzed using simple percentages and hypothesis tested using chi – square statistical method at 0.05 level of significant for validity and to make decisions. From the findings, there was rampant incidence of tax evasion and avoidance in Enugu state due to inadequate, ineffective and inefficient tax administration. The researcher concluded among other things that the apathy of Enugu state people towards payment of tax be checked by involving them in the decision making of tax administration, collection and utilization of the tax revenue.

Oil revenue and economic growth

Chukwuma et al. examined the impact of crude oil discovery, exploitation and exportation on the agricultural commodity export in Nigeria in the period 1970-2011. Annual time series data sourced mainly from the Central Bank of Nigeria (CBN) statistical bulletins for various years were analyzed using co-integration and vector error correction model in a bid to delineate the long run relationship between agricultural commodity exports and oil export. A 1% increase in oil exports depressed agricultural commodity export by 16%, that is, the more Nigeria produces and exports oil, the lower the output and less competitive the traditional tradable agricultural sector becomes. The paper recommended that policy makers should make considerable investments in developing other economic sectors, re-channel the extra revenue from oil to accumulate income-producing foreign assets, and come up with a number of tax and import duty waivers, import substitution and diversification measures in order to boost productivity in the "lagging" traditional tradable sector and develop other agro-allied industries to improve the value chain.

In a study, Aliyu adapted graphic descriptive statistics and the one-way analysis of variance technique to investigate whether the neglect of agricultural sector was as a result of the discovery and exploitation of oil in Nigeria [28]. The study found a significant increase in the quantity of capital expenditure allocated to agricultural sector during the oil boom period and that more capital expenditure was allocated to agricultural sector than was allocated to either of health, education or defense sector in Nigeria during the period. The study concluded by rejecting the hypothesis that the neglect of agricultural sector was as a result of oil boom.

Henry in Bitrus, indicated that in the mid-1980s, Nigeria emerged as the sole country out of six (Nigeria, Indonesia, Algeria, Iran, Venezuela, Trinidad and Tobago), where the standard of living had fallen below par [29]. As such, Henry summarized the performance of Nigerian economy into three basic categories as follows:

- ❖ The specific uses to which petroleum revenue was put conditioned the structure of socio-political sharing. The social interest and class contrast were low because the state was under pressure to render services to the people which continued from military government to military government.
- ❖ There was no much pressure to use petroleum revenue to ameliorate the agricultural sector productivity. This is where Nigeria differs from Indonesia in the study. In Indonesia, petroleum revenue was used to ameliorate the agricultural sector. In Nigeria, that was not done. Thus, Indonesia progressed, while Nigeria declined economically.
- ❖ Macroeconomic adjustment of Nigeria led to declining national revenue, and this differs from other petroleum exporting countries. Indonesia adopted a rapid exchange rate between 1978 and 1980 in form of devaluation. Venezuela, Trinidad and Tobago experienced a large devaluation in 1981 without any hesitation on such adjustment.

Government's external borrowing and economic growth

Imimole, Imoughele & Okhuese examined the extent to which Nigeria's external debt related to indices of ability to pay in order to ascertain the sustainability of it and to identify the main determinants of her external indebtedness for the period 1986 to 2010 [8]. The result from the cointegration test showed evidence of long run relationship between external debt and its determinants. The study also discovered that the main determinants of Nigeria's external debt are gross domestic product, debt service and exchange rate. To reduce the adverse effects of external debt on the Nigerian economy and make it sustainable the study recommended that an analysis of the economic and social profitability of all external debt financial projects be carried out to ensure that the returns would be in excess of the interest and principal repayment.

Folorunso & Falade examined the relationship between Fiscal Deficit and Public Debt in Nigeria [30]. In what follows, the public debt was divided into domestic and external debt with a view to analyzing the causal relationship and relative effect of both categories of debt on fiscal deficit. Bi-directional relationship was confirmed between fiscal balance and public debt as well as its domestic component, while causality only run from external debt to fiscal balance in the country. Both domestic and external debt portends positive effect on fiscal deficit in Nigeria. The study showed that domestic debt has greater impact on fiscal deficit than external debt. Hence, it was advocated that the Nigerian government should consider appropriate mix of domestic debt and external debt as a means of financing budget deficit.

Ezike and Mojekwu opined that the main issue that worsened the Nigeria debt problem is that some of the debt service obligations were in the form of contingent liabilities resulting from Government guarantee of private sector trade transaction that had to be taken on board without adequate planning, due to mismanagement, wide-scale corruption and default by private sector operators, obligations fell on the Federal Government as explicit contingent liabilities in those instances where it had guaranteed the loan [31].

Bader and Magableh noted that the high public debt in Jordan, along with its servicing burden, was obviously hindering the government's efforts to maintain higher and sustained economic growth rate [32]. It was found that real exchange rate, the financial position of the government and the size of foreign aids significantly affect the outstanding balance of external debt, but real exchange rate is the most effective among all explanatory variables. The study also showed that the increase in savings gap and fiscal deficit plays a key role in domestic debt accumulation since the government resorts to borrow to finance it.

Osinubi and Olaleru examined how the use of budget deficits as an instrument of stabilization leads to the accumulation of external debt with the attending effects on growth in Nigeria between 1970 and 2003 [33]. Their study concluded that if debt-financed budget deficits are operated in order to stabilize the debt ratio at the optimum sustainable level, debt overhang problems would be avoided and the benefits of external borrowing would be maximized.

Alshara, Khateeb, and Maitah appraised the size and composition of Jordan external public debt and its effect on some macroeconomic variables such as private consumption, public consumption, gross investment, gross tax revenues, direct tax revenues, indirect tax revenues, imports, Gross National Product (GNP), and disposable income [34]. They reported that external loans positively affect consumption, investment, imports and gross national product (GNP).

Theoretical Framework

Theories of taxation

The three theories of taxation to be reviewed in this paper are:

- **The cost of service theory:** Following the assertion of this theory, the cost incurred by government in providing certain services to the people must collectively be met by the people who are the ultimate receivers of the service [12]. This theory is of the opinion that tax is similar to price. So if a person does not utilize the service of a state, he should not be charged any tax. Some criticisms have been leveled against this theory. If the theory is applied, the state will not undertake welfare activities like medical care, education, social amenities, etc. furthermore, it will be very difficult to compute the cost per head of the various services provided by the state, again, the theory has violated the correct definition and tenets of tax, finally the basis of taxation as propounded by the theory is misleading.

- **Benefit received theory:** According to this theory, the tax expected from citizens should be in proportion to the benefits they enjoy from the services rendered by the government. The theory assumes that there is exchange relationship or *quid pro quo* between tax payers and government. The government confers some benefits on tax payers by providing social goods which the tax payers pay a consideration in the form of taxes for using such goods. The inability to measure the benefits received by an individual from the services rendered by the government has rendered this theory inapplicable.

- **Socio-political theory:** This theory of taxation states that social and political objectives should be the main factors in selecting taxes. The theory advocated that a tax system should not be designed to serve individuals, but should be used to satisfy the desire of the entire society [7]. Hence, this theory forms the basis for this study following the Nigerian case characterized by rate of inequality.

Theory of debt finance

The theoretical framework that justifies the need for external borrowing by developing countries as adapted by Imimole et al. links the increase in gross external debt to (current account deficit - direct and long-term portfolio capital inflows) + (official reserve increases + other private capital outflows) [8]. The model started by summarizing the determinants of the current account (CA) balance, where CA is the difference between items that generate foreign exchange and those that require foreign-exchange expenditure.

$$CA = X - M - ILF - OTP \tag{1}$$

Where,

X=Exports

M=Imports

ILF=Interest paid on loans from foreigners

OTP=other net factors payments and transfers to foreigners

$$CA = \Delta NIR + \Delta BF - \Delta LF - FDI \tag{2}$$

According to Imimole et al. Eq. (2) is another way of writing the current account surplus of equation (1). This time, the current account is the difference between changes in the international reserves (ΔNIR) and foreign bonds placed domestically (ΔBF)), and an increase in loans from foreigners (ΔLF) and foreign direct investment (FDI) [8]. Then, the change in loans from foreigners (ΔLF) is basically the difference between new foreign loans (N) and payments of foreign loan principal (PLF). Then, demand for new foreign loans (NFL) would be:

$$NFL = PLF + ILF + \Delta NIR + \Delta BF - FDI - OTP - X + M \tag{3}$$

Eq. (3) implies that the demand for new foreign loans is an increasing function of payments of foreign loan principal due (PLF); interest paid on loans from foreigners (ILF); ΔNIR; ΔBF; OTP; and imports; and a decreasing function of exports (X) and foreign direct investment (FDI).

Now, the sum of interest (ILF) and principal (PLF) payments paid is nothing other than total debt service paid (DSP). The DSP is also nothing else other than the difference between total debt service due (DSD), which incorporates also past arrears outstanding and current arrears (A). Substituting these relationships into equation (3), equation (4) was found, which represents the demand for new foreign loans.

$$NFL + A = DSD + \Delta NIR + \Delta BF - FDI + OTP - X + M \tag{4}$$

Mebere (2009) postulated that the assumption followed here is that countries prefer to protect their reputation by rolling over their external debt rather than by arrears. This gives an equation for a one period –ahead ex ante demand for new loans, which satisfies:

$$NL_D = DSD_e + \Delta NIR_e + \Delta BF_e - FDI_e + OTP_e - X_e + M_e \tag{5}$$

Where, NL_D stands for new loan demanded, and the superscripts e stands for expectations and other variables are as defined above. From eq. (5) it implies that the demand for external borrowing is an increasing function of total debt service (DSD), the change in international reserves, the change in foreign bonds placed domestically (which partly reflects capital flight), net transfers to foreigners, and imports of goods and services. In contrast, capital inflows in the form of foreign direct investment and export revenues reduce the demand for external borrowing.

Research Methodology

Research design

By definition, a research design is a blueprint which guides the researcher in his scientific inquiry, investigation and analysis. In this study, *ex-post facto* research design was adopted in obtaining, analyzing and interpreting data relating to the objectives of the study. *Ex-post facto* study or after- the-fact research is a category of research design in which the investigation starts after the fact had occurred without interference from the researcher [35].

Nature and sources of data

The data relevant for this study is exclusively secondary as no attempt was made to include primary data in the data set. The data comprises of annual time series spanning from 1986 to 2014. The data set was sourced from Central Bank of Nigeria statistical bulletin 2014 edition, international financial statistics and National Bureau of Statistics (NBS).

Method of data analysis

The method of inferential statistics was adopted in the analysis of data, and it involves the statement and testing of scientific hypotheses. The Vector Error Correction Model (VECM) model was employed using Econometric View (E-view) 8.0 software package for the data analysis. Prior to the regression analysis, diagnostic tests were carried out to ensure the validity of data. The test for stationarity was carried out using the Augmented Dickey-Fuller (ADF) unit root test, while the test for the long run equilibrium adjustment was accomplished using Johansen co-integration test (for the first model in equation 6) and Augmented Engle-Granger co-integration test (for the second model in equation 7).

Model specification

Econometric models aimed at capturing the relationship between sources of public funds and economic prosperity in Nigeria, in line with the theoretical framework and literature reviewed was developed. Hence, the present model was adapted from the works of Ojong et al., Ayinde, Kuranga & Lukman and Ujunwa [12,26,27]. The model is specified below as follow with some modifications.

$$RGDP_t = \beta_0 + \beta_1 TAXR_t + \beta_2 OILR_t + \beta_3 EXTD_t + \beta_4 NASV_t + e_t \quad (6)$$

$$RGDP_{t=}\beta_0 + \beta_1 TGVR_t + e_t \quad (7)$$

Where,

$\beta_{o=}$Constant

β_1 -$\beta_{4=}$Population parameters

RGDP=Real gross domestic product

TAXR=Tax revenue

OILR=Oil revenue

EXDT=External debt

NSAV=National savings

TGVR=Total government revenue

e=Estimated error term or Stochastic term

Description of variables

The variables used for this study are briefly described below as follow.

Dependent variable

- **Real Gross Domestic Product (RGDP):** This is an inflation adjusted measure that reflects the value of all goods and services produced by an economy in a given year, expressed in base-year prices and is often referred to as "constant-price." The growth rate of real gross domestic product was taken for this study. The growth rate of real gross domestic product was calculated as follow.

$$RGDP = \frac{RGDPc - RGDPp}{RGDPp} * 100 \quad (8)$$

Where,

RGDPc=Current year's Real gross domestic product

RGDPp=Previous year's Real gross domestic product

Independent variables

- **Tax Revenue (TAXR):** Tax revenue entails the aggregate government revenue generated through all form of taxes available.

- **Oil Revenue (OILR):** Oil revenue comprises of the aggregate revenue available to government via the export of oil produce to the rest of the world.

- **National Savings (NSAV):** National savings denote the sum of nation's public and private savings. National savings equals a nation's income minus consumption and government expenditure.

- **Total Government Revenue (TGRV):** This refers to the sum of revenue generated from all the sources (excluding savings and debt).

Discussion of Results and Hypotheses Testing

Descriptive statistics

The descriptive statistics was used to describe and summarize the basic features of the time series data used for the analysis. The results for the descriptive statistics were presented in Table 1 below.

From the results of the descriptive statistic, the mean values of the variables shows that on average, total government revenue (TGRV) has the highest rate of 20.09655%, followed by oil revenue (OILR) with an average of 15.59379%, with external debt (EXTD) having a mean of 14.46552, while national savings (NSAV) recorded a mean value of 8.793102%. Real gross domestic product growth rate (RGDP) maintained an average rate of 5.204483, with the least average value of 5.50% being for tax revenue. Having gone through these mean values, it was found that the difference between the mean values of total government revenue (TGRV) and external debt (EXTD) is 5.63103% which indicates that the Nigerian economy is dominated by debt finance. Also, the gap between the mean values of total government revenue and oil revenue is 4.50276% which further shows that the Nigerian economy is dependent on oil revenue. The overdependence on oil revenue and high rate of external debt is justified by the low level (mean) of national savings (NSAV) and tax revenue (TAXR), respectively.

With respect to the maximum values, total government revenue recorded its highest rate of 37.97% in 2001, followed by oil revenue reached its highest of 32.59% in 2005, external debt outstanding maintained a maximum rate of 29.12% in 1994, national savings witnessed its highest point of 23.25% in 2009, with highest growth rate of real GDP and tax revenue being at 17.59 and 13.10%, respectively. The minimum values of 8.33, 3.34, 6.02, -0.82, 2.81 and 9.36% for external debt, national savings, oil revenue, real GDP growth rate, tax revenue and total government revenue in 2010, 1996, 1986, 1991, 1993 and 1986, respectively.

In terms of volatility of the variables, the standard deviation in Table 1 showed that total government revenue is more volatile with an index point of 8.523388 being followed by oil revenue (7.430735), external debt (5.299178), national savings (4.144220), real gross domestic product growth rate (3.943143), and tax revenue (1.996282).

The trend of the variables (oil revenue, tax revenue, external debt, national savings, total government revenue and real gross domestic product growth rate in Figure 1. That is, a figure showing how the various sources of public funds identified in the study has fluctuated over the years (1986-2014) (Figure 1).

Test for stationarity using augmented dickey fuller (ADF) unit root test

To test for the presence of non-stationarity of a data set, it is necessary to investigate the order of integration of the individual time series before any other tests. For this purpose, standard unit root tests were conducted using Augmented Dickey–Fuller (ADF) test (Dickey and Fuller 1979). This test results was presented in Table 2 below.

In summary, from Table 2, the variables (external debt, national savings, oil revenue, real gross domestic product growth rate and total government revenue) were found to have a single unit root or are integrated of degree one I(1) and they are stationary at their first difference, while tax revenue was stationary at level . These results imply that the regression results that would be obtained from the models specified in (Equation 1 ans 2) would return spurious results if there is no long-run relationship among the variables in the model. As such, cointegration properties were investigated.

Empirical Results from Model 1 (Equation 6)

The result obtained from the analysis of data associated with equation 6 was presented in Tables 3-5. The results include the Johansen cointegration test for long run causality, lag selection criteria and vector error correction mechanism (VECM); that is, a model that combines both the short-run properties of the economic relationships in the first difference form of equation (6), as well as the long-run information provided by the data in level form.

Johansen cointegration tests

Johansen co-integration test determines whether a long-term relationship exist between the variables or not. The Johansen test of co-integration uses the likelihood ratio to test for co-integration. The hypothesis of co-integration is accepted if the number of co-integrating relationships is greater than or equal to one. Consequently, the Johansen co-integration results are presented below in Table 3.

From the Johansen cointegration test results presented in Table 3 above, the Trace statistic indicates two cointegrating equations judging from the P-values at None* and 1* which are both significant at 1% level. Likewise, the Max-Eigen statistic indicates two cointegrating equations following the P-values at None* and 1* which both showed a significant level of 5%. Sequel to this result, the number of cointegrating relationships is greater than one, and the null hypothesis of no cointegration was rejected in favour of the alternative hypothesis that the variables used in model 1 (equation 6) are cointegrated.

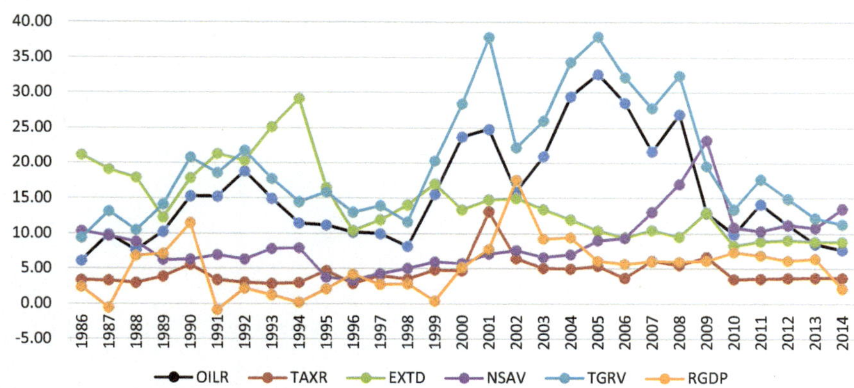

Source: Plotted by Author's (2016) using Microsoft Excel.

Figure 1: Trend of oil revenue, tax revenue, external debt, national savings, total government revenue and real gross domestic product growth rate.

	EXTD	NSAV	OILR	RGDP	TAXR	TGRV
Mean	14.46552	8.793103	15.59379	5.204483	4.500000	20.09655
Maximum	29.12000	23.25000	32.59000	17.59000	13.10000	37.97000
Minimum	8.330000	3.340000	6.020000	-0.820000	2.810000	9.360000
Std. Dev.	5.299178	4.144220	7.430735	3.943143	1.996282	8.523388

Source: Author's Computation (2016) using Eviews 8.0.

Note: All the explanatory variables are expressed as a ratio of Nominal GDP.

Table 1: Summary of descriptive statistic.

Variables	ADF @ Level	ADF @ 1ST Difference	Order of Integration
EXTD	-3.075467	-4.966114	I(1)
NSAV	-2.732451	-5.483560	I(1)
OILR	-3.566754	-6.022959	I(1)
RGDP	-3.233282	-7.201507	I(1)
TAXR	-3.782137	-----	I(0)
TGRV	-1.741058	-5.501452	I(1)

Source: Author's Eviews Computations (2016).

Table 2: Summary of Augmented Dickey Fuller (ADF) Test Results.

Vector error correction mechanism

Having ascertained that the variables are cointegrated, the information provided by the lag order selection criteria was used to generate a set of error correction model (ECM) to capture the short run and long-run behaviour of the GDP growth relationship. The changes in the relevant variables represent the short-run elasticities, while the coefficient of the error correction term represents the speed of adjustment back to the long-run relationship among the variables. Tables 4 and 5 provides the results for the real gross domestic product (RGDP) growth rate and government revenue relationship for the period 1986 to 2014 (Tables 3 and 4).

From Table 4, it can be observed that the lag length suggested by Akaike Information criterion is one lag which is attributable to the size of the observations (Table 5).

From the result presented in Table 5, the coefficient of the lagged value of tax revenue (TAXR) entails that real gross domestic product growth rate increased by 17.1% due to 1% change in tax revenue in the short run. However, the variable was neither significant at 5% nor 10% level judging from the P-value (0.7364). The finding supports Ojong et al. and Ayuba who concluded that non-oil revenue (predominantly tax revenue) was insignificant in affecting growth of the Nigerian economy [7,12]. However, literature abound that tax revenue is the main source of government finance, and is significant to economic growth [5,6,27]. Hence, the insignificance of tax revenue in this regard could be due to the findings that non-compliance to tax laws, lack of skilled tax officers, capital flight, and corruption among tax collectors has a negative effect on tax revenue [13,14,36].

With respect to the one period lagged value of oil revenue (OILR), the coefficient shows that a unit change in oil revenue resulted to 11.5% increase in real gross domestic product (RGDP) growth rate in the short run. This relationship is not significant at 5% level, and lends support to the findings of Ujunwa and Ayinde et al. [26,27], but contradicted the findings of Mustapha who found a negative and significant relationship between oil exports and economic growth in Nigeria. A plausible reason for the non-significance of oil revenue could be attributed to the volatility in oil prices, exchange rate volatility, oil bunkery, oil pipeline vandalism in the Niger-Delta, and misappropriation of oil revenue [21].

In line with literature and theory that a country which is unable to mobilize adequate savings and revenue resort to external borrowing to fill the resource gap. The results reveals that the lagged value of external debt (EXTD) exerted a negative effect on real gross domestic product (RGDP) growth rate in Nigeria. The coefficient suggests that a unit change in external debt caused real gross domestic product (RGDP) growth rate to depress by 28.5% in the short run. This negative effect could be due to the debt burden hanging on the shoulders of the government to clear. Judging from the p-value of external debt, the variable was not significant at 5% level. As such, the null hypothesis of no significance was accepted.

The national income accounting theory suggests that savings is key to investments and economic growth. The results obtained for

Hypothesized No. of CE(s)	Trace Statistic	Prob**	Max-Eigen Statistic	Prob**
None*	92.45167	0.0003	36.33728	0.0249
At most 1*	56.11440	0.0069	29.64541	0.0268
At most 2	26.46899	0.1153	13.82053	0.3799
At most 3	12.64845	0.1284	10.56526	0.1774
At most 4	2.083197	0.1489	2.083197	0.1489

Source: Eviews computations (2016).

Table 3: Johansen cointegration test results.

Lag	LogL	LR	FPE	AIC	SC	HQ
0	-373.98	NA	1069823.	28.07222	28.31219	28.14357
1	-320.56	83.09216*	135350.0*	25.96730*	27.40712*	26.39543*
2	-306.94	16.13881	389260.9	26.81048	29.45015	27.59539

*Indicates lag order selected by the criterion.

LR: sequential modified LR test statistic (each test at 5% level).

FPE: Final prediction error.

AIC: Akaike information criterion.

SC: Schwarz information criterion.

HQ: Hannan-Quinn information criterion.

Table 4: Optimal lag selection criteria.

Variables	Coefficient	Std. Error	t-Statistic	Prob.
D(TAXR(-1))	0.17107	0.49748	0.34386	0.7364
D(OILR(-1))	0.11506	0.17291	0.66547	0.5174
D(EXTD(-1))	-0.2851	0.21698	-1.3138	0.2116
D(NSAV(-1))	-0.246	0.27724	-0.8874	0.391
C	-0.3642	0.60207	-0.6048	0.5557
ECM(-1)	-0.8102	0.28772	-2.8158	0.0146**
Adj. R-squared	0.47559			
F-statistic	2.88942			
Prob(F-statistic)	0.034610**			

Source: Author's computation (2016) using Eviews 8.0.

**Significance @ 5 percent level.

Table 5: Vector error correction model (VECM) results.

this study is contrary to this view. The coefficient of national savings shows that a 1% increase in national savings resulted to approximately 24.6% decrease in real gross domestic product (RGDP) growth rate. This result appears to be due to low investments which resulted to low income, and low income resulting to low savings. Also, the low savings rate could be due to capital flight [19]. On the other hand, the P-value suggests no significant relationship between national savings and economic growth (proxied by real gross domestic product growth rate) in the short run.

The constant (C) entails that *ceteris paribus* (if all the explanatory variables are held constant, real gross domestic product will be reducing by approximately 36.41% in the short run. This is an indication of low economic prosperity in Nigeria.

The long-run error correction mechanisms (ECM) proved to be statistically significant in correcting the disequilibrium at lag one in the two models. It shows that about 81% correction is made to the disequilibrium result from the co-integrating vector, at every one year to position real gross domestic product (RGDP) in Nigeria to its equilibrium root. This also means that real gross domestic product adjusts rapidly to changes in the explanatory variables. The long-run factor in the model has the right sign of negative, showing that at every disequilibrium in the real gross domestic product in Nigeria, there is positive adjustment mechanism at every one year to put them back to equilibrium track, provided other factors are controlled.

Going through the results, the overall regression model is significant judging from the F-statistic. The Prob (F-statistic suggests that the overall regression is significant at 5% level. This means that the explanatory variables jointly have a significant effect on real gross domestic product (a proxy for economic growth).

The adjusted R-squared indicates that the explanatory variables (tax revenue, oil revenue, national savings and external debt) explained approximately 47.55% of the total variations in real gross domestic product, while the error term (e) accounted for the remaining 52.45% of the variations unexplained by the explanatory variable used in the study.

Empirical results from Model 2 (Equation 7)

The results obtained for model 2 are presented in Tables 6 and 7. It comprises of the Augmented Engle-Granger cointegration test for simple regression, and error correction model (ECM). The results are presented as follow (Table 6).

Table 6 shows that the t-statistic associated with the Engle-Granger cointegration test is significant at 5% level judging from the P-value (0.0250). The implication is that there is evidence of cointegration or long run linear relationship between total government revenue (TGRV) and real gross domestic product (RGDP) growth rate. Consequently, the error correction model (ECM) was adopted as shown below (Table 7).

The long-run error correction term proved to be statistically significant in correcting the disequilibrium at lag one in the model.

Augmented Dickey-Fuller test statistic		t-Statistic	Prob.
		-3.9109	0.0250
Test critical values:	1% level	-4.324	
	5% level	-3.5806	
	10% level	-3.2253	

Source: Eviews Computations (2016).

Table 6: Augmented engle-granger cointegration test results.

Variable	Coefficient	Std. Error	t-Statistic	Prob.
D(TGRV)	-0.0596	0.10985	-0.5422	0.5925
ECM(-1)	-0.6804	0.18054	-3.7689	0.0009
C	0.0352	0.65775	0.05351	0.9577
R-squared	0.38027			
Adjusted R-squared	0.3307			
F-statistic	7.67016			
Prob (F-statistic)	0.00253			
Durbin-Watson stat	1.90006			

Source: Eviews Output (2016).

Table 7: Error correction mechanism (ECM) for model 2.

It shows that 68.04% correction is made to the disequilibrium result from the co-integrating vector, at every one year to position real gross domestic product in Nigeria to its equilibrium root. The error correction term in the model has the expected negative sign, showing that at every disequilibrium in real gross domestic product (RGDP) in Nigeria, there is positive adjustment mechanism at every one year to put them back to equilibrium track, provided other factors are controlled.

The constant (C) is not significant at the three levels of 1, 5 and 10%, respectively. However, the coefficient suggests that real gross domestic product (RGDP) growth rate will increase by 3.51% if the explanatory variable (total government revenue) is held constant. This implies that without aggregate government revenue, the domestic economy will be positive.

The overall goodness of the model as shown by the coefficient of determination is 0.38027 which shows that the variations in the regressor (total government revenue) explained about 38% variations in real gross domestic product (RGDP) growth rate, while the error term (e) accounted for the remaining 62% having taken degree of freedom into consideration. The F-statistic, a measure of the overall significance of the regression, shows that the simple regression model (model 2) is significant at the 1% level. That is, total government revenue have a significant effect on real gross domestic product in Nigeria.

The results presented in Table 7 explained the relationship between total government revenue (TGRV) and real gross domestic product (RGDP) growth rate in Nigeria. Going through the results, changes in total government revenue (TGRV) depressed real gross domestic product (RGDP) growth rate by 5.95% in the short run. This is a clear indication that the aggregate revenue generated by the Nigerian government cannot be trusted for running the economy. This is linked to high cost of debt servicing, overdependence on the oil sector coupled with corruption of tax officers, capital flight, and the rest of them [3,36]. As such, it obviously means that the aggregate revenue generated from oil and non-oil sources have not been able to increase domestic production in Nigeria.

Conclusion and Recommendations

Generally, a government of various countries (developed, developing and under-developed) requires financial resources to boost the economic and social wellbeing of her citizens. Consequently, this pressing need of finance have propelled the government of many nations to introduce various means of raising finances for economic growth and development. Sequel to this, this study examined the effect of various sources of government revenue on the growth of Nigerian economy. Consequently, having collected and analyzed the data on yearly real gross domestic product growth rate, aggregate government revenue generated from oil and non-oil sources, oil revenue, tax revenue, external debt and national savings. It was observed that revenue from taxes and oil had a positive effect on economic growth in Nigeria, while the effect of national savings and external debt were negative. On the other hand, the aggregate government revenue was not sufficient enough to foster economic growth in Nigeria, which was assumed to be due to capital flight, leakages of tax revenue, corruption, tax evasion, misappropriation of oil revenue.

Based on the findings of this study, the following recommendations were preferred.

- To boost tax revenue in Nigeria, government should ensure that the citizens willingly comply with tax laws. To achieve this, the government should provide the necessary welfare needs of the citizens. As such, they will find reasons to pay their taxes due to the services they enjoy from the government.

- With respect to accelerating national savings, the monetary and fiscal authorities should ensure that the investment climate is favorable. This can be done by maintaining a stable exchange rate, domestic prices, and interest rate. This will amount to greater investment domestically, and the savings rate will accelerate as a result.

- There is need to develop the agricultural sector to function alongside the oil sector following the recent decline in oil revenue. Hence, the government should lift tariff on the importation of technology that will help expand the agricultural sector in Nigeria. As such, the economy will be well diversified to accommodate other sectors, other than the oil sector solely.

- Also, since the government resort to external borrowing due to the fiscal deficit, there is need to appraise the potential benefits of all external debt financial projects by ensuring that the benefits would offset the debt servicing cost.

Finally, the government should put up policies that would prevent the leakage of available resources out of the country. As such, there should be close monitoring on the use of public funds from various sources in order to avoid siphoning of public wealth.

References

1. Okpanachi U (2004) Government Deficit and the Inflationary Process in Nigeria, 1986-1998. A Thesis in the Department Of Economics, Faculty of Social Sciences Submitted To the School Of Post-Graduate Studies, University of Jos.
2. Wong JD (2004) The Fiscal Impact of Economic Growth and Development on Local Government Revenue Capacity. J. of Public Budgeting, Accounting & Financial Management 16: 413-423.
3. Fagbemu TO, Noah AO (2010) The Ethics of Tax Evasion: Perpetual Evidence from Nigeria. European Journal of Social Sciences 17: 360-371.
4. Oni OE, Daniya AA (2012) Development of Small and Medium Scale Enterprises: The role of Government and other Financial Institutions. Arabian Journal of Business and Management Review (OMAN Chapter) 1: 16-29.
5. Engen E, Skinner J (1996) Taxation and Economic Growth. National Bureau of economic research pp: 1-47.
6. Garba SL (2014) Tax Revenue and Economic Growth. Thesis Submitted to Postgraduate Studies, Ahmadu Bello University, Zaria.
7. Ayuba AJ (2014) Impact of Non-oil Tax Revenue on Economic Growth: The Nigerian Perspective. International Journal of Finance and Accounting 3: 303-309.
8. Imimole B, Imoughele L, Okhuese M (2014) Determinants, and Sustainability of External Debt in a Deregulated Economy: A Cointegration Analysis from Nigeria (1986-2010). American International Journal of Contemporary Research 4: 201-214.
9. Odusola A (2006) Tax Policy Reforms in Nigeria. Research Paper No. 2006/03 United Nations University World-Institute for Development Economics Research.
10. Nzotta S (2007) Tax Evasion Problems in Nigeria: A Critique. Nigeria Account, 40: 40-43.
11. Ogundele AE (1999) Elements of Taxation. (1stedn) Libri Service.
12. Ojong MC, Anthony O, Arikpo FO (2016) The Impact of Tax Revenue on Economic Growth: Evidence from Nigeria. IOSR Journal of Economics and Finance 7: 32-38.
13. Akintoye IR, Tashie GA (2013) The Effect of Tax Compliance on Economic Growth and Development in Nigeria, West-Africa. British Journal of Arts and Social Sciences 11: 222-231.
14. Adeniyi AR (2012) The Effect of Tax Administration on Revenue Generation in Enugu State. (A Case Study of the State Board of Internal Revenue Enugu State). Faculty of Management and Social Sciences, Caritas University Amorji – Nike Enugu State.
15. Folawewo A, Olakojo S (2010) Determinants of Agricultural Exports in Oil Exporting Economies: Empirical Evidence from Nigeria. Journal of Economic Theory 4: 84-92.
16. Stein C (2016) Is Nigeria's Promise a Pipe Dream? U.S. News in Partnership with BAV and Wharton.
17. Akinruwa TE, Awolusi OD, Ibojo BO (2013) Determinants of Small and Medium Enterprises (SMEs) Performance in Ekiti State, Nigeria: A Business Survey Approach. European Journal of Humanities and Social Sciences 27: 1397-1413.
18. Iganiga BO, Unemhilin DO (2011) The Impact of Federal Government Agricultural Expenditure on Agricultural Output in Nigeria. J Economics 2: 81-88.
19. Uremadu SO, Onyele KO, Ariwa FO (2016) The Effect of Capital Flight on Financial Savings in Nigeria Selected. Prime Journal of Administration and Management 6: 2075-2086.
20. Reynolds LC (1966) Peasant Agriculture and Economic Growth in Nigeria. The Economic Growth Center, Yale: Yale University.
21. Chukwuka OI, Uwajumogu NR, Chijioke G, Ebele S (2013) Oil Exploitation and Agricultural Commodity Export in Nigeria: An Empirical Evaluation of the Extent and Impact of the Dutch Disease. IOSR Journal of Humanities and Social Science (IOSR-JHSS) 14: 01-09.
22. Gbaiye GO, Ogundipe A, Osabuohien E, Olugbire OO, Adeniran OA, et al. (2011) Agricultural Exports and Economic Growth in Nigeria (1980-2010). Journal of Economics and Sustainable Development 4: 1-4.
23. Anyanwu JC (1997) Nigerian Public Finance. Joannne Educational Publishers, Onitsha.
24. Adereti SA, Sanni MR, Adesina JA (2011) Value Added Tax and Economic Growth of Nigeria. European Journal of Humanities and Social Sciences 10: 456-471.
25. Obadan MI (1987) The Impact of petroleum on the Nigerian Economy.
26. Ujunwa IF (2013) The Impact of Oil Revenue on the Economic Growth in Nigeria (1980-2010). Faculty of management and social sciences caritas university, Amorji nike, Enugu pp: 1-48.
27. Ayinde K, Kuranga J, Lukman FA (2015) Modeling Nigerian Government Expenditure, Revenue and Economic Growth: Co-Integration, Error Correction Mechanism and Combined Estimators Analysis Approach. Asian Economic and Financial Review 5: 858-867.
28. Aliyu AA (2011) Nigeria's Oil boom Period (1973-1983): Was Agriculture Real Neglected? International Journal of Statistics and Applications 1: 6-9.
29. Henry (1991) Nigeria: From Windfall Gains to Welfare Looses? Sustaining Development in Mineral Economies. The resources curse thesis.
30. Folorunso BA, Falade OE (2013) Relationship between Fiscal Deficit and Public Debt in Nigeria: an Error Correction Approach 5: 346-355.
31. Ezike JE, Mojekwu JN (2011) The Impact of External Debt on Macro-Economic Performance. International Journal of Business and Management Tomorrow 1: 1-12.
32. Bader M, Magableh IK (2009) An Enquiry into the Main Determinants of Public

Debt in Jordan: An Econometric Study. Dirasat Administrative Sciences 36: 181-190.

33. Osinubi TS, Olaleru OE (2006) Budget Deficits, External Debt and Economic Growth in Nigeria. Applied Econometrics and International Development 6: 27-32.

34. Alshara M, Khateeb F, Maitah M (1991) External Debt and its Impact on the Jordanian Economy: An: An Econometrical Study. Abhath Al-yarmouk 7: 231-253.

35. Obasi IN (1999) Research Methodology in Political Science. Enugu: Academic Publishing Company.

36. Uguru LC (2016) On the Tax Implications of Capital Flight: Evidence from Nigeria. Journal of Research in Economics and International Finance (JREIF) 5: 001-007.

20

Multifractal Detrended Cross-correlation Analysis of Gold and WTI Crude Oil Price Time Series

Burugupalli S*

Center for Integrated Studies, University of Hyderabad, Gachibowli, Hyderabad-500 046, India

Abstract

Several papers have documented the cross-correlations across wide range of markets using different methods and the results are being used for the improvisation of market efficiency. In this paper, we have investigated the cross-correlations between Gold market and WTI Crude oil market using MF-X-DFA. Quantitatively, we have employed the recently developed MF-X-DFA method for the data of Gold and WTI Crude oil markets and we have confirmed the existence of cross-correlation between Gold and Crude oil markets. We have also found that these cross-correlations are strongly multifractal in the short term and weakly multifractal in long the term. Moreover, their behavior for small fluctuations is persistent and those of large fluctuations are anti persistent in the short term. Cross-correlations of very small fluctuations and large fluctuations are persistent but whereas for small fluctuations are anti-persistent in the long term. Furthermore, based on multifractal spectrum, we have produced substantial evidences to determine cross-correlation behaviors exhibit multifractal features. Our results have significant implications to market efficiency.

Keywords: Non-stationary time series; Fractals; Hurst exponent; Multifractal detrended Cross-correlation Analysis

Introduction

The multifractality in real world non stationary time series data are described better from scaling exponents. The observed signals of the physical quantities characterizing any complex system like social, financial, ecological, biological or technological are composed of large number of interacting assorted parameters linked each other nonlinearly and they exhibit long-range correlations. It is of crucial importance and significance to quantify such long-range correlations to have a deep understanding of the dynamics of the underlying complex systems. The theory of fractals proposed by Mandelbrot [1] in contrast to the efficient market hypothesis leads to study of complex system behavior through different method development and approaches. Hurst [2,3] proposed rescaled range analysis (R/S), the most popular analysis method for fractals. To overcome R/S analysis method sensitiveness to short-term auto-correlation and non-stationary nature causing bias error; detrended fluctuation analysis (DFA) method was proposed [4] which applied long-range power-law correlation. DFA and its multifractal generalization MF-DFA methods [5] are widely used to describe the fractal properties. Many researchers studied multifractal properties on the different non stationary natural and financial time series data like biological data [6], exchange rate market [7], stock market [8,9] gold market [8,10], crude oil market [9-12]. Two major sources of multifractality which can be found in various time series: one is nonlinear temporal correlation for small and large fluctuations; while the other is fat-tailed probability distribution of increments [8,13,14].

Also multifractality in the daily returns of emerging European stock markets is studied using the Empirical Mode Decomposition (EMD) based Multifractal Detrended Fluctuation Analysis [15]. A comparison study of different fluctuation methods for analyzing non-stationary time series were studied for efficacy of the methods like Fluctuation Analysis (FA); Detrended Fluctuation Analysis (DFA) and Detrended Moving Average (DMA). It was reported that [16] Centred Detrending Moving Average (CDMA) and DFA are the Methods of Choice in determining the Hurst index of time series. CDMA has the best performance while DFA is only slightly worse in some situations. Also CDMA and DFA are less sensitive to the scaling range compared to other methods like FA.

Cross-correlation found to be exists in many simultaneously recorded time series in various real world commodities or financial market data. Therefore, in recent years, many researchers attempted to quantify cross-correlations between non stationary data from complex systems. Detrended Cross-Correlation Analysis (DCCA) was proposed [17] to investigate power-law cross-correlations between two simultaneously recorded time series in the presence of non-stationarity. This new method was applied to different time series for long-range power-law cross-correlations [18]. Subsequently, multifractal generalization of the method was proposed [19] describing the new method as multifractal detrended cross-correlation analysis (MF-DCCA) by combining MFDFA and DCCA approaches. The MFDCCA method was applied [13,20-26] to many different time series for cross correlation analysis.

Efficiency of Brent and WTI crude oil market was analyzed by means of R/S analysis [27]. Dynamics of crude oil prices was studied thru stochastic multi-model approach [28]. Market agent perspective on fractal features in crude oil time series was studied [29,30]. From the analysis it was evidence that the crude oil market is a persistent process with long-range memory effects with multifractal structures. The MFDFA analysis on gold price revealed that multifractality is mainly due to the temporal correlation [30]. But there exist a cross correlation between the gold and Crude oil time series to study market behavior

***Corresponding author:** Burugupalli S, Assistant Professor, Center for Integrated Studies, University of Hyderabad, Gachibowli, Hyderabad-500 046, India, E-mail: satish.burugupalem@gmail.com

and underlying complexity. This article is focused on that study to analyze the cross correlation between Gold and Crude Oil. The section 2 of the article presents the MFD CCA procedure while the Section 3 describes the data. The Section 4 shares the result and its analysis. Section 5 gives our conclusions.

Methodology

Assume that there are two series x(i) and y(i) where i = 1, 2, . . . , N. Now the MFD CCA method is as follows.

Step 1. Construct the profile

$$(i) = \sum \left(x(t) - \bar{x}\right)$$

$$Y(i) = \sum (y(t) - \bar{y})$$

Where $\bar{x}$ and $\bar{y}$ are the average of the two time series x(i) and y(i).

Step 2. The profiles X(i) and Y(i) are divided into N_s=[N/s] non-overlapping windows of equal length s. Since the length N is not always a multiple of the considered time scale s hence in order not to discard the section of series, the same procedure is repeated starting from the reverse end of each profile. Thus, $2N_s$ non-overlapping windows are obtained together.

Step 3. The local trends Xv (i) and Yv (i) for each segment v (where, v=1, 2, 3, . . . , $2N_s$) are evaluated by least squares fits of the data, then the detrended covariance is determined by

$$F^2(s,v) = \frac{1}{s}\sum_{i=1}^{t}\left|X\left((v-1)s+i\right) - X^v(i)\right|\blacksquare\left|Y\left((v-1)s+i\right) - Y^v(i)\right|$$

Here for each segment v, v=1,2,...N_s hence,

$$F^2(s,v) = \frac{1}{s}\sum_{i=1}^{t}\left|X\left(N-(v-N_s)s+i\right) - X^v(i)\right|\blacksquare\left|Y\left(N-(v-N_s)s+i\right) - Y^v(i)\right|$$

Here for each segment v, v=N_s+1, N_s+2,..., $2N_s$. The trends $X^v(i)$ and $Y^v(i)$ are the fitting polynomial with order m in each segment v.

Step 4. Hence the qth order fluctuation function would be,

$$F_q(s) = \left[\frac{1}{2N_s}\sum_{v=1}^{2N_s}\left[F^2(s,v)\right]^{q/2}\right]^{1/q}$$

If $q \neq 0$ then the qth order fluctuation function would be,

$$F_0(s) = \exp\left\{\frac{1}{4N_s}\sum_{v=1}^{2N_s}\ln\left[F^2(s,v)\right]\right\}$$

When q=2 the MFD CCA is as like CCA

Step 5. Analyze the scaling behavior of the fluctuations by observing logarithmic plots between $F_q(s)$ and s for each values of q. If the two series are long-range cross-correlated then the $F_q(s)$ will increase for values of s and we can obtain a power-law expression as

$$F_q(s) \sim s^{H_{xy}(q)}$$

Hence taking log on both sides, we could represent this as

log $F_q(s)=H_{xy}(q)$ log(s) + logA (8)

Here the scaling exponent $H_{xy}(q)$ is known as the generalized cross-correlation Hurst exponent, describing the power-low relationship. Especially, if the two time series are equal then MFD CCA is the same as MFDFA. When the scaling exponent $H_{xy}(q)$ is independent q, the cross-correlation between two series is monofractal while if the scaling exponent $H_{xy}(q)$ is dependent on q, then the cross-correlation between two series is multifractal. If the scaling exponent $H_{xy}(q=2)>0.5$ then the cross-correlations between the return fluctuation from the two series related to q are long-range persistent. If the scaling exponent $H_{xy}(q=2)<0.5$, the cross-correlations between the return fluctuations of the two series related to q are anti-persistent. If $H_{xy}(q=2)=0.5$, there are no cross-correlations between the two series. Further for positive q, the $H_{xy}(q)$ describes the scaling behavior of the segments with large fluctuations. On the contrary, for negative q, $H_{xy}(q)$ describes the scaling behavior of the segments with small fluctuations. According to the multifractal formalism, the Renyi exponent $\tau_{xy}(q)$ can be used to characterize the multifractal nature of the time series which is expressed as,

$$\tau_{xy}(q) = qH_{xy}(q) - 1$$

If the Renyi exponent $\tau_{xy}(q)$ is linear of the q, we can conclude that the two correlated series is monofractal, otherwise, it is multifractal. The multifractal spectra $f_{xy}(\alpha)$ describes the singularity content of the time series which could be derived through the Legendre transform:

$$\alpha_{xy}(q) = H_{xy}(q) + qH'_{xy}(q)$$

$$f_{xy}(\alpha) = q(\alpha_{xy} - H_{xy}(q)) + 1$$

Data Analysis

Although crude oil prices possess long-range dependence, the degree of long-range has decreased in short time horizons, although the market is tending towards efficiency regime at long. Crude oil is called the blood of industries which plays an important role in all economies driving backbone of financial system. Oil price, as one of the main focal points in many countries, has become an increasingly essential topic of concern to governments, enterprises and investors. Therefore, understanding the dynamics of its price time series seems to be crucial, since it may allow one to assess the potential impacts of its shocks on several economies and on other financial assets. Similarly Gold price fluctuation and trading is directly related to market inflation in any country. So it becomes evident for a cross correlation study and analysis on Gold and Crude Oil time series.

Global crude oil pricing benchmarks Brent and WTI price hence its price volatility become a hot research topic recently. The US's imported crude oil is priced in accordance with WTI price, so the change of WTI crude oil price reflects the US's crude oil demand. Crude oil outside the US market is priced in accordance with Brent price, so Brent price can reflect international crude oil demand more deeply than WTI. For two markets, maybe Brent market is affected more by Gulf Wars than WTI hence to avoid impact of gulf war onto Crude oil price we had chosen WTI Crude oil time series for cross correlation study with Gold time series.

We choose the daily closing data of West Texas Intermediate (WTI) crude oil obtained from the Energy Information Administration, US Department of Energy (http://www.eia.gov/dnav/pet/pet_pri_spt_s1_d.htm) and the Gold data obtained from (http://fx.sauder.ubc.ca/data.html) for the period of 3rd January 1995 to 13th August 2013 with total 4486 data points. The return of daily price is calculated as, $r(t) = \log(P_t) - \log((P_{t-1})$ where P_t being the daily closing price index at time t (Figure 1).

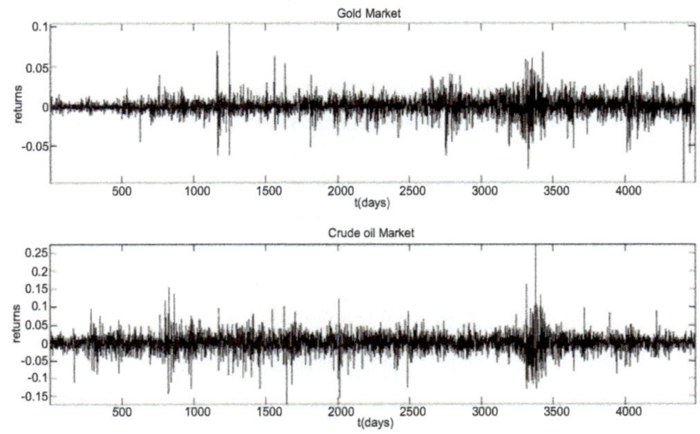

Figure 1: Returns of Gold and WTI Crude oil markets.

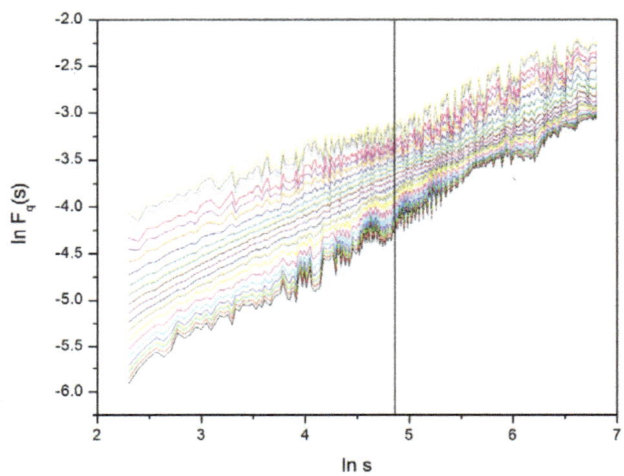

Figure 2: Fluctuation function.

	Mean	Min	Max	Stand dev	Skewness	Kurtosis
Gold	2.78E-04	-0.0960	0.1031	0.0113	-0.1481	10.665
Crude oil	4.04E-04	-0.1709	0.2756	0.0256	0.0673	10.4602

Note:*min, max, stand dev denote minimum, maximum, standard deviation respectively.

Table 1: Descriptive statistics for the returns of Gold and WTI Crude oil markets.

	Hxx	Hxy	Hyy	[Hxx+Hyy]/2
-10	0.53304	0.59079	0.75124	0.64214
-9	0.53012	0.58538	0.73839	0.63425
-8	0.52744	0.57946	0.72295	0.6252
-7	0.52538	0.57318	0.70445	0.61491
-6	0.52455	0.56682	0.68255	0.60355
-5	0.52596	0.56077	0.65727	0.59161
-4	0.53088	0.55523	0.62929	0.58008
-3	0.53938	0.54979	0.60003	0.5697
-2	0.54723	0.5435	0.5711	0.55917
-1	0.54767	0.53551	0.54309	0.54538
0	0.54064	0.5253	0.51443	0.52754
1	0.53083	0.5119	0.4809	0.50587
2	0.51905	0.49334	0.43573	0.47739
3	0.50321	0.46782	0.37323	0.43822
4	0.48355	0.43678	0.29869	0.39112
5	0.46283	0.40544	0.22774	0.34529
6	0.44344	0.37852	0.17026	0.30685
7	0.42639	0.35743	0.12695	0.27667
8	0.41176	0.34142	0.09488	0.25332
9	0.39929	0.32921	0.07097	0.23513
10	0.38863	0.31968	0.05279	0.22071

Table 2: Short term H(q) vs q for Gold and WTI Crude oil markets.

Q	Hxx	Hxy	Hyy	[Hxx+Hyy]/2
-10	0.63574	0.55373	0.497	0.56637
-9	0.6284	0.5448	0.49182	0.56011
-8	0.61945	0.53428	0.48663	0.55304
-7	0.60832	0.52205	0.48167	0.54499
-6	0.59415	0.50826	0.47732	0.53573
-5	0.5758	0.49353	0.47414	0.52497
-4	0.55202	0.47918	0.47301	0.51252
-3	0.52238	0.46722	0.47534	0.49886
-2	0.48898	0.46001	0.48333	0.48616
-1	0.4564	0.45973	0.50016	0.47828
0	0.42773	0.46786	0.52902	0.47837
1	0.40273	0.48374	0.56865	0.48569
2	0.38038	0.50259	0.60833	0.49435
3	0.36056	0.51691	0.63479	0.49768
4	0.34357	0.52214	0.64496	0.49427
5	0.3294	0.51916	0.64383	0.48661
6	0.31769	0.51136	0.6369	0.47729
7	0.30797	0.50168	0.62774	0.46785
8	0.29982	0.49186	0.61818	0.459
9	0.29289	0.48267	0.60908	0.45098
10	0.28691	0.4744	0.60076	0.44383

Table 3: Long term H(q) vs q for Gold and WTI Crude oil markets.

Results and Discussion

To test the presence of cross-correlation quantitatively we need MF-X-FA method which can estimate the cross-correlation exponent. We show the log-log plots of fluctuation function $F_q(s)$ versus time scale *s* for Gold and WTI Crude oil markets. In Figure 2 we can find that only one line cannot fit the log-log plots of $F_q(s)$ versus time scale *s* well. Hence we define the "crossover" s^*, as the turning point when the linear trend of the curves underwent a fundamental change. The short-term behavior of financial market is easily influenced by the market external factors such as the major events while the long-term behavior is determined by the internal factors. With the time evolving, the short-term shocks gradually decay for the effects of long-term supply and demand mechanism in the markets. The scaling exponents for s<s* can reflect the short range correlation also imply the correlated behaviors in the short-term. Then, the scaling exponents for s>s* imply the correlated behaviors in the long-term (Table 1). Thus, we can say that the "crossover" can reflect the lasting period of the effects of the factors which determine the market short-term behavior. We found the "crossover" at about ln (s*)=4.8 (i.e. 130 days). We provide the slopes of each line, just the scaling exponents for s<s* and s>s* in the Tables 2 and 3 respectively.

For q=2, the scaling exponent is the Hurst exponent calculated from the method of DFA. When q=2, the scaling exponent for Gold and WTI Crude oil markets is markets is 0.49334 for s<s* indicating that Gold and WTI Crude oil markets are weakly cross-correlated in the short-term. For s>s*, the scaling exponent for Gold and WTI Crude oil markets is 0.50259, larger than that for s<s* indicating that they are moderately cross-correlated in the long-term.

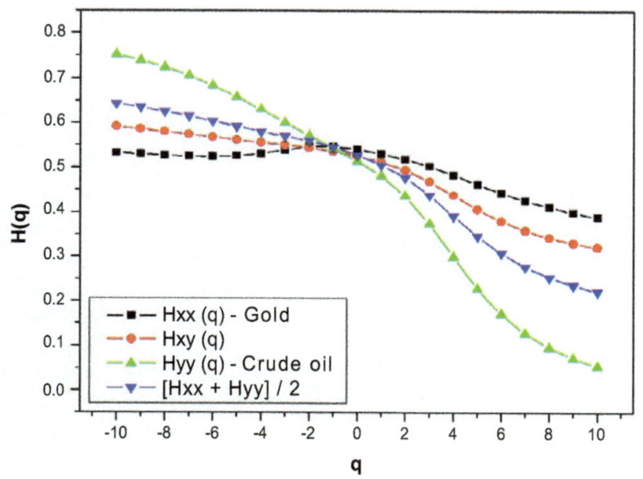

Figure 3: Short term s<s*.

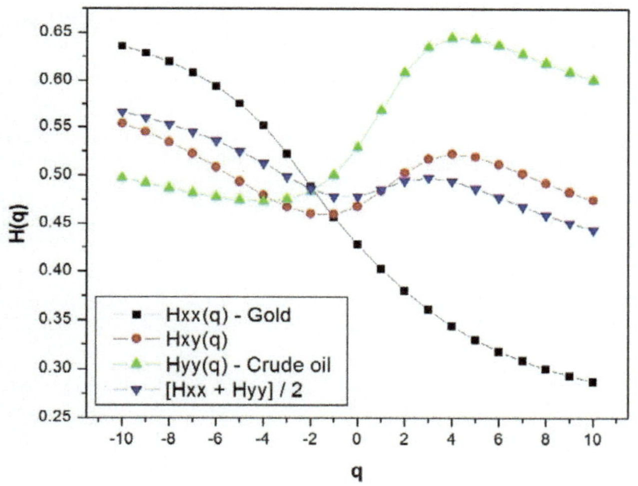

Figure 4: Long term s<s*.

For other values of q, the scaling exponents indicate the cross-correlated behaviors between the kinds of fluctuations related to q showing multifractlity behavior. We provide the scaling exponents with q varying from −10 to 10 for $H_{xx}(q)$, $H_{xy}(q)$, $H_{yy}(q)$, and the average scaling exponents $[H_{xx}(q)+H_{yy}(q)]/2$ for short term and long term in Figures 3 and 4 respectively.

From Figure 3 for s<s*,we can find that $H_{xx}(q)$- Gold market scaling exponents are decreasing from 0.53 to 0.38 indicating that it is exhibiting moderate multifractal features in short term where as $H_{yy}(q)$-WTI Crude oil market scaling exponents decrease from 0.75 to 0.05 indicating it is exhibiting strong multifractal features in short term. While the cross-correlated scaling exponents $H_{xy}(q)$ decreases from 0.6 to 0.35 indicating that cross-correlated behaviors are multifractal in short term. Moreover for q<0 we can find that for $H_{xy}(q)$, the scaling exponents are greater than 0.5 indicating that cross-correlated behaviors of small fluctuation are persistent (positive) in the short term. The scaling exponents for q>2 are less than 0.5 indicating that cross-correlated behaviors of large fluctuations are anti-persistent (negative) in the short term.

From Figure 4 for s>s*, we can find that $H_{xx}(q)$-Gold market scaling exponents are decreasing from over 0.63 to 0.28 indicating it is exhibiting high multifractal features in the long term. Similarly $H_{yy}(q)$-WTI Crude oil market scaling exponents increase from 0.5 to 0.6 indicating it is moderately multifractal. While the cross-correlated scaling exponents $H_{xy}(q)$ are not varying considerably indicating cross-correlated behavior is weakly multifractal in the long term. Moreover for q<-5 the scaling exponents are greater than 0.5 indicating that cross-correlated behaviors of small fluctuations are persistent (positive) in the long term. Congruently for q>1 the scaling exponents are greater than 0.5 indicating that cross-correlated behaviors of large fluctuations are also persistent (positive) in the long term.

For q<0, the scaling exponents $H_{xy}(q)$ are always less than the average scaling exponents $[H_{xx}(q)+H_{yy}(q)]/2$ and for q>0, the scaling exponents $H_{xy}(q)$ are greater than the average scaling exponents $[H_{xx}(q)+H_{yy}(q)]/2$ in the short term.

For q<1, the scaling exponents $H_{xy}(q)$ are always less than the average scaling exponents $[H_{xx}(q)+H_{yy}(q)]/2$ and for q>1,the scaling exponents $H_{xy}(q)$ are greater than the average scaling exponents $[H_{xx}(q)+H_{yy}(q)]/2$ in the long term.

Conclusion

Historically gold retains its value during times of crisis and is used as a hedge against inflation, deflation or currency devaluation. Gold also most popularly used as an investment. Crude Oil is a vital source of energy for the world hence higher crude oil prices drive fuel inflation as crude oil demand is inelastic. Diversity of participants like producers, government, extreme socio-political events and speculators drive crude oil market price.

The results demonstrate the overall significance of the cross-correlation based on the analysis of multifractality. We found that the global Hurst coefficient varies with the q and there is multifractality evidenced through the multifractal spectrum also. We get the cross-correlation exponent 0.48. We found that there exists a power-law cross-correlation between the Gold and Crude Oil time series and the multifractal features are significant. The analysis throws light on the structure of crude oil and Gold market as well as its link to macroeconomic conditions and socio-political extreme events.

In this paper, we used multifractal detrended cross-correlation analysis to investigate the cross-correlation properties between Gold and WTI Crude Oil. We find that the cross-correlations display the characteristic of multifractality in the short term. Moreover, the cross-correlations of small fluctuations are persistent, and those of large fluctuations are anti-persistent in the short term, while the cross-correlations of all kinds of fluctuations are persistent in the long term.

Finally, when q<0, the cross-correlation exponents are smaller than their average exponents, but larger than the average exponents when q>0.

From our analysis we found Gold price has long term correlation with crude oil price. That is the reason why gold is sold off during economic weakness as it's also used as a kind of proxy currency. Currencies tend to lose their purchasing power over years due to inflation and as time passes it can't buy the same amount of oil which could have bought years ago while gold could. The main idea behind the gold-crude oil cross correlation is the one which suggests that prices of crude oil partly account for inflation. Increases in oil price increases prices of gasoline which is derived from oil which drives transport of goods costly hence the Good prices rises. As a final result inflation hence gold price tend to appreciate with inflation rising. So, an increase in the price of crude oil can eventually translate into higher gold price.

References

1. Mandelbrot BB (1982) The Fractal Geometry of Nature, W H Freeman, New York.
2. Hurst HE (1951) Long-term storage capacity of reservoirs, Transactions of the American Society of Civil Engineers 116: 770-808.
3. Hurst HE (1957) A suggested statistical model of some time series which occur in nature, Nature 180: 494.
4. Peng CK, Havlin S, Stanley HE, Goldberger AL (1995) Quantification of scaling exponents and crossover phenomena in non-stationary heartbeat time series, Chaos 5: 82-90.
5. Tabak BM, Cajueiro DO (2007) Are the crude oil markets becoming weakly efficient over time? A test for time-varying long-range dependence in prices and volatility, Energy Economics 29: 28-36.
6. Buldyrev SV, Goldberger AL, Havlin S, Mantegna RN, Matsa ME, et al. (1995) Lang-range correlation properties of coding and noncoding DNA sequences: GenBank analysis, Physical Review E 51.
7. Podobnik B, Stanley HE (2008) Detrended cross-correlation analysis: a new method for analyzing two nonstationary time series, Physical Review Letters 100: 084102.
8. Wang YD, Liu L (2010) Is WTI crude oil market becoming weakly efficient over time? New evidence from multiscale analysis based on detrended fluctuation analysis, Energy Economics 32: 987-992.
9. Manimaran P, Pal M (2012) Dynamics of Fluctuations in Foreign Exchange Rate Time Series through Wavelet Analysis, Journal of Wavelet Theory and Applications 6: 1-10.
10. Bolgorian M, Gharli Z (2011) A Multifractal Detrended Fluctuation Analysis of Gold Price Fluctuations, Act A Physic A Polonica B 42: 1
11. Lo AW (1991) Long term memory in stock market price, Econometrica 59: 1279-1313.
12. Alvarez RJ, Cisneros M, Soriano A (2002) Multifractal Hurst analysis of crude oil prices, Physica A 313: 651-670.
13. Barabasi AL, Vicsek T (1991) Multifractality of self-affine fractals, Phys Rev A 44: 2730-2733.
14. Bunde A, Havlin S (1995) Fractals in Science, Springer-Verlag, Heidelberg, Germany.
15. Mantegna RN, Stanley HE (2000) Introduction to Econophysics: Correlations and Complexity in Finance, Cambridge University Press, Cambridge, UK.
16. Zhou WX (2008) Multifractal detrended cross-correlation analysis for two nonstationary signals, Physical Review E 77: 066211.
17. Wang YD, Wei Y, Wu C (2010) Cross-correlations between Chinese A-share and B-share markets, Physica A 389: 5468-5478.
18. Kantelhardt JW, Zschiegner SA, Koscienlny BE, Havlin S (2002) Multifractal detrended fluctuation analysis of nonstationary time series, Physica A 316: 87-114.
19. Manimaran P, Panigrahi PK, Parikh JC (2006) Difference in nature of correlation between NASDAQ and BSE indices, Physica A 387: 5810-5817.
20. Ma F, Wei Y, Huang D (2013) Multifractal detrended cross-correlation analysis between the Chinese stock market and surrounding stock markets, Physica A 392: 1659-1670.
21. He LY, Chen SP (2011) Multifractal Detrended Cross-Correlation Analysis of agricultural futures markets, Chaos, Solitons & Fractals 44: 355-361.
22. Horvatic D, Stanley HE, Podobnik B (2011) Detrended cross-correlation analysis for non-stationary time series with periodic trends, EPL 94: 18007.
23. Xue C, Shang P, Jing W (2012) Multifractal Detrended Cross-Correlation Analysis of BVP model time series, Nonlinear Dyn, 69:263-273.
24. Wang F, Liao G, Zhou X, Shi W (2013) Multifractal detrended cross-correlation analysis for power Markets, Nonlinear Dyn 72: 353-363.
25. Li Z, Lub X (2012) Cross-correlations between agricultural commodity futures markets in the US and China, Physica A 391: 3930-3941.
26. Cao G, Xuc L, Caoa J (2012) Multifractal detrended cross-correlations between the Chinese exchange market and stock market, Physica A 391: 4855-4866.
27. He LY, Fan Y, Wei YM (2009) Impact of speculator's expectations of returns and time scales of investment on crude oil price behaviors, Energy Economics 31: 77-84.
28. Bernabe A Martinaa E, Alvarez-Ramirez J, Ibarra-Valdez C, (2004) A multi-model approach for describing crude oil price dynamics, Physica A 338: 567-584.
29. Shao YH (2012) Comparing the performance of FA, DFA and DMA using different synthetic long-range correlated time series, SCIENTIFIC REPORTS 2: 835.
30. Caraiani P (2012) Evidence of Multifractality from Emerging European Stock Markets, PLoS ONE 7: 7 e40693.

Personalized Temporal Trading Functionalities Engaged in Calendar Market Anomalies: Empirical Evidences from the 2007 and 2009 Financial Crises

Vasiliki A Basdekidou*

Special Research Fund Account (ELKE) Aristotle University of Thessaloniki, Greece

Abstract

In volatile markets -like the calendar market anomalies- institutions, traders and speculators constantly search for predictable security's price action patterns; and their trading plans disturb security prices when they attempt to exploit the uprising trading opportunities. Generic forecasting patterns once become known to public are, therefore, unlikely to win for long periods of time and they will self-destruct when discovered by a large number of traders and speculators. Therefore, this gives rise to non-stationarities in the time series of financial returns and complicates formal tests and evidences of market efficiency, market anomalies and the search for successful and profitable forecasting approaches. Obviously, the need for adapted (i.e. no generic) strategies in trading the calendar market anomalies is apparent. This personalization is complicated and is referred to particular calendar market anomaly (seasonality), to trading instrument characteristics (e.g. beta functionality), and to the traders' profile (investors, swing traders, intraday speculators, etc.). Hence, in the calendar market anomalies domain, the personalized (adaptive) temporal dynamic approaches could improve trading returns by incorporating temporal trading functionalities. The main target of this paper is to investigate, analyze and document the personalized trading functionalities enclosed in calendar market anomalies. These functionalities are characterized as temporal because of the "time" function involved by default in calendar market anomalies. In particular this article is focused on the identification of monthly calendar anomalies on the Greek and Bulgarian stock markets. Empirical evidences, before and after the 2007 and 2009 financial crises, are presented in support of the hypothesis that small and less liquid markets tend to exhibit market anomalies. In the case of Greece these anomalies are so strong that they are not influenced by the recent crises. Empirical evidences also show that crises may change the long-run calendar anomalies trading functionalities and therefore lead to an improved Market efficiency as a short-run effect. Paper's innovation is related to the introduction and discussion of the personalized (adapted) temporal trading functionalities encapsulated in markets inefficiency, as far as the calendar markets anomalies is concern. Actually, the presented analysis, in this article, enhances the existing portfolio of approaches and knowledge about the impact of financial crises on real firm behavior during the calendar market anomalies periods.

Keywords: Efficient market hypothesis; Calendar market anomalies; Temporal trading functionalities; Personalized trading; Liquidity management; Financial crisis

Introduction

A market anomaly (or market inefficiency) is a price and/or rate of return distortion on a financial market that seems to contradict the efficient-market hypothesis [1-3]. The market anomaly, as empirical observational evidence, is referred to: Structural factors (such as unfair competition, lack of market transparency, regulatory actions, etc.); Behavioural biases by economic agents [4-6]; and Calendar effects, such as the "January effect" [7-9].

Market anomalies, as hypothetical theoretic evidences, are related to the economic fundamentals of the security (fundamental anomalies); to technical trading rules (technical anomalies); and to economic calendar events (calendar anomalies). Fundamental anomalies include value effect, small-cap effect (low P/E stocks and small cap companies do better than index on an average) and the Low-volatility anomaly, technical anomalies include momentum effect [10], while calendar anomalies involve patterns in stock returns from year to year, month to month, day to day [11-13].

According to the so called efficient-market hypothesis, regulated security markets are viewed as efficient[1] [1-3,7] and there is a logical justification in that respect. These markets have competitive structure, their transaction costs are minimal, their infrastructure is well organized and the information is usually equally accessible to all market agents. In light of these circumstances, it seems only logical to expect that these markets should be efficient.

Therefore, whenever a security market is being analyzed in trading strategies, one of the most frequently studied aspects concerns the possible availability of market anomalies. The empirical study of such market anomalies represents a constant interest and researchers often refer to it whenever there are new empirical observations accumulated. The reason is that the identification of market anomalies implies that, for some reason, the respective security market is not efficient, and the lack of market anomalies would confirm the efficient-market hypothesis.

Besides the theoretical problem for the availability or the lack of market efficiency there is also another reason that makes anomalies

[1]A security market is efficient if at all times prices of all securities are equal to their investment value reflecting fully and immediately all of the information available.

***Corresponding author:** Vasiliki A Basdekidou, Special Research Fund Account (ELKE) Aristotle University of Thessaloniki, Greece
E-mail: Vasiliki.Basdekidou@gmail.com

a focus of interest. When market anomalies are being observed, they are typically related to the existence of unfair competition, regulatory restrictions, and issues with relevant information access, structural factors or behavioral reactions not related to information about stock fundamentals. At the same time, anomalies, should they persist long enough, could give rise to trade strategies that investors might make use of. On the one hand, they indicate some market imperfections, and, on the other, they could represent a commercial interest for investors.

Despite of the theoretical arguments in favor of the efficient-market hypothesis for the regulated security markets there are numerous evidences that market anomalies existed in different periods on many markets. This is an empirical fact and it could be expected that if there are anomalies smaller and less liquid markets will tend to exhibit more market anomalies than larger and more liquid ones.

The focus of the present study is on the calendar effects on the Greek and the Bulgarian stock exchanges. Unlike many of the developed and a number of the emerging markets, these two stock markets have been relatively poorly studied with respect to their empirical characteristics. This justifies a study trying to bring in additional arguments for or against stock market efficiency from the point of view of comparatively small and less liquid markets such as the Greek and the Bulgarian ones.

The period under investigation includes the last two financial crises[2], which influenced and had a significant impact on both these markets. This further allows for an additional research perspective which deals with the question – how and in what way was the efficiency of these two markets influenced by the crises?

Articles innovation note

Paper's innovation is referred to the introduction and discussion of the personalized (adapted) temporal trading functionalities encapsulated in markets inefficiency, as far as the calendar market anomalies is concern. Actually, the presented analysis adds to the portfolio of approaches and knowledge about the impact of financial crises on real firm behaviour.

The rest of the paper is organized as following. The "Calendar Market Anomalies" section provides literature review on calendar anomalies. Then, the "Methodology and Data" section explains the methodology of the study and the data used in it. Following, the section "Empirical Observational Results" presents and discusses the main results obtained on the basis of the application of the chosen methodology. Thereafter, the "Discussion" section interprets, explains and describes paper's findings and the new understandings of the trading opportunities involved in market anomalies; and finally in "Conclusions" section a synopsis of the introduced methodology and innovation is presented and discussed.

Calendar market anomalies

A number of calendar temporal market anomalies, related to the monthly returns of the underlined securities, were discussed so far in the economic literature. These cases were analyzed in detail for the US markets [14,15]; the developed markets [9,16,17]; the emerging markets [18-21]; and the transitional economies markets, such as those of Poland, Romania, Hungary and Slovakia [22-24].

[2]The two crises are the following: the first one is the international financial crisis that started at the end of 2007, due to the subprime mortgage crisis on the American market. It practically spread out to all international markets. The second one is the sovereign debt crisis within the Eurozone, which began during the fall of 2009 and spread out mainly to the countries from the so-called EU periphery (Greece, Italy, Portugal, Spain, Ireland), but also to the rest of the EU countries to a varying degree.

The most widespread calendar anomalies are the so-called: "Weekend effect", "January effect", "Halloween effect", "November effect" and "December effect". Obviously, these effects could not be identified on all markets and at all times [25,26]. In particular, the "January effect" is a calendar anomaly which manifests itself through higher stock returns in the month of January relative to the other months of the year. This phenomenon has been well documented by empirical data in numerous studies. It was first identified in [14] - in their research they find that in the period from 1904 till 1974 the mean return for the month of January for the New York Stock Exchange was three percentage points higher than the mean return for the other months. In fact, more than a third of the annual return was realized in the month of January in particular. Another research on the New York Stock Exchange [15] indicates that most probably this effect was mainly due to low-cap companies' shares, since, on average, half of their annual returns have been accumulated in the month of January.

Later on, a lot of research has documented that such an anomaly could be observed not only on the American market. It was identified on other developed markets, too – in Japan [16], in Canada [17], Great Britain, Italy, Hong Kong [9]. It was also identified on a number of emerging markets such as Malaysia [18] and Turkey [19], as well as in transitional economies such as those of Poland, Romania, Hungary, and Slovakia [22].

As for the Greek stock market, economic literature offers inconsistent results. On the one hand, [25,27,28], ascertain a powerful "January effect", whereas Floros [29] finds no such effect. The reason for this discrepancy is in the different periods that researchers analyze. In the context of the present study it should be taken into account that the time series considered by these researchers stretch at latest until year 2002.

The body of economic research offers various possible explanations to the "January effect", and yet none of them has been commonly accepted. Most frequently, the phenomenon is being explained through the behavior of institutional investors who do "tax-loss selling". In other words at the end of the tax year they sell their loss-making positions. The aim of such behavior is to realize capital losses at the end of the tax year that could compensate for the capital gains from the profit-making positions, so that investors could achieve a particular tax effect. This type of behavior at the end of the year causes an increase of the supply of shares that have registered poor performance over the year, which results in an additional tendency for reduction of their prices. Such a decline is caused by calendar reasons (the tax-year end), and not by fundamental factors or some new information. Then, at the beginning of the next year (in January), the pressure on the supply side and on prices of these shares, respectively, dies out and they manage to realize abnormal high returns since they recover their fair market price.

The tax effect sought is one plausible explanation and it has been accepted by many researchers, but, at the same time, it could not be the only explanation. A lot of research indicates that the "January effect" has also been observed on markets as the Canadian one, where there is no capital gains tax [17], or as the Japanese one, where netting capital gains with capital losses is not allowed [16]. Another plausible explanation of the "January effect" is also the release of new information. For many companies, the first announcements for the financial results for the last fiscal year are released in January [14]. Yet another possible explanation is the existence of a positive relationship between risk premium and portfolio returns in January [30].

Similarly to the "January effect", the so-called "December effect" is a market anomaly according to which stock returns in December are systematically higher compared to other months of the year. This effect is most commonly observed during the last trading days or during the last week of the year, and is, therefore, often referred in the literature as "the turn-off-the-year effect". This anomaly has been identified on markets such as the Australian [31], the Indian [32], the ones in Belgium, Canada, Japan, Switzerland [9].

The explanation for this phenomenon has also been sought in several directions. One of them points out tax arguments just as with the "January effect". If it is rational for investors to try to liquidate positions with losses in December in order to compensate capital gains, it is also rational for them in December to delay the selling of stocks that have generated capital gains throughout the year. By postponing the selling of such stocks for several days, investors could delay paying taxes for an entire fiscal year, and therefore they usually restrain from such selling. In this way, the supply of stocks, which have generated capital gains throughout the year, is weak in December in particular which in turn leads to an additional tendency for increasing their prices.

Some other explanations to the "December effect" focuses on making investments awaiting the "January effect", or a targeted restructuring for reporting and accounting purposes of institutional investors' portfolios. It is often the case that at the end of a particular reporting period many portfolio managers aim to fill in their portfolios with stocks that have performed well during the past period. This could be observed by quarters when reporting has that frequency, but it is most well observed at the end of the year.

It should also be noted that monthly calendar anomalies have been observed not only in the months of January and December. Although much rare, such anomalies have been identified in other months as well. For example, some markets have documented anomalies related to the month of November [33-35].

Yet another calendar market anomaly is the so-called "Halloween effect". That is the name of the phenomenon under which stock returns are significantly higher for the period November-April compared to the period May-October. If that is actually true, it would be profitable for financial investors to buy shares at the end of October[3] and sell them at the beginning of May. Therefore, sometimes such a strategy is referred to as "sell in May and go away".

This effect has also been observed on a number of markets. The first investigation of the problem was conducted by Bouman, and Jacobsen [36]. In their paper they present evidences that the "Halloween effect" was present in 36 of the 37 countries they studied for the period from 1970 till 1998 (18 countries) and for the period from 1988 till 1998 (19 countries). One of the 36 markets that displayed the effect was the Greek market between 1970 and 1998. The authors also found out that the effect was the strongest on the European stock markets. Later on, those same countries have been studied in Andrade et al. [37], and they arrived at the conclusion that the effect also persisted during the years following the period analyzed by Bouman and Jacobsen [36]. The analysis of Andrade et al. [37] indicates the availability of the "Halloween effect" in these countries also for the period up to April, 2012.

The effect is manifested in the fact that the mean return for the six months from November till April was about 10 percentage points higher than during the other six months of the year, and such size of the effect allowed for the application of a successful trading strategy. What is more, the authors also demonstrate that the effect manifested itself not only in aggregation for the market as a whole, but also in separate classes of shares (e.g. according to size or according to book value-price ratio).

For the Greek market in particular, the availability of the "Halloween effect" has been studied in Siriopoulos, and Giannopoulos [38]. The authors find such effect but explain it by atypical, "extraordinary" returns during specific months.

There is no commonly accepted view with regard to what factors could actually cause the "Halloween effect". The economic literature offers mainly two hypotheses. According to Bouman and Jacobsen [36] this seasonal effect is caused by the holiday season for the market participants. Kamstra et al. [39], on the other hand, offer an explanation related to behavioral reactions. By analyzing the geographical location of markets, controlling for other factors, they find a correlation between returns' cycles and the duration of the light part of day, which is shorter during the fall-winter season. Thus, they arrive at the hypothesis for the possible influence of the duration of the light part of the day on the mood of some of the investors, on their readiness to take on risk, and on their ability to estimate that risk. This in turn could cause cyclic recurrence in their behavioral reactions which follows the change of the fall-winter season by the spring-summer season.

Finally, the "Weekend effect" is a phenomenon in financial markets in which stock returns on Mondays are often significantly lower than those of the immediately preceding Friday. Some theories that explain this effect attribute the tendency for companies to release bad news on Friday after the markets close to cause depressed stock prices on Monday. Others state that the "Weekend effect" might be linked to short selling, which would affect stocks with high short interest positions. Alternatively, the effect could simply be a result of traders' fading optimism between Friday and Monday [40-44].

The weekend effect has been a regular feature of stock trading patterns for many years. For example, according to a study by the Federal Reserve, prior to 1987 there was a statistically significant negative return over the weekends. However, the study did mention that this negative return had disappeared in the period from post-1987 to 1998. Since 1998, volatility over the weekends has increased again, and the phenomenon of the weekend effect remains a much debated topic.

In this paper, I document regularities in trading patterns of individual and institutional investors related to the day of the week. I find a relative increase in trading activity by individuals on Mondays. In addition, there is a tendency for individuals to increase the number of sell transactions relatively to buy transactions, which might explain at least part of the "Weekend effect".

Methodology and Data

The study of the calendar effects on the Greek and the Bulgarian stock markets has been performed through the application of regression analysis. The following econometric models have been specified, based on the market indices of the Athens Stock Exchange (Athens) and the Bulgarian Stock Exchange (Sofia):

$$R_t = \sum_{1}^{12} c_i D_{it} + u_t \tag{1}$$

$$R_t = c_0 + c_1 DHt + u_t \tag{2}$$

[3] The famous holiday "*Halloween*" is celebrated at the end of October in the USA. This coincidence gives the name to the aforementioned effect.

The following symbols have been used:

R_t: return in period t;

D_{it}: dummy variable which takes the value 1 for the ith month and 0 otherwise;

DH_t: dummy variable which takes the value 1 if the relevant month falls within the November-April period and 0 if the relevant month falls within the May-October period;

C_i: parameters of the model subject to estimation;

u_t: residual, random error of the model.

The applied models are standard for the study of calendar effects. These models and their modifications have been used, for example, by [26,31,32] for the monthly calendar effects, and by Siriopoulos, and Giannopoulos [38] for the "Halloween effect".

These models have the following logic. Model (1) reflects the influence of returns in different months. It allows for testing the null hypothesis that there are no months whose influence on market return is statistically different from the other months of the year. The alternative hypothesis is that there are such months, whose return, other things being equal, is systematically different from the return for the other months of the year.

From a formal point of view, the null hypothesis is that $C_1=C_2=\ldots=C_{12}$, and the alternative is that it is not true - not all coefficients are equal. If the null hypothesis is rejected, then the returns exhibit month-of-the-year effect. In this case during the respective month there is a recurring over time, statistically different return in comparison to returns in the other months. So, a monthly calendar effect is being observed, while the size and direction of this effect are determined by the respective parameter C_i for the particular month.

Model (2), on the other hand, reflects through the variable DH_t, the aggregated influence of returns for the months from November till April on the return of the market. It tests the null hypothesis that during the period between November and April return does not significantly differ from the return during the period from May to October, i.e. there is no "Halloween effect" observed. The "Halloween effect" will be observed if the return during the periods November-April is systematically different and higher than the return during the periods May-October. The constant term in the regression equation C_0 corresponds to the mean return for the months from May to October, while the parameter C_1 corresponds to the difference between the return for the months from November to April and the return for the months from May to October. From the point of view of the formal apparatus, the null hypothesis is that $C_1=0$, and the alternative is that C_1 is a positive number.

The data related to returns on the Greek market is calculated on the basis of the GD Index, which is the main composite index of the Athens Stock Exchange. The data regarding returns on the Bulgarian stock market is calculated on the basis of the main index of the Bulgarian Stock Exchange (SOFIX). Both indices are capitalization-weighted, they are calculated and officially published by the stock exchanges in Athens (for the Greek market) and in Sofia (for the Bulgarian market). Monthly data has been used and in the graphs and tables later in the text, monthly returns for the Greek market are indicated by GDMR, and monthly returns for the Bulgarian market are indicated by SOFIXMR. The period under investigation is Jan.1991-Dec.2014 for the Greek market and Oct. 2000-Dec. 2014 for the Bulgarian market since the later is a very young one and this is the longest possible data period.

Figures 1 and 2 show returns by months for the Greek and the Bulgarian stock markets, respectively. The graphs are organized in such a way that they indicate what the return for the respective month was for all the years included into the analyzed period. As it is well seen in these graphs, there is justification to analyze the possibility of a probable calendar market anomaly. For the Greek market the months of January, March, June, and December apparently often register higher returns compared to the other months of the year. The month of May is characterized by significantly low returns. For the Bulgarian market the months of January, February, July, and December stand out with higher returns. The question is how systematic those differences are - are they random or do they have a systematic nature, i.e. are they statistically significant.

Personalized trading is referred to adapted trading approaches as far as the trading instruments (e.g. stocks or 3x leveraged ETFs; bonds, Forex), time-frame (e.g. 30-min; daily; weekly) and strategies (e.g. intraday or swing trading) is concern [10-13]. Also, the term "Temporal Trading Functionalities, TTF" was introduced for the first time in financial literature by Basdekidou and Styliadou in [10-13].

Personalized temporal trading functionalities involved in calendar market anomalies and affects markets inefficiency as far as the various "effects" is concern. These "effects" are well known to traders and speculators, so stable forecasting patterns are, therefore, unlikely to persist for long periods of time and have been already self-destructed because they have been "discovered" by a large number of traders and speculators. Therefore, this gives rise to non-stationarities in the time series of financial returns and complicates formal tests and evidences of market efficiency, market anomalies and the search for successful

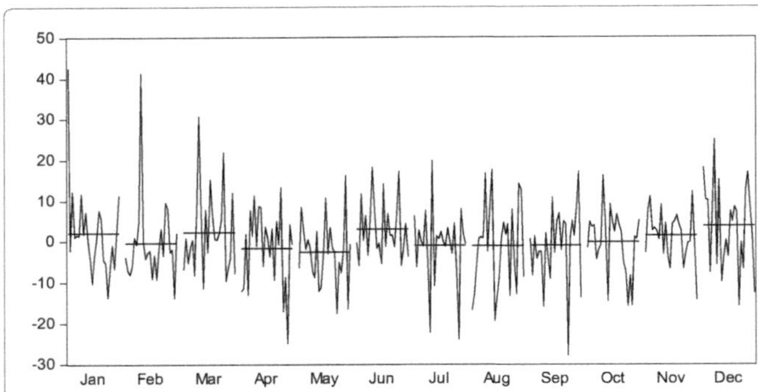

Data source: Athens Stock Exchange (Athens, GR)

Figure 1: Stock market returns (%) in Greece by months: 1991-2014.

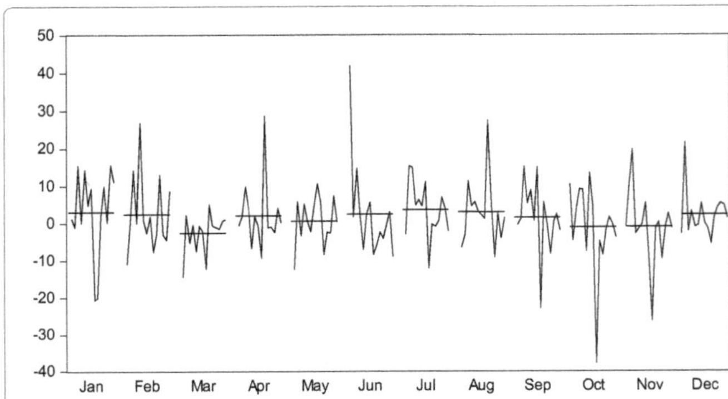

Data source: Bulgarian Stock Exchange (Sofia, BG).

Figure 2: Stock market returns (%) in Bulgaria by months: 2000-2014.

forecasting approaches. In this domain, recent bibliography introduces temporal price action patterns which can be easily adapted to support particular personalized regulations, forms and plans [10-13]. Hence, the personalized (adaptive) temporal dynamic approaches could improve trading market anomalies returns by incorporating temporal trading functionalities.

Empirical observational results

Each of the Models (1) and (2) has been evaluated in three different time periods. For the Greek market those are the periods 1.1991-11.2007, 1.1991-9.2009, and 1.1991-12.2014, respectively. The point of having these three periods is to capture the influence of both crises; the international financial crisis and the debt crisis in the Euro zone. The international financial crisis hit the Greek market after December, 2007, and the debt crisis started in October, 2009. Therefore, by separately analyzing those periods before the beginning of the aforementioned crises, together with the period from 1.1991 till 12.2014 as whole, there is the opportunity to make comparisons and draw the respective conclusions with regard to the possible influence of the crises on market efficiency.

The same logic has been applied to the selection of timeframes for the Bulgarian market. The following periods have been analyzed: 10.2000-11.2007, 10.2000-9.2009, 10.2000-12.2014 taking into account the fact that the month of October, 2000 is the earliest period for which there is official data for the SOFIX index.

The possible influence of the crises on the efficiency of the markets could be analyzed by another method as well. For example, Siriopoulos, and Giannopoulos [38], as well as Dash et al. [32], introduce into the equations additional dummy variables for months where unusually large price changes are observed. This allows for direct isolation of the influence of these observations and for a separate analysis from the rest of the data.

This approach, however, is purely technical and presupposes a certain degree of subjectivism in making the decision according to which observations should be considered as "outliers" and should be isolated from the main sample respectively. If just the "large" (following some formal criteria) deviations are isolated from the algorithm for estimation of the parameters, it could also happen that data might be isolated, which is not part of the period of the respective crisis and was not caused by it, or the sample could keep such data which was caused by the crisis, but did not register large enough deviations. In this study, the exact time and the reasons for the crises are well known, so the analysis of separate periods in general, by taking into account the crises, is more justified from an economic stance.

Before evaluating the parameters of the respective models, the data about returns on the Greek stock market (GDMR) and about returns on the Bulgarian stock market (SOFIXMR) have been tested for stationary. This has been done by applying the Dickey-Fuller test and the results are presented in Table 1.

As the results indicate, the coefficients before the lag values DGMR(-1) and SOFIXMR(-1) are statistically significant and negative. In this way, the hypothesis for non-stationarity is rejected with a very high confidence level (over 99%) for both markets.

Table 2 presents the results of the econometric estimation of model (1) for the Greek market. It demonstrates, for each of the three analyzed periods, the values of the estimated coefficients for the relevant months and student's t-statistic, which is used to estimate the statistical significance of the coefficients.

The empirical results demonstrate that within the three periods there is justification to reject the null hypothesis, i.e. there is the justification to accept that there is a calendar anomaly. If we analyze the period before the two crises, such anomaly is observed for the months of January and December. In both cases the parameters of the model for the respective months turn out to be positive and statistically significant. The parameter for the month of January is significant at a 95% confidence level, and the parameter for the month of December is significant at a 99% confidence level. Consequently, during a period of

GDMR, No. of Observations: 287				
Variable	**Coefficient**	**Std. Error**	**t-Statistic**	**Prob.**
GDMR(-1)	-0.86556	0.056708	-15.26358	0
C	0.145228	0.526153	0.276019	0.7827
R-squared	0.449783	Mean dependent var		-0.19202
Adjusted R-squared	0.447852	S.D. dependent var		11.9851
S.E. of regression	8.905727	Akaike info criterion		7.21821
Sum squared resid	22603.91	Schwarz criterion		7.243712
Log likelihood	-1033.81	Hannan-Quinn criter.		7.228431
F-statistic	232.977	Durbin-Watson stat		1.952941
Prob(F-statistic)	0			
SOFIXMR, nbr of observations 170				
Variable	Coefficient	Std. Error	t-Statistic	Prob.
SOFIXMR(-1)	-0.75667	0.074606	-10.14223	0
C	1.009249	0.70354	1.434531	0.1533
R-squared	0.379764	Mean dependent var		-0.05334
Adjusted R-squared	0.376072	S.D. dependent var		11.48355
S.E. of regression	9.070755	Akaike info criterion		7.259683
Sum squared resid	13822.8	Schwarz criterion		7.296575
Log likelihood	-615.073	Hannan-Quinn criter.		7.274653
F-statistic	102.8648	Durbin-Watson stat		2.020519
Prob(F-statistic)	0			

Data source: The respective stock exchanges.

Table 1: Results of the tests for stationary.

Variable	Jan. 1991-Nov. 2007		Jan. 1991-Sept. 2009		Jan. 1991-Dec. 2014	
	Coefficient	t-statistics	Coefficient	t-statistics	Coefficient	t-statistics
D1	4.0532**	1.9286	2.6288	1.2760	2.0510	1.0833
D2	-0.4617	-0.2197	-0.0913	-0.0443	-0.4216	-0.2227
D3	2.5125	1.1955	3.7035*	1.7977	2.2748	1.2016
D4	-0.2641	-0.1257	0.4182	0.2030	-1.6386	-0.8655
D5	-1.7759	-0.8450	-2.7832	-1.3509	-2.6505	-1.4000
D6	3.2424	1.5428	3.1950	1.5508	2.9466	1.5564
D7	-0.1816	-0.0864	-0.0887	-0.0431	-0.9994	-0.5279
D8	-1.3446	-0.6398	-1.4842	-0.7204	-1.1721	-0.6191
D9	-0.9515	-0.4527	-2.2693	-1.1015	-1.0331	-0.5457
D10	1.9994	0.9514	1.4925	0.7052	-0.2494	-0.1317
D11	2.7684	1.3173	2.2459	1.0611	1.3340	0.7046
D12	5.2826***	2.4385	3.7983*	1.7945	3.6919**	1.9501

Data source: Athens Stock Exchange (Athens).
*statistically significant at a 90% confidence level.
**statistically significant at a 95% confidence level.
***statistically significant at a 99% confidence level.

Table 2: Econometric estimation of Model (1) for the Greek stock market.

almost 17 years, which preceded the world financial crisis, the Greek market has had a market anomaly and the returns in December and January were systematically higher compared to returns for the other months of the year. Therefore, within this timeframe the market was inefficient since phenomena were observed that contradict the market efficiency hypothesis.

After the world financial crisis hit at the end of 2007, the market also demonstrated calendar anomalies. Until the beginning of the debt crisis in 2009, the months of March and December indicate statistically significant and higher returns than the other months of the year. The calendar anomaly in December for the realization of higher returns was preserved and the world financial crisis did not have any influence on it. The January anomaly, identified before the crisis, however, did not manifest itself and it was replaced by the anomaly in the month of March. It was probably caused by the negative trend of price drops induced by the crisis which lasted from December (2007) until February (2009) and included two January months with strongly negative returns. As a result the average effect for the month of January decreased. Simultaneously, March (2009) marked the strongest market recovery in the period between the two crises.

When analyzing the entire period from 1991 till 2014, it turns out that the December anomaly was preserved. The 2009 debt crisis, just like the previous financial crisis, did not influence this anomaly. For a period of 24 years, encompassing four full market cycles, and two dramatic crises on the Greek market, a calendar anomaly expressed as the "December effect" was preserved. The stock returns in the month of December were systematically higher by 3.7 percentage points than the mean return for the rest of the months. In other words, the empirical data about the Greek market does not support the hypothesis that it was efficient during the analyzed period.

Table 3 indicates the results for the Bulgarian market. They, however, tell a different story. In the period before the start of the international financial crisis there were market anomalies with regard to four months of the year. In January, June, July, and September there was a statistically significant and higher return compared to the mean return for the rest of the months. The effect was the strongest in the month of June, expressed by 2.7 percentage points higher return, and for the other three months the return was 1.9-2.4 percentage points higher.

After the start of the international financial crisis, these calendar effects disappeared. They did not recover after the debt crisis as well. That is to say that during the years before the crises, it could not be accepted that the Bulgarian market was efficient. There were calendar effects, which contradicts the hypothesis for market efficiency.

At the same time, when the entire period of market development is analyzed, including the period after the crises such effects are not registered. Thus, there is empirical justification to accept that the market efficiency improved because calendar anomalies dropped out. Nevertheless, this conclusion should be taken with a certain degree of attention. The reason is that the time series for the Bulgarian market is significantly shorter than the time series for the Greek one. Therefore, the effect of the crisis periods has more "weight" compared to the other data. Obviously, the low or negative values of returns during the crisis periods have caused a decrease of the otherwise systematically higher returns during specific months within previous periods.

Table 4 indicates the results from the econometric estimation of Model (2) and the testing of the "Halloween effect" hypothesis for the Greek market. For each of the analyzed periods, the values of the estimated coefficients of the model, as well as the standard regression coefficients of the model, the standard errors of the estimation, empirical student's t-statistic are seen, noticed together with the possibility such statistics to be realized, lead to the conclusion that the null hypothesis is true.

As it is seen from the table, during the period preceding the beginning of the international financial crisis and when data for the period following is added, the regression coefficient for DH turns out to be statistically significant at 90% and 95% confidence levels, respectively. Therefore, the hypothesis for the lack of the "Halloween effect" during those periods should be rejected.

This result is compatible with the conclusion of Bouman, and Jacobsen [36], who document the availability of the "Halloween effect"

Variable	Oct. 2000-Nov. 2007		Oct. 2000-Sept. 2009		Oct. 2000-Dec. 2014	
	Coefficient	t-statistics	Coefficient	t-statistics	Coefficient	t-statistics
D1	6.3600**	1.9588	0.4288	0.1136	3.0590**	1.2120
D2	4.1760	1.2862	2.6005*	0.6890	2.5079	0.9937
D3	-3.9705	-1.2229	-3.8754	-1.0268	-2.5929	-1.0274
D4	1.4625	0.4505	3.3094	0.8768	2.1351	0.8460
D5	-0.1741	-0.0536	1.7027	0.4511	0.7146**	0.2832
D6	8.7832***	2.7052	5.2277	1.3851	2.4782	0.9819
D7	7.7990**	2.4020	4.6995	1.2451	3.6728	1.4552
D8	2.5726	0.7924	5.2089	1.3801	3.0910	1.2247
D9	6.6517**	2.0487	3.2678	0.8658	1.5850	0.6280
D10	4.9138	1.6179	0.1574	0.0417	-1.0120***	-0.4150
D11	2.7698	0.9120	-0.4481*	-0.1187	-0.8974	-0.3681
D12	3.4792	1.0716	2.5864	0.6853	2.3836	0.9776

Data source: Bulgarian Stock Exchange (Sofia).
*statistically significant at a 90% confidence level.
**statistically significant at a 95% confidence level.
***statistically significant at a 99% confidence level.

Table 3: Econometric estimation of Model (1) for the Bulgarian stock market.

Periods and Variables	Coefficients	Standard error	t-statistics	P
		Jan. 1991-Nov. 2007		
C0	**0.1647***	**0.8589**	**0.1918**	**0.8481**
DH	**2.1211***	**1.2177**	**1.7418**	**0.0831**
		Jan. 1991-Sept. 2009		
C0	**-0.3390**	**0.8437**	**-0.4018**	**0.6882**
DH	**2.4401****	**1.1958**	**2.0406**	**0.0425**
		Jan. 1991-Dec. 2014		
C0	**-0.5263**	**0.7731**	**-0.6808**	**0.4965**
DH	**1.7415*****	**1.0933**	**1.5929**	**0.1123**

Data source: Athens Stock Exchange (Athens).
*statistically significant at a 90% confidence level.
**statistically significant at a 95% confidence level.
***statistically significant at a 99% confidence level.

Table 4: Econometric estimation of Model (2) for the Greek stock market.

for the Greek market for an earlier period that ends in 1998. It is also compatible with the results of Siriopoulos, and Giannopoulos [38], who also find this effect within the timeframe from 1986 until 2004. The continuation of the effect after that and its presence even after the end of the international financial crisis indicates how rigid it was.

During the period from 01.1991 till 11.1997, the "Halloween effect" indicates that the monthly return for the six months from November till April was on average 2.12 percentage points above the monthly mean return for the other six months of the year. The effect is similar for the period from 01.1991 till 09.2009. In this timeframe the monthly return during the six months from November till April was on average 2.44 percentage points above the monthly return for the other six months of the year.

When the results of model (1) are also taken into consideration, it could be argued that the identified "Halloween effect" was mainly caused by the months of January and December for the period from 01.1991 till 11.1997 and by the months of March and December for the period from 01.1991till 09.2009. This result is not compatible with the conclusions of Siriopoulos, and Giannopoulos [38]. They found out that the "Halloween effect" was caused not by a systematic calendar influence of particular months, but rather by separate "unusually" high negative returns during the market crash in October, 1987 and in August, 1998, during the Russian crisis. The results in Table 4 rather support other hypothesis; namely that the largest systematic influence was caused by the monthly effect in December, together with the monthly effects in January and March. All of these months fall within the period November-April and this is the probable cause for the appearance of the "Halloween effect" for the Greek market.

The results in Table 4 also indicate that the hypothesis for the lack of a "Halloween effect" after the start of the debt crisis could not be rejected with a 90% confidence level. The empirical data is very close to the critical value for rejecting the hypothesis, but, nevertheless, it remains. The market crash caused by the debt crisis, beginning in November 2009 and continuing till May, 2011, reduced and obliterated the otherwise systematically positive "Halloween effect" that was observed before that.

Table 5 shows the results regarding the estimation of Model (2) for the Bulgarian market. As could be seen in this case, the hypothesis for lack of "Halloween effect" could not be rejected with a meaningful confidence level.

In analyzing the seasonal effects by months, it turns out that during

Periods and Variables	Coefficients	Standard error	t-statistics	P
		Oct. 2000-Oct. 2007		
CO	5.0869	1.3145	3.8699	0.0002
DH	-2.4323*	1.8700	-1.3007	0.1970
		Jan. 1991-Sept. 2009		
CO	3.3773*	1.4972	2.2558	0.0261
DH	-2.6104**	2.1173	-1.2329	0.2203
		Oct. 2000-Dec. 2014		
CO	1.7224	1.0138	1.6989	0.0912
DH	-0.6315***	1.4296	-0.4417	0.6593

Data source: Bulgarian Stock Exchange (Sofia).
*statistically significant at a 90% confidence level.
**statistically significant at a 95% confidence level.
***statistically significant at a 99% confidence level.

Table 5: Econometric estimation of model (2) for the Bulgarian stock market.

the first analyzed period (preceding the international financial crisis) there was a positive calendar effect for the months of January, June, July, and September. Three out of these four months fall out of the period November-April and the higher returns for them hindered the appearance of a possible "Halloween effect".

Discussion

Traders constantly search for predictable security's price action patterns and affect prices when they attempt to exploit the uprising trading opportunities. Stable forecasting patterns are, therefore, unlikely to persist for long periods of time and will self-destruct when discovered by a large number of traders and speculators. Therefore, this gives rise to non-stationarities in the time series of financial returns and complicates formal tests and evidences of market efficiency, market anomalies and the search for successful forecasting approaches. Hence, the personalized (adaptive) temporal dynamic approaches could improve trading returns by incorporating temporal trading functionalities. Paper's innovation is the introduction and discussion of the temporal trading functionalities encapsulated in markets inefficiency, as far as the calendar market anomalies is concern.

The empirical study of the Greek and the Bulgarian stock markets demonstrates the presence of market anomalies, related to calendar effects. It turns out, that for the Greek market for a period of 24 years (1991-2014), including four full market cycles and two dramatic crises, a calendar anomaly was preserved and was expressed as a "December effect". Stock returns during the month of December were systematically higher compared to the rest of the months of the year. This applies for the time before the 2007 financial crisis and between this crisis and the following 2009 debt crisis, and for the period following it. The two crises did not have any influence on that effect. This conclusion represents a particular interest as far as previous studies on the Greek market have mostly demonstrated the availability of a "January effect".

If one analyzes the period before the two crises on the Greek market (1991-2007), calendar anomalies would be observed for the months of January and December. During a period of almost 17 years, preceding the international financial crisis, the Greek market had had calendar anomalies and returns in December and January were systematically higher compared to the other months of the year. This conclusion and the "January effect" in particular support the results of Fountas, and Segredakis [25], Mills et al. [27], and Koutianoudis, and Wang [28], who find the "January effect" in previous periods, and respectively it does not support Floros (2008) [29], who does not identify such an effect for a previous period as well.

As far as the "Halloween effect" is concerned, the empirical study of the Greek market demonstrates that this effect was also present in the period before the start of the debt crisis. This result is compatible with the conclusions of Bouman, and Jacobsen [36], who also find this effect for an earlier period. The continuation of the effect after that and its presence even after the international financial crisis indicates how rigid it was.

The identified "Halloween effect" is mainly caused by the systematically high returns during the months of January and December for the period from Jan.1991-Nov.1997 and during March and December for the period from Jan.1991-Sep.2009. This result is not compatible with the conclusions of Siriopoulos, and Giannopoulos [38], who believe that the "Halloween effect" on the Greek market is caused not by a systematic calendar influence of particular months, but by particular phenomena; "unusually" large negative returns during the market crash of October, 1987 and of August, 1998 during the Russian crisis.

The conclusions presented above indicate that within the analyzed timeframe the Greek market was inefficient, because empirical evidence had been observed, which contradicts the market efficiency hypothesis. This situation was rigid and the international financial crisis and the debt crisis had had a comparatively low influence on it.

The Bulgarian market shows market anomalies with regard to four months of the year within the period before the start of the international financial crisis. In January, June, July, and September there was a statistically significant higher return in comparison to the other months. The effect was most powerful in the month of June. Or in other words the market hasn't been efficient during this period. This result is consistent with calendar anomalies and seasonality as identified by Stoica, and Diaconasu [40] for the period 2000-2010, by Guidi et al. [41] for the period 1999-2009, and by Tilica, and Oprea for the Romanian stock market (the day-of-the-week effect, DOW) [42][4]. When data for the period after the start of the international financial crisis is added, these calendar effects disappear, since low returns during the crisis period compensate for the high returns in particular months before it. The monthly calendar effects did not reappear after the debt crisis as well.

The analyzed data does not justify the identification of the "Halloween effect" for the Bulgarian market neither before, nor after the two crises. There were monthly calendar effects before the international financial crisis. At the same time, taking into account the period after the crises such effects could not be registered. Therefore, there might be a formal empirical justification to accept the fact that market efficiency

[4] These studies employ daily data which usually show larger random fluctuations.

was improved because the monthly calendar anomalies disappeared. Nevertheless, such a conclusion should be taken with caution since it may not be a correct one. The time series for the Bulgarian market is comparatively short and therefore data for the crisis periods have a lot of "weight" in the data set.

I survey 500 Chief Financial Officers (CFOs) in the Greece and Bulgaria to directly assess whether their firms are credit constrained during the global financial crisis of 2007 and the local south-Europe crisis in 2009. We study whether corporate spending plans differ conditionally on this survey-based measure of financial constraint. Our evidence indicates that constrained firms planned deeper cuts in tech spending, employment, and capital spending. Constrained firms also burned out through more cash, drew more heavily on lines of credit for fear, banks would restrict access in the future, and sold more assets to fund their operations.

Ialso find that the inability to borrow externally caused many firms to bypass attractive investment opportunities, with 72% of constrained Greek and Bulgarian CFOs claiming that their investment in attractive projects was restricted during the credit crisis of 2007. Also, more than half of the respondents declared that they canceled or postponed their planned investments. This analysis contributes to the portfolio of approaches and adds some knowledge on the impact of financial crises on real firm behavior.

Finally, the presented empirical evidences are in support of the hypothesis that small and less liquid markets tend to exhibit market anomalies [45-47]. For both the Greek and the Bulgarian markets calendar anomalies are identified for the period before the international financial crisis in 2007. Such anomalies may be so strong that they could be stable enough, so that they could not be influenced by deep sovereign crises (the case of Greece). At the same time periods of crisis may change long run calendar anomalies (the case of Bulgaria). Crises usually bring relatively large negative returns which could compensate for systematically higher returns in particular months in previous periods. Such changes may formally lead to the conclusion of the improvement of market efficiency, but this may not be the case. It may just be a short run effect of the crisis while in the long run the relevant market may continue to exhibit anomalies [48-50].

Conclusions

The main target of this paper is to investigate, analyze and document the trading functionalities enclosed in calendar market anomalies. These functionalities are characterized as temporal because of the "time" function involved by default in calendar market anomalies. In particular the paper is focused on the identification of monthly calendar anomalies on the Greek and Bulgarian stock markets. Empirical evidence, before and after the 2007 and 2009 financial crises, is presented to support the hypothesis that small and less liquid markets tend to exhibit market anomalies.

In the case of Greece these anomalies are so strong that they are not influenced by the recent crises. Empirical evidence show, also, that crises may change the long-run calendar anomalies trading functionalities and therefore could lead to improved market efficiency as a short-run effect. Traders constantly search for predictable security's price action patterns and affect prices when they attempt to exploit the uprising trading opportunities. Stable forecasting patterns are, therefore, unlikely to persist for long periods of time and will self-destruct when discovered by a large number of traders and speculators. Therefore, this gives rise to non-stationarities in the time series of financial returns and complicates formal tests and evidences of market efficiency, market anomalies and the search for successful forecasting approaches. Hence, the personalized (adaptive) temporal dynamic approaches could improve trading returns by incorporating temporal trading functionalities.

In this paper, I document regularities in trading patterns of individual and institutional investors related to the market anomalies ("Weekend, January, Halloween, November, and December effects"). In particular, we find a relative increase in trading activity by individuals on Mondays. In addition, there is a tendency for individuals to increase the number of sell transactions relatively to buy transactions, which might explain at least part of the "Weekend effect" [42-44].

As paper's innovation could be regarded the introduction and discussion of the personalized (adapted) temporal trading functionalities encapsulated in markets inefficiency, as far as the calendar market anomalies (various "effects") is concern. Actually, the presented analysis improves the existing portfolio of approaches regarding the impact of financial crises on real firm behavior.

Conflicts of Interest

The author has not declared any conflict of interests with the Greek and Bulgarian stock market data and trading strategies discussed herein. What is presented in the article is as balanced, unbiased, objective and evidence-based as possible.

Author's Bio Profile

Vasiliki A. Basdekidou holds a B.Sc. degree in Economics from the Aristotle University of Thessaloniki (Greece, 2002), a two-year master's degree in Economics (major: Financial Economics) from the University of Macedonia (Greece, 2005) and a Ph.D. in Corporate Finance from the Bulgarian Academy of Sciences - Economic Research Institute (Bulgaria, 2015). She is working at the Special Research Fund Account of the Aristotle University of Thessaloniki for the last 10 years.

References

1. Malkiel BG (2003) The Efficient Market Hypothesis and Its Critics. Journal of Economic Perspectives 17: 59-82.
2. Timmermann A, Granger CWJ (2004) Efficient Market Hypothesis and Forecasting. International Journal of Forecasting 20: 15-27.
3. Laffont JJ, Maskin ES (1990) The Efficient Market Hypothesis and Insider Trading on the Stock Market. Journal of Political Economy 98: 70-93.
4. Branson C, Duffy B, Perry C, Wellings D (2012) Acceptable behaviour: Public opinion on behaviour change policy. London: Ipsos MORI.
5. Camerer CF (2003) Behavioral game theory. Princeton, NJ: Princeton University Press.
6. Camerer CF, Loewenstein G, Rabin M (2011) Advances in Behavioral Economics. Princeton, NJ: Princeton University Press.
7. Basdekidou VA (2015) Functionality, Returns and Efficiency before and after the Debt Crisis: An Empirical Analysis of the Greek Stock Market (Unpublished doctoral dissertation). Bulgarian Academy of Sciences – Economic Research Institute, Bulgaria.
8. Chiraz A (2016) Does the Index Futures Destabilize the Underlying Spot Market? Some Evidence from Frensh Stock Exchange. Bus Eco J 7: 244.
9. Agrawal A, Tandon K (1994) Anomalies or Illusions? Evidence from Stock Markets in Eighteen Countries. Journal of International Money and Finance 13: 83-106.
10. Basdekidou VA (2016) IPO Trading with Short-term and Intraday Temporal Functionalities. Bus Eco J 7: 257.
11. Basdekidou VA (2017) Seasoned Equity Offerings as Technical Market

Anomalies: Long-term Temporal Trading Functionalities. International Journal of Economics and Finance 9(1).

12. Basdekidou VA (2016) Nonfarm Employment Report Trading with Binary Options and Temporal Functionalities. Annales Universitatis Apulensis series Oeconomica 18(2).
13. Basdekidou VA, Styliadou AA (2017) Technical Market Anomalies: Leveraged ETF Trading with Daily and Intraday Temporal Functionalities. Bus Eco J 8: 275.
14. Rozeff M, Kenney W (1976) Capital Market Seasonality: The Case of Stock Returns. Journal of Financial Economics 3: 379-402.
15. Keim DB (1983) Size-Related Anomalies and Stock Return Seasonality: Further Empirical Evcidence. Journal of Financial Economics 12: 13-32.
16. Kato K, Schallhaim JS (1985) Seasonal and Size Anomalies in the Japanese Stock Market. Journal of Financial and Quantitative Analysis 20: 243-260.
17. Berges A, McConnell JJ, Schlarbaum GG (1984) The Turn-of-the-Year in Canada. Journal of Finance 39: 185-192.
18. Nassir A, Mohammad S 91987) The January Effect of Stocks Traded on the Kuala Lumpur Stock Exchange: An Empirical Analysis. Hong-Kong Journal of Business Management 5.
19. Balaban E (1995) January Effect, Yes! What About Mark Twain Effect? Discussion Papers, 9509, Central Bank of the Republic of Turkey.
20. Nassar S (2016) The impact of capital structure on Financial Performance of the firms: Evidence From Borsa Istanbul. J Bus Fin Aff 5: 173.
21. Kabeer MA, Iqbal A, Najaf K, Najaf R (2016) The Influences of MacroEconomic Factors on Capital Market Performance in Pakistan. J Bus Fin Aff 5: 176.
22. Asteriou D, Kovetsos G (2006) Testing for the Existence of the January Effect in Transition Economies. Applied Financial Economic Letters 2: 375-381.
23. Davcev L, Hourvouliades N (2013) The Influence of the Greek Economic Crisis on FYROM Exports. J Bus Fin Aff 3: 115.
24. Asiedu E (2016) A Study of use and Impact of Market Segmentation Practices on Bank Performance: With Special Reference to Commercial Banks in Colombia. J Bus Fin Aff 5: 162.
25. Fountas S, Segredakis KN (2002) Emerging Stock Markets Return Seasonalities: The January Effect and Tax-loss Selling Hypothesis. Applied Financial Economics 12: 291-299.
26. Maghyereh AI (2003) Seasonality and January Effect Anomalies in an Emerging Capital Market. The Arab Bank Review 5: 25-32.
27. Mills TC, Siriopoulos C, Markellos RN, Harizanis D (2000) Seasonality in the Athens Stock Exchange. Applied Economics Letters 10: 137-142.
28. Koutianoudis T, Wang S (2003) Is the January Effect Economically Exploitable? Evidence from Athens Stock Exchange. Working Paper, University of Manchester.
29. Floros C (2008) The Monthly and Trading Month Effects in Greek Stock Market Returns: 1996-2002. Managerial Finance 34: 453-464.
30. Corhay A, Hawaini P, Michel P (1987) Seasonality in the Risk-Return Relationshp: Some International Evidence. Journal of Finance 42.
31. Marret G, Worthington A (2011) The Month of the Year Effect in the Australian Stock Market: A Short Technical Note on the Market, Industry and Firm Size Impacts. Australian Accounting Business and Finance Journal 5.
32. Dash M, Dutta A, Sabharwal M (2011) Seasonality and Market Crashes in Indian Stock Markets. Asian Journal of Finance and Accounting 3.
33. Bhabra H, Dhillon U, Ramirez R (1999) A November Effect? Revisiting the Tax-Loss-Selling Hypothesis, Financial Management 28: 5-15.
34. Geske R, Subrahmanyam A, Zhou Y (2016) Capital structure effects on the prices of equity call options. Journal of Financial Economics 121: 231-253.
35. Johnston K, Paul C (2005) Further evidence of the November effect. Journal of Economics and Finance 29: 280-288.
36. Bouman S, Jacobsen B (2002) The Halloween Indicator, Sell in May and Go Away: Another Puzzle. American Economic Review 92: 1618-1635.
37. Andrade SC, Chhaochharia V, Fuerst ME (2012) Sell in May and Go Away Just Won't Go Away. Financial Analysts Journal 69: 94-105.
38. Siriopoulos C, Giannopoulos P (2006) Market Efficiency in the Greek Stock Exchange: The Halloween Effect. SPOUDAI, University of Pireus 56: 75-88.
39. Kamstra M, Kramer LA, Levi MD (2003) Winter Blues: Seasonal Affective Disorder (SAD) and Stock Market Returns. American Economic Review 93: 324-343.
40. Stoica O, Diaconasu DE (2011) An Examination of the Calendar Anomalies on Emerging Central and Eastern European Stock Markets: Recent Researches in Applied Economics. Proceedings of the 3rd World Multiconference on Applied Economics, Business and Development (AEBD '11), Iasi, Romania, 16-121.
41. Guidi F, Gupta R, Maheshwari S (2010) Weak-form Market efficiency and calendar anomalies for Eastern Europe equity Markets. MPRA.
42. Tilica EV, Oprea D (2014) Seasonality in the Romanian Stock Market: The day-of-the-Week Effect. Procedia Economics and Finance 15: 704-710.
43. Alexakis P, Xanthakis M (2006) Day-of-the-Week Effect on the Greek Stock Market. Applied Financial Economics 5: 43-50.
44. Ajayi RA, Mehdian S, Perry MJ (2014) The Day-of-the-Week Effect in Stock Returns: Further Evidences from Eastern European Emerging Markets. Emerging Markets Finance and Trade 40: 53-62.
45. Hossain SA (2015) An Empirical Analysis to Assess the Impact of Inconsistency of Exchange Rate on Share Market: A Case Study of London Stock Exchange. J Bus Fin Aff 4: 154.
46. Athanassakos G (2014) Is Volatility Risk? The Bad Influence of Academia to the Discussion. J Bus Fin Aff 3: 127.
47. Najaf R, Najaf K (2016) Impact of Crude Oil Prices on the Bombay Stock Exchange. J Bus Fin Aff 5: 216.
48. Gurloveleen K, Bhatia BS (2015) An Impact of Macroeconomic Variables on the functioning of Indian Stock Market: A Study of Manufacturing Firms of BSE500. J Stock Forex Trad 5: 160.
49. Vargas-Hernandez JG, Echeagaray JES, Echeagaray TIS (2016) Analysis of the Organizational Eco-Systemic Change in a Cooperative Society of Fishing Production. Bus Eco J 7: 230.
50. Jarrett JE, Li Y (2016) A Data Analytical Study of the Japanese Equity Market over a Lengthy Period. Bus Eco J 7: 241.

The Simple Long Volatility Trade

Chaturvedi V*

Chaudhary Charan Singh University, Meerut, India

Abstract

Based on the fact that researchers are only just beginning to address the question of what we mean precisely by risk or volatility, and how best to model it, investment opportunity is clearly indicated. This opportunity reflects the potential for generating abnormal returns through identifying and executing trades based on volatility. The evidence to support this in favors of traditional portfolio strategies is that volatility processes are eminently more persistent and forecast able than asset return processes. Following this, there is a view that volatility arbitrage is likely to prove one of the most fruitful investment opportunities in the next decade, providing adequate means can be found to describe and model the underlying process.

Keywords: Volatility trade; Investment opportunity; Traditional portfolio

Introduction

Based on the fact that researchers are only just beginning to address the question of what we mean precisely by risk or volatility, and how best to model it, investment opportunity is clearly indicated. This opportunity reflects the potential for generating abnormal returns through identifying and executing trades based on volatility. The evidence to support this in favors of traditional portfolio strategies is that volatility processes are eminently more persistent and forecast able than asset return processes. Following this, there is a view that volatility arbitrage is likely to prove one of the most fruitful investment opportunities in the next decade, providing adequate means can be found to describe and model the underlying process.

I) Asset class: FTSE-20 index futures, options on the FTSE-20 index

ii) Strategy: Volatility Arbitrage

While standardized exchange traded options only started trading in 1973 when the CBOE (Chicago Board Options Exchange) opened; options were first traded in London from 1690. Pricing was made easier by the Black-Scholes-Merton formula (usually shortened to Black-Scholes), which was invented in 1970 by Fischer Black, Myron Scholes and Robert Merton [1].

Literature Review

Despite their importance to well-functioning derivative markets and their popularity among option traders, volatility trades have received little attention in the financial research literature. While every derivatives textbook discusses such volatility trades as straddle, strangle and butterflies, to my surprise there was no paper devoted to their design or trading. Furthermore, to my knowledge no one has used real time data to construct a volatility trade portfolio in practice, assuming transaction cost and margin requirements. Without a doubt, the most important "imperfection" of real financial markets is the existence of transaction costs. Broadly speaking, transaction costs create bounds around the theoretical price within which the market price may fall without giving rise to a profitable arbitrage or volatility trade, large enough to cover the cost of exploiting it [2]. The main scope of this paper is to fill this gap by examining Volatility Trades on a recently established market, the Athens Derivatives Exchange. In the following chapters we will introduce some of the market's most liquid products and the common practices used by major financial institutions acting as market-makers/traders in the ADEX.

Volatility Trading vs Traditional Investment

In considering traditional investment most of the people think of stock or equity. Whether an investment on a stock or equity will produce profit or not, depends on the direction of the market. If the stock rises then the investor can capitalize on this price and accumulate the profits. On the other hand if the price of the stock falls the investor is accumulating losses. Only by using derivative products the investor could establish a short position and benefit from the falling prices. In both cases the investor has to have a clear view on the direction of the price [3].

Most fund managers will agree that despite the progress made in technical and fundamental analysis, view takers can hope to be on the winner side more times 4 than they lose.

On the other hand volatility trading offers another dimension to investing, which is trading the volatility of the price and not the direction. The volatility trader is not interested in whether the price is going to rise or fall; since he can benefit from both and can almost completely ignore the first dimension. He is primarily interested in whether the market is going to be volatile or not. The very position of the volatility trader is based on exploiting the volatility of the portfolio constructed. In order to do this, the portfolio will have to be fully hedged and this way has no exposure to the market. This is a crucial point to the volatility trade when constructing volatility portfolios. The most attractive feature of trading volatility is that, volatility portfolios often produce gains at times when directional strategies are performing poorly. For this purpose, in the following section we will introduce the concept of volatility and introduce its numerical and statistical significance.

***Corresponding author:** Varish Chaturvedi, Ph.D, Researcher, Chaudhary Charan Singh University, Meerut, Uttar Pradesh, India, E-mail: drvctlc@gmail.com

Volatility

Almost everyone has a concept of volatility when used in connection with finance or investment. For example, volatile markets or stocks involve higher risk since volatility is used as a measure of uncertainty about the returns provided by the stock or the market.

Measuring volatility: The volatility of a price series is a measure of the deviation of price changes around the trend. One use of the volatility measure is to make probability statements about the approximate likely range of the range of the stock price in the future. According to the strict mathematical terminology, volatility represents the standard deviation of the lognormal distribution. If a volatility of a series is x%, then in one year's time:

- 68.30% of all stock prices that are expected to occur under the lognormal distribution within the limits set by the mean +/- one standard deviation (volatility) are covered.
- 95.40% of all stock prices that are expected to occur under the lognormal distribution within the limits set by the mean +/- two standard deviation (volatility) are covered.
- 99.70% of all stock prices that are expected to occur under the lognormal distribution within the limits set by the mean +/- three standard deviation (volatility) are covered.

Different types of volatility

When discussing volatility we have to be aware that there are different types of volatility. To avoid confusion, we should look at the different types and their main characteristics.

Future volatility: This is the type of volatility every market participant would like to know, because it describes the future fluctuation of stock prices. If we knew a way of exactly determining the future volatility, we would be in a position to calculate correctly the theoretical options price applicable in the future already today. This information edge would among other things; enable a trader to sell overpriced options and buy underpriced ones.

However, since market participants cannot foretell the future, they are equally dependent on forecasts when it comes to determining future volatility. Many different models have been developed for this purpose although the pace of theoretical development has slowed somewhat in the last decade.

It should be noted that Economists have become increasingly intrigued of late by the possibilities afforded by the high frequency data. The key point is that precise estimation of volatility does not require long spans of data, but volatility can be measured arbitrarily well from return series that are sampled sufficiently frequently. The tendency towards the use of high frequency data to construct volatility estimates is now becoming standard research practice.

Historical volatility: Historical Volatility on the other hand is the volatility that can be calculated by the price series of the past. The purpose of this paper is to provide a detailed analysis of volatility.

The importance of historical volatility is that this volatility is used for the fair pricing of an option as input in the Black-Schools formula to calculate the fair value of an option as shown in Figure 1.

Implied volatility: Historical as well as future volatility are associated with the price of the underlying and say something about how the prices of the underlying are distributed over time. On the other hand, a different type of volatility, the implied volatility, is derived from the option price itself.

In Figure 2, the calculation method for deducing the implied volatility from an option's price in the market is presented.

Outline of this dissertation

In starting we begin with an introduction to the notion of the simple Long Volatility Trade. This chapter explores the meaning of volatility trading as well as provides numerical examples of the long volatility trade using puts or calls. We then present the sensitivities of the long volatility trade to parameters affecting its returns. Finally, in order to illustrate the profitability of such trades, we construct a long volatility portfolio using at-the-money puts and evaluate its performance when transaction costs and margin requirements are taken into account. In mid we investigate the price profile of the Short Volatility Trade. We begin by illustrating how a short volatility portfolio can be constructed in order to exploit the lack of volatility and illustrate where the profits of this trade come from. We continue by presenting how time decay and volatility affects the profits of this trade and construct a short volatility portfolio for this purpose. The return of this portfolio is then evaluated. By using real-time data from the settlement prices of the Athens Derivative Exchange, the profitability of the long and short

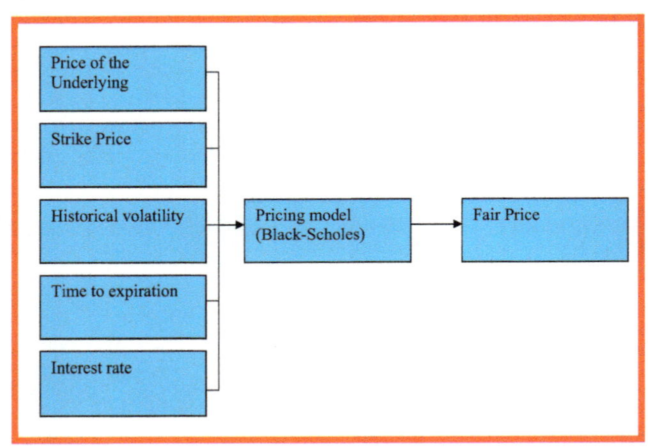

Figure 1: Historical volatility.

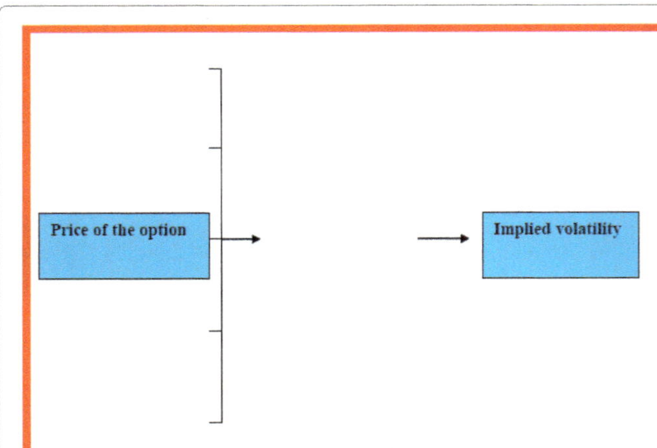

Figure 2: Implied volatility.

volatility trading scenarios are compared. The effect of transaction costs and margin requirements in these returns is also illustrated.

We explore the use of combinations of options of different series in volatility trading. Following this, we illustrate the price profile and sensitivities of the commonly used volatility strategies to parameters such as theta and Vega. We conclude by implementing trading scenarios using at-the-money straddles and strangles and examine their returns. This way the reader can compare the performance of the two trading strategies with the returns produced by the simple long and short volatility trade. We identify the functional requirements in order to build a prototype volatility trading system. We continue by introducing the limitations and constraints of the system under development. We introduce the concept of Visual Modeling and graphically illustrate the business domain of the volatility trading system using a class diagram. We document the decision of using Rapid Application Development in constructing the prototype and employ the Dynamic Systems Development Method to develop that prototype. Finally we illustrate the prototypes conceptual level using the entity relationship diagram.

The simple long volatility trade

Outperforming index portfolios: In this chapter we will examine the profile of one the most straightforward volatility trade in the market [4]. The trade consists of a long position in a call option and shorts the underlying instrument in such a ratio in order to achieve delta neutrality. It is due to the curved profile of options that a volatility trade can profit in a rising as well as a declining market. The ratio of two options to one future is dictated by the delta of the at-the-money call, discussed in later chapters. The profile of this trade is presented Profit/Loss in index points as mentioned earlier the profit of the trade comes from the different rate of increase/decrease of the price of the option responding to changes in the underlying asset. As the index rises the option price outperforms the loss from the short position in the future. In a decreasing market, the short side of the future outperforms the decline in the options price, thus producing profit to the volatility trader. In a nutshell, the option portfolio outperforms the future portfolio both in the rising as well as the declining market.

The simplest and most straightforward way of benefiting from this trade is to completely liquidate. Sell the option portfolio and buy the futures in the index to close the two positions set at start point. However, there may be still profit to be made in this trade providing the market continues to be volatile and the investor wishes to capitalize on the option price curvature. By rehedging his position (ratio of option to futures) the investor can not only lock his profit, but also continue to benefit from volatility, without having to exit his position or set up another volatility portfolio.

It appears from our simplified approach that the above out performance will always be achievable by going long on options and short the underlying. The answer to this is that this is not exactly true, as we will witness later. It is the purpose of this chapter to show that several parameters and risks have to be taken into consideration for a volatility trade to be profitable. At this point it would be useful to define basis risk. According to Hull basis risk is defined as follows:

Basis = Spot price of asset to be hedged – Futures price of contract used

In a situation where we are short futures, a strengthening of the base could result in losses, even when the underlying asset exhibits increased volatility. Basis risk can thus easily affect the effectiveness of the rehedging process. According to the Value basis of the front-month contract, basis risk can be as high as 3 percent illustrating the risk associate with the trade and potential losses-profits resulting from the rehedging activity.

Another interesting parameter affecting the rehedging process should also be noted. According to practitioners acting as market-makers in the ADEX, profit and losses can often result from the difference between the implied volatility the ADEX uses to estimate the settlements price of all options and the volatility exhibited intraday (during the day) on which options have been bought or sold.

The price profile of the call: In order to further illustrate where the profits in a long volatility trade come from, it is necessary to examine the price profile of a call. For this we will have to examine what determines the value of a call and how this value changes over time.

The option sensitivities

An option's price is sensitive, having a tendency to change in response to certain key variables. These key variables, called "the sensitivities" or "the Greeks", measure a change in the price of an option or combination of options in response to a change in one of the key variables.

The Greeks (Delta, Gamma, Theta, Vega and Rho) enable, among other things:

- Prediction of a movement in an option's price, given a change in a variable
- Calculation of the number of options required to hedge a change in a variable

Delta: At this point it would be useful to discuss delta, an important parameter in the pricing and more importantly in our case, the hedging of options. Being the first derivative of option price with respect to the underlying, the delta is represented by the formula: change in the option price Delta: change in the underlying price.

According to Hull's definition: The delta of a stock option is the ratio of change in the price of the stock option to the change in the price of the underlying stock. It is the number of units of the stock we should hold for each option shorted in order to create a risk less hedge. Keeping this in mind, a risk fewer portfolios is said to be delta neutral, when having a delta equal to zero. The delta of a call option is positive and can vary between 0 and 1, whereas the delta of a put option is negative and can vary between 0 and -1.

Gamma: As described in the previous section, the trade profits from volatility are a result of the options curvature. And the price profile is only curved because of the kink to expiry. For a given index price move, say x%, the more curved the profile the more significant the rehedging profit. Curvature is so important in the option market that it has also been assigned a Greek letter –Gamma. Since the slope of the curve is the delta, the curvature is the rate of change of delta.

Gamma measures the rate of change for a given movement in the underlying price. Gamma compensates for the convexivity of the near-day option value curve by measuring the rate at which delta changes for an identical change in the underlying value. It equals the increase in the delta of an underlying asset for every increase in the asset's price. Having the following formula, gamma is the second derivative of the option price with respect to the underlying:

$$\text{Gamma} = \frac{\text{Change in option price}}{\text{Change in the underlying price}}$$

Theta: The theta of a portfolio of options is the rate of change of the portfolio's value with respect to the passage of time *ceteris paribus*. In other words, it is the rate of change of the value of a portfolio with respect to a decrease in the time to maturity of the options in a portfolio.

Vega: Vega (ê) (actually a star, not a Greek letter), also known as kappa, measures changes in the option premium per 1% shift in volatility. Vega is always positive and maximum for at-the-money options, decreasing to zero for in the money and out-of the money options. It is the first derivative of option price with respect to volatility.

The sensitivity of options to volatility changes is similar to the sensitivity exhibited to time passage. Near-the-money options are most sensitive and deep out-of the money and deep in-the-money options are less sensitive. The importance of getting volatility right is illustrated. Rising volatility results in additional profits to the long volatility trader [5].

Additivity of sensitivities

Before proceeding to the trading simulations, it would be useful to present a special feature of the price profile of portfolio of options. In deriving the price profile of option portfolios, consisting by many different combinations of different options, weighted for position sizes, we simply have to add them together. This concept of price additively can be extended to even the most complex portfolios, containing large numbers of different series of calls and puts.

Deriving the price profile of a combination of options is very useful and with experience, most volatility players will have a fairly good idea even without the use of software.

Trading scenario

We have identified the trading opportunities in the Athens Derivative Exchange. In order to benefit from the underpriced options, we will perform a long volatility trade for the period from mid-September 2000 to October 2000. Instead of using at-the-money calls in order to construct our long volatility trade, at-the-money puts are preferred since they exhibit lower implied volatility thus are cheaper to buy from the corresponding calls.

Strangles

A strangle involves the simultaneous purchase or sale of an equal number of puts and calls on a given underlying instrument with the same expiration date but different strike prices. Typically the call will have a strike above the current futures price, while the putt's strike will be below the stock price. As with the straddle, the strangle purchase is looking for a large move in the underlying that exceeds either strike level by more than the amount paid for both options.

Sellers of strangles are looking for little or no movement from the underlying. These sellers of short volatility will look for options with higher implied volatilities that provide more premiums. The short positions will be profitable if the stock price stays within the range bounded by the strike prices of the sold options plus the premium collected. Sellers will also benefit if the options implied volatilities decrease, which would make the options cheaper to buy back if the seller wishes to close the position.

Conclusions

Having presented both the long volatility trade and short volatility trade profile and sensitivities of each position, one can see that the worst-case scenario for the short volatility trader is the best-case scenario for the long volatility trader. In a market crash as well as in a market ramp the losses for the short volatility trader can be enormous. The short volatility trade is a strategy, which we can calculate beforehand what the maximum possible profit is but not the extent of the losses. This strategy has a limited profit potential and an unlimited loss potential thus should be used with great caution.

On the other hand in a long volatility trade position a market ramp or crash is the dream of every trader (and nightmare of the short volatility trader). The profit depends on the severity of the price moves. The long volatility strategy provides an unlimited profit potential and this together with the limited loss feature makes it a very attractive strategy.

It is a common ground for both practices that a highly liquid derivatives market is imperative. As the market becomes more liquid larger positions can be built, transaction costs can be decreased and profits increased. Market makers actively involved in the Athens Derivative market are eligible to lower transaction costs and can benefit from smaller movements in volatility or lack of it.

At the end of the day market makers are concerned in being delta neutral and gamma or *Vega* positive having to manage combination of options of different series and classes and numerous positions in futures.

References

1. Bittman J (2008) Trading Options as a Professional: Techniques for Market Makers and Experienced Traders. McGraw-Hill, Business and Economics.
2. Natenberg S (1994) Option Volatility and Pricing: Advanced Trading Strategies and Technique. McGraw-Hill Education, Business and Economics.
3. Connolly KB (1997) Buying and Selling Volatility. Wiley, Business and Economics.
4. Sinclair E (2013) Volatility Trading (2nd edn). John Wiley and Sons, Hoboken, New Jersey, USA.
5. Hsu C (2014) Rule Based Volatility Investment. Press: Financial Times.

Relationship between FDI and GDP: A Case Study of South Asian Countries

Baig MM, Kiran S and Bilal M*

Department of Business Management, University of Sargodha, Sub-campus Mianwali, Pakistan

Abstract

The basic objective of this study is to compute the long run relationship between FDI and GDP for south ASIAN countries (Pakistan, Nepal, Bhutan, India and Maldives). For this purpose, the FDI and GDP data of south Asian countries is collected for the period 1991-2012.the data was analyzed by using technique of unit root test, Johnson co-integration and granger causality test. The unit root test (ADF) augmented test confirmed that data is not stationary at level but it is stationary at first difference. The Result of co integration test indicates that there exist co-integration equations at the 0.05 level. The granger test shows that FDI and GDP in case of Nepal cause a unidirectional causality. The study will help and give guiding principle to policymaker and investor make scheme to prop up economic growth in Pakistan which is suffering from a high ratio of unemployment.

Keywords: Foreign direct investment; Gross domestic product; Unit root test; Cointegration test; Granger causality test

Introduction

In the light of expected benefit of FDI many studies have been conducted the role of FDI in host countries may increase through marketing skills, inflow of managerial know-how, capital with creating new job opportunities, through the inflow of technology, and impact of proficient market. FDI has most established component of capital flows. As a result, FDI has become an important substitute in the development finance process (Global development finance 2001). Inward FDI can increase host countries export which cause to increase foreign exchange earning in developing countries. FDI can also encourage technology transfer and creation of new job and boost overall economic growth. From earlier literature we find that foreign direct investment increase gross domestic product like Falki who lays stress on foreign direct investment. The result shows negative relation of FDI and GDP but positive relation between GDP, domestic capital and labor force. More result of literature deals with relationship between FDI and economic growth, between trade and FDI on economic growth and relationship between trade and economic growth. The important element of cash flow is FDI and important channel through which financial globalization benefit the economy.

Accordingly, some researchers have found either a statistically insignificant or a negative relation between FDI and economic growth and among trade and growth. Current study explores the relationship between trade FDI and economic growth. Our study is different in the way there is little experimental work on this subject in Asian countries. Earlier studies relationship between FDI and economic growth in Middle East and south Mediterranean countries Pakistan found notorious result. The study will help and give guiding principle to policymaker and investor make scheme to prop up economic growth in Asian countries which is suffering from a high ratio of unemployment. The objective of this study is to Identification of the direction of the relationship to understand the changes arise in the trends in the economy so; the relevant scheme shall be devised to overcome any sort of problem at earlier stage.

Literature Review

Borensizein, et al. tests the effect of FDI on economic growth in cross countries [1]. Utilizing data on FDI flows from industrial countries to 69 developing countries over the last two decades. They conclude that if advance technology is available in host country then FDI contributes economic growth.

Robles and Pradhan suggest that According to modernization theory transfer of technology through FDI is important in modern countries. Because most developing countries have many problems like lack of necessary infrastructure, liberalized market, economic and social stability which are needed to promote growth [2].

Adams analyzes the impact of FDI on Domestic investment in sub-Saharn Africa. Data use from (1990-2003). This study explore that Domestic investment has positive effect on economic growth in OLS and fixed estimation but FDI is only positive OLS Estimation. He also fined that FDI has initial negative effect on DI but later on positive effect [3].

Arshad and Shujat establish empirical relationship between FDI and economic growth in Pakistan. The data use from (1981-2008). The result support and has positive effect on output in long run [4]. The most striking result in this study is that FDI cause growth in primary service sector and on other hand growth cause FDI in manufacturing sector.

The linkage between FDI and economic growth has been widely discussed in Literature, studies like; Masnoon and Rafique conclude a study to determine empirical linkage between FDI and economic growth. In this regard, they took the sample from 1981-2010 and conclude with the negative linkage between FDI and economic growth in Pakistan. They further conclude the independent of four other variables like debit, trade, inflation and domestic investment that can affect the ordinary relationship between FDI and growth [5].

Mustafa AMM, et al. has conducted a study on Sri-Lankan

***Corresponding author:** Muhammad Bilal, Department of Business Management, University of Sargodha, Sub-campus Mianwali, University Road, Sargodha 40100, Pakistan, E-mail: bilal_uos@yahoo.com

economy [6]. In this study he used the data ranging from 1998 to 2012. Findings of the study conclude that FDI has positive effect on economic growth. They also suggest that according to statistically endogenous theory FDI is determined by economic factor which are domestic investment and labor force. Makki and Somwaru conducted a study on impact of foreign direct investment on economic growth. The data was collected from the world development indicators (WDI) database by covering 66 countries for the period 1971-2000. The data was analyzed by using a system of three equations by applying Seemingly Unrelated Regression (SUR) method as well as instrumental variable (Three Stage Least Squares or TSLS) approach [7]. The results show that FDI act as a magnet for the interaction in sense of positively with trade and in terms of domestic investment. Furthermore, this study concluded that if the rates of inflation, tax, and government consumption will be decreases then it brings in economic developments.

Berthelemy and Demurger conducted a study on relationship between foreign direct investment and economic growth in china. The data was collected from the world development indicators (WDI) database by covering 24 Chinese provinces, from 1985 to 1996.the data was analyzed by using an empirical test of the theoretical model [8]. The results show that the fundamental role played by foreign investment in provincial economic growth in China, and stresses the importance of potential growth in foreign investment decisions.

Cilar and Altiner conducted a study on relationship between foreign direct investment and economic growth on CCO region. The data was collected from the world development indicators (WDI) database for period of 1995-2011 [9]. The data was analyzed by using a granger Causality Test based on error correction model and Holtz-Eakin, Newey and Rosen Panel Causality Test are applied in analysis. The results indicate that a positive causality from FDI to GDP and a slightly less positive causality from GDP to FDI in ECO region have been perceived.

Matthew and Johnson investigated a study on an Investigation of the Impact of Foreign Direct Investment on Economic Growth in Nigeria. The data was collected published work of Abu and Echegbulu [10]. The data was analyzed by using Granger Causality Test single equation model in their FDI-growth studies. The results ad findings show that the present review will focus more on the relevance of FDI to the Nigeria economy.

Hasnen and Rand conducted a study on Granger causal relationships between foreign direct investment (FDI) and GDP in a sample of 31 developing countries. For this purpose, the data was collected from the sample of 31 developing countries covering 31 years.). The data was analyzed by using Granger Causality Test between the FDI-to-GDP ratios. The results and findings shows that the FDI has a lasting impact on GDP, while GDP has no long run impact on the FDI-to-GDP ratio and concluded that long-run effects from FDI to GDP [11].

Hypothesis

1. **HA:** There is long run relationship exist between FDI and gross domestic product.
2. **H0:** There is no long run relationship exist between FDI and gross domestic product.

Methodology

Data source

This study will base upon the exploration of the relationship between FDI and economic growth in Pakistan. In this succession, uses the annual time series data ranges from 1991-2012. Data will be extracted from world development index (WDI) of World Bank and different volume of international statistic (IFS). The variables of this study include per capita GDP growth for measurement of economic growth, FDI inflows to GDP for foreign direct investment.

This study will focus the linkage between FDI, trade and economic growth in presence of different control variable. In this regard we use the time series data for such determination and for the sake of convenience use the log linear model to eliminate trends in the data. This relationship is identifying to application of new theory of endogenous growth stating permanent role of FDI in economic progress. In any discussion about causation among variables, the first step is the determination of unit roots in the data. Different approaches are used for calculation of panel unit root test like (ADF), (PHILLIP PERON) etc. Among these approaches, the most appropriate approach with respect to data will be employed in this study to determine the level of integration. Similarly, different approaches of co integration are also (JOHANSAN COINTEGRATION) and granger causality was used. Among these different approaches most suitable approach with respect to the level of integration as defined earlier will be selected for determination of long-run relationship.

Descriptive statistic

Pakistan: Table 1.

Sri Lanka: Table 2.

Singapore: Table 3.

Correlation analysis

Correlation of Pakistan: Table 4.

Correlation of Sri Lanka: Table 5.

Correlation of Singapore: Table 6.

Unit root Table 7.

Co integration

Pakistan: Table 8.

Sri Lanka: Table 9.

Singapore: Table 10.

All above Johnson co integration test shows that FDI and GDP for Pakistan. SRI Lanka and Singapore are co integrated. Since GDP and FDI have long run relationship for Pakistan. SRI Lanka and Singapore countries at 0.05 level.

Granger causality

Pakistan: Table 11.

Sri Lanka: Table 12.

Singapore: Table 13.

Granger test explores whether the lagged varies of one variable can significantly explain the changes of other variable. Results explore that there is no causal relationship exist among selected variables (GDP, FDI, and Inflation) for Pakistan, Sri Lanka and Singapore.

Conclusion

The purpose of this study to relationship between FDI and GDP for

	GDP	FDI	INF
Mean	0.018836	0.007156	0.019303
Median	0.021023	0.007873	0.019681
Maximum	0.046995	0.080047	0.349526
Minimum	-0.005225	-0.042872	-0.41868
Std. Dev.	0.016403	0.029167	0.237734
Skewness	0.117157	0.765779	-0.285461
Kurtosis	1.771892	3.950546	2.170182
Jarque-Bera	0.97697	2.030753	0.634094
Probability	0.613555	0.362266	0.728297

Table 1: The descriptive statistic shows that GDP mean value is highest as compared to other variables in Pakistan.

	GDP	FDI	INF
Mean	0.030776	0.007465	-0.077061
Median	0.030204	0.014828	0
Maximum	0.077179	0.125636	0.335182
Minimum	0	-0.090705	-0.733794
Std. Dev.	0.022628	0.05181	0.301151
Skewness	0.457486	0.261201	-0.568309
Kurtosis	2.399129	3.445255	2.642479
Jarque-Bera	0.748888	0.294473	0.887327
Probability	0.687672	0.86309	0.641681

Table 2: The descriptive stat shows that GDP mean value is highest as compared to other variables in Sri Lanka.

	GDP	FDI	INF
Mean	0.015183	0.011042	0.019831
Median	0.01178	0.00258	0
Maximum	0.039297	0.095778	2.604992
Minimum	-0.015637	-0.112023	-1.283384
Std. Dev.	0.016185	0.048375	0.974209
Skewness	0.004554	-0.745565	1.257484
Kurtosis	2.107262	4.483326	4.968272
Jarque-Bera	0.498165	2.580505	5.524547
Probability	0.779516	0.275201	0.063148

Table 3: The descriptive statistic shows that GDP mean value is highest as compared to other variables in Singapore.

	GDP	FDI	INF
GDP	1.000000	-0.37723	0.119012
FDI	-0.37723299	0.371314	1
INF	0.119011944	1.000000	0.371314

Table 4: Above results explore that GDP is negatively correlated with FDI and positively with INF in Pakistan.

	GDP	FDI	INF
GDP	1	-0.07607	0.231587
FDI	-0.07607	1	-0.01373
INF	0.231587	-0.01373	1

Table 5: Above results explore that GDP is negatively correlated with FDI and positively with INF in Sri Lanka.

	GDP	FDI	INF
GDP	1	-0.36152	-0.00684
FDI	-0.36152	1	0.373519
INF	-0.00684	0.373519	1

Table 6: Above results explore that GDP is negatively correlated with FDI and INF in Singapore.

	ADF LEVEL FDI	ADF 1st DIF FDI	ADF LEVEL GDP	ADF 1st DIF GDP
Pakistan	-1.83286	-3.88449	0.842867	-3.85455
Nepal	-2.63991	-4.03797	1.716876	-5.05921
India	-1.89583	-5.55924	0.737368	-4.06182
Maldives	0.297584	-5.05646	-0.83123	-5.72681
Bhutan	-2.98038	-4.99879	0.953694	-4.6471
	Critical values			
1%	-4.4206	4.58265	3.80855	3.80855
5%	3.25981	-3.32097	-3.02069	-3.02069
10%	2.77113	-2.80138	-2.65041	-2.65041

Table 7: Above results explore the unit root values with ADF level and 1st DIF.

No. of CE(s)	Eigenvalue	Statistic	Critical Value	Prob.	
None	0.817795	32.68655	29.79707	0.0226	COINTEGRATION
At most 1	0.480394	10.55245	15.49471	0.2406	NO COINTEGRATION
At most 2	0.145332	2.041546	3.841466	0.1531	NO COINTEGRATION

Table 8: The above result show that there is one co integration at 0.05 level in Pakistan.

No. of CE(s)	Eigenvalue	Statistic	Critical Value	Prob.	
None	0.79876	30.16888	29.79707	0.0453	COINTEGRATION
At most 1	0.379862	9.326544	15.49471	0.336	NO COINTEGRATION
At most 2	0.213068	3.114981	3.841466	0.0776	NO COINTEGRATION

Table 9: The above result shows that there is one co integration at 0.05 level in Sri Lanka.

No. of CE(s)	Eigenvalue	Statistic	Critical Value	Prob.	
None	0.827991	42.71008	29.79707	0.001	COINTEGRATION
At most 1	0.676894	19.8274	15.49471	0.0104	COINTEGRATION
At most 2	0.326596	5.140333	3.841466	0.0234	COINTEGRATION

Table 10: The above result shows that there is co integration at 0.05 level in Singapore.

Null Hypothesis:	Obs	F-Statistic	Prob.
FDI_PAK does not Granger Cause GDP_PK	14	0.0482	0.8303
GDP_PK does not Granger Cause FDI_PAK		4.26861	0.0632
INFLATION_PAK does not Granger Cause GDP_PK	14	1.51749	0.2437
GDP_PK does not Granger Cause INFLATION_PAK		0.01902	0.8928
INFLATION_PAK does not Granger Cause FDI_PAK	14	0.07916	0.7837
FDI_PAK does not Granger Cause INFLATION_PAK		1.68832	0.2204

Table 11: Granger causality of Pakistan.

Null Hypothesis:	Obs	F-Statistic	Prob.
SR_FDI does not Granger Cause SRI_LANKA_GDP	14	0.7383	0.4085
SRI_LANKA_GDP does not Granger Cause SR_FDI		0.93127	0.3553
INFLATION_PAK does not Granger Cause GDP_PK	14	0.00992	0.9224
GDP_PK does not Granger Cause INFLATION_PAK		4.60272	0.0551
INFLATION_PAK does not Granger Cause FDI_PAK	14	2.73239	0.1266
FDI_PAK does not Granger Cause INFLATION_PAK		0.34283	0.57

Table 12: Granger causality of Sri Lanka.

Asian countries (Pakistan. Nepal, Bhutan, India and Maldives). For this purpose, the FDI and GDP data of south Asian countries is collected. The augmented test confirmed that data is not stationary at level but it is stationary at first difference. The Result of co integration test indicates that there exist co-integration equations at the 0.05 level. The granger test shows that FDI and GDP in case of Nepal cause a unidirectional

Null Hypothesis:	Obs	F-Statistic	Prob.
SINGA_FDI does not Granger Cause SINGA_GDP	14	0.30235	0.5934
SINGA_GDP does not Granger Cause SINGA_FDI		3.11723	0.1052
SINGA_IF does not Granger Cause SINGA_GDP	14	1.35239	0.9224
SINGA_GDP does not Granger Cause SINGA_IF		0.71349	0.4163
SINGA_IF does not Granger Cause SINGA_FDI	14	1.42325	0.258
SINGA_FDI does not Granger Cause SINGA_IF		0.20824	0.657

Table 13: Granger causality of Singapore.

causality. The study will help and give guiding principle to policymaker and investor make scheme to prop up economic growth in Pakistan which is suffering from a high ratio of unemployment.

References

1. Borenszteina E, Gregoriob J, Lee JW (1998) How does foreign direct investment affect economic growth. Journal of International Economics 45: 115-135.
2. Telatar OM, Genc MC, Keser HY, Ay S, Deger M (2011) The causality relationships between FDI and R&D in european union. Journal of Economic and Social Development 1: 106-114.
3. Aqeel A, Nishat M (2004) The Determinants of Foreign Direct Investment in Pakistan. The Pakistan Development Review 43: 651-664.
4. Atique Z, Ahmad MH, Azhar U (2004) The Impact of FDI on Economic Growth under Foreign Trade Regimes: A Case Study of Pakistan. The Pakistan Development Review 43: 707-718.
5. Bourdon MH, Mouël CL, Vijil M (2009) The relationship between trade openness and economic growth: Some new insights on the openness measurement issue. Inra, UMR 1302 SMART pp: 1-27.
6. Mustafa A, Santhirasegaram D (2012) The Impact of Foreign Direct Investment on Economic Growth in Sri Lanka. Journal of Management 11: 27-32.
7. Gürsoy F, Sekreter A, Kalyoncu H (2013) FDI and Economic Growth Relationship Based on Cross-Country Comparison. International Journal of Economics and Financial Issues 3: 519-524.
8. Kastrati SK (2013) Impact of FDI on economic growth: an overview of the main theories of FDI and empirical research. European Scientific Journal 9: 56-77.
9. Alfaro L (2003) Foreign Direct Investment and Growth: Does the Sector Matter. Harvard Business School pp: 1-32.
10. Bussea M, Hefekerb C (2005) Political Risk, Institutions and Foreign Direct Investment. Hamburg Institute of International Economics (HWWA), Neuer Jungfernstieg 21: 1-25.
11. Carp L, România I, Popa D (2013) The relationship between foreign direct investment, trade and economic growth in Bulgaria and Romania under the impact of the globalization. Conference of Informatics and Management Sciences pp: 168-173.

The Impact of External Environment on Export Performance

Jamshidi H* and Moazemi M

Department of Business Management, Faculty of Management and Accounting, South Tehran Branch, Islamic Azad University, Tehran, Iran

Abstract

The aim of this study is to evaluate the effect of the external environment on the company's strategic behavior, taking into account the psychological distance and the role of market orientation of export activities. Presence and continuity of presence in the turbulent of international markets need to take smart approach, considering the differences in internal and external markets. To Increase export performance in complex environments and greatly varied with the degree of market orientation is possible. Effectiveness and continuity of presence in foreign markets requires a level of adopting the design of the marketing mix.

The method of this research is based on practical objective and descriptive-survey. The study population of research consists of experts, Supervisors and managers of international commerce exporting companies that their companies are excellent and food sample in 2015 Tehran province. To analyze the data collected, the researcher has used SPSS software and Excel.

The results show that export market orientation positively affects the marketing mix adoption strategy and both positively associated with export performance. Also export marketing modifies the relationship between the export marketing mix adoption strategy and export performance. Psychological distance and external environment positively affect marketing mix adoption.

Keywords: External environment; Psychological distance; Export market orientation; Marketing mix adaptation; Export performance

Introduction

What distinguishes the recent decade from previous decades is globalization and competitiveness in businesses. Consumer products markets and industrial goods and services are highly integrated at the global level. Internationalization is caused by providing a context for change. In fact, companies' growth provides a platform for them to move toward internationalization, to the extent that "growth" and "international" have become two intertwined words [1]. In order to prevent the companies' backwardness in the competitive market, it is necessary to enter the international market and prepare the ground for knowledge promotion and create knowledge networks. On the other hand, shifting to different foreign markets always causes increasing the complexity of the environment [2].

The success of firms operating in a given environment depends on the strategic orientation of the organization, and this success has to do with the degree of market orientation [3]. In the context of export activity, many authors assume that export market orientation (EMO) plays a key role in export activity because EMO controls the strategic behavior of organizations, the achievement of sustainable competitive advantages in foreign markets, and EP [4]. EMO permits the analysis of the ability of an organization to predict, respond to, and capitalize changes in the export environment. Firms with a solid EMO will be more dynamic in their search for—and better able to identify and take advantage of opportunities emerging in external markets than firms lacking this capability [5].

The concept of psychological distance (PD) is essential to assess the differences between cultures and markets and to drive international market selection [6].

Export is a vital tool for countries to achieve their goals of prosperity and economic growth [7]. Export promotion is one of the main objectives of the non-oil economy. Non-oil exports positively impacted on economic growth [8]. This is an important issue for countries like Iran, where the bulk of their exchange earnings is obtained from oil exports. Market-Orientation as an organizational competence can successfully facilitate exports performance (EP) [9].

The aim of this study was to investigate the impact of the external environment and the moderating role of export market orientation on export performance in the food industry.

The rest of the paper is organized as follows: first, the study reviews the literature which is followed by hypotheses. Subsequently, it discusses in detail the research methodology employed in this study. This is followed by the results of the analysis. Finally, the study findings are presented, discussed, and concluded.

Literature Review

External environment

Three components of the external environment are particularly pertinent to export activity [10]. Market turbulence refers to the level of insecurity in the external environment, which obliges companies to change their strategies keep abreast of changing customer needs [11]. Technological turbulence represents the high rates of technological change in the manufacture of products and the technology intrinsic to the product itself. Businesses competing in industries with high levels of technological turbulence have a greater inclination toward adaptive marketing and operational strategies than businesses in more static industries [12]. Competitive intensity refers to the extent

***Corresponding author:** Hooman Jamshidi, Department of Business Management, Faculty of Management and Accounting, South Tehran Branch Islamic Azad University, Tehran, Iran, E-mail: St_hoo_jamshidi@azad.ac.ir

of rivalry among different players in an industry. As the number of participants in a market increases, the volume and unpredictability of strategic changes may increase dramatically [13]. In the field of export activity, some authors find a positive relationship between the level of competitive intensity of a country-market and the degree of adaptation in the marketing mix program [12].

Psychological distance

Many managers are influenced by their perceptions of hardness of entering to the foreign markets regarding the selection of the target market. In international marketing literature, the "psychological distance" construct has been used to explain the cultural differences or similarities between the domestic and foreign markets [14]. Psychological distance as the distance between the domestic and foreign market is caused by understanding the cultural and business differences, which refers to the similarity or difference in the degree of separation between the export domestic and foreign market of the company. Empirical studies show that a company needs more adaptation in its marketing strategies for entering to markets with more psychological distance than entering the markets with less psychological distance [15]. According to Sousa and Lages, the definition of PD is the individual's perceived differences between the home market and that of the foreign country [6]. PD includes two dimensions: (1) “country” refers to the features of the modernization of a country; and (2) people relates to the degree of separation between people from different countries. In this context, Sousa and Lages find a positive and significant effect of PD on marketing strategy adaptation [6].

From the international marketing point of view, differences between the two countries include differences in marketing infrastructure and legal environment, that causes considering the great psychological gap by the market manager of the target destination. Sousa and Bradley defined psychological gap as the difference perceived by the managers between the origin and destination country. A manager, who intends to enter a foreign market, perceives less psychological distance when he/she perceives more similarities between his/her country and destination country [16].

Marketing mix adaptation

Adaptation or standardization is the first question which arises for the firms that have reached to stage of deciding on overseas marketing programs. Standardization of the marketing mix in all target markets or adopt different methods comply with the conditions of each market are two options for the organizations that selecting each one brings different level of utility for each organization. Standardization is a response to the increasing homogenization of the global markets in which, the market differentiation in marketing becomes less and less important [17].

Adaptation is only associated with a positive target-group specific upgrading of product features. We defined adaptation as any modification of the product standard due to certain market conditions [18].

Some authors like Morgan, O'Cass, Julian maintain that developing a differentiated marketing strategy in foreign markets requires the firm to adapt to the needs and desires of the target markets [19,20]. The adaptation of export marketing tactics brings about several benefits: (1) they allow the firm to adjust its offer to the specific characteristics of each market, which decreases foreign consumers' uncertainty, or PD; (2) they improve relationships with local intermediaries and (3) the firm can attain a greater profitability as a better product market match can result in greater customer satisfaction [19,20].

Export market orientation

Market orientation includes a set of beliefs that puts customers at the center of the attention to provide long-term profitability; it also emphasize on launching effective and efficient business to create the highest value for the customer and competitive advantage [21]. Export market orientation is a technical term that has been used to describe the market orientation level of the company in its export markets [22]. Export market orientation is consisted of three behavioral components (exports intelligence generation, dissemination and responsiveness) in addition to an integrated dimension (a coordinating mechanism) [23]. Market intelligence means identifying the customer's needs and desires faster than competitors [24]. Intelligence dissemination means that the effective response to market needs requires the participation of all parts of the organization [25]. Responsiveness means to respond to the created and released market intelligence [26]. Coordination mechanism is made up of several areas; communication and shared understanding, organizational culture with an emphasis on responsibility, cooperation and assistance; lack of inefficient conflict and goal orientated collaborative work [23]. Export market orientation behaviors is focused on current and future needs of export customers, competitors active in the export market of the company and other factors such as legal and political factors affecting export performance. Thus, the concept of marketing is not different whether a company participates in the domestic or foreign market; however the focus quality of market orientation activities in the foreign market is different from the market orientation activities in domestic market [22]. On the other hand, Rose and Shoham recognize that EMO provides an integrative insight for evaluating EP [9].

Hypothesis

H1. Turbulence (market and technology) and the competitive intensity of foreign markets positively influence the degree of adaptation of the marketing mix program in export activity.

H2. PD positively affects the marketing mix adaptation of the international strategy of firms.

H3. Adapting elements of the export marketing mix has a positive effect on EP.

H4. EMO has a positive effect on the adaptation of the marketing mix strategy in foreign markets.

H5. EMO relates positively to EP.

H6. EMO moderates the relationship between export marketing mix adaptation strategy and EP.

Figure 1 shows the conceptual model.

Methodology

Sample and data analysis

The study population of research consists of experts, Supervisors and managers of international commerce exporting companies that their companies are excellent and food sample in 2015 Tehran province; the list of these selected companies are issued every year by the Iran Trade Promotion Organization. The number of the selected company is 10 and the population is consisted of 45 companies. Census method is used in the present study instead of sampling in order to investigate the population. The researcher managed to collect a total of 32 questionnaires with the response rate of 71% of the whole society.

Table 1 presents the profiles of the respondents.

Measures

In this study, the researcher made questionnaires and has been prepared according to the articles Cadogan, Kaleka and Berthon, Theodosiou and Leonidou and Sousa and Lages [6,10,23,27]. Respondents were asked to indicate their level of agreement on 5-point Likert-type scales, anchored by 1=strongly disagree and 5=strongly agree.

To analyze the inferential statistics, the researcher has used SPSS22 software.

In the present study, calculating Cronbach's alpha in SPSS software was used to estimate the reliability; the final coefficient value obtained for the studied hypotheses is according to the following table after distributing 25 questionnaires in order to conduct initial test (Tables 1 and 2).

Churchill and Malhotra acknowledged that the minimum amount of Cronbach's alpha coefficient for the research questionnaire is 0.6 and as can be seen, the calculated alpha coefficient for the hypotheses and the entire questionnaire is more than 0.6 in the designed questionnaire [28,29]. So, it can be concluded that the questionnaire used has the necessary level of reliability.

To use most of the statistical techniques, we must firstly determine that the data collected follow normal distribution or not. Skewness and kurtosis values are very important indicators for normality. Skewness is a measure to indicate the symmetry. Kurtosis is a measure to test if the data are peaked or flat in accordance to a normal distribution. From the results illustrated in the Table 3, it can conclude that all hypotheses meet the normality conditions.

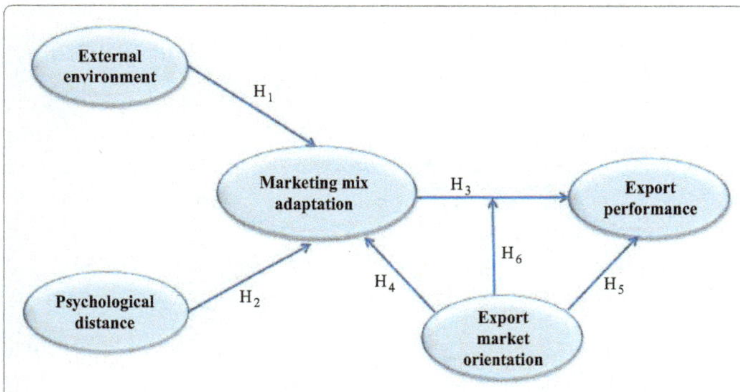

Figure 1: The conceptual model (Navarro et al. [46]).

Demographic profile	Category	Frequency	Percent
Age	25-30	11	34
	31-40	14	44
	Over 40	7	22
Work Experience	Less 4 Years	12	37
	4-10 Years	16	50
	Over 10 Years	4	13
Export Status	Less 10	12	37
	20-Nov	6	19
	Over 20	14	44
Organizational Level	Expert	22	69
	Supervisors or Managers	10	31
Education	Bachelor degree	16	50
	Masters	15	47
	Ph.D.	1	3
Total Respondents		32	100

Table 1: Comparative demographic profile of respondents.

Hypothesis	Reliability
H1	0.635
H2	0.833
H3	0.822
H4	0.662
H5	0.732
H6	0.789
Total	0.905

Table 2: Reliability analysis.

Hypothesis	N	Skewness	Kurtosis
H1	32	0.343	-0.601
H2	32	-0.101	0.281
H3	32	-0.829	0.9
H4	32	-0.322	0.483
H5	32	0.108	0.422
H6	32	0.403	0.196

Table 3: Normality test.

Hypothesis	N	Mean	Std. Deviation	Std. Error Mean
H1	32	3.9062	0.54368	0.09611
H2	32	3.8594	0.48438	0.08563
H3	32	4.0781	0.5497	0.09717
H4	32	3.9844	0.53104	0.09388
H5	32	3.901	0.50951	0.09007
H6	32	3.875	0.51744	0.09147

Table 4: One-sample statistics.

One sample t-test method is used to examine, approve or reject the research hypotheses. In fact, the test is used to determine whether the average observed in samples which is randomly selected from the population, has an amount equal to the assumed mean of the population or not.

Results

Tables 4 and 5 show the results of one sample t-test for the research hypotheses. According to the Table 5, the test values obtained from all assumptions are more than critical value $Z=t>Z_{0.5}$ and so all hypotheses are confirmed at 95% confidence (Tables 3-5).

Discussion and Conclusion

As discussed above, all hypotheses were confirmed and taking into account the research overall model as reference, the following concepts emerge. Our results confirm a positive relationship between the exporting companies' external environment and the strategic behavior of these companies to adapt the marketing mix plan. This result confirms H1, in line with the premises of the contingency approach [30,31]. It can be deduced that due to the type of foreign market, whether in terms of the certain rules and regulations or the level of complexity and environmental sustainability, there is the need for clear and consistent plan of the marketing mix programs to enter and continue participation in the international markets. Furthermore, this turbulent environment forces firms to propose an adequate offer in each country-market and to continue competing against the domestic competitors with certain guarantees in international markets [32].

Hypothesis	Test Value=3					
	t	df	Sig. (2-tailed)	Mean Difference	95% Confidence Interval of the Difference	
					Lower	Upper
H1	9.429	31	0	0.90625	0.7102	1.1023
H2	10.036	31	0	0.85938	0.6847	1.034
H3	11.095	31	0	1.07813	0.8799	1.2763
H4	10.486	31	0	0.98438	0.7929	1.1758
H5	10.004	31	0	0.90104	0.7173	1.0847
H6	9.566	31	0	0.875	0.6884	1.0616

Table 5: One-sample test.

The results also confirm that PD has a positive and significant impact on marketing strategy adaptation, validating H2. This hypothesis is consistent with the results of the other studies [6,15,20,33,34]. It can be argued that different perception level in different societies with different demographic characteristic requires marketing mix consistent with these properties. Therefore, managers ought to be aware of the impact that PD has on their strategic decisions.

The development of a strategic behavior of exporting companies that aims at adapting the elements of the marketing mix to the needs of foreign markets positively influences EP, confirming H3. This result owes to a reduction in the psychological barriers of foreign consumers. It can be concluded that determining type and impact of each of factors of price, promotion, place and product in export position influences market development and strategic and economic goals. The results also indicate that exporters who adapt and adjust their marketing mix elements with their external customers' needs has better export performance than exporters who employ more standard marketing strategies. This hypothesis is consistent with the results of the other studies [19,20,27,35,36].

The results also indicate that the export market orientation has a positive impact on adapted marketing mix strategy in foreign markets that confirms H4. It could be argued that recognition of declared and undeclared customers and market needs and create a new corporate culture to provide superior value for the customer, causes drastic changes, especially in product adapted marketing mix elements. This result is also consistent with other studies [5,7,37-39].

The findings also show that EMO plays a key role in the success of foreign trade operations. Thus, if the exporting company orients itself toward foreign clients, monitors competitors' practices and uses a strong cross-functional coordination on the basis of export market intelligence; the company then improves exporter performance. So, paying attention to the today's needs and demands can be determinant for the organization achieving its goals, as previous studies point out [3,4,26,40,41].

However, the main role of EMO in export activity is as a moderator, as previous studies point out [31,42,43]. In this case, EMO is a vital support element for the company to make appropriate decisions with regard to strategic adaptation to improve its EP, moderating this interrelation. These findings confirmed H6. Therefore, the organizations ability to identify declared and undeclared needs and create superior value for customers can influence on the marketing 4Ps impact in export. This result is also consistent with previous studies [31,43-46].

In summary, this paper contributes significantly to filling an important gap in the research field of exporting. Taking the contingency approach as a reference, the study specifically demonstrates the interrelationships between external environment, PD, strategic behavior and EP. Furthermore, this work shows how these relationships may vary depending on EMO.

Managerial implications

This study has several significant implications for managers to make systematic decisions for their company's export activities. First, external environment and PD of foreign markets are not damaging elements for export activity per se. They will only be harmful when the company refuses to mobilize information systems to study and comprehend their behavior. Fast pace of change in technology requires increasing research and development to provide better and newer products. In this regard, developing systems for monitoring the environment that allows firms to gain insight into the level of turbulence (market and technology) and competitive intensity in foreign markets is advisable.

Export oriented companies periodically review the export environment in terms of the demand structures (growth rate, market turbulence and buyer power), the supply structure (technological turbulence and supplier power) and the competition structure (the competition intensity and entry / exit barriers). Deploying a specialized team in order for continuous visits of export markets and investigating structures and survey of consumers and distribution channels, at least once a year, examine the expedient changes in the marketing mix according to the target market, in terms of export products, changes in competitive price, distribution system, the cost and type of advertising. Also, organizing the valuer groups that constantly review market can lead to the correct pricing, especially in turbulent markets.

Finally, export managers should promote behaviors within their companies with a view to foreign markets. EMO plays a moderating role in the relationship between the strategic decision making of the marketing mix program and EP. Thus, EMO is a key factor for the success of export activity.

Limitations and Future Research

This study offers important and novel contributions to the export marketing literature, but has a number of limitations that could serve as a starting point for future lines of research. This information comes from a certain time period and the results may be different at other times. Therefore, studies at another time intervals, as well as long-term studies to analyze the relationships between the external environment, psychological distance, export orientation and export performance is recommended. Also, this study has been conducted only on a small population and a single country and more companies in a larger geographical area should be included in future research so we can generalize the results. Finally, the potential impact of the other factors in this study is ignored that could be examined in future studies. For example, the quality of relationships with international distributors, evaluating the quality of relationships with customers in shaping the marketing mix, identifying and developing strategies to reduce the products psychological distance for foreign customers and the developing and recognition of the methods of making companies market-oriented.

References

1. Ruzzier M, Hisrich R, Antoncic B (2006) SME internationalization research: Past, present, and future. Journal of Small Business and Enterprise Development 13: 476-497.
2. Zahra S, George G (2002) International entrepreneurship: The current status of the field and future research agenda. In: Hitt M, Ireland D, Sexton D, Camp M (eds.) Strategic entrepreneurship: Creating an integrated mindset, Oxford: Blackwell Publishers pp: 255-288.
3. Navarro A, Acedo FJ, Losada F, Ruzo E (2011) Integrated model of export activity: Analysis of heterogeneity in managers orientations and perceptions on strategic marketing management in foreign markets. Journal of Marketing Theory & Practice 19: 187-204.
4. Cadogan JW, Kuivalainen O, Sundqvist S (2009) Export market-oriented behavior and export performance: Quadratic and moderating effects under differing degrees of market dynamism and internationalization. Journal of International Marketing 17: 71-83.
5. Navarro A, Acedo FJ, Robson MJ, Ruzo E, Losada F (2010) Antecedents and consequences of firms' export commitment: An empirical study. Journal of International Marketing 18: 41-61.
6. Carlos SMP, Lages LF (2011) The PD scale: a measure of psychic distance and its impact on international marketing strategy. International Marketing Review 28: 201-222.
7. Racela OC, Chaikittisilpa C, Thounrungroje A (2007) Market orientation, international business relationships and perceived export performance. International Marketing Review 24: 144-163.
8. Alavinasab SM (2013) Foreign Trade and Economic Growth in Iran: An Empirical Study. International Journal of Academic Research in Business and Social Sciences 3: 508-519.
9. Rose GM, Shoham A (2002) Export Performance and Market Orientation: Establishing an Empirical Link. Journal of Business Research 55: 217-225.
10. Kaleka A, Berthon P (2006) Learning and locale: The role of information, memory and environment in determining export differentiation advantage. Journal of Business Research 59: 1016-1024.
11. Gaur S, Vaudevan H, Gaur A (2011) Market orientation and manufacturing performance of Indian SMEs: Moderating role of firm resources and environmental factors. European Journal of Marketing 45: 1172-1193.
12. Powers TL, Loyka JJ (2010) Adaptation of marketing mix elements in international Markets. Journal of Global Marketing 23: 65-79.
13. Porter M (1985) Competitive advantage. New York: The Free Press p: 70.
14. Ellis PD (2007) Paths to foreign markets: does distance to market affect firm internationalization? International Business Review 16: 573-593.
15. Azar G (2011) Food Culture Distance: An Antecedent to Export Marketing Strategy Adaptation - An Empirical Examination of Swedish and Finnish Food Processing Companies. International Food and Agribusiness Management Review 14: 17-44.
16. Sousa CMP, Bradley F (2006) Cultural distance and psychic distance: two peas in a pod? Journal of International Marketing 14: 49-70.
17. Sheth JN (2001) From international to integrated marketing. Journal of Business Research 51: 5-9.
18. Roland H, Stephanie G (2014) Examining the influence of uncertainty on marketing mix strategy elements in emerging business to business export-markets. International Business Review 23: 418-428.
19. Morgan NA, Kaleka A, Katsikeas CS (2004) Antecedents of export venture performance: A theoretical model and empirical assessment. Journal of Marketing 68: 90-108.
20. O'Cass A, Julian C (2003) Examining firm and environmental influences on export marketing mix strategy and export performance of Australian exporters. European Journal of Marketing 37: 366-384.
21. Dahui L, Patrick YKC, Fujun L (2010) Market Orientation, Ownership Type, and E-Business Assimilation: Evidence from Chinese Firms. Journal compilation Decision Sciences Institute 41: 115-145.
22. Cadogan JW, Paul NJ, Salminen RT, Sundqvist S (2001) Key antecedents to "export" market-oriented behaviors: a cross-national empirical examination. International Journal of Research in Marketing 18: 261-282.
23. Cadogan JW, Diamantopoulos A, de Mortanges CP (1999) A measure of export market orientation: Scale construction and cross-cultural validation. Journal of International Business Studies 30: 689-707.
24. Dodd C (2005) Export Market Orientation and Performance: An Analysis of Australian Exporters. ANZMAX 2005 conference: Marketing in international and cross-cultural environments pp: 28-34.
25. Cambra-Fierro JJ, Hart S, Polo-Redondo Y, Fuster-Mur A (2012) Market and learning orientation in times of turbulence: relevance questioned? An analysis using a multi-case study. Quality & Quantity 46: 855-871.
26. Murray YJ, Gao YG, Kotabe M (2011) Market orientation and performance of export ventures: the process through marketing capabilities and competitive advantage. Journal of the Academy of Marketing Science 39: 252-269.
27. Theodosiou M, Leonidou LC (2003) Standardization versus adaptation of international marketing strategy: An integrative assessment of the empirical research. International Business Review 12: 141-171.
28. Churchill GA (1979) A Paradigm for Developing Better Measures of Marketing Constructs. Journal of Marketing Research 16: 64-73.
29. Malhotra S, Sivakumar K, Zhu P (2009) Distance factorsand target market selection: the moderating effect of market potential. International Marketing Review 26: 651-673.
30. Cadogan JW, Sundqvist S, Puumalainen K, Salminen RT (2012) Strategic flexibilities and export performance: The moderating roles of export market oriented behavior and the export environment. European Journal of Marketing 46: 1418-1452.
31. Calantone RJ, Kim D, Schmidt JB, Cavusgil ST (2006) The influence of internal and external firm factors on international product adaptation strategy and export performance: A three-country comparison. Journal of Business Research 59: 176-185.
32. Qureshi S, Mian SA (2012) Antecedents and outcomes of entrepreneurial firms marketing capabilities: An empirical investigation of small technology based firms. Journal of Strategic Innovation and Sustainability 6: 28-45.
33. Egide K, Etienne M, Amelie P (2012) State of Art: Product Adaptation in Times of Globalization. International Journal of Business and Social Science 3: 19.
34. Katsikeas CS, Samie S, Theodosiou M (2006) Strategy fit and performance consequences of international marketing standardization. Strategic Management Journal 27: 869-890.
35. Omotayo O (2009) Effect of marketing strategy on export performance: Evidence from Nigerian export companies. Annals of University of Bucharest, Economic and Administrative Series 3: 249-261.
36. Koo KR, Kim SJ, Kim KH (2016) The effects of internal marketing capability on export marketing strategy, B2B marketing mix and export performance. Journal of Global Scholars of Marketing Science 26: 51-65.
37. Perez L, Fernando E, Ruzo S (2012) Effects of Export Activity And Market Orientation In Foreign Trade Transactions Effects of Export Proactivity Market Orientation and on Foreign Trade Operations. Spanish Journal of Research in Marketing ESIC 16: 113-133.
38. Julia MA, Ruiz DM, Armario EM (2008) Market Orientation and Internationalization in Small and Medium-Sized Enterprises. Journal of Small Business Management 46: 485-511.
39. Leonidou LC, Katsikeas CSY, Samiee S (2002) Marketing strategy determinants of export performance: a meta-analysis. Journal of Business Research 55: 51-67.
40. Naidoo V (2010) From Ivory Towers to International Business Are Universities Export Ready in Their Recruitment of International Students? Journal of Studies in International Education 14: 5-28.
41. Acikdilli Gaye, (2013) The Effect of Marketing Capabilities and Export Market Orientation on Export Performance. Journal of Contemporary Research in Business.

42. Chung HFL, Wang ChL, Huang PH (2012) A contingency approach to international marketing strategy and decision-making structure among exporting firms. International Marketing Review 29: 54-87.

43. Phattarawan T, Kiran K, Anil N, Anusorn S (2010) The effect of product adaptation andmarket orientation on export performance: A Survey of Thaimanagers. Journal of Marketing Theory and Practice 18: 155-169.

44. Cadogan JW, Diamantopoulos A, Siguaw JA (2002) Export market-oriented activities: Their antecedents and performance consequences. Journal of International Business Studies 33: 615-626.

45. Ahmet KH, Jayachandran S, Bearden WO (2005) Market Orientation: A Meta-Analytic Review and Assessment of Its Antecedents and Impact on Performance. Journal of Marketing 69: 24-41.

46. Navarro-Garcia A, Arenas-Gaitán J, Rondán-Cataluña FJ (2014) External environment and the moderating role of export market orientation. Journal of Business Research 67: 740-745.

The Influences of Macro-Economic Factors on Capital Market Performance in Pakistan

Kabeer MA, Iqbal A, Najaf K and Najaf R*

Department of Accounting and Finance, University of Lahore, Islamabad Campus, Pakistan

Abstract

The key determination of the present research is to examine the impact of selected major variables on stock return of the Pakistani emerging capital market Karachi Stock Exchange. The researches display that capital market is inclined by transform in major economic variables. This study observes impact of three major economic variables i.e. foreign direct investment, foreign exchange rate and inflation at Karachi stock exchange. The monthly data of ten years practice in this study. To reach the objectives, study uses the Ordinary Least Square (OLS) to estimate the correlation and regression model. The Durbin-Watson statistics 1.90 value indication that there are no serial correlations issues in study. And results show that significant negative impact of inflation and Foreign exchange rate and foreign direct investment negative insignificant impact on KSE dependent variable. And overall model good fit by probability of F-statistics which less than 5%.

Keywords: Capital market returns; Macro-economic variables; OLS; Stock exchange

Introduction

In capital markets, the stock price determent by micro factors in short and long run e.g. financial and liquidity position of firm, profit or loss declare and dividend announcement etc. But also, influence on stock returns by some national factors i.e. stock market regulation and tax impose by national government. And some major economic factors furthermore influence i.e. foreign direct investment, inflation, industrial production, interest rate, savings, foreign exchange reserves, gross domestic product, exchange rate, money supply, imports and exports of goods and services and oil and gold prices fluctuation in international markets, used by various researchers. There are one of the most important role of capital market is to act upon as moderator along with investor and borrowers opportunities for investment. In short-term and long run the securities are traded of listed companies in capital market and as well affected by micro and major economic factors. These factor representations study the sensitivity of an equity and debenture return as a role of one or more factors. The capital market and a mixture of variables are directly related with each one other.

Objectives of the study

The specific purpose of this research is following objectives:

i) To look at the macro-economic factors.

ii) To find are there any correlation exist between stock return and major-economic factors.

iii) To study the significant impact of macro-economic factors on stock return.

Review of Empirical Studies

A lot of consequences obtained in the rest of world by researcher used different statistical techniques to affiliation between macro-economic factor and stock return in developed and emerging capital markets and come across impact of these variables on stock market enlargement. The research paper's contribute from poles apart from emerging countries are as follows.

Abbas et al. empirically investigated relationship between five Independent Variables namely Inflation, exchange rate, Gross Domestic Product, gold prices and T-bills rate and Dependent Variable Karachi Stock Exchange 100 index [1]. The study used data on monthly base a period from January 2002 to December 2012. The authors employed Regression and Pearson correlation method find that Dependent variable (DV) negatively co-related with all independent variables (IV), insignificant positive relationship between exchange rate (ER) and stock return, the relationship between inflation rate (IR) and stock return is negative insignificant, Treasury bills (T-bills) is insignificant negatively co-related with Stock Return, Gold prices (GP) is negatively insignificant and Gross Domestic Product has positively insignificant relation with Stock Return in Pakistan.

Khodaparasti [2] examined how exchange rates, inflation, industrial index and M1 as Independent Variables on Tehran Stock Index (TSI) Dependent Variables affect. The authors used secondary data base a period from 2007-2011 [2]. Researcher used Pearson correlation and ANOVA method get that exchange rates and industrial index have more effect on the stock return than inflation and Money supply in Iran.

Ouma and Muriu investigated the impact of macro-economic variables on stock prices [3]. The researchers employed three Independent Variables namely Money Supply, exchange rates and inflation to be tested the dependent Variable Nairobi Stock Exchange (NSE 20). The study worked data a period from January 2003 to January 2013 on monthly base. Applied technique the classical regression model, best linear unbiased estimates (BLUE), Augment Dickey-Fuller

***Corresponding author:** Rabia Najaf, Department of Accounting and Finance, University of Lahore, Islamabad Campus, 89/2-A, Sargodha 40100, Pakistan
E-mail: rabianajaf@hotmail.com

(ADF) and find result that interest rates (IR), there are a significant relation between stock returns (SR) and macroeconomic variables, Money supply (M1) and inflation (IR) are found to be significant relation of the Stock returns. Exchange rates (ER) have a negative impact on stock returns, while interest rates (IR) no relation long-term return. And there is positive significant relationship between Money supply (M2) on stock returns and also negative and significant impact of exchange rate on stock returns, while a positive impact of inflation on stock returns. There is no impact of Interest rates (IR) on stock returns exist in Kenya.

Wasseja et al. analyze the Causal Relationship between Macroeconomic Variables and Stock Prices in Kenya, used Augmented-Dickey Fuller Unit Root Test, Johansen co-integration test, Regression, Granger-causality test and vector autoregressive (VAR) model [4]. These five Independent Variables are namely Treasury bill, Inflation rate, money supply, Real Exchange Rate and Gross Domestic Product and dependent Variable Nairobi Stock Exchange (NSE 20). The study worked historically annual data a period from 1980 to 2012. Researchers used technique Augmented-Dickey Fuller Unit Root Test, Johansen co-integration test, Regression, Granger-causality test and vector autoregressive (VAR) model. The result are that macroeconomic variables no significant effect on stock prices except for inflation rate; exchange rate and change in stock prices also an insignificant factor explaining part of the movement in the macroeconomic variables except for market interest rates. In regression analysis all the macroeconomic variables are jointly significant in explaining the variations in stock prices. The causality between macroeconomic variables and stock prices runs entirely in one direction from inflation rate (IR) and exchange rate (ER) to stock prices (SP) and from stock prices (SP) to market interest rates (IR) in Kenya.

Naik and Padhi have argued that stock return should be affected by five Independent Variables namely industrial production index (IP), wholesale price index (inflation), money supply (M3), treasury bills rates (t-bills) and exchange rates (ER) on Bombay Stock Exchange (BSE). Study collected monthly data a period from April 1994 to June 2011 [5]. Result found by used Johansen's co-integration and vector error correction model that the Indian stock market index formed significant long-run relation with three out of five macroeconomic variables tested. In the long-run, the stock prices are positively related to money supply (M3) and real economic activity represented by industrial production index (IP). Inflation has found to be negatively related to stock price index, the short term interest rate (IR), as proxies by three month government treasury bills (T-bills) and the real effective exchange rate (ER) are not turning out to be the significant determinant of stock prices. In India, the interest rate (IR) does Granger cause to stock prices in the long run but the co-integration results do not show its significant impact on stock prices although the coefficient is negative in India.

Alam and Rashid explore the interaction between Independent Variables namely inflation, industrial production, money supply, exchange rate and interest rate dependent Variable Karachi Stock Exchange 100 index [6]. A period of secondary data collected from 2001 to 2011 on monthly base. Researchers find out result by used Johnson Co-integration test, Augmented Dickey Fuller (ADF) Unit Root Test, Phillip Perron (PP) tests and Autoregressive Conditional Heteroskedasticity Lagrange Multiplier (ARCH LM) test, that there is an impact of macroeconomic indicators on the Karachi stock market (DV) on consumer price index, money supply, exchange rates and interest rates negatively connected with the stock returns, while the industrial production index positively connected with the stock returns. All the variables were significantly connected to stock market returns except inflation in Pakistan.

Osamwonyi and Michael collected annual data a period from 1990-2013 found a positive relationship between Independent Variables namely gross domestic product, interest rate, exchange rate and inflation and dependent Variable Return On Equity (ROE) Listed commercial banks profitability in Nigeria [7]. Researchers practical the Regression technique found a positive relationship of GDP with return on equity (ROE), Interest rate and inflation rate have a negative relationship with return on equity (ROE). GDP significant positive effect on Return on equity (ROE), while interest rate have a significant negative effect on return on equity(ROE) but inflation is not significant at all levels of significance in Nigeria.

Raza et al. study the relation between stock return and macro-economic Independent Variables namely Foreign Direct Investment, Domestic Savings, Exchange Rate and Inflation rate and Karachi Stock Exchange 100 index dependent Variable [8]. The study found result a period worked on 1988-2009, that FDI and Domestic savings are positive significant impact on Stock market development. And exchange rate negative significant impact, while inflation insignificant impact over stock market development in Pakistan.

Ahmad et al. Muhammad identified relation between two Independent Variables namely Per capita income and inflation with dependent Variable Nigerian Stock Market (NSE) [9]. Study conducted annual data from 1970 to 2013. Researcher pertain Zivot-Andrews Unit Root Test, F-Bound Co-integration and Toda and Yamamoto Causality tests. Results found that the variables were non-stationary at levels but were stationary after first differencing. Co-integration established the existent of co-integration amongst all the variables. There is significant positive impact of Structural break (1996) on the Nigerian stock market returns in both short-run and the long-run. The Gross domestic per capita income a Key provider to increasing stock market returns and also positive impact of Gross domestic per capita income and inflation on stock market returns in Nigeria.

Issahaku et al. examines the association between five Independent Variables namely Exchange rate, Consumer Price Index (inflation), treasury-bill rate, money supply and FDI and Ghana Stock Exchange (GSE) as a dependent Variable [10]. The study worked period from January 1995 to December 2010 and collected data on monthly base with used technique Unit Root Test, Co-integration and Granger Causality Test. The researchers found the result that in long run, a significant relationship among stock returns and inflation, money supply and FDI. Also, in the short term significant relationship among stock returns and interest rate, inflation and money supply. There are insignificant relationships between stock returns and FDI in short-run. And a causal relationship existing between in inflation and exchange rate to stock returns has been established in study. Also, a causal relationships appeared from stock returns to FDI, interest rate, and money supply Exists in Ghana.

Yunus et al. evaluate short-term association between Independent Variables and dependent Variable. Authors used five Independent Variables namely money supply, industrial production, exchange rate, interest rates and foreign reserves with dependent Variable Malaysia stock market [11]. Study found result with techniques used Johansen co-integration test and vector error correction model (VECM) that foreign reserves, real exchange rate and industrial production exhibited the significant response to the changes in stock prices in the short run, while money supply and interest rates did not indicate the significant responses to stock prices. A period of data collected on monthly base from January 1980 to November 2007.

Hasanzadeh and Kianvand study the relationship between macro-economic variables namely gross domestic product, nominal effective exchange rate, money supply, gold coin price and investment in housing sector, dependent Variable Tehran Stock Index (TSI) [12]. Researchers worked on quarterly base a period from January 1996 to January 2008. Study used process Co-integration and Vector Error Correction Method (VECM) and found result that Stock prices show significantly negative relation with nominal effective exchange rate and the relationship between stock price and money supply is found significantly positive. With an increase in gross domestic product (GDP) that is positive effect and increases stock prices. And gold coin and housing division act as substitutes for stock market in Iran.

Menike LMCS analyzed the relationship between Independent Variables namely exchange rate, inflation rate, money supply, and interest rate and dependent Variable Sri Lankan Stock Market [13]. Authors worked on monthly data from September 1991 to December 2002. And applied multivariate regression method and try to result that most significant variable the exchange rate is mainly negative to stock prices, a strong negative relation exist the between stock prices and inflation rate, Stock prices react negatively to Treasury Bill rate. The lagged money supply variables become visible to have a negative outcome on stock prices in Sri Lankan Stock market.

Nijam et al. described a relationship between five Independent Variables namely Gross domestic product (GDP), Inflation proxy by wholesale price index (WPI), Interest rate (IR), Balance of payment (BP) and Exchange rate (ER) and Colombo stock exchange as a dependent Variable [14]. Researchers applied practice on Correlation and Multiple Regression techniques on a period from 1980 to 2011. Outcome of study that stock market significantly positively relates to Gross domestic product (GDP), Exchange Rate (ER) and Interest Rate (IR) while it negatively relates to inflation. Insignificant impact of Balance of payment (BP) found to be deterred the stock market performance in Sri Lanka.

Khan MS studied the relation between Independent Variables namely exchange rate, interest rate, inflation rate and GDP (Gross domestic product) growth rate and dependent variable Karachi Stock Exchange 100 index [15]. Study used data from 1992 to 2011 with constructive techniques Pearson's correlation coefficient and multiple regression models found result about exchange rate, inflation and GDP growth rate show in a positive straight line correlation with stock prices of dependent variable. And interest rate show opposite and depressing correlation with stock prices of KSE-100 index. And exchange rate and inflation are statistically significant, while interest rate and GDP growth rate is statistically insignificant. There are relationship survive between exchange rate and stock prices of KSE-100 index show strong positive correlation with stock prices and also statistically very significant in Pakistan.

Venkatraja investigated association between five Independent variables namely the real economic output (Index of industrial production), foreign institutional investment, inflation, gold price and exchange rate and Bombay Stock Exchange (BSE) as a dependent Variable [16]. Author collocated data from April 2010- June 2014 on monthly base. The study practical multiple regression and found that Inflation, inflow of foreign institutional investment, exchange rate and gold price positive influence impact on the Indian stock market performance significantly, While, an increase in gold price is found causing crash in Indian stock market.

Singh P scrutinized relationship about macro-economic factors [17]. The study used Index of Industrial Production (IIP), Wholesale Price Index (WPI), Money Supply (M3), 91 days treasury bills as proxy for Interest Rates (IR), Trade Deficit (TD), Foreign Institutional Investment (FII), Exchange rate (ER), Crude Oil Price (CP) and Gold Price (GP) nine Independent Variables and Bombay Stock Exchange (BSE) as a dependent Variable. Researcher collected data from January 2011 to December 2012 on monthly base. The realistic technique correlation, multivariate stepwise regression analysis and Granger causality test to originate a Significant impact of gold, money supply, exchange rates and foreign institutional investors on the Indian stock market, Another unidirectional causality is from money supply to S and P CNX Nifty which signifies the pressure of variable on the Indian stock market.

Momani et al. also studied the relationship between Amman Stock Exchange as a dependent Variable and four Independent Variables namely Annual Gross National Product (GNP), Annual Money Supply, Annual Interest Rates on the Long-term Deposits and Annual Industrial Production Index [18]. Researchers used data a period from 1992 to 2010 and practical multiple regressions (stepwise method). Result show that a relation create with statistical significance between the all independent and dependent variables. The interest rates variable has an enormous influence on Amman Stock Exchange.

Ali et al. studied the impact of macro-economic variables on Karachi Stock Exchange 100 index dependent variable [19]. The researchers investigated the relationship with respect to Gross Domestic Saving (GDS), Money Supply (MS) and Foreign Remittances (FR) as Independent Variables. Study worked data on annual base start period from 1973 to 2012. Researchers applied Philips and Perron Test and Auto Regressive Distributed Lag (ARDL) to co-integration technique. The ARDL to Co-integration results proved that Gross domestic savings, money supply have positively force on stock market expansion in Pakistan in both short run and long run that are consistent. Foreign remittances have an insignificant effect on stock market development in short run, while in long run the researchers found no any effect on stock market in Pakistan.

Nkechukwu et al. examined the relationship between two Independent Variables gross domestic product (GDP) and broad money supply (M2) and dependent Variable Nigerian stock market [20]. Researchers worked annually data start from 1980-2012. The study used statistical tools the Augmented-Dickey Fuller Unit root test, Co-integration analysis, Normalized Co-integrating Vectors Test, vector error correction model (VECM), Granger-causality tests. A significant found by researchers in the co-integrating vectors indicated that gross domestic product has long-run negative effect on stock market prices contrary to the a priori expectation Money supply has long-run positive effect on stock market prices, Which it is consistent with the a priori expectation. However, the results of the vector error correction model show that both gross domestic product and money supply (M2) have insignificant positive effect on stock market prices in Nigeria.

Hosseini et al. empirically investigated the relationship among four Independent Variables namely crude oil price (COP), money supply (M2), industrial production (IP) and inflation rate (IR) and dependent Variables Bombay Stock Exchange (BSE) and Shanghai Stock Exchange index (SSE) [21]. The study worked on data a period from January 1999 to January 2009 monthly base. The researcher worked statistical technique simple linear regression model, Multivariate Co-integration Test, Vector Error Correction Model (VECM) and Augmented-Dickey Fuller Unit Root Test. The researcher's Result show:

China: In the long-run, the impact of increases in crude oil price in China is constructive force, also Money supply in China it encouraging impact. In china the industrial production (IP) negative. Also in effect of increases in inflation on this stock positive in China. The simultaneous impact of money supply exist Chinese stock market positive. The simultaneous effect of inflation on current Chinese stock index (SSE) positive and significant but this effect lagged one month though positive significant.

India: In the long run, the impact of increases in crude oil price in India this effect is negative, money supply the impact on Indian stock market is negative. In India the effect of increases in inflation stock return positive. In the short run, the simultaneous effect of crude oil price positive in India. The simultaneous impacts of money supply in India it negatively. And the simultaneous effect negative insignificant. However, the lagged effects negative and significant in India.

Sharma and Mahendru found the relationship between four Independent Variables namely inflation rate, foreign exchange reserve, exchange rate and gold price and dependent Variable Bombay Stock Exchange (BSE) [22]. Study examined weekly data a period from January 2008 to January 2009. The researchers used statistical multiple regression model. Result show that Independent variables exchange rate and gold price have a significant relation with stock price, it give the impression to affect the entire stock price while inflation rate significant for only three of the twelve portfolios. Inflation rate and gold price do not become visible to have any significant effect on stock returns. It means that inflation rate and foreign exchange reserve don't influence the stock price.

Ahmad at al. identified the Causal Relationship between Stock Market Returns in Nigerian Stock Exchange as a dependent Variable and six Macroeconomic Independent Variables namely money supply, nominal effective exchange rate, short term treasury bills rate, foreign direct investment, gross domestic per capita income, and gross domestic saving [23]. The researchers used statistics methods Autoregressive Distributive Lag (ARDL) and Vector Autoregressive Model (VAR) and found result that these all six variables have a long-run equilibrium relationship between them, although they may be in disequilibrium in the short-run used time period from 1984 to 2013.

Gay conducted empirical research on exchange rate and oil price as an Independent Variables and stock markets of BRIC (Brazil, Russia, India and China) countries as a dependent Variable [24]. Study effort on monthly data of BRIC (Brazil, Russia, India and China) countries from March 1999 to June 2006. Box-Jenkins ARIMA statistical model used and found the effect of exchange rate and oil price on the stock market return of Brazil, Russia, India, and China did not reveal a significant relationship, Although, the descriptive values of exchange rate, oil prices and the lagged stock market return were not significant in BRIC (Brazil, Russia, India and China) countries.

Akinlo analyzed effect of two Independent Variables foreign exchange reserves and interest rate and dependent Variable Nigerian Stock Exchange. Study worked annual data a period from 1981 to 2011 [25]. Statistical technique unit root tests obtained using the Augmented-Dickey Fuller and KPSS (Kwiatkowski-Phillips-Schmidt-Shin) tests the results show that foreign reserves had positive effect on stock exchange development. And Granger causality show that a bidirectional cooperative association be present between interest rates and stock market development. In the same vein, there was a cooperative association between interest rate and external reserves in Nigeria.

Khan and Ahmed established the relation between macro-economic variables of national Imports and Exports of Goods and Services as an Independent Variables and Karachi Stock Exchange 100 index as a dependent Variable [26]. Researchers worked on Quarterly data start a period from 2005 to 2009. Statistical Regression and Co-integration applied and found result that the Historically stock prices (SP) predicts the current fluctuation in stock prices (SP) and it predict the current fluctuation of National exports while there are no impact on current values of imports by the historically stock prices (SP) or historically stock prices are not predicting the current fluctuation in imports of Pakistan.

Design and Research Methodology

Definition of model

The econometric model under study given the following equation:

$$Y = \alpha + \beta_1 X_1 + \beta_2 X_2 + \beta_3 X_3 + \beta_4 X_4 + \beta_5 X_5 + \varepsilon$$

Where:

Y is dependent variable, "α" is y - intercept and x1, x2, x3, x4, and x5 are independent variables while ε is random error term.

Implementation of the econometric Model:

$$R = \alpha + \beta_1 \text{ LN FDI} + \beta_2 \text{ FR} + \beta_3 \text{ GP} + \beta_4 \text{ IN} + \beta_5 \text{ OP} + \varepsilon$$

Where:

R = return on stock

α = constant term

β_1 = foreign direct investment

β_2 = foreign exchange rate

β_3 = gold prices

β_4 = inflation

β_5 = oil prices

ε = error term

Research methodology

The study has been conducted the secondary data to find the relationship between macroeconomic variables and stock return. In this study, econometric model Ordinary Least Square (OLS) to estimate the particular circumstances and in relation to which other variable quantities may be expressed. Data analysis performed on MS Excel and E-views statistical software. The regression technique makes use of by OLS to identify the significance and direction of relations between Karachi Stock Exchange and major economic factors.

Stock return

Karachi stock exchange 100 index return chosen for the study based on accessibility and also reliability of data. Stock prices are obtained from Karachi stock Exchange official site and experiential on monthly basis stock prices in the period from November 2005 to October 2015. The stock return is calculated as the monthly change in the stock price by the following formula:

R (t) = (P1/P0) -1

Where R (t) the stock price in month t and P1 is current month stock price and P0 previous month stock price.

Foreign direct investment

Foreign direct investment is eminent from assortment foreign investment, a passive investment in the securities of a different country such as public stocks and bonds. Foreign direct investment data collected from State Bank of Pakistan official site on monthly base start a period from November 2005 to October 2015 [27]. FDI calculated as the monthly value by the following formula:

FDI (t) = LN (t)

Where FDI (t) the value at month t and LN (t) is natural logarithm in MS excel in month (t) of FDI value.

Foreign exchange rate

In term of finance, a foreign exchange rate, between two currencies is the rate at which one currency will be exchanged for another. Foreign exchange data obtained from State Bank of Pakistan official site and collected rate monthly base start a period from November 2005 to October 2015. Foreign exchange rate calculated as the monthly rate by the following formula:

FR (t) = 1 / USD (t)

Where FR (t) foreign exchange rate month t, and 1 divided by USD are equal to PKR value at month (t).

Gold prices

All of the valuable metals, gold is the most accepted as an investment. Investors normally buy gold as a way of diversifying risk, particularly through the use of futures contracts and derivatives. The gold market is subject to conjecture and unpredictability as are other markets. Gold prices data collected from World Bank and monthly base start a period from November 2005 to October 2015. Gold price in Pakistan Rupee, 1 Troy per ounce (unit of mass (weight)) is equal to 31.1034 Grams (unit of mass in metric system) weight. Gold prices calculated as the monthly Value by the following formula:

GP (t) = LN (t)

Where GP (t) the value at month t and LN (t) is natural logarithm in MS excel in month (t) of the gold price.

Inflation

Inflation, an increase in the general level of prices reduces the actual value of money, in this manner reducing the expected cash inflow from a benefit, exceptions being inflation indexed securities. The calculation of the inflation rate is the consumer price index (CPI), obtained from the State Bank of Pakistan official site. The twelve-monthly (YOY) change in CPI is given by the following formula:

I (t) = CPI (t) –CPI (t-12)

Where I (t) the annual change in CPI, that is, the inflation in month t, CPI (t) is the CPI in month t and CPI (t-12) is the CPI in the same month of the previous year time period [28].

References

1. Abbas A, Tahir SH, Raza S (2014) Impact of Macroeconomic Variables on Stock Returns: Evidence from KSE-100 Index of Pakistan. Research Journal of economics and Business Studies 3: 70-77.
2. Khodaparasti RB (2014) The role of macroeconomic variables in the stock market in Iran. Polish journal of management studies 10: 54-64.
3. Ouma WN, Muriu P (2014) The impact of macroeconomic variables on stock market returns in Kenya. International Journal of Business and Commerce 3: 11 01-31.
4. Wasseja MM, Njoroge E, Mwenda SN (2015) Investigation of the Granger Causal Relationship between Macroeconomic Variables and Stock Prices in Kenya. International Journal of Business and Economics Research 4: 98-108.
5. Naik PK, Padhi P (2012) The Impact of Macroeconomic Fundamentals on Stock Prices Revisited: Evidence from Indian Data. Eurasian Journal of Business and Economics 5: 25-44.
6. Alam Z, Rashid K (2014) Time Series Analysis of the Relationship between Macroeconomic Factors and the Stock Market Returns in Pakistan. Journal of Yasar University 9: 6261-6380.
7. Osamwonyi IO, Michael CI (2014) The impact of macroeconomic variables on the profitability of listed commercial banks in Nigeria. European Journal of Accounting Auditing and Finance Research 2: 85-95.
8. Raza A, Iqbal N, Ahmed Z, Ahmed M, Ahmed T (2012) The Role of FDI on Stock Market Development. The Case of Pakistan, Journal of Economics and Behavioral Studies 4: 26-33.
9. Ahmad AU, Abdullah A, Abdullahi AT, Aziz UA, Muhammad (2015) Stock Market Returns and Macroeconomic Variables in Nigeria. Testing for Dynamic Linkages with a Structural Break. Scholars Journal of Economics, Business and Management 2: 816-828.
10. Issahaku H, Ustarz Y, Domanban PB (2013) Macroeconomic variables and stock market returns in Ghana: any causal link. Asian Economic and Financial Review 3: 1044-1062.
11. Yunus MM, Mahyideen JM, Saidon R (2014) Influences of macroeconomic variables on stock prices in Malaysia. International Conference on Postgraduate Research 98: 399-416.
12. Hasanzadeh A, Kianvand M (2012) The Impact of Macroeconomic Variables on Stock Prices: The Case of Tehran Stock Exchange. Journal of Money and Economy 6: 171-190.
13. Menike LMCS (2006) The Effect of Macroeconomic Variables on Stock Prices in Emerging Sri Lankan Stock Market. Sabaragamuwa University Journal 6: 50-67.
14. Nijam HM, Ismail SMM, Musthafa AMM (2015) The Impact of Macroeconomic Variables on Stock Market Performance. Evidence from Sri Lanka. Journal of Emerging Trends in Economics and Management Sciences 6: 151-157.
15. Khan MS (2014) Macroeconomic Variables & its Impact on KSE 100 Index. Universal Journal of Accounting and Finance 2: 33-39.
16. Venkatraja B (2014) Impact of Macroeconomic Variables on Stock Market Performance in India: An Empirical Analysis. International Journal of Business Quantitative Economics and Applied Management Research 1: 71-85.
17. Singh P (2014) Indian stock market and macroeconomic factors in current scenario. International Journal of Research in Business Management 2: 43-54.
18. Momani GF, Alsharari MA (2012) Impact of Economic Factors on the Stock Prices at Amman Stock Market. International Journal of Economics and Finance 4: 151-159.
19. Ali R, Haq MA, Ullah S (2015) Macroeconomic Indicators and Stock Market Development. Developing Country Studies 5: 139-149.
20. Nkechukwu G, Onyeagba J, Okoh J (2013) Macroeconomic Variables and Stock Market Prices in Nigeria: A Co-integration and Vector Error Correction Model Tests. International Journal of Science and Research 4: 717-724.
21. Hosseini SM, Ahmad Z, Lai YW (2011) The Role of Macroeconomic Variables on Stock Market Index in China and India. International Journal of Economics and Finance 3: 233-243.
22. Sharma GD, Mahendru M (2010) Impact of macro-economic variables on stock prices in India. Global Journal of Management and Business Research 10: 19-26.
23. Ahmad AU, Abdullah A, Sulong Z, Abdullahi AT (2015) Causal Relationship between Stock Market Returns and Macroeconomic Variables in Nigeria. IOSR Journal of Humanities and Social Science 20: 74-96.
24. Gay RD, Jr, DBA (2008) Effect of Macroeconomic Variables on Stock Market

Returns For Four Emerging Economies: Brazil, Russia, India, and China. International Business & Economics Research Journal 7: 1-8.

25. Akinlo OO (2015) Impact of foreign exchange reserves on Nigerian Stock Exchange. International Journal of Business and Finance Research 9: 69-76.

26. Khan K, Ahmed I (2015) Impact of Stock Prices on Macroeconomic Variables: Evidence from Pakistan. KASBIT Business Journal 8: 42-59.

27. (2015) Economic data –Monetary statistics, State bank of Pakistan.

28. (2015) Country economic data of world economy, data – by country, world Development Indicators.

Sharing Economy and Healthcare Today: ICT, Knowledge, Skills, Projects, Practical Experience in Improving Clinical and Economic Outcomes

Luisetto M*

Pharm D, Pharmacologist, European Specialist in Laboratory Medicine, Hospital Pharmacist's Manager, Italy

Abstract

The aim of this work was to analyze the relationship between professional social media use and the healthcare in sharing economy time when used in healthcare field and specifically in pharmaceutical settings. The innovation introduced with biomedical databases has improved research works with rapid steps in all kind of scientific researches areas tools as Internet, search engines and professional social media in sharing economy time have brought a great development in the way of rapidly connecting with the professionals. The researchers and professionals all over the world in last two decades has been great possibility to sharing their experience more than past with improving in their results. So it is very interesting to see how they are playing a crucial role today healthcare through this rapid development. For example, LinkedIn, Slide share, Research gate, PubMed, YouTube, NCBI, Facebook, Skype etc. This has really brought a revolutionary change in the field. The possibility to bridge researchers and professionals; for example, with similar interests, discipline with more rapid development, never seen in last two decades. We think that using sharing economy instruments we can reduce healthcare costs about 30-40%.

Keywords: Sharing economy; Healthcare; Knowledge; Economic outcome; Social media

Introduction

Even if while some elements of health-care delivery cannot be shared due to safety (dose of a drug and other data), many opportunities for sharing exist in this settings. Technology has the ability to heavy transform the way we works with more efficiency and effectiveness, reducing time and improving also clinical outcomes [1-5]. The results we can have are interesting at different levels such as government, institutions, Insurance, patients and professional [6-9].

Communications between professionals in different hospitals, sharing practical experience and clinical cases, way to improve clinical outcomes or to reduce healthcare costs represent real facts in sharing economy time [10-16]. At the same time patients are extremely interested to be under the hands of Clinical really updates with the best practice or to be treated with the best technologies (the same insurance corporations) [17,18].

Patients like to have the right information in order to choose the best clinical options using also sure web healthcare information database (and in example second opinion in example sharing imaging data or other) [19-21]. An example can be considered the benchmarking management systems never before health care has been as open-minded to new technology as today [22-26].

In example in hospital pharmacy field:

"The development of clinical pharmacy in 1960-70s and pharmaceutical care in 1990 has represented an interesting innovation in pharmacy field [27-31]. However clinical pharmacy and Pharmaceutical care showed some practice critical limits: (a) clinical pharmacy approach is more oriented to clinical population needs or pathology but is not strictly request to manage at the level of every single clinical case. (b) In hospital setting Pharmaceutical care can not to be applied to the entire patient for economic reason (limited number of pharmacist applied). In order to give more rationale priority of actions and to select the patient to be seen in priority way we think a good solution to apply the principle of pharmaceutical care with the instrument of clinical pharmacy into a new management systems" [32,33].

Materials and Methods

We observed relevant literature in PubMed and other database involved in

- Professional social media
- Sharing economy
- Management
- Pharmaceutical care and clinical pharmacy
- Healthcare Costs management
- ICT in healthcare

Results

We have find in literature analyzed a general improvement in some clinical outcomes when clinical pharmacist are stabile part of medical team using the instruments today available (ICT, MANAGEMENT, PROFESSIONAL SOCIAL MEDIA, SHARING ECONOMY) improving in clinical outcomes but also reducing therapy errors or reducing recovery days improving patient quality of life [34-36].

In example in healthcare field using ph. Care and clinical pharmacy added in medical team in stabile way added to modern communication

***Corresponding author:** Mauro Luisetto, Pharm D, Pharmacologist, European Specialist in Laboratory Medicine, Hospital Pharmacist's Manager, Italy
E-mail: maurolu65@gmail.com

instruments as professional social media and sharing economy tools we have observed more than 30% reduction in drugs or medical devices use in hospital setting and we think 10% due to reduction in recovery days or due by therapy errors [37].

Discussion

The results obtained, even if in qualitative ways indicate a general improves in some clinical outcomes or economic that implies a more rapid application of this systems to share information. The reduction of 30-40% in healthcare cost we can obtain using sharing economy instruments is a great economic outcome to obtain in actual economic cycle.

Conclusion

In literature analyzed in this work, there is the need to improve the healthcare systems introducing management and ICT instruments starting from clinical pharmacist university course. All these management instruments must be added to EBM criteria in clinical pharmacy and pharmaceutical care working activities (OSAMA ET AL) [13].

Few ICT instruments can give relevant contribute in management systems and in the same way Professional social media can be considered today as a useful tool to meet between researcher and healthcare professional and a base for a new kind of biomedical database. In professional social media we can find researcher curriculum, professional interest and other relevant information and efficient systems to meet themselves (Luisetto et al. 2016 clinicians teamwork bulletin) Psychological behavior skills for team working [38].

Theory and practical applications to be added to the classic clinical pharmacy programs we submit to the scientific community. We request to introduce this management instruments in the current clinical pharmacist postgraduate course, at the same time we ask public institution to strongly apply this new approach. Management and ICT instruments must be more used in today's healthcare working setting. This will give improvement in health care level.

For example, also use single hospital setting to link all the professionals involved in a single patient or in patient that has been transferred into different hospitals (Acute but also chronic) [37,38].

Undoubtedly, social media will play a crucial role in healthcare. Social media as ICT has brought a great spectrum of efficacy in healthcare as in other working field. It is very simple to say but is interesting at the same time and interesting the economics results we can obtain in more rapid way.

There is a need to have new tools and instruments as scientific social network that add the different characteristics of the social media, biomedical database and other technologies existing today in to have a more useful instrument. In example we think that a new scientific social media that could make easy to find researchers, and professionals and their research activity (related to patients and the society needs) excluding the non-relevant literature.

We submit to the business world "Clinical Pharmaceutical Care" as a new healthcare management discipline. Discipline intended to improve economic and clinical endpoint in pharmacological therapy reducing therapy errors. A more rational application of ECONOMICA resource in medical EQUIPE (clinical pharmacist).

This new approach takes advantages using the Management and ICT principles as well as sharing economy principles.

We also ask International and Business administration schools and organization involved in hospitals accreditation and University to recognize the advantages we can have by using this kind of new health care professional activity. We think that core training must include Management, ICT, Professional social media, sharing economy principles, psychological behavior skills for team working, philosophy, theory and practical applications.

References

1. Tunnecliff J, Ilic D, Morgan P, Keating J, Gaida JE, et al. (2015) The acceptability among health researchers and clinicians of social media to translate research evidence to clinical practice: Mixed-methods survey and interview study. J Med Internet Res 17: e119.
2. Mekaru SR, Brownstein JS (2014) One Health in social networks and social media. Rev Sci Tech 33: 629-637.
3. Thompson MA, Majhail NS, Wood WA, Perales MA (2015) Social Media and the Practicing Hematologist: Twitter 101 for the Busy Healthcare Provider. Curr Hematol Malig Rep 10: 405-412.
4. Kind T, Evans Y (2015) Social media for lifelong learning. Int Rev Psychiatry 27: 124-132.
5. Rodríguez SME, Gómez-RJ, Álvarez MM, Tortolero L, Ribal MJ, et al. (2016) Spanish adaptation of the recommendations for the appropriate use of social networks in urology of the European Association of Urology. Actas Urol Esp.
6. Panahi S, Watson J, Partridge H (2016) Fostering interpersonal trust on social media: physicians' perspectives and experiences. Postgrad Med J 92: 70-73.
7. Jackson J, Kennedy M (2015) Developing a social media platform for nurses. Nurs Stand 30: 45-52.
8. Ranschaert ER, van Ooijen PM, Lee S, Ratib O, Parizel PM (2015) Social media for radiologists: An introduction. Insights Imaging 6: 741-752.
9. Denecke K, Bamidis P, Bond C, Gabarron E, Househ M, et al. (2015) Ethical Issues of Social Media Usage in Healthcare. Yearb Med Inform 10: 137-147.
10. Chan C (2015) A Scoping Review of Social Media Use in Social Work Practice. J Evid Inf Soc Work 15: 1-14.
11. Steele SR, Arshad S, Bush R, Dasani S, Cologne K, et al. (2015) Social media is a necessary component of surgery practice. Surgery 158: 857-862.
12. Steele SR, Arshad S, Bush R, Dasani S, Cologne K, et al. (1938) Society of University Surgeons' Social and Legislative Committee.
13. Kitching F, Winbolt M, MacPhail A, Ibrahim JE (2015) Web-based social media for professional medical education: Perspectives of senior stakeholders in the nursing home sector. Nurse Educ Today 35: 1192-1198.
14. Bond CA, Raehl CL (2007) Clinical pharmacy service, pharmacy staffing and hospital mortality rates. Pharmacotherapy 27: 481-493.
15. Chisholm BMA, Kim Lee J, Spivey CA, Slack M, Herrier RN, et al. (2010) US pharmacist's effect as team members on patient care: systematic review and meta-analyses. Med Care 48: 923-933.
16. Luisetto M, Francesca C, Giovanni B, Behzad NA (2015) Pharmacist Cognitive Service and Pharmaceutical Care Today and Tomorrow Outlook. UKSPB 3: 67-72.
17. Stanley MS (1994) Diagnostic Imaging and Pharmaceutical Care. American Journal of Pharmaceutical Education 58: 2.
18. Howard P (1984) An introduction to the Clinical Laboratory for Pharmacists. Hosp Pharm 19: 425-431.
19. Luisetto M, Sahu RK (2016) Clinical Pharmaceutical Care: A New Management Health Care Discipline in 2016. UKJPB.
20. Luisetto M, Cabianca L (2016) Psychological and Behavior Skills for Ph.Care Practice in Medical Team 2016. IJPPR 5: 1-4.
21. Luisetto M, Mobin IM, Luca C (2016) Professional Social Media: Instrument to Meet Researcher and Healthcare Instruments with a Model for a New Scientific Social Network. International Journal of Economics and Management Science 5: 1-2.
22. Luisetto M (2016) Clinical Pharmaceutical Care, Medical Laboratory Imaging,

Nuclear Medicine: A Synergy to Improve Clinical Outcomes and Reducing Costs. J App Pharm 8: e112.

23. Osama MA, Amer MA (2014) Evidence-based pharmaceutical care: The next chapter in pharmacy practice. Saudi Pharmaceutical Journal 20: 140-141.

24. Ahmed SI (2008) The definition of clinical pharmacy. Pharmacotherapy 28: 816-817.

25. Ahmed SI, Hasan SS (2010) Clinical Pharmacy and Pharmaceutical Care: A Need to Homogenize the Concepts. Am J Pharm Educ 74: 193.

26. Hepler CD (2004) Clinical pharmacy, pharmaceutical care, and the quality of drug therapy. Pharmacotherapy 24: 1491-1498.

27. Keller DR, O'Dell DV, Skochelak SE, Cochran GL, Shull SJ, et al. (2004) Teaching the basics of clinical pharmaceutical care: innovative pharmacy workshops at the University of Wisconsin and the University of Nebraska. Fam Med 36: 89-92.

28. Luisetto M (2016) Open letter to all clinical pharmacists' pharmaceutical care medical laboratory, nuclear medicine and imaging. Clinicians' teamwork 1: 1-3.

29. Luisetto M, Nili-Ahmadabadi B, Cabianca L, Mokbul IM (2016) Steps and Impacts of Pharmaceutical Care and Clinical Pharmacy Development on Clinical Outcomes 2016: A Historical Analysis Compared with Results. Clinicians Teamwork 1: 4-8.

30. Nazir T, Muzzammil S, Zaidi M (2011) Review of the basic components of clinical pharmaceutical care in Pakistan. Teacher Research Journal 1: 1-5.

31. Luisetto M, Sahu RK (2016) Clinical Pharmaceutical Care: A New Management Health Care Discipline in 2016. Journal of Pharmaceutical and Biosciences 4: 63-64.

32. Nedelko Z, Potocan V, Dabić M (2015) Current and Future use of Management Tools. Ekonomika a management 18: 28-45.

33. Slipicevic O, Masic I (2012) Management Knowledge and Skills Required in the Health Care System of the Federation Bosnia and Herzegovina. Mater Sociomed 24: 106-111.

34. Garman AN, McAlearney AS, Harrison MI, Song PH, McHugh M (2011) High-performance work systems in health care management, part 1: development of an evidence-informed model. Health Care Manage Rev 36: 201-213.

35. Al-Shaqha WM, Zairi M (2001) Pharmaceutical care management: a modern approach to providing seamless and integrated health care. Leadersh Health Serv 14: 282-301.

36. Bao L, Wang Y, Shang T, Ren X, Ma R (2013) A novel clinical pharmacy management system in improving the rational drug use in department of general surgery. Indian J Pharm Sci 75: 11-15.

37. Jarab AS, Alqudah SG, Mukattash TL, Shattat G, Al-Qirim T (2012) Randomized controlled trial of clinical pharmacy management of patients with type 2 diabetes in an outpatient diabetes clinic in Jordan. J Manag Care Pharm 18: 516-526.

38. Kicklighter CE, Nelson KM, Humphries TL, Delate T (2006) An evaluation of a clinical pharmacy-directed intervention on blood pressure control. Pharm Pract (Granada) 4: 110-116.

Islamic Calendar Effect on Market Risk and Return Evidence from Islamic Countries

Akhter A[1*], Sandhu A[2] and Butt S[3]

[1]*PMAS-Arid Agriculture University Rawalpindi, PhD Scholar, Muhammad Ali Jinnah University, Islamabad, Pakistan*

[2]*Jinnah Institute of Informatics Rawalpindi, Pakistan*

[3]*Bahria University Islamabad, Pakistan*

Abstract

Anomalies remain part of the market no matter it is developed or emerging one. Studies revealed that arbitragers materialize these situations and bring the markets back to efficiency. This study probed the presence of calendar anomalies in stock markets of six Islamic countries. It is empirically concluded that negative Zul-Hijjah effect presents in Malaysian stock market return and has no effect for other sample countries' stock markets. Zul-Hijjah has negative effect on the volatility of Turkish, Morocco and Egyptian stock markets and has no effect on the volatility of other sample countries' stock markets. Investors must consider this phenomenon while making decisions regarding investment and forming a diversified global portfolio. This field will help the investors in taking effective investment decision and for efficient resource allocation because knowledge of calendar anomalies plays a critical role to structure the optimal portfolio.

Keywords: Islamic Countries; Zul-Hijjah effect; Stock market return; Volatility

Introduction

Stock markets provide a platform where financer and borrower interact. In stock markets large number of sellers and buyers are endlessly occupied in trade of securities and stock markets report the progress of securities. Because the prices of securities move up and down depending on performance of companies and countries' economic and political conditions etc. Fama had worked upon informational efficiency and "Efficient Market Hypotheses" is based on the assumption that the prices of securities adjust quickly on the arrival of new information and existing prices completely reflect all available information.

"A market in which prices at any time fully reflect all available information is called efficient market". Finance literature, especially related to capital markets differentiates anomalies into three categories, namely calendar, technical and fundamental. Calendar anomalies mean abnormal behavior of stock markets at and during specific period of time. Calendar anomalies are one component among a number of factors of inefficient behavior of livestock markets [1]. The existence of anomalies criticizes the EMH presence. Gregorian calendar anomalies are investigated by many researchers. However, different communities follow their own religious calendars along with Gregorian calendar for their religious purposes as:

1. Jews follow their Hebrew calendar
2. Christians follow their Gregorian calendar
3. Muslims follow their Islamic calendar

There are different religious months and days in these religious calendars which are celebrated by these communities. Islamic calendar is followed by Muslims in more than fifty countries of the world and Muslims celebrate religious months such as Ramadan and Aashoora and days such as Eid-ul-Fitar and Eid-ul-Azha. The Islamic calendar is based on Hijri tied to lunar. It consists of 12 months according to 12 phases of the lunar.

In most of the previous studies Ramadan and Muharram effect was examined while Zul-Hijjah also most important month from religious point of view remain untested. Zul-Hijjah is the 12th and last the month in Islamic calendar. The duration of first 10 days of Zul- Hijjah carries a great importance in Muslim culture. Hajj is performed in this month which is the fifth pillar of Islam. The 2nd Muslim festival Eid-ul-Azha falls on the 10th of Zul-Hijjah and animals are sacrificed by the Muslims all over the world in the memory of Prophet Ibrahim (A.S). The month of Zul-Hijjah may negatively affect the stock markets of Muslim countries because of the fact that two major religious activities fall in this month that decrease the trading activities. The purpose of present study is to examine the effect of Zul-Hijjah on returns and volatility of six Islamic countries' stock markets indices. The countries of investigation are Pakistan, Malaysia, Indonesia, Turkey, Morocco and Egypt. Most recent time period for every sample Islamic country is used. This study contributes to the literature on market efficiency with respect to the sample Islamic countries.

The remaining paper is organized as: section 2 consists of review of related studies; section 3 explains the data and methodology, section 4 presents empirical results and section 5 summarizes and conclude the empirical results.

Literature Review

Efficiency of stock markets has been most discussed topic of researchers and EMH is most maligned in this regard. Calendar anomalies have been much discussed by researchers with respect to different stock markets for different periods since decades. In most of the world's stock markets Gregorian calendar anomalies were observed

***Corresponding author:** Akhter A, Lecturer, PMAS-Arid Agriculture University Rawalpindi, PhD Scholar, Muhammad Ali Jinnah University, Islamabad, Pakistan, E-mail: uims.adnan@gmail.com

by many researchers. A review of notable literature on the topic of investigation is organized in the following section.

Aly, Mehdian and Perry [2] conducted a research for analyzing the day of the week effect in Islamic emerging Egyptian stock market for the period from 1998 to 2001 by using OLS. According to the results the Egyptian stock market (Capital Market Authority Index) was weakly efficient because Monday's returns were positive and significant but not significantly different from other trading days of week. Furthermore, Monday's higher returns were consistent with risk because Monday's returns standard deviation was also higher. A research for all index of Istanbul stock exchange for the period from 1987 to 2005 was conducted by Dicle and Hassan [3] for examining the day of the week effect by taking the closing values of both morning and afternoon secessions by employing AR and GARCH-M models the results showed that the day of the week effect existed. Higher returns were earned at the end of weak on Thursday and Friday while negative returns were observed on Monday.

Al-Khazali [4] investigated the day of week of effect in UAE stock markets for the period from 30 July 2001 to 30 August 2006 by using stochastic dominance approach because it was useful for making comparisons among distributions. The results indicated that the day of the weak effect was present in UAE stock markets and possible reason of this day of the weak effect was infrequent trading and illiquidity of stock markets otherwise UAE stock markets were efficient. Kamaly and Tooma [5] investigated the day of the week effect in 12 Islamic emerging stock markets (Egypt, Jordan, Kuwait, Dubai, Bhrain, Labanon, Morocco, Oman, Palestine, Qatar, Saudi Arab and Abu Dhabi) by using daily closing values of Monetary Fund index of the period from 2002 to 2005 by using AR and GARCH methodology. The results indicated that the higher returns were earned at starting and ending days of the week. A significant day of week effect on volatility also was observed in ten countries (Egypt, Jordan, Kuwait, Bhrain, Labanon, Morocco, Oman, Palestine, Qatar and Saudi Arab) at starting and ending days of the week.

Malaysian stock market was affected by financial crisis, and a research in this respect was held by Chia, Liew and Wafa [6] by taking Bursa Malaysia Composite index as a Malaysian stock market proxy covering the period from 1993 to 2005 by using GARCH model. The results were in contract to the results of previous researches January effect was not detected in Malaysian stock market. So, investors must purchase and held not sell the securities to get normal profit in long run and on the other hand they could get more profit than normal profit in short run by getting the benefit of misleading prices of securities. Al-Deehani [7] investigated the month of the year effect in Kuwait stock market covering the period of eight years from 1994 to 2004 by applying structural time series model. According to the results April and June effect was observed in Kuwait stock market and most of its sectors for the studied period due to summer holidays. Most of the people of Kuwait move toward cool countries to spend summer holidays and before leaving the country investors trade heavily due to which prices move upward. For the past seven years negative November effect had also been observed because of overlapping of Ramadan. During Ramadan trading activities might become slow.

Iran is an Islamic country and Tehran stock exchange is its major stock market. Nazari and AkbariRad [8] conducted a research for Tehran stock exchange for testing the "Weak form Efficiency Hypotheses" covering the period of eight years from 2002 to 2009 by using regression model. According to the results Tehran stock exchange was an inefficient stock market because calendar effect was examined for returns (Positive Jun effect), trade volume (Negative September, April and August effect) and volatility (Positive August effect). Moreover calendar effect was also observed for the returns of 21 industries out of 37 industries.

Cultural and religious festivals play an important role in the financial markets in increase and decrease regarding returns on investment in different stock markets. According to Al-Ississ [9] there are two reasons due to which equity markets are affected by cultural and religious festivals. First, on religious and cultural festivals' days the followers of a particular religion become absent from stock markets. The impact of their absence can cause a single sided effect if they all have the same attitude towards the investment decisions or have no effect if they differ in investment point of view. Second, the mood of investors is a function of religious events which affects the investment decisions.

Georgian calendar was extremely focused by researchers for the study of behavior of stock markets. A few numbers of studies were conducted to study the impact of Islamic calendar anomalies on stock markets of Islamic countries by some researchers Seyyed, Abraham and Al-Hajji [10], Ariss, Rezvanian and Mehdian [11], Bialkowski, Etebari and Wisniewski, Al-Hajieh, Redhead and Rodgers [12] and Husain [13]. The purpose of this research is to examine the behavior of stock markets of Islamic countries according to Islamic calendar (which is based on the phases of moon) events such as Muharram, Ramadan and Zul-Hijjah.

Pakistani equity market was examined by Husain [13] for the period from 1989 to 1993 to examine the Islamic month of year effect by applying GARCH model. The results of this study showed that during the holy month of Ramadan the returns of securities remained same but volatility decreased may be due to slow economic activity and reduced working hours during the Holy month of Ramadan. Seyyed, Abraham and Al-Hajji [10] examined Ramadan effect in Saudi stock market for the period from 1985 to 2000 by employing GARCH model. The results indicated that weekly returns of Saudi stock market during the Holy month of Ramadan were same as the returns during other months but volatility moved downward might be due to low trading activity or change in investor's attitudes. A number of factors contribute to change in investors attitudes such as reduced working hours and absence of investors from stock market for the performance of religious duties.

Al-Hajieh, Redhead and Rodgers [12] examined the Ramadan effect on return and volatility of Islamic Middle Eastern stock markets covering the period from 1992 to 2007 through Runs test. The results of that study were in line of results of previous studies as positive association of Ramadan and returns but in contract to the results of previous studies positive association of Ramadan with Volatility was detected in Middle Eastern countries' (Bahrain, Egypt, Jordan, Kuwait, Saudi and Turkey) equity markets especially at starting and ending days of Ramadan. Ariss, Rezvanian and Mehdian [11] examined the day of weak and Islamic month of year effect for Gulf Cooperation Council stock markets for the period from 1994 to 2008 by using OLS. The results indicated that like western stock markets Gulf Cooperation Council stock markets showed last working day effect (Wednesday Effect). So, the foreign investors could earn abnormal return on Monday in Gulf Cooperation Council stock markets because it is not first working day in these stock markets. No Islamic month of year effect was present but volatility decreased during the Holy month of Ramadan.

Mustafa [14] examined the Karachi stock market for the period of from 1998 to 2004 by using conditional and unconditional models the results indicated that the returns during Holy month of Ramadan are lower as compared to Ziqad and Shawal because these two months come after the Ramadan. The people may spent money on purchasing new clothes and shoes to celebrate the Eid-ul-fater and did not concentrate on investment in equity market during Ramadan. Bialkowski, Etebari and Wisniewski explored the relationship between Ramadan and stock market returns and volatility of 14 Islamic countries' (Bahrain, Egypt, Indonesia, Jordan, Kuwait, Malaysia, Morocco, Pakistan, Qatar, Saudi Arabia, Tunisa, Oman, Turkey and United Arab Emirates) stock markets covering the period from 1989 to 2007 through event study. The results indicated positive association of Ramadan and returns of stock markets of Islamic countries and negative association of Ramadan with volatility of sample countries' stock markets may be due to positive social attitude of investors during Ramadan which was reflected in their investment decisions.

Gowan and Jakob [15] examined the Malaysian stock market to check Eid-ul-Fitar effect for the period from 2000 to 2003 by employing OLS. The results showed that Eid-ul-Fitar effect was not found but Chinese New year effect was detected. The possible reason of such results was population of Chinese investors is higher than Muslims investors and the amount of cash bonuses granted by organizations at the event of Eid-ul-fiter is less than the amount of those bonuses which are given for the celebration of Chinese New year due to these reasons Malaysia's stock market shows Chinese New year effect.

By reviewing the literature, it has been concluded that stock market returns and volatility do not remain constant. It means that some abnormalities exist somewhere in stock markets such as Monday effect, January effect and holiday effect etc. Cultural and religious festivals also have effect on stock market returns and volatility reviewed in literature such as Chinese Spring Festival and Ramadan effect etc. The present study focuses on exploring the effect of Zul-Hijjah on returns and volatility of stock markets of Islamic countries.

Methodology

Six pure Islamic countries selected for the study to investigate the impact of the Islamic month on risk and return of the stock market. The details of selected stock markets with sample time period are elaborated in Table 1.

The stock market return is calculated with the help of following formula.

$SMR_{i,t} = \ln(Cv_{i,t} / Cv_{i\,t-1})$

Where

$SMR_{i,t}$ = stock market return at day t of i index.

$Cv_{i,t}$ = closing value at day t of index i.

$Cv_{i,t-1}$ = closing value at day t-1 of index i.

A software Calendar Convertor is used for the conversion of Georgian dates to respective Hijjari Calendar dates which may arise to one day error because the beginning of every Hijjari month depending on moon sighting which may be different for different countries by the difference of one day. To study the impact of the Zul-Hijjah on return and volatility of stock markets of Islamic countries Autoregressive Conditionally Heteroscedastic Model has been chosen due to the reason that that assumption of the linear regression model that the variance of the errors is constant over time is violated in our case. If the variance of the errors over time is not constant, an implication would be that standard error estimates can be wrong [16]. In the context of financial time series and prices of securities the variance is not constant that makes sense to consider a model which does not assume that the variance is constant. The most suitable model for such series is GARCH for forecasting volatility because it also includes the lag values of variables.

GARCH (1, 1) Model is used to capture the effects of Zul-Hijjah on stock market return and volatility of Islamic Countries. In order to approximate and quantify the effect, we have constructed index which summarize variable for capturing the impact of Zul-Hijjah for the stock markets of Islamic Countries. The index was constructed to capture the effect of zul-hijjah through dummy variable as;

$$ZHJj \begin{cases} 1 & \text{Zul-Hijjah} \\ 0 & \text{otherwise} \end{cases}$$

$$R_t = \beta_0 + \beta_1 R_{t-1} + \beta_2 ZHJ$$

The mean equation shows that return is a function of lag return.

Where as

R_t = today return

R_{t-1} = return of the previous day

ZHJ = the dummy variable for Islamic Month of Zul-Hajj

$$\sigma^2 = r_0 + r_1 U^2_{t-1} + r_2 \sigma^2_{t-1} + r_3 ZHJ$$

Where as

σ^2 = today's volatility

$\sigma^2_{t-1} + r_1$ = previous day's volatility this is GARCH term.

U^2_{t-1} = Previous day's volatility this is ARCH term.

ZHJ = the Islamic Month of Zul-Hajj

Results

The test results of the ARCH effect are reported in Table 2. The

Sr. No.	Countries	Indexes	Index Symbol	Time Period	No. of Observations
1	**Pakistan**	KSE 100 Index	KSE	7/1/1997 to 5/3/2013	3863
2	**Malaysia**	FTSE Bursa Malaysia KLSI	KLSE	7/1/1997 to 5/3/2013	3909
3	**Indonesia**	Composite Index	JKSE	7/1/1997 to 5/3/2013	3851
4	**Turkey**	Istanbul National 100 Index	XU 100	12/4/2006 to 4/30/2013	1645
5	**Morocco**	Dow Jones Morocco Total Stock Market Index MAD	DWMA	12/4/2006 to 4/30/2013	1665
6	**Egypt**	Dow Jones Egypt Total Stock Market Index EGP	DWEG	12/4/2006 to 4/30/2013	1479

Table 1: details of selected stock markets with sample time period.

p-value of Obs* R-square for all sample Islamic countries is less than 0.05. So, ARCH effect exists in return series of all sample Islamic countries. Therefore, the Null Hypothesis of no Heteroskedasticity is rejected and can proceed with Generalized Auto Regressive Heteroskedasticity Model.

Zul-Hijjah effect on stock market's returns

The results of mean equation are reported in following Table 3. The intercept C shows the average returns of sample Islamic countries stock markets. Higher average return (0.001141) was observed for Indonesian stock market and negative return (-0.00267) was observed for Morocco stock market. The autoregressive term for Pakistani, Malaysian, Indonesian and Turkish stock markets is significant which implies that today's returns depend on previous day's returns. The positive coefficient in case of Pakistani, Malaysian, and Indonesian stock markets show that today's returns are more than previous day's returns. In case of Turkish stock market negative coefficient implies that today's return is less than yesterday's return. For Morocco and Egyptian stock markets the autoregressive term is insignificant which means today's returns have no influence of yesterday's returns. This is a classic case of "Random Walk" and "Weak Form Efficiency Hypotheses" that hold true here specifically for stated countries.

The coefficient of dummy variable of ZHJ for the holy month of Zul-Hijjah is statically insignificant for five sample countries (Pakistan, Indonesia, Turkey, Morocco and Egypt) stock market which means that the returns of these countries stock markets are not affected due to the holy month of Zul-Hijjah. In case of Malaysian stock market the coefficient of dummy variable ZHJ for the holy month of Zul-Hijjah is statically significant. This shows that the return of Malaysian stock market is affected due to the holy month of Zul-Hijjah. The coefficient is negative which implies that the holy month of Zul-Hijjah causes decline in return of Malaysian stock market. The negative Zul-Hijjah effect in Malaysian stock market may appear due to low trading activity during this month. It can be said that due to religious month, investors liquidate their positions to perform their religious duties specifically in that month.

Zul-Hijjah effect on stock market's volatility

The results of variance equation are reported in following Table 4. The coefficient of lagged squared residual is significant for Pakistani, Malaysian, Indonesian and Turkish stock markets which means that previous price behavior prevails in today's volatility. The positive coefficient implies that today's volatility is more than previous volatility. In case of Morocco and Egyptian stock markets the coefficient of lagged squared residual is insignificant which means that previous price behavior has no influence on today's volatility. The p value of lagged conditional variance term in the conditional variance equation is statistically significant for Pakistani, Malaysian, Indonesian, Turkish and Morocco stock markets which means today's volatility depends on previous day's volatility and coefficient is positive which means today's volatility is more than previous volatility. In case of Egyptian stock market the coefficient of lagged conditional variance term in the conditional variance equation is statistically insignificant which means today's volatility does not depend on previous day's volatility.

Country	Index	Observed*R Square	P Value
Pakistan	KSE 100	192.7280	0.0000
Malaysia	FTSE	956.6604	0.0000
Indonesia	Composite	129.1784	0.0000
Turkey	IN 100	127.9352	0.0000
Morocco	DJ MAD	136.6522	0.0000
Egypt	DJ EGP	134.2281	0.0000

Table 2: test results of the ARCH effect.

The coefficient of ZHJ is significant for three sample countries (Turkey, Morocco and Egypt) stock markets this shows that the volatility of these countries stock markets is affected due to the holy month of Zul-Hijjah. The coefficient is negative for these sample countries (Turkey, Morocco and Egypt) stock market which means that volatility decreases during the holy month of Zul-Hijjah. The dummy variable ZHJ is insignificant for three sample countries (Pakistan, Malaysia and Indonesia) stock market which implies that the volatility of these countries' stock markets is not affected by the holy month of Zul-Hijjah. The possible reason of negative Zul-Hijjah effect on volatility is low trading in market. And it can also be concluded that arbitrageurs in this month help market to achieve efficiency which reduces the market volatility and almost market is at its fundamental.

Conclusion

The objective of the study was to investigate the impact of Zul-Hijjah on stock market return and volatility of the Islamic countries. For this purpose six countries (Pakistan, Turkey, Indonesia, Malaysia, Egypt and Morocco) are selected. In most of the previous studies Muharram and Ramadan effect was examined while Zul-Hijjah is also most important from religious point of view. For the purpose to examine the impact of Zul-Hijjah on return and volatility of Islamic countries' stock markets daily closing values of selected Islamic countries' stock markets indices were taken.

GARCH (1, 1) Model is used for capturing the impact of Zul-Hijjah on return and volatility of stock markets of selected Islamic countries. The results reveal that Zul-Hijjah has negative effect only for the Malaysian stock market return and has no effect on the Pakistani, the Indonesian, the Turkish, the Morocco and the Egyptian stock market return. This shows that Malaysian society is devoted Islamic society and members of Malaysian society are less actively involved in corporeal pursuits and spent more and more time in prayers during this holy month. It is obvious that Malaysian society is closer to the Islamic practices.

In case of volatility negative Zul-Hijjah effect exists for the Turkish, the Morocco and the Egyptian stock market. There may be a religious furor in these countries and investors focus on religious duties and avoid from speculation which is prohibited in Islam due to which volatility moves downward. Zul-Hijjah has no effect on volatility in the Malaysian, the Pakistani and the Indonesian stock market. In Pakistani and Indonesian stock markets Zul-Hijjah has no effect on return and volatility this shows that everything goes on as usual during the month of Zul-Hijjah as it is before. These societies may be in process of change where people are getting away from religious practices and only paying lip service to Islam.

It is beneficial for the investors of sample Islamic countries, to invest in Pakistani stock market because Morgan Stanley declared Pakistan market as the most attractive market across the Asian markets. And we have also seen that the average return of the Pakistani stock market is 0.0011 which is slightly less than the average return 0.001141 of the Indonesian stock market but higher than the other stock markets. The coefficient of dummy variables ZHJ for the holy months of Zul-Hijjah in mean equation is negative for all sample Islamic countries except the Pakistani and Morocco stock markets.

	Pakistan KSE 100	Malaysia FTSE	Indonesia Composite	Turkey IN 100	Morocco DJ MAD	Egypt DJ EGP
C	0.0011	1.46E-05	0.001141	0.000512	-0.00267	0.00902
Ar (1)	0.0614	0.145176	0.116619	-0.48877	-0.03283	-0.0346
P Value	0.0004	0.0000	0.0000	0.0000	0.9405	0.9004
ZHJ	0.000199	-0.00135	-0.00046	-0.01053	0.002465	-0.0024
P Value	0.7806	0.0005	0.6149	0.8859	0.9601	0.9505

Table 3: results of mean equation.

	Pakistan **KSE 100**	**Malaysia** **FTSE**	**Indonesia** **Composite**	**Turkey** **IN 100**	**Morocco** DJ MAD	**Egypt** DJ EGP
C	7.26E-06	1.65E-06	6.03E-06	0.001124	0.002511	0.003517
$(Resid_{t-1})^2$	0.16491	0.219789	0.132395	0.02667	0.064989	0.062855
P Value	0.0000	0.0000	0.0000	0.0001	0.3619	0.1240
GARCH(-1)	0.81607	0.822768	0.854766	0.789794	0.461452	0.354053
P Value	0.0000	0.0000	0.0000	0.0000	0.0186	0.0622
ZHJ	-2.67E-07	7.83E-07	1.55E-06	-0.00140	-0.008353	-0.005694
P Value	0.9116	0.1075	0.2438	0.00000	0.0000	0.0000

Table 4: results of variance equation.

References

1. Abu-Rub N, Sharba T (2011) Calendar effects in the Palestine securities exchange analysis and investigation. World Review of Business Research 1: 52-66.
2. Alya H, Mehdian S, Perry MJ (2004) An analysis of day of the week effect in the Egyptian stock market. International Journal of Business 9: 301-308.
3. Dicle MF, Hassan MK (2007) Day of the Week Effect in Istanbul Stock Exchange. Scientific Journal of Administrative Development 5.
4. Al-Khazali OM (2008) The Impact of Thin Trading on Day of the Week Effect: Evidence from United Arab Emirates. Review of Accounting and Finance 7: 270-284.
5. Kamaly A, Tooma EA (2009) Calendar anomalies and stock market Volatility in selected Arab stock exchanges.Applied Financial Economics 19: 881-892.
6. Chia RJ, Liew VK, Wafa SAWSK (2006) Calendar anomalies in the Malaysian stock market. Munich Personal RePEc Archive. 516.
7. Al-Deehani TM (2006) Seasonality as an unobservable component: The case of Kuwait stock market. Applied Financial Economics 16: 471-478.
8. Nazari M, AkbariRad M (2011) Analysis and Diagnosis of Calendar Effect in Tehran Stock Exchange. Journal of Basic and Applied Scientific Research 1: 854-862.
9. Al-Ississ M (2010) The Impact of Religious Experience on Financial Markets. Working Paper.
10. Seyyed FJ, Abraham A, Al-Hajji M (2005) Seasonality in stock returns and volatility: The Ramadan effect. Research in International Business and Finance 19: 347-383.
11. Ariss RT, Rezvanian R, Mehdian S (2011) Calendar anomalies in the Gulf Cooperation Council stock markets. Emerging markets review 12: 293-307.
12. Al-HajiehH, Redhead K, Rodgers T (2011) Investor Sentiment and Calendar Anomaly Effects: A Case Study of the Impact of Ramadan on Islamic Middle Eastern Markets. Research in International Business and Finance 25: 345-356.
13. Husain F (1998) Seasonality in the Pakistani Equity Market: The Ramadhan Effect. The Pakistan Development Review 37: 77-81.
14. Mustafa K (2011) The Islamic calendar effect on Karachi stock market. Global Business Review 13: 562-574.
15. McGowan CB, Jakob NA (2010) Is there an Eid-Ul-Fitr Effect in Malaysia? International Business and Economic Research Journal 9: 11-19.
16. Gujarati D (2003) Basic Econometrics Fourth (4thEdn). McGraw-Hill.

Permissions

All chapters in this book were first published in JBFA, by OMICS International; hereby published with permission under the Creative Commons Attribution License or equivalent. Every chapter published in this book has been scrutinized by our experts. Their significance has been extensively debated. The topics covered herein carry significant findings which will fuel the growth of the discipline. They may even be implemented as practical applications or may be referred to as a beginning point for another development.

The contributors of this book come from diverse backgrounds, making this book a truly international effort. This book will bring forth new frontiers with its revolutionizing research information and detailed analysis of the nascent developments around the world.

We would like to thank all the contributing authors for lending their expertise to make the book truly unique. They have played a crucial role in the development of this book. Without their invaluable contributions this book wouldn't have been possible. They have made vital efforts to compile up to date information on the varied aspects of this subject to make this book a valuable addition to the collection of many professionals and students.

This book was conceptualized with the vision of imparting up-to-date information and advanced data in this field. To ensure the same, a matchless editorial board was set up. Every individual on the board went through rigorous rounds of assessment to prove their worth. After which they invested a large part of their time researching and compiling the most relevant data for our readers.

The editorial board has been involved in producing this book since its inception. They have spent rigorous hours researching and exploring the diverse topics which have resulted in the successful publishing of this book. They have passed on their knowledge of decades through this book. To expedite this challenging task, the publisher supported the team at every step. A small team of assistant editors was also appointed to further simplify the editing procedure and attain best results for the readers.

Apart from the editorial board, the designing team has also invested a significant amount of their time in understanding the subject and creating the most relevant covers. They scrutinized every image to scout for the most suitable representation of the subject and create an appropriate cover for the book.

The publishing team has been an ardent support to the editorial, designing and production team. Their endless efforts to recruit the best for this project, has resulted in the accomplishment of this book. They are a veteran in the field of academics and their pool of knowledge is as vast as their experience in printing. Their expertise and guidance has proved useful at every step. Their uncompromising quality standards have made this book an exceptional effort. Their encouragement from time to time has been an inspiration for everyone.

The publisher and the editorial board hope that this book will prove to be a valuable piece of knowledge for researchers, students, practitioners and scholars across the globe.

List of Contributors

Mohammed Tarabay
American College of the Middle East, Kuwait City, Kuwait

Jamil Hammoud
Rafik Hariri University, Mechref, Lebanon

Kokobe Seyoum Alemu
Lecturer and Researcher, Ambo University, Ethiopia

Bjorn P
Department of Int. Management and Economics, Copenhagen Business School, Denmark

Matteo A
School of Business Society and Engineering, Malardalen University, Sweden

Onikola HO
ALBA Graduate Business School at the American College of Greece, Athens

Oluwapelumi A and Olaride OB
Department of Mathematics and Statistics, Rufus Giwa Polytechnic, Owo, Ondo State, Nigeria

Mujeeb Ur Rehman Rahimi
Graduate School of Economics and Management, Ural Federal University Yekaterinburg, Russia

Tao Zeng
School of Business and Economics, Wilfrid Laurier University, Waterloo, Ontario, Canada

Naimi EA and Ghafeli A
Management Department, Islamic Azad University, The International Center for Persian Gulf, Iran

Novatorov EV
Department of Management, Higher School of Economics, National Research University, Russia

Abrha FW
Aksum University, Aksum, Tigray, Ethiopia

Abdullah M
Assistant Professor, Independent University, Dhaka, Bangladesh

Raghavendra RH, Velmurugan PS and Saravanan A
Department of Commerce, School of Management, Pondicherry University (A Central University), Pondicherry, 605 014, India

Bushara MOA and Ahmed AMM
Department of Agricultural Economics, University of Gezira, Wad Medani, Gezira, Sudan

Sung-Sup C
Graduate School of Business Administration, Gachon University, Seongnam-daero, Korea

Giannikos IC
Department of Economics and Finance, Zicklin School of Business, Baruch College, City University of New York,USA

Rabia N and Khakan N
University of Lahore, Lahore, Pakistan

Khaliq IH
Pacific Western University (USA), Warid Telecom, Pakistan

Naeem B and Abbas Q
Department of Management Sciences, COMSATS Institute of Information Technology, Lahore, Pakistan

Khalid S
Lecturer, Department of Education, University of Sargodha, Sargodha, Pakistan

Atyeh MH and Khatib AM
School of Business, Australian College of Kuwait

Yasin J
School of Business, Australian College of Kuwait

Rezaei M
Department of Management, Islamshahr Branch, Islamic Azad University, Islamshahr, Iran

Neghabi ZH
Faculty member of Islamshahr, Azad Islamic University, Islamshahr, Iran

Onyele KO and Nwokoacha EB
Department of Banking and Finance, College of Management Sciences (COLMAS), Michael Okpara University of Agriculture, Nigeria

Burugupalli S
Center for Integrated Studies, University of Hyderabad, Gachibowli, Hyderabad-500 046, India

Vasiliki A Basdekidou
Special Research Fund Account (ELKE) Aristotle University of Thessaloniki, Greece

Chaturvedi V
Chaudhary Charan Singh University, Meerut, India

Baig MM, Kiran S and Bilal M
Department of Business Management, University of Sargodha, Sub-campus Mianwali, Pakistan

Jamshidi H and Moazemi M
Department of Business Management, Faculty of Management and Accounting, South Tehran Branch, Islamic Azad University, Tehran, Iran

Kabeer MA, Iqbal A, Najaf K and Najaf R
Department of Accounting and Finance, University of Lahore, Islamabad Campus, Pakistan

Luisetto M
Pharm D, Pharmacologist, European Specialist in Laboratory Medicine, Hospital Pharmacist's Manager, Italy

Akhter A
PMAS-Arid Agriculture University Rawalpindi, PhD Scholar, Muhammad Ali Jinnah University, Islamabad, Pakistan

Sandhu A
Jinnah Institute of Informatics Rawalpindi, Pakistan

Butt S
Bahria University Islamabad, Pakistan

Index

A

Abnormal Returns, 1-10, 135, 173

Acquisitions, 1-5, 7, 9-10, 91, 132-137

Agriculture, 50-53, 68-69, 84-86, 102, 110, 114, 116, 120-121, 147-148, 156, 196

B

Bank, 2, 9, 11, 33, 35, 42, 50, 53, 61, 71, 90, 93-101, 110, 114, 116, 120, 138-140, 145, 147, 149-150, 152, 172, 178, 191-192

Bank Profitability, 90

Banking Sector, 90-91, 100, 138-140

Bankruptcy, 2, 90-93, 99-101

Biotech, 63

Brain Drain, 48, 50, 55-62, 85, 88

C

Causality, 33, 35, 39, 41-44, 46-47, 104-105, 109, 131, 150, 153, 177-180, 188-190

Characteristics, 2, 4, 19, 56, 64, 68, 70, 75, 79, 86, 127, 132-133, 135-137, 142, 163-164, 174, 182, 194

Cointegration, 37, 43-44, 47, 102, 104, 107-109, 147, 150, 153-156, 177-179

Collectivist Sociology, 72

Commitment, 31, 33, 68-71, 78, 185

Companies Size, 141

Cotton Gezira Scheme, 110

Credit Risk, 90, 100, 139

Cronback Alpha, 48, 58-60

Customer Behavior, 17, 31

Customer Metrics, 17-18

E

Earnings Management, 141-146

Economic Growth, 33, 42-44, 47, 49, 85, 127, 147-150, 154-156, 177-178, 180-181, 185

Economic Indicators, 110-111

Emerging Market, 33, 42, 101, 132-137

Equity Premium Puzzle, 122, 124-125

Event Study Methodology, 1, 3-5

External Debt, 50, 147-157

F

Facial Policy, 126

Finance, 1-2, 9-12, 14, 16, 35, 42, 49, 64, 91, 93-94, 101, 109, 114, 120, 122, 125, 130, 137, 140, 145, 149, 152, 157, 162, 172, 174, 177, 187, 192, 196, 200

Financial Crisis, 2, 33, 37, 41, 138-146, 163-164, 167-171, 197

Financial Performance, 13, 90-92, 94, 99-101, 138, 140, 172

Financial Ratios, 13, 90-91, 100-101, 138-140

Firms, 1-7, 9-10, 14, 17, 19, 63-67, 73, 90-94, 101, 132-137, 145, 148, 171-172, 181-186

Futures, 60, 102-109, 162, 171, 173, 175-176, 191

G

Gdp, 34-36, 43, 45-47, 49-50, 53-54, 61, 63, 110, 126-130, 148-149, 152-154, 177-179, 188-189

Granger Causality, 35, 39, 43-44, 46-47, 104, 177-180, 190

Growth Ratios, 138-139

I

Industrial Production, 33-42, 187-190

Inflation, 11-12, 34, 42, 44, 119-120, 126-131, 152, 159, 161-162, 177-178, 187-191

Intangible Assets, 63-64, 66-67

Interest Rate, 103, 124, 126-131, 139, 156, 174, 187-190

Interest Spread Rate, 138

International Acquisitions, 132

Iom, 82

J

Johansen Co-integration, 43-46, 104, 108, 152-153, 188

L

Liquidity, 2, 12, 14, 67, 90-93, 100-101, 103, 125, 127, 137, 140, 145, 163, 187

M

M&A, 1-2, 9-10, 132-133

Management, 2, 9-13, 15-18, 25, 32, 48, 65, 68, 72, 76, 80, 93, 102, 104, 109, 112, 114, 119, 132, 147, 156, 163, 172, 177, 181, 185, 191, 195

Marketing, 17-22, 31-32, 63, 72-81, 109, 113, 177, 181-186

Mean Reversion, 122, 124

Mergers, 1-5, 7, 9-10, 132, 137

Mint Economies, 33-35, 37, 41

Monetary Policy, 126, 130

N

National Company, 68

National Savings, 147-148, 152-153, 155-156

Net Present Worth, 110-111, 115, 117, 119-120

Nonprofit Marketing, 72, 74, 79-80

Nonprofit Sector, 72

O

Oil Revenue, 147-150, 152-156

Ownership, 2, 63-67, 113, 133, 137, 142, 145, 185

P

Pension, 11-13, 15-16

Personality, 68-71

Pharmaceutical Firms, 63-66

Physical Retail Stores, 17-18, 21-22, 24, 29-30

Price Discovery, 102-104, 109

Profitability, 1, 13, 15-20, 22-31, 64, 66-67, 90-94, 101, 115, 121, 138-141, 143-145, 150, 174, 182, 188, 191

Project Analysis, 110, 121

Public Interest, 72, 76-77, 79

R

R & D Activities, 63

Reciprocity, 72, 77-79

Regression Model, 3, 24, 28, 35, 64-65, 102, 104, 108, 142-143, 155, 187, 190, 197-198

S

Sales Growth, 141, 143-145

Social Pressure, 48, 50, 56, 59-61

Social Security, 11-13, 15-16, 48, 69

Social Security Fund, 12

Socio-economic, 43-47, 83, 89, 115-116

Stock Prices, 4, 9-10, 33-35, 37-39, 41-42, 125-131, 145, 165, 174, 187-192

Structural Breaks, 33, 37, 39

Svar, 33-36, 39, 41

T

Tax Revenue, 147-150, 152-156

Total Government Revenue, 147, 152-153, 155

Tracking, 17, 22, 31

V

Volatility Puzzle, 122-123, 125

W

Wealth Creation, 1, 4-5, 11

Y

Youth Migration, 82-83, 89

Z

Z-score, 90-92, 94-101